RUSSIA IN FLUX

THE MACMILLAN COMPANY
NEW YORK · BOSTON · CHICAGO · DALLAS
ATLANTA · SAN FRANCISCO
MACMILLAN AND CO., Limited
LONDON · BOMBAY · CALCUTTA · MADRAS
MELBOURNE
THE MACMILLAN COMPANY
OF CANADA, Limited
TORONTO

RUSSIA IN FLUX

By
SIR JOHN MAYNARD

Edited and Abridged by
S. Haden Guest, from "Russia in Flux" and
"The Russian Peasant and Other Studies"

With a Foreword by
Sir Bernard Pares

NEW YORK
THE MACMILLAN COMPANY
1951

615905

Foreword

By Professor Sir Bernard Pares, K.B.E., Litt.D., Founder and Director Emeritus of the London School of Slavonic and East European Studies. Author of "Russia and Reform," "A History of Russia," "Russia and the Peace," etc.

I have before me the picture of a peculiarly pleasant personality, a tall quiet spare man, often sitting inconspicuously in a back row at one of our meetings in the young and budding School of Slavonic and East European Studies in the University of London, where we were all beginners and in a sense conspirators. This was Sir John Maynard, whom I first knew as having made an honourable career among those Englishmen of our Civil Service in India who have done so much to give respect and continuity to our service there, as for a time caretakers and not as masters. At first all that I knew about this modest man, relating to Russia, was that he had written for us perhaps the most valuable of our series of monographs on the collectivisation of agriculture, especially from 1930 onward.

Therefore, it came later as a complete surprise to me to learn that he had first visited Russia for a period of ten months as far back as 1895-96, when he thoroughly mastered the Russian language (he knew twelve languages in all in the end). In 1895 he had gone as far as Turkestan and Tashkent at the back of India, and later was present at the coronation of Nicolas II in 1896. On his return to India, he had continuously kept up his close touch with Russian thought and literature, till his return in 1933 for his studies of collectivisation. That year he made one of the Intourist journeys covering Leningrad, Moscow, Crimea, Kharkov and Kiev, and found it difficult under the conditions imposed by the Communist Party to get any extensive talks, except on boats and trains; but in 1935, returning to southern Russia, he was able to break away from official guides and to get into close touch again with the peasants; he thought that they looked much happier and more contented. In 1937 he went once more; but this journey was made much more difficult and produced far less results. His work on collectivisation is second to none that has been published in English on this subject.

When I read *Russia in Flux* * (the writer was already over

---

* I.e., the English volume of that title. The present work is based upon a combination of it with the longer, and later, *The Russian Peasant and Other Studies.*

v

seventy), I realised that this book altogether superseded my own knowledge and understanding of Russian social thought; and we must not forget that this has always been the absorbing subject for all Russians, young and old, and that Russian public opinion, first expressed in any volume after the great reform of the emancipation of the peasants, was built up not on political questions but on social. To take an example: I had always felt especially indebted to the *History of Social Thought* by Ivan Razumnik, and especially admire anyone who is capable of charting justly and intelligibly this most complex subject. But Ivan Razumnik, never, as far as I know, translated into English, is only one of very many purely Russian sources with which Maynard is entirely at home. He is equally familiar and sympathetic both with theological Russian thought, which is in itself a labyrinth, and with atheistic, which inevitably in Russia's case is a kind of reverse side to the theological. I cannot help wondering how he managed to do this in his long stay in India, except that one has often noticed that those who know India, for instance Sir Charles Eliot, have a special light on the subject of Russia.

Russia in Flux charts the main currents of Russian thought up to the "October" Revolution, which is, for the present, its most important outcome. Maynard's own position is that of a deeply intelligent and by no means doctrinaire socialist (he was a member of the Fabian Society). He has not the fluency of a frequent writer, and I read the book very slowly twice; but this was well spent time, for the content of every sentence expressed a broad, just and full judgment of the question he was treating. I would venture to compare it with Bishop Westcott's marvellously full though not lengthy commentary on the Gospel of St. John, of which I have always thought that anyone who read each compact sentence slowly enough might be able to write a good sermon on each text.

The whole edition of *Russia in Flux* was destroyed in the blitz, like all the reserve copies of our *Slavonic Review*; it was more fortunate in being reissued in 1941. In October, 1942 followed the second of Maynard's great studies of contemporary Russia, under the title *The Russian Peasant and Other Studies*. This title is rather misleading. It is true the peasant is the main subject of Russian history; in our School we never allowed a thesis for the Ph.D. degree on anything relating to it to proceed without a year's preliminary study of the history of serfdom. But Maynard's book covers far more ground than the peasantry. It is, in my view, far and away the best book written in English on the Soviet period.

To say this means to call in question the entirely undeserved authority accorded so readily to the work of the Webbs, *Soviet Communism: A New Civilisation.* I will not challenge that definition; but Maynard's book towers above theirs. I cannot help regarding their belated and naïve study as an example of the great danger of transferring a reputation deservedly won in one field to another quite different. Though it includes, without doubt, a mass of useful and often trustworthy information, it contains a number of misapprehensions on primary subjects which would not have been possible if the authors had known Russia and lived long in Russia. In Maynard, on the contrary, I find the justest and wisest summary of one question after another which has been the subject of my own study. It is Maynard who has found the acknowledged right emphasis on the main result of the Revolution in his phrase, "the release of energy," which has since been accepted and adopted by all serious thinkers who have had actual live touch with Russia since the Revolution. He has also squarely put the main contrast between Western and Russian social thought when he sets opposite to each other the "political democracy" of the first and "the economic security" of the second. Every serious student of Russia of the Revolution should read and digest this book before he tackles any other.

❊ ❊ ❊

In his very last years Maynard was engaged in collecting a number of firsthand materials on the history of the relations between Poland and Russia. This work after his death was completed by Professor Konovalov of the University of Oxford, and republished in America by Princeton University.

The *Russian Peasant and Other Studies* was reprinted three times in England:—in December, 1942, July, 1943, and later by the Left Book Club, but in two volumes. The book was printed in small type and is difficult to read. Its main substance, together with *Russia in Flux* is now published under the latter title in America, as edited and abridged by Mr. S. Haden Guest.

BERNARD PARES

Prefatory Note

From the Preface by Sir Ernest Barker, Emeritus Professor of Political Science in the University of Cambridge, formerly President of Kings College, London, to *The Russian Peasant* and Other Studies.

It was in 1918 that I had the honour of writing an introduction to a volume published by the Oxford University Press on the history of Russia from the Varangians to the Bolsheviks. Today I am honoured by my old friend, Sir John Maynard, with an invitation to write a fore-word to this volume, with its study of the Russian peasant and its other essays. Friendship imposes on me a command to obey. A deep respect for the learning and the judgment of the author adds an incentive to that command. He brings to the volume which he has written singular gifts both of experience and of sympathy. A long experience in India, and particularly in the Punjab, from 1886 to 1926, has given him a background and a basis of first-hand knowledge of peasant life. He has seen and studied—and not only studied, but helped to administer—"another great agricultural Empire, having some remarkable resemblances to the Russia of the opening twentieth century." This experience is reinforced, and quickened, by a natural gift of social sympathy. An old member of the Fabian Society, who has more than once contested a constituency as a Labour candidate, Sir John Maynard brings to his studies of the Russian peasant, and of Russian labour, an instinctive and understanding spirit of sympathetic comprehension.

There is another great qualification which Sir John Maynard brings to his interpretation of Russia. He has studied, with a quiet patience and unflagging industry, both the literature and the social philosophy of Russia (so great and so influential) and the process of her historical development. Too often we begin our study of Russia with the triumph of the Communist Party in the November Revolution of 1917; too often we forget that Russia, with all her changes, still largely remains the same. To study this volume is to receive a valuable lesson in depth—the depth which comes from an historic outlook added to personal experience enriched by social sympathy. It is this combination which makes the author so safe a guide. The historic outlook, by itself, might lead to mere conservatism. Social sympathy, by itself, might lead to uncritical laudation. When the two are mixed, and personal experience is added to both, the reader can feel a just confidence.

Some words may be quoted from the author's last chapter, which illustrate admirably what has just been said. "Russia is in flux; but it is the same Russia, though with a new and important psychological addition made by the Revolution. . . . A single example will show the continuity of the agrarian problem . . . The Mir dipped under the surface, and again reappeared in the form of a Collective Farm Committee . . . an example of democracy on the lower plane, which may yet prove to be one of the germs of democracy on the higher." That is well said. Equally well said are these words which come at the conclusion of the volume. "There is no real danger of this people becoming obsessed by dogma, despite the rigidity of their quasi-philosophers. *When they find that a rule does not fit life, they give the preference to life;* in other words, they fall back on more primitive and more enduring convictions. Their gift for breaking rules will save them from being pedantic. For the same reason planning will not hurt them, for they will change the plan whenever it has gone amiss. . . . Fate gave to this people a great inheritance; and they have learned to believe that they can dominate it."

The reader will observe that almost half of the chapters in this volume (some twelve out of twenty-seven) are concerned with the peasant. That is natural and just when the author is dealing with a "great agricultural Empire." But there are other riches; and it is permissible, and even proper, for the writer of this foreword to draw the reader's attention to the chapter on "Religion in the Revolution" (for here is a vital issue), to that on "The Nationalities" (another vital issue), and perhaps most of all to the concluding chapter on "Personality out of Collectivism" (perhaps the most vital of all issues). Not that these are the sole "other riches" that deserve the reader's attention. He will do well to study the chapters on "The New Respectability" and "The Constitution of 1936"; and indeed he may be advised, if his time is brief and he is eager to get to fundamentals, to begin at the end and to read the last five chapters first. He may well find that his appetite grows; that his time is less brief than he thought; and that he ends by beginning at the beginning and paying the whole body of studies the whole compliment they deserve.

"I have sought to banish from these pages," the author writes in his preface, "wolves, angels, and predatory fat gentlemen with a gift for arithmetic." There are no wolves, capitalist or communist, in these pages; there are no angels, communist or capitalist; there are not even any predatory fat profiteers. The author has written *Sine ira aut studio,* loving, indeed, his theme ("the tolerance and the all-humanitarianism in a melting pot of peoples in the illimitable space of Europasia"), but loving most of all justice.

ERNEST BARKER

Author's Preface

"There will be an enormous squandering of resources, of labour, and even of human lives; but Russia's strength, and the secret of her destiny, have always in great part consisted in the will and the power to disregard costs in view of the results to be achieved."

WALEWSKI, "Peter the Great"

The Tsar had been the patriarchal house-father to a Great-Russian peasant family, which tilled its fields under his benevolent eye, fought at his command, and yielded obedience to those of the family to whom he vouchsafed authority, temporal or spiritual. The family was replaced by an empire of many races, in which the Great-Russian element was only the largest. The levelling rule of the house-father shifted, by successive steps, into a half-German Court, on a Finnish marsh, outside of Russia: with an official gentry, isolated by a widening gulf, a group of intellectuals troubled by cursed questions, a new capitalism which it was convenient to favour, and a peasantry no longer convinced of the duty of submission to its lords: a State which was not organically one with its people, and a people not organically one with itself. Great reforms, half carried through, were frustrated by reactionary misgiving. The denatured head of the new Russian State, obsessed by an illusion of proprietorship in human souls, made his people puppets in a game of empire: discarded his best, and set the unable in places of power. Two wars, the first disastrous but reparable, the second carrying ruin into the foundations of the State, exposed the sham behind the pageant of Orthodox Autocracy. As when Rehoboam's malcontents broke up the congregation with the cry: "To your tents, O Israel!" the people of Russia, by a common but unconcerted impulse, stood out from this State, of which they no longer had need: and, almost in a moment, it was not. What followed was the beginning of a reconstruction on foundations new to the world's experience.

The fall and the reconstruction must be exhibited as continuous. Otherwise we are in peril of applying the wrong standard to the new achievement: and of missing the true significance of such changes as the removal of the capital to Moscow; and of the federal association of the nationalities.

This study aims at presenting a clue of social and political history, along with a glimpse of the currents of thought that had existed in the Russia of the Tsars.

❊　　❊　　❊

It is inevitable that one who writes about Russia should have his mind focussed upon the ultimate relations of the Western Powers with the vast federation of peoples who form the bridge between Europe and Asia. Whatever these relations are to be, certain things are plain. Neither group must try to force its own ideas, political, economic, or social, upon the other. Propaganda by example is all very well. Propaganda by argument is merely irritating, unless a near platform of agreement can be found. The nagging bitterness of Marxian controversy is to be compared only with that of the Christological disputations of the early Church. People do not believe what they do not wish to believe, particularly where questions of property rights are involved, and logic is only fuel for quarrel. There must be complete self-determination in the sphere of what is now called ideology.

On the other hand, there must be agreement upon foreign policy: not agreement upon basic ideas, for the attempt at reaching that leads straight back to the wrangling of the philosophers: but agreement, if I may so describe it, upon the necessity of agreement. If, for instance, there should be a struggle in Germany between a Marxian and a Fascist group, there must be agreement between the West and the U.S.S.R. as to the limits of intervention. It is not beyond the powers of diplomacy to achieve this, while securing guarantees against the return of the Nazi régime. Without this kind of agreement on practical principles of joint political action abroad—a sort of *solvitur ambulando* rule—the danger of serious clash is evident.

Association in war and in the beneficent tasks of rebuilding is the path to peaceful co-operation. At present there is a long history of ignorance and misunderstanding in the relations of England and Russia. I think it must have been the statecraft of Bismarck—that astute sower of dissension—which created the atmosphere of suspicion. With the present knowledge of facts, it is easy to see what a lantern in a hollow turnip was the fear of Russia on the north-west frontier of India. The wretched organisation of the Russian Empire was a complete guarantee against a successful attack across the Hindu Kush.

Sheer ignorance has helped the task of those who wished to keep the two countries apart. England was to Russia "*kovàrnaya Anglia*," a sort of Slavonic edition of *perfide Albion*. Her exploits in the Napoleonic Wars became something which had been done "*dyenizhkami, dyenizhkami*", by the eternal doles of pence to induce others to fight her battles for her. Then followed the picture of the Englishman "ready to fight to the last drop of Russian blood," and still later the hideous caricature of the monied city man, the "*burzhui*," oppressor of his own and all other peoples: which filled the pages of *Krokodil* till yesterday.

On the British side, an assortment of queer stories formed the stock of popular information about Russia. There was the peasant settler, travelling to his new home with a hat full of bugs from the old one, so that all might be friendly and familiar. And there was the traveller in the cold, suddenly seized by the friendly passer-by, who rubbed his nose with snow to avert frostbite. And there was the imaginary figure of the dispenser of "Russian gold," dating from Crimean days: and the "bear" whom we had fought before and who—while we were Britons true—"should never have Constantinople": though why the German was to be preferred, few took the trouble to enquire. Finally, there was the torch and the dagger, and all the histrionic accompaniments of bloody and godless revolution, and the horrors of the Zinoviev letter.

Russians have an immense appreciation, on a wider and more popular scale, of Shakespeare and Dickens, than we of Gogol and Tolstoy: but they keep their literature in a separate compartment from their sense of national character: and it is a myth that they know more of us than we of them. Both are extremely ignorant and extremely prejudiced: and the ignorance and the prejudice are very likely to do harm, and ought to be dispelled.

It has been my ambition to contribute to the lessening of ignorance and prejudice about Russia, and about the federation of peoples which —as is now made plain—share a Soviet patriotism with the Great-Russian people.

* * *

In the earlier chapters of these studies I have wanted to give an account of the Russian peasant, who, till a century ago, and even later than that, was Russia: and it could not be made intelligible by starting it at the Revolution. A single example will show the continuity of the agrarian problem. The legislators of 1861 were doubtful whether they would make an end of the characteristic institution of peasant life, the *Obschchina* or *Mir*, familiar to us as the Russian village community, and an influential section of them was disposed to individualise landed property. Those of 1893 were still discussing the same question, but inclined rather to the opposite solution of it. When Peter Stolypin assumed the task of establishing a new order after the Revolution of 1905 he went a long way in the direction of destroying the Mir altogether. It went, as it were, underground, in about one-tenth of European Russia: and in 1917 it once again emerged with every sign of renewed vitality, sweeping away the landlords, but also reasserting its traditional authority as against the individualist peasant land-holder. In the epoch of the New Economic Policy the claim to separate proprietorship was again to the fore. The Right Wing of the Communist Party did not, indeed, speak of the "strong and sober," as Peter Stolypin had done: but they favored the leasing of land and the employment of wage labourers on it, and their theoretician, Nikolai Bukharin, called on the peasants to "enrich themselves." It was Peter Stolypin without the title of Excellency and without the Court uniform. Another turn of the kaleidoscope sent the strong and sober, under the new name of *kulak* (or the new application of that name), into exile, gave their land and houses and cattle to the poor and middling peasantry, and made an end of small-scale cultivation and, externally at least, of the Mir also. But the Mir dipped under the surface, and again reappeared in the form of a Collective Farm Committee. It was, and it remains, subject to the superposition of the Communist Chairman (nominally elective, but actually an official nominee), an example of democracy on the lower plane, which may yet prove to be one of the germs of democracy on the higher.

What sort of a picture of the peasant would it be, then, which began with the Revolution? Russia is in flux: but it is the same Russia, though with a new and important psychological addition made by the Revolution. What this psychological addition to the old Russia is, will be one of the aims of these studies to show.

The treatment of religion in the Soviet Union is a vital question for the nations who are allied with her. For something like forty generations, two great religions—Orthodox, or Eastern, Christianity, and Mohammedanism—have intertwined themselves with the thoughts and lives of the vast majority of the peoples of the Union. Character and habits are profoundly affected by the conceptions which these religions—both of them congregational and collectivist rather than individualistic in their outlook—have introduced or perpetuated; I have therefore described the official treatment of them, and have sought to forecast the possibilities of a more cordial attitude.

❃   ❃   ❃

On the ceiling above the grand staircase of the House of Archives at Buda Pesth is a painting which represents the episode of the Communist revolt in Hungary. A mother draws to her heart the frightened children whom snarling wolves attack. Above the group are angels bringing the protection of Heaven to the threatened family.

The angels are capitalist angels, and the wolves are Communist wolves.

If the Communists had won, the angels would be Communist angels—possibly decorated with the whiskers of Karl Marx—and the wolves would be capitalist wolves—unless, indeed, they were fat men, with silk hats, greedy leers, and gigantic cigars.

I have sought to banish from these pages wolves, angels, and predatory fat gentlemen with a gift for arithmetic.

❋ ❋ ❋

I have used the New Style dates, and have therefore called "the February Revolution" *the March Revolution*, and the "October Revolution" *the November Revolution*. As to place-names, which have been changed in large numbers, and in some instances more than once, as individuals came into favour or fell out of it, I have found it impossible to observe any uniform principle. But I have called Peter the Great's capital St. Petersburg up to the outbreak of the first World War; Petrograd from 1914 to the death of Lenin; and Leningrad thereafter.

I am indebted to the Lenin Library at Moscow for access to studies of peasant economy, to Dr. Yakobson, the former Librarian of the London School of Slavonic Studies, for helping me to this access, and to Mr. Jacob Miller for the loan of books from his collection of recent official publications of the U.S.S.R. and for information about the technique of planning. With the kind permission of Monsieur Paul de Hevesy, the author of *World Wheat Planning* (Oxford University Press, 1940), I have made use of statistics of prices in the U.S.S.R. collected by him. I have the permission of the editors of the *Modern Quarterly* to republish part of chapter VI, and of the *Political Quarterly* for parts of chapters XXII and XXIII.

I gratefully acknowledge my numerous debts to Sir Bernard Pares, till recently Director of the London School of Slavonic and East European Studies.

JOHN HERBERT MAYNARD

Contents

		PAGE
	Foreword by Professor Sir Bernard Pares	v
	Prefatory Note by Sir Ernest Barker	ix
	Author's Preface	xi

CHAPTER

I	Historical	1
II	The Peasant in the Nineteenth Century	22
III	Hor and Kalinich	39
IV	The Orthodox Church and the Slavophils	50
V	The Intelligentsia and the Worship of the Plain Folk	63
VI	Some Religious and Anti-Rationalist Thought	92
VII	The Coming of Marx	110
VIII	The Revolution of 1905	140
IX	Counter-revolution and Revolution	157
X	The Peasant in Revolution	178
XI	Hunger in the Towns, 1917-1920	197
XII	The Organisation of Man-power and Production	220
XIII	Civil War. British and French Intervention. Famine	242
XIV	The "Scissors" and the Kulak	250
XV	The Two Disciplines. The Tsarist Inheritance and the Communist Party. Terror and Leadership	278
XVI	The Oppositions within the Party. The Death of Lenin. Right and Left Opposition. The Third International. Trotsky's Arguments	301
XVII	State Economic Planning	327
XVIII	The Old Stones in the New Building	348
XIX	The End of Small-scale Agriculture. Collectivisation	366
XX	The Collective Farm	388
XXI	Urban Labour	412

CHAPTER		PAGE
XXII	Religion in the Revolution	430
XXIII	The Background of the Nationalities: Unity and Disunity	444
XXIV	The Soviet Treatment of the Nationalities: Unity and Diversity	457
XXV	The New Respectability	474
XXVI	The Constitution of 1936	496
XXVII	Personality out of Collectivism	515
	Appendices I-VI	530
	Index	553

RUSSIA IN FLUX

RUSSIA IN FLUX

Chapter I

HISTORICAL

"Eternal is the cruel way of life,
In which generations of mankind
Live and perish without trace,
And leave no lessons for their sons."
N. A. Nekrasov, 1821-1877

"Our teaching is not dogma. . . . Life will show us. . . .
We know the direction. . . . But only the experience of
millions, as they move to the task, will discover the road."
Lenin.

"From the intellectual and the moral point of view I react
antipathetically to the Soviet Government. That Government
has stained itself with cruelty and inhumanity: it is steeped in
blood: it holds the people in a deadly grip: but, at the present
moment, it is the one power which provides some sort of
defence for Russia against the dangers which threaten it."
Berdyaev, *Origins of Russian Communism.*

"I accept all: just as it is, I take it.
I am ready to travel the newly broken road.
I give my whole soul to October and May.
Only my beloved lyre I will not give."
S. A. Yesenin.

What have the Russian people been doing since they emerged into
view as something distinguishable from the general mass of the Slav
race?

Let us begin by conceding the claim that the history of Novgorod
and Kiev, and of early trading adventure under Viking leaders and
early contact with Byzantine civilisation, is part of their history. What
we first see is a kingdom founded upon trade, and upon the warlike
prowess which primitive trade demands, and the deliberate choice
of one of the world religions—a choice which looks wise when it is
made, but is destined to erect a secular barrier against brother Slavs,
who made another choice. Then comes the rush of enemies, the road
to wealth and civilisation is cut, and the Russian people are back in

I

the twilight from which they had hardly emerged. We have glimpses of them stealing off north-eastward, along the rivers and into the forests, where they meet another race destined to add a new and strange element to their blood.

Brave and much-enduring soldiers though they have always been, neither then nor at any other time were they of the fighting sort. They had fought when they must. Otherwise they moved through the wildernesses, where weaker peoples made way or let themselves be absorbed, winning battles, not with man, but with unpropitious nature. Organised kingdoms have always called a long halt to their advance. But there was no natural limit to expansion except the frozen North, the Pacific Ocean, and the mountains and deserts to the South, and the forests were not of the impenetrable sort.

While their withdrawal is still in progress, the Mongol conquest bursts upon them: this time no invasion of barbaric tribes, but of a civilisation better organised than their own. At its best, it gives a Pax Mongolica, which makes the peerless river system of Russia a means of secure access to the trade of Asia and to Genoese settlements on the Black Sea, and supplies to the conquered a Chinese technique of administration and finance, though with no touch of Chinese art. Some of the differences between Great-Russia and the Ukraine take their rise from this epoch, and the Orthodox Church gains strength from the Mongol policy of making it independent of the secular Princes.

Points of light begin to be perceptible in the twilight which covers the Russian people, and these points gradually concentrate upon Moscow. We see her growing rich upon trade, encouraged by the immense authority conferred upon her Grand Prince as the collector of the Mongol tribute from his brother princes, and strengthened by the adhesion of a national Orthodox Church—not yet the minion of an autocracy. The wise policy of able rulers helps this growth, till Ivan the Great, contemporary with the English Wars of the Roses, absorbs Novgorod and what is now North Russia, marries the niece of the last of the Byzantine Emperors, and makes Moscow the throne of something which idealists will call the third and last Rome. And, while Moscow has been growing in greatness and unity, the unity which gave the Mongols their strength has been cracking. Undramatically, almost imperceptibly, we see the Mongol Empire crumble, leaving behind a barbarous offshoot in the Krim Tartars, destined to remain for centuries as effective an obstacle between Russia and the Black Sea as the Swedes and Poles between her and the Baltic. To the

East, Ivan the Terrible confirms the end of Asiatic domination by his conquest of the Volga valley down to the Caspian Sea.

Now that the Mongol Empire is gone, we see more clearly that Russia's isolation was due to other and more lasting causes than her subjection to conquerors from the East. Teutonic Knights, Lithuanians, Poles, all of the Roman Confession, and easily aroused to a crusading hostility against the adherents of an Eastern Church, stand in the way of access to the west and the civilisation of which it is now the centre, and the same sovereign who put an end to the last vestiges of Mongol rule finds himself balked when he tries to make a way through the cordon of opponents in that direction.

❋   ❋   ❋

Russia had a golden age of painting, before ecclesiastical decorum standardised the icon. It owed much to Greek, and something to Italian influence. Strangely enough, it was left to the Bolsheviks to discover and reveal the noblest examples of it. There was an indigenous and very attractive architecture, still to be seen in the wooden churches of the north-west and in the brick ones influenced by them. This was a genuine popular creation: for it seems that the villages built their own churches, and dictated full specifications to the builder guilds. The Church stopped the creative spirit in architecture, as it had in painting, by prescribing a standard form. Later on, Russia acquired unequalled architectural landscapes in her great cities. The craft was the craft of Italians, but there is nothing Italian in the results. The semi-iconoclasm of the Church, which allowed representation of saints in the flat, but not in the round, explains why sculpture has never flourished.

❋   ❋   ❋

Western civilisation owed enormously to Greek thought, whether it travelled in an Arab dress from Spain, or more directly in native form. Byzantium might have sent to Kiev or to Moscow the scholars and the manuscripts which she sent to Italy, thereby making possible the revival of learning. Perhaps there was no Lorenzo de Medici to welcome them, or the cold north smiled no invitation. Instead, Russia received what the Byzantine court and the monks of Athos and Sinai and the Oriental Churches could give: a conception of sovereignty in part late Roman and in part Biblical, but in all respects absolute, and confounding the Tsar's property with his authority; the Canon Law; a religious not secular art; an ecclesiastical education; and the habit of secluding women, which the Mongols did not practise.

Russian clerics did not even learn Greek, because Slavonic was the liturgic language. Russia missed the Renaissance.

She had already missed the contact with that earlier and conquering Rome which gave so much to southern and western Europe: and she missed the other Rome, the ecclesiastical continuation of the first, which was the Roman Church. Thereby she went without the Latin language, the common tongue of European thought and learning, without the rationalistic training of the Roman mentality, which gave its colour even to religion in the west: and without the scholastic philosophers who applied reason to doctrine. That is perhaps why, at a later date, a Russian Churchman could boast, "The Russian Church knows no development." There was no Reformation, because the unity of civil ruler and Church was too complete, and the abortive attack which was made upon the wealth of the Church and its enslavement of peasants at the beginning of the sixteenth century was easily crushed; and there was no Counter-Reformation, so that Russia missed an educative influence such as the later and reformed Roman clergy exercised in the west, while her own clergy neither studied nor taught.

Russia had her magnificent rivers—the most perfect of inland waterways, if ice did not obstruct and if man did not stand hostile at the exits: but the seas were closed to her. Her physical isolation has been paralleled by spiritual. Having chosen her religious orientation to Byzantium, and thereby incurred the hostility of western neighbours, she lost her civilising sun when the Ottoman conquest eclipsed it. From the early sixteenth century the country was practically closed to Roman Catholics, though its architecture was for long in Italian hands. Only the English—precariously, by the difficult approach of the White Sea, where they established themselves as merchants—and Germans, Scottish and Swiss, as mercenaries, obtained access. Russia was cut off, almost as completely as the mythical realm of Prester John, from the influences which might have enriched her life. When the free flow of thought from without begins, we shall see that there comes a belated season of blossom and of fruit: but in the meanwhile a division has come between two sections of her people, which prevents the mass of them from sharing in the harvest.

From Peter the Great's time Russia—or Russia's upper stratum—has always had some European country as its fashion and its idea. In Peter's time the admiration was for technique and the economic life: and Holland, Sweden and Germany were imitated. France attracted admiration under the Empresses Elizabeth and Catherine the Great. After 1815, England, the House of Commons, Bentham, Byron, the dandies and Adam Smith, had their turn. Under Nicholas I, Germany became the ideal: her absolutism and bureaucracy attracted the official mind, her philosophy opened a new world to the intellectuals. But under the admirations and the imitations has always run a current of adverse sentiment resenting innovation, and claiming a primitive and non-European source. The isolation, and the struggle to overcome it, and the resistance to that struggle, make up the web of Russia's history in earlier as in later years. They still make it to-day, when the loom clangs with the exchanges between rival political and economic thinkers on the theme whether Socialism can be built in Russia alone. Upon the shuttles of that loom, the fingers of Russia's people are not often visible. The people are the raw material from which other hands weave the fabric, not the weaver but the wool. But there have been moments when they have taken their place beside the loom, have sent the shuttles flying with a mighty clangour, and changed the pattern and the fabric. There is one such moment when Ivan the Terrible, after great thoughts and great deeds, smitten by that madness which seems the nemesis of unchecked power, destroys his own dynasty by the destruction of his heir. He leaves to his people the legacy of the "Time of Troubles." In the Red Square at Moscow, near to the black and red marble of Lenin's tomb, stands, and has stood for more than a century, the monument to Minin and Pojarski, a butcher and a noble, who called together the popular forces and drove the Poles from Moscow. In the group, it is the butcher who is pointing the noble to his duty: and always (and not only since the revolution) it is the butcher who is named first, though the two are remembered together.

It was not to be imagined that Russia should be without a Tsar, and greatly to be desired that he should be of the old stock. Young Michael Romanov, son of the Metropolitan, was set on the throne by popular acclamation. Tsar and Church were the institutions which typified national existence for the Russian, and gave him his ever-deferred hope of redress and deliverance: till each in turn shrivelled into a lifeless husk.

❋   ❋   ❋

It is now that we begin to distinguish clearly that feature in Russian life which has done most to make Russian destiny. The land is wide: eastwards, almost boundless: and empty. Hands, whether for weapons or the plough, are precious. There is a struggle to keep the labourer in his place: and, on the other side, to find more freedom

or a larger life by flight. The Cossacks have their origin in settlements of runaway peasants: and the economics of under-population
and of labour flux, as a modern economist might express it, are apparent from an early date. The "Time of Troubles" gave special opportunities and motives for flight, and the new dynasty's needs made it
inevitable to bring the elusive peasant under control. Elsewhere,
where similar restrictions on human liberty have established themselves, the historian is dependent upon uncertain inferences and hypotheses. In Russia we can see and hear the successive blows which
rivet the chains: until the sale of the peasant, without the land on
which he works, is recognised by law; and finally the gentry are set
free from the obligations which were the original justification of the
restrictions put upon the people. In the meanwhile, and long before
the establishment of serfdom is completed, Russian colonisation,
started by a Cossack brigand, has reached the Pacific, with Government limping heavily behind it: a people's conquest.

We see a succession of fierce struggles to throw off the yoke. The
manifesto of Stenka Razin—the ballad of whose deeds is still sung—
calling upon all broken men and debt-slaves to join him has the true
Spartacus ring. Emilian Pugachev—the Revolutionary Government
has named a town in south-eastern Russia after him—kept the Russian armies occupied for two years, and Moscow itself was in terror.
It is significant that he hanged priests as well as gentry, for by this
time the Church was no friend. It had played a noble part in earlier
Russian history, confirmed, if it did not create, the greatness of Moscow among the lesser principalities, pointed the way into the fruitful
wilderness for the advancing pioneer, offered in its walled monasteries
centres of refuge and resistance. A Metropolitan dared to rebuke
Ivan the Terrible and died for it. It was another Metropolitan who
uttered the trumpet call to which Minin and Pojarsky responded.
But there were deep causes for alienation. Then as later there must
have been among the clergy humble and pious followers of Jesus the
carpenter, and zealous successors to Paul. But the monasteries were
great landowners, and had at least their full share of debt-slaves and
serfs. The power and the glory of the Church—as later of the State—
rested upon the necks rather than upon the hearts of the people.

✻   ✻   ✻

When Peter the Great begins that tremendous career in which he
wore out the heart and muscles of a superman, we seem to see what
was the choice which lay before Russia. She might have been an
amorphous mass of village communities, laborious, peaceful, sundered

from contact with European civilisation, open to the raid of every man-hunting horde, and to the ambitions of every vigorous ruler on her borders. Something like this is what Leo Tolstoi would have had her be, meeting oppression with the Christian virtues. Peter was not the first to decide against this alternative, but, the decision being made, he was completely ruthless in his acceptance of the consequences. The primary need for him is the military need: and from this flow all his reforms. His people must bear the burdens of a race without natural frontiers: must stretch out hands to Europe, reach and use the sea, build up a great military power, and (since industrialisation was an essential to war then as now) must acquire and apply the technical arts. Hence a more rigorous serfdom, and a people divided into occupational castes. All must work: the gentry as educated leaders in civil and military tasks; the people, even the beggars, monks and nuns, in their humbler functions; and he himself hardest of all. It was an early vision of the Totalitarian State, in which every part must be sacrificed to the greatness of the whole. When Peter became Tsar, his dominion, landlocked except to the frozen north, included the old Russian realm, the conquered Tartars of the Volga, and some nomad tribes of the north, east and south-east, all of them inferior in culture to the Russians themselves; and his capital lay at the heart of the Great-Russian people. He was the ruler of Muscovy, and of the half-waste places on the skirts of Muscovy, not of subject peoples equal or superior in civilisation to his own. The Orthodox Church was still actually, as in theory, the Church of his people, and the Great-Russian language its speech. With his foundation of St. Petersburg, his acquisition of Baltic lands and his adoption of the title of Emperor, he began the fateful change which converted the Tsardom into an empire over many peoples and many cults, in which the original kernel of Great-Russians was less than half, and not the most cultured half of the whole, and the unforced followers of the Orthodox Church perhaps not more numerous.

What was it that made Peter an unforgettable figure, so that his Bolshevik successors spoke of him with admiration as "the real one"? For one thing, he put an end to the Church as a State within the State. Not an originator, he yet carried adaptive energy to the point of originality and did what less audacious predecessors had only thought of. He tried everything, and failed in much: yet much remained accomplished. He made an administrative machine, and brought the women of the capital out of the Asiatic Terem, and tried, but failed, to build a middle class with self-governing institutions. He left the still living, but for him barren, glories of Moscow, to found a new world on a Finnish marsh, and it was no mad folly, but the inspiration of a statesman's genius. He made a new script, almost a new and more flexible language, founded the first newspaper, began the first great navigation canal, developed the mineral resources of the Urals, taught the peasant to plant potatoes, acclimatised the vine, bred sheep, started the protection of forests, tried to establish industries: but where is the list to end? The superman proceeded by trial and error: unmade and remade everything: left a partially ruined Russia, and forgot to provide for a successor. To uncertain heirs, more German than Russian, he leaves a great idea, partially realised, of a Russia in Europe, the inheritrix of the arts and wisdom of civilisation; of an Empire more than and different in quality from the old Muscovy; of an imperial machine immensely strengthened and organized; of a Church without voice against the errors and excesses of autocracy; foreigners in the high places of the realm, and a people groaning under burdens not understood, and already divided into two nations, beardless and bearded, gentry and serf.

The prominence of Germans in the Russian State was increased by Peter's personal predilection for skill and capacity, and by his Baltic acquisitions, with their large upper stratum of German landowners and townsmen, until it reached proportions which gave point to the desire for a return to ante-Petrine conditions. Repressed, yet vital, the protest of the older Russia found an outlet in the next century in the race-worship of the Slavophils. Germanism passed into the ruling dynasty when Peter's daughter Anne married the Duke of Holstein-Gottorp, and their son, afterwards Peter III, married a German princess.

It was in this German princess, selected with unconscious perspicacity by a Prussian King, that Peter the Great found the true continuator of his own westernising policy, and the most resplendent of his successors, "great Catherine, whom glory still adores." A genius of many facets, she writes incomparable letters and shows the qualities of a brilliant diplomat: forestalls the centuries by keeping Russia and herself in the world's news: has dazzling dreams and realises some of them: conquers and colonises: shares the plunder of a Slav Poland which should have stood, one and inviolate, by Russia's side: tolerates all confessions and, in a magnificent vanity, introduces the germ of liberal thought, while rebel Pugachev is hanging priests and gentry and the generals sent against him find a "universal indignation" which hampers their task; and then—abandons her project of freedom of the press in the terror caused by the French Revolution, and falls sick with the news of Louis XVI's execution. A dazzling orgy of pyrotechnics, leaving the ground strewn with the sticks. What are the people doing while it proceeds? Some, of course, are gaping and whooping at the fireworks. But the mass is painfully wresting from nature the wherewithal to pay for them, in the black distance, outside the circle of light.

❋   ❋   ❋

Something—accident, and yet more than accident—confirms after Catherine's death the accession of prestige which her dazzling personality has given to Russia, and creates a legend of invincible latent strength. Her grandson, Alexander I, finds his country invaded by the greatest army of the centuries before our own. A battle in which the Russian soldier shows heroic capacity for self-sacrifice is followed by Napoleon's occupation of Moscow, with the confident expectation of a treaty of peace such as his entry into other capitals had obtained. The Russian people at first show little national feeling: they use the confusion of war to rebel against authority and plunder the estates of the gentry. But when Alexander rises to his great decision, to hold no parley while an enemy remains on Russian soil, Tsar and people speak one language, and work together with Generals November and December to inflict on the invader such ruin as Xerxes suffered. It was an uprising of a people. Herzen tells us that, six months after the evacuation of Moscow, bands of men from the depths of Siberia were still appearing to defend the ancient capital.

Raised to splendid heights as the arbiter of admiring Europe, Alexander's generous impulses spent themselves in sentiment. His policies at home passed into those measures of compulsion in spiritual and intellectual activities for which the name of his friend Arakchéev has become a Russian byword. His Holy Alliance became a league of sovereigns against the aspirations of peoples, and his dream of emancipating the serfs ended with freedom—without land—to the peasants of the Baltic Provinces; that is to say, with nothing for the peasants of Russia. His reactionary brother Nicolas, sworn foe to the philosophers, did far more for the serfs, though he smothered in blood the revolutionary movements which flared at his accession.

The most judicious of the foreign observers of nineteenth-century Russia, Donald Mackenzie Wallace, writing in the seventies, tells us that Russia has accomplished, and can accomplish again, political and social evolutions of a dangerous kind, *provided the autocratic power is preserved* and the people remain politically passive. He goes on to probe the weaknesses of English Liberalism. Russians, he says, believe that they are champions of social equality and enemies of feudalism, and that they will come as deliverers to the lower classes in a country organised on English principles: and he asks whether "the present Liberal principles of liberty and reform may one day come to be regarded as somewhat superficial." To this question he gives a topical application by observing that the Russian peasantry have reason to congratulate themselves that they are emancipated by a Russian autocrat and not by a British House of Commons.

The Emancipation Law was superior to what a British Parliament would have done, because it recognised, in principle, that freedom is not freedom without the means of subsistence. A British Parliament, at all events one of the nineteenth century, would have rejoiced in an opportunity of emancipating the serfs. But unless they had been under the influence of some such exotic genius as Disraeli, in a mood of exceptional illumination, can we doubt that they would have given them the status of agricultural labourers, free in the British sense, with legal but not economic liberty, at most with a modest provision of quarter-acre allotments? The Russian autocrat did better than that. Perhaps he should have done either less or more: and have made either proletarian workers without rights in land, or a nation of peasant proprietors. It was a fateful decision: for it was the peasants and their grievances that made all the Russian revolutions.

There were palace revolutions enough in Russian history to remind the autocrat that his strength was not his own. A Marxian might say that he was the trustee of a class, and that the class removed him when he disappointed it. The Tsar Liberator, though he headed a revolution of his own subjects, freed the serf, gave him land, and carried out some of the complementary reforms—a herculean task—was no Peter, to force the fulfilment of his will against all opposition. The work remained half done.

❋   ❋   ❋

The newly emancipated were burdened with redemption dues, often in excess of the value of the land, and in reality the price of their own thews and sinews. These dues fell upon an illiterate people, most of them unaccustomed to cash obligations of any sort, and delivered them into the hands of those to whom arithmetic was not a mystery. The land would have fed them if the systems of tenure and agriculture had progressed with the growth of the population. But it was less by a fifth than what had been enjoyed by them before, and the portions taken from them consisted largely of grasslands, without which the cattle—the heart of agriculture—cannot fulfil their function. The lack of the balanced holding was an even worse disability than the scantiness of arable. The emancipated serf retained much, though not all, of the old legal inferiority, the old liability to special and degrading punishments, the old insecurity against the arbitrary treatment of official oppressors, the old status with its deprivation of opportunities; with a new multiplicity of masters to replace the old serf-owner. He had become the dependent of the Commune—the Mir—of which he was himself a member; unable to move without its consent, he still worked for his old proprietor, because he needed the wages of labour to supplement the earnings of a scanty holding, and hired from him the grasslands which he had looked upon as his own, though the law assigned them to the landlord. The need of advances often caused him to bind himself for a period of service, which was a temporary renewal of the obligations of serfdom. These were not conditions in which a large and rapid improvement of peasant agriculture was to be expected.

The defects of the great emancipation, after the first flush of disappointment over the redemption dues was over, were not immediately apparent to the mass of the peasantry. It was otherwise with the eager radical publicists. They could not forgive the disappointments of hopes which had been pitched so high: and a passion of sympathy drove them into the countryside, and fostered the growth of a bitter revolutionary conviction. To the peasant it seemed— vaguely and inarticulately—that the Tsar had meant something better, and the gentry had thwarted him: even that the gentry were seeking to injure the Tsar because of the good that he had done. It was not long before the countryside was full of rumours of a new "black partition," which would give all the land to those who worked it.

In the meanwhile, amid the misgivings and tergiversations of timidity and reaction, with the most influential classes clamouring that the emancipated peasant had fallen into drunkenness and laziness and must be disciplined, the Tsar Liberator carried through reforms which produced the equivalent of County Councils in Russia years before they were set up in Britain, made the judges independent of the executive authority, established a corporation of the bar, set up new law courts with a public procedure and a jury system, and put the army on a democratic basis, at least on paper, with equal liability of conscription for all. But the appetite grew faster than what it fed on: or the emancipation had removed a keystone, and made the work of reconstruction too heavy for a weakening resolution. Reactionaries took back with one hand some at least of what was given with the other. The realities of oppression and inequality clashed irreconcilably with the ideals which concessions had encouraged. The most dangerous moment for a bad Government, writes de Tocqueville, is when it begins to reform itself. A Turkish war, made by Panslavist sentiment, ended with a military victory and a humiliating diplomatic defeat. A terrorist party pursued with self-sacrificing fanaticism the Tsar who had done much, but not enough, for liberty, and something, but not enough, for discipline.

❋   ❋   ❋

We are left with the sense that this much-enduring people is suffering, and not making, its own history, and that there is no contact or sympathy between them and the protagonists, whether these are to be found in the machine of the autocracy, or among the Liberals, or in the ranks of the terrorists. On a superficial examination, the Russian public seems to be like the audience in a theatre, perhaps laughing or weeping with the actors, but not dreaming that it is for themselves too to play a part on the stage.

But is it nothing to have occupied a sixth of the earth's dry surface? A peasant people have filled these great spaces, kept at bay their nomad enemies, and brought under tillage so much as is culturable by primitive methods. Nature had made a testament in their favour, and attached a condition to it: that they must earn their inheritance by occupying it, be fruitful and multiply, and replenish the earth. The fulfilment of the condition was the restless labour of centuries. With immensely added quality of performance, with motor and airplane and ice-breaker and steam and electricity, it continues to be the labour of to-day. Over all of us hundreds of thousands of years passed without emergence into history: but great preparatory tasks were performed in that seemingly dead interval. Russia has been a few centuries later in passing out of the stage of unconscious instinctive preparation. In the meanwhile, there have been rare moments when tragic crises have compelled attention, and life itself appeared to be at stake. All else, except the call of the land, has passed over the heads of this peasant people.

It is a people which the rigours of still unconquered nature and the cruelties of man have schooled into an infinite capacity for suffering: not into a love for it, as some fanciful interpreters have asked us to believe. Tolerant, pitiful, Christian in the spirit of the Sermon on the Mount, it has yet been capable of outbreaks of savage and horrifying violence, when the cup of unconsciously accumulated rage was full.

Certain rudimentary social institutions it has made its own: the family: the village commune: the working partnership with chosen comrades. Beyond these it has been non-political: and towards the institutions of the State, with one exception, it has been anarchical, submitting only to the sense of helplessness and to fear.

Round and over this people, but not of it, was sketched the political fabric, State and Church in one, with the most imposing of façades, and with foundations, partly Byzantine, partly Tartar, partly German, whose strength was still taken for granted. The Emperor Pope, as—not correctly—he has been called, was still the benevolent Father and Protector, who would set all things right if the cry could reach him. He had first made, and then unmade, a nation-wide bond of service discipline. The ground was still strewn with the ruins of this outgrown system, and the eye detected the beginnings of another in which landlord and factory employer were taking the place of the serf-owners, and economic pressure was replacing patriarchal or feudal compulsion. The task of government had grown vastly more complex. The ruler was to be judged by a more exacting standard. The abolition of serfdom had left a void into which would rush spirits of evil worse than the first, unless it were filled with a new kind of wisdom and a new kind of justice.

❊ ❊ ❊

If anyone should hope to find in this book definite forecasts of future developments, he would better close it at once. It is enough that there is a new dynamic at work in Russia. For the rest, I refer to that declaration of Lenin which is quoted above: "Our teaching is not dogma. . . . Life will show us. . . . We know the direction. . . . But only the experience of millions, as they move to the task, will discover the road." The leaders themselves do not know each turn in that road.

Why do I sometimes quote from the story-writers and the satirists when I want to show what manner of men they are who pass across the stage of my story? I am inclined to answer with another question. Why did the Imperial University of St. Petersburg make Nikolai Gogol, the author of *Taras Bulba* and *Dead Souls*, its professor of Russian History? Not for any learned work, but for his memorable pictures of Russian character and manners. Statistics may (and do) lie. They may be (and are) suppressed. But the picture of manners by the hand of a master outlives brass. The artist holds up his mirror to nature. It is his own mirror that he holds up: for it is the ownness of the mirror that makes him an artist. By means of it he shows to others a facet of the truth which they would otherwise miss. And that is, at bottom, the reason why the artist must be free. What is here said of the freedom of the artist is true of the freedom of every original teacher—of every one, that is, who makes, or seeks to make, an addition to human knowledge. The gift is precious and the garnering of it means progress, and the wasting, stagnation. The waste happens everywhere: but is least where freedom is greatest, freedom economic and social as well as political.

A thesis of these studies, in so far as they can claim to have a thesis, is that freedom is divided between the Western democracies and the U.S.S.R., part to the one and part to the other. It is incomplete in both.

What does a Russian mean when he says—and he does say it—that the Revolution has made him free?

Free? And what of the passport and the penalties for "flitting" and the difficulties put in the way of visiting foreign countries? It is an observation of the present writer that the Russian is a natural-born roamer, a sort of land-sailor, who was galled by serfdom into a suppressed irritation, which occasionally issued in outbursts of anarchical violence. How do these contradictions find a synthesis?

Russia is wide and the obstacles to foreign travel do not affect more than a very limited number. But this explanation does not solve our problem.

There is no privileged class, except in so far as superior brains or working power confer privilege. The career is open to the talents, and the advantage with which an individual can start (over and above his natural advantage, if any) is reduced to the minimum. Anyhow, there is no born gentleman to take the wall of the ordinary man, and labour is honoured. The white-collar bureaucracy is something of a fly in the ointment, and recent measures for the discouragement of the literary courses of education suggest that the desk begins to make an appeal greater than that of mechanical skill.

But here we are perhaps talking of equality rather than of freedom. What does the Russian mean by his freedom? Is it merely freedom from subjection to another class, or a common servitude which looks like freedom because all share alike in it? These things are part of it, I think. Equality has always made a great appeal.

But there is more than this in the idea of freedom: and it seems to have been Marx—Marx, apparently so unintelligible to the ordinary man—who brought the conviction of it, and ended the domination of fate. Man is not bound to a pitilessly revolving wheel, but can contribute to the making of his own history. Put that thought into his mind and he is awakened to new hopes. It is with deliberate intention that I have repeated more than once this explanation of the dynamic of the November revolution.

The simpler an idea, the wider its potential operation. The Prophet Mohammed gave the Arabs a great empire by implanting in them the notion of unity to replace that of the perpetually recurring feud. The idea which came into action in Russia in 1917 was capable of being exalted into a conviction that science gives creative powers. It is the very essence of the new Russia, of its invincible optimism, of its condemnation of despair, of its readiness to undertake the impossible. Man can fashion nature to his purposes: he can even remake himself. He translates the conception into the task of education: and naturally condemns the pedologists who divided the children into capable and incapable, and sent the latter into special schools suitable to their weakness. He translates it again into the language of the controversy between nature and nurture, and finds for the economic botanist Lysenko against the biologist Vavilov. He translates it again into the enormous undertaking of the Five-Year-Plans and, of course, pitches the task according to his hopes rather than narrows it down to the merely possible. He is in a hurry for practical results, and feels that a thing is as good as done when he has planned to do it.

It cannot be too strongly emphasised that the business of the Bolsheviks—in contradiction to doctrinaire conceptions of what a revolution should be—was reconstruction, not destruction. It is true that the ruin which they found grew worse in the first three years of their domination. If there had been no civil war, or no foreign intervention on behalf of the opponents of the revolution, it is likely that the myth of destructiveness would not have established itself. Russia fell to pieces, shaken down by its own internal weakness. The task of rebuilding was delayed by the attempt, aided by foreigners, to restore upon the old foundations. But the true rebuilding began as soon as this attempt was abandoned. How solidly the work was done we now begin to see.

❋   ❋   ❋

Russia's theologians, philosophers, and poets set the pillar of guiding flame alight for the builders.

Ivanov Razumnik, and the "Scyths," decried, in the spirit of Ibsen's Brand, the middling aim, the small and petty deed. Shestov declared that God demands everywhere and always the impossible. The Bolsheviks, rejecting the transcendent source of the demand, pitch the scale of their effort no less high. The fear of the Lord is no longer, for them, the beginning of wisdom. It is Man himself who is set upon the pinnacle. Vladimir Mayakovsky, in his *Mystery Bouffe*, shows us the Host of the Unclean clambering upwards into the Seventh Heaven and defying the lightnings which threatened them there. The spirit is like that of the builders of Babel, represented as awakening the jealousy of the Gods by the arrogance of their claim.

A spirit of confidence such as this is made possible by the sense of unlimited space in which to grow, of boundless natural wealth to be developed, of endless human fertility to work the soil and exploit the riches. Hope and energy once released, from the Pripet marshes to Kamchatka, from Novaya Zemlya to the Oxus, there is a New World, a new North America, to be occupied and tamed: and optimism is fortified by new sources of conviction.

Are we to dread the possible consequences of some great setback to the extravagance of these expectations? Is there a risk that the dashing of high hopes will be succeeded by a corresponding mood of depression? On the contrary, the imminent peril of a German conquest having been staved off by the valour and sacrifice of this awakened people, it seems that they are confirmed in their unmeasured anticipations. After the devastation of the war there will inevitably be widespread suffering, famine, and disease: but this is a people which has learnt fortitude in the school of recent adversity, and has patience as well as hope.

One thing seems plain. You cannot reproduce the conditions of the U.S.S.R., ancient and yet in a sense still virgin, in older and more fully developed lands by an attempted inoculation with those ideas which are quickening her to conception. A Communist Revolution in France or Germany or Italy would be something different from what it has been in Russia of the open spaces.

The American West of a century ago, with its forests and prairies, made accessible by motor-car and airplane, its arctic partly conquered by meteorological stations, ice-breakers, and anti-scorbutic science, is the truer parallel. But neither the material conditions alone, nor the revolutionary idea alone, would have achieved the result. It is the combination of the two that has made this new world.

It would be a fanciful picture which omitted to show the intervals of weariness and relaxation which have from time to time suspended the heroic strain of reconstruction in the U.S.S.R. They have recurred and are likely to recur. They reflect quite naturally the fluctuations of the seasons in a country of primitive agriculture and a climate of extremes: where tremendous back-breaking toil was succeeded by sleep on the stove. The leading example of relaxation is the period of N.E.P. (the New Economic Policy of 1920-1923). But youth is for ever arriving and renewing the wasted energy. In the most literal sense of the word, Russia is young. The Census of 1939 showed that over 45% of the population of 170 millions were under 20 years of age; 61 millions were children under 15, and 71 millions were men and women between 15 and 39. This left only 38 millions for the middle-aged and the old.

There are dangers, of course, in the immense self-confidence which is characteristic of the Bolshevik régime. At intervals it leads to the perpetration of grave mistakes, as when the Red Armies were hurled to disaster at Warsaw in 1920: or the channels for the irrigation of the food supply were dug up and levelled for the growth of cotton before the Turk-Sib Railway was ready to carry the food: or the cattle were despatched in thousands to ranches as large as provinces, without arrangements to shelter and feed them. It leads sometimes to the merciless punishment of failures: and even to the making of scapegoats: and so to the fear of responsibility which co-exists alongside of it. For the two things, over-confidence and dread of being called to account, are mutually compatible, according as character takes the one or the other turn: and each type tends to exaggerate the other. The centralisation of authority which is a marked feature of the Soviet system does not, however, in fact exclude the existence of a great deal of initiative from below.

The supreme example of willingness to stake all upon the success of an untried course is to be found in the field of agrarian policy: and this is one of the reasons why I dwell so insistently upon the part played by the peasant in Russian history. He is no strategist and lacks the qualities of leadership: but he has shown more than once that he can say No with conclusive emphasis. When Stalin decided upon general collectivisation and on the liquidation of the kulaks (who, despite their unpopularity, came nearest to being leaders of the peasantry, because of the influence which their material resources gave them, and a sneaking admiration of their success), he incurred the risks of that incalculable No from the provider of food: and the history of the early thirties shows how real these risks were. He succeeded—at a cost greater than he had calculated—but how easily a less unbending resolution, sustained by a less invincible self-confidence, might have accepted failure, or shrunk from the final cost!

I would not be understood to suggest that this enormous achieve-

ment was the result of a reckless gamble. As will be seen from a later
chapter, the policy had been before the Social Democrats, and later
before the Bolsheviks, for many years, and the discussion on the precise issue had lasted for three. The pre-1914 level of agricultural and
industrial production had been reached before the blow was struck.
Ruthless though it was, it was not unconsidered: and it is easy now
to see that the dangers of external attack which furnished the occasion were not baseless pretexts, but realities.

All Russian régimes have been sudden and arbitrary and, in their
dealings with the land, in particular, have been entirely free from
scruples regarding the sacredness of property. A more cautious and
less self-confident administration would have seen to it, before five
million human beings were taken from their homes and sent to labour
in exile, that something more reliable than popular sentiment should
make the choice of the victims, and that steps should be taken to
minimise the wholesale destruction of livestock, which repeated itself
in successive waves over the length and breadth of the Union, and for
a whole decade neutralised the gains of agriculture. Ivan the Terrible,
or Peter the Great, might have done the same things, but Catherine
the Great would have shrunk from them: and the reasons for this
difference suggest an interesting reflection. Catherine the Great was
less supremely confident of herself. She would have considered what
Voltaire, or Grimm, or Diderot, would say about it. It is partly because Catherine was so sensitive to European opinion, while the Bolsheviks have isolated themselves from it, that the European reputa-
tions of the two vary so widely. And that reticence of the revolutionary régime, which has grown upon it so markedly during the past
decade, alongside of its propagandist activities, has been aggravated
by the feeling that the squeamish West will be shocked by policies
that are inevitable in Russia.

Russia has her own ethical standards, and her rulers must conform
to them, but they are not those of the West. The West could tolerate
the slow ousting of a class from common rights in land by a century
of Enclosure Acts, because it was gradual and because the process was
regularised by law. It would be shocked by an Ukaz which carried
out the change at a stroke. To the Russian it seems that he who cul-
tivates the soil is entitled to the fruits of it. The ruler must have his
share because he has his task to perform. There was nothing shocking
in the assignment of a task, along with land and souls to help in the
performance of it, to a service noblesse. But rent and serfs, without
service, were an outrage to his conception of God's law; and the in-

justice remained when the serf had become a legally free man, if he paid for his freedom, and if the landlord was a mere rent-receiver, as he often was.

When the Communist Party ousted the *kulak*, it came very close to the edge of a violation of popular standards, because the *kulak* was himself generally a cultivator. The line between him and the middling peasant was very fine. In practice there is little doubt that the line was sometimes crossed. That is why the struggle was so long sustained and its issue sometimes seemed doubtful. I do not doubt that the label *kulak*, with its hateful associations, helped to turn the scale, or that the material gains of collectivisation to the mass of the poorer peasants, in particular the supply of machines and the ending of indebtedness for horses and equipment, made it easy to ignore questions of right and wrong.

❋ ❋ ❋

Is the organisation of fear, the practice of systematic Terror by the Government, as distinct from the normal *deterrence* of every penal jurisprudence, to be classified as a new thing in Russia?

Old Russia was always rough, with its Siberian exiles, its judicial floggings, and its free use of the knout. But its penal law in the nineteenth century was mild, or at any rate respectful of life. Something like Terror made its appearance with "Stolypin's neckties," in the repression which followed upon the revolution of 1905, and, with intervals of relaxation and complete suspension, has continued ever since. It reached its worst after December, 1934, when the murder of Stalin's right-hand man (and perhaps designated successor) Kirov, followed in 1936 by the intervention of the Italian and German dictators in Spain and by Trotsky's announcement of the intention to make a new revolution in Russia, gave solid grounds of fear for the Stalin régime. It was more undiscriminating than it needed to be: but war is undiscriminating too: and when civil strife reaches a certain pitch of bitterness, it must be classed along with war, and justified—or condemned—on similar grounds.

❋ ❋ ❋

Planning, a characteristic feature of the new régime, is not as new as at first glimpse it looks to be. Minute regulation of human activities on some sort of traditional plan was, in fact, normal to mediaeval Europe. The agricultural routine of the three-field rotation is only one of many instances. What was new was the abandonment of regulation, and its replacement by *laisser-faire, laisser-aller*. The Bolsheviks have gone back to the principle of regulation, and put a new con-

tent into the idea. It is done on behalf of the community generally
instead of being directed to the advantage of particular classes: it is
scientific instead of being traditional: and it is deliberately varied
according to circumstances instead of being fixed for an indefinite
period. The execution is as yet in arrears of the idea: thus far, it has
taken the form rather of a production drive than of a co-ordinating
plan: and it is in part responsible for the growth of an excessive official apparatus. But it points the way to a satisfactory technique for the
administration of the world's wealth in the interests of those who
produce it: and is a contribution of extraordinary value to those
gradually accumulated devices—the wheel, the arch, the internal-com-
bustion engine, the representative system, the financial budget, and
the rest of them—which make life easier for Man.

Even the "Party"—that unique misnomer—is not really new: but
rather a new application of an ancient institution: the priesthood.
Think of it as a lay Church, beside which all rivals are but heretics;
having a monopoly of teaching; supplying the personnel of many
offices of State, as the mediaeval Church did; bound to certain abstentions, as were the mediaeval Churchmen; accessible to ability from
all social strata, as was the Church; marked off from the rest by
the dedication to particular tasks, as were the priests; liable to be
unfrocked, as perhaps the Churchmen were not. The parallel extends
even to insignificant details such as the marking of the head by the
shaving of a portion of it. The Communist shaves the face as the priest
shaved the crown.

Like everything else, the "Party" is in flux, and it has seemed to me
during recent years that the direction in which it has been moving
is towards a stricter authoritarianism. The loopholes remaining for
freedom of discussion have been narrowed and the occasions for its
exercise have been limited.

This is not of good augury for freedom in Russia, if we are thinking
of the political half of freedom.

But there is another way of looking at this question, and that involves the frank admission that the Russian peoples need a longer
political education before they are freed from tutelage, and that the
leadership of the "Party" is a necessary condition of such an education. In so far as it is possible to regard that leadership as coming from
within, it is not essentially contradictory of the growth of the conditions of democracy: and on the lower plane, where each man's and
woman's daily experience serves to guide them, democracy exists
already. If we ask ourselves whether a truly democratic system in all

the Russias would have given to these peoples the achievements of the years up to 1941—the rapid industrialisation without foreign debt, the agrarian revolution which made the industrialisation possible by ensuring the delivery of the necessary food and materials, and the effective defence of the country against the greatest military powers in the world—I think the answer must be no. There are emergencies to which the untrained democracy is unequal: and the question, how long a particular emergency is to last, is one of practice, not of theory.

Chapter II

THE PEASANT IN THE NINETEENTH
CENTURY

If we exclude the northernmost third as generally unfitted for agriculture, most of the remainder of Russia in Europe falls into two regions: a region of food deficit, where the crops do not—perhaps we shall soon be able to write, did not—suffice for the food of the inhabitants: and a region of food surplus to the south and south-east of it. The region of deficit is, as regards soil and the length of the open season (in the north, as little as five months), the less favoured by nature. But it has the more equable climate and the greater supply of moisture. It contains the capitals and the manufacturing centres, a larger proportion of the people have learned to supplement agricultural earnings, first by home industries and later by factory labour, and the agriculture is not so nearly universally concerned with cereals, because the nearness of industry has encouraged dairying and the growth of special crops, including flax. The region of surplus includes the famous Black-Earth zone. With a far better soil and a longer agricultural season, extending in the south to nine months, it has wider variations of cold and heat, and suffers from recurring deficiency of rainfall, tending to be more acute towards the east. Historical reasons have made a portion of it, especially north-eastern Ukraine, a land of small holdings and overpopulation, and much of the soil has been exhausted by excessive cereal cultivation. Almost one might say that man has done better where nature was less kind: but this is not the whole truth, for the hot winds and the drought, which periodically bring famine to the so-called granary of Europe, have hitherto been beyond the control of man, whatever the future may have in store in the way of dry farming, drought-resisting plants, afforestation, and irrigation canals.

The region of surplus has been the scene of the worst famines. It was also the scene of the most violent agrarian outbreaks of the early part of the twentieth century. We arrive at a rough demarcation between the two regions if we draw a line, much curved and much indented, from south-west to north-east, starting from a point just south of Kiev, to the junction of the Volga and Kama rivers south of Kazan, and prolong it across the Urals into Siberia.

As in all countries before the scientific engineer gets to work on them with his artificial drainage and artificial irrigation, his communications and supply of power, land and water in Russia are unevenly mixed and badly distributed. Ample moisture, extending to swampiness, prevails in one part, while drought parches another. Rivers carry unused floods to the sea, while deserts adjoin their banks. Here is room for large-scale remedies such as only the highly developed State has the knowledge or the means to apply. The causes of agricultural poverty are partly explained by this inevitable postponement, partly by institutions and practices which affect the processes of agriculture. The Commune, known to many Englishmen, but to fewer Russians, as the Mir, plays a large part among the latter.

This institution was latent, or at least happily concealed from the eyes of administrators, till the forties of the last century, when a German traveller, Baron Haxthausen, under the inspiration of Slavophil friends who yearned for something characteristically Slavonic, dragged it to light. Whatever its true history and origin, it was an inevitable accompaniment of the open-field system of agriculture, which demands an authority for the determination of the leading agricultural processes and their dates. It had an Executive in the Elder, and it expressed itself through the Village Meeting, an assemblage of heads of families, not numerous in the days of the patriarchal household, but multiplying, and becoming more widely representative, as the large joint-families broke up after emancipation. It proceeded by a rough method of acclamation, not by formal voting, and, in its palmy days, enjoyed confidence and commanded acquiescence. It must often have been overruled by the squire or his manager when the members were serfs: but, more often, it must have been found a convenient and representative instrument. One of its prime functions was the redistribution of land, to adjust burdens and rights to changes in numbers and working power. General redistribution had entirely ceased over a third of Russia and had become rare elsewhere: but partial redistributions were constantly occurring.

When we first get our view of the Mir—for this is the name by which I shall call it—rights in land are held in common: but possession and cultivation are individual. There are no private grazing grounds, but some private hayfields, and no practice of stall-feeding of peasants' cattle except in winter. Since all the cattle must graze together over the stubbles of all, and over the fallow land, and since the hay of the common hayfield was generally cut by the joint labour of all, the village meeting decided when to plough, when to mow, when to reap, and was the means of perpetuating the almost universal three-field rotation, which obstructed novelties such as the growing of clover.

Whatever further functions the pre-emancipation Mir may have discharged in addition to the redistribution of the land and the regulation of agricultural processes and dates, we see it, in its nineteenth-century form, acting as an organ of village self-government: distributing among its members the customary peasant duties of repair of roads and bridges, escorting of holy icons and the like, forming by collection from all a reserve of corn for insurance against need, allotting his subsistence farm to the priest, managing the communal field when there was one, organising fire-fighting and protection against thieves, enforcing the patriarchal authority upon contumacious sons, and settling minor disputes among its members. It even made separation orders for quarrelsome spouses, regardless of the law, which gave the monopoly of divorce to the ecclesiastical courts—but the peasants were always half outside the law. It was the maid-of-all-work for the miscellaneous demands of a busy administration, and we are not surprised that more tasks were soon laid upon it by the State.

Before Emancipation (and indeed after it too) the peasant—of course without any clear conception of the juridical meaning of ownership—believed that he, or his Mir, was the owner of the land which he cultivated.* This belief was expressed in the famous plea of the

* Both serfs and serf-owners were disappointed by the Edict of Emancipation. The onlookers, the thinkers, who had hoped so much, felt they had been cheated of a cherished dream. Some of the peasants thought that the true edict was being kept back from them by their late owners.

The essential facts were simple. The plan of emancipation *without land* had been adopted in the Baltic provinces of the Russian Empire. Alexander II decided that the peasantry should not be an agricultural proletariat, such as has been created in Great Britain, but should enjoy rights in the land it tilled. The law said that the land—or that part which did not belong to the Crown or the princely appanages—belonged to the squires; and justice forbids that owners be ousted without compensation. The peasantry believed—and believed it with their blood, as something which God's law and eternal tradition made self-evident—that the land belonged to those who worked it. But compensation, if there was to be compensation, could only be taken from the people. The peasantry must pay; and to them it inevitably seemed that they were to buy back what it was the gracious will of the Tsar that they should receive as a gift. The fact that the name given to the payment—*obrok*—was identical with that formerly borne by the serf's commutation fee, such as old Hor paid to Mr. Polutkin in the story which is translated in Chapter III, must have confirmed the impression.

The legislation provided that the redemption dues might be commuted for annual payment on a 6% basis. Ultimately commutation became compulsory. The peasant could avoid the payment of redemption dues by accepting one of serfs to their squire: *We are yours, but the land is ours.*

Nicolas Berdyaev puts it that the peasant regarded the land as God's,

the pauper lots of one-fourth of the normal, and nearly two-thirds of a million households took this course.

The lana was distributed by local commissions on principles which varied in different regions. In the outcome the average allotment for each male soul was, in acres, roughly 23 for the State peasants, for the most part outside the fertile black earth, 15 for the Appanage peasants, and 9 for the serfs who had been owned by private landlords. These areas, or rather the differing local areas which together made up these averages, were supposed to represent the normal peasant holding; and the theory was that the norm should be completed out of the landlord's remaining estate when land was otherwise insufficient. Generally speaking, the serfs received less land than they had held before Emancipation. In Russia as a whole the reductions amounted to a fifth. These reductions (the *otryezki*, or "cuttings") played an important part in subsequent history. In the north-central part of Russia where meadows were the most valuable part of the estate, the "cuttings" consisted largely of pasture land. The balance of a holding is as important as its size, and the fact that the landlords controlled so much of the area which was essential to balance, either prevented the peasant from putting his arable to its most effective use, or helped to make him dependent on the squire who held the pasture. Often he had to labour for the squire in order to have access to the pasture. The emancipated serf's liberty was a qualified liberty, and it is the qualifications that compel attention.

In the first place, there was the pressure of economic necessity.

Then there was that corporate entity, the Mir, to put limits on his liberty. That he was generally conscious of the restriction is open to question. No doubt many took the control of the community for granted and gave no thought to the matter, unless some check on individual enterprise brought the servitude home to them. But the control was close, and its limits were uncertain. What was certain was that the liability for the dues was (till 1903) a joint one, and, that being so, the Mir was virtually the master, whatever the law might decide. In Great-Russia it continued to redistribute the land, and to do it according to labouring capacity, as indeed seems to be the logically inevitable consequence of the enforcement of joint responsibility for dues. In the Ukraine the joint liability extended only to the common, but even then the open-field system must have involved a considerable degree of control by the community, and everywhere the Mir was a species of residuary authority for all questions affecting village life.

But the most intimate and comprehensive of the restrictions upon the freedom of the liberated serf was the absence of any demarcation of his legal rights and duties. He was as completely at the command of every representative of the executive power as the bullock or horse which he drove to the fields was at the command of the switch he carried. He was expected to do what he was told, and he was beaten if he failed to do it. And yet he was a juror in the new Courts: and in that capacity passed judgment upon his fellow men.

There is plenty of evidence of the reality of this semi-servile status in the stories of peasant life which begin to pour from the literary world in the ferment of thought following upon the epoch of the emancipation. And now the irony of circumstance presents us with an amazing contrast, even more amazing than that furnished by the arbitrary whipping of men who exercised quasi-judicial functions. This poor and ignorant being, as an individual despised and slighted, became, in his corporate capacity, the mystical object of a sort of mass-pilgrimage from a class of cultivated persons who sought to find in him the repository of truth, the source of a salvation which was of this world, not of the next. Was there ever and the right of using it as belonging to the man who gave his toil to it. In this conception there was no room for the rent-receiving landlord. Whatever the historical justification for this, the law held that the land, or rather the land which was not the property of the Crown or the Church or the appanage of a member of the Imperial House, belonged to the squires.

The Mir was the darling of the Slavophils for its specifically Slavonic character. The Populist-Socialist loved it because he saw in it the germ of a peculiarly Russian Socialism, which would give the go-by to the proletarianism of the towns and the capitalism which oppressed Western Europe. The conservative politician saw in it the hope of keeping the peasant (presumably loyal and religious) apart from corrupting influences. But, all the time, life—or death—was too strong for all three, and the object of their affections was decaying before their eyes. The vitality of the Mir depended upon a virtual economic equality among its members, which made a reality of village democracy. The cash-nexus which established itself with the introduction of cash obligations, put an end to the equality, by giving scope to the talents of the more astute for self-aggrandisement: and the end of the equality meant the domination of the village meeting by the more prosperous, and the beginning in the village of a class-struggle. After it had lost its equalising function, the Mir retained that power of obstructing agricultural innovations which made it odious to the agricultural reformer, and its tendency to hold back the more active and enterprising of its members. But we shall err if we suppose that it was unpopular with the mass of its members. Most peasants did not expect to benefit by the withdrawal of restrictions, and had neither energy nor cattle nor implements to do so. To the poor there seemed always the possibility of benefiting by a redistribution and, even when landless, they retained their rights of common pasture and feeding, though it were only for goats or poultry. The Mir remained

anything more startlingly bizarre than this movement of "going to the people" which came upon the intelligentsia of Russia—irreligious or at least un-Christian to a man—within a decade of the emancipation? The serf has become something holy, a source of inspiration and prophecy. But has not this transformation had something like a parallel in a world-shaking event of the past, with which we are too familiar to see it in its true perspective and proportions: the change which placed the obscure felon, agonising on the gallows, at the right hand of God the Father Almighty, coming to judge the quick and the dead? To this transcendent image, to the likeness of the Christ upon the cross to the tormented and suffering people, the poets of Russia for ever revert, and neither sin nor sordidness obscures the vision.

in idea what it had long ceased to be in fact, an agent of equalisation; and equality made a stronger appeal than freedom: a fact which explains some things which would otherwise be unintelligible in the more recent history of Russia.

The love of equality is illustrated by the tenacity with which the peasant has clung to a practice which has greatly embarrassed his agriculture. It is not exclusively Russian, nor even exclusively Slavonic, except in its exaggeration. When the crops were standing, the traveller of yesterday, in areas where collectivisation was not complete, noticed a streaky appearance about the cultivation. These were the "strips," often not more than three or four paces wide, and maybe a quarter of a mile long. They were particularly narrow and numerous in the north, where soil is of uneven quality, and in the agricultural centre with its dense population and small holdings. They were wider and less numerous in the more uniform steppes of the south and south-east: but the scarcity of water there and the necessity of locating the village near the source of supply made the distances to be travelled by the cultivator long and exhausting. A monograph on a village in the Valdai hill area, compiled in the early period of the revolution, says that each peasant in each of the three "fields," winter, spring and fallow, has seventy strips of arable and seventy-six of hay, and each strip is only one-seventh of an acre for a whole "soul," and half of that for half a "soul." In such conditions, one-fifth of the whole land went in boundaries, and it was hard to get the plough round at the end of each strip. The peasants said you could take the hay of one strip under your arm, and carry it across to the next one. Mistakes, and cultivation of the strips of others, were very common. It was calculated by a revolutionary commission that a man had to walk twelve hundred miles, on an average, in the agricultural season, to get round his own holding. But the tradition, and the passion for equality, were so strong that, when the peasants got their additional allotments at the expense of the landlords and other individual owners in 1917 and 1918, most of them divided the new areas into strips— and re-established the inconvenience.

The love of equality naturally shows itself most in those who are not confident of possessing the means to excel. It is negative rather than positive, and is perhaps at bottom a hatred of being surpassed, combined with a doubt of the fairness of the competition, in which particular qualities are marked too high. It existed in the peasant, if we are to trust our authorities on peasant life, along with an admiration for the man who had emerged from the mass, whatever the means which he had employed. There is something of the *kulak* in every peasant, we are told. He is a stubborn individualist who will not share his resources with anyone, will not take part in common tasks, and as soon as he becomes more successful than his fellows, finds the Mir a fetter upon his energies and wants to leave it. But these facts have to be reconciled with others which apparently contradict them. The workers' fellowship of chosen comrades—the *artel* as Russians call it— was a well-established institution, extending to agriculture as well as to industrial and other tasks: and co-operation in production, consumption and credit attained widespread success in the twentieth century. It seems plain that the peasant, in spite of his individualism, was capable of being convinced by the prospect of tangible advantage: but that he preferred the voluntary association, from which the less eligible were barred, to that in which custom gave equal rights to all members of the community.

The history of Russia in the past has been for the most part that of an underpopulated country: and land, at all events arable land, was less important than labour, in the region of deficit. But a part of the Black-Earth zone has suffered from the contrary evil. The serfs here had very small holdings, because their masters wanted all their labour on their own rich estates, and many of them were shortsighted enough to accept the "pauper lots," of one-fourth of normal area, without obligation for redemption-dues, which the Emancipation Settlement offered to them.* This is why we see the peasants of Poltava and Kharkov burning the houses of squires, and dividing up their cattle, implements and grain stores in 1902: and why the seizures of land in 1917 and 1918 came near to doubling the peasant holdings of Ukraine, while they added but a small additional fraction to those of some other regions.

Beside the taxes, there were other liabilities such as attach to the ownership of land in all mainly agricultural countries, where there is no reserve of general wage-labour: the mending of roads and bridges, the clearing of snow from railway lines, the breaking up of blocks in the timber floating down the rivers, the cutting of drains for the escape of floods, the running of official messages; at which no one dreamed of grumbling so long as the customary limits were not seriously overstepped. There was virtually no law for peasants. They did what the Elder, or the Meeting, or the Police told them to do, or

* See Appendix VI: Dr. Shingarev's account of two villages in the Black-Earth zone in the early years of this century.

suffered the usual physical admonitions for recalcitrance. The vagueness of the law for peasants extended to more serious matters than these. In the great majority of cases questions of succession were settled on the spot. But if they reached the Courts, the law of succession showed itself to be completely chaotic: and the decisions of the Supreme Court were so confused and contradictory that the fundamental question, who is the owner of a peasant holding on which the redemption-dues have not been paid in full, was practically insoluble before the Stolypin legislation of 1906.

Some of the serf-owners had been sadistically cruel. Still more had lost their mental balance from the exercise of a virtually unrestricted power. In a few, the very best, power had developed a grandeur and generosity of soul. Dostoievsky's picture of old Karamazov and his sons shows how isolation and irresponsibility worked upon human nature. It seems that the human will needs to have fixed limits set to it, if it is to be saved from over-balancing; for power, like solitude, makes a man either a god or a beast.

Some of the squires, particularly in the region of deficit, where labour was all, were hard hit by the Emancipation. These withdrew to the towns to take up Government service, which had begun to be better paid during the period of Alexander II's reforms. A considerable number sold their land, sometimes to peasants, but sometimes to new owners who were often no improvement on the old. In the region of surplus the terms of emancipation were more favourable to the squires, who continued to cultivate their estates, and "drank beer and kept accounts," as the saying was, that is to say reduced the old lavish scale of their establishments. But everywhere difficulties of labour embarrassed the farming squire, particularly in good seasons when the peasants were occupied with their own land and not hard put to it to find a living. Towards the end of the nineteenth century there was a great extension of the practice of short leasing to peasants in the surplus zone, particularly in the central agricultural and middle Volga regions. This practice exhausted the soil, because the lessee had no motive for sparing it. It also encouraged the notion, already firmly established among the peasants, that the landlord, a mere parasite, had no rights in the land; and it must bear its share of the responsibility for the peasant disturbances of 1902 and 1905.

✳ ✳ ✳

Famine in old Russia was endemic. Famine is not a sudden apparition out of the void, but rather an intensification and extension of normal conditions. There always is typhus. There always are weeds mixed with the bread to adulterate it. Some degree of scarcity, affecting a smaller or larger number of individuals, is endemic. You no more get rid of famine, inchoate, incipient, demonstrating itself among the more helpless and incapable, from a purely agricultural country, than you get rid of the relieving officer and his unlucky applicants from modern industrial England. Good times show a shorter list. The name of famine, the name of slump, is kept for the worst times. But the spectre is always at the door, for some.

Poverty, bitter and grinding poverty, was always present in peasant Russia. The books are full of it: the landless peasant, perhaps not the most ill-starred, for he at least was not tied to a farm and its obligations: the peasant with a non-economic holding, which does not yield a living, without a change of methods beyond the wits and the means of the occupant: the horseless peasant, who must lay on the backs and arms of himself and his wife burdens too heavy for any but animal strength: the peasant in arrears, and the peasant in debt: the peasant at the drink shop: and, at the back of it all, the miserably inadequate yield, rarely as much as six or sevenfold of the seed, and smaller than in any other long-settled and populous country, including India. Even the occupant of an average holding of twenty to thirty acres of good agricultural land in the Black-Earth zone had to look for outside earnings: and numbers in the rural areas could not find employment. The break-up of the joint-family, to which Emancipation gave an impetus, increased the economic strain by adding to the cost of living.

In judging the Russian standard of living, both at the time with which this chapter deals, and at a later stage, we must begin by banishing from our thoughts all comparisons with the United States of America, with Britain, and with Western Europe. Northern India, indeed, is more germane to the case, despite the contrast of temperature which makes the needs in housing and clothing widely different. There were gleams of something better: as when flax cultivation introduced a comparative prosperity into central Russia. Incipient industrialisation, which formed nuclei of special types of consumption, was the principal cause of improvement. Accessible markets for something other than cereals were a condition of a better life for the peasants.

A monograph of a village eighty miles from Moscow, and sixty from the nearest railway station, shows us the people in the 1860's living in wooden huts with a floor space of about 240 square feet, thatched with straw. Prosperous villagers had two such huts, separated

by doors with wickets. The poor had one. The stoves were great erec-
tions of clay, upon which some of the family slept. Many had no
chimney. There was a little opening over the door near the roof, which
let out the smoke after it had warmed, and blackened, both walls and
people. The hut was lighted by burning splinters of fir. The kerosene
lamp (without a globe) came in during the eighties. Clay was the
material for cooking vessels, and clay or wood for plates and dishes.
China was a rarity for holidays. Splinters of wood supplied the function of forks. The general sleeping place was the floor, on straw, which
was brought in each night and taken out in the morning. All clothes
were home spun. The men wore blue linen or hempen trousers and
shirts with gussets under the arms, red ones for holidays, and the
women wore *sarafans* (sleeveless dresses) of printed linen, without
buttons, but fastened by strips of stuff and girdles of coloured yarn,
and bodices of home-made stuff, either wool or linen and wool mixed.
For winter they wore trousers of the same material. Both men and
women wore jackets of untanned sheepskin. The usual footgear was
birch-bark sandals: leather boots only on holidays, and to church, and
a pair lasted more than ten years. In the seventies, when the village
had taken to flax-growing, felt boots also made their appearance. For
a long time there was only one cloth coat in the village: it was borrowed by friends for festive occasions.

The bridegroom had to pay a bride-price (a practice which was
still common in 1934). The bride brought with her a linen bed-cover
and bedding of coarse materials. After the marriage feast, a whip was
given to the bridegroom as an emblem of power. At meals the women
stood while the men sat down to eat, and kept their heads bowed and
their hands folded, not speaking till they were spoken to (survivals
of this practice also are to be found).

The first samovars appeared in the seventies, but tea was only
drunk on holidays. An infusion of dried apple-strips and St.-John's-
wort was often used as a substitute. About 1890, when a dairying economy was being introduced, and the standard of prosperity was rising,
the practice of daily tea-drinking began in this village. Meat was a
rarity. The rye-bread was supplemented by cabbage-soup and barley-
porridge. In autumn they added mutton fat or hemp oil to the porridge; in the spring, milk. Crushed hemp-seed was eaten with radishes;
steamed turnips and a *purée* of oats and peas were eaten; herrings,
biscuits, and sweets, *were only dreamed of* says our informant.

The profits of the dairying brought about changes. In 1898 all the
huts had a stove-pipe and some of them had two rooms. The only

furniture, except the benches fastened along the walls under the icons, was a table. About 1900, wooden beds for the children made their appearance. After the Japanese war manufactured goods spread more widely, and returning soldiers introduced certain luxuries.

❊ ❊ ❊

We have said that bread is the Russian staff of life: but it is not the bread, "water taught to stand up," which passes for such in Britain or the United States of America. At its best it is of excellent rye flour, not deprived of its nutritive constituents, stiff, solid, with an acid tang in it: stuff for unspoiled digestions. Two pounds of it are a fair daily ration, but larger amounts are eaten during heavy field work, and the soldier's ration is more. Baron Haxthausen, after a journey made in 1843, says that five pounds was the harvest ration, and that, in White-Russia, a man would eat seven pounds. As we learn that harvest work often lasted eighteen hours out of the twenty-four, this occasional heroic consumption is not impossible.

Bread kept a man in working, or in fighting, trim—if there was enough of it. There is abundant testimony in our writers on Russian peasant life to show that there seldom was enough, even if statistics of the balance remaining after exportation did not raise a suspicion of deficiency. The first question which is put to the peasant jurors, in a story cited later on, by their fellow villagers who have taken up work in town, is about this primal need. "Is there bread?" Precisely this question was put to the present writer in 1933 by an old woman in a Moscow church, who wanted to know conditions in England. She moistened her lips as she put it. In the story the answer is: "By God's blessing, it will last till the Great Feast (Christmas) if we are careful with it." There was no question of it lasting all the year round till the next harvest, at least in the deficit provinces. Some exhausted their supply within a few weeks after harvest: some had enough till Christmas: some till Lent. Bread was a thing to be treated with respect. The loaf must be stood upright on the table. It must be broken, not cut.

The most provident began from the outset to mix adulterants (sometimes bran, sometimes a bitter weed which our dictionaries translate as pig-weed) with their flour. In a bad season all had to do this.

When the bread supply failed, the household, or some of its members, began to "go out for morsels," to wander and ask their more fortunate fellows to supply their need. This was not regarded as ordinary beggary. All the poorer peasants did it in their turn. It almost approached to a system of mutual insurance.

In the villages of central and north-central Russia cottage handicrafts were well established and had been exploited by merchants from the eighteenth century onwards. Baron Haxthausen, nearly twenty years before the Emancipation, found whole villages of smiths, curriers and linen makers, who received advances on condition of supplying the dealers. Even at this early date there were complaints that the Government was favouring the factory at the expense of cottage industry: and it is not long before we hear of the handicraftsmen falling hopelessly into debt to the merchants. The Populists, who believed that Russia would circumvent the economic developments which had created the capitalist system in the West, disliked the factory and hoped much from the small handicraft. But it seems likely that in Russia, as elsewhere, cottage industries could survive only in so far as they possessed special artistic value, or supplemented factory production with cheaper goods for local consumption. The numbers finding employment in this way continued, however, to be large at the end of the period with which this chapter deals and, as late as 1911, Monkhouse puts them at three and a half millions in summer and eight millions in winter.

We are not surprised to find that the peasant was brutalised by the conditions of his life. One of our writers, whose Siberian stories had great vogue in the seventies, describes the roasting, by their captors, of horse-thieves over a slow fire. This was the revenge for losses caused to peasant transport-drivers. Fire-raisers were often beaten to death, and this was in the comparative civilisation of the Moscow region. The treatment of women was coarse and cruel. The woman was "unclean," and many of the old men would not enter the bathhouse after her. Wife-beating was entirely approved by public opinion, and a particular kind of possession or hysteria, supposed to be due to grief and ill-treatment, was common among women. Life, and the land, made such pitiless demands that there was no chance of the growth of any finer feelings. "Peasants marry their girls in autumn, rather than in the spring, for the same reason that they sell a cow in autumn rather than in spring—to save winter keep."

It is a relief to turn to a picture, by Tolstoi's peasant protégé, of the high jinks of the young people in the Moscow region, in the dead season between spring sowing and hay-cutting. They did not worry themselves with the hoe, or indeed with weeding in any form. They meet at Church after mass and on holidays. It's all picnicking and dancing in the open, to the music of the concertina, with the lads from the factories coming home for the Easter holiday and, with their fine city ways and smart city clothes, disturbing the hearts of the village lasses, and arousing the emulation of the boys. Then comes the hay-cutting, and with it the beginning of the summer's heavy tasks, when manual work often lasts longer than the sun. Admirers of the peasant life, who have never felt the ache in their shoulders, nor the calluses on their hands, have talked of the joy of work. If there ever was such joy, it was not for the Russian peasant, when once his time of "suffering," as he calls it, that is of harvest work, was upon him. It was a time of dust and heat, when the children, neglected for many hours, fell ill and languished. All but the strongest were at the very end of their strength, and those pretty dancing girls aged cruelly fast. It often happened that grain was left uncut or uncarried, when the short open season came to its end.

The rough and inconsiderate treatment of women did not mean that they had no influence in the peasant home. Under the patriarchal system of the joint-family, the house-mother was as much the queen, as the house-father was king, of the household. She had her way over the marriages of the young people, and ruled the daughters-in-law with a rod of iron. A Smolensk landlord tells us that in introducing any agricultural novelty, such as flax cultivation, it was essential to look closely to the interests of the women. Woman had her separate pecuniary interest, because the "woman's box," as it was called, was by custom her inviolable property, and even the husband was punishable, by the practice of the rural Court, if he took anything from it without permission. The wages earned by a woman in summer, when she worked in the field alongside of her husband, belonged to the household: but winter earnings went into the "woman's box." Englehardt got the women on his side over the flax cultivation, because the kneading or stripping of the product to extract the fibre was done after St. Philip's Day, in the winter. One of the factors of the Bolshevik success in collectivisation is similar. It secures a separate dividend to the woman for the work which she does.

The "darkness" of village life was proverbial: a darkness which was more than ignorance, for it included a mass of false knowledge. It was worse, of course, in the women: for the woman's path was "from stove to threshold": she came into contact with no outside experiences, except the gossip of her kind. We see her at her darkest in that horrifying tragedy of peasant life, Count Tolstoi's *Power of Darkness*. The man murderer in that drama can have the consciousness of sin, and can repent. The women show an animal-like unawareness of wrong: but a skill in planning and executing it which no animal could possess. This was one of the unintended revenges which woman took, upon man and his offspring, for domestic slavery and brutal treatment. She became a citadel of darkness in his household, and made a prison for her captor.

❀   ❀   ❀

What did the Church do for the peasant? The Black Clergy, who filled all the important posts in the hierarchy, hardly touched the village. But every village, that is to say every Church-village, for villages within a radius of a dozen miles or more were grouped round a settlement having a Church, had its married parish priest. At some time in the past he had been an elected functionary, and there was a traditional memory of his status as a servant of the Mir. Once by law a member of a hereditary class, he continued for long to be in practice the successor of his father or his father-in-law in "the living." There was normally no salary, the State's subvention for priests' pay being mainly expended *in partibus infidelium*, or among those whom the law recognised as unorthodox. He lived on the land allotted by the Mir, and Englehardt tells us he was often a very good farmer and a "knowledgeable" man. For the rest, he received fees for his spiritual ministrations, and there was notoriously much bargaining over these. He was weak in the article of preaching, and did not make a great success of the pedagogic function which began to be thrust upon him by the State in the latter part of the period which we are considering. He was not quite a representative of civilisation in the village, and yet his ways were a little superior to those of the peasants about him. His reputation, if we are to believe the proverbial philosophy of the people, included greed (be it remembered that he was very poor) and drunkenness (life was hard and dull). Gleb Uspensky perpetrates the somewhat cruel epigram that the priest is wanted, as the postmaster is wanted, drunk or sober, to send off the letters. In the period of repression which began after the murder of Alexander II, he was used for police purposes, to report political secrets discovered under the seal of confession, and to watch the schoolmaster of the rural Council school. But the ecclesiastical seminaries were themselves hotbeds of revolution, and the poverty of theological students and of priests fomented discontent in the class. Stalin was a student in the Tiflis seminary in the middle of the nineties. The village priests were open to bribes, and often attested, for a consideration, the participation in the sacred rites of persons who neglected them or belonged to other confessions. As to their cost to the people, one of the few budgets which we possess shows us the middling peasant of the Black-Earth zone, about the turn of the century, paying six per cent of his income in Church charges.

The same authority who gives this budget says that the children are rapidly infected with freedom of thought and do not take the priest's denunciation of the wrath to come very seriously.

The contribution made by the village priest to peasant civilisation was not, on the whole, a great one: and he did not hold very high the banner of the Church. But he was very human, and very like his flock; perhaps a little better; and he dealt humanly and not oppressively, very rarely refusing the consolations of the Church to the really poor. A little sin makes for the virtue of humility, and perhaps for that of charity too: and a little sin was quite common among the parish clergy.

*   *   *

A great reform is often followed by a tendency to rest upon the reputation of what has been achieved. After the Emancipation and the accompanying reforms, the conscience of statesmen was not entirely asleep over the backwardness and poverty of nine-tenths of the population: but neither was it entirely awake, or at least not awake till mischief had already been done. In 1880 the repeal of the Salt Tax, and two years later that of the Poll Tax, were important measures of fiscal relief. Soon after, the Peasant Bank was established to facilitate purchase of additional land, and the more enterprising and thrifty of the peasants benefited greatly by the opportunity, though, for the mass, this meant only the growth of inequality in the village. The remarkable growth of internal colonisation in Russia attracted the notice of foreign observers. Nicolas II himself intervened to support emigration to Siberia. But the great developments there fall outside of the period of the present chapter. In 1893 a special Ministry of Agriculture was set up. It had a miserably inadequate budget: but Russia was not the only country slow to recognise agriculture's needs and opportunities. Up to 1897 agricultural cooperation, which at a later date extended itself very widely, was suspected by the Russian State of a dangerous political tendency: but a start had been made with it before the Revolution of 1905. If industrial development was the remedy for agricultural poverty, as the historian of Agriculture before the Revolution says it was, Count Witte's work during the eleven years of his administration of finance laid a solid foundation for agricultural prosperity. Not only the material, but also the moral and civil disabilities of the peasant began at this time to receive the attention of the more far-seeing: and, in 1898, Witte, then at the zenith of his career, addressed to Nicolas II a letter in which he recounted the grievances of the class. His list included corporal punishment, arbitrary taxation by the Mir, arbitrary restrictions on leaving the home-village, the entire absence of legal definition of rights and liabilities, and even of the laws of peasant inheritance, and oppression by the Land-Captains and other officials. It was only for those included in the legal category of peasant that these grievances had their full significance though arbitrary, and extraordinary, laws existed for the whole population.

The Rural Councils established by Alexander II, or, more correctly, some of them, were zealous in their attempts—sometimes thwarted by the State—to ameliorate the lot of the peasant. Those of the Moscow province busied themselves with the encouragement of the cultivation of grasses, a fundamental need of an agriculture dependent on cattle. An expert who had distinguished himself by his success with clover found himself in prison. We are not told why, but, recalling some of the things which have happened to the experts and the "intelligents" of a later and less orthodox epoch, we may be pardoned for thinking that we can guess. The State, then as now, is a jealous State: and it changes less than some suppose.

❋   ❋   ❋

We may now sum up some of the reasons of the peasant discontent, which expressed itself in ever-present rumours of an impending redistribution of land by the Tsar, before it took violent form. There was an actual shortage of land in part of the Black-Earth zone: in all parts there were many peasants with non-economic holdings or with no land. Over large areas the landlords seemed to have abdicated all responsibilities for the land except the collection of its rents. The unbalanced holding, deficient in pasture or in hayfields for cattle, was, to the deficit zone, what the smallness of arable holdings was to the surplus zone, a means of reducing the amount of fruitful labour which the peasant could expend on his land. The yield of the land, owing to general economic conditions, among which was the still backward though advancing state of industry, was so low that an average holding was insufficient to keep a family in well-being. Rural unemployment and under-employment, except in the neighbourhood of the manufacturing centres, were rife: though excessive work, at busy seasons, was usual owing to the scanty supply of animals and improved implements. Indebtedness was widespread. There was no capital for improved methods, except at the command of the squires and a minority of prosperous peasants. There were few centres of demand for any variety of local products, outside of the market for cereals. Up to the time of the remission of the Redemption dues in 1905, the imposts on the peasant were heavy, and the method of collecting them was harsh and inelastic, varied by spasms of wholesale remission at coronations and the birth of heirs. Not least important, though not most frequently mentioned, were the outrages upon human dignity which the legal and extra-legal status of the peasantry continued to tolerate. The law for the peasant was the will of the official and of the landlord.

Such were the grievances which, taking the compendious form of a demand for more land (very much as the early English peasants asked for "the Laws of King Alfred"), set in motion the elemental force which was to shake and finally overthrow the fabric of Tsarism. That force might have exhausted itself, as formerly in the rebellions of Stenka Razin and Emilian Pugachev, in a temporary orgy of ill-directed destruction, if it had not been supplemented and guided by another, far weaker, but also far better organised, than itself. The town-workman, himself part peasant, or at most a townsman of not more than a couple of generations' standing, is now on the point of emerging as the leader of the malcontent peasantry; and the intellectuals have for some time been doing for the peasants a better thing than idolising him: they have been attempting to understand.

❊   ❊   ❊

An unsurpassed description of peasant types in the mid-nineteenth century has been given us by Turgeniev in his "Hor and Kalinich," first published in 1847. The present author's translation follows in the next chapter.

Chapter III

HOR AND KALINICH

(Translated from I. S. Turgeniev: first published in the Contemporary, St. Petersburg, 1847.)

Anyone who has travelled between the two provinces must have been struck by the difference of man in Orel and Kaluga.* The peasant of Orel is of low stature, round-shouldered, sullen, downward-looking, lives in a tumbledown hut of poplar wood, does personal service to his squire, does no trading, eats poorly, wears birch-bark sandals. The Kaluga peasant commutes his service for cash, lives in a spacious cottage of pine, is tall, has a bold and jolly look and a clean, bright face, deals in greases and tar, and wears boots on holidays. In the eastern part of Orel the village generally lies among cleared fields, near a ravine which has been somehow turned into a dirty pond. Except a few bushes which serve every purpose, and two or three gaunt birches, you won't see a tree for a mile round; cottage clings close to cottage; the roofs are thatched with rotting straw. The Kaluga village, on the contrary, is generally surrounded by wood; the cottages stand free and plumb, roofed with scantlings; the doors close tight, the fence at the back has no gaps and is not tumbling outwards and does not invite each passing sow to enter. The sportsman too does better in the Kaluga province. In Orel the last woods and large thickets disappeared five years ago, and the swamps don't survive even in memory. In Kaluga the woodlands stretch for hundreds, the swamps for dozens, of miles; that noble bird the woodcock has not perished, the generous snipe is frequent, and the busy partridge rejoices and startles gunman and dog with his whirring flight.

When shooting in the Kaluga province, I met and made friends with a petty squire of that neighbourhood, Polutikin, a mighty sportsman, and, by consequence, a good fellow. True, he had some weaknesses; for instance, he courted all the heiresses of the province, and, when he was turned down, confided his sorrows to all friends and acquaintances, and continued to send to the parents of the girls presents of sour peaches and other fresh garden produce; he loved to re-

* This is the country over which Germans and Russians were fighting in November, 1941, and January, 1942.

peat one and the same anecdote, which pleased *him*, but failed to raise a laugh in anyone else; he admired bad novels; he stuttered; he called his dog *Astronomer*; he said *"be out"* instead of *"but"*; and he had a French chef, whose art and mystery, according to the Russian cook, consisted in changing the natural flavour of every food: from this artist's hands, meat was like fish, fish was like mushrooms, macaroni was like gunpowder; not one carrot entered the soup except in the form of a rhombus or a trapezium. But, save for these few and trifling defects, Polutikin was, as already stated, a capital fellow.

On the first day of my acquaintance with him, Polutikin invited me to spend the night.

"It is five miles to my place," he added: "too far to walk. We'll drop in first on Hor." (The reader will permit me not to reproduce his stutter.)

"Who is Hor?"

"He's my peasant: quite near here."

We walked off. In a cultivated clearing in a wood was the solitary farmhouse of Hor. It consisted of some frame-houses of fir, connected by fences; in front of the principal building there was a verandah supported by thin props. We entered. A twenty-year-old lad, tall and handsome, met us.

"Hullo, Fedya! Is Hor at home?" asked Mr. Polutikin.

"No, Hor has gone to town," replied the lad, showing a row of snow-white teeth: "shall we harness the waggon for you?"

"Yes, my boy, the waggon: and bring us some *kvas*."

We went in. Not a single daub was stuck on the clean beams of the walls; in the corner, before a heavy icon in a silver frame, a lamp glimmered; the limewood table was freshly scoured and scrubbed; between the beams and on the window-posts no active cockroach scurried, no pensive spider hid. The young man soon appeared with a great white crock filled with good *kvas*, with a huge lump of wheaten bread and a dozen salted cucumbers in a wooden basin. He set all these provisions on the table, leaned against the door, and looked at us with a smile. We hadn't finished our luncheon when the waggon rattled into the porch. We went out. A fifteen-year-old boy, curly haired and rosy cheeked, sat in the driver's place and held with difficulty a well-fed piebald colt. Six young giants stood around the waggon, the images of one another and of Fedya.

"All Hor's children," remarked Polutikin.

"All Hor's," chimed Fedya, who had come out behind us to the porch: "and these are not all: there's Potep in the wood, and Sidor has

gone with old Hor to town. Look out, now, Vasya," he added, turning
to the driver. "Go quick: thou'rt driving gentlefolk. But carefully over
the ruts, or thou'llt spoil the cart and upset the gentry's insides."

The rest of Hor's youngsters burst out laughing at Fedya's sally.

"Put Astronomer in!" said Mr. Polutikin with a majestic air.

Fedya, looking as though he liked the job, lifted into the air the
constrainedly grinning dog, and put him at the bottom of the waggon.
Vasya gave the horse the rein, and we were off.

"There's my counting-house," said Mr. Polutikin suddenly, pointing to a little low building. "Would you like to see it?"

"Yes, please."

"It's empty now," said he, getting down: "but you may as well see
everything."

The counting-house consisted of two empty rooms. The watchman,
a bent old man, ran up from the yard.

"Good-day to you, Minyaich," said Mr. Polutikin. "Bring us some
water."

The bent old man disappeared and returned with a bottle of water
and two glasses.

"Taste it," said Polutikin to me. "It's good spring water."

We drank a glass apiece, while the old man bowed to us down to
his waist.

"Now, I think we can be off," said my new acquaintance. "At this
counting-house I sold eleven acres of woodland to the merchant
Allelyuev for a good price."

We took our seats, and in half an hour entered the yard of the
Squire's house.

"Tell me, please," I questioned Polutikin after supper, "why this
Hor of yours lives apart from all your other peasants."

"I'll tell you why. He's got a head on his shoulders. Twenty-five
years ago his cottage was burned down. He comes to my deceased
father and he says: 'Nikolai Kuzmich, allow me to settle in your wood
on the marsh. I'll pay you a good commutation fee.' 'Why dost thou
want to settle on the marsh?' 'It suits me, only be so good as to set me
to no work, but fix the fee that suits you.' 'Fifty roubles a year.' 'As
you please, sir,' 'And no arrears, mind.' 'Certainly, no arrears.' . . .
And so he settled on the marsh. From that day they called him Hor
(Weasel)."

"And he got rich?" I asked.

"Got rich. Now he pays me a hundred silver roubles: and I'll make
it more, perhaps. I've said to him more than once: 'Buy thyself off,

Hor!' But he, the brute, assures me that he hasn't the money. . . .
A likely story. . . ."

Next day, directly after morning tea, we went out shooting. Passing
through a village, Mr. Polutikin told the driver to stop at a little low
cottage and cried sonorously: "Kalinich."

"Ready, master, ready," said a voice from the yard. "I am fastening
my sandal."

We went on at a foot's pace.

Beyond the village we were overtaken by a man of forty years of age,
tall, thin, with a little head carried rather to one side. This was Kalinich. His good-tempered, swarthy face, marked here and there with
pock-marks, pleased me at the first glimpse. Kalinich, as I afterwards
learned, went shooting every day with the Squire, carried his bag and
sometimes his gun too, watched where the bird came down, brought
water, picked strawberries, made shelters, ran behind the carriage;
without him Mr. Polutikin could not stir a step.

Kalinich was a man with the merriest, pleasantest ways, forever hum-
ming under his breath, carelessly glancing all about him, talking a
little through his nose, smiling and wrinkling up his bright blue eyes,
and often putting his hand to his scanty, wedge-shaped beard. He
walked, not fast, but with long strides, leaning slightly on a long, thin
stick. During the day he spoke to me more than once; was helpful to
me without servility, but he looked after the Squire like a child. When
the unbearable heat of noontide forced us to seek shelter, he took us
to his bee-hives in the very depths of the wood. Kalinich opened a little
hut for us, hung with bundles of dry, sweet-smelling grasses, made us
lie down on the fresh hay, put on his own head a sort of bag of netting,
took a knife, lit a splinter, and went out to a hive to cut us some honey-
comb. After a sup of clear, warm honey, we drank some spring water,
and went off to sleep to the monotonous buzzing of the bees and the
prattling whisper of the leaves. A light breath of wind awoke me. . . .
I opened my eyes and saw Kalinich: he was sitting on the threshold
of the half-opened door and carving a wooden spoon. I looked long
with admiration at his face, benignant and clear, like an evening sky.
Mr. Polutikin also awoke. We did not at once get up. It was pleasant,
after the long walk and the deep sleep, to lie moveless on the hay; the
body relaxes and yields to weariness, the face glows with a slight
warmth, a sweet drowsiness seals the eyes. At last we got up and went
out to tramp till evening.

At supper I talked again about Hor and Kalinich.

"Kalinich is a good peasant," said Mr. Polutikin: "a zealous and a

serviceable one, but he can't keep his farm in order. I distract him
from it. He goes shooting with me every day. . . . What sort of farming is that?—judge for yourself."

I agreed with him, and we lay down to sleep.

Next day Mr. Polutikin had to go to town on business with his
neighbour, Pichukov. Pichukov had trespassed on his land and slapped
his serf woman. I went shooting alone, and returned at evening to Hor's.
An old man met me on the threshold, bald, short of stature, broad-
shouldered and stout; Hor himself. I looked at him with curiosity.
The shape of his face recalled Socrates: the same high, lumpy brow,
the same little eyes, the same snub nose. We entered the cottage
together. My friend, Fedya, brought me milk and black bread. Hor sat
on a bench, and, quietly smoothing his curly beard, entered into talk
with me. It seemed that he was conscious of his dignity; he spoke and
moved slowly and smiled occasionally behind his long moustaches.
We talked of the sowing and the harvest and of the peasant life. He
said "yes" to it all; but presently I had an uneasy sense that I was not
getting home to him with my talk. It sounded somehow unnatural.
Hor expressed himself indirectly sometimes, probably from caution.
Here's a bit of our talk.

"Tell me, Hor," said I. "Why dost not buy thyself off from thy
gentleman?"

"Why should I buy myself off? Now I know my gentleman, and I
know my fee. . . . He's a good gentleman."

"It's better to be free," said I.

Hor looked at me sideways. "That's certain," said he.

"Well, why dost not buy thyself off?"

Hor cocked his head a little. "What wouldst thou have me pay with,
sir?"

"Oh, come. I can't believe that."

"If Hor became one of the free folk," he continued under his breath,
as if to himself, "every man with a shaven face would be a bigger man
than Hor."

"Then shave thy beard too."

"What's a beard?" said Hor. "A beard is grass; one can mow it."

"Well, what then?"

"Seems as though Hor would just be one of the merchants. The
merchants do well enough with their beards."

"Well, isn't buying and selling thy job too?" I asked.

"We deal in a small way in grease and tar. Shall I bid harness the
waggon, sir?"

You've got a tight hold on your tongue and keep your thoughts to yourself, thought I. "No," said I, aloud. "I don't need the waggon. I shall be round thy farm tomorrow, and I'll spend the night in thy hay-barn, please."

"Welcome to thee. But will it be quiet for thee in the barn? I'll tell the women to make a bed and lay a pillow. Ho, women!" he cried, getting up from his place. "Here, women. Go with them, Fedya. Truly women are silly things."

A quarter of an hour after, Fedya with a lantern led me to the barn. I threw myself on the sweet-smelling hay, the dog rolled himself up at my feet. Fedya wished me good night, the door creaked and slammed. For a long time I could not sleep. A cow came to the door and breathed loudly twice; the dog growled at her with a sense of decorum; a sow passed, grunting pensively; a horse somewhere near began to munch hay and whinny. . . . At last I nodded.

Fedya woke me at dawn. I liked the gallant lad; and so far as I could see he was a favourite with old Hor too. They chaffed one another in a friendly way. The old man came out to meet me. Whether because I had spent the night with him or for some other reason, Hor behaved more friendly to me than yesterday.

"The samovar is ready for thee," said he with a smile. "Let's have tea."

We sat round the table. A wholesome woman, one of the daughters-in-law, brought a crock of milk. All his sons entered the cottage in turn.

"What a well-grown lot!" said I to the old man.

"Yes," said he, sucking a tiny lump of sugar. "They've no cause to complain of me or my old woman."

"And do they all live with thee?"

"All. They all wish it, so they live with us."

"And they are all married?"

"There's one young scamp won't marry," he replied, pointing to Fedya, who was leaning against the door. "Vaska is young yet. He can wait."

"Why should I marry?" objected Fedya. "I'm all right as I am. What should I want a wife for? To squabble with her, is it?"

"Thou—I know thee! Wearest silver rings. . . . Runnest after the house-wenches. Ha' done with thy impudence!" continued the old man, mimicking the chamber-maids. "I know thee for a whiteheaded lazy-bones that thou art!"

"What good is there in a woman?"

"A woman is a woman-worker," said Hor with dignity. "A woman is servant to a peasant man."

"And what do I want with a woman-worker?"

"Aha, wouldst fain rake out the hot ash with another's hands? We know thy sort."

"Then, find a wife for me, if it be so. Aha! Why dost thou say nought?"

"Enough, enough, thou jester. Now we're disturbing the gentleman. I'll marry thee, maybe. Don't be vexed, sir. Thou seest, 'tis a young child. I can't get sense into his head yet."

Fedya shook his head. . . .

"Is Hor at home?" I recognized the voice at the door; and Kalinich came in with a handful of wild strawberries which he had picked for his friend Hor. The old man greeted him genially. I looked with surprise at Kalinich. I admit I did not expect such delicacy from a peasant.

That day I went shooting four hours later than usual, and spent the next three days with Hor. I was taken up with my new acquaintances. I do not know how I earned their confidence, but they talked to me now without constraint. I was glad to listen to them and observe them. Hor was positive, practical, a business head, a rationalist; Kalinich, on the other hand, was one of the idealists, of the romantics, of the enthusiasts and the dreamers. Hor understood reality, made a place for himself, saved a bit, got on with the Squire and the other powers; Kalinich wore birch-bark sandals, and rubbed along anyhow. Hor fathered a large family, obedient and united; Kalinich had a wife once, whom he was afraid of, and never had a child. Hor looked askance at Mr. Polutikin; Kalinich venerated his master. Hor liked Kalinich and patronised him. Kalinich liked and respected Hor. Hor said little, smiled and talked to himself; Kalinich expressed himself with warmth, but did not talk your head off like a bold factory lad . . . But Kalinich was gifted with excellences which Hor himself recognised: for instance, he charmed away giddiness, hysterics, and the horrors; drove away worms; bees yielded themselves to him: he had a light hand. I was there when Hor asked him to lead a new-bought horse into the stable, and Kalinich with unassuming assurance did as the old sceptic asked. Kalinich stood nearer to nature; Hor to men and society. Kalinich did not like argument, and believed all blindly; Hor rose to the ironical view of life. He saw and knew much, and I learned much from him. For instance, I learned from his stories that every summer before hay-cutting time there appears in the villages a little cart of a particular appearance. In it sits a man in a caftan and sells scythes. For cash he charges a rouble and twenty-five copecks; for paper a rouble and a half; for credit three roubles of paper and one of silver. Two or three weeks later he appears again and asks for his money. The peasant has just cut his oats, and probably has the money to pay; he goes into the liquor-shop with the merchant and settles with him there. Some landlords had the idea of buying scythes for cash and selling them on credit to the peasant for the same price, but the peasants didn't like it and turned shy; they were deprived of the pleasure of tapping the scythe, listening to the sound, turning it over, and asking the rogue of a townee a dozen times: "Now, lad, isn't there something wrong with this scythe?"

The same game is played at the buying of sickles, with this difference only, that the women take part and sometimes worry the dealer into giving them a slap for their own good. But the thing which gives the women most to do is this. The suppliers of material to the paper factories entrust the buying of rags of a particular kind to men who, in some parts, are called *eagles*. An *eagle* gets a couple of hundreds of roubles from the merchant, and sallies out for his quarry. But, in contrast to the noble bird from whom he got his name, he does not attack openly and boldly, he has recourse to stratagem and cunning. He leaves his cart somewhere in the bushes round the village, and himself goes by back ways, like a casual arrival or a lounger. The women scent his approach and steal out to meet him. The deal is made in high haste. For a few coppers, the woman gives to the *eagle* not only all her useless rags, but often also her husband's shirt and her own petticoat. Latterly the women have found it profitable to steal from themselves and dispose in this way of the hemp crop and even their bits of finery, which adds a great deal to the *eagle's* business. The peasants, in their turn, wake up to the job, and, on the least suspicion, the remotest whisper, of the *eagle's* appearance, set to work to get their own back and be even with their wives. And is it not a real challenge? It is their business to sell the hemp—and they do sell it—but not in town, for that means a long tramp; but to travelling dealers, who, having no scales, reckon a *pud* as forty handfuls—and you know what sort of a handful and what sort of a palm a Russian has, particularly when he puts his heart in it!

Such stories I—an innocent creature and a "furriner" (as our Orel people say)—heard galore. But Hor did not only tell me much, he also asked many questions. He learned that I had been abroad, and his inquisitiveness was excited. Kalinich was not backward in his curiosity, but he was more interested by descriptions of nature, of hills, of waterfalls, of extraordinary buildings, of great cities. Hor was taken up with questions of administration and of state. He went over every point in order:

"Now do they do this as we do, or in another way? Tell me sir, yes?"

"O Lord, thy will be done!" cried Kalinich when I was speaking; Hor was silent, knitted his thick eyebrows, and only occasionally observed:

"Seems like this wouldn't work with us, but that other is good, and that is the way to keep things straight."

I cannot repeat all his questions; it's not worth it; but from our conversation I was convinced of one thing, which my readers would probably never suspect; that Peter the Great was *par excellence* a Russian, Russian particularly in his reforms. The Russian is so convinced of his own strength and power that he is ready to risk a fall, he cares little for his past and looks boldly forward. He likes what is good; give him what is reasonable, he does not mind where it comes from. His good sense makes easy fun of the dry-as-dust German reasoning; but Germans, says Hor, are clever people, and he is ready to learn a bit from them too. Thanks to his exceptional position, to his practical independence, Hor talked to me of much which, as the peasants say, you wouldn't lift out of another man with a lever, or grind out of him with a millstone. He thoroughly understood how the land lay. Talking to Hor, I heard for the first time the plain, wise speech of the Russian peasant. His ideas were broad enough in his own way, but he could not read; Kalinich knew how to read.

"This lazy fellow knows his books," said Hor, "and he never lost his bees."

"Did you teach your children to read?"

Hor was silent for a moment. "Fedya knows how."

"And the others?"

"The others don't know."

"Why is that?"

The old man did not reply and changed the conversation. But however wise he was, he had his prejudices and his fixed ideas. For instance, he despised women from the bottom of his heart, and in merry moments laughed at and mocked them. His wife, old and cross, never left the stove, and constantly grumbled and scolded; the sons paid no attention to her, but she kept the daughters-in-law in the fear of God. Not for nothing does the mother-in-law sing in the Russian ballad: "What sort of a son art thou, what sort of a father . . . that beatest not the wife, that beatest not the young one?"

I once thought to intercede for the daughters-in-law and tried to awaken Hor's sympathy; but he quietly stopped me, saying:

"Thou art pleased to trouble thyself with trifles; let the women squabble. . . . Why separate them? It makes things worse. It's not worth soiling thy fingers."

Sometimes the cross old thing left the stove, called the housedog from the passage, saying: "Come here, dog," and brought the poker down on its thin back; or stood under the eaves and scolded at all who passed, as Hor expressed it. But she was afraid of her husband, and went back to the stove when he ordered her.

It was particularly interesting to hear the dispute between Kalinich and Hor when they spoke of Mr. Polutikin.

"Now don't thou say anything against him," said Kalinich.

"Why doesn't he give thee a pair of boots?" Hor objected.

"Boots! What would I do with boots? I'm a peasant."

"Well, am I not a peasant too?"

With this word Hor raised his foot and showed to Kalinich a boot cut out of belly leather.

"Art thou and I of a piece?" replied Kalinich.

"He might at least have given thee enough for sandals. Surely, thou goest shooting with him; and a pair of sandals is gone in a day."

"He gives me enough for sandals."

"Yes, last year he granted thee a ten-copeck piece."

Kalinich turned away vexed, and Hor burst into a laugh so that his little eyes disappeared completely.

Kalinich sang sweetly and played on the balalaika. Hor listened, listened, suddenly turned his head on one side and began to hum in a doleful voice. He particularly liked the song: "Thou art my fate, my fate." Fedya never missed a chance of chaffing his father.

"What are thou grieving for, old man?"

Hor rested his cheek on his arm, closed his eyes, and continued to regret his fate. . . . But at another time not a man was more practical than he; he was perpetually at some job: mending the cart, propping up the fence, looking after the harness. But he did not keep things particularly clean, and to my remarks he once replied that it was "necessary for a cottage to smell of life."

"Just look," said I, "how clean it is at Kalinich's hives."

"The bees would not put up with this," he sighed.

"Hast thou an estate of thine own?" he once asked me.

"Yes."

"Far from here?"

"A hundred versts."

"thou live on thy estate, sir?"

"Ye...

"But the.... chief pleasure?"

"I admit that ... is."

"That's good, sir. Shoot woodcocks for thy health and change thy steward often."

In the evening of the fourth day Mr. Polutikin sent for me. I was sorry to part with the old man. I got into the waggon with Kalinich.

"Good-by, Hor; good health to thee," said I. "Good-bye, Fedya."

"Good-bye; don't forget us."

We started off. The sunset glow began to redden.

"It will be fine weather tomorrow," said I, looking at the bright sky.

"No, there will be rain," objected Kalinich; "the ducks are splashing, and the grass smells too strong."

We went into the wood. Kalinich hummed under his breath, bumping on the driver's seat, and gazed, gazed, on the red glow.

Next day I left the hospitable roof of Mr. Polutikin.

Chapter IV

THE ORTHODOX CHURCH AND THE
SLAVOPHILS

"For where two or three are gathered together in My name,
there am I in the midst of them."

Gospel according to St. Matthew.

"The soul of Orthodoxy is *sobornost*. . . . The Church, as
truth, is not given to individuals, but to a unity in love and
faith it reveals itself."

Father Sergius Bulgakov, *The Orthodox Church.*

"Simple peasants feel that their sufferings are, in part, an
expiation of the universal sin, and they must bear it, as Christ
bore His cross, to redeem all humanity . . . That does not
prevent them from being brutal, lazy, liars, thieves, carnal,
incestuous. . . ."

A Russian lady, quoted by M. Maurice Paléologue.

"The holy words of the Scripture, in which we heard the
voice of the Seven Thunders, sounded to them like catechism
texts learned by heart."

D. S. Merezhkovsky, describing a meeting between
clerics and laymen in 1902.

I offer no apology for the space which I shall devote to the Orthodox
Church. In its strength it was a fundamental element in the life of the
Russian people. It was the builder of the Moscow realm. In its weakness we must seek the explanation of the facility with which—to all
appearance—a people believed to be instinctively religious abandoned
religion when the rulers ceased to support it. Both in its strength and
in its weakness it has established habits of mind which profoundly
affect the outlook and the actions of men and women who have
repudiated all Religion, and are indignant at every suggestion that it
continues to survive in them. It is in the history of the Orthodox
Church and of its downfall, and of the revival of Orthodox thought
in the twentieth century, that we must seek for light upon the ques-

tion whether Religion is actually disappearing from Russia, or destined to reappear in new forms.

All the world-religions, and Christianity most of all, have taken different forms among different peoples and at different times, as emphasis happened to be laid upon one or another group of doctrines or practices. The variation of emphasis often depended upon profound differences of mental habit antecedent to Christianity. It has always issued in differences of what we call national character. It is not the only cause of such differences, but it is a potent one: and we shall be on the track of at least some distinguishing qualities of the Russian people if we are able to find the characteristic features of their religion.

To Eastern Orthodoxy the spirit in Man is a gift from outside, illuminating his darkness and creating in him the possibility of deification. But it is not a gift to the individual: it is a gift to all the faithful, a gift to the congregation, whether marked off by the acceptance of the sacraments or otherwise. It illuminates, and therefore it conveys the knowledge of Truth. The consensus of the congregation becomes the criterion of Truth. In virtue of the spirit which has been communicated to them, they reflect the ideas which are laid up, as patterns, in heaven. Since the faithful are not only the living faithful, but also the dead, the consensus tends to identify itself with tradition. Thus conceived, it is a strongly conservative influence. But it is not always thus conceived. It has been interpreted, again, as the consensus of the Bishops, as representatives of the whole body of the faithful, and in this form explains the authority attaching to the decisions of the early Councils of the Church. But those are not wanting who define the Councils as declaratory organs, rather than authoritative interpreters: and the claim to the rights of the laity, as those upon whom, equally with the apostles, the spirit descends at Pentecost, has been very vigorously asserted at different epochs of Russian Church history.

The most significant feature in the gift of the spirit as conceived by Orthodox thought, and the one which has most affected character and outlook, is that it is an undivided and indivisible whole, present in the council or the congregation. There is no room here for individual differences of opinion. Truth, and along with truth, love, reside in the brethren: not in any of them taken separately. For the individual, the gift means will-less submission. By himself he is nothing, and, in the words of a character of Dostoievsky's, all are responsible for all. The spirit is one, a part of the Godhead communicated by the Word: and there is no distribution of it into a number of separate inspirations.

Nor does it express itself in the agreement of a majority, but only in the agreement of all. The most that the individual can do is to interpret in humility: and to submit.

More than this. The truth, which is the reflection of a pattern laid up in heaven and made visible by the gift of the spirit, is an integral whole. It is one with righteousness. There can be no valid distinction between spiritual and temporal. The claim is upon the whole of life: by contrast with that rationalistic fragmentariness which is characteristic of the West. If the Russian Church seemed to have travelled away from this conception, by the nineteenth- and twentieth-century claim of some of its members for the separation of Church and State, the old totalitarian integrality has reappeared in the Communist demand for the whole of man's allegiance: a combination in a new form of the union of spiritual and temporal.

How much the Russian character owes to the conception of the undivided gift of the spirit to the congregation, I cannot attempt here to determine. Nothing less than a whole history would suffice. One obvious consequence is the idea of *sobornost*, of which I have more to say presently. Another, I think, is the worship of the plain folk, that "going to the people," as one would go to an oracle, to discover the truth which is in its keeping. Another is the merging of the individual in the mass, and the weakness of the individual will. Yet another is that absoluteness in Russian thought which brooks no compromise. He that is not with them is against them. To differ with the brotherhood—*even when the brotherhood has taken the form of the Party*—is to pass away into outer darkness, isolated both from truth and love. There are patterns laid up in heaven, to which the life of the congregation must conform, till it issues in the transfiguration of the world. It was for this that the transcendent and unapproachable Godhead sent His Word to dwell among men. Not atonement, the satisfaction of the justice of God, but love, seems to be the authentic note of this Eastern Christianity.

One of the patterns laid up for realisation was—from the fifteenth century onwards—the idea of the Third Rome: of a Messianic mission of the Russian people. Holy Russia was a God-bearer. The Church of Constantinople—so it seemed—had apostatised when, at the Council of Florence, its representatives accepted reunion with the West under the supremacy of the Pope, and had been punished by the Turkish conquest. Ivan III of Moscow married the niece of the last Emperor of Constantinople, became the champion of the Orthodox Church, and claimed the new title of Sovereign of All Russia. As the mystical

successor of Constantine, the ruler of Moscow became identified with
the Messianic mission of his people. He must be absolute because the
spirit is integral. There was unity of Church and State, because the
conception of a separation between the two had never come into
existence. We learn from Nicolas Berdyaev that Ivan IV thought it
part of a Tsar's duties to save souls. At least, it was his task to create
and maintain an Orthodox society in which souls could be saved, or
man raised to participation in divinity. A great icon, now in the Tretiakov gallery at Moscow, representing the triumph of Ivan the Terrible
over the Tartars at Kazan in 1552, shows us the sixteenth-century conception of the Orthodox Tsars. Above, in the right-hand corner, is a
burning city. Opposite, on the left, is a representation of holy Moscow,
surmounted by the Mother of God and the Divine Child. From right
to left, across the picture, from burning Kazan towards Moscow,
marches an army led by a young Commander. In front of him rides the
Archangel Michael: behind him the Emperor Constantine. In the
army are the Saints Vladimir, Boris, and Gleb. Above and below the
earthly army is the Heavenly Host, surrounding and protecting the
Orthodox warriors. The young Commander is the Tsar Ivan: his succession from the Emperor Constantine, and his alliance with Heaven,
are symbolised by the scheme of the picture. To the theme of victory
is added that of the inheritance of power, and the sanctity of the office
of Tsar. It is the Third Rome triumphant, with its ruler: in whom the
spiritual and temporal powers are indistinguishable, because they have
never been conceived as separate entities.

The Churchmen were the servants of the Tsars. When they lifted
up their voices against tyranny, and they sometimes risked and incurred the pains of martyrdom in doing so, it was as Elisha spoke to
Ahab, as a dutiful servant, impelled by conscience or the spirit, speaks
to an erring master, not as exercising the spiritual authority of a dominant Church. Monks, especially in the north and east, played a civilising and even a political part. Going out into the wilderness they
founded and fortified monasteries which became centres of population and trade, served as outposts of Russian nationality, and sometimes as places of refuge for Russian princes. The Holy Sergei blessed
the expedition of Dimitry of the Don against the Tartars, and so inspired in the army the hope which won the victory. Many monasteries
were founded in the fourteenth century in the period of the Black
Death, and one of these was the famous Troitsa Lavra, north of Moscow, a camp and a fortress as well as a shrine. But these movements
were inspired rather by the nomadism which has been part of the

Russian nature, or by the desire to escape from the world, than by any challenge to the authority of Russian rulers.

There was a period, in the seventeenth century, when it might have seemed that the Russian Church was about to enter upon a more ambitious rôle. Ivan the Terrible had destroyed his own line, anarchy loosed the bonds of the Russian State, the secular enemy, the Pole, established himself in Moscow. The Church inspired the armies of the Russian people which drove out the enemy, and the picture of the Redeemer, which long hung over the Saviour's Gate of the Moscow Kremlin, was carried at their head. Philaret Romanov, then Patriarch of the Russian Orthodox Church, might, it would seem, at that time have established a temporal power. But he claimed no power for the Church. His minor son Michael was elected Tsar, and the relations between the Patriarch father and the Tsar son became the Church's traditional ideal of the relations between Church and State: the secular power being with the son, while honour, reverence, and the obedience of affection, were given to the father.

Peter the Great handled the Church as he handled most other things, like a rough master. It was a part of his policy with secular ministries to put them into commission: and the replacement of the Patriarch by a Holy Synod headed by a lay Procurator had nothing extraordinary about it, if once we take it for granted that there is no valid distinction between temporal and spiritual. Peter's successors were as little troubled as he, by any doubt of the right to use the Churches, Orthodox and other, as an instrument of temporal aims. But it was in the period of deliberate Russification that this policy became most intimately galling to the non-Orthodox.

There was no Ministry of Cults in Tsarist Russia. Each non-Orthodox confession—if it was recognised—had a governing body of its own, including civil representatives of the State on the analogy of the Holy Synod which governed the Orthodox Church; and the Ministry of the Interior had the final control over all of them. Civil control of the Roman Catholic Church was particularly inimical to the principles of the Papacy. It was so exercised as to limit the supply of priests, to restrict the pastoral visitations of bishops, and to hamper communications with the Vatican. In Poland sermons had to pass the censor before delivery. In the west of the Russian empire, Roman Catholics were not allowed to acquire immovable property, and had great difficulty in obtaining employment in the schools or under the State, and the attempt was made to insist on the use of Russian in the Churches even where the mother-tongue of the congregation was Polish. The non-recognised Confessions were treated worse, for they, according to the theory of the State, were Orthodox who did not discharge their Orthodox duties. The so-called reconciliation of the Uniats with the Orthodox Church in 1874-75 was accompanied by persecution which stopped short only of capital punishment. The aim was to assimilate the nationalities by assimilating the religions, and the possibility that pressure might widen the separation does not appear to have presented itself.

In the Orthodox Church the clergy was divided into black and white: the black, celibate and exclusively eligible for high ecclesiastical office, the white, married, and serving for the most part as parish priests.

In thinking of Orthodox Monasticism we must dismiss from our minds ideas of beneficence, learning and preaching, such as we attribute to the Benedictines, and of statecraft, energy and policy such as we find in the Jesuits, and we must realise that the East has not that rich variety of monastic orders, each created to meet a practical need, which exists in the West. There are no monuments of collective intellectual labour comparable with the "Acts" of the Benedictines. The spirit of Orthodox Monasticism was something quite other than this. Humility and purity of heart are the ideal Orthodox virtues, and it was these which the monks were cultivating.

When the Rev. William Palmer was seeking peace for his troubled conscience in a reconciliation of the Anglican with the Orthodox Church, the Sergievsky monks told him that vermin have a use, to teach one patience. They wondered at the questions put to them by the eager seeker, and especially at his wish to turn some of the monasteries into working and learned communities. In reply they kept on repeating that prayer and holiness have more efficacy than learning or work of any kind. It is precisely what a Tibetan monk might say. The White clergy, they said, were all overburdened with work and families: and the academicians (meaning the higher monastic clergy, whose ecclesiastical education had gone further than that of the monks) were equally taken up with work and instruction. The monasteries, they said, were little thought of by anyone, though they had more than once saved Russia—a reference to the splendid past of institutions such as the Troitsa Lavra. They added that the secular clergy were infected with Liberalism (a dangerous fault in the days of Nicolas I) and that they read Lutheran and other bad books. Their aim was to avoid all contact with bustling Martha, and to sit with Mary at the Master's feet. To this statement of the objects of the Orthodox monks we ought in justice to add that, beside their personal salvation, the monks had in view—when they remembered it—the expiation of the sins of the age. Ideally, at least, the conception that each is responsible for all, and must expiate the sins of all, runs like a golden thread through all Russian religious thought, and sets the nobler spirits to their prayers for all.

In the reign of Alexander III, and under the influence of Konstantin Pobiedonostsev, an attempt was made to extend the functions of the priesthood into lay education, in order to combat the liberalising tendencies of the District Council schools. With a similar political motive, priests were required to disclose secrets of the confessional, where the interests of the State were touched. The Church exercised a judicial authority over ecclesiastics, and had its own prisons in which to carry out its sentences. The ecclesiastical prisons were emptied in the periods of reforms which accompanied the revolution of 1905. We are told that they were soon refilled, and that some of the new occupants were priests who had deserved ill of State and Church by their protests against the capital sentences inflicted by the Field Courts-Martial set up in the reaction. This is not the only instance which we find of parish priests championing the dangerous doctrines of Liberalism, or risking their own livelihood to defend the innocent. There were many cases of interference to protect Jews in the pogroms which disgraced the later days of the Empire. But the higher clergy were not in general concerned with these things. "Serfdom and cruel punishment are not contrary to the spirit of Christianity," said a Bishop, "for physical suffering does not interfere with the salvation of the soul, which is our sole concern."

There was an ecclesiastical Censorship separate from the civil. It was a timidly nervous institution, which let nothing pass to which anyone could possibly object. How it dealt with some of the best and noblest work in theology, even where no heresy was suspected, we shall see when we come to deal with the writings of the lay theologian Khomiakov. It was impossible for him to print anything in Russia, and communications to his address from abroad were intercepted and withheld. So he wrote in French, and published abroad, commenting upon his harassers with a Christian restraint. The Eparchial Consistory, the ecclesiastical Council of the Bishops, had jurisdiction in cases of clergy discipline, and of the marriage and divorce of the laity. Though the Bishops themselves had ordinarily a blameless reputation, these Courts, as well as the ecclesiastical offices through which the business of the Church passed, were commonly reputed corrupt as well as dilatory.

The Orthodox Church had a legal monopoly of conversion, and published official statistics of its achievements. The Rev. Mr. Palmer tells us of a priest who converted two thousand persons in the Aleutian Isles, and of the pectoral cross with which he was decorated for this service.

Nicolas Lyeskov, who satirised Nihilists and Churchmen, radicals and conservatives, alike, and was consequently kept out of his deserved literary fame for more than half a century, has left us a satire on the missionary enterprises of the Church. In his story the interference of the Holy Synod takes the form of a sudden order, due to a change of the policy towards indigenous religions, increasing the number of Buddhist temples and doubling the number of licensed Lamas. The Lamas spread the rumor that the Tsar and the Metropolitan had been converted to Buddhism. The Baptizers come back from the wilds, dirty and in tatters, the civil authorities protect the Lamas, and the people refuse supplies and transport to the discredited servants of Christianity. But—as usual—headquarters speaks with two voices, perhaps with more than two. Pectoral crosses continue to be bestowed upon successful missionaries, and fashionable St. Petersburg society continues to give dances on behalf of mission funds. A young and energetic Bishop starts off on a sledge journey, first with reindeer and afterwards with dogs, to learn how a certain Baptizer achieves his successes in the mission-field, and hears some queer stories from his sledge-driver. It seems that the sledge-driver's brother is a professional convert, and accepts repeated Baptism on behalf of others who have scruples. But enough. The story is extant, and translated into choice English.

The position of the Autocrat as Head of the Church did not give him authority to define or modify dogma. Nothing less than an Oecumenical Council of the Eastern Churches could do so. It was a Council of the Eastern Patriarchs, meeting at Moscow, which degraded the Patriarch Nikon: and the Oecumenical Patriarch had approved of the abolition of the Patriarchate by Peter, and was asked to approve its restoration by the Provisional Government after the March Revolution. But it was not till after the Bolshevik Revolution that anyone in Russia had the enterprise to propose the summoning of a full Oecumenical Council of all the Orthodox Churches. The plan broke down owing to diplomatic difficulties: but its initiation in the post-revolutionary atmosphere is instructive.

❋　❋　❋

At the heart of Slavophilism was Russian Orthodoxy and the Orthodox mysticism which is the essence of all Christian culture in the East.
The first Slavophils were men of the ancestral life, typical Russian
landlords, racy of the soil, who had sucked along with their mother's
milk their living convictions. They were bred in the ideas of the old
Orthodox way of living, of the Christian peasant commune, and of the
Christian patriarchal State, in which all things are framed, in ideal at
least, to the pattern of father with children. In their Orthodoxy there
was something of the spirit of the Schism and of the Old Believers,
the same convictions of Russian Messianism which began with the
idea of Moscow as the Third Rome, and was so deeply outraged when
Tsar Alexis and the Patriarch Nikon adopted the Greek tradition in
the liturgy, and again when Peter the Great established an upstart
capital in a non-Russian land. It was expressed in Konstantin Aksakov's apostrophe to Peter: "Thou hast despised Russia and all her past.
Therefore a seal of malediction is imprinted on all thy senseless work.
Pitilessly thou hast repudiated Moscow and hast gone out to build,
apart from thy people, a solitary city. For thou and they could no
longer live together."

In the reverence of the Slavophils for the patriarchal head of the
Russian community there was mingled a dislike for intruding Byzantine and German elements, and in particular for the bureaucracy and
the machinery of State which Peter had imported. They had their ears
attuned to the Liberty Bell of Novgorod the Great, and their eyes fixed
on the parliament of Kiev, or on the independent Communes, and
the free assembly of the Zaporozhian Cossacks writing their outrageous
letters of challenge to the Sultan of Turkey. They idealised the life of
the people, of the plain folk. They held that they should return to the
people and be made whole by them on the soil of a common faith.
They were the first of the worshippers of the people, of the Narod, as
the Russians call, not the nation, but the plain folk: and, anti-revolutionary themselves and upholders of a patriarchal autocracy, they were
first to institute that "going to the people" which played so large a part
in subsequent revolutionary movements.

The most characteristic feature of the Slavophils, in their first and
best inspiration, was their religion. In the face of an ecclesiastical censorship, which made it impossible to publish anything for Russians in
the Russian language, a retired officer of Hussars made a simple but
far-reaching revival of the thought of the Orthodox Church. This was
the doctrine of sobornost, "congregationalism," apparently in no way
schismatic, and certainly not new, but rather a rediscovery, in the

Slavophil spirit, of a fundamental conception which had been overlaid with later accretions of ecclesiastical habit. Put in its simplest form, the idea was that the Church consists of all its members, lay and clerical, gathered together in mutual love, and that truth is to be found there where love is. The Prayer of St. Chrysostom: "where two or three are gathered together in Thy name Thou wilt grant their requests," seems to breathe the same spirit.

The first use of the word *soborny*, which we have translated by "congregational," is by way of distinction from "catholic" in the description of the Western Church, now separated and out of communion. The Latin translation *"conciliaris"* would naturally mean "based upon the oecumenical councils." The word *sobornost* has often been translated by "conciliarity." The idea reappears in the nineteenth century in the reply of the Eastern Patriarchs to the Encyclical of Pope Pius IX to the address of the Eastern Churches. They disclaim all control over the dogmas of Orthodoxy. "We have no sort of worldly inspectorship, or, as His Holiness calls it, sacred direction, but are united only by the bond of love and zeal for our common Mother in the unity of the faith. . . . With us neither Patriarch nor Councils (sic) could ever introduce anything new, inasmuch as with us the body itself of the Church is the guardian of Orthodoxy."

It was Aleksei Khomiakov's task to rediscover and interpret further this fundamental idea in its application to the Orthodox Church of Russia. He tells Mr. Palmer that the gift of truth is separated from the hierarchical functions, is attributed not to individuals but to the totality of the Church, is considered as the corollary of the moral principle of mutual love, and he draws the distinction between the position of Orthodoxy on the one hand and Romanism and Protestantism on the other, in the following remarkable passage: "Romanism is an unnatural tyranny. Protestantism is an unprincipled revolt. Neither of them can be accepted. But where is unity without tyranny? Where is freedom without revolt? They are both to be found in the ancient, continuous, unadulterated tradition of the Church. There a unity is to be found more authoritative than the despotism of the Vatican, for it is based upon the strength of mutual love. There a liberty is to be found more free than the licence of Protestantism, for it is regulated by the humility of mutual love There is the Rock and the Refuge." And again, in an address of the year 1855 to the German Churches: "Romanism has a man, Protestantism has a book. Replace these by the whole Church, as in the doctrine of the Orthodox, and you have the whole difference of Life against Death."

Some of us, recalling unpleasant facts, may feel doubtful about the truth of this picture. But a Church must be judged by its ideals as well as by its practice: and here surely we have the ideal at its noblest. As expressed by a recent historian of the Russian Church, the function of the laymen was a reality. He says they had at all times refused to the hierarchs the sole right to represent the Church and her doctrine. Laity and ecclesiastics possessed, and should exercise—note the should —an equal right to participation in the internal·life of the Church, in her teaching and the maintenance of her doctrine and her canons, and in her glory and her universal triumph. Only when the people took a "counselling" * part in the affairs of the Church, could that Church become truly the Church of Christ. Perhaps the writer is doing what many Russians have done and still do, mix up their wish with its fulfilment.

From the "congregational" or "conciliar" character of the Church, Khomiakov deduces the consequence that there is no division, similar to that in the Western Churches, between the teaching Church and the Church of the disciples. There is no teaching Church in the true Church: which means, no doubt, that the clergy have no monopoly of teaching, and explains why the Slavophil theologians, and the later religious thinkers of whom they were forerunners, were laymen. All the World-Religions had their origin outside of the official representatives of older cults, and, in Asia at least, almost all the great reformers of religious thought were not priests or of priestly caste. In this respect the Slavophils, and the later theologians of the Orthodox revival, were of the Asiatic tradition, with Sakyamuni and Zoroaster and Confucius, with the authors of the Upanishads, with Jesus and Paul and Mohammed and Guru Nanak.

Khomiakov was a historian as well as a theologian, but there is much of religion in his history. As he saw history, the idea of legal right lay at the foundation of the thought of Rome, which passed it on to the Germanic conquerors, not only in the life of the State but in the life of religion. It was this which, in the Roman Catholic Church, gave to the relations of man with God the character of a perpetual law-suit, or as we should perhaps put it, of a perpetual running- account, in which good deeds and bad figured with meticulous accuracy on either side of the ledger. Orthodox Russia, on the other hand, preserved freedom of the spirit, attaching little importance to the material, the formal, the judicial. She had not that pre-Christian culture which prevented the

* This is the same word which I have translated "congregational." From *The Russian Church* by Nicolas Brianchaninov.

West from becoming truly Christian, but received her civilisation along with her Christianity. The aristocratic spirit which came along with the conquerors to the West was alien to her. The communal spirit exists in the Russian people from the beginning. They are organically Christian. Power to them is a burden and a duty, not a right. They reject power as they rejected it (according to legend) when they invited the Varangians to rule over them. Equally they reject formal guarantees of their liberty. Such things are needed in the relations only of conqueror and conquered. Where the power of the State is organic, popular in origin, there is no need of a Constitution. None of the Slavophils were constitutionalists, and Konstantin Aksakov declared that the fullness of power and action was for the Government, while the people should have the fullness of thought, and freedom of the spiritual life. But we find the Slavophils prominent in the struggle for the emancipation of the serfs, and for its accompaniment by the allotment of land and the retention of the Mir, their palladium.

Tyutchev was a diplomatist, as Khomiakov was an army-officer. He has left, in poetry of a lofty inspiration, a running commentary on the affairs of Europe from the revolutions of 1848-49 to the fall of Napoleon III and the establishment of the German Empire. In 1854, when the Crimean War is beginning, he has a vision of midnight and moonlight, in which, over the walls of Istanbul—the Tsargrad of Slavophil dreams—he sees the shield of Oleg gleaming. It is a call to the Slavs to win back Imperial Byzantium. Sometimes he bursts into the language of a purer patriotism, nearer home. Here is the authentic note of love of the much-enduring, for ever tormented, people of Russia—

> "Over the dark crowd of this unawakened people
> When wilt thou rise, O Freedom?
> When wilt thy golden light gleam over them?
> Thy light will gleam and make alive,
> And the sun will drive away the clouds,
> But the old festering wounds,
> The scars of outrage and insult,
> The corruption and emptiness of souls,
> That gnaw the mind and ache in the heart,
> Who shall cure these, who shall cover them?
> Thou, pure vestment of Christ."

It is no mere Liberal emancipation of which the Slavophils dream when they talk of Freedom.

Generally it is something outside of Russia, some event in the field of ecclesiastical or State politics which awakens Tyutchev's muse, and often it awakens her to the glorification of the Orthodox Tsar. In December 1866: "The East is smoking with fresh blood: out upon our evil age. Yet one mighty refuge remains, one holy altar for Truth. In thy soul it is, our Orthodox, our Glorious Russian Tsar."

A later poem describes the triumphal feast of the Padshah at Tsargrad, while, somewhere in the shadows, millions of his Christian victims are bleeding to death.

At the formation of the dual Austro-Hungarian Monarchy in 1867, by which the Austrian Slavs were divided between the Austrian Empire and the Hungarian kingdom, there is an angry outburst against an Austrian minister. He had said that Austria must pin the Slavs to the wall, and Tyutchev replies: "The wall to which the Slavs will be pinned is Russia herself: a wall in which every stone is alive." He is no less bitter on the declaration of the Papal infallibility, which touches his Orthodox Russian soul to the quick: "The Vatican Dalai Lama will not be recognised as the vice-regent of Christ." Britain, the opponent of Russian designs in the East, comes in for the lash:

"Why is the British leopard so wroth with us, why lashes he his tail, why roars so furiously . . . our northern Bear, our all-Russian peasant, will not give up his right to defend himself, nay sometimes to snarl back. . . ."

Already, in Tyutchev, there is a note of something cruder and more flamboyant than the pure Slavophil music. Dostoievsky's excursion into imperialist politics, in the concluding portion of his address on the Pushkin anniversary, made that note yet harsher. We begin to see that mere jingoism is no impossible issue from patriotism of this kind.

Chapter V

THE INTELLIGENTSIA AND THE WORSHIP
OF THE PLAIN FOLK

"The whole history of the Intelligentsia was a preparation
for Communism. Into Communism there entered the well-
known traits of the Intelligentsia—thirst for social righteousness and equality, a recognition of the working classes as the
highest type of humanity, aversion to capitalism and the
bourgeoisie, the striving after an integrated outlook and an
integrated relation to life, sectarian intolerance. . . ."

BERDYAEV, *Russian Communism.*

"He clacked away about something or other, wanted to
stretch his tongue a bit. Of course, he's a gentleman: what
does he understand?"

TURGENIEV, *Fathers and Sons.* The peasant's comment
on the Nihilist Bazarov.

"The peasants have seen in us only strangers. We have
avoided them with contempt. A terrifying abyss separated us
from them."

The cholera doctor, beaten to death by villagers,
in Veresaev's story.

It was in the University of Moscow that the ferment began to work.
The Government, instinctively aware of the perils of Philosophy, but
unaware of the Prussian remedy of employing a philosopher with principles favourable to the autocratic state, abolished the chair of that
study. Whereupon the Professor of Physics used his lectures to satisfy
the young men's thirst for the forbidden subject, and physics became
unprecedentedly popular. Discussion circles sprang up, to which the
thinking élite of all Moscow brought its contribution of thought: and
in these circles we first see grouped together the men of the type to
which the label of *Intelligentsia* afterwards attached itself. They were
of all classes, but their ideas and interests were not those of a class.
They were the Hamlets and the Quixotes, the men of sensitive conscience and of injured pride, men of compassion, "without audacity
and malice," agonising over the problem of the justification of suffering, and convinced of Russia's mission to all mankind; capable of a

lofty heroism, with heads full of cursed questions, and often in direct conflict with art and aesthetics, because art and aesthetics were a distraction from the task of social reform: planning revolution on behalf of a people which was to reject them when revolution was achieved. From the philological standpoint, their label should apply equally to Khomiakov and Dostoievsky, even to Leo Tolstoi. Actually, the religious thinkers are by usage excluded from the class. The "Intelligents" are agnostic, materialist, positivist, anything but formally religious, until, in the first decade of the twentieth century, religion finds itself for the first time associated with liberalism, and with even more advanced forms of political thought.

We have said that they are not religious; and yet the influence of religious tradition and habit upon their whole moral and mental make-up is unmistakable. There is the sick conscience, the sense of sin and the passion for expiation, the moral austerity, the readiness for martyrdom—all surviving the belief in God and the hope of immortality.

They had their faults: and one of these was a contempt for manual labour or at any rate a feeling that manual labour was not their task. Perhaps there was a physical softness, encouraged by sedentary occupation and too much of midnight conversation round the samovar.

But let there be no misapprehension. Weak people, who resolve to be strong, may become stronger than the strongest. The annals of the revolutionary Intelligentsia abound in records of an iron heroism. We see this, in the making, in Chernyshevsky's picture of the "rigorist," Rakhmetev. He abstains from alcohol and from indulgence of the natural appetites, sleeps on a straw bed studded with nails, rations himself as to conversation (that sweet sin of Russia), studies deeply and travels widely. It is a new and non-Christian form of the religious hermit training his will for some great task—what we are not told. But this was written in 1863, and we can guess.

In the early thirties, the two most interesting of the Moscow circles represented two different intellectual tendencies, and at first looked askance at one another as "Germans" and "French" respectively. The "French" circle discussed history and the social sciences. The leading figure here was Alexander Herzen, destined at a later date to edge his way past the censor, and to influence, though not to conquer, Imperial and official opinion. The social sciences were dangerous ground, and Herzen and others were exiled in 1835. The "German," or philosophical, circle included many names afterwards of note: among them K. S. Aksakov, the Slavophil, Vissarion Belinsky, and Michael Bakunin, the anarchist, at this time known as a quixotic young army-officer with a turn for philosophy. Literature, particularly poetry and the drama, as well as philosophy and philosophy in its application to literary criticism, occupied this group of ardent seekers. Sometimes they met in the house of Peter Chaadaev, Nicolas I's "madman," who deserves a book to himself.

Vissarion Belinsky was the moral enthusiast of the philosophical circle. From the start he was a worshipper of Peter the Great, and (if we may anticipate the name), was never anything but a Westerniser. He loved literature, and had a natural gift of ruthless logic, as well as a passionate devotion to truth as, from time to time, he saw it. He was no linguist, and no great reader even in his own language. He got his philosophy by word of mouth, in the heat of conversation. For his literature he was largely indebted to the current journals, which were active in the translation of foreign masterpieces. He never wrote a book, after the tragedy which was his first boyish effort. His writings are to be sought in his correspondence and his reviews.

Belinsky's circle was sympathetic with Chaadaev's condemnation of backward Russia, but it had no politics, and his own inclination at that time was towards a conservative quietism deduced from first studies of Hegelian philosophy. He changed: and it is certain that, like his intellectual descendants, he was never a profound philosopher. Rather, he took from philosophy what harmonised with his moral instincts, and changed both opinions. and the friends who preached them, when the ardent life within him burst the bonds in which abstractions had enmeshed it. The successive changes were preceded and accompanied by an internal struggle, whose bitterness testifies to the sincerity of his passion for truth. The change which has permanent interest for the study of Russian thought was consummated when he turned his back on Moscow and went to St. Petersburg to take up the editorship first of the *Sketches of the Fatherland*, and afterwards of *The Contemporary*, magazines. From the conservative who came near to holding (as did Hegel himself in his defence of the Prussian monarchy) that whatever is, is right, or at all events that the actual is the reasonable, he becomes the reformer: from the champion of art for art's sake and of the self-regarding development of human personality, he becomes the protagonist of social usefulness in literature. In a passage which anticipates Ivan Karamazov's famous challenge to the Almighty on behalf of innocently suffering humanity, he declares that if he could climb to the highest rung of self-perfection, he would call from that height upon his old idol Hegel to answer to him for all the victims of life and history. Otherwise he would throw himself down headlong from the ladder. He does not desire happiness, even gratuitously, unless he can be at peace for each and all of his brethren. It is difficult to believe that Dostoievsky had not this declaration in mind when he made his Ivan Karamazov respectfully decline his ticket to Paradise, unless he could be satisfied of justice done to all his fellowmen. Here the religious and the irreligious thinkers meet.

Nature could hardly have designed a more complete example of the Russian Intelligentsia, and it is easy to understand why Belinsky has been called the father of it. In him we have the westernising, the humanism (which he called anthropology), the idolisation of science, the attraction to the doctrines of Socialism, not always very clearly defined, the replacement of orthodox Christianity by a sort of idolatry of the popular masses, the sublimation of the monastic sense of sin into a spirit of repentance and expiation for past wrongs to this collective human deity, the tendency to philosophise without a profound study of philosophy, and to find in every philosophy only material for the moral passion, the depreciation of mere aesthetics, the utilitarian criterion applied to the work of writers and artists, the ascetic surrender of personal joys, the exaltation of moral and political duty over the religious or cultural developments of the personality —all the qualities and ideas which are characteristic of the Intelligentsia for the next six decades.

When Belinsky had passed completely out of the phase of old Hegelian conservatism, he and his friends found themselves naturally fused into a new circle, which began to be called by the name of the Westernisers, in contradistinction to the Slavophils, and he plunged into the fray with that enthusiasm for extremes which earned him his friendly epithet in the days of the Moscow circle. But there was something of the Slavophil in him too: for he was convinced that Russia was better qualified than western Europe for dealing with the social problem.

Herzen, less extreme, and indeed powerfully attracted by certain aspects of the Slavophil doctrine, travelled between the two camps, and tried to moderate the passions of this battle of the books, persuading Belinsky to drop his violent talk of "the nationality of birchbark sandals and peasant smock." But when the quarrel reached its crisis in 1844—characteristically enough it was a series of lectures on the history of the Middle Ages which topped the climax—even Herzen had to give up some of his friendship on the Slavophil side of the fence.

Those were days—even before the intensified repression which followed on the European revolutions of 1848—when poets and literary men lived a precarious life, under a system half bureaucratic, half paternal, which did not spare the rod. "Society," which combined a large part of the wealth of the country with the whole of the ecclesiastical, official, and court influence, had a tremendous solidarity, and was able to take care of its friends and to avenge effectively all invasions of its dignity and authority.

Judged in the light of freer and more outspoken days, Belinsky, cautious of the censor and careful to avoid the expression of opinions on the practical issues of politics, seems the most innocent of journalists. But some of his Slavophil opponents had friends in high places, and it is evident that he ran risks. There is a story of the Governor of the Peter and Paul fortress, in which political prisoners were detained, meeting him on the Quay and, pointing across the river to the fortress, saying, with a hospitable grin: "When are you coming to us? I have a nice warm cell ready for you."

Belinsky had not that special form of bigotry which is the result of the possession of a rival body of systematic doctrine. Rather, to borrow the words of Herzen about him and his friends, they opposed to the Slavophil idolatries of the past "a lively sympathy for all which agitated contemporary man, a love of freedom of thought and a hate of all that limited it." These were the contributions to the Russian mind of the men of the forties: largely destructive and tending towards that complete denial of authority which later on received the name of Nihilism. It was a true instinct which caused Nicolas, when Belinsky died, to prohibit all literary references to his memory. He supplied the solvent which began the process of eating away the foundations of the old order. He also laid a foundation-stone of his own in the encouragement of a realistic literature. This literature prepared the way for social changes by undermining the moral position of the gentry, whose virtues would not bear a too lively description.

Alexander Herzen, the illegitimate son of a noble whose wealth he inherited, was one of those men "of no class in particular" to whom, along with the "conscience-stricken gentlemen" ashamed of their privileges; has been attributed the creation of nineteenth-century revolutionary ferment. It was he who introduced Socialism into Russian thought, and the cause of woman's emancipation made a particular appeal to him. From the Slavophils he took his admiration of the Russian village Mir and the Russian co-operative workers' fellowship, and his ideal of the Russian people, which assumed for him the form of the Plain Folk, distinct from the nation. His dislike of the modern formalised State must have come to him from the same source. He compared it to Chingiz Khan, plus the telegraph, and thought the military camp of the fighting Cossacks, the Zaporozhian Syech, the most suitable form of State for the Slavonic peoples. In particular he despised the political forms of western Europe, as an inheritance from a Roman religion of property and legalism, involving the swallowing up of personality by society, and he put aside the demand for constitutional reforms. As with the Slavophils, there was not a little of anarchism in his political, or anti-political, thought: and he expressed this clearly enough when he wrote that it was "time for man to challenge republic, legislation, representation, and all the ideas regarding the citizen in his relation to the State."

His early discussions with Belinsky led him to German philosophy, where he soon discovered that "double-facedness" in Hegel, which made some of his disciples into conservatives and others into reformers. Out of all these elements, together with a culture wider than that of Belinsky or the Slavophils, he wove a system of his own which supplied the Populists of the seventies and the Social Revolutionaries of a later date with their staple ideas. It was that synthesis of Westernism and Slavophilism which went by the name of Populism, with its idolisation of the Plain Folk, principally of the Peasant, and its plans of agrarian socialism based upon the Mir, to which the progress of rural capitalism pitilessly gave the lie. The attitude to the Mir was Slavophil, with a difference: for the Slavophils emphasised the ethical, the Populists the economic, aspect.

He conceived Russia as a federation of free communes into which the Romanovs had introduced serfdom and a noblesse and, later, a bureaucracy, radically foreign to the people and their institutions. All but Tsar, peasants, and clergy, are strange and unassimilable elements. Liberalism is an exotic flower. All that is necessary is for Russia to throw off serfdom, noblesse, bureaucracy and the Byzantinised Church and, basing herself upon the Mir and the Workers' partnership, to achieve her free and peaceful revolution. The West has a heavy task of construction before it: Russia has only to clear away mischievous accretions upon her original structure. In the final words of his *History of Revolutionary Ideas*, he appeals to the Slavophils to join with the Westernisers in clearing these away. The task, it will be observed, is one of destruction.

The reforms of Peter the Great are always a touchstone of Russian opinion. Herzen, true to the broad outlook which makes him a sharer equally in Slavophil and Westernising ideals, sees two sides to these reforms. Peter broke away from the Byzantine conception of the Tsar as a remote and mysterious figure, and made his people (and himself with them) a nation of workers. He destroyed the prestige of the Byzantinised Church, which has never had any hold on the people, except through their ignorance—so says Herzen—and at that time threatened the creation of a State within the State. He let in the light and forced the Boyars' ladies out of their oriental seclusion. But he detached the nobility from the people, and made two nations, the bearded and the beardless, serfs and masters, and added a German bureaucracy to the structure of the State. Since that time the history of Russia is the history of Tsar and noblesse—with only parasites and officials between the two. Only the Mir and the Workers' fellowship resisted these changes. Otherwise the people disappeared from history except for the brief moment of national upheaval at the Napoleonic invasion. The division, he continues, accounts for a profound uneasiness in Russian life. Europeanised Russia desires one thing: old Russia desires another. Hence the prevalence in literature of the "superfluous man," the hopelessness of the poet Lermontov, and the ineffectiveness of much of Russian character. The Decembrist revolt was unsupported because the nation knew nothing of what its self-appointed champions hoped to attain.

He goes on to the revival of the mind brought about by Belinsky's championship of the freedom of thought, and the outburst of wholesome laughter provoked by Gogol; but brings down the clouds again in 1848, when European reaction caused Nicolas to drop his project of emancipation and to substitute for it the regimentation of the Universities, a severer censorship and the closure of the frontiers against travel. This was written in 1853, and Herzen seeks to frighten Europe with a picture of a world dominated by an irresistible Russian empire absorbing the mediatised princes and the petty sovereigns.

Perhaps the bugbear really caused some alarm. If so, it was only one of a long series of miscalculations of the military power of Russia, based on the destruction of Napoleon's *Grande Armée*. Within two years, the scandals and the humiliation of the Crimean War (1854-1856) had disclosed the feet of clay in the Imperial image. With all the mediaevalism of serfdom and the choking of thought, the Tsar could not win his country's battles against the free and more industrialised West.

His successor relaxed the reins, and Russia's Troika, held too long and too tightly, broke into what looked for a time like a runaway gallop. There was a rush to the Universities, no longer restricted. Journalism came into its own, and, in close harmony with educated opinion, began to express itself with a new freedom. Beside the central question of serfdom and emancipation, every kind of project was debated by an eager public. We are told that a drama was written in defence of free trade, and a poem in defence of a method of taxation, and proposals (which the Bolsheviks have since carried out) were put forward for the elimination of unneeded letters from the Russian alphabet. A picture of a St. Petersburg salon in Dostoievsky's novel *The Possessed* may be taken as depicting the excitement of these days. "They talked of the abolition of the censorship, and of phonetic spelling, of the substitution of the Latin characters for the Russian alphabet . . . of splitting Russia into nationalities united in a free federation, of the abolition of the army and navy, of the restoration of Poland as far as the Dnieper, of the peasant reforms and of the manifestoes, of the abolition of the hereditary principle and of the family, of children, of priests, of women's rights." When a strong-minded and enterprising lady, anxious to feel herself in the swim with all these men of the moment, proposes to found a magazine to give utterance to their thoughts, "charges of being a capitalist and an exploiter were showered upon her to her face," from which we gather that Socialism was fashionable, and that capitalists were out of favour in advanced society. From abroad Herzen was sending his magazine *The Bell* into Russia, and seeking to convert the Emperor himself and his leading officials to his own principles of reform. In rural areas there was a movement for temperance—not normally popular with the Russian peasantry. Nominal marriages, to secure the freedom of the girls from parental control without involving conjugal obligations, became common. Count Tolstoi, who had met Froebel on his European travels, was establishing his school at Yasnaya Polyana on the principle of freedom for the young, and Turgeniev was depicting in *Fathers and Sons* the gulf between the older and younger generations, the pathos, from the elders' standpoint, of the children's crusade, and the appearance of the new type of Nihilist.

N. S. Chernyshevsky shared with his comrade and pendant Dobroliubov—a pair of Radical Saints they have been called—the kingdom of criticism in this new epoch.

He was an original thinker of powerful calibre, not to be classified under a particular label. He was indeed a Westerniser, a follower of Belinsky, and an agnostic. But he was no Populist, for he did not idealise the Plain Folk, regarded the peasants as barbarians, and expected little or nothing from the proletariat. In the friendliness of his attitude to the Slavonic peoples, he went in one respect beyond the Slavophils: for the Slavophils had no love for Roman Catholic Poland, and Chernyshevsky regarded the Polish influence on Russia as one of enlightenment, and was—if all tales be true—prepared to co-operate with the Poles when they revolted. Unlike Belinsky, whose harsh criticism of the Ukrainian poet Shevchenko, written in the un-compromising Great-Russian spirit, was a blot upon his reputation for literary acumen, he was sympathetic to the Ukrainians when they set up an organ to defend the national cause in the period of the relaxation of the censorship. On the other hand he opposed the Slavophil ideal of an asylum for all the Slavs under the wings of the Russian eagle. He valued the Mir for the sake of the spirit of association which it repre-sented, but was not one of its unconditional devotees. The Slavophils supported the Galician Ruthenes in their struggle against the Poles. But Chernyshevsky saw that they were playing into the hands of the common enemy, and sought to bring all the Austrian Slavs together in combined opposition to Austria.

The temptation to classify thought in definite categories has led to the division of Socialist thinkers into the Utopian and the Scientific, the Scientific being those who hope only for that of which the course of historical development appears to guarantee the attainability. Marx is the leading example of the so-called Scientific type. Chernyshevsky is remarkable among the Russian Socialists for having in him some-thing of the Scientific as well as of the Utopian element. Unlike Marx, he did not ask himself whether the objective environment guaranteed the attainment of the ideal, but only whether the ideal was good. Unlike Marx, he believed, at least for a time, that fundamental changes in economic relations could be brought about without vio-lent revolution, by the demonstration of their utilitarian value, and he was prepared to co-operate with the Imperial power, and hoped that one of the old parties would make peace with Socialism. Unlike Marx, he had no thought of any effective initiative by the urban proletariat, or indeed of any section of the common people, and along with the other idealists, believed that the world was ruled by ideas, and that the small circle of the "best" people would guide the mass.

It is interesting to note the points upon which he does anticipate Marx, of whose works, except by hearsay, he can have known little before his imprisonment. Like Marx, he saw that a Socialist society could not be based merely upon a revised distribution of wealth, but demanded the fuller development of the means of production which technical resources have placed at the disposal of man, and looked hopefully to the machine and the factory and all the devices of capitalism, when the Russian Socialists were still expecting Utopia from the wooden plough and the handiwork of little groups of co-operative workmen. Like Marx again, he thought in terms of the State when the Utopians were planning voluntary colonies, supported by private means and embracing only groups of enthusiastic individuals. Like Marx, he had no expectation of human altruism, and defended Socialism as a product of economic necessity. In short, as the first Russian expositor of Marxism put it a generation later, he was a Socialist with a method, he was "travelling on the right road though he had not time to get there"; and the Marxians are nearer to him in spirit than are his own fancied followers.

Chernyshevsky had fought for a solution of the Emancipation problem which would give land as well as liberty to the serf, without pecuniary obligation. His article was published a month before the Emancipation Decree of 1861, when it was already evident that the peasants would be burdened for an indefinite term with large redemption payments. The cup of bitterness for the "bilious ones," as Herzen had dubbed Chernyshevsky and Dobroliubov, was full.

There is nothing surprising in the imprisonment of Chernyshevsky, or in the later suggestion of the police that he was responsible for the attempt on the life of the Emperor in 1866. What is surprising is that he was able to publish, from prison, a work which affected behaviour and ideals for a whole decade. The ideas put forward in his novel, *What Is to Be Done?* are not original. They are all to be found in Owen, Fourier, Georges Sand, Godwin or John Stuart Mill. Florence Nightingale had recently given, in her own activities, an example of one side of them. The Rochdale Pioneers, and their successors in Co-operation, had been at work for nearly twenty years. Belinsky had been talking of some of these ideas in the forties, and Herzen's "Circle" had been deeply absorbed in others. Nor was there anything remarkable in the literary presentation, in regard to which the critics express themselves with coldness. But something in the book, aided perhaps by the personality of the author and his recent misfortune, caught and fixed popular attention. Henceforth all the original young men were emulating the husband who shot himself to make room for a friend in his wife's affections. All the advanced young couples were emulating the companionate marriage, in which each has his or her own sanctum, and each treats the other with all the respect of a stranger. All the girls were planning to earn their own living and to form Co-operative Producers' Associations, and the Swiss Medical Colleges were filled with Russian women studying medicine, "like Vera"—till the Government ordered them home; on moral grounds, of course.

The Fourierist features of the book show themselves in one of Vera's dreams, where we see the community of the "phalanstery" living in a palace of aluminum and glass (it is impossible to resist the suspicion that the Exhibition of 1851 and the Crystal Palace have something to do with this picture, for Chernyshevsky is a great Anglomaniac), and Russia converted into a paradise of fertility, beauty and healthfulness by the subjection of nature to the needs of man—a glimpse of Socialism as a systematic development of productive resources which anticipates the Bolsheviks.

Lenin's widow tells us that the works of Chernyshevsky were among her husband's favourite books. He was very plainly a forerunner of the Bolsheviks, he was inspired by English Utilitarianism, and hardly, if at all, in the regular Populist succession.

Nihilism—not a new word when Turgeniev applied it to his famous hero Bazarov—was the natural revulsion, carried to the extreme, from the authoritarianism of Nicolas I. He had set up the brazen image of authority and called upon all the people to bow down to it. The Nihilists denied all authority—of the State, of Religion, of the Family, even of Science; for there were particular sciences, no doubt, but no Science in general. Pisarev, the successor of Chernyshevsky in the leadership of the Intelligentsia, called himself and his followers "thinking Realists" but he was quite willing to accept Bazarov as his prototype. Among the things denied was the existence of any valid canons of art (on the ground that everyone has his individual notion of beauty, and no science can reduce this variety to unity) and of any inspiration in poetry not accessible to the ordinary man; and education was condemned as an outrage upon personality.

These negative convictions did not prevent Pisarev from appreciating the poet who writes "with the blood of his heart and the juice of his nerves," a class in which he included Heine, Goethe and Shakespeare. But after being in prison in 1863 he attacked aesthetics in general: none but a philistine and aesthete can allow himself personal pleasure from art while the hungry and unclothed are with us. It is the frequently recurring strain in Russian thought which—long before the Bolsheviks—demands social value from art and condemns art for art's sake.

Pisarev denied the existence of any valid science of history, because

it is inevitably a theoretical justification of the historian's personal convictions. This denial, by a singular irony, has earned for him the title
of the Father of the Subjective method, of which he probably never
dreamed. The Subjective method, practised by Mikhaidovsky and the
later Populists, was a frank acknowledgment that the only way of
describing man as a social being was to give up the pretence of objective detachment, and to feel as a man feels, suffer with his pain and
weep with his tears.

If there was extravagance in Pisarev, it was carried very much further
by his followers. They launched a campaign against verse, which all
but drove Russian poetry from the bookstalls. They denied the distinction between good and evil, and, as is hinted in Dostoievsky's novel
The Possessed, some of them were sexual perverts. The elders were
naturally shocked, and, of course, employed the term "Nihilist" as a
label for everything which they did not like, including young ladies
with bobbed hair who lived in communal boarding houses and tried to
earn their own living. Katkov—once a member of one of the "Circles"
and thereafter a journalist of liberal sympathies—went completely over
to the reactionaries. The Slavophils found themselves allied with the
Government against their own aspirations to liberty, and were drawn
towards Byzantinism. As Nicolas made the Nihilists, so the Nihilists
made the reaction.

✳ ✳ ✳

A more active revolutionary than any of the thinkers hitherto mentioned was Michael Bakunin, one of the "conscience-stricken gentlemen," who inevitably spent all of his mature life in Siberia or out of
Russia.

After a few months as an officer and a gentleman, he left the army
and passed into the circle of philosophical undergraduates of the
Moscow University. Belinsky described him as a profound, unique,
lion-like nature, but said that his pretensions made friendship with
him impossible. "He loves ideas, not people: desires to exercise his
authority but does not love." And again: "Bakunin has many faults
and sins. But there is something in him which outweighs his defects: the *perpetuum mobile* in his soul." Associated with Richard
Wagner in the German revolution of 1848-49, he was probably the
original of the musician's Siegfried, destroyer of gods. But his earlier
life seemed to prognosticate for him a very different future. Converted from early learnings towards French philosophy, he became
an ardent, but not very penetrating, student of the Germans, particularly of Hegel, was convinced that all reality is reasonable, and thus

acquired philosophically conservative opinions. In this intellectual attitude he continued for a whole decade, but the Young Hegelians of Berlin converted him about 1842. He had the reputation of an acute logician, seeing all life through a prism of abstractions, and able to deal with facts only after they had been fused into an idea. An element of abnormality was contributed to his personality by the fact, stated upon apparently good authority, that he was sexually impotent, in spite of his powerful physique. When we look at what came afterwards it is difficult to believe that we are not dealing with two different men whose biographies have been accidentally confused. From 1848 or thereabouts what we see in Bakunin is a Russian giant of enormous vitality, who roared and swore and rushed about Europe, devising conspiracies against Russia, against Austria, against the German and Italian rulers, getting the police on their guard by sheer inability to restrain himself, telling everyone that the first thing in every outbreak is to set fire to the townhall, advising the Communards of Paris to destroy half the city. This second personality is suggestive of a huge will-o'-the-wisp, that not only blazes but buzzes. But the fire which he carried was a real fire, and no mere marsh vapour, and did its work on combustible hearts: and he established a school of insurrectionary action which at times had the upper hand of the school of propaganda, and contributed an important influence to the policies of Lenin. It was impossible to ignore such a portentous firework, and among his own associates he was the subject of many descriptive witticisms. A Frenchman, who had seen him at work in Paris, said he was a treasure on the first day of a revolution, but "*bon à fusiller*" on the second. Herzen, the most delightful of commentators, said he had a way of mistaking the second month of gestation for the ninth, and that he enjoyed all the preliminary bustle of the Polish revolt "as though he were getting ready a Christmas tree." The reactionaries called him the Old Man of the Mountain, after the famous head of the Assassin sect, who inspired terror and agitation from Cordova to Bactria. "*C'est un brave garçon*," said Nicolas, "but we must keep him locked up." In essence the method which he advocated was for a small body of conspirators to seize and hold power till the mass of the people should be drawn into revolution: not into political revolution, for that is superfluous, but into the destruction of the State, and the substitution for it of a purely economic organization. He was for making a clean sweep of existing institutions, as Siegfried destroys Wotan and Valhalla. He may have got his Anarchism from Weitling or Proudhon, if he did not get it from something very deep down in Russian nature or history, something which reveals itself as clearly in Count Tolstoi as in the most ardent of avowed revolutionaries. Something he took from the Slavophils, the hatred of the foreign brand—Byzantine, Tartar, German, or Holstein-Tartar as Herzen called it—upon the Russian State. His aspiration was for a free Slav federation—to include Poland, which the Slavophils excluded—even though it should involve war to the knife with all Germans, Magyars and Turks, after the Government of Russia herself had been transformed to an appropriate amorphism: a somewhat highly spiced dish for the foreign offices, not to mention the ministries of home affairs. Like more than one of the nineteenth-century revolutionaries, and like all of the early Slavophils, he hated the apparatus of government much more than he hated the personal autocrat. It is this which explains the abject confession which he made to Nicolas, and his subsequent declaration that he "would gladly follow Romanov, if Romanov would transform himself from Petersburg Emperor to National Tsar."

He made enormous mistakes, and sometimes acknowledged them. He never understood, or not in time, that the Polish malcontents had the mentality of the aristocrat and the landed proprietor, that they desired the extension of the Polish frontiers into Russian lands, and that co-operation with Russian revolutionaries was impossible to them. He ruined the circulation of Herzen's *Bell* by his collaboration over the Polish question, when all sections of Russian opinion had turned against the Poles. Herzen told him frankly that he did not know Russia, either before his imprisonment or after his exile, and that he had lived for half a century in a world of ghosts and dreams. Herzen's brother editor begs him "to conquer the enthusiasm which carries you away, and even bring yourself to make a preparatory study" of the subject, before hurling his mighty bulk upon the Russian agrarian question. He knew how to answer back, for he vigorously criticised Herzen's attempt to conciliate Alexander II and the reactionaries around him, and found a powerful phrase in which to crystallise his rebuke: "Cease to be Erasmus, and become Luther!"

His official jailors in Siberia, who went to work to make him talk, must have smiled at his easy illusion that the Governor-General there was a revolutionary at heart, and only awaited a suitable opportunity to bring about portentous changes, including the general war on behalf of the suffering Slavs. But his most colossal error—this was one that he himself discovered—was his surrender to Nechayev, a sort of Jesuit of the Revolution, to whom all means were lawful. At that time

Bakunin was attracted by the power and vitality of the Society of Jesus, which he attributed to the complete effacement of the personal will of the individual and the perfection of the collective organisation, and he was ready to abdicate his own personality for the sake of such a force in the revolutionary field. Nechayev's plan—it gave to Dostoievsky the material for his account of the conspiratorial five in *The Possessed*—was to create a small circle bound to a rigid discipline by mutual fear and the possession of one another's secrets; to strengthen the hold upon each member by seductions and other measures of intrusion into private life; and to enforce loyalty and obedience by murder. In pursuance of this design, he actually arranged, in Russia, for the murder of a student who was suspected of the intention to turn informer, and carried off a mass of papers belonging to Bakunin and others, with the apparent aim of using them for purposes of blackmail. Bakunin, a generous, even noble, character, with something of the boy eternal in him, repented of his delusion, which incidentally gave to the political police an opportunity of claiming from foreign Governments the extradition of political offenders as common criminals.

One feature of permanent interest in Bakunin's career was his origination of the first conception of an institution which played a prominent part in later history. When at Naples in 1865-67 he founded a secret society called the International Brotherhood, divided into two categories, to be known respectively as the International Family and the National Families. The former was to be the directing organ, with members bound to strict discipline, and engaged both in open propaganda and in secret revolutionary preparations. How much of this design was realised at that time is doubtful, but, somewhat later, we find Bakunin establishing an International Social Democratic Alliance, for the training of propagandists, apostles, and finally of organisers. He intended this organisation to be a secret one, and, in idea at all events, it seems to have continued the germ of the future Social Democratic, or Communist, Party, in the select and disciplined form conceived by Lenin.

This International Social Democratic Alliance, or certain of its branches, was designed by Bakunin to be incorporated in the International organisation of Karl Marx, without losing its own separate identity. In other words, he desired to enter the International at the head of his own following. Defeated in this design, he continued to pursue the aims of securing for himself a dominating position in the International, and of forcing upon it the adoption of his own prin-

ciples of policy. The difference between these and the principles of
Marx was radical. Bakunin regarded the State as something to be
destroyed, and his strategy was of the conspiratorial and insurrectionary type. A small minority should destroy the power of the State, in
full assurance that the people would give their support to the successful conspirators. He entirely despised the political weapon and
regarded the political revolution, except in the sense of the destruction of the State, as superfluous. Still less did he conceive that change
was dependent upon a gradual ripening of social conditions for it, and
that the revolutionist's share in it was no more than the discovery
and seizure of the appropriate opportunity. In these matters he was
at the opposite pole from Marx. There was an additional cause of
difference. For Bakunin, the German was the eternal oppressor of the
Slav. Marx thought that the German school was a good one for the
backward fragments of the scattered Slavonic race, who had neither a
common language nor a civilisation comparable to the German. The
controversy was fought out upon charges against Bakunin, in connection with his association with Nechayev, of fraud and intimidation,
and he was expelled from the International.

Russian Revolutionaries were divided at this time between allegiance to the conspiratorial and insurrectionist Bakunin and to Peter
Lavrov, who by his *Historical Letters* published in 1868-69, sent the
élite of Russian youth into the villages to teach and help and awaken
the peasant masses of Russia. Lavrov's is a trumpet call, to the few
who are endowed with the capacity for thought, to take their part in
the realisation of an ideal of progress. Progress for him meant two
things: the physical, moral and intellectual development of the individual, and the realisation of truth and justice in social institutions;
the two being so balanced one with the other as to be in perfect
equilibrium, so that neither individualism nor socialism may prevail.
Ideas rule the world, and the society which suppresses the few who
have the faculty of criticism dooms itself to immobility. This leaven
was to become operative in the Russia of the seventies by that process
of "going to the people" by the intellectuals which assumed the
proportions of an Intelligentsia's Crusade in 1872. In order to give
perfect freedom for the work of those who possess this faculty of
critical thought, the rôle of the State as a coercive authority must be
reduced to a minimum: so that we arrive at an ideal of political
anarchy, regulated by a reciprocal exchange of contractual obligations,
and guided by a natural aristocracy of the intellect. The many, who
lack the gift of critical thought, must recognise that their subordina-

tion to the few that have it is the price of their progress: and upon the few rests the sacred duty of diminishing the cost, and increasing the progress attained in return for it, in the greatest degree possible. Nothing like the dictatorship of a gifted minority was contemplated. As Editor of the *Forward* in 1874, Lavrov argued that dictatorship spoils the best of men, that only a second revolution can tear power from a dictator, and that power belongs to the people and the people only.

Lavrov was from the beginning a revolutionist, but he stood for propaganda and the gradual ripening of ideas, as opposed to the abrupt methods of the insurrectionary school of Bakunin. For a time he was the editor of the magazine *People's Will*, which stood for terrorism. The distinction between the two schools is not between revolution and terrorism on the one hand, and peaceful persuasion on the other. Both were revolutionary, and both were terrorist, the propagandists directing their attention to a sort of punitive terrorism against oppressive and unpopular officials. Both stood for action by individuals, whether propagandist or insurrectionist, whether terrorist, educational or agitational, and did not contemplate mass action of the kind which involved prior organisation, such as the Bolsheviks practised later.

The contrast is between propaganda for ultimate revolution, on one side, and agitation for insurrection, whenever possible, on the other. The Lavrovist held that the revolution must come from the instruction of the plain folk by the intelligentsia: the Bakuninist, that the revolutionist is not to teach the people, who already know better than he, and have an instinctive appreciation of the methods of Socialism: he is to combine isolated protests into united action, and find occasions for action, and the people will join him spontaneously. The one expected delay in the revolution: the other thought it might come at any time with luck and courage.

Little though Russians at this time knew about Marx, the fact that the nickname for the Lavrovist party was "Marxists" shows that the Marxist teaching was at this time recognised to be propagandist and gradualist.

In spite of the failure of the Commune in Paris in 1871, the fact that it had established, and maintained for several weeks, an actual Workers' Government, greatly encouraged the Insurrectionist section in Russia, and profoundly influenced the plans of the revolutionaries both in December 1905 and in November 1917. As early as 1869, Breshkovskaya's Co-operative Bank and School had been closed by

authority with the cynical observation: "We want no apostles here."
This was a fair example of the attitude of the Russian police, and since
many, if not all, of these intellectual missionaries had aims ultimately,
if not immediately, subversive, we cannot affect surprise. The "going
to the people," without the subversive accompaniment, has its parallel
in England at a somewhat later date, in the University Settlements in
the poor quarters of cities; in the fashionable craze for slumming; in
"Darkest England"; in Bernard Shaw as a vestryman; and in Charles
Booth's study of London. What happened in Russia has been depicted in Turgeniev's *Virgin Soil*. Rural Russia could make nothing
of its missionaries, did not understand what either insurrectionists or
propagandists were aiming at; probably connected them with Antichrist; and often delivered them to the police. But there is a figure
in *Virgin Soil* of a new and significant type. This is the engineer-
manager, Solòmin, who has succeeded in setting up a little school and
a little hospital, very much against the wishes of the owner of the mill,
and is occupied in organising the men. The literary critics depreciate
Solòmin as a literary creation, and call him a wooden and unconvinc-
ing figure. The Maximalist Socialists despise him as a gradualist and a
man of little deeds. He is a portent, for all that: a quiet man who really
knows the workers, and knows the job, and is a forerunner of Bolshevik
organisers.

Organisation, as distinct from either propaganda or insurrectionism,
began with Zaslavsky, an intellectual, who in 1875 drew up a statute
for the Southern Union of Workers. Stepan Khalturin, very like a
Solòmin come to life, did similar work for the Northern Union in
1878-79. He was a joiner, who started chain-libraries and circulated
books among the workers, deprecated terrorism and looked forward
to a revolution to be brought about by a general strike—a plan which
was realised in 1905. His comment upon the activities of the intellectuals is interesting. "As soon as we have started something going, bang
—the intellectuals have killed somebody, and the police are on us.
Why don't they give us a chance to organise?"

The police broke up his union, he became a terrorist, and was executed in 1882. So much for propagandist gradualism!

In the meanwhile work of a very different kind was being done by
a group of Populists who aimed at depicting the lives of the Plain
Folk, for whose emancipation the revolutionaries were risking life
and liberty. They centred in *Notes of the Fatherland*, one of those
periodicals which have played so great a part in the expression of Russian thought. The "Letters from the Country" of Englehardt, former

military officer and agricultural professor, which I have more than once
had occasion to quote, were published first in *Notes of the Fatherland* which continued and developed further the ideas of Chernyshevsky's *Contemporary*. The *Notes* were the instrument for the creation
of that conception of the peasant which was the characteristic basis of
Russian Populism. In the sixties, the editorial group of the *Notes* included the poet Nekrasov, Saltkov-Schedrin, author of The *Golovlev
Family*, a picture of the life of poor provincial squires, and Mikhailovsky, the maker of the later Populist philosophy, which was inherited by the Social Revolutionaries of the twentieth century.
Nekrasov had been writing poetry since 1838, when he received encouragement from the king of critics, Belinsky, and devoted himself
in particular to poems of peasant life. *Who Can Be Happy and Free
in Russia?* is an account of the wanderings of seven peasants, who
put the question to all and sundry. The Censor's hand was heavy on
the poem, but there is enough of it to give us a distressing picture.
Most poignant of all is the answer of the old woman who, after nar-
rating the cruel sorrows by which she has been visited, says:—

> "The keys to the welfare
>   And freedom of women
> Have long been mislaid:
>   God Himself has mislaid them.
>
> And which fish has swallowed
>   Those treasures so priceless:
> In which sea it swims:
>   God Himself has forgotten."

In 1868 the literary group of the *Notes* was joined by Gleb
Uspensky, who is typical of the realistic portrait-painters of the humbler Russian life, starting with the country town, the inn, and the
posting station, and finally concentrating on the peasant.

He was no idoliser of the peasant as were so many of the Populists,
but sought to describe him as he was, without any of that magic
which transfigures Turgeniev's *Sketches of a Sportsman*, and rarely
rises to the heights of great literature. The title of one of his own
tales, *Figures Come to Life*, suggests the function which he sought to
fulfil. He filled out the jejune outline of the statistical tables, and
showed what manner of man he was of whom the averages and the
decimal points and the column of remarks recorded the skeleton. But
he did it with the vision and the sympathy of one who might have
been an artist if he had been content to be less of a publicist. His was

one of those cases of sick conscience, so common in the Intelligentsia, and the period of his activities was one of disequilibrium in social ideas. Most of the older men and women had been brought up in the traditions of serfdom. The former serf-owners had not forgotten their privileges and had not yet learned to "drink beer and keep accounts" —to adjust themselves to the conditions of a less ample life. The former serfs were free, and yet not free, economically dependent on their former masters, or on the new men (Uspensky describes one who had kept a maison tolérée in St. Petersburg) whose money had won them the succession. The new cash-nexus and the heavy demands for redemption payments, for poll tax, and for other imposts, have set all the peasants plotting and planning to find money: flattering the holiday sportsman from town who has roubles to spend: admiring the clever rogue who has grown rich, no matter how. The old type of official, who had supposed that it was sufficient to be polite to his superiors and have his gaiters brightly polished, is disconcerted by the discovery that "honest earnings"—the charming euphemism of happier days—are no longer permissible: and still more by the further discovery that there are peasants who will not offer them. The times are out of joint. And Uspensky yearns for the restoration of a harmony even though it be a barbarous one.

The truth was that the equalitarian Mir was a Populist ideal, and that it was perishing before the eyes of this Populist investigator. The agricultural banks and the cottage industries, beloved of Uspensky and the Populists, could not stop the devouring progress of capitalism. Now and again we hear from him a cry of the heart, as when he has a sudden vision of his loved villages passing under the yoke of a German master. This vision came to him because he had realised the weaknesses of his people, or the compelling power of the life of agricultural toil, which determined the form of every institution and dictated every action. In a powerful simile he describes them moving all together, like fish into the net; and he makes one of his characters say that they "live without will of their own, without thought of their own, live only in obedience to the will of their work: only to the tasks which the work lays upon them."

This sense of sacrifice to an inexorable fate was expressed in poetical form by his friend and colleague Nekrasov, when he wrote of the eternal repetition of that cruel way of life, "in which generations live and perish without trace, and leave no lesson to their sons."

There was, of course, another way of regarding the life of the farmer, and another peasant poet, Koltsov, puts a happy song into the mouth of his ploughman. But the "cursed questions" were not so insistent when Koltsov piped his bird-songs.

The idealist must always be in despair. He is debarred from optimism, as soon as he finds a gulf between his own ideas and those of others, by the belief that ideas rule the world. The Marxist finds the hope of a remedy in the knowledge that not ideas, but the relations of production, determine the course of events. He knows that there is at all events a possibility of putting things right. This is what a Marxist critic of Gleb Uspensky said, and the observation has the merit of suggesting one way in which the arrival of Marx changed the current of Russian thought: by putting optimism in the place of pessimism, even for those who cannot be content with existing realities. He taught that man can make his own history.

The sick conscience found a satisfaction in expiation, and the character who takes this sort of pleasure in suffering is almost as much of a favourite with Uspensky as with Dostoievsky. One character is the brighter in soul, the more he is humiliated, and the worse he suffers from cold and hunger. Another, in the *Power of the Earth*, is happy after the beating which the magistrate orders for him. If Uspensky has these bonds of union with Dostoievsky, he has also bonds with Tolstoi. There is work which is good for a man and there is work which is bad. The work in the field, wringing subsistence straight from nature, is the good. The work of civilised life, and especially the work of the official, which is done merely to earn the means of living, is the bad. Here we are in company with the simplifiers and the natural anarchists, of whose thought Tolstoi gave us the supreme expression. And yet the peasant, as described in Uspensky's most elaborately drawn figure of Ivan Ermolaevich, is the very reverse of an anarchist. Rather he is the convinced conservative and individualist, taught by nature and by the agricultural life to obey and to command. Nature is to be obeyed, and obeyed under penalty of starvation and death. But to obey nature and do her work, Ivan must rule his family and his animals, the human and the non-human agents of toil, with an absolute rule. When his daughter-in-law falls ill, he and his family treat her harshly. The needs of the farm are too urgent, and he can't spare a single hand from work. These things teach him to understand the Tsar, and to regard the revolutionaries as of Antichrist. He will not listen to Uspensky's well-meant efforts to persuade him that co-operative effort would cure the troubles of the peasantry. A good manager will never lend his horse to a stranger. As to putting a stop to the depredations of a one-armed horse-thief by combining with others, to give him an honest job, "I should do better to break his other arm, so that he shouldn't steal." He is even inclined to leave the Mir, for "I once made a clearing, and, as soon as I had done it, they made a fresh distribution of the land." To every suggestion of changing anything he has one answer only: "We can't do without it." Religion is part of the necessary order, and Ivan teaches his son to pray in a jargon of half-remembered scraps from the creed and the liturgy. That we have in Ivan Ermolaevich at least one type of the actual Russian peasant, and perhaps the type most frequent in the successful farmer, we cannot doubt, and Uspensky thinks Ivan would hand him over to the police as an agitator if he were less kind-hearted than he is.

One of the colleagues of Gleb Uspensky on the *Notes of the Fatherland* was N. Mikhailovsky, a worker true to the type of Vissarion Belinsky: not a profound philosopher, not a writer of books, after his first essay, *What Is Progress?* and not a systematic finisher of anything; a journalist and a reviewer, whose thoughts lie scattered over many volumes. A Marxian critic warns us that a not too high opinion of the works of Mikhailovsky is the beginning of wisdom; and yet his influence was prolonged and profound.

In the first edition of *The Leviathan* of Thomas Hobbes of Malmesbury there is a picture of a crowned giant, with a sword in his right and a crozier in his left hand, standing above a landscape of towns, villages, castles, and churches. All that part of the body which is visible is made up of innumerable minute figures, the clergy, it seems, filling the place of the heart. Below are representations of diadem and mitre, cannon and spiritual lightnings, battle-field and council-chamber. In his introduction Hobbes tells us that the Commonwealth is but an "Artificial Man," the Sovereignty an "Artificial Soul," the Magistrates "Artificial Joints;" Reward and Punishment are the Nerves, and so on: the conception of society as an organism being completed by the statement that Concord is Health, Sedition is "Sicknesse and Civil War, Death." The Brahmins had the same idea when they located their own origin in the mouth of the Deity, and the other castes in less honourable parts of Him; and Menenius Agrippa used it to explain to the Roman Plebs why, for their own sakes, they, the arms and legs, must continue to serve the Patricians, the Belly of the Organic Commonwealth. It was no better than a picturesque metaphor, which Bluntschli reduced to an absurdity when he located in the navel of the organism—the point of severance of child from mother—the function of capital punishment in the State, and made that a reason for the maintenance of the institution.

Herbert Spencer put the conception of society as an organism into terms of Darwinian evolution, when he argued that evolution consisted of differentiation in the social as well as in the natural sphere. This meant that social evolution was the increasing division of labour, allotting progressively discriminated functions to the individual. Herbert Spencer's works were being translated into Russian towards the end of the sixties, and Mikhailovsky, then a young man of twenty-seven, fell with hostile ardour upon the theory. It was the apotheosis of the factory system, which sets one man eternally on the performance of a single operation for the making of a pin's head, and so—it is argued—destroys his integral humanity. If it does not go so far as this, it at all events tends to divide men into those who work with their muscles and those who work with their brains, and has in it the makings of an Indian caste-system. Mikhailovsky argued that, though the English working man is on a higher plane of civilisation than the Russian peasant, the Russian has a higher type of civilisation because it presents to him a wider range of activities. He saw that the Mir was decaying under the impact of a growing capitalism. But the Mir and the Workers' Fellowship were precious to him, as to all the Populists, as a refuge for the individuality of the common man, fleeing from the menace of an industrial revolution. He therefore advocated the maintenance of the Mir by the action of the Government.

He wanted to save the treasure of individuality from the predatory host that threatened it, by substituting simple for complex co-operation. But he got into difficulties, and had to shift his ground, when he came to define what he meant by these expressions. At first he evidently meant that the desirable form of co-operation was that in which all the workers engage together in the doing of a common task, as in the common cultivation of a particular crop. But someone naturally asked whether he proposed to sacrifice all the triumphs which industry has attained by specialisation: and he found it necessary to adopt a different definition. Simple co-operation became for him henceforth the co-operation of equals, complex co-operation the co-operation of unequals. The military camp of Zaporozhian Cossacks on the Dnieper—always a favourite example—was a case of simple co-operation, despite the differentiated functions of its members, because there was equality. He seems therefore, to the present writer, to have abandoned his objection to the excessive specialisation which condemns a man to the eternal performance of a single contribution to the making of a pin's head, and to have adopted in lieu the principle, excellent in itself but irrelevant to the original aim, of a classless society: in which the Marxists would heartily concur with him.

He missed the way out of the difficulty which was suggested by a less well-known Populist colleague, who saw that the production of a surplus, by giving leisure to the workman, would solve the problem. A man may still continue to work at the single process which contributes to the making of a pin's head, but if he needs to work at it only for a limited number of hours, the rest of the day is available for the development of personality along more varied lines. This is the solution of the industrial division of labour, to which the Bolshevik attempt to achieve an immensely increased production points the way.

Progress, for Mikhailovsky, meant not an improvement in an imaginary social organism attained by the sacrifice of the personalities of the individuals who make it up, but a tendency to proceed from the simpler to the more complex in the development of the individual. The struggle for individuality was, for him, a universal principle, beginning in the inorganic and gradually penetrating the organic world. "Every whole, blindly, elementally, in virtue of the immanent laws of its being, strives to subordinate to itself its parts, to convert them to service for the fuller perfection of its existence." The Darwinians are right that man is not the centre of the universe and that Nature has no aims, is not teleological, as the jargon goes. But man can make himself the centre. He can say: Nature is pitiless to me and knows no distinction between me and the sparrow so far as right goes. But I will be pitiless to her, and by my blood and sweat will subdue her, and compel her to serve me. I am not the aim of Nature nor has she any other aim. But I have aims and I will attain them. This is how Ivanov Razumnik, of the Maximalist "Scythian" school of socialists, paraphrased the meaning of Mikhailovsky. It is the conception of creative evolution, of the primacy of personality in a socialist society, because man fights the brute law of competition by means of co-operation.

Mikhailovsky, and his Populist followers, had at heart the interests of human personality. Work was not only necessary but was also that which completed and ennobled personality. Therefore the interests of personality meant, more concretely, the interests of labour, and, more concretely still, those of the Plain Folk, and in particular, but not exclusively, those of the peasant.

They did not think of the urban worker as something separate from the peasant, as the Marxists did: and the idea of the proletariat, property-less by definition, as the leader of labour would have been re-

pellent to Mikhailovsky, who looked upon property, or rights analogous to those of property such as the peasant had, as necessary to
the completion of personality. The hegemony which the Populists
envisaged was that of the men of ideas, of the intelligentsia.

If Mikhailovsky seems to us to involve his thought unnecessarily in
abstractions, to speak of simple and complex co-operation where we
should speak of equality, of the development of personality where we
should speak of freedom, let us remember that he was writing in
Russia and that there was a Censor to be evaded: a Censor with a
meritorious but not too penetrating staff, which might be deceived
by a judicious publicist into missing the point of the lesson. Nothing
is more remarkable in the history of the revolutionary thinkers than
the vast amount of thought, dangerous to the existing order, which
they succeeded in publishing: and nothing more strikingly illustrates
the comparative efficiency of the present régime than the success with
which subversive doctrines, as distinct from mere criticism of methods
and details, are kept away from the public.

Unlike Herbert Spencer, Mikhailovsky as an investigator of social
conditions placed himself mentally in the position of the man whom
he observed, suffered with his sorrows and wept with his tears, assumed
or created an aim for man and society and passed moral judgments
upon it; was subjectivist and teleological, as the learned say. He made
no bones of it and called himself a subjectivist, denying that objective
enquiry into such matters was fruitful or even possible. He recognised
with the positivists that only relative truth is accessible to man. He
gets the elements of it through his five senses. If he had more than
five, truth would present itself to him differently. The criterion of a
scientific sociology must therefore be the same as the general criterion of truth, the ideas of a normal, integral, all-round developed man,
totus, teres atque rotundus. As this perfect rotundity is rare, as there
is always a preconceived opinion, there is always a bias to the rolling
of the ball. Tell me, he says, to what social union you belong, and I
will tell you how you look upon things—a conclusion that is surprisingly near to the Marxian.

Mikhailovsky's popularity was at its height in the second half of the
seventies, when revolutionism was at its apex. Even earlier he had
been demanding the summoning of a constituent assembly, for he was
one of the first to preach the combination of the political with the
social struggle, an idea strange to the earlier Populists, but shared with
the Marxists. In the *People's Will* magazine he appealed to the revolutionaries to support the demand for a constitution. "You fear the

constitutional régime because it will bring with it the hated yoke of the bourgeoisie." (There was a fear that a constitution meant a middle-class domination as in England and France.) "Look about you! That yoke already lies upon Russia. To the European bourgeoisie, autocracy was an obstacle: to our bourgeoisie, it is a support. By standing apart from the political struggle did you stay the growth of the bourgeoisie? No, you helped it on: because the more autocratic the Police officer, the easier for the man of money to steal."

It has been convenient in this chapter to restrict our purview to the revolutionaries and their likes, but we must not forget the existence of a background of very different elements. In the middle seventies the Rural Councils were busy, and they had been followed by bodies of a similar kind, but with a more restricted franchise, in the towns. The Government was remodelling the army on a theoretical basis of complete equality for all classes in the matter of military service. Leo Tolstoi, not yet "converted," was writing *Anna Karenina*. Dostoievsky was at work on *The Brothers Karamazov*, which was to contain the germs of a religious revival. Khiva had been stormed by Russian troops, and Britain and Russia were glaring at one another across a would-be scientific frontier. The Panslavonic enthusiasts had jealous eyes upon the Turk in the Balkan peninsula, and Michael Katkov— high in favour with bureaucracy and nobility—was calling for a reversal of the engines of State. The reactionary novel, with the patriotic hero who fights the Poles and the Nihilists, was popular in the towns. A certain Evgeny Markov, of whom we know nothing else, was regretting the mistake of the Emancipation of the serfs, and remembering the good old times.

The prosecutions of 1874 had thinned the ranks of both the insurrectionist and the propagandist sections of the Populists, and in 1876 the surviving leaders united in a programme of "Land for the People," in an organisation which called itself *Land and Freedom*, after an earlier society of the same name in the sixties. This group seems to have included the northern Populists only; in the south the revolutionaries continued to wander, without plan or discipline, between Kiev, Kharkov and Odessa till a skilful police officer used their disorganisation to effect captures which put an end to their activities, and incidentally taught the lesson of the necessity of discipline in a revolutionary party—which Lenin was to assimilate with notable consequences.

In the meanwhile, in 1877, Russia was again at war, and at war in the Panslavist cause: and, as usual, war, or its result, was for Russia the occasion of intensified revolutionary ferment. Activity against the revolutionists increased, and thousands were put on their trial for political offences. The embarrassments of Government were increased by its diplomatic failure, and by the anger of its patriotic and orthodox supporters, who saw the fruit of Russian sacrifice enjoyed by Austria. The rejoicings which marked the acquittal of Vera Zasulich on the charge of shooting General Trepov, and her easy escape, show the half-convinced attitude of Russian Society in the struggle between Government and the revolutionaries. *The "Haves" were not sure of themselves and their rights.* A month after the Treaty of Berlin was signed, Stepnyak shot the Chief of Police in the capital, and Courts-Martial were set up to deal with attacks upon officials. The war was followed by a long crisis of unemployment, which sufficiently suggests the economic background of the years of revolutionary crisis.

Vera Figner, propagandist and revolutionist, has left us a record of the differences which now divided the revolutionists. The city members of *Land and Freedom* thought that those in the villages were doing nothing, because there was nothing to show. The Populists in the villages thought "that the city members were neglecting the real business of agrarian terror." One terrorist who had already attempted the life of the Tsar, is introduced as advocating his murder "as a means of producing greater activity in the movement." We shall clear away some misapprehension if we examine for a moment the different aims and methods of those whom we class together as terrorists. There were terrorists who stood for punitive or deterrent acts of terror against oppressive officials. This was what was meant by the Populists in the village when they talked of "agrarian terror." Entirely different aims were in the minds of those who demanded terroristic attacks on the Head of the State in order to secure political change.

By 1879 almost all sections of revolutionaries were in agreement with Mikhailovsky that the aim must be a political constitution, as a preliminary and an instrument of social change. Even Tkachev, the successor of Bakunin in the conspiratorial and insurrectionary section, was convinced that it was necessary to seize and use the machinery of the State, not merely to destroy it. A new body, calling itself the *People's Will* was brought into existence to pursue the political aim. The dissentients, among them George Plekhanov, soon to stand forward as the champion of Marxist doctrines, formed a separate group called *Black Partition.* As usual, in times of distress or strain, the countryside was seething with wild rumours of a coming redistribution of land, of the coming of Antichrist, and of the Day of Judgment. *Black*

Partition aimed at using the peasant's apocalyptic hopes to win his support for a social programme, and rejected the political weapon. It placed its trust in the workmen of the cities, was prepared to co-operate with the State, and founded groups for the study of Karl Marx. Zheliabov, the leader of *People's Will*, on the other hand, advocated the overthrow of Tsarism and the summoning of a constituent assembly. His programme included nationalisation of the land, but he deprecated present discussion of this or other economic questions, as likely to alienate the support of landlords and bourgeois liberals.

An inner ring of *People's Will* planned the murder of Alexander II, and achieved it on March 13th, 1881. The letter which was addressed to his successor demanded an amnesty for political crimes and a constitution in accordance with the findings of a free constituent assembly, and threatened "inevitable revolution" if these were not conceded; but the actual course of events was very different. The revolutionary parties were broken to pieces and revolution was reduced, as an able official boasted, "to a cottage industry." The heroism of the Terrorists, now killed or in exile, had behind it no popular resolve. Ivanov Razumnik, from the height of his Maximalism, calls the eighties the period of small deeds, and of political indifferentism erected into a principle, of a revolutionary intelligentsia which had decayed into renegades and *agents provocateurs*. Of this epoch, and its continuance into a later decade, Chekhov, with his pictures of aimlessness and futility, was the satirist. But it was as much an era of the birth of new forces as of the death or eclipse of old.

Before leaving the subject of Populism, apparently stricken to death by the failure of the eighties, and the absence of any response from the Plain Folk to the sacrifices of its champions, we must note its remarkable revival in the Social Revolutionary party. The peasant disturbances in the opening years of the twentieth century gave renewed hope to those who had believed in the revolutionary appeal of the land for the people. Victor Chernov, afterwards one of the successive Ministers of Agriculture in the Provisional Government of 1917, took up the mantle of Mikhailovsky, and set himself to prove the essential identity of the interests of the peasant with those of the town proletarian, and the solidarity of the whole working class. The idea was in essence identical with the "two-class party of workers and peasants" which reappears in the Oriental and Colonial policy of the Third Communist International, and is the subject of some of Trotsky's destructive analyses. Chernov's thesis was directed against the contention of a famous Austrian Marxist, that the peasant was a property owner and, as such, an unconditionally hostile element in a socialist revolution. The Bolshevik view was rather that the peasantry fell into two groups, one of which was proletarian, while the other was virtually capitalist, "petty bourgeois," as the jargon runs.

Victor Chernov, who published a full statement of the Social Revolutionary position in his *Constructive Socialism*, after the Bolshevik Revolution, stood for a triple alliance of the workers: at the plough, at the factory bench, and at the writing desk. He wanted a *Green International*, and he fixed his hopes for agriculture on small independent working farmers, a union of labour and property with a collective superstructure in the form of agricultural co-operation, and on individual farming. Instead of the nationalisation of land, and the centralised machinery of administration which that involves, he wanted its *socialisation*. That is to say, he wanted the land to be inalienable, and the right to it to be based on labour, and to be equal for all. But the forms of management were to be as various as local sentiment might demand and the methods were to be those of democratic self-government in each locality, with the right to appeal to a central authority against the deprivation of equal rights of enjoyment.

Such a policy could not but make a wide appeal to the peasantry, at all events until it was actually put into force, and the Social Revolutionaries received a majority of the rural votes for the Constituent Assembly of 1918, and actually dictated the main lines of the first Communist Decree on the employment of the land. The subsequent history of the party, known familiarly as the Eseri (S.R.'s) falls outside the scope of this study. It had not the definiteness of principle nor the rigor of internal discipline that characterised the Communist Party, and the reasons of its failure are the explanation of Lenin's success.

Chapter VI

SOME RELIGIOUS AND ANTI-RATIONALIST
THOUGHT

"Le niveau de notre âme est trop bas sur la terre!
Il faut monter encore, il faut monter toujours."
MADAME ACKERMANN.

I shall fail in my aim of providing a glimpse of the currents of thought in pre-revolutionary Russia, if I do not supplement my sketch of the pre-Marxian rationalists with some account of the religious and anti-rationalist thinkers other than the Slavophils. Few of these are revolutionary in intention, in the sense of proposing the overturn of the Russian State—though Leo Tolstoi comes near to that in his advocacy of elimination by negation—but all, with perhaps one exception, are preparers of the soil of revolution, and symptomatic of the coming harvest. More than one of them strike the note of religious expectation: that Man must surpass himself.

There were shocks in the early life and youth of Fyodor Dostoievsky sufficient to account for morbid lesions. One, of which we do not know the precise nature, affected him in childhood and produced a nervous disease which took the form of lethargic crises. When he was eighteen years old his father was murdered, and the old disease turned to epilepsy. Having joined a circle which occupied itself with the reading of Fourier and other Socialist writers, he fell into the hands of the police, when the repression, following on the European revolutions of 1848-49, was most active. He and other young men were led out for execution. Perhaps there was never any intention of carrying out the death-sentences. Anyhow they were commuted on the execution ground. The revulsion of feeling drove one of the youths mad, and Dostoievsky's mind probably received a lasting shock. Four years were spent by him in penal servitude in Siberia, followed by service in a disciplinary battalion, and it was not till 1859 that he was allowed to return to Russia. The experiences of the ten terrible years bore fruit in his story *The House of the Dead*.

Sigmund Freud has analysed his history and tells us more of the causes of the neurosis which affected him. A diabolical woman figures in more than one of his stories, and he thought ill of love, and ill of women in general, regarding them as a pit for men. He was married twice and had four children, of whom two survived him.

It is obvious that psycho-analysis must find in him a case of absorbing interest, for strange twists of soul manifest themselves in his work. Into one of these a political opponent, Mikhailovsky, "the great Doctor of the Populist Church," fixed his powerful intellectual teeth. In a long article entitled *A Cruel Talent* he showed that Dostoievsky not only loves suffering but takes a pleasure in inflicting it. It was easy to substantiate the charge by quotation. The man from the underworld who torments, quite causelessly torments, the girl Lise, tells her that one may intentionally torture a person out of love, and that love, for him, always meant to tyrannise. In fact he sometimes thinks that love consists in the right, freely given by the loved object, to tyrannise over it. He says he *always began love for hate*, and finished it as a piece of moral enslavement, and afterwards could not even imagine what one could do with the conquered object.

And then follows the startling reflection: what if these monstrous feelings are not monstrous at all, but only deep unknown secrets of the human soul, in which love and tyranny flourish side by side—or perhaps of the educated soul of the nineteenth century?

He discovered—or he rediscovered—the irrational element in man which philosophers—or at all events recent philosophers—had overlooked. It is as the great irrationalist rather than the anti-rationalist, that his title to originality is established. His Shatov, in *The Possessed*, says: "science and reason have from the beginnings of time played a secondary or subordinate part. Nations are built up and moved by another force, which sways and dominates them. It is the force of the persistent assertion of one's own existence, and a denial of death. It is the spirit of life, as the Scriptures call it, 'the river of living water,' the drying up of which is threatened in the Apocalypse."

Dostoievsky's interest in suffering seems sometimes a mere sadist delight in it. Sometimes it seems a passionate desire for regeneration by means of it, a religious conception of expiation for sin. And he believes, and frequently says, that the Russian people (in that limited sense which excludes the gentry and the educated) loves and desires it. Salvation is conceived as something corporate rather than individual, and the sins of all are to be expiated by each. As Khomiakov jested, "even into paradise the peasants enter only by communes." It follows that the cleansing fires are to be sought and endured communally, each for all and all for each.

This means a profound and general conviction of sin, a sense of the Fall, as a theologian might put it. Perhaps the psycho-analysts would tell us that the age-old prevalence in Russia of the patriarchal family, and the savage tyranny over the women and children which this institution meant, had created a universal sense of guilt in all, who had desired the removal of the ever-present tyrant.

It is certain, at any rate, that the passion of self-chastisement was common, and that Dostoievsky looked deep into the soul of his countrymen when he revealed it. What else he saw in that daring analysis, an analysis which takes us far beyond and below the bounds of reason, into some lower stratum of unconscious will, he himself could tell only by fits and starts. There are in him all the contradictions and unevennesses of the prophet, now at the zenith of his power, now at the nadir of depression and banality. But he clearly saw, or believed he saw, something which was new to the knowledge of mankind, or had been forgotten by it: and that was the polarity of the human soul, seeking for opposite things, even yearning for opposites, correspondences the conjunction of which should produce new powers and new values. The story of the peasant who betted that he would shoot at the Eucharist—a believing peasant too—is an illustration of this fluctuation between extremes. Why has man a passion for destruction and for chaos—evidently Dostoievsky feels this in himself as well as in others —though he also has the wish to make a new path through the wilderness? There is doubling, or a cleavage, of the spirit. Perhaps it is new, something which has appeared as the soul has grown more complex. Perhaps it is a struggle as of the butterfly within the chrysalis. Perhaps it is a prophecy of the changing of man into the God-man, the contention between the human and the divine which are in the end to be mutually complementary. That Dostoievsky himself saw something like this in the antimony which he revealed, seems certain. This particular thought was not new, for the Greek theologians did not regard the natures of God and Man as fundamentally separate, though they used the word Θεος in a sense which is not adequately translated by our word God.

It has frequently been noticed that Dostoievsky's religion is more concerned with Man than with God. This present life on the material earth is, in fact, the great opportunity in which Man is working out the possibilities of a great destiny. The Elder Zosima, in *The Brothers Karamazov*, speaks of the agony of the man who has missed this opportunity, even after he has risen up to the Lord. "Once, in infinite existence, immeasurable in time and space, a spiritual creature was given, on his coming to earth, the power of saying: I am, and I love. Once, only once, there was given him a moment of active living love. And that happy creature rejected the priceless gift." So that thereafter he must say to himself: "there is no more life for me and there will be no more time. Even though I would gladly give my life for others, it can never be: for that life is past which can be sacrificed for love, and now there is a gulf fixed between that life and this existence." Perhaps it was of the infinite preciousness of this earthly opportunity that Dostoievsky was thinking when he said that he belonged to a people capable of making a religion out of materialism.

In the Near East there is something holy about a madman, though whether the madness came from god or devil is not clearly settled. There is inspiration in his very folly. Dostoievsky, if he does not repeat this idea, at least raises the question whether disease is the necessary condition of the reception of the transcendent. For him, will must have the primacy over reason, and, it seems, the weakening of reason sets the will free. This is why he detests utilitarianism and the conformity of action to calculated advantage, and all that he describes under the satirical name of the *Crystal Palace*: presumably Chernyshevsky's Fourierist picture of the life of the Phalansteries, and organised Socialism in general, even happiness—or at least the deliberate search for it. If man's will could be completely subjected to his judgment, he would become a machine; whence the dionysiac side of Dostoievsky, the desire to break away from all restraints, the anarchical element which many have noted in him. In the ordinary sense of words he is the very reverse of a revolutionary: but there is in him revolution under the mask of reaction. As one of his successors said, he carried within him the principle of the great overturn, though he desired to fortify the structure. It is in his successors, in the school of thought which proceeded from his influence, that we find the extravagance into which the irrational tends to plunge, when the firm ground of reason is left behind.

Dostoievsky is no systematiser; perhaps he is not even a believer: but he passionately desires to believe. He even passionately loves orthodoxy, and says that no one can love or understand the Russian people who does not love orthodoxy. But his orthodoxy is not the orthodoxy of dogmas, but rather that "congregational" conception of the Slavophils (and of the Old Believers), the conception of mutual love and trust among brethren, in which, as Khomiakov taught, truth resides. For him, the atheist and the unorthodox were not those who disbelieved this or believed the other, but those who had torn themselves away from the native soil which nourished the orthodox Russian folk. "It's all like an ocean, I tell you," says the Elder Zosima, "and mutual love, and mutual acceptance of responsibility of each for all and all for each, will make the unity which is bliss." For him, as for so many—I had almost written for all—Russian thinkers, but under different terms and phrases, Russia was the "God-bearer," having a Messianic mission. To the reactionaries, the Messianism is one of reaction; to the revolutionaries it is one of revolution. In Dostoievsky's imagination the mission ceased to be one to the Slavs, it became one to all the world; but always a mission of Russia herself: of the Orthodox land and the Orthodox folk. The mission was to be attained by the conversion of the State into a Church, by a Theocracy gathering the peoples under Orthodox wings. In *The Idiot*, Prince Myshkin has a vision of the whole of humanity rising again, renewed by the Russian thought (the idea of Theocracy), and of the "astounded world, astounded and dismayed, because it expects of us nothing but the sword ... because, judging us by ourselves, the other peoples cannot picture us free from barbarism."

In the famous speech in praise of Pushkin, which the Slavophils greeted as a historical event, Dostoievsky spoke of the Russian people as possessing a special gift for embodying in itself the idea of the unity of all humanity, and made the poet's depiction of this all-human quality one of the leading justifications of his panegyric. He even saw in the reforms of Peter the Great the unconscious aim of the attainment of the unity of mankind, and declared that "the task of coming generations in Russia will be, in the end perhaps, to utter the final word of the great universal harmony, of the final brotherly agreement of all peoples in Christ's evangelical word." We must take it as an echo from contemporary politics, that Tsargrad (Constantinople), in Russian hands, was to be the centre of this new all-human federation. The mood was not always the same, and Dostoievsky was quite capable of railing at foreign nations and at Jews, and of declaring the necessity of wars.

He was an intimate friend of Konstantin Pobiedonostsev, of whom we have already heard something in this study. His eyes were not closed to the social evils of Russia. He saw that "money-lenders and devourers of the Commune were rising up: the peasants rotting in drunkenness: and what cruelty to their wives and to their children! I've seen in the factories children of nine years old, frail, rickety, bent and already depraved." He scoffed at the "Liberal" freedom, which was so obviously for the rich man only, having power and means to satisfy his desires. But his remedies for these evils were not, after his early days in the Petrashevsky Circle, which took him to Siberia, the remedies of the Socialists. "Equality is to be found only in the spiritual dignity of man. If we were brothers, there would be fraternity: but without that, men will never agree about the division of wealth. . . . But God will save Russia. Salvation will come from the people, from their faith and their meekness." We note that, as with the Populists, it is the plain folk, the Narod, which is the saviour.

V. Rozanov, one of the successors of Dostoievsky, has been described by a penetrating Russian critic as the greatest writer of his generation (that is, in the purely literary sense). It is with the substance of his writings, not with their form, that we are here concerned. Among his earlier works was an essay on the interpretation of Dostoievsky's legend of the Grand Inquisitor. The Rome which built the lie is the deceiving scarlet woman of the Apocalypse, and her fall is at hand as is there prophesied: "Thus with violence shall that great city Babylon be thrown down and shall be found no more at all." He ends on the note of the sins of the West. Only Eastern Orthodoxy, avoiding alike the universalism of the Roman and the individualism of the Protestant Churches, sits with Mary at the Master's feet. The apocalyptic tone, so truly echoing Russian popular imagination, is absent from the Slavophil writers, but is characteristic of Dostoievsky and of his successors in religious speculation. Antichrist, and the tremendous imagery of the Book of Revelations, are present realities to them, as they are to the masses of the Russian people whenever the strain of life is intensified by suffering and calamity.

Konstantin Leontiev (1831-1891) at the end of his life came to a strange dream of the World Socialist Revolution—from the lips of an aristocratic reactionary—conceived as under the leadership of the Orthodox Autocrat, enthroned at Constantinople, with the blessing of the Orthodox Church! But it was not so strange that none could plan to carry it out. The "police socialism" of Zubatov and Father Gapon, a decade later, was an essay in this very direction. There is something in these anti-revolutionary writers which smells of vast impending change, reflects a general expectation in society of revolution to come. Leontiev, judged by all his earlier utterances, hated Socialism, but he is fascinated by a sense of its inevitability, and hopes, by putting Tsar and Church at its head, to preserve a little of the "organised multiformity" and aristocratism which he loves. It is not the familiar British spirit, astutely willing to meet particular grievances as they become urgent, while holding on with a crusty pluck to the central citadel whence the grievances proceed. We might take it to be merely the failure of the courage of an individual, afraid of Socialism for society, as he was afraid of eternal perdition for himself. But it does not stand alone among the evidences of readiness to compromise with social peril, which was one of the factors in the success of the Revolutions. They succeeded, because the possessing classes had ceased to believe in themselves.

❆   ❆   ❆

A revival of religious idealism in the eighties had found a double expression in Count Leo Tolstoi and in Vladimir Soloviev. The latter had aspirations to the establishment of a Universal Church, and, like Peter Chaadaev, he wished to see the Roman Church at the head of it. The national Church, if it was not to become a mere department of the State, must have a support outside the State and of the Nation, and it was in Rome that this support was to be found. In an apostrophe to the Apostle Peter, he says:

"Thou knowest that the Church has need of an earthly body to manifest herself. Twice already thou hast given her a social form: first in the Greco-Roman world, and then in the Romano-German world, thou hast set under her the empires of Constantine and Charlemagne. She awaits her third and last incarnation."

There must be a Universal Monarchy as well as a Universal Church: for the Church, without a secular power distinct from, but united with her, cannot establish upon earth Christian justice and peace. For the creation of the political power which is to save and regenerate Europe, Russia is historically destined.

Such were the basic theses of Soloviev's theory of Church and State, as expressed in his *Russia and the Church*, which was published in 1888, not in Russia, and not in the Russian language, for the Ecclesiastical Censors could not have tolerated the ecclesiastical supremacy assigned to Rome, but at Paris and in French. We are back among the conceptions of Universal Dominion, spiritual and temporal, which laid the foundations of the Holy Roman Empire. There is a mediaeval flavour too in Soloviev's typification of the twofold government of Church and State by the twofold nature of Christ, human and divine. One heretic, Nestorius, he says, separated the human from the divine nature. Even so, the false liberalism separates State from Church and sets the twain asunder. Another heresy, that of the Monophysites, made the human nature of Christ disappear in the divine. Even so, some to-day abandon the earthly world, the states and the empires, and would absorb the human soul in contemplation of Divinity. The true Orthodox must avoid both of these errors and maintain the bond which links the human state to the Church of God, as the humanity of Christ was linked to the divine Word in Him. The Church must neither dominate nor submit to domination by the secular power, and there can be no question of supremacy as between the two. The line of reasoning may be mediaeval, but the conclusion is clear.

The characteristically Russian conception of *sobornost*, "congregationalism," figures prominently in the thought of Soloviev, and it is a "congregationalism" of the State as well as of the Church. Christians are where Christian society, State as well as Church, is. Christianity is social. There must be a Church and an Empire to enshrine the politically and socially organised world. There is no Kingdom of Heaven for the individual. His salvation must be a corporate one along with his fellows. Christianity has failed, hitherto, for lack of the Church and the Empire, in which the aim is now to enshrine it. The pseudo-Christian, or semi-Christian, doctrine that the Kingdom of Christ, and the teaching of Christ, are for the individual has produced the false ideas of individualism which, in Soloviev's view, are responsible for all the anomalies of history, and, in particular, for the aberrations of the Revolutions. Within this framework of Christian State and Church, Man is depicted as the Messiah, who is to save the world from chaos by uniting it to God, by incarnating in created forms the eternal Wisdom—that Σοφία which has become the object of a special cult within the order of the Orthodox Church. The Russians, says Soloviev, in dedicating their most ancient temples at Kiev and elsewhere to the Holy Wisdom have distinguished her clearly both from the Mother of God and from Jesus Christ. She is the Guardian Angel of the earth, future and definitive appearance of the Divinity, the Soul of the World, as he elsewhere calls her: the feminine principle, to which, in the post-redemption cosmic process, human reason mystically supplies the place of an active and creative principle. The East, while avoiding the temptation of materialism, pride, and aspiration to universal ecclesiastical dominion—typified by the Temptations on the Mount—into which the West has fallen, has been deficient in this active and creative principle. In the union of all humanity, the West will supply what the East has lacked.

This is a rarefied air, which only the adept can breathe with freedom and security. It is dangerous to change the language of a theologian. But it seems plain that, in the thought of Soloviev, Man supplies something which is lacking to God. It is he, not God, who is the Messiah now: it is he, and not God, who completes the cosmic process

in the realisation of the God-man, man made divine by the identifica-
tion—lost at the Fall—of his will with that of the Divinity. The God-
man has already once been realised in Christ—but not by way of an
Atonement, which, for Soloviev, is "a casuistical solution of an impossible law-suit," and a purely juridical idea sprung from the legal
notions of Rome. He is now to be realised in mankind. But the process
is not completed in the individual: it takes place in society, made perfect by the fully Christian State and the fully Christian Church. The
end is the creation of the Kingdom of God upon earth, in a new
cosmos, in which (this is quoted from N. A. Berdyaev, who is the
modern continuator of the thought of Khomiakov, Dostoievsky and
Soloviev) "food shall be the Eucharist, union shall be marriage and
the awful watery element shall be Baptism," all things shall be transformed into the sacraments of which they are the prototypes. It is to
be a universal Salvation, a transfiguration of the Cosmos. *Man must
surpass himself.*

We wonder no longer that each and all must do expiation for all
and each; a notion widely present in all Russian thought, both learned
and popular.

It is not necessary to share these visions in order to see how en-
nobling is the part which they assign to Man; with how much of
Russian thought they are akin in their contemplation of a social, a
corporate, salvation; how closely the issue of them corresponds with
that belief in the Kingdom of Heaven upon earth, which was the object of so many Russian hopes; how they include all peoples in one
transcendent unity. In a society with these infinite potentialities of
ennoblement, as Soloviev sees them, nothing mean or base was to be
tolerated. For the Orthodox Church, as hitherto conceived, serfdom
and barbarous punishment were not contrary to the spirit of Christianity: for physical suffering does not interfere with the salvation of
the soul. But a Christian society, conceived as a union of man with
God, could not be indifferent to the sin of the oppressor. There is no
room in it for distinctions of class, for true social good is union. Baptism is the sacrament of liberty. There must be no serfdom, and no
slavery in any form, to contradict in the social sphere the liberty which
Baptism has given in the religious. Confirmation gives to each Christian the sacred unction of the King. Communion crowns the other
two, making all brothers and sons of God. There is a triple union to
accomplish: that of the individual, by his union with his complement,
woman; this is the sacrament of Marriage, symbolic, it seems, of the
mystical union of human reason with the feminine hypostasis, the

Divine Wisdom: that of social man, by reuniting the individual with human society; the type of this reintegration is given in the ecclesiastical hierarchy by Ordination: and of universal man, by restoring his union with the organic body of humanity in the sacrament of Extreme Unction.

The last words of *Russia and the Universal Church* are these: "The cycle of the sacraments, as well as the cycle of universal life, is closed by the resurrection of the flesh, by the integration of all humanity, by the definitive incarnation of Divine Wisdom."

This is no mere Christian Nirvana. We shall see presently that Vladimir Soloviev, however high his head may be set, has his feet firmly on the solid earth, though it is a transfigured earth. That he does contemplate the immortality of transfigured individual man in a transfigured universe is made plain by another work of his, *The Justification of the Good*. Discussing the spiritualisation of marriage, he says that the children in the present imperfect state are needed to do what the parents have failed to accomplish. But to accept as a permanent condition of the life of man, this succession of mortal generations is to accept the kingdom of death. It is evident that, in the cosmos changed as he expects it to be changed, among men who have raised themselves to participation in the Godhead, marriage as a means of carnal reproduction will cease to exist, because the immortality of individual man will have made the succession of mortal generations unnecessary. This (presumably) represents what Adam and Eve might have been but for the Fall. The Fall brought Death, and it brought Reproduction, inevitable companions unless life was to cease.

※　※　※

Count Leo Tolstoi (1828-1910) was one of the great artists of all time, his vision penetrated to the deepest recesses of the human heart: and he was also a man of the world, a landlord who for many years cultivated a large part of his own estate as a home-farm, and made it pay; he was an enlightened schoolmaster on principles learned from Froebel himself; he served as an Arbitrator of the Peace in the distribution of land at the Emancipation of the serfs; and his account of his distribution of famine-relief in 1891-92 shows that he had all the instincts of a first-class administrator. If to all these things he had added the qualities of an original and coherent theologian and philosopher, the combination would have been without parallel in history. Without any desire to depreciate the quality of his thought, we must be prepared to look at it undazzled by the splendour of his literary reputation. If we do so we shall find, among other things, that, like his own Karataev in *War and Peace*, "he often contradicted what he had said before," though, it may be that "both statements were just."

Though he himself talks of having lived a vegetable life for fifteen years, he was never one of the peaceful souls who are untroubled by questionings. Rather he belonged to the type which Russians recognise under the name of "wanderer," and was for ever agitated by moral problems, for ever spiritually on the move: like his Pierre Bezukhov, who wandered from the life of the man about town to Freemasonry, and thence passed under the influence of a peasant ideal. His final departure from his home, in search of something that in his eighty-second year of life he still had not found, is typical of him.

Like all the clever young men of the forties who were not Slavophils or in training for the Episcopate, Tolstoi abandoned Christianity at an early stage: and he was not reconverted till he began to be obsessed, towards the end of his fifth decade, by the realisation of death. In the interval the great novels were written, and they show two influences which persist throughout his life. One, as we have seen elsewhere, was present in the air of Russia. It was the worship of the Plain Folk, and in particular of the Peasant. The other was a strain of Buddhistic or Hinduistic thought, which he derived through Schopenhauer, and which was only modified, not eliminated, by a third influence, that of the ethical teaching of Jesus Christ.

The so-called ethical Christianity is not Christianity in the ordinary sense. There is no original sin, and man's nature is essentially good. Christianity, as professed and practised, is regarded as a heresy far removed from the teaching of Jesus Christ. That teaching, taken from the teacher's recorded words, and sometimes with the interpreter's own corrections of text and translation, is the religion of Tolstoi, and the aim of it is the establishment of the Kingdom of God upon earth.

It is in no way surprising that the authorities of the Orthodox Church excommunicated him in 1901. The surprising thing is that they waited more than twenty years to do it, and that they allowed the publication of so many subversive books: of the *Confession* which rejected the authority of the State and Church, and denied personal immortality: of *What I Believe* and *The Kreutzer Sonata* and *The Kingdom of Heaven Is Within You* and *The Christian Doctrine* and *Resurrection*. All through these years Tolstoi had been preaching the doctrine of anarchy: of the destruction of both State and Church by a system which his Indian follower, Mahatma Gandhi, would describe as non-co-operation, but, to be directed, not only against a bad State and a bad Church, but against every kind of State and every kind of Church, as in their essence bad. His is the complete individualism which leaves everything to the conscience of each. His anarchism is unqualified by those beliefs in "orthodoxy" and "congregationalism" which modify the anarchism of Dostoievsky, or by the acceptance of the immemorial substratum of Hindu doctrine which modifies that of Mahatma Gandhi. Its quietism and non-violence may have seemed to take the danger out of it: and this may be why he was left for twenty years in nominal communion with the Church, and suffered to publish the most subversive of political doctrines.

And yet when the Revolution of November came, it was much closer in type to the negative conception of a Tolstoi than to the insurrectionist dreams of a Bakunin. True, it was an insurrection in Petrograd which carried the Bolsheviks to power. But the Revolution was something greater, and widely different in kind, from that insurrection. Society is like a building which stands by the compulsion of its own weight: so long as the natural thrusts continue to be met by the resistance which the architect has prepared against them. Something perishes or is withdrawn; and eventual collapse becomes inevitable. States exist because men believe and obey; because the social machine divides up the social responsibility so that no one feels to what extent the acts and abstentions required of him are contrary to what his individual desire or conscience would prescribe. If and when each comes to say, as Tolstoi bids him say, "For me, I have no need of the State," and takes his own path accordingly, the belief and the obedience are gone, and the State is at an end. In its essence, the Revolution in Russia was precisely this. *The keystone came out of the arch.* The armies became a crowd of individuals on their way home; the peasants were dividing up the land of the lords.

When such things happen—and they have happened often, and we call them the fall of empires—there is a painful and sometimes infinitely prolonged process of rebuilding, during which a portion of the world reverts to barbarism, and mingles regression with restoration. I take it that this is what we are witnessing in the modern Union of Soviet Socialist Republics; so there is no ground for surprise that friends and enemies both find, in their contemplation of the rebuilding operations, ample material to justify their own sympathies and convictions.

I do not say that Leo Tolstoi made the collapse. Rather he bore witness, with all the power of the artist, to the existence, in the Russian

State and in the Russian people, of those fissures which made the collapse imminent. Strongly anti-revolutionary, he was nevertheless a prophet of revolution.

The doctrine of non-resistance was held by him before, as well as after, his so-called conversion. Dostoievsky satirised it in 1877, in an imaginary conversation with Lévin, Tolstoi's representation of himself in Anna Karenina. He puts to Lévin the case of a child on the point of being killed by a Turk (these were the days of the Bulgarian atrocities and of the Bashi-Bazuks). Lévin is made to say: "How can I kill the Turk? It is better that he should gouge out the eyes of the child. But I'll be off to Kitty." (That is, to Kitty Sherbatskaya, Lévin's wife.)

A revolutionary view of Leo Tolstoi has been given by Boris Pilnyak, who has never shown servility to the men of the moment and was recently in trouble for his independent views. He has himself declared that he is a non-Bolshevik, but he likes to associate with Bolsheviks "because they have buoyancy and cheerfulness." He speaks of the "holy and idiotic philosophy of Tolstoi's Karataev" as something diametrically opposed to the aims of the Bolsheviks. They desire to regulate life by conscious rational purpose, while Karataev represents an elemental, senseless automatism. Indeed, if we attempt to picture a nation of Karataevs, we find ourselves returning to Gleb Uspensky's simile of the shoal of fish rushing together into the net.

There are, however, no signs that the present Government of Russia desires to limit the circulation of War and Peace. On the contrary it tolerated a Tolstoyan school at Yasnaya Polyana, gave some measure of support to Tolstoi's daughter against the hostile zeal of local Communists, erected a monument to Tolstoi himself, and still pays a small pension to one of his relatives. Only the books which preach anarchy are banned: for the Bolshevik State is a powerfully organised one, and greatly does it need its power and its organisation, if the task of rebuilding is to be performed.

Marxian doctrines were widely current in Russia throughout the greater part of Tolstoi's work on social and religious questions. Their influence upon him, particularly in the story of Resurrection, is evident. Nekhludov, the hero, after living the life of a man about town, repents, and follows to Siberia the woman whom he has seduced. In his visits to the prison he sees plainly that peasants are being punished for offences to which they have been forced by economic oppression and for hindering the officials and the rich generally from enjoying the property which they have taken from the people. He discusses the question of punishment with a lawyer, and when the lawyer says it is just, he interjects: "As if justice were the aim of the law!" "What else?" asks the lawyer, and Nekhludov replies: "The upholding of class interests. The law in my opinion is only an instrument for upholding the existing order of things to the advantage of our class." It is the conception of the class-war, and of Government as the instrument of the dominant class. In 1905 he is appealing to the Emperor to make an end of private property in land.

Vladimir Soloviev, who had faced the terrors and splendors of a transfigured cosmos, had enough versatility to write a manual of practical social ethics in which, without naming either Karl Marx or Leo Tolstoi, he discussed and criticised some of the doctrines of both which were exercising the brains of the nineties. Soloviev stood for that social Christianity which is the natural outcome of the doctrine of *sobornost*. The spirit is not a gift to the individual, but to the congregation. It is something undivided and indivisible. Man—not the individual man, but Man organised in the fully Christian Church and the fully Christian State—is the necessary complement and helper of a God who needs that complement and that help. N. Fyodorov, author of *The Philosophy of Common Work*, carried the same reasoning to a conclusion more immediately affecting the State. The gift of the spirit has been torn into fragments, and must be reunited in the common and active task of the reconstruction, economic and social, of society. This conception of religious duty brought the author so near to the Bolsheviks that his work retained some of its popularity after the Revolution.

A movement which can be clearly traced to Dostoievsky and Soloviev is the religious-philosophical movement of the early part of the twentieth century. Kartashev, afterwards Minister of Cults in the Provisional Government, advocated the liberation of the Church from the tutelage of the State. He found an associate in D. S. Merezhkovsky, who, after an early period of Hellenism, in which he sought for a synthesis of flesh and spirit, turned to a more definitely Christian inspiration. The two together founded the *Society of Religious Philosophy*, which brought together such laymen as Rozanov and Shestov (of whom there is something more to be said below) with cultivated churchmen. The aim in ecclesiastical policy was freedom for the Church, but some of the members at least were adepts of the mystical teachings of Soloviev, and looked for an imminent revelation of the feminine hypostasis, the Divine Wisdom, and the transfiguration of the cosmos. Projects for the revival of the Patriarchate, abolished by Peter the Great, were in the air, and the reactionary newspapers talked spitefully of a plot to create two Tsars and destroy the Orthodox Autocracy. Merezhovsky and his wife Zinaida Hippius, a gifted poetess, dabbled in Revolution in 1905, and the Tsarist Government doubtless had reasons for looking with some suspicion on the *Religious Philosophical Society*. Indeed the idea of the more complete freedom of the spirit, unless allied with a distinction such as Leo Tolstoi drew, between the inner and the external freedom, was not a comfortable bedfellow for Autocracy. In it we see yet another of those influences which seemed to be making for revolution among non-revolutionaries.

The Christian Revival (for it is not too strong an expression) extended into another and a very unexpected sphere. Hitherto not only Socialism, but even Liberalism, had been associated with the negation of the Christian metaphysics. Now religion passed into the ranks of the political reformers. A group of religious Liberals, including such distinguished names of former Marxists as Peter Struve and N. A. Berdyaev, published, in 1907, a volume formulating the new political philosophy; but it will be convenient to postpone an account of their views to the chapter in which we shall consider the coming of Marxism.

In the years immediately preceding the First World War, there were further indications of the activity of religious thought in the establishment of the Imaslaviye movement, for the worship of the Name of God, which, Berdyaev says, is characteristic of Orthodox Mysticism. The Holy Name, he tells us, contains the divine energy which penetrates and changes the heart of man; and he assigns the cult to the influence of Platonism, which was preserved by the Eastern Patristic tradition when St. Thomas Aquinas and the Scholastic philosophers turned to Aristotle, and affirmed that man and the world belonged exclusively to the natural order. In Platonism, as the Eastern Fathers conceived it, the earth is only the symbol of the heavenly and spiritual. The Holy Name, in the same way, is the symbol of something not otherwise to be grasped or formulated, the vehicle of the incommunicable. In the worship of the Name, I cannot but recognise a kinship with the religious conceptions and practices of Asia, and catch a glimpse of something which Western thought has lost—or escaped: for I prefer to leave open the question whether it be loss or gain.

The gigantic figure of Nietzsche, who owned Dostoievsky for one of his masters, had for long loomed large upon the Russian imagination, but it was not the most characteristic ideas of the master which had the greatest influence. The idea of the Superman was not new. Madame Ackermann had already made Nature apostrophise her creature Man with the warning:

Tu n'es pas mon but, il faut que tu périsses.

But it was the notion of surpassing man by something greater which contributed to Soloviev's conception of the evolving God-man in a transfigured cosmos, and inspired a group of Russian poets and writers with a contempt of small deeds and gradualism, and a demand such as that of Ibsen's Brand for the heroic and the impossible. This group, calling itself the Scyths, combined the influences of Dostoievsky and Nietzsche. In Leo Shestov we see God depicted as transcending human standards of morality and reason, as "demanding always and only the impossible"; only to be achieved by a dionysiac escape from common sense, such as the monks of the Thebaid sought by asceticism, and by the second sight of unreason, such as comes just before death and came to Dostoievsky in the underworld of prison. The Master's order is more imperious than that of Reason, says Shestov. For, having destroyed Reason, you will only be a fool; but, having disobeyed the Master, you will lose your soul. It is precisely reason and common sense which block the vision, because that which is to be perceived is beyond reason and common sense. The natural vision must be confuted by the supernatural vision, which is the gift of the Angel of Death.

This maximalism of the Scythian group, demanding always and only the impossible, was championed and expounded by Ivanov Razumnik, the despiser of smugness and respectable philistinism, and it passed into Russian poetry, where it grew into a revolutionary messianism, as entirely foreign to Nietzsche's outlook on the world as was the racial and the nationalistic maximalism of which he was the unintentional parent in Germany. What was new in Nietzsche, or what was newest in him, was that he was a revaluer of values, neither immoral nor amoral, but the sceptic of an old morality and the seeker of a new. Previous philosophy had left Christian ethics alone, while striking deadly blows at Christian metaphysics. But Nietzsche placed himself beyond good and evil, in order to ask whether that which has long been held to be good and evil is really good and evil. He saw the old morality as something fit for *slaves*, and insisted on the creation of a new one fit for *masters*. By an irony of circumstance, which is perhaps less rare than we suppose, these Russian Nietzscheans, trans-

formed into revolutionary Messianists, found themselves championing the older morality which their master despised and rejected. For,
if we tear from our minds the veil with which anti-clericalism and
the jargon of irreligious profession have obscured them, we shall see
the Bolshevik revolutionaries in the true line of succession of the
Christian moralists: seeking, in the language of the Canticle, to cast
down the mighty from their seat and to exalt the humble and meek.
The revolutionary ethics were those of which Nietzsche had sought to
make an end; and when the poet Blok set the stamp of eternity upon
his vision of "the twelve" with the figure of Christ marching at their
head, he was denying him whom the Scyth Maximalists took to be
their master.

We have Ivanov Razumnik's own account of the central idea of
these Scythian revolutionaries. The introduction of Christianity to
the world, nineteen hundred years ago, was a revolution, but a revolution which the old world captured and brought to naught. Christianity made a new man, and the new man was spiritually free. But
his spiritual freedom was left uncompleted by physical, economic
and social freedom, because the victory of the old world marred the
work. A new revolution has now come to complete the old. The gospel
of the new is the gospel of the old, that is of the liberation of man.
But, this time, there is to be a complete liberation, physical, economic
and social, as well as spiritual. It is the mission of the Scyths, of the
newer nobler Russia which they represent, and indeed of all the
Scyths in spirit, of whatever country they be, to break up the smug,*
respectable, philistinism of Europe, and effect this apocalyptic transformation. As we might expect, these ideals found a natural home
among the poets.

✻ ✻ ✻

If we are to attempt to summarise the attitude of the Russian people to Religion at the time of the Revolution, we must begin with
the definite affirmation that the Church, as an organised institution,
had lost all religious influence. She collapsed, as the State collapsed.
She was to be rebuilt, on new foundations, before she could become
again the God-bearer. Dostoievsky and Vladimir Soloviev were, per-

* The word which I have tried to convey by smug, respectable and philistine is
Myeshchantsvo, which might literally be translated by townsmanship or bourgeoisie. It seems to mean the opposite of the heroic spirit of Ibsen's Brand, a pursuit
of comfort as an end in itself, lack of courage, smallness, meanness: the sort of
thing which some artists have had in mind when they expressed a wish to épater
le bourgeois. Gradualness and small deeds are part of the idea. Courage and
activity are its negatives.

haps, the beginners of the new construction. Because the Church, as such, made no appeal to man, the religious cry in the Civil War never roused the masses. There was nothing similar to the Pilgrimage of Grace in sixteenth-century England, or to the use made of the clergy in the revolt of the Right in twentieth-century Spain. On the one side there was the desire to recover property and domination, on the other side the determination to cling to what had been won; and not even the pretence of a spiritual import illuminated the struggle on the side of the reactionaries.

But when we have said this, we are left with the deeper question of Religion apart from the Church. Merezhkovsky, describing a meeting of clerics and laymen in 1902, says: "The holy words of the Scripture in which we heard the voice of the seven thunders sounded to them like catechism-texts learned by heart." Little though we may be convinced by those who discover a profound religiousness in every peasant, the Russian people were more religious than their Church. Of the brotherhood of all the "orthodox" they had a profound sense, and the ethics of the Sermon on the Mount, however frequently ignored and flouted, were their ethics. It is questionable whether they gave any thought to personal immortality. In this respect, as in many others, Count Leo Tolstoi is a mirror of the Russian people. For the rest, the rites of the Church were a piece of necessary and salutary magic, which it was imprudent to omit.

Berdyaev's epigram was: "The people has given up Christianity and the Intelligentsia is coming back to it." There were certainly some grounds for the second half of this dictum. In the nineteenth century, outside of the Slavophils and the aspirants to ecclesiastical careers, religion had no following among the youth of the Universities or in Russian society. In the twentieth century, the tide was setting the other way, and the poets and the philosophers, even the politicians, had turned with it.

Chapter VII

THE COMING OF MARX

"However strange it may appear at first sight, yet it is actually Marxism—at first critical rather than orthodox Marxism—which has supplied us with an idealist, and, later on, a religious, current of thought."

BERDYAEV, *Origins of Russian Communism.*

"There are parts of what it most concerns you to know that I cannot describe to you; you must come with me and see for yourselves. The vision is for him who will see it."

Plotinus, as quoted by DEAN INGE.

"Marx introduced into revolutionary theory and practice the order, method, and authority, which had hitherto been the prerogative of Governments, and thereby laid the foundations of the disciplined revolutionary state."

PROFESSOR E. H. CARR, *Michael Bakunin.*

"The living core of Marx's doctrine was that he transformed a demand for economic justice into a demand for a just organisation of society; for a society so constituted that, in it, justice would, in virtue of its very structure, be done."

PROFESSOR HEREFORD, *Contemporary Review*, May 1927.

The Hebrew prophets proclaimed a vision of history and of its inevitable continuation into the future. There was in Karl Marx something of the passion for justice which inspired their utterances. But he was more than a Prophet, because he initiated the world into his method. He claimed to be scientific where the Hebrew Prophets claimed to have a revelation, and to show how Man could carry the work of Prophecy further, and play a part in its realisation. He had a close friend and collaborator in Friedrich Engels, who made large contributions to the joint work. It is possible to separate the contributions of the two, but for my purposes I shall not attempt the separation, but shall continue to call the joint work by the name of Marx.

Earlier Socialists had for the most part depicted the desirable, and had assumed that the idea of the desirable would win its way to acceptance, and reform the world according to its own image. They had not asked for the help of history to tell them what conditions were in process of development, and therefore actually capable of realisation. Marx called his own Socialism scientific, and the earlier Socialism utopian, because he made a new departure in this respect. He plotted the curve of history, as mathematicians say, and his prophecy was its continuation. Whether the curve was correctly or incorrectly plotted can only be decided by the event.

It is this plotting of the curve of history that is the essence of the Marxian method. And the method is more important than any of the results so far attained by it. For, without the method, prophecy degenerates into dogma, and, if right, is only right by accident or by inspiration. With the method, if it be sound, there is a vista of further results, ascertaining, perhaps controlling, the evolution of human society. They may even contradict Marx himself, as the Hegelian dialectic, in the hands of the young Hegelians, ultimately contradicted Hegel.

But there can be no plotting of the curve of history without the assumption that history follows laws of its own. At the back of the Marxian method lies this assumption. It adopts from the biological sciences the conception of evolution, and applies it to the life of human societies. History, in the sense of the activity of social man, enters the domain of law and becomes the subject of scientific investigation. Accidents, in the sense of events which have historic consequences but no historic cause (earthquakes, for instance) may deflect its course. Great personalities are accidents, but the field in which they operate has been prepared by history, and is not accidental. Just as we have to assume, for working purposes, that the order of nature continues unchanged, so it is assumed that the "accidents" will not suffice to disturb more than temporarily the working of the laws of history, and that the curve of human affairs can be plotted. But, as an Einstein arose to enlarge the work of a Newton, so some later thinker may teach us that the curve is to be plotted otherwise than Marx plotted it. Neither Marx nor Engels fancied that they had completed their own theory: any more than the theory of the origin of species had been completed by Darwin.

In plotting his curve, Marx went back to a very ancient theory of the universe. He accepted the doctrine that all things are permanently in flux, always in a state of becoming, that every form contains in itself the germ of its own destruction, but that the destruction is only the birth of a new form, which in turn must be destroyed and give place to a newer. This doctrine that all things are in flux he extended to the forms of social life. It is evident that we ought to change our metaphor and, instead of the plotting of a curve, speak rather of observing a stream of historical tendency, and of tracking it where the natural configuration of the country suggests that it must flow; but the nature of the soil offers possibilities of erosion and avulsion, which may modify its course, and sudden alterations of level may quicken it into a destructive torrent.

Behind all this there was a philosophy, going down to the very roots of being and of thought: but Marx and Engels never formulated such a philosophy in separate form. Their followers and commentators have done it for them (as they have done much else): but there is no doubt of its general character. One group of philosophers puts the idea before the thing. The philosophies of the great Religions, at all events of all the Religions which postulate a Divine Creator of the Universe, inevitably put the idea before the thing. Another group puts the thing before the idea, existence before consciousness. Hegel, of whom Marx in his early days was a worshipper, and whom he never ceased to admire even when he had, in his own language, turned him upside down, conceived that there was a logical idea at the basis of life, and that this logical idea developed itself progressively, and was the cause of all change, as a theologian might speak of a power within us, not ourselves, that makes for righteousness. The mature Marx rejected this pre-existent or co-existent idea, and substituted, as the cause of growth and change, social facts of an entirely different order, arising out of social life and social relations, and having no mystical character.

We are now prepared to consider what we mean by Dialectical Materialism. It owes a sad grudge to its godparents for a name wholly unintelligible to most of us, and of doubtful intelligibility to all. How doubtful is its intelligibility is shown by a recent suggestion that *materialistic*, in its application to the interpretation of History, means objective, realist, positive, and not materialistic at all in the philosophical sense of the word. At any rate it does not mean that History is mechanistic, but rather that it is to be treated as a branch of Biology. The present writer takes the materialism of Marx to consist primarily in the fact that he belonged to the group of philosophers who put the thing before the thought, who do not believe in the mystical pre-existence of the idea, who believe that thought grew out of a particular form of motion in matter, that there was no Divine Creator who "thought" of the Universe before it came into existence. It is materialism, secondarily, because it explains social life in terms of economic relations. In the Marxian view, history is, in the final resort, always to be explained by the social relations arising out of material production: though the connection of these relations with the facts is frequently obscured by a layer of intermediate causation.

This is why Dialectical Materialism is materialistic. Why is it Dialectical? We must expel from our minds all association of the word with local variations of language, and get back to its original significance of the art of discussion, of conversation and dispute, of the interchange of arguments, where A takes one view, B takes another, and finally, if they are reasonable people not too wedded to their preconceived opinions, they agree on something which is not precisely what either of them said at the beginning of the discussion. The Dialectic may thus be conceived as consisting of a statement, and a contradictory statement, and of a third statement which reconciles or embodies the other two. Let us now remember that in the view of Marx, to which he succeeded as the heir of a long line going back to the Greek Heraclitus, nothing is static, all things are in flux, in process of becoming. In such conditions a simple Yes, or No, is not the answer to any question. Yes is still true, while No is becoming true, and No is already passing into something that is neither Yes nor No. The Dialectic is the syllogism of a growing and a changing world, where truth also is a rushing river. He who argues dialectically must travel with that river, not stand on its bank and observe it as a stationary phenomenon.

Mr. H. G. Wells, little as he likes the Marxian doctrine, gives us precisely the appropriate metaphor in his autobiography, when he speaks of "running as hard as I can by the side of the marching facts, and pointing to them." We see him, in the light of this metaphor, as an enthusiastic collegian running by the side of his college boat, along the towpath of time, and pointing out from moment to moment how B gains upon A, till C comes from behind and successfully bumps B. At each moment his bulletin of information is correct, and at each moment it is contradicted and made untrue by the next phase of the eternal spectacle, fulfilling perhaps what the intelligent amateur has foreseen of the temporary issue. This is just what happens to the user of the dialectical method. There is indeed a singular correspondence between the method of Karl Marx and the method of Mr. H. G. Wells. The latter is trying to "disentangle the possible drift of life in general, and of human life in particular, from the confused stream of events," precisely the first part of the Marxian undertaking. He is also trying to do what our imaginary collegian can hardly be trying to do: that is, to find "the means of controlling that drift," like Marx, and probably with an equal amount of *parti pris*. When he speaks of the "change from life regarded as a system of consequences to life regarded as a system of constructive effort," he comes even nearer to Marx. Both are prophets, both base their prophecies on an observed curve in human affairs, or an observed stream of tendency; they have the same suspicious outlook on the national State, the same aspiration to internationalism, they have the same determination to help the fulfilment of the prophecy by the addition of human effort to the factors which contribute to it. The method of Mr. Wells is the method of Marx—without the jargon, or shall we say, with the substitution of the jargon of natural science for that of German philosophy—with new inductions from new facts, and without the conception of class-struggle which is no part of the method, but a particular induction from history and coloured and flavoured by the juices of an eupeptic in lieu of a dyspeptic nature.

As the conversation, which gave its name to the dialectic, proceeded by statement, counter-statement and agreement upon a third statement, which reconciled or included the other two, so the dialectic is conceived as proceeding, in this eternally changing universe, by thesis, antithesis and synthesis: each synthesis serving in turn for a new phase in a further similar process. Each successive phase in the process contains in itself a contradiction which must ultimately destroy it, and cause it to give place to the new phase. It is the disruptive force of the eternally repeated contradiction which moves the world and makes its history. If I may be pardoned for adding yet another metaphor to those which I have already ventured to employ, the contradiction is the force which produces the explosion, and the series of explosions is the motive power which impels the machine. Thus if we consider, for the moment from the Marxian standpoint, that particular balance of economic forces known as the Capitalist system, we see that, as the result of an earlier dialectical process, it superseded the Feudal system, because it provided an immensely greater range of economic satisfactions to man. No sooner has it done so, than internal contradiction begins to make itself apparent. The Capitalist system, as Marx sees it, is increasingly unable to find markets for its own products at prices profitable to itself, is compelled to restrict production, and becomes a fetter upon the growth of wealth. It therefore perishes and gives place to a new synthesis, that of Socialism, which does not need to demand a separate profit in each portion of the field of production, so long as outgoings are balanced by incomings over the field taken as a whole.

Truth itself is not something absolute or static. It is a perpetually shifting goal, to be approached only by successive approximations, each of which requires to be verified by practice.

In the particular example taken, the new synthesis, of Socialism, is not an automatic product of self-determining forces, independent of the will and action of man. There must be a concurrent activity of thought, feeling, and will, and Man must, so to speak, fling himself into the balance, in order to determine the result. The Capitalists and their supporters may prefer a smaller output of wealth for society as a whole, in consideration of retaining a larger share of it, and a dominating position for themselves. They may make a fight for it, with the help of the tremendous machinery of modern warfare, and defy the less well-organised majority. In short, they may make the synthesis something other than Socialism, and may be successful in the making of the alternative, *if the conditions are ripe for their success.* This is where the power of man to make his own history comes into the dialectical process. He has that power, but it is not an absolute power, because he can only win that for which the course of history has prepared the conditions. The Capitalist victory will be only a temporary set-back, if a system other than the capitalistic one is the one which fits the conditions of the time and gives the greater scope for development of the productive forces.

If we assume, for the moment, that Socialism is the synthesis, and that, as a further development of the dialectical process, the classless society, which is the Marxian aim, is attained, we are not to infer that this is the end of the process. It was not the affair of Karl Marx or of Friedrich Engels to follow the future of man beyond the termination of his economic antagonisms. Their purview extends to the attainment of a social constitution which gives scope to the forces of production, and their task ends there. But the dialectical process continues to infinity in the development of human personality. Set at liberty from economic pre-occupations, man has before him a limitless future, which it is for other eyes to explore. As Lenin put it, the immanent contradictions will remain, and their continuance is the necessary presupposition of further development. The whole of history is nothing but the progressive transformation of human nature, first unconscious, and afterwards conscious. A perspective of endless possibilities opens before us, with ample room for all the apocalyptic imaginations which for so long have occupied the Russian soul.

But this is not the point which concerns us at the moment. I have tried to convey my notion of what is meant by Dialectical Materialism. The operator—for he is more than an investigator—proceeding with the assistance of the dialectical method seeks to foretell the historical process by using economic relations as his clue through the darkness of the labyrinth, and by observing the internal contradictions whose function it is to produce the new phase by the destruction of the old: and he seeks to complete the process according to his own aim. Human will (it is human will conditioned by economic relations and environment) is one of the factors in the production of change; but only one of them.

Such is the method, which might be described as a method of induction assisted by certain special clues and accompanied by effort. As a method of inquiry it is one which might be used by any investigator, with or without the revolutionary bias, and has doubtless been employed, consciously or unconsciously, by most of those whose attention has been directed by the influences of Marx to the bearing of economics upon history. But the Marxian doctrine covers a much wider field than the Marxian method. In the first place, there are certain of Marx's inductions from his study of history and economics which have virtually passed into dogma. They spring out of his method, and they are presumably liable to be contradicted by the same, but their origin and their possible fate have been forgotten in reverence for the master.*

The most significant of these inductions is the class-struggle. We shall see presently that followers of Marx have not always and everywhere attached equal weight to this induction. It is obvious at all events that the class-struggle is not a permanent factor: for it comes to an end with the establishment of the classless society. A second induction, following closely upon the theory of the class-struggle, is the dictatorship of the proletariat, in the period after the defeat of the bourgeoisie and before the attainment of the classless society. It seems that Marx was indebted for this conception to a Russian source— Michael Bakunin. It has played an enormous part in Russia, where it has merged with the older conception of a messianic mission of the Russian people, and has, under the Constitution of 1936, lost its original significance of the domination of a class. Another induction of importance is the theory of Surplus Value, which shows us the cap-

---

* In this as in the other chapters the editor's sole aim has been to give the clearest presentation of Sir John Maynard's argument, from which his own views may differ in certain particulars.

italist employer taking from his workers an increasingly excessive share of the value of the product of their work. It was valuable to revolutionaries for the theoretical justification which it provided for the expropriation of the expropriator; regarded as the statement of the fact that the worker produces more than he consumes, it is almost a truism; and it has furnished to Russian Marxians one of their firmest principles: that one man must not be allowed to make a profit out of the work of another.

Apart from particular inductions which have found their way in a greater or less degree into dogma, Marx, the revolutionary, embodied in his works a mass of quite avowedly biased advice and instruction. Just as John Tanner, in G. B. Shaw's *Man and Superman*, wrote a Handbook for Revolutionaries, expanding Mrs. Poyser's thesis that "we must be born again and born different," so Marx provided, and intended to provide, the materials for a Revolutionaries' Manual: not a manual of tactics, but a manual of strategy; not the arithmetic of Revolution, but its algebra. He passionately desired the reconstruction of society on such a principle as would ensure economic justice, he did not believe that this reconstruction could be carried out unless it fell within the curve of history as plotted; but he believed that it did fall within that curve, and he wished to convince men that this was a true forecast. How far he thought that it could be brought by the conscious will of man within the curve, is one of the controversies. The elements of human will and activity being once introduced into the chain of causation, it seems impossible to resist the conclusion that the same method, in different hands, may lead to different results. At any rate there was no pretence of the enquirer's impartiality, on this side of his work. He wrote his Revolutionaries' Manual with the intention of teaching Man how to think, and whither to direct his energies, *if he desired the Socialist Revolution*. A natural consequence of this combination of intentions, of the provision of a method of enquiry along with a manual of revolutionary strategy, but clearly differentiated one from the other, is that the critics have questioned the value of the method. To announce, as some of his successors and commentators have announced, that the Marxian method is a means to a particular result, is to discredit it entirely as an instrument of scientific enquiry. That this is precisely the method of the representatives of the mystical philosophies, who demand the activity of the enquirer's will, as well as of his thought, in the search for ultimate reality, would not appear to invalidate the criticism, I suggest that method and handbook are separable, and ought to be separated; but to abandon the method, while retaining some of its results, is to invite dogma to run riot; and, man's brain being what it is, he is already only too willing to spare himself pains, by making a dogma and clinging to it. We must therefore retain the method, while leaving open the question of its results.

※ ※ ※

We are dealing with Russia: and the point which interests us is not so much what Marx himself meant as what his Russian followers and expositors understood him to mean. Michael Bakunin had been in close touch with Marx for some years before the publication of the *Communist Manifesto,* and he published a translation of it into Russian in Herzen's *Bell* in the early sixties. *Das Kapital* was first translated into Russian in 1872, and from this time there was a slow, very slow, infiltration of Marxist ideas among the Russian revolutionaries. The followers of Lavrov were popularly described as Marxists, presumably because he stood for propaganda, against the Bakuninist doctrine of conspiratorial insurrection, which was anathema to Marx. An illustration of the difference of the ways in which the works of a master may be interpreted is given by the notion, current in Russia in the early eighties, that the Marxists were the friends and supporters of Capitalism. A story was published in one of the magazines in which a disciple of Karl Marx was represented as glorying in the provision of agricultural machinery on an estate of which he is manager, and in the capitalistic developments there. The picture was not drawn without a reason. To the Marxian, or to the Marxian of one type, the capitalist system was one of the links in the chain of history, a desirable successor to feudalism, and an inevitable predecessor to Socialism. He really desired the fuller growth of capitalism: so much so that, at the time of the disastrous famine of 1891-92, some of the orthodox Marxists of the day protested against assistance to the peasants, on the ground that the growth of capitalism must not be impeded. Engels had said something similar much earlier, but, in informing the capitalist of the services which were expected of him, he had added the significant reminder: "But the executioner is at the door."

There was even a tendency to identify Marxism with the Manchester School of economics, which perhaps accounts for the Tsarist Government's long toleration of what was known as "legal Marxism," that is, Marxism expressed in the columns of the press legally published within Russia. This legal Marxism became the philosophy of the new class of managers and engineers brought into existence by the developments of economic policy by Count Witte. The non-terroristic character of the Marxian doctrine was doubtless a recommendation, but the Tsarist Censors were never remarkable for perceiving the ultimate tendencies of any teaching: and were evaded with an ease which strikingly illustrates the comparative efficiency of the present Government of Russia.

We have seen that Marx supplies a method of social enquiry, and also—quite separate from the method—a manual of strategy for the revolutionary in making the revolution. He also supplies some scattered hints which help the revolutionary in deciding what to do when the revolution has been effected. But he is quite misunderstood if he is supposed to supply a scheme of policy for the Dictatorship of the Proletariat when the Proletariat has come into power. The general aim is plain enough; the attainment of a classless society. But that is scarcely more definite than the Kingdom of Heaven upon earth, to which it has some remarkable resemblances. The Dictatorship of the Proletariat, in conducting its affairs towards the dimly envisaged goal, has a thousand things to do each day, and it is not part of Karl Marx's function to give instruction how they are to be done. Certain lines, mostly negative, are made plain. An end is to be made of exploitations of class by class, of man by man, and of woman by man. An end is to be made of private profit, whether it be made out of direct labour or out of the exchange of commodities. Socialism depends primarily upon the system of production: only secondarily upon the system of distribution. Production is to be recognised as a social function. Whether it is to be in the hands of some central organisation, or of local organisations, or of voluntary, co-operative societies, or even of individuals socially controlled and prevented from exploiting others, there is no attempt at definition. Engels did indeed suggest co-operative farming as the best method of dealing with peasant agriculture, but that hint stands alone. Distribution is left undefined, except that it is quite clear that it is *not to be egalitarian*. The worker's share will depend upon the work he does. Later on, when the classless society is attained, and the increase of production has removed the difficulties in the way of gratifying all desires, it will depend upon his needs. The factory is to be the centre of social and political, as well as of economic life. Woman is to be in every respect the equal of man, and the family is to take the new form which her emancipation and her work side by side with man will dictate.

These are important principles, supplying the foundation for a commonwealth aiming at the attainment of Socialism: but they leave the whole architectural superstructure to the wisdom and taste of the builders. For dogma in the conduct of day-by-day business, the teaching of Marx offers no justification: and its crystallisation into dogma, if that were to take place, would be fraught with results only comparable with those of the petrification of religious teaching, and more immediately ruinous.

Marx does not present his followers with an ethical system. He provides a method of ascertaining what will happen, not what ought to happen. But an ethical system based upon social justice must inevitably flow from the Marxian doctrine; and it will not be a Nietzschean system, built upon the exaltation of the superior few, but rather one in which all humans count equally as social units.

❊   ❊   ❊

The first systematic explanation of Marxist doctrines in the Russian language was given by George Plekhanov, whom we last saw as the exponent of the *People's Will*, in its new determination to use the political weapon, and work for a political constitution. His alternative hopes of a "Black partition," that is of the allotment of additional land to the peasantry, were disappointed, and he went abroad and plunged into Marxist studies, the fruits of which were seen in a series of publications and in the formation of the *Liberation of Labour Group*, the first Russian Marxist association. In his *Socialism and the Political Struggle*, 1883, he took as his point of departure the decision of the Revolutionaries to aim at a political constitution for Russia, and showed that the logical consequences of the departure had not yet been appreciated by its authors. If the State is to be used to effect economic change, it must be a State inspired and worked by those who understand and sympathise with the spirit of the change. In other words, the political weapon must be used. Though each country has its own economic peculiarities, one and the same scientific Socialism supplies for all the strategic principles by which the change is to be effected. This doctrine is the head of the movement: and the property-less workers of the cities are its heart. Their merit as a class lies precisely in the fact that they have none of the prejudices created by the possession of property. They, therefore, are the instruments of the change, and they must be fitted for their task by participation in political life. It is a slow and gradual process: but economic justice is not to be produced by the mere transfer of land and the instruments of production to new hands; it is only to be achieved by the socialistic organisation of production. Even if momentarily achieved by more summary means, it will be rapidly undone, unless those who constitute the State understand and are in sympathy with the aim.

Still less will any sudden seizure of power, before the necessary education has been effected, produce the results which are sought. Those who obtain power by such means, before their natural supporters are ripe for it, will find themselves inevitably using the power in the interests of those who are ripe for it, that is of another class.

The book opens with a quotation from Marx on the class-struggle: "Every class struggle is a political struggle," and Plekhanov tells us that history shows a political struggle between classes, wherever classes exist, having their economic interests as their ultimate aim. But his emphasis is on the need of the political struggle rather than on the existence of a class-war. He does not deny the need of the ultimate capture of power on behalf of the revolution, but he denies its immediate possibility or desirability. He regards the peasant as an ally, because the peasant desires the land: but reliance is placed upon the property-less worker of the town, because his interests are not warped by the possession of property.

In the following year, 1884, Plekhanov published a second exposition of Marxism, entitled Our Disagreements. It is interesting to observe in it the modest pretensions of the Russian Marxians at this stage of their preaching. Marxism, says Plekhanov, is the true algebra of revolution, and "though it includes defects and impracticabilities, it is a first attempt to apply scientific theory to the analysis of complicated and involved social relations." He only points to the solution, and hopes that People's Will, the organisation of the revolutionary Populists who aimed at a political constitution for Russia, will itself become Marxist. In hoc signo vinces. Marxism will show how to utilise the progressive aspects of the Liberal revolution, while remaining true to the worker class.

Plekhanov is writing with the object of converting Populists to Marxism, and he deals tenderly with the peasant-worship which was a central feature of their social thought: but he points out that the Mir is in process of decay. He damns with faint praise the practice of terrorism, which "does not widen the sphere of the revolutionary movement, but on the contrary narrows it down to the heroic acts of small partisan groups."

The same ideas are embodied in the programme of the group of Liberation of Toil, which was established in 1884, but the latter is more definite in regard to the political institutions which are to be set up. The workers are to conquer political power, and to make a democratic constitution with a popular legislative assembly and organs of local self-government. They are to be organised for struggle, both with the existing Government and with the future bourgeois parties which may be expected to arise under a democratic system. This clause provides for the "Permanent Revolution"—we should rather call it continuous than permanent—of which Karl Marx foresaw the necessity. The classes are to be eliminated; economic emancipation is to be attained by means of collective ownership of the instruments of production, for which the present development of technique is already preparing; the coercive State is to wither away and to be replaced by purely economic organisations; the coming economic organisation is to be international: all Marxian anticipations. The standing army is to be replaced by the general arming of the people; the land is to be divided among the peasant communes; and reforms of taxation and factory inspection and State aid to producers' associations are specified as desirable. The value of the revolutionary movement in the villages is recognised, but "Populist traditions are to be maintained only in so far as they do not contradict scientific Socialism." The new group recognises the need of the terroristic struggle against absolute Government, but differs from *People's Will* in respect to the seizure of power, and in respect to the direct activity of the Socialists of the working class (by which is meant insurrectional adventure). Except the reference to the elimination of classes, the document contains nothing about class-war and it puts forward the Intelligentsia rather than the proletariat as the leader in revolutionary activities. The process is evidently to be a gradual one, and it is contemplated that the revolution will in the first place be one which will place the bourgeois in power, but the workers are to be active in preparing for their own succession to the first place.

The general result of these discussions of 1883-84 is to show us a Marxism somewhat different from the one with which we are most familiar, especially in the small prominence assigned to the class-war, and noticeably gradualist in temper. Neither of these two points appears to the present writer to be absolutely vital to the Marxian system. One vital question is the attitude to human freedom. If the historical process works itself out according to inevitable laws, and man's interventions are entirely predetermined by similar laws, the philosophy is one of apathy at the best, despair at the worst. But if man can make his own history, subject only to the limitations imposed by the historical process on the range of possibilities and by social environment on the direction of his own will; if he can make it, in the same sense in which he can boil a kettle, by moving the sticks which make the fire, and by placing the water where the fire will make it hot:

then the philosophy is one of hope. George Plekhanov does not appear to me to emphasise the freedom of man, so much as he emphasises the inevitability of history. In this his interpretation was at one with the general interpretation given in Germany, where it was probably the cause of the final defeat of the Marxist party. It passed into the Menshevik doctrine, where it threw a pallor over the native hue of resolution. The Bolsheviks on the other hand transferred the emphasis to the freedom of man. They interpreted Marx as meaning, not that Communism is fated to be realised, but that, if society is to survive, Communism is the only way of escape from Capitalism's inability to provide a good life for its wage-earners. Marxism in this form, or thus coloured, is a call to man to make his own history, and the enthusiasm which it ultimately evoked in Russia becomes more easily intelligible.

A second vital question is that of the ultimate economic aim: whether it is a redistribution of good things on a principle of justice, or the establishment of a society so constituted as to provide a guarantee of justice; whether the keynote is distribution, or production. Plekhanov seems to stand for the latter interpretation, which is indeed the inevitable one for the close student of Marxian teaching. Mere redistribution does not take the world beyond the stage of a generalised poverty. Production, freed from the fetters imposed by the condition of a separate private profit to be achieved in each section of the field, and from the quarrel between employer and employed, is capable of giving the material security and the leisure which man requires. As I have already noted, but venture for the sake of emphasis to repeat, it is production, not distribution, which the form of Marxism adopted by the Bolsheviks emphasises. The assumption is made that when the artificial limits, imposed by the individual entrepreneur's need to make a profit in his own section of the field of production, are removed, and when full and free use is made of the possibilities of science, by a society in which no motive for restriction persists, production will advance in an infinite degree, and it will actually become possible to give to everyone in accordance with his needs. Until this stage is reached, Communism is not attained: and since some, or even all, must continue to go hungry of material satisfactions, all the old conflicts must continue. That is to say many will grab, and some will steal, and all the old apparatus of the State with its coercive authority and its policemen (however they be named) must persist. Only when all can find satisfaction, can the State wither away, as Marxians anticipated that it would.

I diverge here for a moment to point out the possible effects on these anticipations of a shortage of certain raw materials such as the rarer metals. In so far as these should prove to be irreplaceable, a perfect organisation of production might still leave the world with causes of friction and dispute. But this difficulty was not present to the mind of Plekhanov.

By 1887 Marx's *Capital*, in a Russian translation, was the most widely read book among Russian students. The Populists continued their terroristic attempts, for this was the year in which Ulianov (the brother of Lenin) made his attempt on the life of Alexander III and suffered the death penalty. Tolstoyan influences were strong, and somewhat depressing. The Maximalist Ivanov Razumnik calls the eighties a period of contentment with little deeds and smug philistinism. A disastrous famine in 1891-92, and the evident failure of the administration to cope with its destructive effects, ushered in a decade of great intellectual and economic activities, which was contemporaneous with Count Witte's financial administration. Labour began to use a new means of defence and to make larger claims. About 1893 the name of *Social Democrats*, already in use in Germany, began to be applied to the Russian Marxists, to distinguish them from the Anarchists, and to emphasise their acceptance of democratic methods. They stood for the combination of Socialism with the political struggle, but used the day-to-day economic needs of the workers to press the political lesson upon them. In 1895 a Petersburg Fighting Union was formed, with Lenin as one of its leaders. It was the germ of the Russian Social Democratic Party. The Textile workers' strike of 1896 confirmed in Lenin and Plekhanov the Marxian conviction that the proletariat would be the instrument of revolution. A year later the Jewish Social Democrats, always well in the van, formed the union known as the Jewish Bund, and in 1898 the first general Social Democratic Congress was held at Minsk, and formally inaugurated the Party which Plekhanov had advocated.

※　※　※

This was the decade in which Maxim Gorky rose to literary fame. Though he was far from being a Marxist in these early years the spirit of his writings, buoyant and combative, and the source of his inspirations in street and field, were sympathetic to the Marxian outlook. His faith in life attracted youth, to which Tolstoyan principles made no appeal. His robust and cheerful engine-driver Nil, in *Townsmen*, may be drawn with something less than the highest of dramatic gifts, and may have in him a good deal of that satisfaction with small deeds against which the Maximalists protested, but he is the New Man, the portent of a new era, and the forerunner of the Bolshevik worker, convinced that "he who works is master of the house," and with some of the narrowness of his class. He has his bitter fling at the "swine, fools, and thieves, who command honest men," but says "they will pass like boils from a healthy body." He comes in with a lot of young people who have been rehearsing a play to be shown to soldiers, and someone says: "It is pleasant to be with them. There is something healthy, such as you feel out in the forest." Speaking to a young lady, with a very different turn of mind, the turn of mind of the intelligentsia which Chekhov satirised, he says: "I love to live. I love noise, work, jolly simple people. But do you live? You are perpetually groaning for an unknown reason, and complaining. Against whom, why and for what? I don't understand." He goes on to describe his own particular hobby: "I'm awfully fond of forging metal. In front of you is the red formless mass, malicious, fiery. To beat the hammer on it is a joy. It spits at you with fizzing, blazing sparks, seeks to burn out your eyes, blind you. . . . It is living, malleable . . . and with mighty blows from the shoulder you make of it what you need." All this is an unmistakable anticipation of the Bolshevik attitude to life.

Again, in an argument with the educated and restless youth, who tells him that "we shall see what answer life will give," he says: "I will compel it to give the answer which I want. Don't try to frighten me. . . . I know that life is a serious thing, and all my capacities and powers are needed to order it. And I know that I am no hero, but only an honest healthy man, and yet I say: Never mind! We shall win. And with all the powers of my soul I satisfy my desire to plunge into the very depth of life, to knead it this way and that, to prevent this and help the other. This is the joy of life."

To which the educated youth replies: "Devil knows what he means: it is as though he were drunk."

It is the New Man, unintelligible to the old Intelligentsia, and, let us add, failing in turn to understand it: and the New Man is, at bottom, on the side of the Marxists, at all events of those Marxists who believe that man can make his own history. Meanwhile Anton Chekhov depicts the old, and leaves us in little doubt of its weakness: it turns to futility, boredom, and despair of life.

The epoch of Count Witte's financial reforms was also that of a new interest throughout the world in the problems of industrial labour, of the adoption of the Erfurt programme by the German Social Democrats in 1891, of the Encyclical of Pope Leo XIII dealing with the condition of workers. In Russia, Tolstoi's gospel of non-violence and non-co-operation with the State was still a living force. Religious thinkers were straining the eye of faith to follow the flights of Soloviev into the empyrean where the realisation of the God-man was awaited. Poetry was awakening from a long contempt. The triumphs of the Moscow Art Theatre were being prepared by its greatest dramatist, Chekhov, and its greatest producers, Stanislavsky and Nemirovich-Danchenko. New wealth seemed to promise the growth of new branches on the tree of civilisation, and more insistent political claims by the enriched middle class seemed imminent.

Socialist thought was divided between the opposite camps of Mikhailovsky and the Populists on the one hand, and of the Marxians on the other. The former stood for democracy and the federal form of the State, the rights of personality and of the individual, for an ethical basis of legislation, for the claims of Labour in general and for land for the peasant. The Russian Marxists laid no emphasis for the present on the rights of personality, but much on the struggle of classes, denied the validity of any distinction between evolving reality and right, and aimed at the hegemony of the urban working classes. The more fatalistic among them were willing to co-operate in the expropriation of small proprietors in order to hasten the advent of capitalism. Those of them who emphasised human will, while recognising the inevitability of the capitalistic phase, were intent upon active revolutionary intervention in human affairs. To all appearances the Marxian doctrine was marching triumphantly upon the broken forces of Populism, and about to secure the undivided allegiance of the progressive Intelligentsia. A turn of opinion reversed this anticipation. By the time that Kerensky, for a few months of 1917 to hold supreme power in the Russian State, was a University student, the first ardour of enthusiasm for Marxism was at an end, and the Social Revolutionary Party, which had revived Mikhailovskyian Populism, was gaining ground against it.

Peter Struve was the author of the first Marxian work legally printed in Russia and of the manifesto of the first Social Democratic Conference. But his "legal" Marxism proved to be a stepping-stone to the revision of Marxian theory, and ultimately to a religious Liberalism. The revisionist movement originated in Germany, with Eduard Bernstein, who, while still an orthodox Marxist, held that the economic revolution works itself out automatically. This theory contained the germ of quietism and conservatism. It explained away the most characteristic features of the Marxian doctrine: its materialism, the primacy which it assigned to economics as a motive force in history, its lack of emphasis on the claims of the individual. In Peter Struve's hands, revision took the form of criticism of the dialectic as a method of enquiry. He declared that social evolution proceeds by gradual steps, not by leaps, thus eliminating the expectation of a violent revolution; that the theory of surplus-value is subject to revision and to ultimate negation; and that a State rising superior to the influence of class is possible, so that a conflict of classes is not inevitable, and the withering away or destruction of the State is not necessary. In 1899 he was demonstrating that the standpoint of Marxism is not unconditionally anti-individualistic: on the contrary, that it tends to the elevation of real personality, social and economic organisation being only the means, while the all-round development of personality is the end. This was another way of putting the truth, too seldom understood, that the removal of economic anxieties is the way to set man free for the pursuit of true individuality. Struve had previously (in 1894), in his *Critical Observations*, minimised, in the orthodox Marxian fashion, the part to be played by the Intelligentsia, the mere men of ideas, who have no part in production and do not constitute "a class." He still holds that they are powerless from the social and economic standpoint, but recognises their political value, and, by implication, the power of ideas. The orthodox Marxist does not deny the power of ideas, but he minimises it, by his insistence upon the fact that ideas are conditioned by the state of economic relations. To emphasise the power of ideas is to return to Populist conceptions, and to adopt an idealistic rather than a materialistic standpoint. Orthodox Marxians recognised no absolute ethical standard, and no such thing as natural right or natural law. In 1901 Peter Struve was claiming that natural right, rooted in the ethical idea of personality, is the criterion of all positive law. "No objective law," he wrote, "denying the freedom of the expression of thought and will, can be recognised as in accordance with right, even though it be reduced to the form of law, with every formality, and receive the sanction of universal suffrage." N. A. Berdyaev, a brilliant member of the Struve group, who has for many years continued to illuminate the dark places of religion and philosophy, was arguing, like Mikhailovsky (and like Kant), for man as an aim in himself, and claiming that every new form of social organisation must justify itself as a means of realising the ideal aim— the natural law of personality, freedom and equality.

Revisionist Marxism became the doctrine of a large part of the Intelligentsia and of the majority of the University students, who accepted the historical justification of Capitalism given by Marx, while dropping his expectation of revolution. About the same time, 1898, the new Social Democratic Party was divided by the emergence of a section which called itself Economist, returning to the earlier doctrine of the Populists, disclaiming the use of the political weapon, and the aim of a political constitution, and limiting the activities of the working class to the economic sphere. It found its theoretical support in "legal" Marxism purged of the revolutionary spirit.

The stars in their courses were fighting for the stability of the Tsarist State by robbing its most dangerous enemies of their ideological basis. Policy carried the advantage further, by the establishment of the peculiar system of Police Socialism known by the name of Zubatov: which offered the prospect (precarious, perhaps, but temporarily real) of robbing political agitation of its grievance. The quarrel between Bolsheviks and Mensheviks, of which I shall have occasion to speak presently, was quite unintelligible to working men, and played into the hands of the authorities. But the Emperor, and the camarilla which surrounded him, unconscious of what the future had in store, threw these strategic advantages away by the Far Eastern policy which led to the Japanese war in 1904.

❋   ❋   ❋

Lenin sought to make good the weak places in the Social Democratic armour by pressing upon his colleagues the fateful policy which is responsible for the existence of the Communist Party—a disciplined order of devoted adherents more nearly resembling the Society of Jesus than any of the lax aggregations of political sympathisers to which we are accustomed to apply the name of political party. There was nothing characteristically Marxian in this idea. We can trace the germs of it to Bakunin, Nechayev and Tkachev. But, almost certainly, it is to this idea, realised by Lenin in fact, that the Bolsheviks owed their emergence at the top of the revolutionary wave in November 1917. As described by Lenin in *What Is to Be Done?* (1902) the plan is one for a "small compact core, consisting of reliable and hardened workers, with responsible agents in the principal districts, and connected by all the rules of strict secrecy with the organisations of revolutionists. Let the roots go as deep and wide as they can, but the struggle against the political police can only be conducted by professional revolutionists who can keep secrets, and whose organisation demands far greater training than that of Trade Unionists. A strong and disciplined revolutionary organisation can alone prevent the danger of premature outbreaks, before the ferment and anger of the working class are ripe for them. It is because of the need of restraint and of secrecy that democratic management is inapplicable to a revolutionary organisation."

Lenin was aware of certain weaknesses of his countrymen: the perpetual discussion, and the fissiparous tendency, the loose talking and the premature action, which (as Khalturin said) brought down the police upon them and ruined organisation. The disciplined "Party" was the remedy for these things.

The "Economist" group stood for subservience to the spontaneous action of the mass as well as for the elimination of political aims. Lenin's pamphlet insists that without leadership from above, the movement must degenerate into the use of such weapons as lie ready to hand, in particular of terrorism, which is a mere waste of forces: and that the aim must be the political aim, the seizure of power. Economic grievances must be used to illustrate the necessity of the political aim: for only a Workers' State will redress them. Unity of object must be secured by the establishment of an all-Russian newspaper—a plan not fully realised till the publication of *Pravda* in 1912. The Jewish Social Democratic organisation, the Bund, was at this time claiming autonomy, and Lenin, true to his instinct for discipline and organisation—qualities not often to be found among his fellow-countrymen—insisted upon unity.

At the Second Party Congress, in 1903, begun at Brussels and finished in London, the battle was joined between the "softs" and the "hards" on the subject of party discipline. The youthful Trotsky was on the side of the "softs." He tells us that he "did not at that time fully realise what an intense and imperious centralism the revolutionary party would need, to lead millions of men in a war against the old order." The looser formula, requiring mere co-operation or sympathy from candidates for membership, was temporarily victorious: and the "softs" shortly obtained control of the *Spark (Iskra)*, which was the journal of the party. George Plekhanov almost immediately joined the "softs," with whom the general trend of his writings had already shown him to be in sympathy. The formal separation of the sections took place on the issue of co-operation with the Liberals, which Lenin condemned. The "softs," hereafter known as *Mensheviks* (Minority Party), were defeated by the "hards," *Bolsheviks* (Majority Party), on this issue: and the former abstained from attending the Third Party Congress in 1905.

As might be expected from the favour which they showed on this occasion to the policies of co-operation with the Liberals and of elasticity in the organisation of the party, the Mensheviks represented reformism and gradualism rather than revolution. With the typical Marxist, it was an axiom that the first theatre of the Socialist Revolution would be one of the advanced capitalist countries. The Mensheviks were gradualist and opposed to the seizure of power, and, in the Revolution of 1905, they desired the summoning of a Constituent Assembly and deplored the armed rising at Moscow. They distrusted the peasantry as allies in the struggle for revolution, thought that Russia was ripe only for democratic, that is for parliamentary institutions, and stood for co-operation with Liberal non-socialists. Trotsky, young and fiery, can never have found his spirit's home in so much moderation, and he tells us himself that he left the Mensheviks in 1904, after vain attempts to dissuade them from their alliance with the Liberals, though he did not join the Bolsheviks till August 1917. Lenin and the Bolsheviks, already clear in their conception of the class-struggle and its logical consequences, hoped for nothing from Liberals or from middle-class politicians. To them, as to the newly-formed party of the Social Revolutionaries, peasant disturbances had brought home the value of the peasantry as a revolutionary ally. But they saw that the industrial proletariat must lead, because the peasantry is attached to rights similar to those of property, from which the town-worker—perhaps only until he acquires vested interests in social insurance—is completely dissociated. Inspired by that particular brand of Marxism which calls on man to make his own history, and, as we shall presently see, also by something which was Bakuninist rather than Marxian, they looked forward to armed insurrection; ultimately for the conquest of power, and immediately for the creation of a historical example: having before them the memory of a heroic failure, that of the Paris Commune. Where such differences of temper and outlook existed, the division between the Bolshevik and the Menshevik groups of the Social Democratic Party explains itself. It may be that the Mensheviks were the truer Marxists, but controversy over such a question is barren.

It will help us to obtain a correct perspective if we realise how small was the *apparent* importance of the Bolshevik section, and indeed of the Socialists in general, at the time of the Revolution of 1905. Even eleven years later, M. Maurice Paléologue, the French Ambassador in St. Petersburg, admirably informed though he was on most aspects of Russian life, believed that the leader of the Bolsheviks was Alexander Kerensky, who was actually a member of the Labour group of the Social Revolutionary Party. The Bolsheviks were the stronger in the industrial north, in the centre, and in the Urals, the Mensheviks in the south and in Georgia. In November 1904 the Bolshevik Party numbered only three hundred, and in September 1905 only eight thousand. The Mensheviks had a stronger hold upon the upper ranks of the workers, as we shall see by their predominance in the St. Petersburg Soviet of 1905, and, if we may judge by the fact that the Teachers' Conference in 1906 excluded the Bolsheviks altogether, also upon the rank and file of the Intelligentsia. The Social Revolutionaries made a wider appeal in rural areas than did either section of the Social Democratic Party. As all Socialists alike boycotted the elections for the first Duma, we can draw no inference from the voting for that body, in which the Kadet Party (representing the educated middle class in general) won a hundred and fifty seats, and Aladin's Labour Group won ninety. But, for the second Duma, when the policy of boycott had been dropped, and the franchise was still a wide one, thirty-five Social Revolutionaries and fifty-four Social Democrats of both sections were elected. In the second Duma, from which a large number of Kadet and Labour deputies had been excluded for their participation in the Viborg manifesto, the Kadets won a hundred and twenty-three, and the Labour Group two hundred and one seats. We gather that all the Socialists taken together were not able to win one-third of the number of seats captured by the parties which stood less far to the Left.

The St. Petersburg Soviet of 1905, which became the original example of an afterwards famous institution, was not a Marxian, nor even a Socialist, invention, but rather a spontaneous device brought by the factory hands from the villages, something quite as genuinely Russian and popular as the Mir, or the workers' co-operative association, though not so early discovered by the sociological student. The Soviets, in this their earliest form, consisted of representatives of the workers in the factories. At a later date they included also representatives of peasants and of soldiers. Lenin being absent in Finland, a section of the Bolsheviks mis-applied his canon of a limited and disciplined party organisation, and threatened to secede from the Soviet unless their terms were accepted. This incident provided a new descriptive nomenclature for the tendency to dictate to the non-party masses, which Lenin envisaged as having a far wider degree of freedom than the disciplined party. Those who showed this tendency were described as Ultimatists, pronouncers of the Ultimatum, or Otzovists, from the Russian word which means to recall: and it was vigorously resisted by Lenin, as destroying the basis of non-party co-operation with the party. In so far as the Party, at a later date, has taken up a dictatorial attitude, beyond its guiding and inspiring functions, it is likely to be charged by the Bolsheviks of the older school with an Ultimatist, or Otzovist, deviation from the principles of Lenin.

Even if Lenin had been in Russia when the St. Petersburg Soviet was set up, there are reasons for doubting whether he would have given it a particularly warm welcome. But, as usual, he learned from the facts and, having seen how the Soviets of St. Petersburg, and of the score of other towns which followed suit, served in practice to embody the will of the workers, he recognised them as "organisations of power, despite all the embryonic, unorganised, scattered elements, in their make-up and functioning." In October 1915 he is still speaking with some reserve about the value of the institution. The Soviets must be looked upon as "organs of insurrection and of revolutionary power. But only in connection with a mass strike of a political nature and with an insurrection can such institutions be of lasting value."

＊　　＊　　＊

The leading facts about the institution of the Soviet are: that it represents not a geographical constituency, but is a microcosm of a particular class, that is, of a body of workers engaged together on common work, who have intimate knowledge of their fellows; that there is a power of recall as well as of election; and that the function of the elected is administrative as well as legislative, resembling rather that of a county council than that of a parliament. But perhaps the most significant fact about the Soviets is that they involve the creation of a series, or successive tiers, of administrative authorities: the lowest of which is directly chosen by the workers, while each higher body is chosen by the body below. It thus brings the workers, or their representatives, into immediate executive touch with every kind of public business, from the humblest of everyday concerns up to the supreme tasks of the head of the State. These characteristics fit it better than a parliament for a rapidly changing situation, but the Soviets of 1905, as of 1917, were far from keeping pace with the impatience of revolutionaries, and represented the moderate man rather than the extremist. The first chairman, Khrustalev Nosar, was an orator rather than a leader. Trotsky, who succeeded him, was criticised for attention to economic objects when he should have aimed at securing the power of the State. But the temper of the members was not such as to support extreme measures. The Mensheviks never lost the advantage which they gained from the aloofness of the Bolsheviks at the establishment of the Soviet. Its measures were moderate because its temper was moderate: perhaps because it was really representative of a working

class which at that time (1905) did not contemplate the overthrow of
the Tsarist Government, and contained large elements of the purely
"economist" way of thinking. It went nearest to attacking the régime
when, doubtless under the inspiration of Trotsky, it repudiated Romanov debts, and called on the people to withdraw their deposits from
the Savings Banks. It was convinced that Count Witte aimed at pro-
voking disorders, in order to crush them effectively, and it desired to
disappoint him in this aim.

The opportunity of joint action with the really dangerous agrarian
movement was missed. When that was over, and the Soviet had been
broken up, and its leaders imprisoned—in other words when the advantage was already on the side of law and order—the Moscow insurrection occurred, against the wishes of the Menshevik section. The
tactics of this rising were deplorable. Mr. Maurice Baring says it was
conducted by boys and girls. But a more important question here is
that of its policy, which was evidently deliberate. It was an imitation
of the Paris Commune, deliberately "insurrectionist" in design, in the
sense in which Bakunin and Tkachev might have used the expression. It was intended to give to Russia and to the world an example of
what the proletariat could do, in the hope of establishing a provisional
government of the city of Moscow, for a time; but without the expectation of overthrowing the Tsarist Government. This interpretation is supported by former utterances of Lenin himself. In May 1901
he proposed preparation for armed insurrection in connection with
the massacre at the Obukhov works. In November 1904 he wrote
that the working class must extend and strengthen its organisation and
prepare for insurrection. In May 1905, having said that the people
could not defeat the army, he continued: "that the people may rise,
together with a small handful of the army, against despotic rulers, is
a reality of to-morrow." And, after the mutiny on the battleship
Potëmkin in June 1905, he pointed out that the call for insurrection
was timely, and urged Social Democrats to study military questions.
After the Revolution of 1905 had been defeated he told the Mensheviks that "it was really a great revolution, and not a chaos . . . not because the Tsar was compelled to proclaim a constitution, and not
because the bourgeoisie began to show signs of life, but chiefly because, abortive though it proved, there was an armed rising of the
workers in Moscow, and because the world proletariat has for one
month had a glimpse of the Soviet of Workers' deputies at St. Petersburg. . . ." He called the rising the greatest historical movement of
1905 and "the signpost to future victory." In other words he was, at all

events at this time, an advocate of what we may call *exemplary* in-surrection, which is certainly not Marxian.

When Engels gave his advice about insurrection in his *Germany in 1848* he said it must seize the moment when the activity of the van-guard of the people is at its height and the vacillation of their oppon-ents at its extreme. Neither of these conditions was satisfied in De-cember 1905, nor can anyone have supposed them to be satisfied. The timing and preparation of the rising of November 1917 were very different.

All the Socialist parties boycotted the first Duma, probably because the Witte franchise had not then been brought fully into effect. Their participation in the elections for the second and later Dumas was in harmony with the Marxian principle of taking part in politics, and with Lenin's translation of it into the use of legal as well as illegal methods. His line was to co-operate in the election, but to refuse to carry out the Menshevik plan of forming an alliance in the Duma with the Liberal Kadet party. An attempt, classified as Ultimatist, or Otzovist, in tendency, to recall the Social Democratic deputies from the third Duma, because of its reactionary tendencies, was resisted successfully by Lenin.

The counter-revolution was a period of extreme depression, and there was a moment when even he was pessimistic. In the reaction the Mensheviks stood for a legal Workers' party, and for legal Trade Unions, with reformist demands. The party had lost faith, and there were many deserters, intellectuals as well as working men. The prac-tical differences between the different groups of Social Democrats centred at one time in the question of the "expropriations," violent seizures of money and property for party funds. In a single half-year of 1907 there were over a hundred of these "Exes" in Lodz alone, and Stalin distinguished himself at Tiflis by the cool audacity of his seizure of bank funds. The attitude of the groups towards "Exes" was char-acteristic. The Mensheviks disapproved, the Bolsheviks approved, sub-ject to the maintenance of strict party discipline and control. The London Social Democratic Congress of 1907 forbade the practice: and it is said that Lenin organised a secret Bolshevik centre to maintain relations with the perpetrators of the seizures, because of their value as a source of funds.

* * *

The fissiparous tendency of Russian thought was in the meanwhile receiving a new manifestation. At the beginning of the last quarter of the nineteenth century, German philosophy took a turn away from

Hegel and back to Kant, and produced what seems to have been in its origin a critique of pure experience. The argument was that only sensations exist, and the name of empirio-criticism (which presumably means that experience is the only source of knowledge) was invented for it. Whatever the originators, Avenarius and Mach, may have intended to convey by the doctrine, it was seized upon by Russian thinkers nearly thirty years later, by some to defend the materialistic interpretation, and by others, including Victor Chernov and the Social Revolutionaries, as a useful weapon for the idealists. A Marxist philosopher, P. A. Bogdanov, partly alone, and partly in collaboration with other Machians, expounded the principles of the Machian doctrine as understood by Russians, and A. V. Lunacharsky, afterwards Minister of Culture and Education in the revolutionary Government, took to what was slightingly described as "god-building" on the basis of it. He spoke, for instance, of "deification of the highest human potentialities," of "religious atheists," of "scientific socialism in its religious significance," and said that "for a long time a new religion has been maturing within me." The Immanentist group in Germany, who were close associates of Mach and Avenarius, were preachers of Theism, and the tendency in this direction was no mere accident. The Christian revival in Russian thought, under influences which descended from Dostoievsky to Vladimir Soloviev, had created a soil which was favourable to such developments, and the old days when intelligence was regarded as synonymous with disbelief seemed to have passed away. The writings of N. Fyodorov (who died in 1903) combine the Orthodox conception of *sobornost* with that of an active socialism as a Christian duty.

❊   ❊   ❊

Under the ministry of Peter Stolypin the Government policy was a combination of vigorous repression of disorder, with the creation of a (presumably) conservative class of peasant land-holders independent of the Mir, and the maintenance of a constitution made safe by a restrictive electoral law. There are signs that this policy might have been successful in averting revolution. One of the results of a constitution—even a restricted constitution—was the growth of a capable and influential Liberal group. If it was not precisely a party, in the sense of an organisation having roots in the people, it was at any rate a body of enlightened and high-minded politicians, who showed themselves capable of useful public work. It received a powerful reinforcement in the realm of ideas from a body of former Marxists, for by this time the Russian revisionist group had passed over to a religious liberalism, the principles of which were embodied in a collection of essays published under the title of Landmarks in 1907. In this volume Peter Struve takes the revolution of 1905 as the text of his sermon, and blames the principles of the Intelligentsia for the mischief which it caused. The Intelligentsia, or the Socialists, for to him they are one and the same, deny the personal responsibility of man, and attribute all suffering and all crime to economic and social conditions. They preach the idea of service to the people, with no corresponding obligations. But progress can only be the fruit of the inner perfection of man and of the growth of his sense of responsibility. Only religion can supply what is missing. For lack of it, the Revolution of 1905 ended in a harsh reaction as soon as agitation ceased.

N. A. Berdyaev, another of the contributors, is scornful of the Intelligentsia for the weakness of their philosophy, and compares them to Dostoievsky's Grand Inquisitor, who aimed at giving happiness to man at the cost of truth. They have never understood Hegel, nor Kant, nor Mach, nor even Marx. They have only asked how they can use these philosophies to help their idol, the people. They have admired Positivism, because it deifies humanity. Their love of man is not respect for man as the child of God. It has turned to Man-Idolatry. Chaadaev, Dostoievsky and Soloviev are neglected because they offer no support to Socialism. He complains of the philosophers of the Right, including Merezhkovsky and Rozanov, for an anarchical denial of philosophical reason, and sees a tendency for mysticism itself to become an instrument of social aims (probably a reference to the mystical anarchism of Vyacheslav Ivanov and the Christian revolutionism of Merezhkovsky). He calls for a synthesis of knowledge and faith, for the recognition of the independent value of truth, and for "congregationalism," sobornost of the consciousness, which can only be realised in the soil of the national tradition. In this last we hear an echo of Slavophil teaching.

One criticism by Berdyaev and by another contributor, Frank, is that the Socialists aim at a purely distributory system. This statement was true of most of the earlier Russian Socialists except Chernyshevsky. But Marxism, as has already been pointed out, laid stress upon production rather than upon distribution. In his Critique of the Gotha Programme, Karl Marx was very definite in his repudiation of egalitarian distribution, and his Russian followers have been generally steadfast in their emphasis on production as the key to scientific Socialism.

Bulgakov, another contributor to Landmarks, and now a leading publicist of the Orthodox revival, analyses the qualities of the Intelligentsia, and notices the large contribution of Religion to these. Their aversion from the world, their rigoristic morals, their penitence for supposed sins against the plain folk, their eschatological dream of the kingdom of heaven upon earth, their desire to save man from suffering, if not from sin, are all traced to religious training, and the writer exclaims: "How often, in the debates of the second Duma, did we hear from atheist lips echoes of orthodox thought!" These are very just observations. Many of the advanced thinkers had been trained in the religious seminaries (as was Stalin), and among their thoughts are the reflections of religious teaching. Though the Bolsheviks completely repudiate Christian cosmogony and dogma, their ethics are fundamentally Christian, by contrast with the Nietzschean doctrine of a "master's" morality, and their habits of thought continue to be profoundly influenced by Orthodox conceptions.

There was a time when the doctrines of Mach and Avenarius seemed likely to establish themselves as the standard philosophy of Bolshevism. The Party might have become confirmed in an idealistic, even in a fideistic, tendency which would have altered its history. Lenin, after a period of thought and study, published his one philosophical work, *Materialism and Empirio-criticism* (1909), which was an effective intervention on the side of materialism. The work is more important as a historical fact than as a body of philosophical argument. The choice of a philosophy was vital to the Party, just as the choice of a theology was vital to the early Christian Church: and deviations, or heresies, were fraught with unforeseeable consequences. In the long run, Lenin's intervention determined the abandonment by Russian Marxists of theories which might have led back to idealism and to religion. But the Communist school at Capri, which was founded by Maxim Gorky and Lunacharsky, and conducted largely under the auspices of Lunacharsky and Bogdanov, continued to pursue the tendencies which Lenin repudiated, and Gorky declined to supply funds for the rival school which Lenin established at Paris. The great leader's attitude to the teaching of Capri is illustrated by the story of his remark to the new-comers from Capri to Paris: "You won't find intellectual liberty, and right of private judgment, here." On the question of discipline on the party-line, there was no compromise for Lenin.

As a statement of Marxian philosophy and fundamental theory, George Plekhanov's *Fundamental Problems of Marxism*, the date of which suggests the intention of a reply to the Machians, is more important than Lenin's philosophical work. Thought is conditioned by being: as the influence of cattle upon Kaffirs, or of camels upon Arabs, clearly shows. The Deed came first, says Goethe. This is the essential of Materialistic philosophy. Dialectic is a theory of social evolution, with recognition of the occurrence of sudden changes. It explains the end of a social order, as well as its existence. Whatever is, is right: but it is coming to an end for all that: and what next is, is also right. History is made by human beings and therefore by great men among the rest. This is not merely Chanticleer helping the sun to rise, or the beating of tomtoms to end an eclipse. In sociology, causal necessity is made up of many items, one of which is the conscious action of men making their own history. A dualist, who separates thought and being, can only imagine one kind of necessity, which compels us to act against our wishes, and only one kind of freedom, which enables us to act in accordance with them. But a Marxist, who identifies being and thought, recognizes the freedom, which is limited by the necessities of natural law, in the social as in the physical world. One decides to boil a kettle: and it is done by putting the vessel full of water where the fire is. The means of ending the ills of society must be sought in the material relations of production, not invented as a Utopia. History, in its entity, is nothing but a continuous modification of human nature. Such, in brief summary, is Plekhanov's outline of the fundamental problems of Marxism. The struggle of classes is not forgotten, but it is not emphasized as fundamental. As we should expect, Plekhanov soon figures in the opposite camp to Lenin, as a patriot, a "defensist," concerned primarily with the defence of his country in war: which is precisely the reverse of the mental attitude of those to whom the essential problem was the struggle of classes.

※   ※   ※

I do not attempt to give an exhaustive account of the successive divisions in the Social Democratic Party. But one of them, which took place in the period of counter-revolution, is important because of its effect on the policies pursued during the First World War. This was the movement known as *Liquidationism*, which gave up illegal work, and was supported by the legal magazine *Our Dawn*. The Georgian Chkeidze, who afterwards distinguished himself by his courage in opposing the vote of the Duma for war credits, was at one time its leader, and it included many intellectuals. During the war the *Liquidators*, who had been expelled from the party, became Defensists, stood, that is to say, for the prosecution of the war to a successful issue, without annexations or indemnities, against the Defeatism which aimed at converting the war into an international one of classes.

In spite of the gulf between the Bolshevik and the Menshevik Social Democrats, no separate and independent Bolshevik Party existed before 1912. A Conference at Prague in that year formed a Bolshevik Central Committee, and thus completed the split in the Social Democratic organization. This conference also decided upon Bolshevik participation in the election for the fourth Imperial Duma, and upon the foundation of a legal daily newspaper in St. Petersburg. Such was the origin of *Truth* (*Pravda*), which, often suppressed but re-established, continues to-day as the organ of the Party now called Communist. Stalin was associated with Malinovsky (afterwards discovered to be an agent of the Tsarist Police) in the editorial management. The economic depression which had been heavy over Russia up to 1910 had now lifted, strikes recommenced in the period of comparative prosperity, and the Revolutionaries began again to hope.

Chapter VIII

THE REVOLUTION OF 1905

"An incompetent Government is being opposed by an ineffectual Revolution."

A Japanese Observer, quoted by MAURICE BARING.

"Russia was and still is being played with like a top. In the eyes of our rulers was not the Japanese campaign itself a war with toy soldiers?"

COUNT WITTE's *Memoirs.*

The pastoral life makes men companions of the stars and wild associates of their own cattle. Agriculture brings them nearer to one another and, as soon as the earliest stage of the woodland-clearing is past, combines them into communities. But the communities are small and scattered because, until much has been learned of the means of controlling nature, a square mile can barely hold half a dozen families. Industrial tasks draw them closer. But the final concentration comes with the rise of the factory, and is most complete when machinery begins to be operated by power. In this new phase of human existence, man lives in a crowd of other men doing like work and having common interests. If the farmer learns by looking over the hedge, the factory hand sees more and at closer quarters across his bench.

It has been calculated that there were ten millions of male non-agricultural workers in the Russia of 1905. They were for the most part scattered over the rural areas, and employed in small handicrafts. But a substantial fraction was employed in factories of exceptionally large size, and these workers were more closely massed together than those of any of the great industrial countries. The proportion employed in large works having more than a thousand hands apiece was in Russia three times as great as in Germany. The less industrialized country had the larger proportion of the largest-scale industry.

Karl Marx, who got his industrial facts from England, noted that the factory was a potential centre of social life, of play and study and thought and action, as well as of industrial production. In the early days of the industrial revolution in every country, when hours were too long for play or study or thought, it was, at least, a centre for exchange of grievances as well as for work, and that formidable weapon, the strike, was forged on its stithies.

In Russia the factory originated with serf-labour, but Emancipation gave to its growth a greater impetus. Moscow became a centre of the textile industry, and iron and steel established themselves in St. Petersburg. In 1884 George Plekhanov was demonstrating to the Populist Revolutionaries that the Capitalism, which they believed that Russia could evade, was already upon them both in town and in village. Between 1887 and 1898 the output of iron and steel almost trebled, and that of textiles almost doubled itself. A prosperous class of owners and middlemen came into existence, having no concern with their workers except as instruments of profit. The factory worker, at first a seasonal hand more interested in his land than in the factory, and returning periodically to his village, became, in an increasing degree, particularly in the metal trades, a permanent, even a hereditary, townsman. The abuses which characterise the early stages of industrialisation were not less gross in Russia than elsewhere: exploitation of female and child labour; hours of enormous length; wages on a tropical scale in a rigorous climate; no guards on the machinery, and accidents common, with no compensation; heavy and capricious fines; an oppressive truck system; housing which was not housing at all, but meant, at best, a share in a common barrack, at worst, sleep beside the machine: all the familiar accompaniments of the worst wage-slavery, relieved only by the possibility of return to an even more precarious existence in the village. There were higher and lower grades of labour, and some of this is not fully applicable to the iron and steel workers of St. Petersburg or to the railway men, but such was the lot of the mass, and the luckiest fared little better. Much of the capital was foreign and its owners absentees.

The workmen were not allowed, before the Revolution of 1905, to form their own organizations. But they actually adopted a practice brought from the village, and elected their own elders (Starosta), who became the germ of the later Soviets. From the seventies strikes became frequent, generally for the payment of withheld wages or by way of protest against excessive or capricious fines. In the latter half of the nineties they were declared on a large scale, and the demands included the limitation of hours.

There is nothing surprising about bad conditions in factory labour. Most of them can be paralleled in present or very recent Bombay, and they tend to come into existence everywhere till the operations of large-scale industry are brought under control. One competitor cannot afford to be more considerate than another. Only the public authority can force them all to be considerate. The indictment against the Tsarist Government is that it did not, except spasmodically, attempt to deal with the evils of industrialisation. Nicolas Bunge has left behind him a noble memory of his tenure of the portfolio of Finance in the eighties. Beside the abolition of the poll-tax and the foundation of the Peasant Bank, he set limits to the practice of fining factory hands, provided for fortnightly payments of wages and for a fortnight's notice of dismissal, and secured liberal factory legislation. The legislation was made nugatory by inadequate inspecting staff. It is said that there were only two inspectors for the two thousand factories of the Moscow region. To propose additions was regarded as sympathy with subversive tendencies, as Count Witte found when he broached the subject with Nicolas II. Bunge was dismissed, "for socialist leanings."

Count Witte was Finance Minister from 1892 to 1903, a period of extraordinary developments in the railway system and in industry, with the establishment of a gold standard, the encouragement of foreign and domestic capital, and the intensification of protective tariffs. Wages rose and strikes multiplied. Two large strikes in 1897 led to legislation for the limitation of hours. Adults were to work not more than eleven and a half hours, or not more than ten if nightwork was included. But secret instructions nullified the law. The temptation to pursue "prosperity" (for the rich were growing richer and the resources of the State were being doubled) was too great to allow of interference with the freedom of employers. By this time the young Lenin was busy in the St. Petersburg factories, illustrating the teachings of Marx with the every-day occurrences of working life: and we can imagine the reactions of him and his hearers to the secret instructions.

The boom of 1897 was succeeded by the slump of 1899, and the Novoye Vremya, most conservative of newspapers, said that unemployment was reducing the workers to despair, and called for reforms "from above, as in 1861" (the year of the emancipation of the serfs) — and was punished by suspension for a week. The first political strikes came after 1900. In 1901 the demand for an eight-hour day put the onus of decision not upon individual employers but upon the Government itself. The first general strike, which took place in South Russia in 1903, and included the great oil centre of Baku, shows how far general organization had progressed. The movements of rural and urban discontent were converging upon one another.

Alexander III was a man of steady convictions, though not of steady nerves, who followed with tenacity the policies with which Pobie-donostsev, his most reactionary tutor, must have inspired him. In an age when the Empire of all the Russias had grown far beyond its primitive kernel of Great Russian Orthodoxy, and included nationalities of older and superior cultures, and other faiths and confessions having claims not less venerable than those of Orthodoxy, he sought to bring all alike within the framework of a sort of glorified Orthodox Muscovite Tsardom. Autocracy, Orthodoxy, Nationalism, were the bases of his policy, and Russification was his instrument with the non-Russian people, who were more than half of the whole. The Russian language is everywhere imposed. Cathedrals of the Russian type are built in all non-Orthodox centres of culture, none but Orthodox can acquire land in the western provinces, Catholicism is the worst treated of all the tolerated confessions. Russian administration and justice are introduced into Poland and the Baltic Provinces. Even the Armenians, the most pro-Russian of the subject nations, are driven into opposition. Cultivators of the non-Russian races are ousted from their lands to make room for Russian colonists. When, at a later date, we find that the non-Russian nationalist is often the most active in the revolutionary field, we see the fruits of a policy which attempted to thrust Russian Orthodoxy and nationhood upon unwilling peoples.

In Alexander III these policies were accompanied by a foreign policy firmly resolved upon peace. The dynasty would have survived—who can say for how long?—all the weaknesses of Nicolas II, if he could have kept out of war. But from the first he played with fire. He had hardly come to the Imperial throne when he accepted a plan to bring about in Constantinople a situation which would have given a pretext for the landing of Russian troops. Fortunately he wavered, or Europe would have been at war in 1896. The miserable story of the Japanese war cannot be retold here. But those who fancy that autocracy is a guarantee of continuity of policy may well glance at the events which led to it. For years, military preparations had been directed against the dangers of war on the western front, and the railway policy had been largely, though not exclusively, inspired by that prospect. But Nicolas, as Heir Apparent, had visited the Far East and became interested in its possibilities. It was the policy of the German Kaiser to divert Russia from too close an attention to European affairs. A camarilla, having corrupt interests in Korea, established itself at the Russian court. The Ministers stood for one policy, and that a cautious one. An adventurer —we need not enquire how his influence began—stood for a different and a rasher policy. The Foreign Minister lost all influence upon diplomacy in the Far East, and the Emperor corresponded direct with a man of little judgment or experience who had been made Viceroy of the Eastern territories. After an attempt to reach a settlement at St. Petersburg, the Japanese began the fighting in 1904, used their sea-power to cut the Russians off from Korea, inflicted a series of military defeats, obtained the surrender of Port Arthur, and destroyed the Baltic Fleet at Tsushima. By the Peace of Portsmouth in August, 1905 the Empire of Peter and Catherine abandoned Korea and Southern Manchuria, and ceded half of the great island of Sakhalin, to a power which Nicolas had been convinced would not dare to proceed to the extremity of war against him. The issue of paper money in Russia had been doubled, the credit of the Empire abroad was impaired, and when Count Witte passed through France he saw signs of the disgust and contempt with which the collapse of the great ally was regarded. An unnecessary and filibustering war had exposed to the nations the weakness of Russia, had imperilled the dynasty, and, but for the hasty conclusion of peace, might have come near to overthrowing it in 1905.

The lack of co-ordination in the body politic is not less apparent in internal than in external affairs. The idea of a Social Revolution from above had for some time been in the air of Russia. It was a police officer named Zubatov who put in practice the plan of harnessing the workers' movement to the police-machine. Co-operative Societies, like Trade Unions, had hitherto been discouraged by authority. They smacked of self-government. Now they were established under the patronage of the Police, who also assisted the workmen in their preparations for the general strike of 1903 in Southern Russia. This was no momentary escapade of an individual, but a policy aimed at convincing the proletariat that the Government was their friend. The employers were so much alarmed by this disconcerting reinforcement to their workers, that they begged for the legalisation of strikes, and of election of shop-stewards by the men, as the lesser evil. Only the second of the two requests was granted, and the practice of keeping one foot in each of the two camps of capital and labour was continued for some time.

Another bizarre device of the administration was the patronised *pogrom*. In its origin the *pogrom* was the smashing of the window of a pawn-broker's shop by any angry borrower, promptly punished and having no political importance. The Minister von Plehve, who first rose into distinction as the efficient prosecutor of Alexander II's murderers, and had, in 1903, prescribed a "small successful war" as the remedy for internal troubles, used the pogrom as a lightning conductor for diverting popular discontent upon Jews. The pogrom of Kishinev in 1903 led to the murder of von Plehve himself in the following year. The murder was organised as an act of vengeance by a Jew named Azev, whose history is a compendium of the ramifications of the police administration. He was a police-agent, and, when the peasant disturbances of 1902 encouraged the formation of the Social Revolutionary party, which succeeded the Populists in the championship of peasant rights, the police secured his nomination as the head of the new Socialist organisation. For years he hovered between the revolutionaries and their natural enemies, effecting selected betrayals, and alternately, or simultaneously, deceiving both.

Immediately on the outbreak of the Japanese war internal troubles began with Polish resistance to mobilisation. Peasant disturbances followed in March, and continued at intervals, inspiring terror among the landlords.

Von Plehve's murder was followed by a swing of Government to the left when his successor, Prince Svyatopolk Mirsky, "opened a ventilating hole for public opinion" by the relaxation of the censorship. The Holy Synod proposed the convening of a Church Assembly to discuss the restoration of the Patriarchate, always a symbol of the freedom of the Church from the domination of the State. A decree of December 12, 1904, gives us a glimpse of some of the burning questions of the day. The Committee of Ministers was required by it to make proposals for the *establishment of legality* (that is to say, for the removal or limitation of arbitrary and extra-legal powers), for the extension of freedom of speech, for religious toleration and self-government, for diminution of the disabilities of non-Russian nationalities, and for the abrogation of extraordinary laws. The only legal measures which resulted from this inquiry were an alleviation of the position of the dissenters and the removal of some Roman Catholic grievances in respect to schools in the western provinces. At the same time a conference of rural Councils was permitted to meet, and to make proposals which included an elective national assembly with legislative powers, but without responsible government in the British sense of the phrase.

This swing to the left was soon followed by a swing to the right. One of the "Police Socialist" agents was a priest known as Father Gapon, who exercised a great influence with the workers of St. Petersburg. They had recently suffered a fall of a quarter to a fifth in their real wages, and Father Gapon, though evidently vain and accessible to flattery, was moved by a genuine sympathy for their cause. When Bolsheviks and Mensheviks were at logger-heads over a plan for a grand demonstration of workers, the priest assumed the leadership, and in January, 1905, took a procession to the Winter Palace, with a petition for a general amnesty for political offenders, a Constituent Assembly to be elected by universal suffrage, and an eight-hour day. There is evidence that he contemplated a disturbance in the event of the rejection of this petition, but there were no preparations for anything more than unorganised violence. Some arms were taken by the crowd from policemen. The Emperor was absent at Tsarskoye Selo, and the Grand Duke Vladimir had been entrusted with the preservation of order. There was some firing on the crowd at the city gates but there were no preventive arrests; the procession was not prohibited; when a considerable part of the workers reached the Palace Square there was no summons to disperse. The troops were posted to receive the demonstrators, a bugle sounded, and firing began. Dr. Dillon, who was present, estimated the dead at seventy odd, and the wounded at two hundred and fifty. Afterwards, there were attacks upon individual police officers, and barricades were erected on Vasilievsky Island, but were easily captured by troops and police. This "Bloody Sunday" may be taken as the beginning of the Revolution of 1905.

Popular indignation was already high owing to the surrender of Port Arthur in circumstances pointing to treachery. It rose to fever heat. A general strike was proclaimed in Poland, always in the van of the workers' movement. Such respectable bodies as the Moscow Agricultural Society and the Unions of professional men joined in the demand for a Constituent Assembly. In February the Grand Duke Sergius, Governor-General of Moscow, was assassinated by a Social Revolutionary. In March western Georgia expelled the Russian officials and formed a local government of its own which lasted till December. Peasant disturbances of a violent type were chronic throughout the year, in the seasons for such disturbances, which are always limited by agricultural conditions. In the industrial areas, strikes demanding a Constituent Assembly and an eight-hour day culminated in the formation of a Union of Unions, which acted as a Central Strike Committee. On arrival of the news of the destruction of the Baltic Fleet at Tshushima this Union of Unions demanded an end to the war, and the crew of the battleship *Potëmkin*, mainly Volga peasants, mutinied in the Black Sea, and carried the ship to a Roumanian port. A gesture of conciliation, ill-judged in the opinion of Count Witte, granted self-government to the Universities, and the students' meetings in these asylums of free speech attracted revolutionaries from outside and became centres of agitation.

In August, the Government disappointed the demand for a Constituent Assembly by proclaiming the intention to convoke a consultative assembly so composed as to establish the preponderant influence of landed proprietors—the so-called Bulygin constitution.

The war with Japan was now over; but its authors and conductors were not forgiven. From September the newspapers, even the conservative *Novoye Vremya*, were in open revolt against what remained of the censorship, and by tacit agreement ignored its orders. A Peasant Union, with a programme of expropriation without compensation, began to meet at Moscow under the eyes of the authorities. Lenin was not then a name of power, but the fact that he was able to return from exile, to address large audiences at St. Petersburg, and to publish articles in a daily newspaper founded by Maxim Gorky in the interests of revolution, is an illustration of the hesitant temper of the authorities.

Count Witte says that they were frightened, and that terrorism played a part in frightening them. He adds that the administration was in a state of chaos. For instance, during the demobilisation and the return of the troops from the Far East, the military authorities themselves did not know where their men were, and in some places, at the very height of the troubles, there were no police at all. What contribution the new rich, who had drawn their wealth from his economic policy, were making to the solution of the difficulties of Government, is suggested by his story of the chairman of the Stock Exchange who asked him to use his influence with the Imperial Bank to reduce the rate of discount. Witte said he could not interfere with the Bank's rules: whereupon the worthy financier affected an attitude of despair, and said: "Give us the Duma!" Some millionaires contributed to revolutionary funds, and the general attitude of employers, at this stage of the revolution, was hostile to the Government, or hopeful of extracting concessions from its difficulties. Later, when the interests of employers appeared to be threatened, they too became frightened, and withdrew their support from strikers and agitators.

The remaining, and the most important, events of the first Revolution fall under the headings of the formation of the St. Petersburg Soviet of Workers' Delegates, of which Trotsky was first the Vice-Chairman and afterwards the Chairman, with corresponding Soviets in almost a score of other towns; the General Strike, the issue of the October Manifesto, and the withdrawal of middle-class support from the strikers; the insurrections of the peasants in the Black-Earth zone in October to December, of the Baltic peasants in November, and of the Moscow workmen in December 1905; the announcement of the Witte franchise; and the assemblage of the First Imperial Duma in an atmosphere of counter-revolutionary triumph.

Of the Soviet I have spoken elsewhere. The General Strike was effective in securing what may be called an ostensible surrender on the part of the Government, mainly because the organisation of the Railway workers prevented traffic, even between St. Petersburg and Peterhof, except by water: but it was effective only because it was backed by a renewal of peasant disturbances. Officials of the most reactionary complexion were at this time discussing plans of expropriation of the large estates in order to restore order among the peasantry, which was plainly the most urgent consideration. Witte had not, of course, the advantage which we have, of knowing the subsequent course of the urban workers' movement. But he had all the sources of contemporary information at his disposal, and he is quite clear in the opinion that the peasant movement, which wrecked two thousand estates in 1905 and spread terror in the most influential part of society, and not the Soviet of Workers' Delegates, now established at St. Petersburg and directing the General Strike, was the cause of the Emperor's Manifesto of October 30th. The one was a nation-wide danger, the other only a serious inconvenience. Trouble with urban workers seemed a normal occurrence, and was in some degree discounted in advance. But the peasantry was still regarded as the backbone of the Empire, and its defection as a peril to the Orthodox Autocracy. There is no doubt that this was a just estimate of the two forces.

The Manifesto of October 30, 1905, was not a Constitution. As ultimately interpreted it was not even the promise of one. It promised civic freedom on the basis of inviolability of the person, freedom of conscience, of speech, of assemblage, of association, and it promised an elective Duma with legislative power (without mention of legislative initiative), and with a real participation in the control over the legality of the behaviour of the officers of State. As to the franchise, it promised, but without stopping the elections appointed under the previous Bulygin constitution, "to admit to participation in the Duma those classes of the population which have hitherto been deprived of the franchise, so far as this is feasible in the brief period remaining before the convening of the Duma, leaving the further development of the principle of general suffrage to the new legislative order." Whatever may have been the precise meaning of these words, they seemed to concede a Duma, with at least a veto on legislation, and with a right to public discussion of the conduct of officials, to be elected on a very wide franchise, and to be authorized, subject to the concurrent authority of the Council of State, to widen the franchise yet further. There was no mention of any reservation of autocratic authority. On the other hand there was clearly no concession of legislative control over the executive power. It was far from being the Constituent Assembly for which the strikers and a large part of articulate Russia were asking, but it seemed, and perhaps was, much: and the St. Petersburg Soviet—under moderate Menshevik influences—at once called off the General Strike. The manifesto made no reference to the land question, and when it reached the peasants their disappointment was the occasion of additional disturbances and either this, or a general impression of the abrogation of authority, may account for the outbreak in the Baltic Provinces, where the worst outrages of the revolution were committed, between the Lettish population on the one hand and their German masters on the other. Political autonomy was restored to Finland, but the working class, which had formed a Red Guard there, remained under arms. Measures of Russification generally were withdrawn, all claims on account of the redemption-payments required by the Emancipation law were cancelled, and the reorganisation of the Peasant Bank, to allow of the more extensive purchase of land, was promised.

What did Nicolas II actually mean by the Manifesto of October? When a deputation from the *Union of the Russian People* (recently formed under the patronage of the Grand Duke Nicolas to support the principle of autocracy) visited the Emperor and asked for assurances, he told them that the religious principle of absolute autocracy remained intact. The new fundamental laws published before the opening of the first Duma were issued by the absolute Autocrat, and a chapter of them expressly reserved the validity of the ancient Statutes relating to the Coronation, the Anointment, and the Faith. Within a year an example of the significance of these reservations was given by the publication, when the Duma was not sitting, of the Ukaz establishing the basis of the highly controversial agrarian reform of Peter Stolypin. It has been suggested—and such must have been the early teaching of Pobiedonostsev to his imperial pupils—that the Tsar could not have abandoned his Autocracy without violating his religious oath, and that the manifesto could only have ended absolutism, for the imperial conscience, if it had been accomplished by a corresponding declaration of the Tsar as head of the Orthodox Church.

The *Union of the Russian People*, which interested itself so deeply

in the preservation of the Autocracy, had other items in its programme. It claimed a superior status for Russians over non-Russians
in the Empire, and represented the Jews to be the main source of its
troubles. It turned back to a patriarchal ideal of the Russian State and
deprecated the influence of the bureaucracy: points which seem to
have a Slavophil origin. It appealed to religious reformers by a demand
for the convening of a Church Council to restore the Patriarchate,
placed in commission by Peter the Great; to the peasantry by the
claim to access to more land; and to the general public by asking for
equalisation of taxation. It is easy to detect resemblances to what was
elsewhere and later called National Socialism. The programme seems
to have been very well-considered, as a reply to revolutionary tendencies, and on the surface at least, the Union was a sort of Primrose
League, enjoying conservative and official countenance of an unim-
peachable respectability. But it had a Mr. Hyde to its Dr. Jekyll, in
the shape of the so-called Black Hundreds, which were the agents of
the pogroms. By no means all officials, not even all Ministers, were
aware of the aristocratic and official backing to these activities. Witte
has described to us the shock with which he, the chief Minister of the
Empire, received the information that a hidden hand was behind the
hooligans. He is so malicious in his comments upon his sometime
master, Nicolas II, that we must not overrate the value of his statement that, at heart, the Emperor's ideals were those of the Black
Hundreds; but the highest quarters were not unsympathetic to the
"loyalists" who beat up "the disloyal."

A Ukraine landowner tells us how a Jew of his—landowners had
their Jews who did business for them, and were regarded as a useful
sort of dependants, receiving protection in return for dirty work—was
beaten up in a pogrom. The landowner went to the local Governor to
ask for protection for his Jew. The Governor reflected, and then said,
with a cynical grin: "Go and complain of me at St. Petersburg. I shall
get credit as an energetic officer in my dealings with Jews. And you
will get the protection that you ask." We recognize the old official
hand here.

The Black Hundreds started their operations on the very morrow of
the constitutional manifesto, and over a hundred pogroms took place,
the worst being at Odessa, where seven hundred persons were killed,
and at Tomsk, where many perished in a conflagration. Maurice Baring
tells the story of a Moscow police officer who, being asked to stop an
attack on the funeral cortège of a dead revolutionary, replied, with a
shrug: "Liberty." One consequence of the non-interference of the

Police was that it was impossible to enforce the restrictions upon the sale of arms, and many persons obtained supplies which contributed to the disorders of the period which followed. It was said of Ivan the Terrible—perhaps by a chronicler whose interests he had offended—that he had "become a rebel in his own land." Something like that was true of Nicolas II, or of his government as represented by Von Plehve.

The war was now over, and resentment over a humiliating peace was not so effective a grievance as war. The Manifesto had taken the edge off popular feeling. Many thought a constitution had been granted. When the Soviet attempted to renew the general strike, the response was a cold one. The employers and the monied people were satisfied, or frightened, and withdrew their support. At a later stage, under the evident influence of the youthful Trotsky, the Soviet declared a repudiation of Romanov debts and called on the people to withdraw their deposits from the Savings Banks. But it was clear that neither this body, nor the workmen whom it represented, would have supported any attack upon the authority of the Tsar, and that the town-workers had shot their bolt, for the present at all events.

The peasants resumed rioting in 1906, and again in 1907, producing renewed panic among landlords and a rush to sell estates. But there are well-recognised limits to peasant disturbances, since agriculture is literally the life of the people, and the seasons will not wait for man. Peasants can be active in the dead time, between spring sowing and hay cutting. They can act again with effect when the harvest is cut and carried. The winter limits their activities to their own near neighbourhood, and the thaw makes roads and rivers impassable, and reduces the country for a time to an archipelago of mud. They are irresistible rioters till the troops arrive, but there is no organisation, and they are overpowered in detail—free, of course, to resume action when the military detachment has passed on, unless spirit has been completely crushed by the terror. Armed resistance to punitive columns in 1906, when the Government had recovered the initiative, was rare and feeble. With the months of October and November 1905 the moment of combination between town and country had gone by. Between peasant and Government the position was almost one of stalemate.

The soldier, in the mass, is a peasant in uniform, and his grievances are the peasant grievances, with the addition of some of his own, among which delayed demobilisation played a great part. Like his brother peasant, the soldier did not dream, in 1905, of the displacement of the Tsar, or even of his replacement by another member of the Imperial family. He wanted land, and he wanted an end to arbitrary officials and to the special civil disabilities and inferior legal status of the peasant. There were eighty-nine outbreaks in the Army in November and December 1905, accompanied with much disorder along the line of the Siberian Railway. Troops at Sevastopol fraternized with the revolting Black Sea Fleet, a military gathering at Irkutsk demanded a Constituent Assembly, as well as military concessions, and threatened a peaceful strike. But the Army, however undisciplined, was loyal, as it was soon to show in the crushing of the belated, ill-judged, and ill-managed rising at Moscow in December, when the authorities, for once, showed both judgment and energy.

The interest of the Moscow insurrection, which lasted only ten days, lies in its illustration of revolutionary tactics. While it was in progress, Count Witte's franchise law was published on December 24, 1905, giving effect to the promises of October 30th.

Expecting that the new legislature would meet in an ugly mood, Count Witte borrowed largely both in Russia and abroad before the elections were held: a piece of judicious hedging which expresses the extent of his confidence in the new institutions. But we need affect no surprise that a statesman trained in a school so entirely dissimilar from the parliamentary one was cautious. The Constitutional Democratic party—the Kadets—made no secret of their intention to propose the expropriation of landed property, and there was an understanding among the Ministers that the Duma would be dissolved if this question were touched. In an atmosphere of punitive expeditions, with the "loyal" Black Hundreds co-operating with military and police to restore order, the elections took place, and the first Duma began its sittings on May 10, 1906, in the Tavrida Palace at St. Petersburg.

Maurice Baring, a candid and careful observer, tells us that, in 1914, Russia was being worse governed than under Alexander II. Count Witte, always bitter against his successors in power, writes about the same time that the concessions of the revolutionary years existed only on paper, or had been retracted. There are those, on the other hand, who point out that it is not the worst, but the weakest, rulers upon whom the nemesis of bad government falls, and that the Tsarist Government had made, and was making, substantial improvements in itself when it fell. The truth, as it appears to the present writer, is something different from either of these opposite opinions. The appetite comes with eating: and the standard which people apply to their Governments is a progressive one, advancing with the amelioration of the administration. The achievements of the year which centred upon the Revolution of 1905, some temporary, some permanent, were real, and the administration of 1914, with some qualifications, was absolutely better than that of twenty years earlier, but not better relatively to the expectations of the Russian people. In particular they had ceased to regard the power of the Autocrat to involve them in war as a part of the necessary order of things.

First among the benefits conferred by the Revolution of 1905 was the existence of the Duma, even after the limitation of the franchise, which deprived it of its claim to speak for the whole people. It fell far short of the hopes of those whose eyes were fixed on the Parliaments and Congresses of the West. That was inevitable, since the so-called political parties were mere bodies of thinkers having no organic root in the electorate. But it was a training-ground for a limited class, and that an important one, capable of representing a portion at least of the aspirations of the people. It was a platform of free speech, giving opportunities for the ventilation of abuses and the exposure of highly-placed offenders. The support given by some of the authorities to the hooliganism of the Black Hundreds was revealed in the Duma in 1906, and the prosecution of a former Director of Police followed the disclosures. On this platform Alexander Guchkov could denounce the Court favourite, Rasputin, Paul Miliukov could ask whether the conduct of war by the Ministry was madness or treachery, Grand Dukes could be told that they were out of place in high Army-command. That the speeches in the Duma caused alarm in the highest quarters is made plain by the letters of the Tsaritsa begging the Tsar to prevent it from meeting. Finally, the elective body gave an opportunity for the free play of a moderate Liberalism, capable of carrying out valuable, if minor, reforms. Another change of the period was the establishment of the office of Prime Minister, which introduced an element of potential—not always of actual—coherence and stability into public business.

※   ※   ※

The peasants, proverbially "dark" and "deaf," suffered under wrongs for which they could not find the right name. Their demand was expressed as a claim for the land held by the landlords. That would not have solved the problem of their poverty, as subsequent history showed. One cause of their poverty was excessive demands from the State, another a primitive system of land holding and of agriculture, a third was the national character. Character is the product of history and institutions, and an element in the Russian peasant character was certainly the inferior legal and social status which had survived serfdom. These things were remediable, if only slowly: and the period of the first Revolution brought some palliatives. The landlords kept their land but, frightened by the attacks upon their estates, increased their sales of land and reduced their rents. The reorganisation of the peasant bank was carried out. The way was opened to a wider policy of colonisation. If the mass remained as poor as ever, the "strong and sober" received a magnificent opening in the Stolypin legislation of which we speak in the next chapter, and in the encouragement of Agricultural Co-operation. If it be true that the best way to help the poorer is to make the less poor prosperous, then the first Revolution and its sequelae helped the peasantry as a whole. If we calculate the burdens on the peasantry at different epochs—the thing was done by a qualified Russian economist in 1924—we find that they were not, taking a general average, excessive in the years immediately preceding the Great War, and the old reproach against the Tsarist administration of over-taxation of the peasants had been by that time removed.

The moral burden upon the peasantry, the inferior legal and social status, the liability to arbitrary treatment and to exceptional punishment, was only in part removed by the Revolution of 1905. From 1906 they ceased to be debarred from the higher institutions of learning, and were able to rise in the services to posts from which they had previously been excluded. The Land-Captains remained, and continued to exercise illegal and arbitrary powers. The rural Courts remained unchanged, and corporal punishment, though restricted by law, continued to be practised on the peasants. But that they themselves saw in this Revolution some improvement in their status, is shown by their name for it, "ravneniye," the levelling.

❋ ❋ ❋

It was not only the peasant who needed assurance of inviolability of person. The ordinary citizen was also subject to arbitrary interference, and the promises of 1905 did not put an end to these. In 1913 Stephen Graham tells us that "anyone is liable to arrest at any hour of the day or night at the instance of a stupid or corrupt police." The exceptional-status regulations of Alexander III, which expired in 1906, were renewed by an Imperial Ukaz for an additional period of three years, and exceptional laws and exceptional jurisdictions continued to be a cause of complaint up to the outbreak of war in 1914. In 1912 Count Witte tells us that the police still have unlimited authority, including the right of administrative exile; that correspondence is still unreasonably examined; that laws regulating association and meeting exist on paper only. It seems, indeed, to have been impossible to any Russian police, then or afterwards, to accept, in practice, any limitation upon their authority. We shall miss some of the lessons of Russian history unless we realise that the outlook on law, and on the liberty of the subject, is fundamentally different from that which, in theory at least, prevails in the Anglo-Saxon world.

The guardians of civil rights—without which, anywhere and every-where, such rights exist upon paper only—are the Courts and the Press. The Bar, at least the Bar of the great cities, had always enjoyed a high reputation since its organisation by Alexander II. Judges were made inviolable by Imperial decision under the Fundamental laws of 1905: but it was the practice to make temporary, instead of substantive, appointments to the Judicial Bench, so that removal was a simple matter. On the other hand there was a real relaxation of the censor-ship. Maurice Baring tells us in February 1906 that "every case of oppression is now reported in the newspapers as it happens," and that "some of the comic and satirical papers might have Marat for their editor." Before 1906, Kluchevsky's history of Russia could be circu-lated only in manuscript notes, like Peter Chaadaev's Philosophical letters seventy years earlier. The relaxation was no merely transient feature. Books now begin to appear which were formerly unprintable, and the Bolshevik newspaper *Pravda* (*Truth*), though often sus-pended, begins to have a continuous life as a legal journal from 1912.

Except as protégés of the police, during the bizarre episode of Zubatovist Socialism, both Trade Unions and Co-operative Societies had been frowned upon by authority, as likely centres of disaffection and conspiracy. Both now received authorisation, which in the case of the former was precarious and short-lived, though the law was on the Statute book. But the strikes of 1905 secured a ten-hour day to the metal workers and an eight-and-a-half hour day to the textile workers. Sick benefit funds, established under a law of 1912, were more fortu-nate than Trade Unions, and had two million members by 1914. Co-operation obtained more than a nominal blessing. In the forms of Producers' and Credit Co-operation it rapidly demonstrated its adapt-ability to the conditions of the Russian peasantry and was more swiftly successful than in any other country. In 1914 there were 33,000 socie-ties with twelve million members, and the butter of the Siberian Co-operatives had become famous on the western markets.

In the early phases of the Revolution of 1905 religious teaching was declared to be free, and certain remissions were conceded to the Jews. The position of the Old Believers was alleviated, and we see them hereafter holding regular annual religious conferences, attended by delegates from North Russia, the Urals and the Caucasus. Some of the grievances of the Roman Catholic schools were removed. The prison at the Suzdal monastery which was used by the ecclesiastical tribunals for clerical and dissenting offenders, was emptied of prisoners after the Manifesto of October 1905: but soon began to be occupied again by priests who had denounced the death-sentences pronounced in the Field Courts-Martial of the counter-revolution. Self-government was granted to the Universities.

The non-Great-Russian nationalities also benefited by the temporary liberalism of the Government. Autonomy was restored to Finland, and was, for a time, a reality, so that Finland became a refuge for the disgruntled politician and the revolutionary, beyond the reach of the Tsarist police. Poland was also to have enjoyed political concessions, but these were declared, as early as November 14, 1905, to be postponed, because of the renewal of unrest after the issue of the October manifesto. Active measures of Russification were generally withdrawn, but up to 1906 the use of the Ukrainian language was prohibited in schools, courts, and public offices and, even after the withdrawal of this prohibition, books in the language were not allowed in public and school libraries.

The Revolution and the repression that followed it had a demoralising effect both upon officials and people. The habit of resort to exceptional laws, and of employing irregular auxiliaries in suppressing disturbances, affected the official balance. Violence is not discipline, any more than a man is a good rider because he jerks at his horse's mouth. The agrarian disturbances, continued into 1907 and 1908, the violence of the Black Hundreds, and the practice of revolutionary "expropriation" of funds, which melted imperceptibly into unashamed robbery, were equally demoralising to the population. In the words of a peasant, quoted by Sir Bernard Pares, respect for the State was gone, and only fear of it remained. Even the fear must have been partly gone: for the people had seen that ministers and officials, as well as landlords, could be frightened. The experiences of the first General Strike of 1905 and of the operation of workers' Soviets in St. Petersburg and other important towns were fraught with lessons which the revolutionaries did not forget. 1905 was a step towards 1917.

Chapter IX

COUNTER-REVOLUTION AND REVOLUTION

"Be more autocratic, my very own Sweetheart, show your mind. . . . Ah, my Love, when at last will you thump with your hand upon the table? . . . Oh, Lovey, you can trust me. I may not be clever enough—but I have a strong feeling, and that helps more than the brain often."

> The Tsaritsa's letters to the Tsar.

"As poor peasants, how happy, how worthy, had ye two been! But, by evil destiny, ye were made a King and Queen of: and so both are become an astonishment and a by-word to all times."

> THOMAS CARLYLE: writing of Louis XVI and Marie Antoinette in *The Diamond Necklace*.

"When I think that our autocratic régime ends in this impotence, I become republican."

> *A Russian Grand Duke*, quoted by M. MAURICE PALÉOLOGUE.

"Russia, alas, is the classic model of a state where many people are not where they belong. It is a country where there is a general complaint about the lack of good men, but where no attention is paid to the good men who exist."

> Speech in the Duma, Aug. 14, 1915.

When a people enters upon a career of industrialisation, it has two primary needs, besides that of technical skill: the need of capital and the need of consumers to take the products. If it is fortunate enough to find a world of consumers open to it, before the competition of rivals has developed, the two needs are solved together, by the profits derived from the great open markets. Russia, when she commenced industrialisation in earnest in the eighties of the nineteenth century, had neither capital nor consumers. It was necessary to borrow the capital largely from abroad, and to find the effective demand for the product largely in the State's own needs of railway development and in further industrialisation; which involved the encouragement of industry by subsidies and protective tariffs. Her own peasants, however greatly in need of the products, could offer no considerable effective demand for them. In such conditions, if the process of development received a check, the restriction of demand was likely to hold up industrial production altogether. A normal demand for the products of industry could only be established by an addition to the purchasing power of the peasant: which might mean a solution of the agrarian question in terms of political change, and a loss of support for the autocracy among the landlord class.

Who paid for Russian industrialisation, for the service of the foreign debts, for the gold reserve which was necessary to stabilise the currency and establish Russian credit, for the lag between outlay and realisation? There was only one source of payment, and that was the product of the soil: the grain, the flax, the timber, the oil. Of these things, the grain was the largest item, and the burden of Russia's great export trade, by which a "favourable" trade balance was maintained continuously from the eighties onward, in bad years and good, lay ultimately upon the peasant, whose daily ration was the less because of it. There was a long tradition in Russian history of heavy exports of grain. In these latter days when, to the luxury needs of a small circle and the elementary equipment required by a primitive State, was added the vast growth of railways and industry, the strain upon the food supply even in favourable seasons was much increased. Economists may tell us that the export of grain increases production by developing a market for surplus, and therefore does not diminish the amount available for home consumption. But Russia, an exporting country, was producing less grain per head of its population than other European countries which were importers. Either the latter were wasting their food, or the former was going short.

The compulsion which reduced the ration was the heavy drain of payments to the State and to property owners. Before the abolition of the redemption-payments this drain was enormous. A trustworthy calculation made for the year 1912 shows that it was still eighteen per cent of the gross income of the peasant, of which less than twelve per cent was on account of taxation levied by the State. The latter figure corresponds with remarkable closeness to the general average of the land revenue and cesses raised in British India. In return for this the peasant received the potential benefit which extended industrialisation was likely to bring to agriculture by the enlargement and variation of its markets.

For the extension of industrialisation, and for the abolition of redemption-payments, he was indebted to Count Witte, an economic and financial genius who showed, in the later days of his power, that he might have saved the Tsardom, or postponed its fate. He was not ignorant of the danger of stripping his country of her food to pay for his policy of industrialisation. But he saw that a country which lacks industries is at the mercy of its neighbors, because there is neither wealth nor successful war without them, and he held that it was necessary to build up national industry before dealing with the agrarian problem. In effect, his policy for his country was one of compulsory saving, taking the form of investment in railways and in industrial plant, similar in kind, if not in degree, to that pursued under revolutionary planning.

Witte, seasoned administrator as he was, and evidently not too skilful a manager of political parties, had no liking for Constitutions. But he was a realist, and a statesman and, when he returned from making the Peace of Portsmouth and found all Russia in dangerous turmoil, he told his Imperial master that he must choose between a constitution and a military dictatorship. He was premier when Nicolas issued the Manifesto of October 30, 1905, and must have advised him to yield whatever that manifesto did in effect yield. In December he issued the regulations which made the franchise all but universal, and took the wind completely out of the sails of the revolutionary movement: and was never forgiven for it by his Imperial master and mistress. Then he set to work to minimise the danger of the impending Duma, by issuing the fundamental laws, by making the Council of State into a Second Chamber alongside of the democratic assembly, and by protecting the military budget against political interference by a very large foreign loan. Given the disbelief in democracy and parliamentarianism—and it would be absurd to affect surprise at this disbelief for such a country as Russia—this was statesmanship. Witte's way was to establish a fresh basis for the Imperial authority by economic development, and, in the meanwhile, to maintain peace, to avoid quarrels with the Jews and with the non-Great-Russian nationalities, and to frustrate the encroachments of politicians upon the executive power, while giving them the consultative assembly which could no longer be withheld. Think as we may about the ultimate wisdom of this policy, if carried out it would have given to Russia a very different history in the twentieth century.

We hear nothing of a broken heart. Rather, Witte withdrew into a corner to snarl, to dip his pen in gall and to dissuade the Japanese ambassador from the proposal to send a Japanese army to Europe to help the Allies: and to die when the economic machine which he had equipped and set going was already being driven to destruction.

* * *

None of the Socialist parties took part in the elections to the first Duma. Otherwise there was general participation, and no more interference than the sporadic operations of punitive forces made inevitable. According to all the rules of the game—as practised in the West—the legislative assembly should have had widespread support in the country. The largest party in it consisted of the Constitutional Democrats, the "Kadets"—the Liberals, we may call them—versed in the best models of western Constitutionalism. The Duma discussed the Black Hundreds and their pogroms, the abolition of capital punishment, an amnesty for revolutionary offences; and the programme of the Kadet party showed that they had other proposals unpalatable to Government, including the abolition of administrative punishment, of extraordinary Courts, and of the passport system, and the incorporation of guarantees in the fundamental laws. The Emperor had not pretended to concede responsible government, but the parliamentarians endeavoured to make the Government responsible to the Duma by passing a vote of censure on the Tsar's Ministers, as a majority in the British House of Commons might have done, in the days when majorities were not subservient to ministries. The Ministers ignored the claim, and walked out. The critical struggle was over the land. The Kadets proposed expropriation, and rival proposals of a less drastic kind were put forward on behalf of the Government. The Duma was dissolved: and the Kadet and Labour members retired to Finland, and appealed to the country to withhold co-operation and to repudiate foreign loans concluded without the Duma's consent.

There was no response. Liberalism had called spirits from the vasty deep. They did not come when called. All the power was on the other side, and the constitutional forms were no more than forms. Externally, the protesting members had reproduced the constitutional procedure of the western democracies. The vital difference was that they had no roots in the electorate, which did not regard them as its own, but looked on, as at a spectacle.

The Minister who was selected to carry out the dissolution of the first Duma was Peter Stolypin. A lesser brain than Witte, he was nevertheless the monarchy's second chance of escape, and the second chance that the monarchy threw away. As a Minister he resisted a proposal for the appointment of a Liberal ministry from the ranks of the recalcitrant Duma—which would have conceded the claim for responsible government—and was made Premier to carry out his own alternative policy. He took up with vigour the task of restoring order in a desperately disordered country, and established, under the authority of the fundamental laws, the Field Courts-Martial, known as *Stolypin's neckties*, which summarily tried and hanged robbers within twenty-four hours of capture. This was the period of the expropriations, the "Exes" as they were familiarly called, acts of brigandage for the collection of revolutionary funds, which were not in practice, nor always even in motive, distinguishable from ordinary crime. The number of executions on account of these expropriations, and of armed resistance, is variously put at figures ranging from six hundred to three thousand five hundred. Liberal opinion was indignant and the Emperor Nicolas himself was perturbed. It is said that there were ten thousand victims during the repression of the disturbances in Latvia in November 1905. But, as usual in Russia, executions in legal form, even when the procedure was that of a Field Courts-Martial, were more shocking than mere slaughter in hot blood with no form at all. People talked of a Stolypinshchina, as they had talked of a Pugachevshchina in the days of the great rebellion. But, if we admit that Governments must either maintain order or abdicate, it does not appear that Stolypin's Courts-Martial were unnecessarily severe. Over eleven thousand persons were condemned to various penalties in 1907, the largest number of cases being in the Baltic provinces and in the regions of St. Petersburg and Moscow, and we hear of villages in which every tenth man was whipped.

This drastic visitation was only a fraction of Stolypin's policy: which, viewed from the standpoint of the revolutionary, was a doubly dangerous one. Not only did he seek to repress disorder by severities (which, in a greater or less degree, is the way of every Government) but he aimed at finding a new basis of strength for the monarchy in a class of new rich, reinforced by the addition of a well-to-do peasantry. It was to this that his agrarian legislation was directed.

At the height of the disturbances in 1905, the Emperor's own entourage was discussing the compulsory expropriation of the large estates to meet the peasant demand for more land. Such a measure would have been quite in keeping with the methods of the Tsarist Government, which had sequestrated the landed property of the Church under Catherine the Great, bought out the squires on a large scale at the Emancipation Settlement, and, at a later date, reduced the holdings of the old-established settlers in Siberia to forty and a half acres per male soul in order to make room for new colonists. The conception of the sacredness of property, subject to certain strictly limited overruling rights of the State, was replaced in Russia by that of expediency, and in this respect the revolutionaries were in the legitimate order of succession to the Tsars. The advocates of expropriation were naturally met with the argument that more land was not the remedy for the troubles of the peasant. If we are content with bare averages, we find that in 1900 the peasants had just under seven acres per head for men, women and children. So far from this average being inadequate, it was, on the peasant scale of subsistence, almost handsome. We may agree with those who tell us that, for one reason or another, it was impossible to utilise more than a third or a half of this area in any given year. But this is an argument, not so much for adding to the land, as for adding to the means of cultivation and improving its conditions.

If we leave general averages, we find a different story. The word *peasant* was an elastic one. A man might be legally a peasant when he had become a large proprietor. The historian of Russian Agriculture before the Revolution tells us, in connection with the large purchases made by "peasants" after the establishment of the Peasant Bank, that a whole third of the area was bought by men who held from a hundred and thirty-five to two thousand seven hundred acres apiece. Again, the regional averages go down below five acres per head and up to twelve or thirteen: and the provincial averages very much more widely. M. Köfod, who made the Stolypin Settlement, tells us of 560,000 whole households which had no more than five and a half acres apiece, that is, perhaps, a little more than an acre per head, and of two and a quarter millions of households in which the average per head would range from this figure up to two and a half acres. Prima facie, there was need here for more land: but the question was complicated by the fact that many of the non-economic holders lacked cattle and equipment, and many more had no intention of living by agriculture, so that the best solution for them might be to be bought out.

The nature and value of the large estates proposed for expropriation were also to be considered. In 1905 the panic among the landlords was already causing many of them, especially in the Black-Earth zone, where holdings were smallest, to sell their land to peasants. It has been calculated that, even if the expropriation of the landlords had been complete, the addition of new cultivation to be made to the average peasant holdings would have been less than thirty per cent.

The quality and nature of the farming on landlord's estates differed widely. Much of their land was already leased to peasants, who cultivated it in peasant fashion, with peasant knowledge and peasant means and, because of their transient interest, produced yields smaller than they obtained on their own allotments. But some of the larger estates were valuable to agriculture. The general average of the yield upon them, taken in the mass, was substantially higher than that on peasant holdings, and the best of them observed superior methods. Wholesale expropriation would therefore injure the interests of agriculture, and reduce the food surplus with which Russia paid for her imports and met the service of her foreign debt. These considerations led M. Chuprov, a contemporary advocate of expropriation, to limit his proposals to estates upon which no measures of improvement had been taken. It was the same distinction which the Bolsheviks proposed in 1917-18 to observe between ordinary estates at the disposal of the local land authorities, and improved estates and superior stock which were to form the nucleus of model State farms. But, in proportion to the amount of such reservations, the area available for increasing peasant holdings would be reduced, and the addition to be made would therefore be nearer to fifteen than to thirty per cent of the existing average.

In his provincial government of Saratov, Peter Stolypin had been in contact with peasant disturbances only less threatening than those of Ukraine, and with a body of landlords ready to defend their rights. He conceived the idea of calling in a new world of individualist peasant proprietors, freed from the control of the Mir, consisting of "the strong and the sober," to strengthen by their self-interest the principle of landed property, and of thus putting an end for ever to the talk of expropriation. What he expected to happen to that unfortunately large section which was neither strong nor sober, we can only guess. Presumably he expected it to sink into the ranks of the rural proletariat, which already existed in considerable numbers. It is plain that he attached no value to the Mir, which had played its part as soon as common responsibility for taxes was gone, and that in his condemnation of it to extinction, he made no difference between its agrarian functions and its work as an organ of village self-government, in which it was difficult to replace. His aim was not less political than economic: to create a new and stable conservatism in the village.

Those who are accustomed to the gingerly approach to great problems of Governments of a different type can only gasp at the speed with which Stolypin flung himself into the task of revolutionising the agrarian system of an Empire, while conservatives and socialists alike protested. It was only a few degrees less drastic than the Bolshevik plan of the general collectivisation of holdings: and its revolutionary swiftness helps us to understand some subsequent history. Within

five months of his appointment for the purpose of dissolving the first
Duma, an ordinance was issued, under a clause of the Fundamental
Laws, without reference to either House of the Legislature, which envisaged the end of the Mir and the establishment of individual peasant property in land, and entrusted a Land Settlement Commission
with the task of consolidating the new farms out of the old strips. The
Revolutionaries of November 1917 were less bold, for, in their first
agrarian legislation, they at least acted upon the ascertained wishes of
the great mass of the peasantry.

The Stolypin legislation would be wrongly described as establishing
free trade in land, for it maintained the existing restriction upon the
sale of peasant land to non-peasant and, by a clause inserted by the
third Duma, forbade the acquisition of more than a limited maximum
of peasant land by any one purchaser in any one district. The social
danger of the buying out of poor peasants by richer peasants, or by
non-peasants, was thus provided against, in so far as legislation on such
a matter can be effective.

Like most Russian legislation of the Tsarist, no less than of the
revolutionary, epoch, the law showed less regard for individual rights
of property than is normally shown in Britain. The rights of the peasant in land had been—so far as Russian law was definitely ascertainable—rights of the whole household. The new law transferred them to
the head of the household. The old rights in land were subject to
redistribution, general or particular, carried out by the Mir. At the
moment of the operations under the new Settlement, a peasant might
have more or less than his normal share. But the measure of his new
rights was his actual possession, subject to payment for any excess
on a scale fixed in 1861, when the value of land was very different.

There was another respect in which the Stolypin legislation, as completed in 1910 and 1911, treated existing rights in a more summary
way than a British legislature would be likely to treat them. In a
considerable part of European Russia, peasant land covering nearly
a quarter of the whole area of peasant allotments had already become
separate heritable property, not subject to redistribution by the Mir.
This would normally have stood in the way of the consolidation of
holdings which it was desired to effect. The law of 1910, which was
passed by the third Duma, provided that the owners of such separate
heritable property in a village might decide by a bare majority in
favour of the consolidation of their separate strips into integral holdings. It will be noticed that the dissentient minority might thus be
compelled to exchange land which they had hitherto, on solid

grounds, considered to be their separate heritable property, not liable to redistribution. The law of 1911 went still further in the direction of authorising the compulsion of minorities.

During the brief currency of the Stolypin Settlement and probably, at least in part, in consequence of it, agricultural statistics show improved conditions. There was an increase in the importation of agricultural machinery and artificial fertilisers, a general increase in the acreage under crop, apparently indicating that land formerly regarded as unproductive was being tilled, and a slight increase in the yield per acre of rye, oats and barley, but not of wheat. Emigration to Siberia and Central Asia which had previously been very active, amounting to seven hundred thousand a year both in 1908 and 1909, fell off between 1909 and 1914, presumably in consequence of improved conditions at home. In spite of an industrial slump which lasted till 1910, industry produced, between 1905 and 1914, double its earlier production.

The second Duma, which met in March, 1907, a more extreme body than the first, because of the exclusion of the constitutionalists who had appealed for non-co-operation with the Government, was soon dissolved in an atmosphere of police prosecutions. A large proportion of its Socialist members were exiled, to return in triumph at the fall of the monarchy ten years later. Then followed the new Electoral law, which made the conservative "Octobrists" the leading party in the third Duma which met in November the same year and gave predominance to the propertied and Great-Russian elements of the population. This was characteristic of Stolypin's policy of political and economic nationalism, with a constitutional or quasi-constitutional monarchy, but without responsible government. He leaned, or wished to lean, upon the Duma, whose support he ultimately used for his agrarian legislation, and upon the middling landowner and the middling capitalist, and upon the patriotism, not to say the chauvinism, of Great-Russians against the federating tendencies of the other peoples of the Empire. The reactionaries might have recognised the constructive statecraft which framed these plans, but they were not grateful to their second potential saviour. The Court, always blind to its friends, and having perhaps an instinctive sense of the tendency of his measures to convert the Orthodox Autocracy into a sort of Louis Philippe monarchy, could not abide Peter Stolypin: and when he was murdered in 1911, the Tsaritsa said: "He is gone: let us hear no more of him." As for the inchoate class of capitalists and bourgeois, whose interests would seem to have dictated a warm support, they did not at any time show willingness to put up an energetic struggle either for themselves or for their friends. Throughout this period of revolution, attempted or achieved, the middle class in Russia seems to have expected to have its battles fought for it by the official machine. Its activities did not go beyond those of the *Union of the Russian People* and the less reputable performances of the Black Hundreds.

The period of the third and fourth Dumas, starting in 1907 and carrying Russia into the beginning of the First World War, is one which leaves the inquirer with a sense of contradictions. It begins with a spiritual depression and disillusionment, along with which violent disorder continues to prevail, so that something like stalemate appears to be reached, between a Government which cannot enforce peace and a people which will not submit to repression. The counter-revolution is so far successful, that many socialists are in despair and withdraw from their activities. The literature either does not serve as a mirror for the life out of which it springs, or truly represents a chaos of conflicting tendencies. There is a revival of religious thought and interest springing from Dostoievsky and Soloviev. A band of liberals, former Marxians, bring religion, without reaction, for the first time into politics. Artsybashev publishes *Sanin* and preaches in it a kind of anarchy of sexual behaviour—which at a later date proved too strong a dose for Bolshevik ethics, so that *Sanin* was excluded from circulation and Artsybashev expelled from Russia. Vyacheslav Ivanov, mystical anarchist and adept of the cult of the Divine Wisdom, demands, like Dostoievsky's Ivan Karamazov, the non-acceptance of the world. The poet Andrei Bely immerses himself in a mystical eschatology with all, and more than all, of the imagery of the Book of Revelation. It is, in part at least, a literature of escape, from which the realism of an earlier generation has entirely departed: perhaps an interval of sultry hush and tension before the breaking of a storm.

In the meanwhile the Duma has ceased to be representative of the population as a whole—if indeed it ever was so—and yet is doing work of an effective kind: co-operating in the land-settlement; improving the schools and the pay of teachers; making itself felt in the administration of finance, and improving Russian credit by the publicity of accounts and statistics.

In 1912, with the disturbances at the works of the British concessionaries on the Lena gold-fields, there is an unmistakable revival of Labour activities, long repressed. The officials responsible for the bloodshed are brought to trial, and a young Labour member of the Duma, Alexander Kerensky, uses the opportunity of the prosecution to attack the régime. The number of strikers rises to nearly a million in a year, and in July 1914 labour disturbances become gravely menacing.

This renewal of Labour demonstrations coincides with a period which we have already described as one of prosperity, at least for some, with foreign capital entering Russia in ever-increasing volume, and the accompanying symptoms of boom. In the meanwhile, the police have been continuously active, and a legal state of emergency has been continuously in force in the greater part of the Empire. If Witte's gall is not too much for his veracity, the letters even of the Dowager Empress are being intercepted and copies of them transferred to the appropriate *dossier*. Hardly have the Field-Courts-Martial brought their operations to a close when in 1910 the British Ambassador, Sir George Buchanan, is writing of political difficulties, particularly in the Universities and High Schools, with Professors delivering their lectures under police protection. The Duma thunders against exceptional laws and administrative exile, and its Chairman, the conservative Octobrist, Alexander Guchkov, resigns the chair. The conservative reconstructor, Stolypin, is murdered. In 1912 Buchanan tells us of political strikes, of mutinies in the Baltic and Black Sea Fleets and among the troops at Tashkent. In 1913 the fourth Duma, with its Octobrist majority gradually taking up an attitude less and less friendly to the Government, censures the Ministry for the continuance of a state of exceptional law: and Guchkov tells Buchanan that there has never been a time when Russia was so deeply permeated by the revolutionary spirit. It has been suggested that one of the considerations which took the Government into war was the wish to escape from revolution at home.

How are we to account for the existence of this menacing unrest in the Russian people, despite "prosperity" and a respectable and efficient Duma, before the war and the attendant maladministration had brought hunger and destroyed confidence in the capacity and even in the good will of the rulers?

There is a school of thought which denies that anything was wrong, or at least that anything was so wrong as to call for cure by a drastic operation. The autocracy was, in essentials, like every other Government which is concerned with the defence of property. It had abolished it in its most obviously objectionable form, of property in men and women, and had secured to the emancipated a proportion of the land which amounted, from the first, to half of the whole, and was steadily advancing by purchase. It was doubtful whether any other system would have ventured so far to ignore vested interests or to achieve so much. It had shown itself conspicuously of the best European quality in Catherine the Great's offer of an asylum to the Jesuits, in Alexander I's contribution to the European settlements of 1815, a far wiser one than that of a century later; and in the initiation of the Hague Court of Arbitration for international disputes. It had established peace and the primary essentials of good government over vast areas of Asia, and had ended the raids of the man-stealing Turkman, as at an earlier date those of the Krim Tartar. It had suffered the birth of a literature of world-wide appeal, at the very moment when its assertion of discipline over its subjects was most uncompromising. Since the remission of the redemption-dues, its imposts on the peasantry were no longer excessive. Its courts were modernised, the jury was at work in them, and, whatever might happen in the repression of revolt, its normal jurisprudence was the mildest in Europe. The industrial revolution was still at an early stage: and there had been similar abuses in that stage in all the industrialised countries. Elective organs for the consultation of public opinion had been brought into existence, and were producing administrative reforms. If all was not well, at least it was as well as in the rest of Europe, with its slums and work-houses and prisons for one section of its peoples, and its palaces for another.

Russians—thus the argument continues—are dreamers. The peasants hear of a country of warm streams, as in Tolstoi's War and Peace, or of a Land of Truth, such as that of which Gorky's wanderer tells us in Down and Out: and at once leave their homes to seek for it. They are no wiser when they are educated, and Utopian theories exercise an irresistible attraction for them. Liberal concessions only set their imaginations off in riot, and make them greedy for more. There are no rigid traditions, no respect for history, no sense of reality, to keep them from harnessing the Winged Horse. They are incorrigible talkers, and the talk intoxicates them. They are not concerned with the dull routine of cause and consequence, and even their interests do not make a determining appeal to them. They claim the impossible from life, and are the natural and easy prey of revolutionary propaganda. With such a people the fatal error, for a Government, lies in the first beginning of concession. It was the slackening of discipline, not in 1917, but at an earlier date (some seem to suggest, even as far back as the Emancipation), which made the Revolution. The meritorious and experienced officials who were convinced that there was still much to be said for the knout must have argued somewhat on the lines which I have suggested. I will only note that a good deal of it is true of human nature in general. Many of us would be far safer under lock and key. But—*quis custodiet?*

There was plenty of discipline in the Russian empire, but it was not an even discipline, with laws intelligible to all, and it was not equally applied. I will not say that there was one law for the rich and one for the poor: but there was certainly one administration for the rich and another for the poor. It seems nearly certain that to the vast mass of the Russian people, then and perhaps now, autocracy was the only conceivable form of government, in everything outside of the routine of village life, where the tradition was truly democratic. If anything was wrong with the autocracy, anything, that is, which could not be cured by the well-tried method of a palace revolution, and a change of the person of the autocrat, it was that the autocrat had in some measure ceased to be the *leveller* which public opinion expected him to be: that, in the words of Pobiedonostsev, "wealth, acquired by rapine, over-mastered power itself"; that the true tyrant was not the Tsar himself, but the exploiters who sheltered behind him and mastered his governing machine.

The increase of wealth and its uneven distribution, the development of the cash-nexus, the rise of the money-lender of all types, squire, merchant, churchman, and peasant, the power of the industrialist and the harsh conditions which he enforced upon the worker, with the frequent co-operation of the police, had ended the old patriarchal supremacy of the Tsar, and made obvious the existence of gross and oppressive inequalities which his power did not avail, even if he desired, to level. The fancy that the Tsar, if you could reach him, would always do justice, was long in dying. Perhaps it died finally when the Grand Duke Vladimir fired on the crowd outside the Winter Palace on Bloody Sunday in 1905, and the participants in the demonstration were expelled from the capital, to spread the news over thousands of villages. Even the Constitution, particularly in the form which was given to it by the restrictive electoral law, seemed to create political privilege (as perhaps most constitutions do): for some were to be consulted, and many not: a very wide departure from the dream of equal *accessibility* for all, never realised in practice, but always surviving in tradition. Perhaps the appropriate cure was a different way of choosing the autocrat, with more exacting tests of his capacity for the tasks of a superman, and the Revolution has hit upon this: the substitution of a ruler for a *fainéant*. But we are anticipating.

On the policy of the War there was from the outset a radical difference of opinion in governing circles. Not only was Germany the main support of the autocracy, and her overthrow by the western democracies a likely prelude to the further liberalisation of Russia, but she was the principal source of supply for machinery and for the half-manufactured articles which were completed in Russia. Many, like Witte, must clearly have foreseen the economic consequences of the closing of Russia's frontiers and western and southern outlets, have hoped for an early settlement, and been half-hearted or sceptical over the measures necessary for the prosecution of such a struggle to victory. Suspicion, if not of German leanings, at least of lukewarmness to the war and of animosity to the Russian Commander-in-Chief, attached from an early date to General Sukhomlinov, Minister for War. The catastrophe of the Galician retreat threw an odious glare upon his responsibility. He was removed from the Ministry, and the Duma demanded that he be put on trial. But obstacles were placed in the way of the case, and the Empress interceded with her husband to hush it up, referring mysteriously to stories which might bring disgrace upon important personages if the trial takes place. The Empress's letters convey, in connection with this scandal, messages from "Our Friend," upon whom she always bestows initial capitals, and who is no other than Gregory Rasputin.

Rasputin (the name signifies debauchee, and acquaints us with the bearer's reputation in his native Siberian village) was neither priest nor monk, nor in any sort of religious orders, but a wandering "man of God." He was lucky enough to exhibit curative or mesmeric powers over the precious and only son, who wrung his mother's heart by being a sufferer from haemophilia. Then he became something for which our western experiences have no parallel, but readers of Dostoievsky may recognise in the part which he plays with the Empress, some resemblance to the *Elder*, to whom Alyosha Karamazov entrusts his spiritual life. The devoted wife and mother, grand-daughter of Queen Victoria, and of life not less strict than her grandmother, surrenders her soul to the guidance of this religious adventurer and presses all his political counsels upon her Imperial husband.

Rasputin is something of an enigma, because he started with a few simple and great ideas which multitudes must have shared with him: an immense sympathy with his fellow-peasants and their sufferings, a religious devotion to the autocracy as the hope of Russia, and a passion for peace. He foresaw (perhaps he had no need of exceptional qualities for this perception) the confusion which would come upon Russia during or after the war. Kerensky (no friend of his) speaks of his "wonderful intuition" and it is evident that he possessed some sort of animal magnetism. Those who are aware of the wilder orbits of the Russian spirit may not be surprised that he regarded sin as necessary to salvation, because without sin there is no repentance. Some highly-placed ladies lent themselves to his orgies, religious and other, or visited him to intercede for their husbands. Probably his head was turned by the enormous influence which he found himself to possess. In the later stages of his life at Court, a knot of financiers provided him with money and gave him a weekly dinner, at which he generally became drunk. It cannot be said that the Empress was blind to all of this. On one occasion she writes to her husband: "Our Friend was very gay after dinner: *not tipsy*." The italics are mine. When he was tipsy, he talked, and what was said by him was used for the Stock Exchange, or reported to Berlin. He had not the brains to carry through any systematic intrigue, but he easily became an instrument for the intrigues of others, and he had plenty of cunning to protect his own interests. A final and particularly effective device was to convince the Empress that his departure would be followed by the death of the Tsarevitch and the fall of the dynasty.

In April 1915 he got very drunk at a dinner party, and boasted to his fellow guests, with obscene gestures, that he did what he liked with "the old woman." The police reported this at Court, and one might have supposed that it would have ended his career. But the Empress only thought that the Devil had set a snare for the holy man, she complained of the Commandant of Gendarmerie who had given the information, and used all her powers of persuasion to forestall any opportunity of interpellation about the scandal in the Duma. On this occasion, Guchkov, the head of the Octobrist party, figures as her particular *bête noire*, no doubt because he had already exposed Rasputin in 1912. She asks angrily: "Cannot Guchkov be hanged?" We get the full significance of this interjection when we recall that, at the March Revolution, Guchkov was prominent among those who struggled for the monarchical principle against Kerensky and the republicans. When it is a question of giving effect to the promise of autonomy in Poland, she tells her husband: "Our Friend begs you to wait. . . . His love to you and Russia is so intense and God has sent Him to be your help and guide." When a comrade of Rasputin's, who had been foisted into a Bishopric, wants to have a certain person canonised, so as to attract pilgrims and their money, and the Procurator of the Holy Synod, a man of great weight in Orthodox and conservative circles, stands firm against the trick, the Empress writes indignant letters, the Procurator is displaced from his lay headship of the Church, and—*the false Saint is duly canonised.*

The Commander-in-Chief, the Grand Duke Nicolas, was suspected by the Empress of intending to use his influence with the troops to secure his own position (possibly as Regent), in the event of the death or removal of the Emperor. There is a blank in the letters from July 11, 1915, because the Emperor was at this time with his family: but we soon discover how the time was being spent. The Empress writes a paean on the "great decision" which the Emperor has taken, and two days later he assumes the supreme command of all the forces of the sea and land armies operating in the theatre of war, with General Alexéev as Chief of Staff.

What the armies thought of the new High Command we learn from Major-General Knox, British military attaché. Misgiving was almost universal. Foreign Minister Sazonov said: "The only way out is to go and drown ourselves." It was not only the military situation which was prejudiced. Henceforth, and more particularly after Stürmer became President of the Council of Ministers in February 1916, the Empress was in control of the civil government of the rear, and distrust of authority permeated all classes.

Nicolas II was jealous of his authority, jealous of it even against the encroachment of his own wife: and he did not always yield to her insistence. Paradoxical though it may appear, his judgment was good. It was not on every occasion that he showed lack of will-power. Rather it would seem that he was the victim of a sort of morbid apathy, perhaps the result of fatalism. He felt himself born for suffering, a feeling which presently deepened into a sense of being a destined sacrifice. M. Paléologue, the French Ambassador, has left us an account of a conversation of 1909 in which Nicolas told Stolypin that his birthday was the day of the Patriarch Job, and quoted the despairing words: "Let the day perish wherein I was born, and the night wherein it was said there is a manchild conceived." There is a figure in Tennyson's *Princess* who, in moments of crisis, at grips with enemies of flesh and blood, has the hallucination of fighting with shadows, and collapses before them. Some such neurosis affected the life of Nicolas.

He was not, like his wife, under the direct influence of Rasputin, and it has been suggested that the murder of the latter, in December, 1916, came to him as something of a relief. The three persons who carried it out were Prince Yusupov (who married the Emperor's niece), the Grand Duke Dimitry, and Purishkevich, prominent in the reactionary *Union of the Russian People*—all men of the Court and of the extreme Right. There was joy in Petrograd because Rasputin met his death by drowning (the drowned cannot be canonised), and the Churches were filled with candles burning before the icons of St. Dimitry, in honour of the Grand Duke's namesake. But, lest we should forget the contradictions in Russian life, the murdered Man of God became a martyr for the peasants. "He caused the Tsar to hear the voice of the people"—doubtless because he spoke for peace.

The murder did not end the influences which were carrying the dynasty to ruin. Rasputin had had his predecessors in the function of fooling the Imperial pair; some other would have stepped into the place if he had ceased to fill it, and, when he was dead, the Court or its satellites were busy raising his ghost to consult him, up to the very night of Revolution.

✳   ✳   ✳

Alongside steady Socialist propaganda among soldiers and work-men, it had long been known that members of the Romanov family contemplated the deposition of the Tsar and the removal of the Tsaritsa to a convent. There was another plot for the deposition of the Tsar only and the appointment of the Tsaritsa as regent for her infant son, and yet a third for the removal of the Tsaritsa only: the former designed to facilitate a separate peace with Germany, the latter to make possible a more vigorous prosecution of the war. Palace conspiracies, or the talk of them, continued after the murder of Rasputin. The odium of Russian defeats and of Russian sufferings was concentrated largely on Alexandra Feodorovna, whose sobriquet, "the German woman," recalls "L'autrichienne," the name by which Marie Antoinette was known to Paris when the Austrian armies were advancing against France. There was an attempt on her life in January 1917 by an officer in the Imperial Hospital at Tsarskoye Selo. She was naturally in correspondence with her German relatives, was grieved at mob attacks upon Germans, protested against the changing of German place-names, of which Petrograd itself was an instance, and against a foolish proposal of the Holy Synod in 1914 to prohibit the German custom of the Christmas tree; sympathised with German prisoners of war, and urged the Tsar to allow Americans to inspect the prison camps. The suggestion of treachery to the country of her adoption is without foundation. But that she became an instrument in the hands of men who sought to bring about a separate peace with Germany is probable.

✳   ✳   ✳

The assistance given in the prosecution of the war by Town and County Councils and by unofficial bodies was always a cause of jealousy and suspicion to the Empress, as indeed to the official machine in general, and some of her most insistent letters urge the Emperor to "shut up that rotten War Industries Committee," or complain of the doctors and nurses employed by the Union of Town and County Councils. In September she is conveying a message from Rasputin begging earnestly for the nomination to the Ministry of Home Affairs of one Protopopov, who was perhaps the worst selection made even in this period of infatuation. He had been a member of the Duma but had recently visited Stockholm where he met a German agent, and had returned to Russia under the suspicion of secret negotiation with the enemy. His health—even his sanity—was doubtful, so that we find the Empress explaining in a letter, in which she asks the Emperor to put the food supply into his hands, that her protégé is "not mad." Probably he was suffering from something like inchoate general paralysis of the insane. He was an accomplished necromancer, and was the person who subsequently gave himself the pains of raising Rasputin's ghost. He at once set to work to reorganise the Black Hundreds for an attack upon the Duma, and to plan with the Empress a method of circumventing the bodies which were co-operating with the Government over military supply, but his courage failed him when he was asked to take the food and fuel supply into his own hands.

By this time economic conditions were reaching a crisis. Germany was blockaded and, with her usual efficiency, planned and executed counter measures. Russia was blockaded in fact, and soon she had lost Poland, and with it a large part of such industry as she possessed.

Food was scarce and dear. Hitherto the peasants had cut down their consumption of food, partly in order to pay their dues to the State and their rents and interest to squires and moneylenders, partly to buy industrial goods, partly to indulge in vodka. By a self-denying ordinance at the declaration of war, the Government had prohibited, except for industrial purposes, the sale of spirit, of which the State had a monopoly. M. Paléologue makes the interesting suggestion that the deprivation of alcohol accounts for the depression which is so evident in Russia during the greater part of the war. However this may be, it went far to cut off exchange between town and village. This tendency was aggravated by the short supply and high price of industrial goods. The villages suffered from the lack of these, and the cities and industrial centres were, by consequence, short of fuel, flour, but-

ter, eggs, milk and vegetables. The holders of diminished stocks of
marketable foodstuffs effected a corner in them, and raised prices to
an unconscionable figure. Rationing began in 1916 and was steadily
extended till it covered all the more important articles of food. But
the maximum prices fixed for grain and fodder were made ineffective
by official and general corruption—the Government's own purchasing
agents often paid more than the prescribed maximum. The British
Ambassador told his Government in August 1916 that the civil population "had had enough of an administrative system which, in a country so rich as Russia . . . rendered it difficult for them to procure many
of the first necessaries of life even at famine prices."

✤   ✤   ✤

The flush of enthusiasm which greeted the declaration of war had
faded into depression and suspicion after the disasters in East Prussia.
There was a brief recovery during the Galician successes: to be succeeded in the summer of 1915 by a mood of tragic heroism, when
munitions failed, and the slowly retreating troops offered their bare
bodies to the cannonade of General Mackensen. But already the desertions, which afterwards assumed such catastrophic dimensions, had
begun, and confidence in the military administration could not
survive so severe a shock. The Government was now compelled to
abandon its policy of excluding the Rural Councils and other public
organisations from co-operation in the tasks of military supply, and a
magnificent effort to supply deficiencies was temporarily successful, so
far as the direct object of fitting out the armies was concerned. But in
this effort it seems that the need of husbanding resources in machinery, plant, and means of transport was overlooked.

In the meanwhile the working population of the towns was being
subjected to an extraordinary strain by overwork and underfeeding,
with severe penalties for every sign of resistance to the exaction of
heavy tasks. The Government had been forced to raise wages and in-
flate the currency and so to set in motion the vicious succession of
economic and financial evils which these measures entail. Trotsky
has given us a picture of the conditions in the factories in the latter
days which preceded the revolution: when nerves were in such a state
of tension that an unexpected whistle might at any moment start a
strike. The garrison of Petrograd, unduly large and demoralised by
inaction, became restive and undisciplined. At the end of October,
1916, there was a rising in the Viborg quarter of the city, where the
great iron and steel works were situated. Infantry of the line fired on
the police engaged in restoring order. Cossacks drove the infantry back

to barracks, and a hundred and fifty soldiers were shot by the authorities—all very like an anticipation of the events of March, 1917, except
in the fidelity of the Cossacks and the consequent success of the
repression.

A police officer in the capital about this time sent to the Minister
of the Interior a remarkable report on the conditions existing both in
the city and the country. He spoke of the disintegration of the rear as
threatening to throw the country into anarchy, of the uncontrolled
profiteering, of the unfair distribution of foodstuffs and articles of
prime necessity, of the rapid increase in the cost of living and of the
inadequacy of the sources of supply, of the extreme anxiety everywhere
prevalent, and of exceptionally strong feelings of opposition and hostility to the Government in every section of the capital. "These hostile feelings have attained a power among the masses which is without precedent even in 1905-6 . . . complaints of the dishonesty of
the administration, the unbearable burden of the war, the impossible
conditions of everyday life. The inflammable statements of the radicals, that one must first get rid of the Germans at home, and then
proceed against those abroad, are meeting with more and more approval. . . . Wholesale disturbances may arise anywhere . . . events
of primary importance are approaching. . . . The peasants lease no
more land because they feel sure that, after the war, land will be distributed to them free of charge. At the beginning of the war, the very
idea of revolution seemed preposterous, but now everyone is sure
that it is inevitable."

Such was the situation, with an angry Duma about to meet, when
Protopopov asked to be excused "for a fortnight" from undertaking
the task of victualling.

The Duma met in November, 1916, and Professor Paul Miliukov,
afterwards Minister of Foreign Affairs in the Provisional Government,
launched a tremendous attack upon Stürmer and Protopopov. He
charged Stürmer with treason, on account of the provocative action
of the police in the strikes in the munition factories, of his secret
correspondence with Germany, and of Protopopov's conversations
with a German agent at Stockholm.

The Censorship—without warrant of law—forbade the publication
of the whole text of this speech. But it is a testimonial to the effect
of representative institutions, even in conditions such as those of
Russia in November 1916, that the intriguers were thoroughly frightened by the publicity thus given to causes of public indignation. The
Empress wrote to her husband that "both Protopopov and Our

Friend" thought it would be wise for Stürmer to "go for a rest for three weeks." The Emperor removed Stürmer, but the Empress was able to save Protopopov from a similar fate. Her letters interceding for him, and begging that the Duma be not allowed to claim the success of expelling all the ministers, show morbid excitement. ". . . It's a hunt against wify. . . . I am fighting for your Reign and Baby's future." The same note reappears: "We must give a strong country to Baby . . . else he will have a yet harder reign, setting our faults to right." In the yearning for the preservation of the life of her son and of his full inheritance we have the key to her infatuations. And what a revelation it is of the intimacies of that tenderly affectionate, yet fate-stricken household, when she writes: "Be Peter the Great, Ivan the Terrible, Emperor Paul—crush them all under you—*now don't you laugh, naughty one!*"   •

Protopopov kept his post, had bogus telegrams despatched from the country daily to the Empress to confirm in her the illusion that she had the support of the Army and the peasantry, gave occasion to Buchanan (who never minced his words) to tell the Emperor, in January, 1917, that his Minister of the Interior was bringing Russia to ruin, arrested the Workmen's group in the War Industries Committee—probably as loyal a lot as he could have found in the whole working class—and fitted out the police of the capital with machine-guns, anticipating—some say, desiring to provoke and crush—a revolution from below.

The Duma had been summoned for the 27th of February, and on that day, though the only crowds on the Petrograd streets were the food queues, a proclamation threatening the use of force against demonstrators was issued by the Commandant of the garrison. Then came a sudden reduction in the supply of bread. The bakers were dissatisfied with the officially fixed price, and were selling rye flour for horses' food. Some shops were ransacked, and some were closed by the owners.

The Cossacks riding through the streets went through all the apparent motions of suppressing riot. But a junior French diplomat took note of a trifling incident. He saw a Cossack wink to the rioters.

Chapter X

THE PEASANT IN REVOLUTION

"To whom, dear Nicolas, should belong
The land, the fields, and the villages?"

"To you, my brothers and sons, to you alone."
BORISOV. The peasants' talk with St.
Nicolas the Miracle-worker.

When we consider the crucial year of 1917, with fourteen millions or more of Russians under arms, we become conscious that the soldier is only the peasant in uniform. It is he whose reactions to agrarian change put an end to the proceedings of the Stolypin settlement; he who, cantoned in restless idleness in the capital, makes the first abortive essay of revolution in October, 1916; who finally tilts the unstable balance of the State in March, 1917; who discusses thereafter in his committees the dangerous question whether it remains necessary —after three years of war—that he shall die; who figures in September in the mobs which seize land or prevent the removal of food, murder landlords and their agents, and destroy property and stock.

But it is with the peasant, the peasant without the uniform, that the stirring of the Titan began. The economic machinery for the satisfaction of the primal needs of man falls somehow out of gear. As it were, the driving-belt of the conveyor slips from its place, and the wheels which convey the grain to the hungry cease to function.

The process is so simple, and has become so familiar, that we have almost forgotten to ask ourselves what it is which keeps the towns alive, and what are the forces which cause the cultivator to produce more food than he and his family can eat. Partly, of course, it is the compulsion of tax and rent and mortgage payments. These items seem to have forced some 18% of the Russian peasants' gross production into the market. What was the peasant's motive for producing or for delivering more than the machinery of compulsion could extract from him? Normally it was his need of certain commodities and minor luxuries (including vodka). For the rest, the Government had fixed the price of grain—the peasant's real currency—but had left the price of manufactured articles—the subject-matter of the peasant's demand

—to the higgling of the market. The normal motive ceased to operate on the peasant because he was asked to accept less than the normal reward.

In other words, there was a virtual anticipation of what subsequently came to be called the "Scissors" crisis.

It was Trotsky who devised the name. Studying the graph of agricultural and industrial prices, his eye was caught by the uneven divergence of the two lines from the norm, and he saw that they resembled a steadily widening expansion of a pair of scissors. The "Scissors" was to play a great part in revolutionary history: and it was in active operation in 1917.

If it was the "Scissors" which kept back the grain in the surplus-producing south and south-east, it was something even more intimately disturbing which raised temperatures to fever point among the deficit producers whose holdings were of the non-economic type. The Food Committees, which had been established by the Government, sometimes tried to wring grain from sources which had no surplus: the threat of hunger was present for the small producer.

Let us turn back for a moment and see how the agrarian situation of 1917 differed from that of 1905, when for a time it had appeared almost equally threatening.

At the earlier date the old communal and egalitarian agriculture was already of the past. A reliable calculation of the year 1894 puts the numbers working as wage-paid cultivators at nearly 2½ millions, not including the women who went into the harvest-field. The Bolshevik historian, Pokrovsky, tells us that there were 5 millions of agricultural workers unemployed in 1905—perhaps he means rather underemployed. The peasants having non-economic holdings, who were calculated as being 30% of the whole on the morrow of emancipation, now formed a much larger proportion. The rise of agricultural prices after 1896 hit them hard, and partial dependence upon earnings for a livelihood was widespread, especially in the northern half of the Black-Earth belt and adjoining areas. Large-scale industry was developing: but its growth had not gone far enough, and the absence of an effective peasant consumer created a vicious circle. The two types of capitalist agriculture—the enterprising squire and the thriving peasant—had, indeed, come into existence: but the demand was for cereals for export, not for that variety of products which is stimulated by a well-distributed local industry. M. Pavlovsky, whose facts command confidence, has nothing but praise for the cultivating squire, but he emphasises the mischief, material and moral, done by the widely extended practice of leasing land for short periods to peasants who cultivated with their own stock and implements. It has been described as the key to the agrarian movement of 1905, because it exhibited the landlord as a mere burden upon the land.

It was against the landlords that these earlier disturbances were directed, and the aim was to drive them from their estates. Many squires' houses were ravaged and burned. We hear nothing at this time of any action against well-to-do peasants. Punitive expeditions visited the scenes of the disturbances, and "restored order." The restoration of discipline was partial and precarious: and some degree of disorder lingered obstinately on.

At the second of the two epochs, in 1917, the differentiation in the peasantry (and indeed in the squires too) had gone a good deal further. The economic contrast was now more distinctly between the enterprising landowner and the thriving peasant on the one hand, and the old-fashioned go-as-you-please squire and the non-economic holder and the feckless person on the other. Even at this stage Pavlovsky's observation, that the alienation of peasant land for poverty and similar causes had not gone far enough to be a serious danger, warns us against exaggeration. What had actually happened was stated by a writer in *Ruskaya Muisl:* "A powerful petty bourgeoisie is being created in the village." In the language which was current ten years later, the *kulak*—not as a mere money-lender or dealer, but as a holder of land—had come into existence, and a new agrarian problem with him.

The "separator" or "seceder," as his enemies called him, under the Stolypin settlement—the Otrubnik or Khutoryanin, to give him his official appellation, the individualised peasant, as we might say—was obviously the typical figure of this new portent. It is he who, along with the enterprising squire, makes a commercial business of agriculture, increases the swelling figure of cereal exports to a whole half of the product taken to market, helps the State to a "favourable" balance of foreign trade, accounts for the increased (but still not large) total of steel ploughs, drills, and harvesters, roof iron and other amenities. It is he who is "strong and sober," and wise and capable enough to benefit by the increased attention given by Government and District Councils to agricultural improvement; who causes the figures of horned cattle in European Russia to rise by 8% between 1904 and 1914 (and, on the other hand, the figures of sheep to fall by 20%, because of the extension of cultivation and reduction of pasture); who swells the record of what Pavlovsky calls the "product as well as the corollary of capitalism," rural co-operation. Who would not share the enthusiasm of those who see in the advance- ment of the "strong and sober" the best hope of the progress of all? certainly gave a most admirable jolt to production and conferred ......mense economic benefits—at a certain stage of growth and at a certain cost.

In the later of the two epochs of agrarian disturbance passions ran much higher than in 1905. The landlords endeavoured to dispose of their land by actual or fictitious sale, and there was an organised de- termination on the part of the peasants to prevent this. The move- ment was directed not only against landlords, as in 1905, but also against "separators," who were forced back into the communes and made again to pool their land. It was much more like the reassertion of the primitive authority of the Mir, against a State whose rights were denied, than an anarchical outbreak against all order. The people did not seize land which had not been cultivated by their communes or owned by squires whose serfs their forbears had been. As Lancelot Owen puts it: "The Mir was living and active though the State was in suspension." The observation is profoundly true, and the interpre- tation of it is significant for the comprehension of Russian history. It was the upper, the artificial, one might almost say the foreign, storeys of the building of State, which were shaken down. The lower, the native, parts of the structure stood firmer than ever. It was not only that the Mir reappeared in all its pristine vigour: other alternative authorities having an underground existence certainly from 1905, and probably even from earlier years (for the Soviet had its origin in un- recognised organisations set up in the factories), were the Soviets, which assumed overt activity everywhere as soon as the façade of State power had collapsed.

The incidents which together constituted the revolution of March, 1917, need only be briefly summarised here. The trouble began with a shortage of food in the capital—at that time named Petrograd—and a reduction of the bread ration: but behind these overt grievances was a long story of incompetence, suffering, and mistrust. The capital was crowded with troops, inactive and restless. The fourth Duma was sitting at the Tavrida Palace. Its President, Prince Lvov, warned the Tsar, then at General Headquarters of the field army, that the capital was in a state of anarchy, and asked him to appoint a minister "pos- sessing the confidence of the country," according to the approved formula of parliamentary government. In reply, he received an order dissolving the Duma. On the same night (March 11-12) a part of the Emperor's own Guard mutinied, and next morning mutinous troops fraternised with workers in attacking police and breaking into arsenals. The arrival of mutineers, accompanied by civilian crowds, at the Tavrida Palace caused the Duma—which had been technically dissolved—to decide to sit again in unofficial session and to appoint a Temporary Committee: which became virtually the revolutionary authority. The Ministers of the old régime were arrested or surrendered. Seventy-three policemen lost their lives in attacks by soldiers and workmen. The rest surrendered or disappeared, and no Police Force—under that hated name—has ever come into existence since. The Army everywhere fraternised with the Revolution.

It remained for events to show what—in positive terms—the Revolution meant. The negative intention, that neither Nicolas II nor Alexandra Feodorovna—the "German woman," as the people called her—should rule, was clear enough. For a generation to come, perhaps for longer, Russia was to search for her intention. For the moment, at least, the intention was definite enough: the land for the working commune, with an end alike of landlords and "separators", and—peace. But it was soon evident that these apparently simple demands involved the whole structure of the State, and constructive change extending to limits as yet unforeseen.

In explanation of what happened in rural Russia, let me again emphasise the virtual disappearance—outside of the Mir and the Canton Committee—of all authority. Tolstoi had counselled his countrymen that each should say: "For me there is no State." They had taken his advice, and the State had vanished into air. We learn from a pamphlet of 1920 that a few landlords survived even then, but these were local accidents of a country of huge distances.

A militia with heads chosen by popular election had replaced the police, and there is abundant evidence that this militia, hastily formed, ill-trained, and uncertain of its ground with the people, was not efficient. The lack of an adequate Police must be placed high among the causes of the overthrow of the Provisional Government, for rural disturbances involved virtual severence of the economic tie between town and village, and cut off supplies from the capital and from the army at the front.

After a short interval in which an attempt was made to make use of the Chairmen of Rural Councils as local governors, Provincial and District Commissars were appointed by the Provisional Government, and the demands of these functionaries for military help in the maintenance of order, and the exhortations of the central authorities to

them to put down anarchy, fill a large place in the official correspondence. It is evident that they lacked machinery for the work of administration, and that the locally elected bodies, the Soviets in the towns,
the Canton Committees in the rural areas, and the village Mirs
(which exhibited all the vitality of their indigenous origin) took their
own course, without much regard to orders from above.

Canton Committees, of the nature of Soviets, were formed with
the acquiescence of the Provisional Government, and played a prominent part in the agrarian movement, till the new bodies provided by
the legislation of May 1917 came into existence in September. We see
them, in the Tver province, collecting grain and money for war requirements, organising a Canton library, and ultimately arranging for
the elections to the new legally authorized body. But a good deal
of their activity was more strenuous and less innocent than this. Both
the Canton Committees and the village Mirs clashed, often violently,
with the Committees set up by the Central Government for dealing
with food-supply and with the land. The Food Committees were
organised in connection with the grain monopoly which the Provisional Government found it necessary to establish. The Bolsheviks
raised the slogan: Down with the Food Committees, and there were
cases of destruction of local food offices, due to dissatisfaction with
the fixed price or with the method of requisition. The Land Committees were established to settle disputes between peasant and landlord, or peasant and peasant, with respect to land, rent, and wages,
and to help to secure seed, implements, animal and machine power.
Where they took their colour from local influences, the Land Committees joined vigorously in the movement for the seizure of land.
Where they stood aloof, as representatives of the central authority,
they often found themselves virtually set aside by the purposeful determination of the locally elected bodies. The picture is, in general,
one of centrifugal tendencies too strong for the Central Government.

The opening of the sowing season of 1917 raised in an acute form
the questions of the land, and rumours of a "black redistribution,"
which had been of chronic recurrence since the Emancipation, with
its disappointing provision for the cultivator, were at their height. In
April the Provisional Government decided that the right of occupation should depend upon the cultivator's labour: but our old acquaintance, Doctor Shingarev, Kadet Minister for Agriculture, advised voluntary agreements between landlords and peasants, and contemplated
compensation for the former, and postponed legislation to the Constituent Assembly. Disorders had already begun, and the plan of

compensation was particularly obnoxious to the peasantry. In April trespass and unauthorized ploughing, illicit removal of timber, destruction of boundary marks and appropriation of cattle were becoming frequent; and cases of robbery, riot, and incendiarism were occurring. Trotsky cites a telegram received from Tambov province, which always took the lead in agrarian enterprise. The gist of it is a demand for the prohibition of the sale of land by landlords: "or we will shed blood." The peasants wished to stop sales because alienation was an obvious device to put the land beyond their reach. The Provisional Government boggled over prohibition; while the village Mirs were interfering with the cultivation, in the interests of peasant claims.

The Army had been embarrassed by the deficiency of fodder in March. It was now necessary to decree that all surplus grain should be sold to the State at fixed prices and, though there may have been a moment when the fixed prices were profitable to the owner of grain, they rapidly lost attraction as the products of industry became harder to obtain.

In May a fuel crisis was added to the existing crises of food and fodder. Cases of violence and destruction were nearly five times as numerous as in April. Attacks began to be made on spirit-depots, and 5,000 soldiers joined in a great raid on one of these in the town of Mtsensk: a fact which sheds light on the discipline at the rear.

Chamberlain has pointed out that more than half of the agrarian disturbances registered in 1917 happened in the Central-Agricultural and Middle-Volga regions, in the provinces of Tambov, Voronezh, Orel, Kursk, Tula, Ryazan, Penza, Saratov, Simbirsk, Nizhni Novgorod and Kazan, areas in which the leasing system was particularly prevalent and the squire was regarded as a parasite. In the west, and in Ukraine, where there were home farms, simple seizure predominated over violence and destruction.

In May Shingarev had been succeeded as Minister of Agriculture by Victor Chernov, a Social Revolutionary, the theorist of Populist Socialism. The Social Revolutionaries were the party most influential in rural Russia, and half of the members of the all-Russian Congress of peasant deputies which sat in May and June were of this party, only fourteen seats falling to the Bolsheviks. This congress approved a statement of agrarian principles which were virtually those of Chernov. His scheme was the socialisation, as opposed to the nationalisation, of the land: that is to say, its removal from the processes of private ownership and exchange, and its treatment as public property under the administration of the organs of self-government; the right of cultivation being earned by toil, and regulated by a calculation of the needs of a consuming family. The landlord was to receive no compensation. A rent was to be levied from the cultivator and devoted to social needs. The local Land Committees were to settle disputes, and the Central Land Committee was to act as final Court of Appeal, and to prepare for the agrarian legislation which was still postponed for the meeting of the Constituent Assembly. In order to facilitate the work of these bodies, private alienations—unless sanctioned by Provincial Land Committees—were prohibited. (July 25, 1917.) But nothing was done to expedite the meeting of the Constituent Assembly, or to reassure the peasantry by formally declaring the land to be public property and taking possession of it. Thus, while offence was given to the champions of private property, not enough was done to stop the progress of agrarian crime by tangible guarantees of the enforcement of legal expropriation.

The demands of the peasantry included safeguards for agricultural labour, the fixing of wages, in some cases also of hours, and cessation of the employment of prisoners of war, whose competition kept wages down. Those who had left the *Mir* under the operation of the earlier legislation for the creation of separate peasant property in land were, in the Central-Agricultural and Middle-Volga zones, which were strongholds of the *Mir*, as well as storm-centres of agrarian disturbances, often forced to return to it. In the earlier stages the Social Revolutionaries exercised a moderating influence in the villages; but, as the excitement grew, and violence was stimulated by the return of deserters from the armies, this influence was lost. Agrarian crime became immensely worse as soon as the harvest was in, and the Government deferred till too late the preparation of the decree for immediate expropriation. In the meanwhile, as we learn from Monkhouse, the position of employers in industry was increasingly difficult. The men made a practice of placing unpopular managers and foremen in wheel-barrows and wheeling them off the premises. There were more serious cases, of beating, even of murder: but savage violence was noticeably less than in the rural areas.

V. A. Rudnev, economist and philosopher, who worked later in the State Planning Commission, was publishing at the end of May a vigorous and instructed attack on war-profiteering, showing that capital was held back in the hope of still higher prices, that fixed prices were being evaded, that wild speculation by middlemen was going on in coal and metal, that useless factories were being erected at Government expense, and that industrialists were deliberately creating anarchy in production. W. G. Groman, a Menshevik statistician and economist, was pointing out that everywhere, except in Russia, the pressure of war-needs was bringing about the State organisation of economic life and labour. The Social Revolutionary and Menshevik organ was demanding the State monopoly of some, and the State control of other, industries, and the State control of credit institutions to prevent speculation, and was hinting at compulsory labour for all. The Executive Committee of the Petrograd Soviet was urging the acceptance of a scheme of State control of national economy. But the Government shrank from offending property interests. It appointed an Economic Council, but otherwise did nothing except raise wages: which led to a further rise of prices.

An abortive demonstration (July 16-19, 1917) in which the Bolsheviks took part, under the slogan "All Power to the Soviets," gave the Provisional Government one of several opportunities for getting rid of opponents whom we now know to have been dangerous to it. None of these was grasped. The explanation seems to be that only three or four months ago all the victims of the old régime had been released, and all, including Lenin, warmly welcomed back to their native land, in the glow of exaltation and unity of sentiment which the first days of the Revolution created. In the light of our later knowledge we know that Lenin was dangerous to the Liberal revolution. But we must not suppose that he then seemed very dangerous. The Peasant Congress laughed uproariously when he offered, on behalf of the Bolsheviks, to accept power. He commanded only a tiny minority among the peasants: Bolshevism was not a soldiers' movement, its strength lay in the factories; but the idea that the factories might lead the peasantry was still limited to a few. No doubt a ruthless Government, or even a Government of the old-fashioned police type, would have made sure of Lenin's good behaviour in the old-fashioned way. But any statesman or administrator might, at this stage, have underrated the Bolshevik leader's importance. And the men of the Provisional Government were legally minded, and Kerensky himself a lawyer, disposed to wait for a "case" before taking action, and to believe in the effectiveness of conciliation and oratory.

It is at a later stage, when Trotsky and other Bolshevist prisoners are released on small bail in September, and when the Military Revolutionary Committee disobeys with impunity a formal order of the Government, that we begin to ask whether the long-suffering patience of the Provisional Government does not amount to tempting providence. It may be that Kerensky regarded the Bolshevik leaders, according to the forms of Western Constitutionalism, as "the alternative Government": if so, he would seem to have been misled by a false analogy. There are peoples among whom public order is secured by, the acquiescence of the vast majority in certain fundamental principles of government, and in certain convictions which may be described as rules of the game. It is a rule in this game that a majority vote is accepted as the substitute for the ordeal by battle. Where the necessary conventions are faithfully observed, and the umpires are not too closely related to one of the teams, this mode of settlement is an economiser of time and strength. The preliminary process makes it possible to elicit and consider many opinions and interests, and the need for paying attention to the wishes of all classes prevents grosser types of oppression. But where the conventions are not accepted, or not observed, where the interested spectators are momentarily threatening to break into the ring, and determine the issue of the match by a justice of their own, in which force is the arbiter, government by discussion and majority vote, with the whole apparatus of parliamentarianism, becomes an unreality.

Prince Lvov, who had held the office of Prime Minister since the establishment of the Provisional Government, resigned on July 20, 1917. He was dissatisfied with the projects of agrarian legislation submitted by Chernov, which appeared to him to condone the seizures. It is evident also that he was unwilling to give his support to the measures of "strong" government, which were being forced on the ministry by the July disturbances and the collapse at the front. Kerensky became President of the Council of Ministers, retaining the portfolios of War and Navy. The death penalty, which had been abrogated in March, was restored "for major crimes committed by men on military duty." Military censorship of newspapers and letters was re-established, and power taken to suppress newspapers, prohibit meetings, and arrest by administrative order.

So far as legal authority was concerned, Alexander Kerensky was now at the summit of power, with a Cabinet consisting predominantly of moderate socialists, among whom Chernov was the most radical. If we count out the Socialism which has often been practised by absolute Governments, it was the first Socialist Government in the world: and it might well have seemed that Kerensky had the ball at his feet. But the great questions still remained to be answered. In July the renewed military offensive in Galicia had met with disaster. It was necessary to decide how to restore a routed army, and how to make war or peace; what to do with the insistent demand for land; how to build up the shattered economic life of the country. The setback which the Bolsheviks had received was not of long duration. Early in August the Petrograd workers were mingling with soldiers of the active army, and learning that conditions at the front were returning to those of the Tsarist régime. A week later the influence of the Bolsheviks in the Petrograd factories was already restored, the party had grown from 80,000 in April to 200,000; and the Social Revolutionaries of the Left were beginning to catch up Bolshevik slogans and ideas.

Kerensky's own words show how he proposed to utilise his virtual dictatorship. The Constituent Assembly set for October was postponed to December, and, having thus delayed the opportunity of definite settlement of outstanding questions, he felt the "need of making an inventory of the nation's political forces, and to give the parties, the Soviets and other organisations, an opportunity of appraising themselves." This was not action of the kind demanded by a pressing emergency. For action, Russia was to choose between a military saviour in whom courage and energy were not united with comprehension of the political situation, and the socialist leader at whom she had laughed a few weeks before.

The story of the successive expedients by which the "persuader-in-chief" attempted to establish a government of mutual goodwill and conciliation without grappling with the inescapable problems; of the ignominious collapse of the plan to restore discipline by a military dictatorship; of the suspicion of betrayal to the interests of the Right which the negotiations brought upon Kerensky; of Lenin's deadly sarcasm that Kerensky was "a Kornilovist who had accidently quarrelled with Kornilov"; of the revival of the Red Guard under the name of the Armed Workers' Militia, has already been told too often and too well to need recapitulation here. The Head of the Government, who now combined military with civil authority in his own person, could look for support neither on the Right nor on the Left, and was henceforth hurried, helpless on the stream, towards the approaching roar of the falls.

Meanwhile, the Social Revolutionary Minister of Agriculture, Chernov, had a long struggle over his bill to prohibit sale of land pending settlement of the land question. He succeeded in passing it when the Kadet Ministers resigned in July. Landlords were at this time destroying their own crops to keep them from the peasants, and the Provisional Government had still not put the law into force in September. Chernov then resigned from the Ministry. September showed a great increase in rural crimes of violence, but October beat all records. The disturbances were most intense in the regions of the minority nationalities, where, in some cases, the peasant movement began to merge with the strike movement of the urban workers. We now hear that Churches require special protection by the Mirs, that the lines of communication between the surplus-producing provinces and the towns are virtually cut, that stock is disappearing, and famine threatens the towns. Destruction was widespread. Libraries, works of art, bloodstock, conservatories, and experimental stations, were in many cases destroyed, animals ham-strung, houses burned, masters or agents sometimes murdered. It was now far more than a mere seizure of estates and property.

General Verkhovsky issued an order from the War Office on October 24th which declared that "ruin in the rear, destructive riots, burning of grain in transit, violence and atrocities, threaten the Front Line with hunger and cold, supplies of food and accoutrements being held up." The whole territory of the Republic was now divided into military areas, whose commanding officers were to co-operate with the civil Commissars. In his last days of power, Kerensky was ordering the suppression of disobedient Land Committees, exhorting Commissars to use military force, and, at last, preparing a decree for the legal expropriation of the landowners whom he could not protect.

The bread ration, which had been a pound a head per day in March, was reduced to three-quarters in October. The price of bread had been doubled in September, and the Minister of Supplies in the Coalition Government had resigned in consequence. Three-quarters of a pound is a starvation diet for men to whom bread is the staff of life, as it was, and still is, in Russia. It has been calculated by Chamberlain that real wages in the second half of 1917 were less than two-thirds of what they were in the first half of 1916. The cities were full of queues, shortages, and discontent. In a pamphlet in September Lenin was demanding effective measures to ascertain who was plundering the Public Treasury, a progressive tax properly enforced, and—significantly —the firing squad for profiteers. "It is doubtful whether any revolutionary government can get on without capital punishment applied to exploiters," he wrote.

It was being demonstrated, not for the first time and not for the last time, that, in Chernov's words, "the peasantry is the real autocrat of Russia." For it was the peasantry—working unconsciously through its control of the fuel and food supply, and confronting its rulers with an ill-fed and disordered army and with a hungry mob of city workers— which brought down the Provisional Government.

Certain constitutional changes, including the proclamation of a Republic (which had been delayed till September 16th) and the dissolution of the Fourth Imperial Duma (which had been sitting at the March Revolution and had served as the basis of the Provisional Government), ended with the appointment of a Council of the Republic or Pre-Parliament, and the formation of the last of the coalitions of the Provisional Government. Sir George Buchanan, the British Ambassador, told his Government that the Bolsheviks "alone have a definite political programme and are a compact minority. . . . If the Government are not strong enough to put down the Bolsheviks by force, at the risk of breaking altogether with the Soviet, the only alternative will be a Bolshevik Government." In a few weeks there was a demand for the dissolution of the pre-parliament and for the convening of a second all-Russian congress of Soviets, whose meeting was fixed for the day on which the Bolshevik revolution took place. The Pre-Parliament survived till its dispersal by soldiers on the fateful day of November 7th.

Early in October Kerensky made another attempt to secure the support of all the Socialist parties, including the Bolsheviks. He held a conference at which he said that he was willing to work for a transition to a new system of government, if they would take the responsibility of dissolving the coalition with the propertied classes, represented by the Kadet ministers, and point out a person willing to form a new Provisional Government, "as I personally could not carry out the task conscientiously." But these overtures were not successful.

In the meanwhile the Germans were making their naval advance towards the Gulf of Finland and had occupied the island of Oesel. Since September, the foreign Embassies had been informed of the Government's intention to move from Petrograd to Moscow, which caused rumours of an intended surrender of the capital. Disorders among the troops in Finland had caused the Finns to throw themselves into the arms of Germany. Insurrection had broken out in Turkestan. The Allied Conference on war-aims, for which the Provisional Government had hoped, had been abandoned. Kerensky's attempt to secure his position in the capital by moving troops from the disaffected garrison to the front was abortive. As soon as they had formed for the march, the soldiers dispersed, so thoroughly that some units on arrival at the railway had already lost three-quarters of their effectives. On October 9th, Buchanan, as dean of the diplomatic corps, read to Kerensky and the other ministers a note from the British, French, and Italian ambassadors, warning the Government of the need of measures to restore order both in front and rear. The Soldiers' Committee election in October showed a sharp swing towards the Bolsheviks. Even the Cossack rank and file were moving in that direction. The municipal elections showed similar results, partly because all the garrison, including soldiers merely passing through Petrograd, recorded their votes. Soldiers from the front were declaring that, if peace were not made by a stated date in November, they would leave the trenches and make peace themselves. Officers were being deprived by their men of horses and arms, displaced from their functions, and even murdered. On November 3rd guards were posted by the Government to protect the Embassies in Petrograd.

❋   ❋   ❋

The November Revolution, enormous in its ultimate significance, was, from the military standpoint, so easily achieved, and was so undramatic in itself, that it is natural to ask why insurrection was necessary. In October Bolshevik majorities were secured both in Moscow and Petrograd, and, on a superficial examination, it might seem that the cause was won, and that it was only necessary for the Soviets of the two capitals, now controlled by the party of Lenin, to carry out the peaceful assumption of power.

For the Western constitutionalist, accustomed to the constitutional game, and assuming that majorities will have their way, the answer may seem difficult. But Lenin was not a Western constitutionalist, and did not expect power to be automatically transferred by a change in the balance of votes in a popular assembly: though he might, and did, value such a change, as one of the indications that the balance of opinion—and therefore of opportunity for power—was changing. He had reasons now for believing that the transfer of power would be forestalled or resisted, unless it were clinched by accomplished facts: and that the moment was favourable for the accomplishing of those facts. But he was, in fact, always bent upon insurrection at the right moment, and the variation of tactics at different times merely meant that the right moment appeared to him nearer or more distant.

The reasons were first put before the Bolshevik Central Committee on September 28th, before majorities had been secured in the Soviets of Petrograd and Moscow. On this occasion, Kamenev moved the rejection of Lenin's proposal for the seizure of power, and succeeded in carrying the negative motion. In October, both the external and the internal situation had changed. The German naval advance had taken place: but mutinies had occurred in the German fleet nearer home, indicating to the sanguine temper of the revolutionaries the

early advent of world-revolution. At the same time there were rumours
of a peace between the Imperial Powers at the expense of Russia. The
Provisional Government's plan to withdraw part of the Petrograd
garrison, to make room for other troops less friendly to revolution, had
been thwarted by a counter- order of the Petrograd Soviet, which had
thus demonstrated the Government's weakness. Beside the electoral
successes in the two capitals, the intensification of disturbances in
the rural areas seemed to offer an opportunity. The Bolsheviks were
politically in a strong position, having a legally permitted organisation
and a score of newspapers, and the metropolitan Soviets and a majority
of the masses in the capital on their side. An odd jumble of reasons,
but the great strategist of revolution saw his chance, and backed it.

Lenin's resolution for armed insurrection within an early period
was carried. But some prominent party-men, including—the names are
interesting in view of later history—Rykov and Tomsky, were cool
towards it, and Zinoviev and Kamenev voted against. The two latter
prepared a written protest, arguing that there was no justification for
the Party to stake its existence on a rising. They would get one-third
or more of the seats in the Constituent Assembly, and the Constituent Assembly, when it met, would be obliged to seek support in the
Soviets. Neither the majority of the people of Russia, nor the majority
of the international proletariat, was with the Bolsheviks, and the forces
of the opposing parties were stronger than they appeared to be. The
immediate task, they urged, was to use the Congress of Soviets, summoned for an early date in November, to consolidate the proletarian
party and its organisation, and to establish close relations with the
railway, post-office, and telegraph workers and with bank employees.
In other words, they desired a peaceful and democratic development
of the Revolution, and took their stand upon the strictly Marxian
ground that insurrection, when the time is not ripe for it, is mere
adventurism. This protest of the two dissentients was communicated
to the non-party newspapers, which aroused great indignation as a
betrayal of plans. They also demanded the convocation of a plenum
of the Central Committee to review the decision. Lenin described
the action of the pair in publishing their protest as "strike-breaking"—
an evident appeal to the feeling of working-men against the blackleg
—and threatened to move their expulsion from the party. Evidently
the Government was now aware of the intention to make an early
insurrection, though the date for it was not yet fixed. It could no
longer be supposed that the preparations were being made against the
possibility of German attack.

It seems that the dissentient pair might have done as they pleased if they had not published their protest. The case is interesting as an illustration of the degree of liberty enjoyed by members of the party, within the party: a matter which subsequently played a part in the controversies between Stalin and Trotsky. Another illustration of this liberty was given by the division in the party over the question of boycotting the Pre-Parliament which was set up by the Democratic Conference of September to give a parliamentary basis of government, pending the convocation of the always deferred Constituent Assembly. Lenin, Trotsky, and Stalin stood for boycott, and the rank and file of the party appear to have been with them. But the advocates of co-operation, including Kamenev, carried their point in the Central Committee. (October 31, 1917.) The Bolshevik members appeared in the Pre-Parliament, but they withdrew on the fourth day of its sitting.

The Congress of Soviets had been summoned to meet on November 2nd, but it was postponed to November 7th. The plan of the leaders was to confront this assembly with the accomplished fact of the seizure of power.

Another meeting of the Central Committee of the Party appointed a military political center consisting of Sverdlov, Stalin, Bubnov, Uritsky and Dzerzhinsky. The Military Revolutionary Committee of the Petrograd Soviet, which had been created to co-operate in the protection of the capital against the German advance, already included Sverdlov, Uritsky and others of the most active Bolsheviks. It had appointed its own Commissars to each unit of the Petrograd garrison, and to each arsenal and magazine where arms were stored. By November 2nd these Commissars were in control of all arms and ammunition. On November 5th the garrison of the Peter and Paul Fortress undertook to accept orders only from the Military Revolutionary Committee: so the strategic position of that Committee, acting in complete accord with the Bolshevists, was similar to that in which the Bolshevik Party stood before its losses in July. The Peter and Paul Fortress, along with the Kronverksky Arsenal, which was also in Bolshevik hands, occupies a commanding position on the river above the point at which the Great Neva separates from the Lesser. The western end is opposite the Winter Palace, which was the headquarters of the Government and of Kerensky himself. A second Bolshevik stronghold was the workers' district known as Viborg, in the north-eastern part of the city, above the island on which the Fortress of Peter and Paul stands. The Military Revolutionary Committee had its headquarters further up the river, in Smolny, protected by machine-guns and artillery.

All the preparations were conducted in the full light of publicity. A sort of review was held on November 4th: shooting drill was going on. On November 5th the Viborg District Soviet requisitioned cars and first-aid supplies, and the working-women formed Red Cross divisions. It was not till the night of November 5th-6th that the Government decided to take legal proceedings against the Military Revolutionary Committee, to suppress Bolshevik newspapers, and to summon reliable troops: and the news of the decision was at once carried, through the sentries on duty at the official headquarters beside the Winter Palace, to the Bolshevik headquarters. The Government ordered the cruiser *Aurora* to leave the Neva: and the Military Revolutionary Committee countermanded the order; the Government broke up the Bolshevik printing plant and sealed the office: and the Bolsheviks sent troops and restarted the newspaper. The passing along of the news by the sentries on duty, the slipping away of comrades through the November darkness to carry it to Smolny, and the child-like outbursts of Lenin's laughter, when he heard of the restarting of the newspaper, stand out vividly to our imaginations.

On the early morning of November 7th, without resistance, railway stations, telephone exchanges, telegraph and post-offices, lighting-plant, water-works and other important buildings in Petrograd were seized. The reasons for the Government's long inactivity are made plain by a fact recorded by Buchanan. During the seizure of the buildings, the Cossacks received an order to come out, and disobeyed it. If other evidence of Kerensky's isolation were needed, it is furnished by the fact that his garrison for the Winter Palace, the seat of his government, consisted of military cadets and a shock-company of a Women's Battalion. There were guns but, when the attack came, the gunners could not or would not fire them. Provisions were forgotten. There were plenty of troops cantoned in and about Petrograd—if they had been willing to act: but those of them who were not sympathetic with the Bolsheviks were hostile or indifferent to the Government.

At 10 A.M. on November 7, 1917, the message was broadcast "The Provisional Government is overthrown. The State power has passed into the hands of the Military Revolutionary Committee." Nothing was said about the Soviets in this message: perhaps because the Congress did not meet till that evening. But the insurrection had been called in the name of the Soviets, and the Military Revolutionary Committee was itself a Committee of the Petrograd Soviet.

The members of the Congress of the Soviets were gathering throughout the day, but the session was not begun until nine in the evening, under the name of the Congress of the Soviet Dictatorship. Of the 615 delegates having votes who were present at the opening, 390 were Bolsheviks or Bolshevik sympathizers, presumably Social Revolutionaries of the Left. This Left wing of the Social Revolutionary Party formed a substantial minority of the whole, which had split off from the majority in August over the question of support to the Provisional Government. An eye-witness describes the Congress as consisting largely of young men from the Baltic Fleet and from the front. Most of the peasant delegates were soldiers. Conspicuous by their absence were the middle-aged intellectuals, the old type of peasant with the long beard, and the old Socialist Party leaders. Such was the assembly which assumed the power which the Tsar Of All The Russias had dropped in March 1917.

The Right wing of the Congress protested against the insurrection, and one speaker, Dan, prophesied its collapse and called for a coalition of Socialist parties. Seventy of its members then withdrew and, in conjunction with other moderate Socialists, formed a "Committee for the salvation of the country and the revolution," which became the main organised centre of opposition to the Bolsheviks, with affiliated Committees in the provinces.

Before the dawn of the 8th, news arrived of the capture of the Winter Palace and of the Ministers, except Kerensky, who had left the preceding day. The final capture was an entry, rather than a storm.

How unimpressively, and almost like the finish of a children's game, the great consummation arrived, appears from various anecdotes. The telephone girls, scampering out of the captured telephone exchange— not so much, it appears, from panic as from unwillingness to co-operate with the captors—recall the chorus of Opera Bouffe. On the later afternoon of the 7th, which has passed for ever into the world's calendars as the day of Revolution, the fashionable people were on the Nevsky Prospect as usual, laughing together, and saying that the Bolshevik power would not last more than three days. Rich people in their carriages were scolding the soldiers, and the soldiers "argued feebly, with embarrassed grins."

The news of the capture of the Winter Palace and the Ministers reached the Congress. Resolutions were passed "that the Provisional Government is deposed: that the Congress assumes power: that the Soviet Government proposes immediate peace. It will transfer land to the peasantry, establish control over production, promptly summon a Constituent Assembly; and it guarantees the rights of the nations of Russia to self-determination."

On the evening of the same day, November 8th, it met again; passed, with emotion, the resolution for peace; and then proceeded immediately to agrarian legislation. It voted down a proposal for a coalition, and nominated a purely Bolshevik Council of People's Commissars. The list included Lenin, without portfolio, Rykov for the Interior, Trotsky for foreign affairs, Stalin for nationalities, Lunacharsky for education. It did not include Kamenev or Zinoviev, the two Bolshevik dissentients on the issue of insurrection, nor any of the Social Revolutionaries who had formed part of the Presidium in the Congress of the Soviet Dictatorship: but we shall see that the latter continued for several months to support the Revolutionary Government, and virtually dictated the earliest legislation on agrarian reform.

The Cadets of the Military Schools occupied the Central Telephone Exchange of Petrograd on November 11th: but within a few hours the Bolsheviks were again in possession of the whole city. Kerensky brought a force under General Krasnov to attack the capital. The soldiers melted away, as those of General Ivanov and Krymov had in similar circumstances, and by November 14th, Kerensky was in flight, having narrowly escaped from being delivered up by his Cossacks. In the meanwhile, General Kornilov had escaped from the lenient custody in which he was held by the Provisional Government, and joined Kaledin in the south, where the two laid the foundation of the future civil war. In Moscow there was a fierce struggle for the possession of the Kremlin, ending in the establishment of Bolshevik military control. At General Headquarters at the front, the Commander-in-Chief, General Dukhonin, refused to open negotiations for an armistice, and was murdered by soldiers.

A Revolutionary Government had been established: but none knew better than Lenin that it was easier to establish than to maintain.

Chapter XI

HUNGER IN THE TOWNS (1917-1920)

> "Kalinin, with his dirty feet, has climbed upon the throne
> of the elect. The nobles will not pardon us for this. . . . Of
> course, we made many mistakes, because we did not learn to
> rule before."
>
> "Papa" Kalinin, in October 1919 when White armies
> were threatening Moscow and Petrograd.

If some new Bach, or Beethoven, or Wagner, should seek to convey in music a conception of the Russian Revolution, the leading motive should certainly be the hope inspired by the conviction that man is the maker of his own history. But among the many subordinate motives of that imagined sonata, hunger should be one, hunger passing through the whole gamut of human emotions: the struggle against plundering enemies, the agony of drought and dried-up field and emptied barn, the horror and despair of famine, the killing cold without food or fuel, the weakening and death of loved ones; and then the slow up-building of new strength and resources, under the gracious rustle of returning rain, the rattle of the machine in the harvest-field, the clang of the flail on the threshing-floor, and the anticipation of peace to enjoy the garnered store.

At this early stage there was some reduction of the resources of rural Russia in consequence of the diversion of labour to the purposes of war, but no serious hunger in the villages. But the increasing severance of the towns from their client agriculture, partly by civil war and foreign occupation, partly by the lack of industrial products at reasonable prices to remunerate the peasant, partly by the novelty of the socialist nexus, which had as yet found no substitute for the machinery of the private grain trade, made famine in the urban centres, and drove their population back into the country for the means of life. The way to bring more food to the towns was to coax it out of the barns by an adequate supply of commodities, and this was hindered by the low productivity of industrial labour, which, in turn, was aggravated by the short supply of food. This situation repeats itself, with variations of degree and detail, through a great part of the revolutionary period,

and it was intensified into rural famine in 1921-22. Behind it lie difficulties of agrarian and industrial organisation, only to be solved by
long and doubtful struggle. The collectivisation of the farms was itself
a phase of this struggle, directed towards the mechanisation of agriculture, the more effective application to it of scientific knowledge,
and the organisation of an effective substitute for the machinery of the
private grain trade, which socialism repudiated.

This chapter aims at conveying a picture of the hunger in the towns,
but I make no apology for including in it much that travels beyond
that limited aim. The primary need, the original postulate, without
which neither revolution nor life itself could exist, was food: and on
food were built all the heroisms of high politics and the terrors and
splendours of history. But there is no disentangling this theme from
the story which goes along with it.

Some of the economic conditions at the November Revolution
were these. The cultivated area had been reduced by the war by a
sixth, the number of horses available for agriculture by nearly a third,
the cereal harvest was down by 14%. A very imperfectly industrialised
country had been deprived of its access to foreign manufactures,
except through the north and the far east. The product of industry
was a little more than three-fourths of what it had been in 1913. The
railway system had suffered severely from the strain of war. Most
of it led towards the most highly industrialised regions, and these
had passed out of Russia's hands. Some of the surviving factories
catered for luxuries, for which the Revolution stopped the demand.
The money in circulation was twelve times as much as in July, 1914.
In the country, the paper rouble was worth from a tenth to an eighth
of the pre-war rouble, though the foreign exchange was rather better
than this, doubtless because a virtual blockade had for three years
stopped imports, except of war material, as well as exports.

It was not yet economic exhaustion. The country was to endure
another three years of war and blockade, with the temporary loss of
large portions of its territories, including those which provided its
surplus food, its cotton, and its principal fuels and metals, before that
stage was reached. We have, indeed, cause to feel surprise at its economic vitality. Probably the very incompleteness of the economic
co-ordination, and the inadequacy of the transport system, did something to save it. Duranty has pointed out the intensely local character
of production and trade in Tsarist Russia. There were uncounted
reserves, all small in amount, but important in the aggregate, which
prevented political from producing economic collapse, until the agony

had been prolonged for a longer period of waste and destruction, the marching and counter-marching of armies, and foreign boycott.

We get a glimpse from an informant (who shows some taste for the backstairs) of the men who had to deal with this situation, complicated as it was by a foreign war with a superior enemy, a disintegrated army, the accomplished facts of the seizure of most of the land by the peasants and some of the factories by the workers, by the non-co-operation of expert staffs, by an urgent shortage of food and fuel, and by inconvenient promises which presented themselves for fulfilment. In the early months, before the Revolutionary Government was transferred to Moscow, these men lived together with their families in cramped quarters in the Smolny building, once Peter the Great's tarring yard and thereafter a fashionable school for young ladies. They were all old acquaintances, if not actually friends, who had been in exile together and knew one another's weak points. If we mistrust our informant's statement that the renewal of the old squabbles sometimes led to hand-to-hand fights, there is something convincing (and very human) in the story that the ladies quarrelled over the removal of a saucepan of milk from the common kitchen. We must remember that these men were entirely lacking in experience of statecraft and administration. Will-power had to make up for all deficiencies. They suffered from all the difficulties of a permanent opposition which suddenly finds itself in power, having acquired the perfect technique and habit of rebellion, and none of arts of government: and they found themselves boycotted by the staffs of the administrative offices, including the hospitals and the telephone service. The very keys were in unfriendly hands, and the Banks withheld money from the new Government, while they supplied it to the striking staffs. Marx could not help them here. He had given them a method of historical induction, the clues of economic determinism, and of class-struggle, and the principles of successful revolution. But here were problems of every day, hand-to-mouth, humble and ordinary "carrying on": and his philosophy hardly touched them. Lenin said to Trotsky, "Es schwindelt," "My head swims," and no one who has any inkling, however tiny, of what the torrent of work is like, when political troubles are something more than mere parliamentary crises, will feel any surprise at this pregnant aside. But beside the force of will which the hardships of prison and exile had developed in the revolutionaries, there was intellectual ability of a high order.

Lenin is too great and complex a figure for any description that is not designed on the grand scale. Anything less would add nothing to common knowledge. But I shall sketch very briefly a few of the figures who stood round the leader. Lyov Davidovich Bronstein, known to the world as Trotsky, the name on one of his false passports with which he escaped from Siberia, was a Jew of versatile genius, equally at home in literary criticism, in philosophy, in political pamphleteering, and in administration. Compact of fire, conscious of superiority, free from all self-seeking, contemptuous of opposition, waiting confidently to receive his due, dangerously sharp of tongue and offensive to rivals, he yet showed a noble recognition of the greatness of Lenin, under whom his genius stood rebuked as it is said Mark Antony's was by Cæsar's. At the zenith of his energy, he was a sort of Judas Maccabæus. His creation of the Red Army, and his military administration, made him the idol of the working people. After Lenin's death, a kind of proud negligence made him the victim of a cooler and more calculating rival, and his name is remembered as that of an enemy of the State for which he did great things. Karl Radek called him the Reason of the Revolution, and Lenin its Will. Lenin left a political testament in which, after saying that Stalin and Trotsky were fundamental factors of stability, he proceeded to criticise both. He called Trotsky the most able man in the present Central Committee, and added that he was distinguished also by a too-far-reaching self-confidence, and a disposition to be too much attracted by the purely administrative side of affairs. His enemies have charged him with playing in exile the part of Coriolanus. The conviction which my own study of the man has impressed upon me is, that without a Lenin behind him he would not have made a good leader for a revolutionary Russia.

Joseph Dzhugashvili, the "legendary Georgian," whom Lenin christened Stalin, "the man of steel," is action and pugnacity incarnate. He seemed inept in matters of theory, and unskilful in the use of language, and has yet shown capacity for creative development of Marxian doctrine. His early days were spent in exploits of an extravagant daring. It seems that he has no cruelty or bloodthirstiness in him, but he kills without hesitation, "on necessity." Half Georgian, half Ossetian mountaineer by descent, he forgets neither friends nor enemies. He has much humour of a rough type, is entirely without fear, and quite at home with a city mob. Lenin had something to say about him in his testament. He expressed a doubt whether Stalin knew how to use his power as General Secretary of the party with sufficient caution: and added a postscript in which he said that Stalin was too rude, and "this fault, entirely supportable in relations among us Commu-

nists, becomes insupportable in the office of General Secretary. Therefore I propose . . . to remove Stalin from that position, and appoint to
it another man . . . more patient, more loyal, more polite, and more
attentive to comrades, less capricious, etc. . . . . From the point of
view of preventing a split and from the point of view of the relation
between Stalin and Trotsky. . . ." Trotsky's description of him in
the *Stalinite School of Falsification*, 1932, is interesting because it is
not wholly unfavourable. "Energy, will and decision, are combined
with empiricism and short-sightedness, an organic tendency to opportunist decisions on great questions, personal rudeness, disloyalty, and
readiness to abuse power in order to keep the party in subjection."

As the virtual ruler of Russia, Stalin had the supreme duty of maintaining external peace while the strength of his country was being
built up. He departed from the policy of peace to make a minor war,
which came near to becoming a major one. That his extension of the
frontiers of the U.S.S.R. to the west and north-west was politic, as a
means of postponing and holding off the full terrors of the German
pounce, was demonstrated in 1941. A major war was ultimately forced
on him, but when it came, his policies had secured to his country
both unity and strength. He has earned a place among history's great
rulers.

Grigory Evseyevich Apfelbaum, known as Zinoviev, seemed out of
place among the Bolshevik leaders because he lacked physical courage.
He was a great demagogue, and doubtless useful for his oratorical gifts,
and was a sort of political boss in the city of Petrograd. He worked with
Lenin in exile, helped organise the Third International, and became
its leader. Together with Stalin and Kamenev he controlled the policies of Russia in Lenin's last illness; he had his finger deep in British
politics in 1924, when he wrote, or did not write, the *Red Letter* which
assisted the Conservative Party into power. His divagations and
tergiversations and submissions in Russian revolutionary politics were
numerous. It is difficult to believe that he planned terroristic outrage.
But (if the sentence was actually carried out) in 1936 he suffered the
death penalty for doing so.

Lyov Borisovich Kamenev was, like Zinoviev, not so brave or determined as the typical revolutionary. He belonged to a well-to-do
bourgeois family of Tiflis, was closely associated with Lenin in Geneva,
married Trotsky's sister, and taught in Lenin's propaganda school near
Paris. He became president of the Moscow City Soviet. But he, along
with Zinoviev, had opposed Lenin's proposal of insurrection, and

incurred the reproach of sending his protest to the non-party news-papers and thus betraying the plan. He had a gift for negotiation and compromise, and had a pleasant way with him which earned him the reputation of being genial. It is doubtful whether either he or Zinoviev really warmed to the peasantry. Both were men of the cities. After the revolution he shared the political vacillation of Zinoviev, and finally his fate.

Nikolai Bukharin, a brilliant intellectual, attractive in personality and appearance, on the extreme left in 1918, when he took part in a plot for the kidnapping of Lenin, was afterwards the leading ideologist of Stalin's ruling group, and set on foot the attack against the Trotsky Opposition. On Stalin's turn to the left in 1928, he gravitated to the right, and was sentenced to death in March, 1938, along with the Trotskyist and Rightist conspirators. His last plea is an enlightening document, showing the springs of Party loyalty.

Felix Dzerzhinsky, member of a noble Polish-Lithuanian family, had in him something of the persecuting saint. He was head of the political police, where his work in the reclamation of waif children was particularly good: but his reputation was that of a man who needed a leader.

Georgy Vasilyevich Chicherin succeeded Trotsky in 1918 as People's Commissar of Foreign Affairs: he belonged in spirit to the "con-science-stricken gentlemen" characteristic of nineteenth-century Rus-sia. His great success was the agreement with Germany at Rapallo in 1922.

Michael Kalinin, known affectionately as "Papa," had the gift of talking to humble folk, and was one of the few who had steadily main-tained a leading position since the early days of the revolution. He succeeded Sverdlov in 1919 as President of the Central Executive Committee, and became the ceremonial head of the U.S.S.R. He began life as a metal-worker.

Madame Alexandra Kollontai was appointed People's Commissar of Public Welfare on November 13, 1917. A champion of sexual free-dom, and author of novels on social subjects, she was afterwards Soviet representative successively in Mexico, Norway, and Sweden.

Leonid Krassin had been director of the Russian branch-company of the electrical firm of Siemens, Schuckert, of Berlin, and was unique among the Bolsheviks in having a Big Business training. He was extensively employed after the revolution in economic work, notably as head of the Co-operative organisation and as People's Commissar of Foreign Trade, and was also Soviet ambassador in London.

Nadyezhda Krupskaya, wife and co-worker of Lenin, became, early in the revolutionary period, a member of the Central Executive Committee of the U.S.S.R., and devoted herself to education and the causes of Women and Youth. She always worked for moderation and sobriety in social reforms. On her death in February, 1939, her ashes were immured beside Lenin's tomb in the Red Square.

Vyacheslav Molotov was employed on journalistic work on *Pravda* from the establishment of that paper in 1912, and has always retained his hold upon the positions of importance, though widely different opinions of his capacity have been expressed. He replaced Litvinov as People's Commissar for Foreign Affairs in May, 1939.

M. P. Tomsky was for twelve years (1917-29) President of the All-Union Central Committee of Trade Unions, and a determined champion of Trade Union independence. He was charged along with the Trotskyite-Zinovievite centre, and committed suicide to avoid arrest in July, 1936.

I. M. Sverdlov was one of the five who organised the military *coup* of November, 1917, and was President of the Central Executive Committee when the Constituent Assembly was dissolved and when the Emperor and has family were shot. A leading figure in the most dramatic incidents of the early Revolution period and a capable administrator, he died of typhus in 1919.

A. I. Rykov opposed the November insurrection and resigned from the Revolutionary Government on the issue of the freedom of the Press. Always a man of the Right, he was sentenced to death in March, 1938, as one of the Trotskyist and Rightist bloc.

Such were a few of the men and women who shared the adventure of revolutionary government with Lenin. What they did was largely what they must. Self-preservation made the first claim, as it must upon every Government which will neither abdicate nor be swept away, and food and fuel came at the top of the list. The peasants must have their land, and as much of their demand for manufactured goods as the urban workers, those rival claimants, could be induced to concede. The soldiers, peasants in uniform for the most part, were already making peace in their own fashion by pouring homewards, so that Trotsky, when he travelled to the German headquarters at Brest-Litovsk, found the Russian trenches deserted. The official seal must be set upon that peace which the return of the troops had spontaneously decreed. Of these tasks, the hardest, perhaps, were the supply of food and of commodities: for these demanded positive action, indeed actual compulsion, and not a mere bowing to the multitudinous will.

For sheer anarchy, what the Russians call *Bunt*, was a large element in the November revolution, the merely negative outburst of elemental forces, exulting in the downfall of intolerable restraint, and expressing itself in the popular verses: "There is no God, and no need of the Tsar. We'll smash the Commissars and keep the grain for ourselves." I have already suggested that the Russian character suffered from a maladjustment of institutions to national habit. The nomad was tied down and made into a serf. The misfit was intolerable, and the revulsion expressed itself in a periodical breaking out.

But along with this exultant lawlessness, there was also a theorised anarchy, the anarchy of Kropotkin and Tolstoi, which regarded the State as an evil thing, and sought to make an end of the political bond. When Monkhouse was travelling across Siberia, he found one of the railway stations in the hands of professed anarchists. Makhno, the enemy of all governments in the Ukraine, seems to have been a theoretical anarchist. We shall see later what some of the theoretical anarchists thought of the violence of the revolution as it actually turned out.

Trotsky, from the thick of the struggle, has given us a glimpse of the tasks of the new Government in 1917. These were primarily to extend the revolution to the whole country, and fight the counter-revolution. In December a new political police (not under the name of police) was formed, and placed under the control of the Polish idealist Dzherzhinsky. Under different names this institution repeats itself in Russian history. The Third Section of Nicolas I gives place to the Tsarist Okrana. During the period of the Provisional Government there was a gap in continuity, but Kerensky was planning its restoration, and might have ruled longer if he had achieved it. Under the men of the November revolution it appears first as the Extraordinary Commission (Cheka, according to the initials of the Russian words), then as the Special State Political Institution (O.G.P.U., or Gay-pay-oo), and more recently as the People's Commissariat of Internal Affairs (Narkomvnudel). Under these different names it is, with modifications, always the same, and the Revolutionary Government had re-established it within six weeks of their seizure of power. With a very few exceptions, and those partial and doubtful, all States have it, and perhaps could not live without it. The reason is simple. All, except the most primitive political organisations, are hard upon somebody, and most are hard upon many. They have their enemies, whom they must watch and control, if they would not run the risk of sudden attack from within. The use made of the weapon varies with the

State's sense of its own security, and with the traditional temper and habits of its people. A Government newly established by revolution, and threatened by counter-attack, will strike hardest and most ruthlessly. If it was born in a storm of anarchy, as was the Government of November, 1917, it will not risk waiting till opposition has gathered force and courage. But in fact the new Cheka, under its Polish chief, was not, in the early months, active against political enemies. The killings of this period were outbursts of popular passion and mob law. The Terror, as the organised policy of the revolutionary State, came later, when dangers thickened and nerves were frayed.

When I say that the Revolutionary actors did what they must, I do not forget that they were filled with the expectation of an impending World-Revolution. The Paris Commune of 1871, with its supposedly fatal errors of neglecting to seize the Banks and to fall immediately upon its enemies gathering in Versailles, was both an example and a warning. Its history was a powerful influence, and they sought, in turn, to furnish examples to the world proletariat in the great adventure on which they believed it was about to enter. During the period up to August, 1918, says Trotsky, "our decrees were more propaganda than actual administrative measures." There is the unmistakable ring of propaganda about them: the rulers often prescribe what is ideally desirable rather than what is feasible in the circumstances, or what they themselves know is likely to be done. The decree of November 12th regarding workers' insurance gave the full wage to all wage-earners, at the cost of the employer, in every form of incapacitation and unemployment, without limit of time: but the means for its execution in full did not exist. A formal excuse for such legislation is that all laws at this time were theoretically provisional, pending the convocation of the Constituent Assembly. But the weakness is one which, for long, did not disappear from Communist legislation.

The same idea—that of providing models for a world on tiptoe for revolution—shows itself in the early foreign policy of the new State. The Rumanian gold reserve is held back till it can be handed over to a proletarian State, because the existing Rumanian régime is an oligarchy. It did not matter that a rupture with Rumania followed. Funds are provided by decree for the left internationalist wing of workers in all countries, whether at war with Russia, or at peace with her, or neutral: and a message of December 30th to the allied countries calls on the workers to rise, if the Governments do not take the opportunity of peace. All Muslims, including those of India, are invited to rise and free themselves, and are assured that Constantinople will be left in Muslim hands. The whole of the bad old world in *status quo ante* is challenged, with magnificent disregard of means.

It was in this spirit that the foreign debts of the Tsars were repudiated on February 10, 1918, and that Sverdlov answered a conciliatory letter from President Wilson with an appeal over his head to the people of the United States. The upstart and outlaw State was confident of the coming of something which would turn the forms and courtesies of diplomacy into a mockery. Anyhow it was out for a brave flourish, and rejoiced in the chance of snapping its fingers at the potent, grave and reverend signors of an outworn world. It might go down in blood and fire within a few weeks, but it would leave a challenging memory behind.

The leaders did not forget the possibility of early failure, and of a revolution like that of the Paris Commune, smothered in blood after a few weeks of survival and traduced to posterity by the victor for lack of memorials of its achievement. Lenin insisted, therefore, upon the publication of the classics of socialism and materialism in the Russian language. He would multiply copies of the Communist scriptures while he could. And he aimed at the creation of revolutionary monuments to impress popular memory and make revolutionary experience clear to all. On the same principle we should expect to find the wholesale destruction of the great cathedrals, the statues of the Tsars, and the monuments of the past. Much damage was done by mobs of peasants in the seizure of estates. Particular buildings, including sacred buildings, have been destroyed for practical objects. Many have been taken for secular purposes, but there has been no general or systematic destruction of monuments of any kind. If we were to say that the November revolution destroyed institutions, but not concrete memorials of the past, we should be near the truth. Past cultures are valued, partly no doubt as warnings, but generally as stepping-stones, necessary to the attainment of to-day's ideal.

❋   ❋   ❋

The decree abolishing the inheritance of property (excepting peasants' lands) did not issue till May 1, 1918. But large houses were at once transferred to the charge of town Soviets, to be administered by house-committees selected by the residents: and the housing shortage was relieved by the introduction of the poorer into the houses of the richer. A decree was passed for the recognition of none but civil marriages, for equal rights for all children within and without wedlock, and for freedom of divorce on the application of one party: and another separated Church from State, nationalised Church property,

prohibited all but secular instruction in schools, and gave equal freedom of practice and propaganda to all confessions. The Judges were
henceforth to be elected, and the validity of former laws was to be
determined by the help of the revolutionary conscience. (February,
1918.) Revolutionary tribunals were to deal with sabotage and counter-revolution. Lesser reforms which had been talked of for many
years were not forgotten. The Russian alphabet was deprived of its
superfluous letters, and the old Calendar, which kept the Russian
always well behind the Western date, by an interval increasing in
each successive century, was discarded. This last item was significant
of a change in popular temper. In the seventeenth century such, and
smaller, alterations split Russia into two camps. Now it passed un-
noticed, although the Feasts and Fasts of the Church were displaced
by it.

The Revolutionary Government was far from being a one-man dictatorship. There were important and quite open differences of opinion between the Commissars. On November 17, 1917, the Central
Executive Committee decided by thirty-four votes to twenty-four to
restrict the freedom of the Press. Zinoviev, Kamenev, Rykov and other
members, resigned from the Central Executive Committee, and eight
of the fourteen Commissars also resigned. It was a revolt of the Right,
demanding a general socialist coalition, and protesting against the
muzzling of the Press. At a somewhat later date we shall see the
Bolsheviks of the extreme Left insisting on a more rigorous expropriation of capitalists, and ultimately carrying their point against
Lenin in a nationalisation decree which may be regarded as inaugurating the epoch of so-called War, or Military, Communism. No one influence had the whole of its own way in this stage of the revolution
(if, indeed, it ever had) and the evident signs of wavering between
State-control and workers' control of industry, and a modified form of
both, are to be thus explained.

All this time the preparations for the meeting of the Constituent
Assembly, which had been so fatally delayed by the Provisional government, were proceeding. The Constituent had been the dream and
the hope of all the Liberal, and most of the Revolutionary, thinkers
and workers, from as far back as 1881. It was to be the means by
which the people of Russia were to declare how they desired to be
governed: and all democratic aspirations centred in it. The Bolsheviks and their supporters seemed little more than a stop-gap till the
great Assembly should formulate the people's will. There were warnings that the de facto government might not accept the democratic

decision. Lenin wrote in *Pravda* that the Constituent Assembly must recognise the Soviet régime and its policy for peace, land, and workers' control of industry. But the Central Committee of the Social Revolutionaries, dominated by influences of the Right, was confident that no attack would be made upon the Assembly, and ignored or rejected proposals for precautionary measures, while the Bolsheviks made careful preparations for action.

The first election results, which arrived in mid-December, showed an anti-Bolshevik majority. The Assembly was to determine the constitution, including the position of the non-Great-Russian nationalities, and all vital questions, including that of the land, were theoretically left to its decision. When it met, it claimed supreme authority in the State, and, seeing that it was elected on the basis of universal suffrage, all the constitutional proprieties were on its side when it made the claim. It might even favour continuance of the war, or demand such conditions of peace as would make the conclusion of an agreement unlikely. There was strong feeling in the majority against the adventurism of the Bolsheviks, who had installed themselves in power by insurrection.

A warning of what might be expected was given by the arrest of some of the Kadet members of the Assembly (one of them, Shingarev, first Minister of Agriculture in the Provisional Government) before the Assembly met, for their connection with the underground Provisional Government, which, in defiance of the Revolutionary Government, had arranged a meeting of its own for December 11th. When the Constituent met in the Tavrida Palace in Petrograd on January 18, 1918, it was mainly anti-Bolshevik in its composition. The figures are variously given, but the number of anti-Bolsheviks, and Mensheviks elected, not counting the Social Democrats and Social Revolutionaries from Ukraine, appears to have been nearly double the total of the Bolsheviks and Social Revolutionaries of the Left, who might at this time be expected to act together. On the opening day a demonstration in favour of the Assembly was dispersed by armed force, with nine deaths, and Shingarev was murdered in bed at the Marinsky Hospital by soldiers and sailors. It was thus that the author of *The Dying Village* expiated efforts of reform, which went either too far or not far enough.

When the session opened, armed soldiers and Red Guards were seated among the representatives, and the proceedings were much disturbed by the "invited" persons in the gallery. Sverdlov, President of the Central Executive Committee, read a declaration in favour of

vesting all power in the Soviets, of nationalisation of the land, a democratic peace, the repudiation of the debts of the Tsarist State, nationalisation of banks, and workers' control of industry. Victor Chernov, a Social Revolutionary, was elected President by a majority of
votes over Madame Spiridonova, a Left Social Revolutionary, who was
the Government's candidate. He spoke in favour of an immediate
peace, and of land for the peasants. According to Baron Meyendorff's account, a part of the Government's declaration regarding war
and land problems was supported by a majority, but the principle of
"all power to the Soviets" was rejected by 237 votes to 136, and the
Constituent Assembly expressed regret that negotiations with Germany had been initiated without the previous consent of the allied
democracies. Russia was declared to be a democratic federal Republic.
(January 19, 1918.) At 1 a.m. the Bolshevik representatives withdrew,
leaving only one of their party behind. At 5 a.m. the sailor in charge
of the guard advanced towards the President and, in the name of the
Government, called upon him to close the proceedings: for, he said,
the guard is tired. This was not forcible dispersal, for Chernov had
time to put a motion to nominate a peace delegation, to engage in
negotiations in agreement with the Allies, and to appoint a commission to prepare a land bill. The meeting was then adjourned to the
evening. On the same day the Central Executive Committee of the
Revolutionary Government decreed the dissolution of the Assembly,
and its members were not again allowed to meet.

Some attempt was made to show a technical irregularity in the
constitution of the Assembly. The nomination of the candidates took
place while the Social Revolutionary Party was one and united, and
the election when that party had been divided into "lefts" and
"rights." But it is evident that the double authority of the Constituent
Assembly and the Revolutionary Government based upon the Soviets would have repeated the evils of the dyarchy in the Provisional
Government, and that the dissolution was an act of self-preservation
on the part of Bolsheviks and Left Social Revolutionaries. The struggle over the Constituent Assembly was in effect the same as over
Kerensky's régime.

There was no molestation of the members, many of whom made
their way to the People's Army on the Volga, where the military opposition was gathering head. A statement made by the French ambassador, Noulens, that thousands were killed in the excitement following the dissolution of the Assembly is not supported from other
sources. The military cadets in Leningrad, who sympathised with the

majority in the Assembly, were disarmed and imprisoned, and army and workers alike accepted the accomplished fact with apparently general equanimity. The dissolution by the Revolutionary Government of the Constituent Assembly was remarkable as the definitive assertion of class-rule against the partially democratic and parliamentary institutions which had made their appearance in Russia in 1906. It marked the end of that domination of the Social Revolutionaries of the Right which had been characteristic of the Kerensky régime. For the first time the coalition of Bolsheviks and Social Revolutionaries of the Left, which made up the Revolutionary Government, felt itself firm in the saddle, having put an end to the menace of a democratic restoration. Incidentally we note a second demonstration of the political conditions illustrated in 1906 by the fiasco of the Viborg manifesto. The champions of responsible government had then made a solemn protest against the dissolution of the Duma, and called upon the country which had elected them to withhold taxes and recruits and disclaim responsibility for foreign loans. No one lifted a finger in response. Neither in 1906 nor in 1918 had the elective assembly any roots in the people, nor any organisation in the constituencies to support the elected representatives. Parliamentary institutions imitated in their external aspect the parliaments of the Western world, but missed the living sap. They were plants without a root, which look like living plants only till they begin to wither.

These grim days of mid-winter in the capital were full of hunger, cold, and fear. Ambassadors were mobbed in the streets, and the military guard broke into the cellars of the Winter Palace and plundered the liquors. Private cellars were similarly raided. Red Guards kept a wild kind of order, with rifles unslung, and shooting at sight. Amid the terror and confusion, there was the sense of something great in the doing. Such was the moment which inspired the poet Alexander Blok to his poem of *The Twelve*. Often quoted, it echoes the essential note of the Russian spirit, finding redemption in the very arms of sin.

✳   ✳   ✳

Within a few days of the Revolution, General Alexeiev, Chief of Staff to Kerensky, was on the Don, gathering the nucleus of a Volunteer or People's Army for resistance to the Revolutionary Government. On December 12th the Menshevik Workers' Council at Tiflis captured the local arsenal, and began to take arms and equipment from the soldiers withdrawing before the Turks. A south-eastern Union of Cossacks, Caucasians, and People of the Steppes was formed in preparation for secession or for civil war. Generals Kornilov and Denikin

joined Alexeiev. In the Ukraine a national Assembly (Rada) was
already in existence, and was disarming Red Guards. It refused the
Revolutionary Government's demand for co-operation against the
Don Cossacks, and the Ukrainian Bolsheviks, always a strong element,
though not at Kiev, fled to Kharkov, where they set up an Ukrainian
Soviet Government.

The rival Government at Kiev played an important part in the negotiations with the Germans which led to the treaty of Brest-Litovsk, and
the occupation by German and Austrian armies of the best and richest part of the old Russian empire. The three Social Revolutionary
Commissars who had been appointed in December resigned their
offices on the conclusion of this peace, bringing the Revolutionary
Government nearer to the One-Party system.

Two significant changes were made in the spring of 1918. One was
the moving of the capital: and the other was the changing of the
name of the dominant party. For the Old Believer, and again for the
Slavophil, Peter the Great, who moved his capital to St. Petersburg,
was like Jeroboam, "who made Israel to sin," because he set up a new
place of pilgrimage to divert the tribes from the Temple at Jerusalem.
A visible centre of unity and attractions, such as is Mecca for the
Muslim and Benares for the Hindu, was thereby slighted and robbed
of a part of its imperious claim. The importance of such symbols to
the history of peoples is incalculably great. They are essential to
the beginnings of patriotic sentiment. In Peter's case, the change was a
declaration of a new orientation in his people's life. The semi-Asiatic
Third Rome was abandoned—the Third Rome with its tradition of
succession from Byzantium—and a capital set up in a non-Russian land
with no history and no traditions, an uncertain future and no past.
The autocrat would fain drag old Russia, gasping and rubbing her
eyes, out of Asia into Europe. She obeyed in the body: but the soul
remained behind in the Red Square, beside the unique and impossible Cathedral of St. Basil. It was not only the Slavophils who were
unable to forgive the sacrilege. Moscow remained, for the masses of
the Great-Russian people, the centre of the traditional life and the
symbol of such unity as they possessed. If there was a patriotism among
them, it was a patriotism of Moscow. When the Revolutionary Government decided, in the very heyday of its hopes for a World-Revolution and the formation of an international brotherhood of peoples, to
return to Moscow, it was fulfilling a prophecy made by Herzen in
1853, when he wrote: "If Tsarism falls, the centre of liberty will be in
the heart of the nation, at Moscow." When the November Govern-

ment carried out the change, it gained an emotional foundation for its power, by placing its centre where the affections and imaginations of the people have theirs, and made a restoration of the Romanov tradition for ever impossible. At the same time, in March, 1918, the Seventh Congress of the Bolshevik Party changed the party's name to Communist, thus emphasising the completeness of the breach with the Social Democrats, whose name was associated with the aspiration to a parliamentary régime, and asserting the victory of the non-parliamentary Soviets, based upon a class. It appointed a Commission to frame a new constitution for the party, and pronounced for iron discipline and for universal military training.

There is a close relation between the problem of food supply and the protests of the peasants against exactions of food, on the one hand, and the agitation for the renewal of the war against the Germans, on the other. For the pressure upon resources was in great measure a consequence of the German occupation of the producing areas. The Social Revolutionaries—always the friends of the peasantry —figured, for this reason, prominently in the war-party. An anti-German demonstration in July, 1918, was followed by the murder of the German ambassador and by a Social Revolutionary rising. The suppression of the latter by the Revolutionary Government—which desired peace with Germany in pursuance of the policy of Brest-Litovsk—may be taken as the beginning of the Terror; for Terror was not, for eight months after the Revolution, characteristic of the régime.

In June, 1918, the breathing space from war, which Lenin had endeavoured to utilise to strengthen the administration, was rudely ended by the emergence of an unexpected enemy. A corps of Czecho-Slovaks, consisting at the outset of residents in Russia, and afterwards enlarged by the admission of Austro-Hungarian prisoners of war, seized Chelyabinsk and established themselves along the Trans-Siberian Railway. It was the beginning of the long struggle of anti-revolutionary intervention. It was at this moment that Social Revolutionaries of the Right murdered V. Volodarsky, the People's Commissar of the Press. The Social Revolutionaries of the Right and Centre and the Mensheviks now resigned from the Central Executive Committee of the Soviet Government. Henceforth we see the Social Revolutionaries, under one of those names compounded of initial letters which are so characteristic of Soviet Russia, as the "Eseri" (S.R's), playing a varying, perhaps a vacillating, part in the Civil War. These are elements which may be regarded as representative of the well-to-do peasantry, and their exclusion was a minor revolution, involving a change in the basis of the Government.

As an essential part of the change, Committees of the Poor (which were actually Committees of all except the prosperous) were set up to replace township and village Soviets of more general composition. Their business, in rural areas, was to take possession of machines, to organise common tillage and harvesting, to collect food (of which they themselves were entitled to a share) and to distribute food and implements. There was, in fact, a substantial urban element in them, and this may be the reason why no breach was really made in the village front, and why the Committees of the Poor were not for long in active operation. The struggle for food was waged fiercely on both sides.

The murder, in July, of the Tsar and the Imperial family was determined by the dangerous political and military situation, and the advance of a Czech force on Ekaterinburg (now renamed Sverdlovsk, after the President of the Central Executive Committee, who approved the deed), and the present writer feels no doubt that the Revolutionary Government authorised or endorsed it as a necessary act of state; but twenty-eight persons were arrested in September, 1919, for complicity in it, and five were sentenced to death.

Amid all the troubles of July time was found for the promulgation of a Soviet Constitution based upon the declaration of rights of November 7th. Russia was declared to be a Republic of Workers', Peasants', and Soldiers' Soviets (a strictly class constitution), and the aims laid down were the abolition of the exploitation of man by man, and of the division of society into classes, the suppression of the exploiter, and the establishment of a society organised on Socialist lines. Certain groups were excluded from citizenship. How real was the disability of the disfranchised we are able to judge from another decree of July, by which the *bourgeois* were mobilised for a year's rough manual labour. When the Moscow Soviet made out its scheme of rationing, it divided the available amount into four categories, of which those engaged in dangerous trades received four shares, and professional men and persons living on unearned income received one. The food-card was a weapon which the Government did not hesitate to use against its opponents.

The difference between the basis of representation of urban workers and of peasants is generally mis-stated. For the former the constitution provided for one representative for 25,000 voters, for the latter one for 125,000 of the *population*. This is not a difference of five to one, but possibly a difference of as much as three to one, if we may assume the number of persons under eighteen in the villages to be less than the number at that age and upwards. This electoral favouring of the urban population continued till the promulgation of the constitution of 1936, when both were placed on an equal footing.

In the meanwhile the Ukraine, in the hands of its German and German-protected exploiters, and nominally ruled by the Hetman Skoropadsky, was not less disturbed than the areas required to find food for the Revolutionary Government. In one respect, and that a deadly one for the counter-revolutionaries, it had a profounder cause of discontent. Of all the Governments which were set up in Russia to combat revolutionary rule, only one, that of the Social Revolutionaries at Samara, had the wisdom to assure the peasants that the counter-revolution did not mean the restoration of the land to the landlords. All the rest, in greater or less degree, made plain their policy of re-establishing or compensating them. It was this, and no transcendant virtue in the Bolsheviks, which decided the issue of the three years' struggle, in despite of British tanks and French munitions and Japanese rifles and bayonets. In the Ukraine, Hetman Skoropadsky so earned the hatred of the peasantry by a pro-landlord policy that when he fled, along with his German protectors, not one stone of his palatial mansion was left upon another. In the meanwhile a semi-political banditry prevailed, and German hopes of grain were defeated by drilling holes in the floors of the railway vans. Ludendorff has something in his war memoirs which pours a flood of light upon the character of the separatist movement in the Ukraine. The German Commander-in-Chief formed two divisions from Russian prisoners of Ukrainian origin, and set them to the Ukraine to support German policy. As soon as they arrived they "fell victims to radical influences and had to be disbanded." The events of 1941 confirm the inference. Whatever jealousies and causes of friction may exist between Great-Russia and Ukraine, there is not, in the present writer's judgment, any general desire for political separation.

If July marked a low point in the fortunes of the Revolutionary Government, the nadir was reached in August. Hunger in Petrograd became starvation, for the new grain was not yet in. Extreme penalties were prescribed for withholding grain, and for consuming it—a widespread practice—in illicit distillation of liquor. Death was threatened for armed resistance to collectors. The members of Workers' Food-Detachments numbered tens of thousands. Forty-seven peasant risings took place. On August 21st the Whites captured Kazan, a vital point both in the river and railway system. The territory of the Republic of Soviets was reduced, in the vivid language of Trotsky, to the size of the ancient Moscow Principality. A new counter-revolutionary Government, supported by a British occupation and financed by rouble notes printed in England, had come into existence at Archangel, so that all the seas were now closed to the revolution. At the end of the month the discontent of an important section showed itself in the murder of Uritsky, head of the Petrograd Cheka, by a Jewish student.

The Bolsheviks had their backs to the wall, and the Terror was loosed. During the first days of September more than five hundred *bourgeois* and officers were summarily shot. The British Embassy at Petrograd, empty save for Commander Cromie, who perished in an attempt to defend the records, was sacked, in order to find evidence of British complicity in the murder of Uritsky. Prominent Allied subjects were arrested. Former officers were seized and parked at Kronstadt. Hostages were taken for good behaviour *"Une période où la crainte paralysait tant de volontés,"* says Noulens, the French Ambassador.

Worse was to come: for on September 13th, Fanya Kaplan, a Right Social Revolutionary, who admitted that she was a supporter of the Constituent Assembly and an advocate of foreign aid against the Soviet régime, shot and wounded Lenin.

The fact that discontent at this time centred in the Social Revolutionaries of the Right will not escape the reader. It is not the champions of the Tsarist régime, but the well-to-do peasantry, the source of such strength as Kerensky commanded, the party which constituted the majority of the Constituent Assembly and desired renewal of the war with Germany, from which comes the 1918 opposition to the Revolutionary Government.

The fuel and food difficulties, as we see them in December 1918, were in essence similar to those of an earlier date: that is, they were due rather to maldistribution than to actual scarcity. Madame Britnieva tells us (writing of Lipetsk in the province of Tambov in the Black-Earth zone) that "the peasants brought quantities of food in exchange for salt, cloth, and manufactured goods"; that is, for barter with private persons. But Countess Alexandra Tolstoi, at that time employed in a Museum at Moscow, says that the building was unheated, there was no kerosene and fuel, the food consisted of bread, potatoes and carrots, and the "tea" was made of apples, carrots, and herbs. She adds that "bagmen" went out to the villages with various articles which they there exchanged for food. We are indebted to an agricultural expert compiling a village monograph for the knowledge that villages within a sixty-mile radius from Moscow were full of fine city furniture, bartered in exchange for food. How wretched was the state of the industrial workers, in the prevailing conditions of cold and hunger, we gather from the fall in the population of Petrograd, predominantly industrial in character, from 2,300,000 in 1917 to 700,000 in 1919: a reduction only in part accounted for by the removal of the capital to Moscow. With the single exception of Samara (the Kuibyshev which became the temporary capital in 1941), which may have been affected by being the headquarters of the Social Revolutionary Government in 1918, all the other considerable towns lost a substantial proportion of their population. It was a flight from the foodless and fuelless towns to the villages.

But if life was comfortless for the worker, in spite of a privileged status, it was barely sustained by the *bourgeois*, now the declared class enemy, subject to the performance of unsavoury tasks hitherto reserved for the poor, and with difficulty finding any share in the scanty supplies available. Konstantin Fedin, in *Cities and Years*, has given us a picture: the pencil-written placard announcing "French and German are taught here: stockings are darned: and rabbits also kept"; the anxious eye upon the cupboard lock when a guest arrives; the hammering at the door, at three in the morning, which calls the professor out for the job of digging or scavenging; the march through the cold, dark streets; the unaccustomed strain of the pick and shovel to sedentary muscles. Literary life and activity still survived, thanks in large measure to Maxim Gorky, whose reconciliation with the authorities placed him in a position to find the means of subsistence for many young writers. Paper is short, and of very bad quality, as the pamphlets of the day demonstrate, but authors somehow get hold of it and print their works. Even political journalism, not of purely Communist complexion, continues possible up to 1922, and there is a stir of literary talk in the Moscow cafés, where the poet Sergei Yesenin, ill-fated husband of Isadora Duncan, later to kill himself because, as he says, he is like a frisky colt overtaken by a railway train, lives a roistering life. Most writers find their way, for a short time at least, to prison. There is great activity in the theatres, now free from the thraldom of the box-office and crowded nightly, perhaps as much for warmth and light as for entertainment. It is the proletariat now, in half-sheepskin and home-spun and birch-bark, that fills boxes and stalls.

There will be, somewhat surprisingly, a move for reconcilation between Bolshevik and *bourgeois* later on, showing itself after the ruin of General Denikin and the execution of Admiral Kolchak, when, as Madame Rachmanova, one of our diarists, says, the Government seemed disposed to play the generous and forgiving enemy. The impulse is mirrored in Gladkov's novel *Cement*, where the workman, who has restored the destroyed cement-mills, forgives the engineer who was responsible, under White domination, for getting him a thrashing, and the victorious Communists at Novorossisk welcome back to port a ship laden with their fleeing enemies. It is a typically Russian, and a typically Christian, scene. We learn from Alexandra Tolstoi that there existed at this time a political Red Cross, for the relief of political prisoners, organised by the "intelligent" class under the auspices of the Government. It distributed butter, sugar, oil, and other food to these unfortunates. I do not think that anything similar would have been allowed to exist in 1938. It was a blessed moment: but the causes of struggle were too deep-seated for it to last.

The food decree of December 15, 1918, made no provision for the maintenance of any (outside of the Army and Navy) except State employees and workers in industries, in mines, and in transport. But the Labour Decree of 1919 required all to work, and provided a minimum subsistence allowance—when the food was forthcoming. There is a picture by Sergei Semyonov, who knew the life of the rank and file among the workers and Government servants in Petrograd, of the hunger in the city when General Yudenich was threatening it. The girl who tells the tale is in the post-office, drawing 400 depreciated roubles every month. Her father in a factory gets 800 roubles, and he also gets an iron ration of half a pound of bread daily—for long periods the bread-ration is not received, or not received in full. The shifts and pilferings of hunger bring moral deterioration: and the father's extra half-pound turns his children against him. Ultimately he dies from insufficient nourishment. We have glimpses of the agony of the suffering intellectuals and of the obvious willingness of many to let the Whites in, if they can only get food that way.

There was as much anger and disappointment on the Left as on the Right. Emma Goldman's *Disillusionment in Russia* tells what was felt by the ardent revolutionary deported from the capitalist United States, and arriving in the Promised Land of Socialism to find the body of liberty trodden underfoot in the desperate struggle. Unconsciously she herself pronounces the defence of the Revolutionary Government. All about her she sees unspeakable outrage. But "how could I speak out when the country was still besieged on several fronts? It would mean playing into the hands of Poland and Wrangel. For the first time in my life I refrained from opposing grave social evils." All that the Bolsheviks were doing, or allowing to be done, was done in the necessity of preserving their existence as a Government and of defeating their enemies: and she was forced, by the logic of the situation, into connivance. The ultimate question was "Which rule is to be preferred?" *Inter arma silent leges.* What no one can do with immunity, or without self-waste, is to fight on both sides. That is what war means: class-war no less than national war; and lies, and cruelty, are part of the armaments on both sides.

Meanwhile the Revolutionary Government, like Laocoon in the serpent's coils, was wrestling with half the world. In February, 1919, it attempted to secure an end by offering to pay debts due to Allied subjects and to renounce propaganda: but received no reply. It is probable that France was not alone in her ambitions of economic and political aggrandisement in Russia. But the agreement which her representatives made with Petliura, the President of the People's Republic of the Ukraine (and similar agreements were also made in respect to the Caucasus and with Wrangel), gave France the control of all railways for fifty years; and the control of policy, financial, commercial, industrial and military for five, as security for French debts.

The Bread War was raging more fiercely than ever, but the Government made attempts to restrict the arbitrary action of food-searching parties and to reassure middling peasants, who feared for their stocks.

In the third all-Russian Congress of Soviets a voice from the villages found significant expression: "The land belongs to us: the bread to you; the water to us: the fish to you; the forest to us: the timber to you." The peasants, more than willing to part with their surplus products if commodities were to be had in exchange, were only deterred by fear of the loss of their land in a counter-revolution from showing their resentment towards the Communist rulers. I again emphasise that the ultimate victory of the Communists was due to the fact that their cause represented the land for the peasant, while the Whites declared they would give it back to the landlord.

Meanwhile, in March, 1919, the foundation of the Third or Communist International had been announced. It was a symbol of that confidence in the imminence of World Revolution which explains the untroubled courage of the revolutionary leaders in facing the storms of the early years. The conviction that man had a share in the making of his own history came from the Russian interpretation of the teaching of Karl Marx. Together with the apocalyptic vision of a Messianic mission for the Russian people, it created that sustaining faith which filled the place of a religion. There were high hopes at this time, when Hungarian, Bavarian and Slovak Soviet-Republics, all short-lived, were proclaimed. The expected triumph caused more stringent measures to be adopted towards those Socialists who were not Bolsheviks. Up to now Social Revolutionary and Menshevik newspapers had been tolerated. They were now suppressed. At the Eighth Congress of the Communist Party Lenin announced that the first stage of the Revolution, which was the seizure of power, had passed: and that the second, which was about to begin, would be the separation of the proletarian and half-proletarian elements of the village (that is of the middling and poor peasants and the agricultural workers) from the more prosperous, and their union with the urban proletariat in a struggle against exploiters.

Chapter XII

THE ORGANISATION OF MAN-POWER

AND PRODUCTION

"Only listen and understand the talk of the machines,
You, the future Master, you, the Messiah!
With steam, steel and fire, you are allied!
You will capture the globe."
                                SADOVIEV, *At the Lathe.*

The preceding chapter had for its central subject the question how those who do not produce food are to be supplied, when the motives of exchange established by the compulsions of rent and tax and by the offer of an attractive return for additional labour have ceased to operate.

The early Revolutionary Government approached the problem by awkward substitutes for abandoned machinery. People from the towns, supported by have-nots in the rural areas, were sent out to fetch the grain, as and how they could. The crudity of the method is obvious. While devising more effective substitutes for abandoned methods, it was necessary to revert temporarily to the old: and this is what was done in March, 1921, when the peasants were permitted to trade in their surplus.

But, behind this question of distributing the product, lay the more radical difficulty of stimulating production. The present chapter deals with this more fundamental problem of increasing the productivity of labour, and with the attempts of the revolutionaries to find and to obtain acceptance of that principle of organisation which should best favour the aim. Temporarily, the answer was found in that same policy of March, 1921, which sufficed for the question of distribution: but it involved the abandonment of the socialist ideal, and was evidently not final.

What was to be the driving force which should compel or coax the surplus product into existence? And in the first place, who was to own, or control, the instruments of production? Sometimes they are owned or partly owned by a landlord or entrepreneur, and then we call the system capitalistic. They may be owned or controlled by workers, and then we speak of workers' control of industry and of peasant proprietors in agriculture, or of self-employing co-operative association. They may be controlled, or partly controlled, by a public authority, though owned by an entrepreneur, which is a modified form of capitalism. And they may be owned and controlled by a public authority under a socialist system. And there may be variations and combinations of any of these systems, such as we shall ultimately see in the collective farms.

War on the large scale, such as Russia suffered from 1914 to 1921, compels recourse to public control even in states which have no inclination to socialism in times of peace. It did for Russia very much what it did for the Western countries. Not only did it shake the economic machine out of gear, by the diversion of man-power and the diversion of demand, but it showed up fundamental weaknesses which escaped attention during peace. In the normal course there is much economic waste; producers curtail production, to make sure of profit, workers reduce effort to forestall unemployment; labour and materials are consumed on the less necessary articles for a few, while many go short of the more necessary; speculators corner goods and levy tribute; transport is employed in the long-haul carriage of goods that are available close at hand; ships and vans travel three-quarters empty. There is a chaos of production and distribution and transport. But only the economists and statisticians see it and shake their heads. The principal sufferers may be conscious of a void, but they do not know why, and they cannot mend it. These are the conditions of peace. A serious war puts nations into the position of beleaguered cities, where every scrap of waste must be eliminated. Not only must soldiers and munition-workers be fed and equipped, but the mass of the people must be kept in good heart. Food, fuel, everything, must be rationed, and all used in the most effective way for the achievement of victory. For the moment, the full-fed man sees that the ill-fed man is a danger to himself. Hence the public control of economic operations which characterised in a greater or less degree all the nations in the First World War.

Tsarist Russia was kind to its capitalists—or afraid of them—and did not carry the process of control very far. Nationalisation naturally started with trade, for the first step, when the difficulties of a state of siege arise, is to find a way to distribute existing stocks. The Tsarist Government started and stopped with trade. It fixed a price for grain. The Provisional Government went a little farther, established the grain sales monopoly, but shrank from controlling private industry: thus giving the peasants the grievance that their sales were controlled, while their purchases were to be made in a free market. The November Government maintained the grain monopoly, for the system of requisitioning the surplus at a fixed price is the same thing in different language. But it was, for a long time, in two minds over the form which the control of production ought to take.

The northern half of the agricultural zone of Russia was not self-supporting. The food surplus was in the south, and the north depended upon supplies from it, and upon the communications which brought them. Nearly nine-tenths of the coal, and all the oil, were located in the south. Severance of the south meant a famine of food and fuel. Short of severance by war, such as threatened to repeat itself in the closing months of 1941, the weakness of communications produced, with a difference of degree, similar results. *Deficit* Russia, by which I mean the north and centre, which could not supply itself with food, and with fuel on the commercial scale, was, when at war with its Western neighbours, in the position of a sea-girt country blockaded by a superior enemy, and threatened with starvation in consequence.

Before the fall of the Tsarist Government, some of these adverse factors were already in operation, but the surplus-producing south was in Russian hands, and the sea was open to the north and to the far east. These conditions continued under the Provisional Government, aggravated by the loss of the most highly industrialised portions of the Empire: Poland, the Baltic provinces and autonomous Finland, and in an ever-increasing degree by rural anarchy. It was the lack of food due to this rural anarchy, and not due literally to famine in the country as a whole, which brought the Provisional Government to ruin. There was food in the barns and there was money—depreciated "Kerensky" money, it is true—in the banks. But the economic circulation, necessary to the life of the body politic, was desperately congested.

Kerensky's successors—we must not yet speak of them as constituting a purely Bolshevik Government, for something resembling a coalition with the Social Revolutionaries continued till July, 1918—borne to power by elemental forces over which they had incomplete control, inherited the anarchy and the economic congestion. Their first decree, significantly, was the abandonment of a cherished Bolshevik plan. This was the Land Decree of November 8, 1917, which gave up the general nationalisation of the land, and accepted in lieu of it management by local peasant bodies, who should freely decide the local forms of tenure. It was the Social Revolutionary plan, which had been endorsed by the numerous peasant assemblages of recent months: and it sacrificed, except in a very limited degree, the prospect of cultivation on the large scale to the demands of the people for an addition to their holdings on the old terms.

The peasants had long been demanding fixed prices for manufactured commodities, to balance those already enforced for agricultural products. General State-control of the factories would have been the means of meeting this demand. But here the claims of the workers ran counter to those of the peasants, and the early industrial policy was determined by more influences than one. A vigorous attempt, made in the first days of the Revolution, to get a supply of wares to the peasants was frustrated by the prevailing anarchy. Part of the objects collected were withheld by factory committees, part appropriated *en route* by railway Committees, and part fell into the hands of speculators. Only a fraction reached those whom it had been intended to supply. The Revolutionary Government desired, at the outset, to co-operate with those who owned and managed the factories, and to utilise their services. The owners withdrew funds, the managers and technicians held aloof, and the Bolshevik encouragement of workers' control during the period of preparation for revolution confronted the new Government with a record of promises to be fulfilled. A decree for Workers' Control was therefore passed on November 27, 1917, but it was not everywhere enforced, and a little later we see Lenin examining workers' deputations as to their knowledge of the commercial side of industrial operations, and advising them to be cautious about embarking on the management of their own factories. His wish at this time was for State-control over privately owned capital— that is to say, neither nationalisation nor workers' control, but rather something resembling war-time regulation in western Europe.

About 20 per cent of the factories, more particularly those concerned with war industries, continued in the early months to work as before under their old ownership and management. The remainder were divided about evenly between the centralised system of nationalisation, and workers' control operated by local factory committees: two systems, theoretically separated by wide distinctions, but, in the absence of trained managers and a business staff, less different in practice than in theory.

In one form or another, low productivity both in agriculture and in industry was the root of the troubles of the Revolutionary Government: and in both it was vital to find forms of organisation which should replace those set aside. The leaders never concealed from themselves that in the long run the new order must be judged, without possibility of appeal, by its power of meeting man's material needs: and that if capitalism could successfully undersell it, it would fail. The incentive to effective labour must be found without the landlord and the entrepreneur, or, in one form or another, they would find their ways back.

In so far as Workers' Control held its own against the contrary principle of centralisation, it was inimical to the establishment of a satisfactory work discipline. Or we may put it another way, and say that the State, as the employer of labour, was too dependent politically upon its own labourers to be able to control them. The revolutionary leaders had taught the workers to rebel against both State and employers, and their pupils proved apt to better the instruction. The creation of a new work-discipline was, in fact, one of the greatest, perhaps the greatest, of the tasks of the new régime: because the motive force had to be found within the worker himself, and for a long time that needed to be supplemented by an external stimulus drawn from the old armoury.

A nucleus of trouble lay in the decree of November 12, 1917, for workers' insurance. The provision covered, in theory, all wage-earners and poor persons, and every form of incapacitation and unemployment. The full wage was to be paid, the full cost to be met by the employer, and the fund was to be managed by the workers. As interpreted in practice, this meant full maintenance for all workers without reference to the wages earned by them, and without reference to the social value of their work. The pay was the same whether the work was or was not done. It was a low wage but a sure wage, and attracted the easy-going: but the more energetic returned to the land, where there was at this time much profit to be made. At the same time the Revolutionary Government found it necessary for political reasons to employ as many workers as possible. It is significant that the Railways, which employed just over 900,000 men in 1915, employed over 1,200,-000 in 1921, though no additional construction had taken place, and hundreds of miles of track had passed out of the territory controlled by Russia.

If the industrial leaders and managers of the old régime had been enlisted for co-operation in production on the scale on which Trotsky brought ex-Tsarist officers into the Red Army, some of the faults of labour might have been balanced by skilful direction. But this help, or enough of this help, was not obtained, because of the quarrel with the technical intelligentsia, of which something has been said earlier.

There were other causes also for the low productivity. Capitalist business is provided—in private profit—with a self-registering index for the regulation of supply. With a money economy and normal book-keeping, figures show at regular intervals whether incomings yield a favourable balance over outgoings, and cry a halt, or a change of direction, to the unsuccessful business. The Revolutionary Government had not at this stage learned by a painful experience that it is possible, and indeed necessary, to retain the capitalist system of cost accounting, after abandonment of the capitalist device of private profit: and that figures must be used as pointers to the success or failure of communist undertakings just as meticulously as in private business. In a later chapter I have spoken of the awakening to the need of adapting capitalist devices to socialist economy. It was not, indeed, necessary that each particular industry taken by itself should pay its own way, any more than it is necessary for Army, Navy, or Air Force, to do so: but it was necessary that the degree of the commercial success or failure of each should be registered by figures, so that the controlling authority might know when, and to what extent, it was paying a subsidy: and it was necessary that success or failure over the whole field of industry should be similarly ascertainable, lest a general excess of outgoings over incomings should involve indebtedness or collapse. For all these purposes a stable currency, as well as a system of commercial accounts, was essential. In the period of War-Communism the Revolutionary Government had neither.

A similar inexperience in industrial management led to confusion in administration. When the Supreme Economic Council undertook the nationalisation of a number of manufactures in November, 1918, it set up forty departments to deal with them, without any attempt to co-ordinate their work with that of the local Economic Councils: friction was the natural result. In short, Socialism had not yet discovered its own appropriate technique, much of which must necessarily be adapted from the experience of Capitalism.

In those days there was no regular budget of State receipts and expenditure: but States have lived without budgets for much longer than they have lived with them. It has been alleged that there were no taxes: but the practice of requisitioning the surplus of agricultural production approximated to a tax in kind. No charge was made for the services, such as railways, post, telegraphs, schools, theatres, worked by the State and local bodies. But some of such services, and notably theatres, schools and parks, have been and are, in whole or in part, gratuitous, in States which are not open to the charge of practising War-Communism. The stocks of raw material and the fixed capital inherited from the pre-revolutionary epoch were drawn upon. But this improvidence could easily be justified in a country suffering from civil war within, and foreign blockade without. The State paid wages or workers' insurance largely in kind, a practice common in States having a primitive organisation, and, at least so far as agricultural labour is concerned, widely followed to-day. The theory of State finance, if this expression can be employed, was that provision for the service of the great family of the State could be made, so long as both outgoings and incomings were within that family. The only index to the process was the ever-mounting total of paper money, and the still more rapid rise of the prices of all things that were for sale. But, here again, the western countries furnished an example in their own economy, and the evil was rather of degree than of kind. The most orthodox have since discovered that a gold standard or a gold backing is not essential to economic life.

The radical defect of War-Communism lay, not in its incidental and removable faults, or in an unorthodoxy which may be merely freedom from unnecessary obsessions, but in the low productivity which ultimately ruined it. Because industrial productivity was catastrophically low, at a time when war-needs absorbed a large part of the product, there was little or nothing except depreciating paper to give to the peasants, and therefore no incentive to surplus production. Because grain deliveries were short, a fierce campaign was necessary to make up the deficiency, workers were allowed to go out and obtain food for themselves, and time was lost from the factories. But, worse than this, real wages were inevitably low, because the total divisible product was small, and because grain was withheld by its producers. The lowness of real wages, in spite of the recklessness of a system which paid a nominal full wage for a slack day's work or for none, is illustrated by Farbman's calculation that the worker's food gave him only two-thirds of his normal average calories. Being underfed, his natural tendency to slackness was increased, and another spin was given to the vicious round of low productivity and hunger.

Some theorists justified inflation as a means of destroying the value of savings and of ruining the class-enemy. But this was a clever afterthought. In its essence, inflation, in the sense of an increase of currency out of proportion to the growth in the volume of real transactions, is an attempt to arrive at a goal that perpetually recedes, to catch up with the uncatchable. By progressively diminishing the value of money, the process necessitates its own progressive acceleration. The Revolutionary Government was aware that it expended more than it received, and it made attempts to remove the necessity of printing notes to pay the balance. The capital levy of 1919, if it had been a success, should have checked inflation: but it brought only 10% of the estimated proceeds. The next expedient was to put a high price on manufactured commodities: which still more tightly closed the grain-store of the peasant, and raised wages and the prices of everything that was for sale. The use of money as between the different departments of government was eradicated: but the item was not large enough to be effective. Nothing less than increased productivity could, by giving a function to money other than the raising of prices, have checked the vicious progress. In the autumn of 1919, we are told, 18,000 workers were busy, night and day, printing money. The note-issue, which in January, 1918, was twelve times that of 1914, had reached astronomical figures in 1921.

Civil War and Allied Intervention form the background to the scene—a background which advances, at moments of intense crisis, till it all but crowds the actors from the stage. Germany and Austria, which once loomed so large, are out of the picture from November, 1918: but Britain, France, the United States and Japan, are gathered about what seems to be the perishing body of the Russian State, and the Czecho-Slovaks, though no longer actively campaigning, are still echeloned across Siberia, and playing a part in the confusion of its politics. Skoropadsky has fled from the Ukraine, amid the tempest of popular anger produced by his support of the landlords, but Petliura is in Kiev in his place, and has proclaimed an Ukrainian People's Republic, based upon the peasantry. General Krasnov, the Ataman of the Don Cossacks, has lost the flank support of the Germans, and has ceased to be threatening. But General Denikin, with the Volunteer Army, is on the point of destroying the Revolutionary armies in the country between the Black Sea and the Caspian, and of beginning the great advance which will threaten Moscow in the following autumn. Anarchy, championed by the redoubtable Makhno, enemy of all governments alike, will range over the Ukraine in the rear of both armies, recruiting its green armies from deserters of both sides. Voroshilov and his partisans still hold Tsaritsyn, "the red Verdun," for the Soviets, and the Volga and Kama valleys are in the hands of the Red Army. But the line of the Ural mountains, Orenburg, Ufa, Ekaterinburg, and the railways running eastwards, with the whole trans-Siberian line as far as Vladivostok, are occupied by Whites, with their allies, Czechs, British, French and Japanese, while guerrilla forces range the country behind. Some of the enemies of the Soviets, and particularly the French, in their later operations in southern Russia, will have grounds for doubting the loyalty of their soldiers in the face of Revolutionary Russia. On November 18, 1918, Admiral Kolchak had just been proclaimed dictator at Omsk, overthrowing a government which stood farther to the left, and nearly captured Trotsky himself. In the north British and French are occupying Archangel. The Allied blockade of Russia has begun. In the first half of 1920, after Denikin and Kolchak have had their day, a new centre of danger will develop in the Crimea, while the Poles, in alliance with Petliura, will establish themselves far within the racial frontier of Russia, and demand the boundary line of 1772. Only after the Revolutionaries have first driven the Poles in rout, and then been driven by them in rout in their turn, will there be an end of war for revolutionary Russia: and the end of war will mean the raising of fundamental questions of policy, and a long retreat over the whole economic front.

The fluctuation of the policies of the Revolutionary Government in the organisation of industry shows itself in the long dispute over the functions of the Trade Unions. The second All-Russian Trade Union Congress, in January, 1919, was the theatre of a lively argument against the merging of the Trade Unions in the machinery of the State. Lenin pointed out that industry would break down if each Trade Union and Factory Committee concentrated upon itself, and that the way to give to Trade Unions wider functions in the building of large-scale industry was to assimilate them to the organs of State power. This seemed conclusive so long as the war lasted. But the controversy was only sleeping. Released from the preoccupations of war, Trotsky turned to the organisation of transport and the increasing of the productivity of labour. But the end of war renewed the opposition to centralised control and the militarisation of labour, and raised the demand for proletarian democracy in industry. The Party Conference of 1920 and the Trade Union Congress of that year were the centres of a controversy which agitated both Press and platform. It is interesting to notice that the discussion was to all appearance a completely free one. This phase of freedom did not last.

In October, 1920, orders were issued for a mobilisation of labour on military lines, with instructions that it should be effected "with revolutionary animation." At the opposite extreme, Shlyapnikov, of the Labour Opposition, demanded self-government in the factories and control of the economy of the State by a congress of producers representing the Trade Unions: a logically complete extension of Workers' Control into something closely resembling the Syndicalist organisation of public affairs. Another group complained of the excessive concentration of power in the inner circle of the Communist Party, and demanded greater influence for the rank-and-file members of the Party, and for the constituent organs of the State—claims which anticipated those to be put forward by Trotsky on a more famous occasion of later date.

The Communist Party pronounced for a compromise solution. Each Union must contain a Communist element, and the Unions must accept a position subordinate to Party control, and be converted by degrees into auxiliary organs of the proletarian State. They were to have representation in the economic organs of the State, and to have a voice in the appointment of managers. But managers were to be selected, not elected, on the basis of competence, and one-man management was to be the rule for all factories. These decisions made an end of proposals for a Syndicalist State, and for workers' control of industry, but the relations of the Trade Unions to the State continued to be a subject of controversy.

THE RED ARMY

The organisation of the Army is not the organisation of production: but it has a very close connection with the management of labour, and I make no apology for saying something about it here.

After a short-lived attempt at a voluntary army, which was little different from a body of those armed workers to whom Lenin had often spoken of committing the business of the community, the Revolutionary Government, under the inspiration of its newly appointed Commissar of War, Leon Trotsky, established the principle of conscription for all male citizens between eighteen and forty, with the exception of the disfranchised classes. Training was optional for women. Provision was made later for work at the rear by the disfranchised.

This was the origin of the Workman-Peasant Red Army, for which drafts were gradually called up. On August 1, 1918, it numbered 331,-000, and on October 1, 1920, 5½ millions. Despite grave defects, it bore testimony to the organising gifts of the Commissar. Show me another man, said Lenin, who will create an army in six months and win the respect of foreign experts! The result was achieved, in the first place, by a complete negation of all the principles of army organisation for which the Bolsheviks had stood in the period of their agitation against the Tsarist and Provisional Governments: in particular, by a severer, but more impartial, discipline than that to which the Tsarist armies had ever been subjected. No more was heard of the election of officers. An end was made of the Army Committees. But Trotsky was well aware that to abolish an Army Committee may merely mean to drive it underground, and conceal the initial causes of discontent. The Red Army was, and is, permeated by Communists—that is to say, members of the organised and disciplined party who know what the men are doing and thinking, handle complaints while they are still in the germ, and help to canalise feeling.

Another of the institutions of 1917 was the Political Commissar with the troops. In the Red Army this institution was maintained and extended, forming a complete political department. General Knox has shown that in the Russian army between 1914 and 1917 the men often had no idea why the war was being fought. Whatever the value of blind discipline may be—and in modern armies it does not seem to be worth much—instructed and intelligent discipline is better. The Commissar had a staff of selected soldiers to serve as political guides. He had other functions also and, on a famous occasion, when a unit failed, we find Trotsky uttering a threat to shoot, first the Commissar, and then the Commander. There is evidence that these summary methods have not ceased to operate. When there was suspicion of the loyalty of an officer to the Soviet Government, it was the Commissar's duty to watch him and report upon him. Under the conditions of revolution and civil war such things are obviously inevitable.

Trotsky's greatest contributions to the Red Army were his insistence upon regular organisation and regular tactics, against attempts to put the army upon the footing of partisan detachments using only guerrilla tactics, and his use of military experts, including old Tsarist officers and old N.C.O.'s promoted to officer rank. Over these questions he came into collision with Klim Voroshilov, afterwards the People's Commissar of Defence, and with Stalin, at that time a prominent member of the Revolutionary Council of War, who supported Voroshilov; and the military quarrel was, together with some jealousy due to Trotsky's late entrance to the Party, the origin of the breach between him and Stalin.

In two years 48,000 ex-Tsarist officers were taken into the Red Army, often by methods of compulsion, including the use of the families as hostages for good behaviour and of the State's monopoly of food. Among the earliest of this class who accepted service with the Bolsheviks were Tukhachevsky, Putna, Kork, Uborevitch, and Pimakov: all of whom were executed in June, 1938. Opportunities, withheld under the Tsarist régime, of rising by skill and merit were freely offered. Trotsky said that a revolution "not only permits but creates discipline in an army: but not under the class which the Revolution has overthrown." But he chose and promoted officers without regard to their origin, and was successful in arousing their professional enthusiasm. There were some cases of treachery among ex-Tsarist officers, but most of them served with credit, and some, particularly Tukhachevsky, who became the Commander of the first Red Army in June, 1918, with very great distinction. As to the general superiority of the Revolutionary discipline—in spite of certain outbreaks—there is a good deal of evidence. "The orders of the Bolsheviks go right down to the bottom," said an ex-Tsarist General to Roden Buxton. A lady diarist, who is no admirer of the revolutionaries, is obliged to pay tribute to this quality, by contrast with the observed habits of the opposite side in the Civil War. She finds that "the Whites, too, commit atrocities," and that the Reds maintain discipline but the Whites do not.

Though the Red Army in the Civil War ultimately totalled over five million men, it never had more than half a million rifles, and the maximum number of combatants in it never exceeded 600,000, with 700 guns and 2,800 machine-guns. There was no effective central military administration: most of the recruitment was done at the fronts: and the forces lived almost entirely upon the country. It was a great achievement, after the collapse of the Tsarist armies. But we must not fall into the error of over-estimating Trotsky's success. In the first place, the fighting in the Civil War was not, generally speaking, in any way comparable with the fighting against German armies. The actual fighting was done by armies of 100,000 to 150,000 men on both sides. Occasionally White troops achieved marvels, as in those regiments of the Volunteer army which were composed entirely of ex-officers, who made it a point of honour to advance till they dropped. But most of the operations were in the nature of raiding and counter-raiding, and the enemy was not of the highest military order. The Red Army won, because the country was with them, or rather because the country was against its opponents, and because it held interior lines, and was inspired by a single determined will. In the second place, the number of desertions from the Red Army was so high—and highest when the cause of the Revolution appeared to be losing—that praise of its military virtues must be qualified. The same defect which had shown itself in the Tsarist armies was manifest here also. The men were not prepared for a long struggle and for permanent privations.

In this respect the Civil War presents a marked contrast to the campaign of 1941 against the invading Germans. It is a necessary inference that the Bolsheviks had now won that general confidence and attachment which they lacked in 1918-1920.

In the early period of the Revolution, before, and even for a year or two after, the death of Lenin, there was social equality between officers and men. The officers had no separate mess of their own, and Erich Wollenberg, who served in the Red Army from 1921 to 1936, tells us that in 1925 an officer had to justify himself to the Party for allowing a private to black his boots. The pay of a Corps Commander was only 150 roubles per mensem.

As soon as victory was within sight, it was decided to use a part of the Red Army as an Army of Labour, and from February, 1921, four Labour Armies began operations. In the Donets basin, normally the centre of the supply of the minerals and ferrous metals, a whole third of the enterprises were idle. The Ukrainian army was used: not to work the mines or the foundries, but to make it possible for others to work them. In four months it had repaired 120 major bridges. The Petrograd Army so improved the food and fuel supply that the Putilov metal works in Petrograd substantially increased its output.

The principal changes made at later dates in the organisation of the Red Army have been in the direction of regularisation. Territorials have been replaced by regulars, and military titles have been restored to the officers. There has been some vacillation over the characteristic institutions of Political Commissars and subordinate Political Instructors, but at the time of the German invasion this branch of the Army had been completely restored. It was their business to make sure that the rank and file know what they were fighting for, and to maintain the soldiers' morale. It was widely believed that the tremendous purges of 1936-38 had seriously weakened the Army, but its achievements show that its quality was well-maintained. The youthfulness of the Generals, and the facilities for rapid promotion, have been noticed by many observers.

ORGANISATION OF AGRICULTURE

The reader will have a clue to what, at many points, looks like a puzzling contradiction between intention and performance, if he realises from the outset the existence of a dualism in agrarian policy. The Communist leaders were not masters of the situation. Their ultimate aim was one thing, their policy of the moment was another: generally a compromise between the will of the peasantry and their own convictions. There is always a danger of undue simplification in a summary statement. But if I limit my sentence to the personal convictions of Lenin himself, it is safe to say that, throughout the greater part of his career, his aim was something very closely resembling that which ultimately issued in the collectivisation of the peasants' holdings, together with the institution of State farms by paid labour: but that from a very early stage he intended to secure the alliance of the peasantry, and recognised the necessity of conceding their demands.

The idea of collectivisation—that is to say, of joint cultivation—as distinct from joint ownership or joint management, on a very large scale, first emerges in Friedrich Engel's *Peasant Problems in France and Germany*. He there says that there is no idea of forcibly expropriating the small peasant, as the Social Democrats would be compelled to do in the case of the large landowner, and that the task will first of all consist in transforming individual production and individual ownership into co-operative production and co-operative ownership: not forcibly, but by example and by social aid. Co-operation is not the precise term which I should apply to collectivisation, because the latter involves the acceptance of associates whom one has not chosen for oneself: but that is a distinction which developed later.

We see the notion of State farms, along with the notions of the economic failure of small farming and the need of employing machinery in agriculture, emerging in Lenin's mind in his writings between 1901 and 1906. All these ideas co-exist with the purely Marxian conception of letting capitalism take its course in the villages, with the result of accumulating land in the hands of a few, in the same way that it was to take its course in industry, with the result of accumulating capital also in the hands of a few. Capitalism was to take its course, because it was (from the Marxian standpoint) an essential preliminary to the creation of proletarian conditions and the rise of social democracy. The peasants, as we have no difficulty in imagining, were not troubled by the agrarian theories of Marx and Engels: equally they had no desire for State farms or for collective farms, neither of which came on any considerable scale within the range of their experience. Some wanted the perpetuation of a redistributing *Mir*, some (these were the "strong and sober," together with others who wished to dispose of their land to the best advantage) wanted the consolidation of separate properties in the land. For the time being the new Revolutionary Government "gave the peasant nag its head," leaving all details to be determined by the local will.

The local seizures of 1917 and 1918 gave to the peasant an average addition of 20% to his holding. But the variations from one part of the country to another were enormous. In the Ukraine holdings were almost, but not quite, doubled, and the ultimate attachment of the peasant to the Soviet Government, however great the grumbling by a section, was thereby guaranteed. Comrade Yakovlev, afterwards Commissar of Agriculture, visited in 1923 a village of the Kursk province, and found that it had, between 1917 and 1922, increased its holdings of land by 65%, but was only gradually bringing the new land under cultivation. Roden Buxton has left us an admirable picture of a village east of the Volga, in the province of Samara, where each "soul" got an additional area of thirteen and a half acres, and his host, having a family of seven sons, got ninety-four and a half acres. This was wealth to the peasant, if adequate means of cultivating it existed. On the other hand, one of our village monographists shows us a tract in the Moscow province adjoining Smolensk, where there was no landlord's land to divide and the people had no particular interest in the survival of the Soviet Government.

Each village took, or tried to take, the land which had been cultivated by the predecessors of its present members in the days of serfdom: so that there was no sort of equality between village and village in the seizures. There were "no good landlords," said the people of one village, so all the land was seized: but their particular landlord had been a friend to the peasants, so they gave him his share along with the rest, and left him in undisturbed possession of his house. "You cannot eat land," and many of those who extended their holdings could not cultivate the additional area, because they had not the stock, either live or dead, for the purpose. This, and the loss of the landlord's agricultural example, often not without value, minimised the advantage which the peasants obtained from the seizures. They were also insecure in their new estate. Some of them were desperately afraid of the return of the old landlords, either in the flesh or in the spirit. A certain Count Stroganov had had a terrible reputation in his lifetime for his treatment of offenders against his rights. The local peasants left all the land on one side of the river untouched, lest the Count should return from the grave and flay the trespassers. At last some returned Red Army men mustered up courage, crossed the stream and ploughed up the deserted lands. In the Valdai hills we hear of peasants who were afraid to build on the home-estate round the old landlord's mansion, because that involved a documentary transaction which would stand as evidence against them. They preferred to trespass quietly on the area and plant potatoes there. *No one was certain of the permanence of the Soviet power.*

The seizures which had taken place during the eight months of the Provisional Government included 108 million acres taken from 110,-000 large owners, and 140 millions taken from 2 million individual peasants: mainly, no doubt, those who had secured separate proprietary holdings under the Land Settlement of Peter Stolypin. Some of the landlords were still holding their lands in 1920, as we learn from a pamphlet of that year, and village records furnish us numerous instances of peasants of the more prosperous type who continued to occupy separate farms and to claim independence of the *Mir*. There was a widespread desire for the official confirmation of rights acquired by seizure, along with a demand for measures of equalisation from those sections of the peasantry which found themselves in possession of the smaller holdings: all the makings, in fact, of a bitter class-struggle within the village.

To the general claim for the confirmation of the seizures there was no saying nay. "Let them do it," said Lenin: "if the lands are seized the banks will be ruined (by the loss of the mortgage money). If stock is taken over, the power of capital will be broken. With the control of the proletariat at the centre, the rest will follow of itself. The point is the transfer of the political power to the proletariat." And he went on to that famous disclaimer of knowledge of the turns in the road to Socialism, which I have set at the head of the first chapter of this book as the true motto of the Communist Government, most accomplished of experimentalists and opportunists.

✻　　✻　　✻

The first Land Law of the Revolutionary Government made a provisional settlement. It did lip service to the principle of nationalisation, and declared that the land and its appurtenances belonged to the entire people and that damage to them was a grave crime. Minerals and forests and waters having a national importance were to be in the hands of the State. Orchards, plantations, nurseries, seed-plots and hot-houses were to be preserved as model farms. Cattle-breeding studs and poultry farms were to be the property of the entire people. Dwelling-houses and the gardens belonging to them were to be left to the owners, a notable concession rarely observed by the people. The rest of the land was to be distributed by Canton Land Committees and District Peasant Soviets. Each village was to decide the mode of land-tenure, whether by households, by individuals, by village communes, or by co-operative organisations. The right of user was declared to belong to all who wished to work the land by their own or by family labour, or on co-operative principles, but the use of hired labour was prohibited. The distribution was to be made, on principles of equality, on the basis of the norms of need advocated by Victor Chernov and the Social Revolutionaries. There was to be periodical redistribution in accordance with changes of population and growth of productivity, and the right of heredity was recognised, subject to this.

So far as the great bulk of the land was concerned, this was, in effect, a law of local option: for the application of the principle of equality, and the reservation to the State, were in practice dependent upon a system of survey and settlement not yet provided for.

Up to February, 1919, only thirty-five State-farms had been created, and those of small dimensions. There was evidently no popular desire to make use of local option for the formation of large government estates.

The second Land Law, passed after the dissolution of the Constituent Assembly, might naturally have been expected to mark the triumph of the poorer over the more prosperous peasants, and it did, in fact, declare that the individualistic use of land must be regarded as transitory. It emphasised the aim of increased production and gave preference, in the allocation, to agricultural co-operatives (which would later be named agricultural collectives) over individual applicants, with a view to a transition to socialist agriculture. The dividing of holdings into numerous separate strips was discouraged. Surplus revenue, resulting from superior quality or situation, was to be paid to the Soviets for public needs (a very obvious recognition of the principles of rent and of public ownership); the trades in grain and agricultural machinery were declared to be State monopolies; and paper provision, afterwards to be to some extent realised in fact, was made for State Insurance for sickness, old age, accident, and the various contingencies of agriculture.

We must not fall into the error of assuming that anything like full effect was given to the principles embodied in the decrees at this time. The actual agrarian policy presents a conflict of aims: on the one hand the equalisation of holdings, which means the perpetuation of *petite culture* of the peasant type, and the diminution of the surplus by a backward agriculture; on the other hand, the stimulation of production by the encouragement of *grande culture*, with improved agricultural machinery and the application of agricultural science. The second of these two aims is capable of being realised in different ways: either by Peter Stolypin's plan of encouraging the "strong and sober," of helping the prosperous to grow more prosperous, even though it be at the expense of the poorer; or by building the individual farms into collective entities, and creating State-farms worked by paid labour alongside of them. In pursuance of the last-mentioned plan there were at the end of 1920, about 4,400 State-farms with an average area of 1,150 acres, and 3% of the peasants' land was being jointly cultivated by collective labour. There is yet another and an intermediate method of attaining the second aim, and that is the encouragement of voluntary producers' co-operation, which was carried so far and so successfully before the November Revolution. A trial was given to this method, but it was not swift enough, and not sufficiently all-embracing, to commend itself to rulers in quest of early and large results, and fearful of foreign attack.

The desire to increase production is emphasised during the autumn of 1918 by propaganda against "such a waste of human labour as is involved in small peasant economy", and in favour of "collective tillage." A milliard roubles was provided for agricultural improvement, on condition of the adoption of joint cultivation. Hitherto no provision had been made for a survey and settlement staff to carry out the desired changes. The Land Law of February, 1919, was this provision. It also repeated the principles that all forms of individualistic use of land must be looked upon as out-worn and transitory, and that priority in the distribution of land must be given to State-farms and to "associations," condemned the division of holdings into isolated strips, which wasted land as well as labour, and gave to the Land Department power to assume control of land, in order to prevent exhaustion and increase productivity. The Revolutionary State was not yet in a position to supplement these instructions by the provision of agricultural machinery on a large scale, and of a network of qualified scientific advisers: and the new survey and settlement staff was slow, expensive, and not always above the suspicion of corruption, and directed its labours sometimes to the aim of equalisation, sometimes to the retention of existing conditions.

On the whole, however, the period of War Communism had an equalising tendency upon land-tenure within the village: and some redistribution took place even between adjoining *Mirs*. The teaching of Marx is not egalitarian: but it is opposed to the private ownership or control of the instruments of production, including the land. The Revolutionary Government had surrendered to the peasantry as regards the control of the land, but surrender as regards the *unequal* control of it by individuals was another matter, and resistance to this

further surrender continued, with varying fortunes, against an opposing
section, which emphasised the economic advantage of encouraging
and supporting the more prosperous and thriving peasants; until the
policy of collectivisation propounded a new solution, from which
inequality of individual rights in land, but not inequality of corporate
rights in it, was eliminated.

The period of War-Communism was one in which vast tracts of the
old Russian Empire were from time to time completely inaccessible to
the Revolutionary administration and subject to White military control. Other large tracts were the scene of actual military operations, as
the tide of battle ebbed and flowed across them, and were for long
periods subject to the devastations and requisitions of both sides.
Partisan bands, brigands and deserters ravaged the country behind
the hostile lines. The Ukraine was not free from these for years
after the end of the Civil War. Tambov, and adjoining portions of
the Black-Earth zone, were the scene of a fresh outbreak in 1920-21.
It was the fertile, the surplus-producing, part of Russia, the south, the
east, and the south-east, which suffered most from these conditions,
the existence of which is the perpetual background to all that we have
to say in this chapter on the subject of rural life. The ravages of civil
war and brigandage in the Black Earth, the granary of Russia, were
preparing, throughout this period, the ruin which culminated in the
Famine of 1921-22.

The State's monopoly of trade, and in particular of the trade in
grain, though constantly evaded, embarrassed the economy of the
peasant by the difficulties which it placed in the way of obtaining seed,
cattle and agricultural implements. The system implied a precise calculation which should leave to each a sufficient supply of seed-grain
as well as food for man and beast, and adequate arrangements for
manufactured commodities to be delivered without charge. Such perfection of adjustment was, of course, impossible, and, though the
peasant generally succeeded in keeping back a far larger part of his
product than was contemplated, it was only by some illicit arrangement that he could utilise the surplus to obtain any of his requirements. Such illicit arrangements, if freely practised, were both expensive and precarious. The grain which was withheld from the towns,
except in so far as the requisitions were effective and the campaign of
the food detachments successful, was used for illicit distillation on
a very large scale, as well as to feed the increased village population
produced by the exodus from the half-starved towns, and to com-
pensate for the diminution in the yield of agriculture. There was at

the same time an almost complete elimination of those earnings sup-
plementary to agriculture upon which a considerable portion of the
peasantry had been partially dependent.

You cannot tax a peasant in cash unless you give him a market for
his produce. The abolition of the market necessarily involves taxation
in kind. This simple and obvious fact explains some of the changes
made by the Revolutionary Government in rural taxation. It started
with a theoretically complete monopoly of trade, and therefore abandoned cash-taxation. When the New Economic Policy re-established
the market, it was not long before rural taxation was again levied in
cash. When the peasant's freedom to dispose of his surplus was again
limited, a system of "compulsory sale in the nature of a tax" was
adopted which has virtually restored the system of taxation in kind,
though the remains of taxation in cash continue alongside of it, because the collective farm is able to sell its surplus after the Government claims are met, and the peasant is at liberty to sell the produce
of his own yard, or kitchen garden.*

❊   ❊   ❊

I have already emphasised the fact that the surplus-producing section of Russia, to which the country owes its reputation as a granary,
has the best soil and the longest open season, but also the most ca-

---

* The internal controversies of the Communist Party, a section of which con-
tended that the peasants were undertaxed and demanded that they should be
subjected to heavier burdens for the building of Socialist industry, led, in 1923-24,
to the preparation by qualified statisticians of a comparative calculation of extraordinary interest. This showed, for the whole of Russia, that the proportion of the
peasant's gross income which was absorbed in 1912 by all taxation, direct and
indirect, averaged 11.2% and that the additions of other charges, which were
brought to an end by the Revolution, for rent and land-purchase raised the total
to 18%. If we take tax payments and requisitions in the nature of tax only, the
charges upon the peasant during War Communism and the early years of the New
Economic Policy formed, because of the fall in income, a substantially larger
proportion of the peasant's income than the 11.2% taken by Tsarist taxation.
If we include, along with taxes and requisitions, those pre-revolution payments for
rent and land purchase to which the Revolution put an end, we find that the
change of rulers gave relief in 1918-19; increased the burden in the two years
1920-22; and maintained it, in 1922-23, at approximately the same level as in
1912. The profits derived by the Government from the issue of notes, which
took place on a very large scale between 1918 and 1921, are treated as taxation
for the purpose of this calculation, and one-third of them is debited to the
peasantry, as an addition to their tax payments. Roughly speaking, an equal
proportion—but not an equal amount per head—was taken, on a reduced
income: and the conclusion must be, therefore, that there was some increase
of the burden. Since the calculation was published at Moscow in 1924, we may
safely conclude that the Revolutionary Government regarded it as unobjectionable.
It will be noticed that its conclusions harmonised with those of the Right Wing
Communists who opposed any substantial addition to the burdens of the well-to-do

pricious climate. It is periodically visited by droughts, when hot winds from the east burn up the growing crops. The middle and lower Volga valley suffers very acutely from these visitations, of which the history of Russia is full, but the whole of the Black-Earth zone is also subject to them: and we have the paradoxical result that the richest agricultural area is also the most prone to recurrent famine. The year 1920 was visited by one of these droughts. In spite of the activities of the Food-War, the food-levy brought less than two-thirds of the estimated amount. The shortage of food caused a general reduction of rations, together with measures for speeding up food-trains which led to a dearth of fuel. Food-picketing and food-cordons intensified peasant discontent. Many food-collectors were killed, and troops sent by the Government to repress the malcontents fraternised with them. In other words, the areas of surplus-production were in revolt against the requisitioning of food for the army, the towns, and the deficit areas farther north.

Trotsky had already put forward proposals, which were not at that time accepted, for a limited tax-in-kind and for free trade in the surplus grain. Peasant discontent now began to force reconsideration of them. In February, 1921, the party organ *Pravda* (Truth) published letters which recommended the same plan: and Lenin supported it in a speech made before the Moscow Soviet. Resolutions in favour of a free-trading policy were carried at annual conferences of leather, metal, and railway workers, and there were ominous signs among industrial workers generally of dissatisfaction with Communist leadership. The Tenth Party Congress accepted the principle, and on March 21, 1921, the Central Executive Committee passed the famous decree inaugurating the New Economic Policy: generally described by its initial letters—identical in Russian and English—as N.E.P.

This decree replaced the quotas of provisions, raw materials, and forage delivered to the State by taxation-in-kind on a reduced scale. The tax was to take the form of a percentage of agricultural products, varying according to the economic position of the cultivators. Collective responsibility, reinstituted in 1918-19, was again abolished, but

peasantry. Its authors had no difficulty in showing that the advocates of higher taxation of the peasant were very far astray when they put the demands upon the peasant in the later Tsarist period at 40% of income. Local burdens may have continued to be excessive, owing to bad distribution, after the general rate of taxation had been brought to a reasonable level: but the general rate in Tsarist Russia ceased to be excessive after the abolition of the payments for redemption from serfdom. This result, however surprising, may be accepted as substantially true.

organisations of peasants were to be formed to supervise the handling of the produce collected. Then followed the clause which led to the remodelling of the Communist economy. The surplus left after the payment of the tax was declared to be entirely at the disposal of its producers, to be used for any purpose, including barter against the produce of factories, workshops and small industries, whether through co-operative organisations or in the market. Those who wished to hand over their surplus to the State were to receive manufactured commodities, and a permanent supply of the latter, produced at home or imported from abroad, was to be provided for this purpose. Thus began the great seven years' halt in the progress of the revolution. It seemed like Russia's Thermidor, and for some time the course of its development appeared to confirm that diagnosis.

Chapter XIII

CIVIL WAR. BRITISH AND FRENCH
INTERVENTION. FAMINE

> They came to the pits, and found no water:
> They returned with their vessels empty:
> They were ashamed and confounded and covered their heads:
> Because the ground is chapt:
> For there was no rain in the earth.
> THE PROPHET JEREMIAH.

In arriving at the epoch of the New Economic Policy I have reached the point at which a tremendous calamity, the climax of seven years of war, of which the last half was fought in the very heart of Russia herself, was impending over her people. And before I attempt to depict it I must turn back to some of the earlier links in the chain of causation.

In June, 1919, General Denikin was winning victories for the Whites in the south, with the help of British tanks and his own superior cavalry, and the Order of the Bath was conferred upon him by His Britannic Majesty. In the East, Admiral Kolchak was being pushed back by the Red forces towards the Urals. The question arose whether the Revolutionary Government's forces should follow Kolchak over the Urals, or concentrate against the danger of Denikin. It was keenly debated, and Trotsky was strongly for the latter course, but was over-ruled. The peril in which Moscow stood from Denikin later in the year might seem to have justified Trotsky: but it is probable that Denikin grew weaker the farther he advanced from the sea, where his foreign supports lay. The result of the decision was that Kolchak was being driven back while Denikin was taking Sevastopol, Kharkov and Odessa, and establishing himself north of Tsaritsyn (now Stalingrad) after the capture of that long and well-defended point of vantage on the Volga.

The declared policies of the Whites helped to strengthen the political position of the Soviet Union at this time. Two proclamations, one by Admiral Kolchak, Dictator in Omsk, and one by General Denikin in Southern Russia, showed what the peasantry and workmen were to expect from a counter-revolutionary success. The one left the agrarian question open for a National Assembly, to meet at a future date, but restored the home-farms of the landlords, and disclosed a preference for individualistic farming of the type favoured by the Stolypin legislation of 1906-11. The other contemplated a division of land between former owners and peasants, with compensation to the former, and a general return to the individualistic type of land-holding. General Denikin also proclaimed the restoration of the owners' rights in the factories, while making certain promises of a less definite kind for the satisfaction of labour.

Even the restoration of landlords, however ill-judged as a policy, might have been explained as a measure of equity. But the Denikin administration also attacked the Ukrainian language, newspapers and schools. It hardly needed the drunkenness, corruption, and profiteering of the rear to persuade the people that the Whites were not a good exchange for the Reds. In Siberia we have the testimony of Madame Alia Rachmanova, not ordinarily a friend of the Bolsheviks, that "except the soldiers at the front, no one wants the Whites to win." They were, in fact, daily destroying their own chances of success, by demonstrating how little they cared for the people of Russia, and how little experience had taught them.

In August, 1919, the Red Army, which was now attacking to the southward, had a serious setback owing to the White superiority in cavalry. By the middle of October, it seemed that both the old and the new capitals were in danger. In the north, General Yudenich, based upon British naval support in the Gulf of Finland, had advanced from Esthonia within striking distance of Petrograd. General Denikin, who had announced in July that his aim was Moscow, occupied a triangular area based on the three seas, with a co-operating fleet in the Black Sea and a British flotilla on the Caspian. The White army was from 300,000 to 400,000 strong, but it held a large part of Russia in Europe, and its rear was not safe. There was a sort of armed neutrality between Denikin's forces and those of Petliura, the President of the Ukrainian Republic. The Poles, though established at Minsk and Polotsk, two railway junctions far within the Russian boundary, lay there inactive, because the recollection of Tsarist policy made them doubtful of the political advantage of replacing a Red by a White Government. In the east, Admiral Kolchak was back at Tobolsk in Siberia.

Denikin was only two hundred miles south of Moscow. Yudenich had taken Gatchina, some thirty miles south of Petrograd.

Even Lenin thought of abandoning Petrograd, but Trotsky held out against surrender. A special "Communist Party" week brought many new party members in this moment of acute military crisis. Multitudes in the cities registered for defence. A pamphlet of November, which seems to be a reproduction of a speech by Kalinin, tells us that not only the Patriarch Tikhon, but the Mensheviks and the Social Revolutionaries, who had incited the Czechs against the Bolsheviks, supported the Soviet power at this dangerous moment. Denikin's victory would have meant the triumph of the counter-revolution, and the establishment of foreign Imperialist powers as exploiters of Russia. Russian patriotism was enlisted on the side of the Reds.

By the beginning of November both Yudenich and Denikin were in full retreat. On December 31st the Donets coal-basin was occupied by the Red Army, and the White forces cut in two. The final collapse was due to guerrillas in the White rear, and to indiscipline among White troops. In the meanwhile Kolchak had been ruined by partisan warfare in Siberia, and by risings at Vladivostok and Irkutsk, as well as by the military operations of the Red Army.

It seemed a complete triumph: but the removal of the immediate anxieties of civil war only gave the opportunity of realising the price of victory and the extent of the troubles which remained. France and Britain continued to maintain a rigorous blockade. The Revolutionary Government reached the oil-centres of Grozny and Baku only in March and April, and during this winter oil still remained inaccessible. The Donets basin was reoccupied, but Denikin's forces had ruined the mines, and coal continued scarce. Kolchak's collapse had given access to the iron of the Urals, but the engineers and some of the skilled workers had left the mines with the retreat. The cotton of Turkestan was no longer cut off by an enemy army, but the peasants had ceased to cultivate a cash crop when the market for it was closed, and had grown food instead. Railways were paralysed and factories worked only half time. The old trouble of low productivity, which was the essence of all the difficulties of the Revolutionary Government, continued and was intensified. The consciousness of the need of a more effective work-discipline was attested by a decree in February, 1920, making more specific the labour obligations of all citizens, and two months later by one which changed the system of rationing according to category to one of rationing according to work—an obvious further move in the direction of payment by results. Under the new plan only active workers were provided for, and only for those days on which they worked. There was an appalling epidemic of typhus in

Southern Russia, carried by lice as the armies moved over the stricken land. Sanitation, never of a high order, had been neglected for three years.

In the meanwhile there was a renewal of war from a new quarter. In March the Poles were at Mosyr, east of the marshes of the Pripet, and well within the Russian racial frontier. Towards the end of April they attacked the Red Army at Jhitomir.

A Janus-like attitude in foreign policy is perhaps an inheritance from the dis-coordination so noticeable in Tsarist statecraft. The Revolutionary Government not infrequently sought the friendly co-operation of other States, while organisations tolerated by itself, and even departments of its own, acted in such a way as to defeat that aim. In the spring of 1920 attempts were made to resume commercial relations, and Litvinov and Krassin were sent to western Europe for this purpose, which was favourably regarded by the Allied Supreme Council. In the meanwhile, the League for the Liberation of Islam was arousing discontent in the Mahommedan possessions of Britain and France. Doubtless there were other reasons besides this which determined the Entente Powers to support Poland against the Soviet Government. It was the help they gave, and in particular the despatch of the military mission to Warsaw in July, 1920, which decided the issue of the war in favour of the Poles. They would perhaps have done more for their protégé, if the London dockers had not refused in May to load munitions for Poland.

Allied help was also given Wrangel, who now renewed the Civil War from the Crimea. His Foreign Minister was Peter Struve, sometime Marxist and thereafter religious Liberal. Hitherto no responsible leader of the counter-revolution had ventured to hint at restoration of the monarchy, though plenty of White officers had talked king-making in their cups. But Wrangel's manifesto declared the right of the Russian people to choose its own master and, whatever may have been meant, the language seemed to imply that someone should again be Tsar. He said, or Peter Struve said it for him, that he aimed at making a Left policy with Right hands: and this might have been a very astute method of handling the nettle. But his actual land-policy, as announced, was that each peasant should keep the land which he had seized, as separate hereditary property, on payment of one-fifth of the harvest for twenty-five years as compensation to the owners. This was enough to set the peasants against him, for all that they gathered from such an announcement was that they were to pay a rent, and a fairly stiff one. In short, like all the White leaders except the Social Revo-

lutionary Government at Samara, he put victory into the hands of his
opponents, and nullified his own military efforts.

I deliberately emphasise the part which was played in the determination of the civil struggle in Russia by the White antagonisation of the
peasantry. It has an evident bearing on the conditions existent in the
winter of 1941-42.

We need not follow further the military struggle with Wrangel. On
November 11th the Red Army entered the Crimea after an eleven
days' struggle in the Isthmus of Perekop, the Revolutionary Government offered an amnesty, and all that remained was for the allied
fleets to carry those who did not accept it into exile and poverty.

Russia was employing less than half of the industrial labour employed before the war, and the product, in pre-war roubles, has been
calculated at only 18% of the earlier period. In the most efficient industries the product was less than one-third of the pre-war standard.
Procopovich speaks of an epidemic of unconscious sabotage, caused
by the notion that industry was a Fortunatus purse in which it was
only necessary to dip the fingers. Of the struggle to restore we have a
vivid glimpse in Gladkov's novel *Cement*. The hero, Gleb, twice
brings the factory back to working life, but at every turn he finds in
his way the Industrial Bureau, an impassable outwork of the Supreme
Economic Council, and all his questions rebound from this obstacle
unanswered. In the factory administration he finds waste, inactivity
and sabotage; in the Economic Council a mysterious activity of routine which he is unable to fathom. "The people there were all im-
portantly business-like, carrying fat files about, clean-shaven like Communists, the sort of people whom one used to find hanging about the
cafés and the Stock Exchange." In the factory itself the right people
are not rewarded: and he quotes, from the factory gate, the Bolshevik slogan, "He who does not work shall not eat"—in which some wag
has ironically obliterated the first of the two nots.

What we see here is the good workman, hampered by office routine
and office ignorance, burning to be set free from the trammels of both.
But he recognises that all will be well if he can only get past the mud-
dlers and meddlers to the man at the top. The need of the Soviet
State was for the capable manager, and improved labour-discipline.

❊   ❊   ❊

In such a desperately shattered economy as that of Russia at the
close of the period of civil war, all who were familiar with her past history must have known what they had to expect. Famines have been a
recurring phenomenon throughout the ages, but they have been sus-

ceptible of alleviation by the development of the means of transport, and it has been possible by the organisation of information to obtain early warning of their imminence. The machinery of the market has assisted by the appeal which rising prices make to the speculator in grain, but, where there are very great variations in purchasing power, this influence may rob the poorer country to feed the richer one. In India, which has been a severe sufferer, the famine in which no food is to be had, even at a high price, is virtually of the past: famine has become a phenomenon of agricultural unemployment accompanied by high prices. That is because the means of importing and transporting food is now fairly adequate. An administrative technique has been elaborated for ascertaining the approach of famine by village-to-village records of cropping and other agricultural information; for testing the existence of famine conditions by the opening of experimental relief works; and for the administration of relief by means of local works, of which a permanent programme is maintained in anticipation of the calamity. An exchange of experiences would have been of value to Russian administrators who, in spite of many recurrences of scarcity, had developed no corresponding technique.

War has always been a potent cause of famine. Agriculture depends upon the closest obedience to the calls of the season, and a few weeks of interruption to the processes of husbandry may destroy the food-supply of a year. The requisitions and devastations of war sweep away the results of the peasant's labour, and often drive him from the land, or deprive him of his cattle and seed. In Russia civil war was accompanied and followed, particularly in the south and south-east, by prolonged insecurity and brigandage, which completed the destruction of local resources. Railway communications, always imperfect, and concentrated too much upon the west, had suffered grievously. In a large part of the area which was to suffer from one of the worst of famines, bridges, tanks and stations were gone. Evidence of the deliberate abandonment of cultivation, in consequence of the system of requisition and the prohibition of trading in surplus grain, is absent. What these things had produced was wholesale concealment of cultivation and of stocks, and extensive smuggling and illicit practices, including the distillation of liquor from grain. A far more important result of War-Communism and of the monopoly of grain, inherited in part from the Tsarist, and in its completed form from the Provisional, Governments, was the destruction of the normal machinery of the grain trade. There were no merchants on the large scale, ready to pour imports of grain by boat and rail into the affected tracts. We cannot doubt that the scent of profit would have warned them of scarcity, and have supplied the lack of timely Government organisation. The Soviet Government had not yet built up a system capable of replacing that which had been destroyed, and the tremendous pressure of daily needs had made the accumulation of food reserves an impossibility.

Long severance by war and blockade from the industrial West, and the decay of internal industry, had prevented the renewal of agricultural implements and machinery. There was a wholesale reversion to the wooden plough, and a general reduction in draught animals, which had either perished or been requisitioned for military needs in a great part of the war area. The sown area in the Volga provinces was reduced in 1920 by these conditions and by drought to one half of the pre-war figure, and the yield was a low one: and the whole of the surplus-producing section of Russia suffered in some degree.

The drought of 1921, still more severe than that of 1920, visited a country already swept bare of resources. It was worst in the Volga provinces from Vyatka to Astrakan, and in the Urals and adjoining parts of Asia, but affected in greater or less degree the whole of the Black-Earth zone, and extended far into the south-east. Regarding the Ukraine, there was one of those controversies on question of fact which had already occurred in connection with the famine of 1891. The Central authorities of the U.S.S.R. claimed that the drought was not severe in the Ukraine, and insisted on large deliveries for the relief areas held to be worse sufferers. Half a million tons were therefore sent out of the Republic, against the protests of local statisticians and officials. In fact, there was extraordinary variation in different Urkainian provinces. One did better than usual; two had more than half a normal crop; four had from a third to nearly a half; five had less than a fifth, and three of these five had 5% and less. Of the existence of famine in a large portion of the Ukraine there was no real doubt. The medical report for the first half of 1922 puts the number of deaths from starvation in the Ukraine at 67,126, and those from diseases which follow malnutrition at 741,352.

There has been an unfortunate recurrence in later years of these differences of opinion regarding scarcity in the Ukraine. Nothing less than a system of crop records based on local inspection by a trained staff will reconcile the widely varying estimates which are put forward, or make an end of the suspicions of repeated famine which are widely disseminated by agencies unfriendly to the Soviet Government, and aggravated from time to time by that Government's reticence about facts. For the whole of Russia, Nansen, the best authority on the facts, put the famine-stricken population at 33 millions, of which he estimated that 19 millions stood in danger of death from starvation. The famine among humans was, of course, accompanied by a huge mortality among horses and cattle.

The consequences of this destructive famine are writ large upon the agricultural statistics. For all Russia the cultivated area descends in 1922 to 62% of what it was in 1916. In the Kirgiz country the percentage is 47%, and the cattle diminish from 3,789,000 to only 495,000 head: evidence of a nearly complete holocaust, or of the removal of cattle to distant pastures. In the Kuban-Black-Sea province the losses amounted to 60% of the horses, 46% of the large horned cattle, 70% of the sheep, and 87% of the pigs: though the people did their utmost to preserve horses and horned cattle, sacrificing sheep and swine for the purpose. In the Kuban valley, the seat of the finest wheat cultivation, the diminution of cultivated areas is a whole third, and the number of iron ploughs goes down by half. The Ural has similar losses, and even wooden ploughs and harrows largely disappear. Between 1920 and 1923 the losses of cattle amount to one-third on the Lower Volga. In the Ukraine just upon two-thirds of the total number of peasant households, in the three steppe provinces which had been worst affected, were in debt for purchases of food.

※　　※　　※

Famine itself is a local extension and a temporary intensification of a poverty always existing. Whether in industrial town or agricultural village, some are always on the border line, ready to be pushed across it by the first untoward accident. We call it famine, or we call it industrial depression, when distress extends beyond a certain conventional limit. There is no fundamental remedy till we learn to distribute all risks over the whole body politic, and to make the economics of abundance the aim of our society. With halting steps, with innumerable blunders, it is towards this goal that the U.S.S.R. directs itself, blazing out the pioneer trail along which many corpses lie.

In 1932-33 there was severe scarcity in parts of Russia, particularly in the Ukraine and the North Caucasus. A legend has established itself among writers on Soviet history and economics that this scarcity was comparable with the famine of 1921-22, and that it caused millions of deaths. The present writer, who has had some experience of the phenomena of actual famine, travelled through the Ukraine and the North Caucasus just before the excellent harvest of 1933 was ready for the reapers, when the scarcity must have been at its worst because the stocks must have been at their lowest. He thinks it right to place upon record the fact that he did not witness those phenomena, including crowds of beggars and emaciated children at the river ports and railway stations, which are normally associated with serious famine. He believes that the scarcity of that time was in no way comparable to the great famines, and desires to expunge an error from current history.

Chapter XIV

THE "SCISSORS" AND THE KULAK

"By delay, he restored the state."
QUINTUS ENNIUS. Lines in honour of Quintus Fabius
Maximus, "The Delayer."

"The frogs asked for a new king. Jupiter was vexed with
their solicitations and sent them a stork."
AESOP's Fables.

The New Economic Policy was a victory for compromise and opportunism, as much in the international as in the internal sphere. The Foreign Offices abroad regarded it as the Russian Thermidor, the end of the Revolution. It was accompanied by an Anglo-Russian agreement and by the resumption of trade relations with a number of European countries, followed by the appearance of Soviet Russia at the International Economic Conference at Genoa, and the Rapallo treaty between Russia and Germany. Lenin declared that Russia must no longer sacrifice herself on behalf of the international proletariat, but save her own economic position. But the activities of the Communist International, with its centre and source of financial support at Moscow, continued to be the cause of embarrassing, and sometimes of alarming, complications, culminating in the severance of relations by Great Britain in May, 1927.

If we are to understand the nature of the changes made in 1921, we must see with the eyes of the men who, at least up to the fateful advance upon Warsaw in the preceding year, had believed in the imminence of World-Revolution. While the apocalyptic dream lasted in all its vividness, its prophets were like the early disciples of Christianity, having their eyes on the clouds for the Second Coming of Christ to establish the Kingdom of Heaven upon earth. At any moment the skies might open to disclose the glory of their hopes. What need to measure the strength of Kingdoms, Principalities and Powers, or to determine the lines and the proportions of the work of reconstruction, when such a triumph was at hand, when all the skill and experience of the peoples of the West were on the point of becoming available for the assistance of the daring pioneer? It was sufficient to hold the fort, in the full faith of a better life to come, against the imperialist enemies who were about to melt away like phantoms of the night, and to deal with the necessities of each day as it passed, without facing the question: What, and how, will you build—in this Land of Fragments which revolution and war have left to you?

The vision did not disappear, but its brightness faded, it grew more remote and less certain, faith was more strained, weariness followed upon effort. Not only was World-Revolution postponed, but the peasantry, the allies upon whom the Revolution in Russia itself depended for daily bread, withheld their sympathy, and made it plain that they would not stay the course. The great disillusionment had come. In place of the apocalyptic vision, there appeared the almost-certainty of the long and painful recovery unhelped by the expected sharers in the labour. The question, whose urgency had been obscured by other and more immediate questions—of insurrection, peace, war, self-preservation—now demanded an answer: What, and how, will you build in the Land of Fragments, where the work of destruction is but too well done already?

As yet, there was none but the vaguest of answers. In the Party and its sympathisers there was a hard core of men and women determined to create a Socialist State. But what was the Socialist State, and how was it to be built? Marx could not help. He furnished the philosophy, and in some degree the technique, of revolution: and he furnished certain principles which might guide the builders of a part at least of the new temple. But almost everything still remained to be discovered, in a world where no pioneer had yet established a foothold. The best answer to the insistent question was that of Lenin, which I have placed at the head of the first chapter of this book: "We do not know. Life will show us." It was another way of saying: We learn in doing.

So much at least seemed plain. The material which lay closest to hand must be used. The natural desire of the individual man for his own subsistence and his own gain must be set free to achieve the work of restoration. That, in part, is what the New Economic Policy did. But neither Marx, nor the determination of the idealists that the end should be the construction of the Socialist State, permitted that freedom to be complete. It was inevitable that the system should be a mixed one, in which individualism and collectivism would work side by side, in an uncertain sharing of their separate spheres, amid a struggle which changed from time to time the boundaries of each.

The epoch of the New Economic Policy was therefore an epoch of doubt, vacillation, experiment, contradiction; of groping towards an uncertain goal; and also an epoch of material restoration, purchased by a partial surrender to the old Mammon. Seven years of deterioration were to be followed by seven years of recovery, before a leader could find courage to declare that the path of socialism was found, and to follow it, undeterred by the groans of those over whose bodies it passed. There was to come a further Revolution, greater and more difficult than that of November.

On the economic side, the New Economic Policy (N.E.P., as I shall hereafter call it, according to the Russian practice) was, in a certain sense, a reversion to the methods of capitalism. But it was not a reversion to the methods which Lenin had wished to follow in 1918. He desired at that time, before the introduction of War-Communism, to make use of private capital, controlled by the State. N.E.P., as it presently developed, was to concede a large freedom to the petty capitalism of peasant-agriculture, to retain for the State the monopoly of foreign trade, and the "commanding heights" of transport and industry, and to leave openings—of a width which varied from time to time —to private capitalism in the less important industries and in trade. The essential step was the initial one, which limited the State's demand upon the peasant, and permitted him to trade in the surplus. On that step there followed, by an inevitable sequence, a series of others which caused Lenin to speak at the Eleventh Party Congress, in no uncertain terms, of the *return to Capitalism*. The unwillingness of the peasant to part with his grain for paper money led to a decision to allow the town-worker part of the product of his work. (April, 1921.) This, in turn, led to payment by results, and to the grant of permission to factory-managers to barter part of their out-turn for raw materials and fuel, with the necessary consequences of commercial accounting. The use of money had never been abolished, and the need for calculation put an end to the possibility of abolishing it, and emphasised the evils of inflation, and the inevitability of price and payment for services rendered. A reduction in the number of workers to be fed, and of the factories to be supplied with raw materials, limited the distributing function of the State. The limitation of the State's commitments caused the selection of the factories best fitted for survival, and the grouping of them into combinations managing their business on commercial lines, selling part of their products to obtain working capital, and jointly responsible for commercial success. Interest, banking, money-taxes, budget, and the need of economy in State expenditure, all find their way back, till the economic system becomes one of State Capitalism, in so far as it is not worked by private and co-opera-

tive capital. The familiar phenomena of Capitalism reappear. Since
the requisition of raw materials is stopped, and circulating capital is
short, unemployment increases: and real wages in the summer of
1921 are only half of what they had been in December, 1920.

But the new system was Capitalism *with a difference*, because a
Government was in power which was conscious of intimate dependence upon the support of the workers of the towns, and intensely
suspicious of private capital. Powerful elements in the Communist
Party were shocked and alarmed by the retrogression from Communist
principle. At the third Congress of the Communist International,
a speaker charged the Central Committee of the Party with selling
the proletariat to the peasantry for a mess of pottage. Among the
younger and more idealistic there were cases of suicide. The existence
of this adverse current of sentiment disturbed the smooth course of
private profit-making, and from an early period obstructed and, in
part, set it back. From 1924, when the Twelfth Party Congress decided
on the repression of the Nepmen, because private was evidently stifling
socialised business, the adverse current gained in volume until, from
being two-fifths of the total trade, wholesale and retail, in 1923-24,
private trade sank to one-sixth of it in 1927-28. Taxation, if often
evaded, was crushing when enforceable; a scale of maximum profit,
varying in different localities, and enforced with varying degrees of
rigidity, was fixed by law, and the operator was liable to prosecution for
speculation, if the super-profit exceeded a certain figure. Such a system
inevitably worked with extraordinary inequality and, by multiplying
doubtful risks, gave a stimulus to the wildest speculation. Duranty
tells us, in September, 1923, of stores well stocked, and constantly
shut owing to heavy taxation, but soon reopened. It was a game of
catch-as-catch-can between speculator and Communist. Great fortunes
were made and flaunted, in spite of the social stigma attached to the
Nepman's operations. It was the official cue to worry him. The militia
"always inspected for clean floors on a rainy day," when the shop-
keeper was likely to be caught out. Obstacles were put in his way by
denying to him credits at the State Bank, and refusing transport
facilities; he was "milked" by the House Committees, who made him
pay three-fold for the better apartments which he occupied; he had to
pay high tuition fees for the admission of his children to school, and
a military tax for grown sons barred from the Red Army by their
father's occupation; and, when he died, the inheritance-tax on his
property, if the tax-collectors succeeded in laying hands upon it, was
90% of all sums in excess of 100,000 roubles.

The Nepman found his compensations in a predatory economy and in unbridled indulgence: and avenged himself by infecting with the acquisitive spirit the ranks of the Communist Party itself. We hear of a Saturnalia of corruption, gambling and prostitution, and of police connivance with crime. The sale of wine and beer was legalised in 1922, and the hotels and cafés of the cities were scenes of drinking and dissipation. The weaker brethren, outside of this orgy of profit-making and luxury, began to ask themselves why only the Nepman and his family should be prosperous. "Some of the wives," writes Anna Louise Strong, "even of Communists, began to complain: We endured hunger when everybody was hungry, but now some people make money and live comfortably, and why can't we?" In the spring of 1924, the Soviet authorities were horrified at the corruption which they found among the heads of state-trusts and party members. The general release from the restraints of religion and of popular opinion, which had been brought about by the collapse of 1917, produced a kind of anarchy in sexual morals, of which Romanov's *Two Pairs of Silk Stockings* may be taken as the literary expression. The old principles were outmoded and ridiculed, and rational substitutes, based upon the permanent needs of society, had not yet begun to take their place. Thirsty for the joys of life, men and women plunged downwards to the gutter, where the new stream seemed to flow. Lenin might disapprove the licence which placed the indulgence of the appetites alongside of the drinking of a glass of water, as equally natural and insignificant, and ask whether the dirtiness of the water made no difference. But the time had not yet come for the re-establishment of a rational self-discipline, and nature, for the present, took her own wild way, like a destroying flood before it has found its normal and beneficent channel.

Some have thought that N.E.P. was intended by Lenin to be the permanent course of the Revolution, but the evidence that it was a temporary device seems to me to be overwhelming. In defending his proposals he said that War-Communism had been inevitable in the conditions of war, as indeed it had been, and that, at present, the one consideration was to increase productivity, even though the effort would enable small industry to make disproportionate gains. At a later date (October, 1921), he was more definite. "We have met a great defeat, and are now making a strategic retreat. . . . All of our military successes were preceded by similar retreats. . . . Afterwards we began . . . a cautious advance, finally crowned with victory." On his temporary return to official work after his illness, he told the Moscow Soviet that "if we work hard enough, we can have Socialism instead of N.E.P." (October, 1922.) Trotsky put the point with picturesque brevity when he said that the stop was only that of a train taking on water. That some of the Party were tired out by the terrific strain of revolution and civil war, and ready to take refuge in a prolonged compromise, is in accordance with our expectation of human nature and, in particular, of Russian human nature, which had hitherto shown itself capable of immense temporary effort rather than of continued steady energy. But it is plain that the leader planned in 1921 only a breathing-space for economic recovery, and many stirring spirits were, from the outset, eager to bring the breathing-space to a close.

On the other hand, it was being argued, in the summer of 1921, that N.E.P. was consistent with Communism, so long as the workers were protected against exploitation: a theory which would have limited the scope of Communism to benevolent protective legislation with a full staff of factory inspectors, such as we might imagine to proceed from a Prince Bismarck. Such theorising was quite of a piece with the general spirit of an experimental epoch. In 1924 even Trotsky's speculations took a pessimistic turn, and he was confiding to his friends that American capital had re-established a firm capitalist order in Europe and that the prospects of the revolution promised ill. In the same year Stalin declared that the efforts of one country, especially of a peasant country like Russia, were not enough for the organisation of Socialist production and for the final victory of Socialism: and that the efforts of proletarians of several advanced countries were necessary for the achievement of these results. He spent much pains, later, explaining away this statement, but such was the direction which his thought was taking when he made it. Proposals were on several occasions made, and canvassed, for a modification of the State's monopoly of external trade, which it was natural to regard as the cornerstone of a Socialist system. It was possible for Bukharin to publish an article calling upon the peasants to grow rich quickly, when Bukharin was himself a member of the inner circle of leadership: though Stalin found it necessary to explain away the heterodox slogan, which harmonised only too closely with his own measures authorising the leasing of land and the hiring of labour. Very great freedom was allowed to the opposition to state and discuss its alternative policy in all its many details, and the Government took great pains to formulate its replies. As late as 1927 Stalin was comparing the project of hydroelectric power from the Dnieper to a peasant buying a gramophone when he needed a cow: not foreseeing, at that time, the grandiose developments of his own Five-Years' Plan. He, like everyone else, was still groping.

Groping, experimentation, and a measure of freedom which contrasted strongly with the centralisation of War Communism: these were some of the characteristic features of the eight years' interval between the introduction of N.E.P. and the start of the first Five-Years' Plan. For a whole year a new marriage law was under public discussion; the death penalty was abolished and re-instituted after an interval; a movement of reparation seemed to promise a measure of tolerance for political differences; the free Philosophical Academy discussed without let or hindrance a purified and ennobled form of Christianity; the partisans of a proletarian literature wrangled without interference by Government or Party with another group for which Trotsky found the expressive name of Fellow Travellers, because they went part of the way along the road to Socialism. The satirists of Soviet administration and society dipped their pens in disrespect, and Trotsky declared that this was precisely what the new world of the revolution needed. "How good it would be," he wrote, "if a stage Inspector-General (such as Gogol's famous *Revizor*) would walk across our Soviet life! The Censorship will set upon it if it hints at a return to the old life of the nobility. But if it says: We are building a new life, and yet how much piggishness, vulgarity and knavery of the old and new are about us! Let us make a clean sweep of them . . . then, of course, the censorship will not interfere: *and if it will interfere, it will do so foolishly and all of us will fight such a censorship.*" If it could but have been so! But the quarrel within the party was already preparing the way for a harsher and less tolerant system.

※　　※　　※

It is no part of the aim of these studies to depict the turns and twists of N.E.P., though one would not go far wrong in suggesting that they tell more about the broad Slavonic nature than many pages of graver history. So we pass by in silence many tempting episodes: how Lunacharsky, once dressing like a builder's foreman, took to wearing a "burzhui" top-hat, how Meyerhold, abandoning black bread and eggs, ordered four-course dinners among the champagne-drinking Nepmen, how Bim and Bom, the Circus Clowns, made game of Soviet Red Tape, how the Marxists, forgetting that classes, not individuals, make history, set to work to establish a Lenin cult and, with a subconscious memory of the incorruptibility of the bodies of the Christian saints, achieved the preservation of his remains to be exhibited to pious worshippers; and proceed with no further delay to the part which the peasant played in the new economic liberty which N.E.P. had conferred upon him.

Lenin, whose eye was upon everything, was severely critical of the first efforts of the revolutionaries to investigate rural conditions. They theorised and generalised without a basis of fact. His criticism inspired a remarkable body of enquiry which, following the monographical method instituted by Le Play, supplied to the Soviet Government, before and after Lenin's death, detailed accounts of village life and work in areas scattered over a large portion of Russia. They do not all follow a single plan, and some deal rather with Party work and administration than with the methods of husbandry practised and the standards of material and moral life. But in the result we have something which it is possible to regard as a picture of the Russian village in the first half-dozen years of the Revolution, supplemented in a few cases by material for its pre-revolution history. The enquiries extended to Asia; to the Altai province, the Bashkir Republic, and to Turkestan. The present writer has not been able to obtain the records of these areas, but the descriptions which have been accessible to him include a good deal about the Moscow province and some about Novgorod the Great, Tver, Smolensk, Kursk, Tambov, the Upper Volga valley, Samara, and the south-eastern areas as far as the Mountain Republic adjoining the Georgian Military Road.

The freedom with which some of these monographists reveal and criticise the errors of the revolutionary administration, exhibiting it in certain respects as a retrogression from standards attained in the pre-revolution period, has been to me a constant source of surprised interest. It must be understood that we are dealing, not with works printed and published abroad, but with the output of publishing institutions at Moscow, Samara and Rostov-on-Don, which may be said to have appeared under the auspices of the Soviet Government itself. Here is some criticism from a writer who subsequently rose to a high position under the Soviets. He is describing the administration of the Tambov province.

"Before the revolution, the peasant endured the drunkenness of the Elder, the corruption of the Writer, the rudeness of the Police officer, the high-handedness of the landlord. But the old customs, rudeness, drunkenness, corruption, have not disappeared. Some old hands remain, and the new men have sometimes fallen under the old traditions, encouraged by the ignorance of the peasants. Within three weeks, we of the Enquiry Commission had heard of every such case, for the peasant has a keen flair for official abuses."

Presents of milk, fowls, eggs, to the chairman of one Executive Committee, brought lenient treatment over the taxes. An Inspector of Finances gave his father an abatement. A chairman of a village Soviet cultivated Government land and did not pay. The Militia had confiscated a horse, and their chief let it out for hire to a merchant, and kept the proceeds. A demobilised Red-Army-man met a Militia man drunk, and reproached him. He hiccupped: "We are the Government. We are allowed to get drunk." And so on, and so on. *Plus ça change.* . . .

A writer on a village of the Valdai Hills in north-western Russia contrasts the independent attitude of the peasant there, who has the tradition of the old civilisation of Novgorod the Great, and is in the habit of leaving the village for outside earnings, with that of the typical corn-raiser of Central Russia. He says there is no solidarity among the peasants of such provinces as Orel and Bryansk, and when they grow rich they cease to live like peasants. Among such people as these, he adds significantly, the lower authorities of the revolutionary régime quickly adopted the insolent bureaucratic tone with a too submissive peasantry.

Another writer, describing the conditions of the Tambov province, says that the law does not reach the poor man, and Co-operation only works fairly when there is equality of means. The State-farms of the early period are described in terms of severe condemnation. Not one of our writers has a good word to say for them. They do no good to the adjoining villages, and they are not always able to pay their own workmen. The rural Co-operative shops are burdened with excessive credit charges by the Central organisation, and often force the people to have recourse to private traders, because the elected management treats the work as a routine duty. Schools and local institutions are starved for lack of adequate salaries regularly paid, and of the allotment of funds for equipment. In some places in the south-east the school teachers are "just like peasants, but with less good boots." One teacher "spends his night sewing boots, uses to clothe his body the straw bought for the stove, and looks ill." Everywhere the children of the poorer peasants are kept from school by lack of clothes and boots. In one village there existed before the Revolution a credit society which provided the neighbourhood with loans at 12 per cent interest for agricultural equipment, and now the Integral Co-operative wants 20 per cent, and has very inadequate funds. It is the well-to-do, and not the poor, who obtain advances, and "our Credit practice does not correspond with our Credit policy." The peasants of the Valdai Hills who work in the forests for the Nepmen are grossly exploited. The Labour Code should protect them, but it exists only on paper. A village Communist cell in the mountain republic adjoining Vladikavkas writes a report that is quoted in full as an example of illiteracy. The present writer, deciphering with difficulty, understands the cell to acknowledge the receipt of frames for windows, but to complain of lack of a door: an awkward deficiency in a bitter climate. But poverty, grinding poverty, is everywhere apparent, and takes us back, at every point, to the low productivity of labour, both in town and country, as the radical defect.

A comparison between the conditions of 1908 and 1920 for 223 villages of the province of Tver shows that, in the latter year, the peasants' purchases amounted to less than half of the salt, one-ninth of the tobacco, one-fifth of the kerosene, one-half of the soap, one-thirty-second part of the clothing, one-tenth of the boots, one-twentieth part of the building materials and nails, one-half of the agricultural implements, two-thirds of the carts and wheels, one-quarter of the household implements, which were bought in the former year; and this at a time when the correlation of agricultural and industrial prices were generally favourable to agriculture. Purchase of sugar, tea, vodka, flour and seed (except flax and vegetable seed) had entirely come to an end. The inefficiency of the administration told in more ways than one. There was an immense amount of concealment of cultivation and of grain stores, which defeated the requisitioning policy of the Government. A canton of the province of Tver paid, under pressure, an amount of rye which was just under one-thirteenth part of what it used for illicit distillation in 1913. The gains on illicit distillation and on illicit sales of timber in this area covered all losses, and allowed of much new building in the villages, while the towns were going to ruin. In the period of the strictest nationalisation and of the monopoly of trade there was much underground trading in grain and in boiled butter. Occasionally the watchers confiscated a load: but did not always take it to the authorities. The smart smuggler did very well out of his enterprise.

War-Communism temporarily killed the local fairs, where peasants picked up notions about improved implements and, what was worse, temporarily killed rural Co-operation. Cattle-dealing came to an end too, and some lands remained unsown because seed-grain could not be bought. The revolutionaries have unjustly suspected the schoolteachers of counter-revolutionary sympathies, and so have alienated a valuable agency. The local authorities are eaten up by the tasks of tax-collection and pure administration. There is a significant repetition of the warning that there is too much ink and paper. "Paper eats up the Communist cell." Everything which has no bearing upon taxation is marked, according to the immemorial practice of the Tsarist offices, either "for information" or "for guidance" and—filed among the records.

Facts such as these are frankly recorded, alongside of others which tell in favour of the revolutionary régime, with an admirable objectivity. An ardent spirit of creative reform runs through the work. It is a new "going to the people," repeating the missionary spirit of the seventies, but with far more definite and practical aims, and a better equipment. But the task is Herculean, and the technique of socialist administration has not yet been discovered.

Another feature of these village records is that they set the world-shaking events of November, 1917, in an altogether new light. In the village, at least, we feel that these were not so tremendous as they looked outside of it. There is continuity in some of the rural histories, and the revolutions which actually changed the local life were the adoption of some new technical crop, the beginning of clover cultivation, the change from three-field to many-field rotation, with the replacement of ribbon strips by clock strips, and the redistributions of the land which these changes involved. It was not everywhere that the seizure of landlords' land and stock made important additions to local wealth, and, anyhow, the seizures were largely made before November, and the establishment of the November Government in many cases merely confirmed the accomplished fact. The Civil War affected the South and East, the requisitioning policy and the excesses of the Food Detachments were directed to the provinces of food surplus, not to those of food deficit. Over the vast expanses of Russia there remained many "deaf" districts, many "bears' corners," where the peasant was hardly conscious of the Revolution except as a name. The local flour-mill and oil-press were nationalised, but the only people who could work them were the former owners, and they were still in control, as lessees of their old businesses or in the quality of salaried specialists. The man who formerly ran the Co-operative still ran it: for the excellent reason that no one else knew how. The man who lacked land or, still more common, lacked stock with which to cultivate it, continued to have to hire himself out. The law against employment of hired labour was easily evaded. The labourer was even more anxious than the hirer to conceal that he was a hired man and not a sharer or a relative of the hirer. He held aloof from the Union because he wanted work, and feared that the employer would be shy of a Union man. As ever, "money talked." It was another story when collectivisation was pressed, and the *kulaks* were liquidated. That was the true revolution for the peasant, but the lesson that emerges is that—while the seizure of power by a new class may be sudden and violent—the actual process of beneficent change is inevitably gradual and slow. In the meanwhile it is much if there is a new hope.

The peasant had some specific grievances against the consequences of the Revolution. The dearth of manufactured commodities which resulted from the decay of industry and the Allied blockade was a grievance of the first magnitude. The impossibility of replacing agricultural implements, and the extreme difficulty of getting them repaired, lowered the standard of husbandry. Later, when manufactured articles began to be available, their excessive price in terms of agricultural products was a constant reminder of an injustice, which, it seems, was laid at the door of the town-workman, rather than of the Revolutionary Government. A speech made by "Papa" Kalinin, on the alteration of tax policy at the introduction of the New Economic Policy, shows us what some of the grievances were. "There have been occasions when they (the food requisition officers) have taken from the peasant everything to the last straw. If they (the townspeople) have so far enjoyed almost without recompense the bread of the peasant, it has been because during these years they have had for the most part to work at war-industry." He does not deny the hard measure which the peasant has received, and is frankly apologetic.

During the period of War-Communism, the State, backward and ill-equipped, hampered by internal opposition, by civil war and blockade, attempted to organise universal provision, and inevitably failed to supply to the peasantry either the means of cultivation or the commodities which were the necessary price of food for town and army. It was not yet possible to organise the Russian countryside into manageable units which could be instructed, and controlled, and coaxed, into becoming obedient sources of supply: because the power-driven machines which alone could reconcile the cultivator to such a system were not yet available. It was necessary, therefore, to revert to a measure of *laisser faire, laisser aller*, in which the natural aptitude of Stolypin's "strong and sober" for winning prosperity for themselves would be utilised to advance peasant economy in general. Security of tenure was guaranteed by putting a limit to the successive redistributions of the land, and prohibiting the use of peasants' land for the formation of State and Collective farms. The Central Co-operative organisation was authorized to make purchases abroad, in order that the peasants might be supplied with commodities—a significant breach in the State's monopoly of foreign trade, in so far as Co-operation enjoyed any real independence of the State. These measures involved the surrender of Lenin's design of replacing small peasant tenure by large estates under national or collective management, and the reversal of such tentative measures in that direction as had already been taken. But there is ample evidence that the surrender was never intended to be more than temporary. "Papa" Kalinin, who had a knack of saying simply and directly what some of the revolutionary leaders immerse in a cloud of verbiage, is quite frank on this subject.

"The desire is to meet the wishes of the peasant mass . . . for this purpose, great flexibility and understanding are needed from all our workers. For the success of the planned line of policy depends—it is necessary to say so definitely—on *knowing how to avoid the alienation from us of the individualist, the small farmer.* . . . Marxist principles do not call for the artificial destruction of small farming. It will inevitably perish gradually of itself . . . as the cabmen failed in the competition with the automobiles. . . . We can only persuade the mass of small farmers into collectivisation by showing that it is better and more profitable."

The case of the small holding, he says, is similar to that of the small shop which cannot compete with the factory. "But"—and here he seems to forecast with accuracy the policy of to-day—"I think there will be a certain freedom of trade in small matters."

The leasing of land and the hiring of agricultural labour continued to be prohibited in the first years of the N.E.P., but both were permitted in 1924-25, with a limitation on the term of lease. Neither prohibition had been effective. By 1927 there were nearly as many agricultural proletarians as there had been before the war, and the difficulty of organising or protecting them had proved practically insuperable.

One side of the New Economic Policy in the village was, in idea at all events, to encourage maximum production by a neutral attitude towards the rival forms of landholding. State-farms, and cultivating associations in the nature of collective farms, no longer received, in practice or in theory, special encouragement. Some state-farms were leased out, some were closed, and the remainder were reorganised with an average area of 1,800 acres, and for the most part deprived of subsidies. The number of cultivating associations, of the nature of collective farms, fell by a third between 1921 and 1923. Freedom of choice in the village between the *Mir* and individual holdings caused a partial reversion to the principle of Peter Stolypin's settlement. In 1922 the surveyors consolidated more than 3 million acres of individual holdings in independence from the *Mir*, and in each of the years 1923 and 1924 areas not much less. This was not quite on the scale of 1913, when 4½ million acres were so consolidated, but it was sufficient to show the vitality of the desire of some for separation from the commune. We shall, however, go astray if we infer from these figures that a majority of the peasantry wished for the separation of their holdings. Survey and settlement, with redistribution of land, were taking place on a great scale. By 1927 two-thirds of the cultivated land of European Russia, not less than 150 million acres, had been redistributed. In almost every village there was a struggle between those who desired to maintain the Mir, and those who wished to leave it or break it up: and the number of cases in which it was maintained was far greater than the number in which it was wholly or partly broken up during these three years of activity by the individualisers. There were, however, in addition to the cases of consolidation of holdings, a large number of cases in which individuals registered their titles to the land without claiming consolidation, and a further large number in which voluntary groups of associated cultivators obtained allotments which, under revolutionary law, were independent of the Mir. But when all was done, and when further detachments of individual farms from the Mir had been stopped by the legislation of 1926, the Report of the Central Statistical Bureau dated January 1, 1927, showed that 95% of the land was still within the sphere of these obstinately surviving organisations. In particular instances we have clear evidence of the survival of the old "Mir" and the village-meeting, under the formalities of the new village-Soviet: showing itself in the reference of important questions, such as the internal distribution of the village assessment, by the latter to the former body.

Within the Mir, however, there was a great deal of internal subdivision between households, partly, no doubt, in consequence of the relief from taxation conceded to the poorer household, but due partly also to a revolt of the young against the old which the Revolution had encouraged. There had been 15 million peasant dvors or households before the war. Before the period of intensified collectivisation the number had risen to 26 million: a social and economic change of profound significance.

During the decade of Survey work from 1919 to 1928 the principle of equalisation of holdings was constantly in conflict with the rival principle of permitting, even encouraging, the prosperous to become more prosperous, in order to increase the marketable supplies of food. On the one hand, there were repeated redistributions made at the instance of returning soldiers, or of persons claiming a closer approach to equality; on the other hand, there was legislation to give security of tenure, by insisting on a minimum interval between two redistributions—legislation which was often made ineffectual by the intervention of the local Land-Committees.

There was much controversy over the effects of the New Economic Policy on the stratification of classes in the village, and the disputants on one side deduced from the available statistics that the middling peasant was steadily passing, on the one hand, into the ranks of the poor, and on the other hand, in smaller numbers, into the ranks of the prosperous: in other words, that extremes of fortune were establishing themselves, in accordance with the process which is assumed to be normal under capitalistic conditions. This conclusion was for a long time resisted by the dominant section in the Communist Party. Statistics seem to show, generally, that the equalising tendency noticeable under War-Communism did not persist in the village under the New Economic Policy, and that in certain areas the middling peasant was becoming either poorer or richer. In the Tambov province, for instance, the monographist Yakovlev shows us a marked advance between 1920 and 1923 in the differentiation of economic prosperity. Households with no cultivation have increased, households with cultivation of 27 to 40 acres have increased also, and those which cultivate from 40 to 60 acres have for the first time made their appearance. The same process is to be observed in the records of cattle-owning. Some middling peasants are going down, and others are going up: but the descent of middling into poor is more rapid than the ascent of middling into prosperous.

✳   ✳   ✳

Work at harvest-time was back-breaking. A chronicler of the Upper Volga describes the women at the reaping, under the hot summer sun: bent into triangular shape, can't straighten their bodies, faces like red-hot copper, eyes half-closed from heat and exhaustion, hearts beating hard, backbones cracking. The threshing is yet to come—all with flails and by human muscles. As for the threshing-floor—music at a distance, a torment of cruel labour hard at hand. And this work lasts eighteen hours in the day. "You beat and you beat, and out of it all comes a scrap, with a pinch of butter." If there was illness in a family at the moment of sowing or the moment of harvesting, good-bye to the crop, without the good offices of neighbours or of someone who would do the work—for a consideration. An attempt was made by the Revolutionary Government to ensure the peasant against such contingencies by the establishment of Sowing Committees, whose duty it was to organise help for those in need of it at critical seasons. This, along with the insurance of horses, was a palliative, but not a cure on a great scale.

In conditions such as these, with large numbers owning rights in land of which the alienation was not allowed by law, but lacking cattle, implements, often even seed, to cultivate it, the practice became widely established, on the part of the more prosperous cultivators, of letting out live and dead stock on hire, or of undertaking cultivation on behalf of those who could not do it for themselves. A new profession came into existence, the profession of providing the means of cultivation, which often carried with it the great advantage of immunity from taxation. You had no crop of your own, you helped another man to raise a crop and, as he was the registered right-holder in the land, it was he who met the requisition or paid the tax. Your half, if the payment took that form, was not the proceeds of agriculture but payment for service rendered, and not taxable, or anyhow not easily brought to book by the taxing authority. It is in the Black-Earth zone, in Tambov and the south-east, that we hear most of this practice. Yakovlev says two-thirds of the horseless and a substantial proportion of those having one horse, hired animals. Most of the prosperous and middling peasants did business of this kind. When the lenders had crops of their own, the borrower naturally had to wait till they had finished, and the short season might be dangerously near to its close before his turn came.

Payment for the loan was sometimes, but rarely, made in cash. Generally it took the form of kind, or of labour. The payments in kind might be a share of the crop, or a fixed quantity of grain. A favourite method was halving the crop, but sometimes the lender took as much as two-thirds. We hear of a charge of two bushels an acre for one ploughing and 4 bushels for two, 1 bushel for reaping, and so on. These were the charges for an iron plough; ploughing with a wooden plough was a good deal cheaper. We must bear in mind that 14 or 15 bushels to the acre was a good average cereal crop. We are not contemplating, as in Britain, methods that yield an average of 33 bushels, taking failures along with successes.

Sometimes the use of the plough and harrow was given "without payment," but this meant that the borrower must be prepared to do odd jobs at any time for the lender. Payment in labour seemed easier to the borrower, but it was heavier than it appeared to be, because the work generally had to be done when occupations in the field were heaviest, and the borrower might have to sacrifice part of his own crop to discharge his obligation.

In the south-east it was common for men to work at the harvesting and threshing of an acre, in return for the cattle and implements for ploughing and harvesting an acre; the alternative being the halving of the crop on the borrower's land. Other cases of payment in labour which are cited are: a lad's work for the whole summer in return for the ploughing of 1¾ acres; four man-months of work for the ploughing of 4 acres; half the crop and eighteen man-days of work for the ploughing of 8 acres. In one village the people told the investigator that they had to give up the crop on half or a third of their land to get the rest ploughed.

It is easy to see that it was this practice, so common in the cereal-raising areas, and so often involving the sacrifice of a large portion of the proceeds of husbandry to persons possessing cattle and implements, which suggested to the Government of the U.S.S.R., at a later date, the characteristic expedient of the Machine Tractor Stations, which undertake all the heavy processes by power-driven machines in return for a share of the crop—a good deal less than that demanded by private enterprise for less efficient methods. We shall see that, in return for less than one-fifth of the crop, the heavy work which ought to be done by animals or mechanical means is now increasingly done on the collective farms by machines, with a diminished risk of the arrival of the snow before the crop is carried home. This knowledge of what has gone before will help us to understand why the people's resistance to the process of collectivisation had so little vigour in it. Only the well-to-do were losers, and the natural inertia of conservatism was overborne by a substantial gain for the greater number.

I have more than once emphasised that grievance of the peasantry which consisted in the lack of manufactured commodities and their high price. Next after the subsistence of his family, and himself, it was for town goods that the peasant worked. Money, when it took the form of something not exchangeable for town goods, meant nothing to him. In the period of inflation which lasted till 1924, he made all his calculations in grain, in *puds* and *phunts* of rye or wheat or, as in the Mountain republic, of maize, against *arshins* of printed cotton, and *puds* of salt and kerosene and herrings and iron and nails. The Soviet Government issued graphs, which showed the relative prices of industrial commodities and agricultural produce on the basis of comparison with pre-war rates. I have elsewhere explained how the "Scissors" has come to mean the divergence of agricultural from industrial prices, a disordered correlation between the products of town and country:

a phenomenon which has sometimes extended far beyond the limits of Russia.

There was a time, a short time, in the Revolutionary epoch when the Scissors was favourable to agriculture because, though manufactured goods were short, food was shorter still. The position began to reverse itself after the harvest of 1922, and at the same period in 1923 the Scissors was wide open, with the lower of the two blades representing agriculture and the upper industry.

A pair of man's boots had been worth 150 lb. of rye before the war; they were worth 108 lb. between 1918 and 1920, 450 lb. in the latter months of 1923. The peasant used to get his printed cotton shirt for 36 lb. of rye: in 1923 he had to pay 252 lb. for the same. A yard of printed cotton cost six or seven times, a sack of salt six times, a load of pig-iron six times, a cask of kerosene three and a half times, a cask of herrings three times, a hundredweight of nails more than double, scrap iron nearly double, what it cost in rye or wheat before the war. Maurice Hindus, revisiting his old home about this time, found that the lamp was rarely lighted, because kerosene was too expensive. The high price of salt was particularly hard, for salting was the peasant's way of keeping his vegetables, mushrooms, cucumbers and the like. The girls did not like the deprivation of all means of beautification but, when paint was beyond reach, they used beetroot, we are told. The village was thus economically sundered from the town, because it could not buy, and was therefore unwilling to sell.

It was an impossible position: and it would have been an urgent danger to the Revolutionary Government, if the peasant had not taken into his head to blame the urban worker rather than the Government.

There was another aggravating circumstance in the economic correlation between town and country. Overhead charges on industrial goods were enormous. As is everywhere the case, except in so far as Co-operation redresses the balance, the peasant must sell at wholesale prices and buy at retail. The retail prices at which he bought were swelled by the profits added by each successive government organisation which handled the goods. The Co-operatives, as the agency of retail distribution, took up the grievance with energy, and their first all-Russian Congress (January, 1923) demanded that the costs of industrial production be reduced by rationalisation, and that prices be strictly regulated by the State.

Our village monographists are generally severe in their comments upon the inefficiency of Co-operation. There are whole cantons in

which it exists only as a signboard. The "Centre" charges 25% for
credit on goods supplied. The people often deal with the private trader
"because we are such poor traders, and often we have to sell goods
below the purchase price." The elected management treats the work
as a routine duty. The Co-operative has a difficulty in obtaining credit,
but the private trader has old business relations which make it easy
for him to get it. The private trader has more flexibility and initiative.
One very unkind remark is made in the rural record of the Yaroslavl
neighbourhood on the upper Volga. The Co-operative shops are in the
hands of "former merchants, former *kulaks*, rogues, cheats, and even
clergy." The Co-operatives have a smaller selection of goods, and they
charge too high a rate of profit on articles in which there is no competition. The best that is said about them is that "they don't cheat,
but they like to put something in their pockets."

But over vast areas of rural Russia the shop in any form was a
novelty. The peasant had to rely upon fairs, upon pedlars, upon occasional visits to a town many miles away by the vilest of roads. It was
not much that he wanted, at all events not much that he could hope
to buy. A Russian economist, writing in 1925, calculated that a middling peasant could spend not more than 35 roubles in the year on
town goods, and a poor one not more than 25. The rest must be home-
made or make-shift, as it is in every natural and primitive economy.
Bad though it might be in the eyes of town critics, the arrival of the
Co-operative had been the arrival of a new convenience in village life,
and of a competition with the profiteering private dealer: and when
the "Scissors" reduced the peasant's purchases to little more than
matches and kerosene, it was an advantage to have these near at hand.
The attempts at cultured amenities, such as they were, were appreciated. A Co-operative tea-room was much liked because a cloak-room
was attached to it, in which the peasant could deposit miscellaneous
articles while he did his business. It was a safeguard against petty theft,
always a weakness among the Russian peasantry.

But how easily these joint undertakings went up in smoke! From a
Co-operative inn, leased from a small dealer, every article, plates,
dishes, cups, even chairs, disappeared in turn: till the society gave up
the struggle. Now the *kulak* was installed in it once more, and making
good money out of rubbish. Everybody's business had proved itself to
be nobody's business. Lest the daughters of the Philistines rejoice,
let us point out that the Socialists were still in quest of the right
technique.

While the Tsarist régime had looked jealously upon Consumers'

Co-operation, it had encouraged Credit Societies and Co-operative production, as the means of dealing with rural indebtedness and of allaying agrarian discontent. These Associations had 10 million members in 1916, and the loans from the State Bank to them were between 300 and 400 million roubles. Credit Societies held most of the capital of the central Co-operative Bank at its inception in 1912, but the centre of financial weight shifted to the Consumers' Co-operatives after the Revolution, indicating a relative decline in the importance of the Credit movement. The value of rural Credit Societies, as distributors of credit among a village clientèle with whom the State agencies cannot possibly have a close individual acquaintance, must obviously be diminished by the increase of collectivisation, which substitutes a collective for an individual borrower. The need for rural Credit Societies was, however, as great as ever during the continuance of the New Economic Policy, and the village monographists have much to say regarding them. We learn that in the south-east of Russia there is a crying need of credit, but a failure of the machinery for providing it to the poor, who need it most. After the ravages of famine in 1921 and 1922, working cattle are everywhere lacking, but those most in need find it most difficult to obtain loans. Incidentally we notice a departure from the normal system of rural Credit Societies, which should rely upon personal knowledge of the borrowers' character, and not demand the security of property. These south-eastern Credit Societies, it seems, and perhaps the Russian rural Credit Societies in general, demand security, which the poor man cannot give, and so defeat the principal object of their own existence. Yakovlev, writing of the province of Tambov, quotes the bitter comments of the poor on co-operation: "I know them—these co-operators who have cattle, stock, and machines. They don't take us in the Co-operative. Pay your subscription, and enter: but you get nothing, if you are poor." He tells us how the Government's loans of seeds went to the Co-operatives—because it was desired to encourage Co-operation—and seed was delivered at the nearest railway station: but the horseless poor could not even fetch it home, without paying tribute to their more well-to-do neighbours who had horses and carts, and for the most part they went without. He puts his finger on a weak spot in Co-operation (other than Consumers' Co-operation) when he says that, without approximate equality of means, there is no true Co-operation. In the prosperous dairying tracts of the Moscow province, the Credit Societies worked very well: lent money first at 12% and afterwards at 11% —quite fair rates for rural borrowers. as experience in India shows, because of the risks—and generally lent it for periods which indicate arrangements to carry the borrower over the difficult time between seed-time and harvest. But these were not typical of the Credit Co-operatives in general.

The best-known types of the Agricultural Co-operative Societies are the Creameries of Siberia and the Milk Association of the Moscow Province, of which our monographists give us a very favourable picture, showing them to be real harbingers of civilisation. There were also agricultural partnerships, which cultivated land in common and became the prototypes of the collective farms. But the Agricultural Co-operatives were associations for selling produce, after processing it, and for buying and passing on to their members seed, implements, and their other various requirements. Often they combined Credit functions with these, and commonly they set up Co-operative shops for the simultaneous needs of the peasant household. After their eclipse during the period of War-Communism they recovered their independence of the State under the New Economic Policy, and inspectors continued to test and guarantee their milk products. The agricultural authorities of the Soviet Government regarded them as a second best, pending the formation of agricultural Collectives, with joint cultivation, which alone, they believed, could give the maximum product. Widely established though they were—there were 80,000 of them in 1927—they were neither numerous enough, nor strong enough, to solve the problems of peasant agriculture, and they did not help to convert small-scale into large-scale cultivation. But they helped in the restoration of agriculture to its pre-war standard of productivity, and put the thriftier section of the peasants on their legs.

Co-operation, in so far as it tended to keep down the retail prices of commodities in rural tracts, was a palliative for the hardships of the "Scissors." The more liberal supply of agricultural credits worked in the same direction. The drastic measures which the Soviet Government took in 1923-24 to bring down the prices of industrial goods effected an adjustment which was of very great advantage to the peasant. But the low price of agricultural, in terms of industrial, products was, after the brief interval in which agriculture was even less productive than industry, a permanent disease of the economy of the U.S.S.R., until the effective restoration of industry. The contention of Strauss, in *Soviet Russia*, 1941, that the Soviet Government has favoured agriculture to the detriment of industry, in its more recent policies, is discussed later.

The Scissors is not a uniquely Russian phenomenon. A maladjust-

ment of the correlation between the prices of industrial and agricultural products accompanied, if it did not originate, the world-wide
depression of the thirties. A completely unorganised agriculture continued to produce, when a partially organised industry was putting a
check upon its production, and, because agriculture ceased to be able
to buy, the wheels of industry were stopped. Russian agriculture tried
to meet its difficulty by keeping its products off the market. A part,
at least, of world agriculture applied the remedy of destruction. The
adjustment which shall make plenty no longer a cause of economic
depression is, for the world in general, yet to seek. While the interests
of individuals continue to be contrary to the interests of the community as a whole; while each producer benefits by scarcity in his own
particular line, whereas the whole body, producer and consumer alike,
benefits by the enlargement of the total output—such an adjustment is
not in sight.

❊   ❊   ❊

It is not surprising to find that the Revolution made no immediate
or radical change in the realities of the local rural administration. The
Provisional Government had maintained the Provincial and District
Council (Zemstvo), and had added to it a Canton Council, which
existed only for three months. The November Revolution replaced
these Councils with Soviets, and thereby introduced an element of
less experience, but representative of a much more numerous class.
The institutions which touched rural life most closely, beside the Land
Committees, were the Canton Soviets, or the Executive Committees
which exercised their authority when the full body was not sitting,
and the village Soviets. It was hard to find suitable men for the Canton
Soviet, without going to the larger unit of the district or even of the
provinces, to obtain them. It was hard also to find men willing to take
up the heavier local duties. In critical times, for instance in the southern districts during Denikin's campaign against Moscow, there was
often group-tenure of office and rapid rotation, as one man after another shuffled off the burden. Sometimes a man was elected President
of the village Soviet to spite him. The peasant quite understood the
election of the village Soviet and the working of the Canton Executive
Committee. Beyond these his political ideas did not extend, and he
had only the vaguest notion of his right to influence by his (indirect)
vote the composition of the District Soviet. In villages where many
were poor and a few well-to-do, the latter usually had a dominant
position in the local institutions, and exploited it for their private interests. When the village Soviet offended powerful interests, the well-

to-do sometimes set up the authority of the old *Mir* against it. There was general inability or unwillingness in the local institutions to support the poor against the prosperous. We hear of a village Soviet in the Stavropol area of the south-east which is a sort of Mr. Facing-both-ways. Nearly half the members are Communists, the poor are well represented, the work on paper is excellent. But the well-to-do do not like expenditure on public objects—how strangely familiar it sounds! There is no selection of pure seed, and no milling centre, no joint water-supply, no fire-fighting appliances, no drugs or instruments at the Medical Centre, no step is taken for re-survey of the land in the interests of the poor, the budget is for 10,000 roubles expenditure and 1,478 income. This last phenomenon, of a fictitious expenditure against a tiny income, repeats itself elsewhere.

Why do not the poorer use their numerical strength in the Soviet to obtain what they need? In the village, we are told, people are *afraid of consequences*. It is awkward to quarrel with the man from whom you want to borrow implements or cattle, to whom you may perhaps have urgent need to hire yourself out as a labourer.

It is the old story. Liberty is not liberty for the economically unfree. From the Valdai hills comes the story of a middling peasant—not merely a poor one—who tries to stand out against a dominant clique of the well-to-do. He gets a thrashing, and no redress for it: the true agrarian revolution is not as yet—in 1923—accomplished. Money is still king.

❊   ❊   ❊

We see in the pages of Leonid Grigorov very varying types of the "Popular Judge." One is a sensible, honest, considerate man, with no pretensions to legal training and very little need of any. He sits, with two elected Assessors and the permanent secretary, who records the proceedings, in a rather dirty room decorated with pictures of Marx, Lenin and Trotsky.

Another Popular Judge in a different canton is also a Communist, but he is for ever doing scandalous things.

A third Popular Judge described by Yakovlev in his account of the Tambov province was formerly a village Writer, and was promoted to judicial functions after the Revolution. In his new capacity he decides cases, "for butter and flour," in the old way. But he is a good fellow too, and explains the law, and writes petitions for the peasants, who think nothing of his little foibles. There are some good things too, says Yakovlev, which the new Revolutionary Judges do. They'll punish a prosperous man more severely than a poor one; they'll sentence an official for abusive language; they come down heavily on an embezzling co-operator, and they make the father of an illegitimate child pay alimony to the mother: they take cognizance of a poor man's grievance on an anonymous newspaper complaint, and so on, and so on, things that the Courts of the old régime left alone. It's a more popular régime, for all its foibles, and nearer to the people.

We catch glimpses of the Government Insurance Agent, for ever travelling through all sorts of weather, and pushing insurance against hail, drought, fire, pestilence, cattle-plague, and pressing for protection against fire by the maintenance of hose and pumps. These things saved many from being plunged into horselessness and houselessness. They are the little things which the village values—and by which it judges the Government.

Trotsky, one of the protagonists in a controversy I shall discuss in another chapter, drew up an indictment of the Government's policy in which agrarian conditions played a large part. It was intended to be delivered as a speech against a proposal to expel the author from the Central Executive Committee in October, 1927: but the Committee declined to listen. For the present we are concerned with Trotsky's statement of the facts of rural Russia. He says, in effect, that the Government is deliberately following Peter Stolypin's policy of building "upon the strong and sober" among the peasantry, and strengthening that more thriving element which we have learned to know by the name of *kulak*. All the machinery, land survey, taxation, State-credit, State-determined prices, are being used to help the prosperous, and depress the middling peasant and the poor. The distribution of land is not sufficiently favourable to the poor, and the prosperous get too large a proportion of the rural income. Taxation is not steep enough, and there is too much indirect taxation, which (as everywhere) falls with disproportionate weight upon the poor. State-credits do not reach the middling and the poor peasants, and nothing is done to put an end to that disparity between autumn and spring prices which is one of the causes of the permanent depression of the poor, who are all buying for seed in spring, and all selling under economic pressure in autumn. The slow pace of industry has caused the "Scissors" to draw wider apart, the gap between wholesale and retail prices has widened, and both influences have increased the dependence of the poor upon the prosperous, and stimulated the practices of renting land, hiring labour, and taking usurious interest. Farm labour is badly paid and badly protected. In the result the differentiation of classes is growing in the village, and rural capitalism is becoming stronger, so that the prosperous minority have most of the surplus grain in their hands and are able to hold it up and put a check upon development. This growth of the prosperous minority had received legal sanction in the legislation of 1924-25, by which the hiring of labour and the renting of land had been conceded.

The most important of Trotsky's inferences in the field of agrarian policy are, that industry must produce machines to increase the productiveness of agriculture, and that the Mirs, now controlled by the prosperous few, must be brought under the guidance and control of the State by collectivisation, that is by the pooling of land and labour and their proceeds. As we know, these were the expedients soon to be adopted. If we can clear our minds of the obscurities engendered by angry controversy, we shall find that the facts of the agrarian situation were not seriously in dispute. Even the ultimate remedy was generally foreseen, but the speed and the occasion of the approach to it were matters of heated discussion.

Some, like Bukharin and Rykov, were arguing for the encouragement of the prosperous peasant, because that was the means of promoting the growth—and therefore ultimately, on Marxian principles, the earlier downfall—of capitalism in the village. Bukharin said it was possible to absorb, and therefore unnecessary to destroy, the opposition to Socialism. Trotsky argued that the encouragement had already gone too far. In December, 1927, while the ink was hardly dry on Trotsky's pen, the Fifteenth Congress of the Communist Party decided on the restriction of the leasing of land and the hiring of labour, and accepted, in principle, gradual collectivisation; by example, not by compulsion.

The opening of the "Scissors" to the advantage of industry, and the disadvantage of agriculture, was less exaggerated in 1927 than in 1923, but still remained serious. A hundredweight of rye was exchangeable in 1927-28 for about half of the cotton, sugar, salt, oil, soap and nails, which it sufficed to buy in the pre-war period: rather less than half in the case of private dealers, rather more than half in the case of the Co-operatives.

We have a statistical picture of the stratification of rural classes in 1927. Roughly speaking, 3% of all the agricultural households were employed on State and collective farms. Eight per cent were purely proletarian, dependent upon employment on the lands of others, badly, or not at all, organised in rural unions, and as much subject to exploitation as a similar and perhaps smaller class had been before the Revolution. Over 20% were semi-proletarian, partially dependent on the land of others, but having very small holdings in addition to their cottage gardens or yards. More than half of these had holdings of less than three acres. Nearly 65% were middling peasants who were producing small surpluses without employing hired labour. A large proportion of these were letting out cattle and implements to others. These 15 million middling households, comprising 81 million persons, were the backbone of the peasantry. The petty capitalist farmers, employing hired labour, and corresponding to the class vaguely described as *kulaks*, represented nearly 4% of the total; along with their families perhaps 5 million persons, as estimated later on at the time of their expulsion from the villages.

Rural Russia had preserved her ancient constitution in spite of all that had been done to alter it. Over vastly the greater portion of her agricultural area, the village *Mir*, and the village meeting which represented it, continued to make partial redistribution of the land, to hold by the ancient three-field rotation of crops, to fix the dates for carrying out the manure, sowing, hay-cutting, harvesting, throwing open the stubbles for the common grazing. The strips were preserved, and a man had to walk on an average 1,260 miles in the agricultural season to get round his own holding. But the old large families were broken up, and the number of household units increased, largely as a consequence of the fiscal methods of the first ten years of Revolutionary Government. In the whole of the U.S.S.R., of 26 million households, 8 millions were horseless. In the Ukraine not much less than half the households lacked a horse. The supply of agricultural implements was not much over two-thirds of what it had been before the war, and the efficiency of the existing supply was less. Such machinery as existed was in the hands of the more prosperous few. In the spring of 1928, nearly three-quarters of the area sown was sown by hand. Not much less than half of the harvested area was reaped with the sickle. More than two-fifths of the grain was threshed by the hand-flail. There was acute need of fertilisers and of seed of good quality.

And yet the area under cultivation and its productivity had nearly returned to the pre-war standards, and the area producing raw materials for industry was substantially above that of 1913. Taking 100% as the pre-war standard, agricultural production, which had stood at 69% in 1924, approached 85% in 1927. Horned cattle, of immense importance for manure as well as for draught, were more than pre-war, sheep and swine were about equal to the old figure.

The countryside was back to pre-war days, *minus the landlords*. The peasant had lost one master; his other master, the *kulak*, was stronger than ever. But the *kulak* had fulfilled his function, as bees fulfil theirs in storing the hive.

In February, 1928, an article appeared in *Pravda* (*Truth*) which foreshadowed a change in the Party policy, and explained its cause: the village had expanded and enriched itself, but the principal beneficiary was the *kulak*. Hence the difficulties which had been experienced during the current winter of 1927-28 in the collection of grain for the use of the army and the cities. A second cause, explanatory of the difficulties, was backwardness in the supply of industrial products, resulting in the hoarding of grain by the peasants in general and the *kulak* in particular. The power of the prosperous element had increased, was increasing and ought to be diminished, at the same time that a more rapid development of industrial production must be undertaken. The stage was now evidently set for a great change, a change which, so far as the vast rural expanses were concerned, was a second and complete Revolution.

Chapter XV

THE TWO DISCIPLINES. THE TSARIST INHERITANCE AND THE COMMUNIST PARTY. TERROR AND LEADERSHIP

"From an American viewpoint all Soviet citizens are treated very much like prisoners on parole, especially since the Tsarist passport system was revived in 1932."
LITTLEPAGE AND BESS, *In Search of Soviet Gold*, 1932.

"Account of the trial of the chairman of a Co-operative shop, charged with embezzlement. He confessed 'so objectively that it might be the misdeeds and debauches of someone else, so completely identifying himself with the community that he actually began to grieve with it over the misfortune of having such a president. By a reverse process, his weakness was their weakness. All of them—somehow the Court too—were in the muck together, and somehow all together must get out of it.' "
ALBERT RHYS WILLIAMS, *The Russian Land*.

"He who, at every age, as boy and youth and in mature life, has come out of the trial victorious and pure, shall be appointed a ruler and guardian of the state. . . . They will have to be watched at every turn of their lives, in order that we may see whether they preserve this resolution."
PLATO, *The Republic*.

"The Party is a thong . . . it often cuts into my flesh, but I can't live without it. . . . I need someone to give me orders. I must feel another shoulder next to mine."
PAVEL RAYEVSKY in KIRSHON's play *Bread*.

In an earlier chapter, on Russia before the Revolution, I spoke of the growing sense of indiscipline which was characteristic of the Russia of the later Tsars. It often expressed itself in a Cassandra-like denunciation of political and social evils, and in a call for the restriction of liberties which were being abused. But alongside of it there were the obvious facts of a political system which denied a legal status to the larger half of the population, and conceded it very precariously to the remainder. There was, in fact, as much indiscipline in the Government and its apparatus as in the governed, so that, in the words of a Japanese observer, quoted by Maurice Baring, "an incompetent Government was being opposed by an ineffectual Revolution." A sort of drawn battle was in progress, in which each side inflicted and suffered casualties but could not establish a definitive superiority. The setting up of the Duma was an attempt to adjust the Russian state to the conditions of a new discipline based upon a quasi-parliamentary constitution, and Peter Stolypin was apparently convinced of the need of transforming the Orthodox Autocracy into something like a *bourgeois* monarchy of the Louis Philippe type, resting upon a strong and sober peasantry. But the rulers and the clique which surrounded them would not have it so, and the opportunity was allowed to pass.

Count Leo Tolstoi was already preaching the end of the State and the replacement of its political authority by the religious standards of the individual. "The Kingdom of God is within you." When the Revolution of March, 1917, arrived, it was precisely of the type which Tolstoi had advocated. No one made it, but each said to himself, "For me, I have no need of the State." The magic words shook down the tottering fabric. The army was a crowd on the way home. The peasants were cultivators taking back the land.

But the internal discipline of the individual, which Tolstoi's plan had postulated, had not matured to take the place of the artificial discipline which had collapsed into dust. *The power slipped into the street.* Lenin and his Bolsheviks picked it up. It was now their task to create a discipline, and to give coherence and form to a land of fragments.

But that was not the work of a moment. It was possible, by obeying those wild forces, at once to ride the whirlwind: but not to direct the storm, except by long and patient work, such as demanded administrative genius of a high order, and the practice of creative compromise. In fact, they proceeded by the construction of a two-fold discipline: one an imitation of a semi-barbarous past, the other an inspiration from a more enlightened future. One was Terror, and one was Leadership. One came from without and from above, from the Third Section of Nicolas I, from the Okhrana, and bore various names thereafter, of which Gay-Pay-oo is the best known to the West; the other from within, and by selection and promotion out of the best brains and the best hearts of the Russian people, and calling itself (by a historical accident of revolutionary history) by the entirely inappropriate name of "The Party."

The Gay-Pay-oo—I shall call it compendiously by that name, though the revolutionaries first called it Cheka, and at a later stage the Ministry of Internal Affairs—was something which Alexander Kerensky ought to have established, and, in his later months, thought of establishing, and which the Bolsheviks set up immediately on their arrival in power. In times of profound peace, a long-established Government with no possible rivals may with impunity abstain from the creation of such an agency, or may achieve the feat of making a moderate use of its terrible powers. Normally—because every Government is hard upon someone at some time, and because every Government has a duty to preserve itself or resign its functions to another— the existence of a political police is inevitable, because it is the eyes and the ears of the public authority, and often the hands too.

One distinction, indeed, must be clearly drawn, if we are not to fall into a moral confusion. Every Government makes use of fear as an everyday agency. That is what we mean when we speak of deterring. From the magistrate who fines a motorist ignoring a signal, to the judge who assumes the black cap in passing sentence upon a murderer, punishment is used for this purpose, and the talk of curative or reformatory measures has not made an end of the practice. But we reserve the word Terror for something less discriminating than this ordinary penal jurisdiction. We talk of Terror when the blow is struck at whole groups or classes without regard to the culpability of the individual; and apply the word to the organisation of fear, by Governments, or by parties contending together for supremacy, as a means of eliminating opposition or compelling co-operation. Contrary to a general impression, the Bolsheviks did not employ this method till eight months after the November Revolution, when the Left Social Revolutionaries, who had up to this time maintained an unstable alliance with them, rose in revolt. Over 400 persons were put to death in consequence of the outbreak which occurred at Yaroslavl, and the early period of leniency then came to an end. (July, 1918.) The shooting of the Imperial Family in July, however shocking to the world, was perpetrated to prevent an imminent rescue, and falls into another category. The terror was intensified when the murders of prominent Bolsheviks and the attempt on the life of Lenin, following upon the spread of the civil war, had demonstrated the peril in which the revolutionary régime stood. (September, 1918.) "With what foot-rule," asked Lenin, "do you measure the number of necessary and superfluous blows in a battle?" The Terror, in the sense of mass-execution, or mass-punishment in some form of unarmed persons by organised authority, continued, with certain intervals, throughout the civil war. It seems to have been equal on both sides, and orders by White Generals for the execution of hostages are extant.

The dramatist Alexander Afinogeniev, who lost his life in the bombing of Moscow in November, 1941, wrote in 1931, when the battle over collectivisation was almost at its hottest, a play called *Fear*, describing a struggle in the Institute of Physiological Stimuli between the old professoriate and the new. The old-fashioned Professor finds that fear is the common stimulus, and that the abolition of fear would bring a rich creative life: with the obvious implication that the Soviet Government must change its ways. His woman opponent, a sixty-year-old member of the Commission of Party Control, declares that fear, hitherto the instrument of the class oppressor, is now felt by those who desire a return of the old order. "When we break the resistance of the last oppressor on earth, then our children will look for the explanation of the word *fear* in a dictionary." The lady wins, of course, for the authorities remove the old-fashioned professor; and she hits upon a significant truth when she describes the Terror as something affecting a particular class, and making no difference at all to the psychology of the rank and file of the population. The Terror has been tolerated, because it has not touched the masses. When, and if, it touches them the régime will be in danger.

The Terror took more forms than one. Like war, blockading and starving out the hostile nation, it deprived the "enemy" of food-cards, at a time when the supply depended upon rationing, or left him without the relief made necessary by famine. But its principal form was the killing or physical ill-treatment of persons assumed to be associates of the opposing section.

In 1922 the Soviet Union had emerged from a desperate struggle for existence, and, after the merciless annihilation of the rebel sailors at Kronstadt, had made a vital concession to the peasantry. It seemed that extraordinary measures for internal security were no longer urgent, and—again contrary to general impression—there was, in fact, a period of six years in which the Terror was suspended. The Gay-Pay-oo was deprived of the authority to execute persons without trial, and there was a brief interval in which capital punishment was off the statute-book. How real was the relaxation of tension during the epoch of N.E.P., becomes evident if we contrast the treatment of the various Oppositions within the party at this time with the events of 1936-38. Exile was the worst penalty during the former period, death sentences came thick and fast during the later.

It was a turn in foreign politics which brought back the Terror in 1927. Disappointment after disappointment had fallen upon the Soviet Government, in China and in Britain, and the rupture of diplomatic relations by the latter was followed within a few days by the murder of the Soviet envoy in Warsaw by a Russian refugee. A bomb was thrown in Leningrad, and an attempt was made at Minsk on the life of an officer of the Gay-Pay-oo. It seemed as though the long-threatened danger of attack by the Capitalist states was about to be realised, and that traitors at home would prepare the way for them. The powers of the Gay-Pay-oo were strengthened, and on two successive days twenty White Russian prisoners were executed. Among them was Prince Dolgorukov, a man of seventy-eight, once Chairman of the Kadet Party, and a well-known champion of freedom and democracy. There was no pretence that these persons were personally concerned in any plot. The act was typically terroristic: a demonstration intended to strike fear into opponents.

The Gay-Pay-oo had political prisons of its own, including the famous Lubianka at Moscow. It was more than a political police in the ordinary sense. It included a frontier army; it provided guards at markets, railway stations and river ports; it assumed responsibility for the reclamation of the waif children of whom war and famine had left a terrible legacy; it possessed reformatory prisons for the treatment of ordinary non-political crime, the inmates of which are patients rather than prisoners; we even hear of it establishing dancing clubs for the wholesome amusement of youth in the towns. From 1929 it had the new function of organising penal labour on the building of canals and railways and other work carried out by the agency of deported persons. In this capacity it established human, even friendly, relations with its prisoners, and one of the paradoxes of recent Russian history has been the release of many persons, and the decoration of some of them who had done good work under its auspices in the building of the Baltic-White Sea Canal, and of the Far Eastern Railway.

Part of the reputation of successive Russian Governments for cruelty is derived from the rigours of the journey to Siberia, and from the careless, corrupt, or capricious, administration of the prisons. But before, as well as after the Revolution of November, there has been a marked contrast between the good-humoured leniency with which ordinary offences are treated and the harshness towards crime which attacks the State itself, as an entity distinguishable from the community. Under the Tsars political offenders were frequently tried by special Courts created *ad hoc*, and the Emperor often took a personal part in the administration of justice in such cases. Ordinary theft was very lightly regarded; and Maurice Baring tells a typical story of a policeman who was taking a drunken man "to a friend's house, where he can rest." Under the Revolutionary Government the discipline for ordinary criminals aims at curative results. Yet the theft of the property of the State, including the grain in the fields of the collective farm, is punishable with shooting. I think that the notion of crime, as distinct from sin on the one hand, and from wrong to a particular individual on the other, was, and perhaps still is, imperfectly developed. I shall endeavour elsewhere to make it plain that religious ideas survive the formal abandonment of religion. The thief is a sinner who ought to repent; the person injured by the theft may be expected to retaliate upon him: but other members of the community will naturally pity the sinner and help him to win absolution. How cruel could be the retaliation of the persons directly injured by a theft we learn from Gleb Uspensky, the depicter of peasant life and character. "If he kills the man who took his horse, he feels innocent, because the horse was his helper on the land." Rick-burners and fire-raisers were often beaten to death by the peasants, and we hear of a horse-thief roasted over a slow fire by men who lived by the carrying trade.

Similarly, the State retaliates on the person who attacks it. But the ordinary offences which are treated with such sympathetic consideration and such lenient discipline, at Bolshevo and other similar centres, do not seem to be attacks upon the State, however much they may affect the community of which the State is the embodiment. I have heard an instructive story of the Revolutionary period regarding a man who stole the watch of a foreigner. The law provides a penalty of three years' imprisonment for such a theft. But in this case the offender was shot. He was shot for discrediting the U.S.S.R. in the eyes of foreigners.

We get some light upon Russian conceptions of crime and punishment from the popular attitude towards the capital sentence. Capital punishment for ordinary crimes was abolished by the Empress Elizabeth, daughter of Peter the Great (1753), but flogging, sufficient to cause death, continued for some time longer. The latter was stopped by Nicolas I, and from that time up to the Revolution of 1905 a very high regard was shown for human life. This did not stand in the way of the semi-official encouragement of pogroms—but I speak, for the moment, of the official attitude. Judged by the British standard, the official Russian practice in regard to the capital sentence was, in this interval, remarkably lenient. The Revolution of 1905-6 was drastically repressed, and the Field-Courts-Marshal executed numbers which are variously stated at from 600 to 2,000. The Provisional Government of March, 1917, abolished capital punishment even for soldiers on active service; but soon had to reinstitute it. It was again abolished in 1922, but again restored.

There seems to be, in the Russian temperament, a special horror of the legal enforcement, with all its paraphernalia and solemnity, of the capital sentence. This susceptibility coexists with a high degree of indifference to human life, and occasional extensive destruction of it, as in the pogroms. Kerensky shows that he was aware of the existence of this contradiction, when he says that "killing by terror or mass execution is another matter, but it is practically impossible to carry out a judicial death-sentence in Russia."

It may be that pity finds time to come into operation, and reflection fixes the blame upon a third party, the State, when formal justice does its dreadful work. It may be that a deep-rooted and traditional distrust of the State makes Justice seem to be Injustice when it puts on its robes. I recall a sentence which Bernard Shaw has put into the mouth of his Julius Caesar: "This was natural slaying. I feel no horror at it." Evidently there are those to whom the wilder justice, by its very spontaneity, seems the less horrible.

Dostoievsky makes Prince Myshkin say that murder by legal sentence is more terrible than murder by brigands, because in the case of the latter, hope remains till the final blow is struck. This seems another way of saying that the prolonged torment of despair for the sentenced victim is too great to be justified. A great Russian thinker, Vladimir Soloviev, who has analysed from the religious standpoint the case for capital punishment, asks himself which, of two things, is the greater sin. "The fanatical crowd which, under the influence of a mad anger, kills a criminal on the spot, is to be blamed; but deserves indulgence. As for the Society, which kills slowly, coldly, consciously, it has no excuse." As between the murderer and the Society which executes him, he finds for the former, for the latter "lacks all those physiological and psychological conditions and motives which have obscured and concealed from the criminal the essence of his act." With or without reason, the Russian people appears to agree with this judgment: is capable of mass murder: and pities the condemned criminal. It may be that it pities him less when the execution is summary.

There were indications, during the Terror of 1937, that popular sympathy was awakened on behalf of the victims. This, at least, is how I interpret certain official pronouncements and actions. It was thought necessary to emphasise the solidarity of the executioners with the Red Army, and the frontier guards who protect the Socialist Fatherland from external enemies. The beneficent functions of the political police, as builders of canals and railways, were put prominently forward. The twentieth anniversary of the establishment of the Cheka was accompanied by organised ovations, at which the public demanded the continuance of the good work. A poem in the principal Communist Daily romanticised the function by calling it Razvyedka, which means the military reconnaissance of the enemy's forces, and so has associations with the defence of the Fatherland against armed attack:

> "Day and night, we are on guard,
> Day and night, we keep the fight.
> The foe is wise, we are wiser,
> The foe is strong, we are stronger.
> All the peoples of the Soviets will help us
> To burn to cinders the enemy's nest."

❋   ❋   ❋

With the adoption of the first Five-Year-Plan, and its accompaniment of a revolution in agriculture involving changes greater and more radical than those of November, 1917, the U.S.S.R. entered upon a period of renewed struggle, in which the weapon of Terror has seldom returned to its sheath. Periodically we see Stalin himself impressed by the necessity of moderation. In March, 1930, he tells his followers that they are dizzy with success, and orders them to cease compulsory collectivisation and the removal of church bells and closure of churches. In June, 1931, he cries a halt to the persecution of the intellectuals. Later, a new danger appears on the international horizon. To the danger of Japan in the Far East is added that of Nazi Germany in the West, renewing the fear of capitalist, now renamed fascist, attack. Internally the battle of collectivisation seemed to be won, and the food supply seemed at last to be secured. Suddenly an underworld of insecurity opened at the feet of the victorious Party. S. M. Kirov, the Secretary of the Party in Leningrad, was murdered as he sat in his office in the Smolny to announce the Government's decision to abolish rationing and equalise food prices.

S. M. Kirov, a native of north-central Russia, was deep in revolutionary activities from his boyhood upwards, and was one of the earliest members of what afterwards became the Communist League of Youth. An accident brought him into the inner circle of Stalin's Trans-Caucasus friends. Escaping from the police at Tomsk, in 1909, he helped to edit a revolutionary journal at Vladikavkaz, where he made friends with Stalin's crony, Ordzhonikidze. During all the chances and changes of 1918-22 he played a leading part in south-eastern Russia on behalf of the Revolutionary Government, recovered machine-guns and treasure from under the ice of the Volga, and helped to defend Astrakhan from the Whites. When Trotsky desired to concentrate the Red forces against Denikin's threat to Moscow, Kirov at Astrakhan, like Stalin and Voroshilov at Tsaritsyn, resisted the demand. It was probably bad strategy and worse discipline, but it created a special bond of sympathy between Kirov and Stalin. Stationed in Baku, he distinguished himself by his activity in the restoration of the oil wells, which were only less important than the food supply. In December, 1925, when Zinoviev, the political leader of the Leningrad proletariat, was joining his forces with those of the Trotsky opposition, Kirov was sent to the post of difficulty at Peter the Great's capital, and won the workers to the cause of the Government. In the critical year of 1929, when Stalin had launched the first Five-Year-Plan, he had charge of the north-west. He was a man of exceptional courage, energy, and versatility, and discharged each successive task with distinction. Already a member of the Central Committee of the Party, he became in 1930 one of its inner ring, the Politburo.

I have dwelt thus at length upon Kirov's career, because his assassination is a turning-point in Soviet affairs, and because his past goes far to explain the fierceness of the reprisals which followed. In losing him, Stalin lost not only a valuable instrument but a particular friend, one of those political workers of the Caucasus for whom the General Secretary of the Party has a very warm corner in his heart. It was the first murderous attack for sixteen years on a prominent Bolshevik within the limits of the U.S.S.R., and it profoundly shook the confidence of the Government in the efficiency of its police and in the security of the leaders. The discoveries which led to the trials of 1936-38 were its direct consequence: and an atmosphere of increasing suspicion, aggravated by the danger of foreign attack on two sides, from then on pervaded the U.S.S.R.

* * *

The Central Executive Committee at once decreed a special law for the summary punishment of outrages. This forbade appeals against convictions, and required the immediate execution of death-sentences. Sixty-six persons, including one woman, were executed at Leningrad and Moscow after summary trial, thirty-seven others at Kiev and Minsk. All this happened before the actual assassin of Kirov, a Communist named Nikolaev, was brought to trial, and there appears to have been no allegation that the 103 persons executed were guilty of complicity in the murder. The proceedings fall into the category of demonstrative terrorism, differing only from earlier cases of the same character in that the forms of law were observed. The head of the Leningrad section of the Commissariat of Internal Affairs (which had now taken the place of the Gay-Pay-oo) was put on his trial for negligence, and along with other officials of the Commissariat sentenced to imprisonment.

S. M. Kirov had succeeded Zinoviev in the leadership of the Communist Party at Leningrad on Zinoviev's latest fall from favour. It was now stated, with the support of the Moscow and Leningrad centres of the Party, that Zinoviev and his group were morally responsible for the murder. Zinoviev, Kamenev, and a number of other persons who had been associated with the Opposition of 1926, were arrested, and thirteen of them brought to trial. The indictment stated that an underground counter-revolutionary terrorist group of former members of the Zinoviev group had been formed to disorganise the leadership of the Soviet Government, in order to change the present policy to that of the Zinoviev-Trotsky platform; and that it looked for armed assistance from certain foreign States. A consul of a foreign Power was alleged to have paid money to Kirov's murderer, and to have helped to establish communications between the group and Trotsky, at that time in France. Nikolaev had been separately tried and shot, but no further sentences of death were passed at this trial. (January 17, 1935.) Zinoviev, Kamenev and ten others were sentenced to varying terms of imprisonment. The reflections upon the negligence of what I shall continue to call the Gay-Pay-oo caused great activity among the political police, and a large number of persons were dismissed from their posts and exiled or prosecuted on charges of Zinovievism and Trotskyism. This general heresy hunt was directed largely against teaching staffs and students: and many members of the Communist League of Youth were found to be infected with the views which were obnoxious to the Government.

Many hundreds of arrests, mostly of persons of the dispossessed classes, were made in March, 1935, and an epidemic of crime, much of it of a political character, was in existence in the summer. The local head of the Gay-Pay-oo in a district of the Ukraine was killed, and attacks were made on tax-collectors, newspaper reporters, chairmen of collective farms, factory foremen and shock-workers. Death sentences for thefts of public property were numerous. In the course of their activities the political police arrived at fresh evidence implicating more deeply Zinoviev and Kamenev. At the end of June it was already public property that these two were actual organisers of the Kirov murder, and in full sympathy with Trotsky, who was alleged to have advocated terrorist methods against the Communist leaders.

Over a year elapsed between this date and the institution of the murder charge against the old Bolshevik group, including Zinoviev and Kamenev, in August, 1936. Two events happened in this interval. The revolt of the parties of the Right in Spain occurred in July, 1936, with Italy assisting the insurgents from the very start, and Germany doing the same at an early date in the operations. This certainly increased the anxiety of the Soviet Government regarding the European situation. It seemed that the Central European dictators were staging a rehearsal of further plans to be carried out in Czecho-Slovakia or even in Russia itself. The second event was an attempt, in which Bukharin was employed as an intermediary, to secure the withdrawal of Trotsky's opposition. If there had been no revolt in Spain, encouraged by the European Dictators, or if the attempt to conciliate Trotsky had been successful, there would have been no Zinovievite-Trotskyist trials, and no outbreak of the Terror, at this time. But enquiries by the political police, accompanied by the usual pressure upon suspected persons, were proceeding throughout the interval, and eliciting fresh discoveries.

In August, 1936, Zinoviev, Kamenev and fourteen others, some of them prominent figures in the Trotskyist group of 1924-27, were brought to trial for forming, at the end of 1932, under the inspiration of Trotsky, a united centre for terrorist action against the leaders of the Party and the Government: and organising measures (which were successful in the case of Kirov) for the murder of Stalin and others. In the open trial, which took place before the Military Collegium of the Supreme Court of the U.S.S.R., under the special decree for the summary disposal of political outrages which was passed after the murder of Kirov, all the forms of law were observed. All the accused persons confessed. All were sentenced to be shot, and their property to be confiscated. Of this open trial we know everything. Of the previous proceedings before the investigating officers of the Commissariat of Internal Affairs we know only a single fact, because it happens to be mentioned in the formal indictment; but it is an enlightening fact. Zinoviev, *in spite of obdurate equivocation, was compelled by the weight of evidence to confess.* The language is quoted from the official document. Regarding the confessions generally, in this and the other cases which followed, I have made a suggestion when discussing the survivals of Orthodox Christian tendencies in the Bolshevik psychology.

A character in *The Three Cities* by the Yiddish writer, Sholom Asch, says that it is a positive pleasure to a Russian to confess his sins and beg someone's forgiveness, and that he will, if necessary, gratify this desire by inventing a sin for the occasion; because he is afraid of being alone with himself and has a passion for collectivism. Louis Fischer gives another explanation which will be more intelligible to the British mind. He says that the course of the trials had been arranged beforehand between the authorities and the accused, and it was agreed that confession should be rewarded by the remission of the death penalty. It is possible, of course, that different persons had different motives, or different combinations of motives, for those confessions which presented an apparently insoluble enigma to so many of us.

This was the first occasion upon which any of the old Guard of the Bolsheviks, the revolutionary founders of the Soviet State, had been sentenced to death. In the past, the political police have sometimes spared the lives of persons reported to be executed. If the sentences were actually carried out, the case was a novel and striking departure from previous Soviet practice, which reveals itself in its true light if we contrast the comparatively lenient treatment of Trotsky and his associates in 1928-29. I feel no doubt that the Soviet Government was seriously alarmed by the policy of the Central European Dictators, and therefore decided on the ruthless destruction of an opposition at home which might furnish a foothold for foreign attack. The subsequent course of events, first in Spain, where a Government of the Left was overthrown after a struggle of more than two years by a Right supported by German and Italian troops, and in Russia itself, where a sudden military attack in violation of a recent non-aggression agreement was made by the German armies and explained as an anti-Communist crusade, has justified as a measure of general policy the determination to stamp out resistance to the Communist Government. Whether each of the accused persons in each of the proceedings which followed one another thick and fast between the years 1936 and 1938 deserved his fate is a question which I do not propose to investigate in these studies. That some false charges were made, and that some innocent persons were convicted and punished, was officially admitted at a later date. It was indeed impossible that, in so great a mass of criminal information and prosecution, there should have been no failures of justice. The trials were open, the accused persons generally confessed: because those who were not ready to confess were often disposed of without trial. But there was a mystery regarding these confessions, and there was often a long interval between the arrest of the accused and the commencement of the open trial. Of what happened in those long intervals of silence, during which the accused were in the hands of the political police who prepared the prosecution, we know nothing: but must inevitably imagine much. Under similar conditions in India, a confession made to a police officer, unless recorded with certain special precautions by a magistrate, is not admissible in evidence.

The more serious charges included conspiracy against the lives of the Soviet leaders and against the Communist régime, treasonable correspondence with foreign Powers, and industrial sabotage. As to the general likelihood of such offences in a period of revolutionary changes and strong partisan feeling, I think there can be no doubt. But it is equally likely that there was some fabrication. The plain truth is that, when passions of this kind are aroused, there are some who will stick at nothing, and others whose judgments will be dictated by their prejudices. Seventeenth-century England is full of examples; and the Dreyfus case reminds us how near we are, even to-day, to a similar danger in Western Europe. That industrial sabotage by highly placed authorities was not improbable, I am sufficiently convinced by the evidence of Mr. Littlepage, an American mining engineer, who gave an objective account of his experiences in *Soviet Gold*.

Among the old Bolsheviks and men of long revolutionary service who suffered in consequence of these proceedings were M. P. Tomsky, the consistent champion of the freedom of Trade Unions (shot himself to avoid arrest); Karl Radek, a brilliant Polish Jew, at one time the close political friend of Trotsky, and thereafter principal editor of *Izvestia* (sentenced to ten years' imprisonment); Gregory Sokolnikov, who built up the Soviet currency, was Vice-President of the State Planning Committee, Ambassador of the U.S.S.R. in Great Britain and Assistant Commissar of Foreign Affairs (ten years' imprisonment); Y. L. Piatakov, who had been Chairman of the State Bank and Assistant Commissar for Heavy Industry (shot); L. P. Serebriakov, railway chief (shot); N. I. Muralov, the Bolshevik giant, a famous fighter and the henchman of Trotsky in the Civil War (shot); Marshal Tukhachevsky, a military officer of the highest distinction (shot); N. N. Krestinsky, formerly Assistant Commissar of Foreign Affairs (shot); K. G. Rakovsky, once Chairman of the People's

Commissars in the Ukraine and thereafter Soviet Ambassador successively in London and Paris (imprisoned for 20 years); A. I. Rykov, prominent throughout the revolutionary period, always showed Rightist tendencies and definitely joined the Right opposition when Stalin decided on the liquidation of the *kulaks* (shot); Nikolai Bukharin, a brilliant intellectual, once the leading theoretician of Stalin's ruling group and one of the Septemvirate of 1924; gravitated to the right when Stalin made his leftward turn in 1928 (shot).

Many of the principal accused had been close associates of Trotsky, and no concealment was made that it was upon Trotsky himself that the gravamen of the most serious charges rested. But many of the punishments of this period of terror were inflicted in consequence of accidents and failures of industry, agriculture, transport and trade. A tendency to treat these accidents and failures as deliberate can be traced back to that strike of the intelligentsia against the revolution of which I have written elsewhere, and Stalin's attempt to restore public confidence in the directing class will be described in a later chapter.

Besides these accidents and failures, deliberate or not, there were actual or alleged abuses of power, for which members of the directing group were dismissed or drastically punished. It was upon this directing class, consisting largely of members of the Communist Party, and making up, as a whole, that bureaucracy against which Trotsky had directed so much of his invective, that this part of the Terror fell. Some of the victims were no doubt suffering from lassitude, after the exceptional effort of the Plans, for over-work is notoriously common among Russians in positions of responsibility, and some were indifferent and negligent (for these things are even commoner than over-work). Peter the Great took the same way with his instruments. Whenever he returned from absence in the field he found the administration in such a state that it was necessary to begin at once a series of trials and executions. If, in these general cleansings of the administration, some sacrifices are made to appease the popular sense of justice, by *levelling* the group which has enjoyed more than its share of material advantage and consideration, we need feel no surprise. I have little doubt that Trotsky's denunciations of the new directing class received so much attention as to suggest the need of reminding them that they too were mortal. It would not have been the first time that Stalin had taken a hint from the invective of his adversary. The function of leveller is a very popular one in the U.S.S.R. But in all autocracies it has been a part of the ruler's duty to know "whom to advance, and whom to trash for over-topping." Some light is thrown upon this

part of our subject by the proceedings of October 29, 1937. When the
workers in coal-mining and metallurgy were received at the Kremlin,
Stalin toasted the *lesser leaders*, the men whom he described as the
household managers of the nation's business, addressing himself particularly to the furnace men, and to Father Korolov, the supervisor
of the blast-furnace gang, who was present. The newspaper gave a
portrait of Father Korolov, in West European clothes, complete with
white collar and tie, which helps us to realise the status of the group
to whom these "lesser leaders" belong. Such people, he said, had been
regarded in the days of the Tsars as the dogs of capitalism. Now
they were recognised as workers for the interest of the people. He
continued with the significant remark that "leaders come and go,
but the people remain. Only the people is immortal. All the rest is
transient. We must therefore know how to earn and value the confidence of the people. To the health of our household managers," he
cried, "who will not allow anyone to lower the high calling of a Soviet
economic leader."

The Communist Daily, in crossing the "t's" and dotting the "i's"
of this speech, said that it was an open secret that the Plan of 1937
for heavy industry was not being fulfilled and that there had been
a slowing down during recent months. It called upon what we should
describe as the non-commissioned element in the industrial army,
which is in close association with the masses, to listen to their voices
and carry the work to higher standards with their co-operation. It
went on to blame the "Trotskyist-Bukharinist fascists"—such was then
the approved combination of depreciatory epithets—for the mischief
they had done to industry, and bade the household managers point
the lesson. All this, as I interpret it, was in part a justification of the
blows which had been struck at industrial leaders, in part a reassurance
to those who had escaped from the purge, and also a warning to them
not to hold their heads too high, but to keep in close touch with the
mass of workers. *Closer to the masses*—this was the lesson which
was now being impressed alike upon the Party and upon the leaders
of the Trade Unions and of industry.

At the beginning of 1938 the Central Committee of the Communist
Party discovered that innocent members of the rank and file had suffered unjustly, and ordered the rapid disposal of their appeals and
their early reinstatement. The natural result of wholesale prosecution
and punishments is a crop of false charges, and the Press has contained evidence of the activities of the informer. But the rank and
file had been little touched, and their sympathy with the sufferers had

on the whole been small. The Soviet Government did not lose the support of the masses by the drastic proceedings of 1936-38, for the masses believed that the punishments had been deserved: as—in general—they probably were.

※　　※　　※

It is a relief to be able to turn from the discipline of terror to the discipline of leadership: a sphere in which the achievement of the Soviet Government has been new and great. The leadership comes from what historical accident has named the "Party": but the Webbs * have taught us to describe it as a *vocation of leadership*. It serves to induct a politically uneducated people into an understanding of public duties, and now that the function has been pointed out by an appropriate definition, it is natural to ask oneself whether any democracy can be brought rapidly into existence without it. It was planned as a narrow circle of disciplined and chosen spirits working in secret for the overthrow of the Tsarist State. But it has become something entirely different. By 1942 it existed as a public association of two millions of men and women exercising the vocation of leadership in a population which, at the outbreak of war in June, 1941, fell not far short of 200 millions. It may be that it is in process of undergoing a further metamorphosis at which we can only guess.

Let me begin by a statement of the obvious. There have been and are some very bad Communists. The records of the village monographists abound with such. It is also true that there have been some very bad Popes and some very bad Cardinals. No useful purpose would be served by multiplying particulars about individuals.

Evidently the Party is not a communion of saints, nor for the purposes for which it was founded did it need to be such. P. N. Tkachev, who succeeded Bakunin as the head of the Revolutionary organisation, agreed with his predecessor in his schemes of insurrection, but differed from him in his desire to preserve instead of abolishing the State. He wrote a letter to Friedrich Engels in which he advocated the creation of a strong revolutionary organisation with a rigid discipline. It was an idea which he inherited from Bakunin, and it was the germ of Lenin's conception of the Party. In his European exile Lenin digested his experiences with the workers of St. Petersburg, and published the famous pamphlet *What is to be Done?* In this he formulated the conclusion that only a strong and disciplined organisation can prevent the danger of premature outbreaks, before the fer-

* Beatrice and Sidney Webb, founders of the Fabian Society, and authors of "Soviet Communism: A New Civilisation."

ment in the working class is ripe for them. It is because of the need for restraint and for secrecy that democratic methods are inapplicable to such an organisation. This was not a denial of democracy, but the exclusion of democracy from a particular sphere, as a fighting sea-captain would exclude it from the control of a battleship. The paradox of the Party's evolution is that the organisation planned to carry through a revolution has survived into the post-revolutionary period, and has taken a form in which it must guide and instruct the mass and furnish a reservoir of energy and good-will from which the leaders of all grades are to be drawn.

Those who made the Party seem to have had before their minds certain faults of human nature, or of Russian human nature, and to have determined to change them. One of Lenin's favourite authors, Chernishevsky, imagined a regicide-in-training, who set himself to harden his body and his spirit by abstaining from indulgence and by sleeping upon iron nails. The Russian is a loose talker. The Communist must keep the Party secrets. The Russian is a natural anarchist who respects no rules. The Communist must observe a rigorous discipline, must be ready to go anywhere, and to do anything. The Russian is hesitant and tolerant and wavering and introspective; looks before and after and pines for what is not; doubts all things, easily tires, easily despairs; has a poorly developed instinct of self-preservation and readily resorts to suicide. The Communist must be and do none of these things. He must have faith, active faith, and the buoyant optimism which faith gives; must have his eyes firmly fixed upon the external realities about him, must have no sympathy with, or mercy for, those who hold heretical views, must spare neither himself nor others, must set an example of untiring work; must protect health and life as instruments of achievement on behalf of the Party.

There must be no sentiment; no introspection; no melancholy nor subjectivism: above all, none of those qualities of the Russian lie-abed, which have passed into·proverb in the name of Oblomov, the sluggard hero of a famous tale. It is a setting back of the current, a determination to turn the impossible into the possible. Pope Hildebrand attempted something like it, when he demanded celibacy in all priests, and required those of them who had wives to abandon them.

Formerly the qualifications required for entry to the Party varied according as the candidate belonged to the urban workers, the peasantry, or the *intelligentsia*. From 1939, when the Party made changes aiming generally at increased democracy, security against arbitrary procedure, and elimination of Party interference in industry, the qualifications were made uniform: a gain to the technicians. The candidate must still accept the Party's programme (but need not, it seems, be a profound student of principle); must be a producer, free from the mentality of property; must not exploit the labour of another for profit; must be engaged in some civic activity, and must be politically active too; and must be a militant atheist, for religion is one of the unpardonable sins for the Party man.

Above all things, the Communist must have that stirring activity of temperament which brings a man or woman to the fore among their fellows: something which we vulgarly denominate "push." Self-confidence, self-assertion, ambition, are all facets of this quality, without which the latent gifts remain undiscovered and unutilised. The first postulate of recognition by others is recognition by oneself. There must be a conviction of capacity to shoulder a task, and a readiness to face the trouble and risk of undertaking it; and this conviction and this readiness are the conditions of acceptance by the mass of mankind. The party man and the party woman are, in a sense, self-recommended to their fellows. They are ready for a duty for which most people are not ready: and in this sense they constitute a sort of natural elite. They may disappoint expectation hereafter, and in that event they may be purged at a later stage but, anyhow, they have won their start in the life of ambition.

This explanation is not the mere platitude which it may at first appear to be. I have sought to emphasise the distinction between two disciplines, the discipline of terror and the discipline of leadership, and to suggest that the one comes from without while the other comes from within. The men and women who find themselves enlisted in the vocation of leadership, as it expresses itself in the so-called Party, are recruited from the mass of the people in virtue of a specific quality, which does not separate them from their fellows, and distinguishes them solely by their willingness to accept an additional and heavier task. No doubt, they may tend to become separated hereafter in proportion as the achievement of official ambition removes them into an official class: but that is merely to say that no method is available for the sublimation of human material into something which is superior to human motives. Mrs. Seema Rynan Allan, in *Comrades and Citizens*, has given us a good reason why people may safely trust a Communist more than they trust an ordinary man. It is an answer given by a non-Communist worker, when asked why he voted for Communists to represent him on the Trade Union Committee. "When a

Communist does not do what he undertakes to do, he has to answer for it." This is so, and the Courts and all the authorities demand a higher standard from the man or woman who has joined the Party.

Stalin himself has been a severe critic of the Party. During the period which followed upon the murder of S. M. Kirov in December, 1934, admission to its ranks was temporarily closed. At the elections which followed upon the introduction of the new Constitution in 1936 emphasis was laid upon the alliance between Party and non-Party, with the evident intention of dimming the line of distinction between the two. During the prosecutions, which were numerous at that time, the members of the Party received a reminder that they had been holding their heads too high, and themselves too much aloof from the mass of the workers; and at the end of October, 1938, Stalin was again lashing the leaders of the Party, as well as the heads of the official departments, with accusations of negligence, corruption, and incompetence, and holding them responsible for insufficient food and defective industry.

That there exists a popular notion of Party privilege is plain enough from current stories of disgusted comments proceeding from *voces populi*, on fur coats and other similar luxuries. There certainly is a possibility of access to certain exceptional comforts and amenities—better apartments, even motor-cars—obtained not by means of money, but rather in the form of what the French call *frais de représentation* in consideration of the special needs of the recipient's work, and, of course, there are openings for the gratification of the ambition of the Communist man or woman: but there is access to these openings for the non-Communist also, if he or she has the energy and capacity to use them, and no obstacles are interposed by the lack of means or social influence to advancement of these kinds. There is a career opened to the talents in the Western countries too, but money paves the way to it; in the U.S.S.R. membership of the so-called Party—attainable by certain special sacrifices and efforts by those in whom nature has implanted a turn for public work—gives the opportunity. In so far as success is dependent upon the conditions of early life and the position of parents, its conditions are more rigidly determined in the West than in the U.S.S.R.

Privilege is dependent not so much upon membership of the Party as upon the degree of success which a man or woman is able to attain in consequence of that membership. Stalin expressed this graphically in a description which he gave of the stratification of the Party. He put it in military language. There were—out of the 2 million or more members—from 3,000 to 4,000 who constituted the General Staff; from 30,000 to 40,000 whose functions were parallel to those of an Officer Corps; and from 100,000 to 150,000 comparable to non-commissioned officers. The rest form the rank and file of the *corps d'élite*. The non-Party mass pass into the ranks of this Army, without let or hindrance, subject to their willingness and capacity for public work, and they earn promotion—or suffer demotion—by the sort of show which they are able to make thereafter.

What are the virtues which are rewarded by success? I have already given some hint of their nature. Along with activity, discipline is the essential need. For it was discipline—a quite un-Russian virtue—by which the Bolsheviks broke and scattered the other parties in the State, as a Roman Legion broke and scattered Gauls or Egyptians. The Social Revolutionaries, a party with an inheritance of ideas systematised by the Populists of the past, and adjusted to later needs by Victor Chernov, a thinker of constructive ability, were the controlling force in the State after the Revolution of March. They commanded large majorities among the soldiers and among the peasants, they dictated the first agrarian legislation of the November Government, they had a majority in the Constituent Assembly of January, 1918, they formed the anti-Bolshevik Government of Samara, which was unique among counter-revolutionary organisations in propounding an agrarian policy acceptable to the peasants, they contributed a large element to the Omsk Government, before Admiral Kolchak established his own dictatorship there in November, 1918. By all the rules—excepting one —it was they who should have been the successors of the Tsars. But they lacked the unity and the discipline which made the Bolsheviks a stone in the sling of Lenin: and they degenerated, as a political force, into vacillation and ineptitude.

Another group which illustrates, by contrast, the reason of the success of the Communist Party, is that of the Anarchists. To the American and the Briton the name evokes the image of the fanatic with the dagger and the torch. Actually, the Anarchists are advocates of an extreme decentralisation, of a peaceful federation of self-governing villages, and economic associations, such as Mahatma Gandhi appears to contemplate for India. They started in Russia with a great natural advantage, the widespread dislike of the organised coercive State, which was a marked characteristic of the Russian people, and their outlook upon the State differed from that of Marx only in contemplating an earlier and more summary destruction of it. The great successes of Co-operation among the peasantry showed the general readiness to accept economic, rather that political, bonds of association. Prince Kropotkin, one of the leading thinkers of Anarchism, spoke feelingly of the openings which the revolution had seemed to offer to the anarchists. The Co-operatives, he said, would have bridged the gap between the peasants and the workers, and, together with the Syndicates, would have filled the place of the coercive institutions of the Police-State. The energies of the people, released by revolution, instead of being imprisoned by a centralised system of government, would have worked wonders. Anarchism found a militant champion in Nestor Makhno, who for a short interval dictated terms to the Communist Government in Southern Russia. The *Nabat*, a general Anarchist organisation of the South, seemed, in the summer of 1920, to have a chance of carrying out the unification of separate Anarchist factions at which it aimed. Far-Eastern Siberia was for a time controlled by anarchists, and a well-known anarchist was its railway chief. All was in vain, and the theorists of libertarianism, lacking unity among themselves, and deficient in the very principle of discipline, were dispersed and swept away by the solid phalanx which Lenin had created. After the overthrow of the Kronstadt rebellion of 1921, in which anarchist influences had participated, anarchist book-stores and printing-offices were closed and leading anarchists imprisoned, and all vestiges of organised combination of the anarchist groups were destroyed. Discipline had triumphed, and had brought back the organised State, in despite of the Marxian principle that the organised State must wither away. True, it was not—in theory—the organised State, but a transitional Dictatorship of the Proletariat, destined to disappear in the Classless Society. But time has not brought any nearer the disappearance, and has immensely consolidated the structure. In this organised State, the Communist Party is the nucleus of Power.

＊　　＊　　＊

The military metaphor employed by Stalin to describe the differentiation of the functions of the various groups in the Party inevitably suggests a question whether the discipline is literally that of an Army bound to obedience to its Commander. In 1934 the Party Congress discussed the basis of democratic centralism, which is the technical expression for the freedom (or limitation) of discussion within the Party. The conclusion was that freedom of discussion is an inalienable right: but may lead to schism unless it is limited to cases in which either several local parties think discussion necessary, or there is not in the Central Committee an evidently strong majority for the proposal, or the Central Committee thinks discussion necessary. After the tremendous winnowing to which the Party was subjected in 1937, and the wholesale removal first of the offenders, or supposed offenders, and then of those who had been too reckless in their accusations, we hear Stalin's trumpet-call for vigilance against the secular enemy, and for freedom of criticism as a means of ensuring supervision from below over erring leaders: followed by a decision of the Central Committee that judicious leadership must guide freedom of discussion.

It is a fair inference that the critic must read warily.

Yet the intention of Stalin seems plain enough. He wanted the rank and file to elect freely all party organs by secret ballot, and to speak their minds. Up to the spring of 1937, the voting had been by show of hands, there was a convention of unanimity, and after the expulsion of Trotsky and others ten years earlier, there was no instance in the Party Congress of even a minority vote against an official proposal. In March, 1938, we find the Central Committee insisting on the principles of the election of Party functionaries, not by list, which was a way of slurring over differences of opinion, but by separate voting for individual candidates: and of the election of delegates by secret ballot. The forms of democracy "within the Party" were evidently to be observed. In the words of the Leader, who declared that "ordinary people are found at times to be closer to the truth than some exalted institutions," Bolshevism was to draw its strength from the humble earth "like Antaeus when he wrestled with Hercules."

I suspect an unconscious reminiscence of an Orthodox religious conception. Truth resides in the congregation—not in a majority of it, but in its aggregate whole. To square this perfectly with the modern parliamentary notion which postulates a determining voice for the majority, after due consideration of the views of the minority, is a hard task.

That Orthodox conception of the brotherhood has played a great rôle in the cementing of Party bonds. It is responsible for some of the agony which the victims of the trials for treason and sabotage have shown at parting from their comrades. The last plea of Nikolai Bukharin on March 12, 1938, is eloquent of this sentiment. "When you asked yourself: if you must die, what are you dying for? There was nothing to die for, if one was to die unrepentant. . . . And when you asked yourself: suppose you do not die. . . . Again, what for? . . . *isolated from everything that constitutes the essence of life. . . .*" A character in Kirshon's play *Bread* puts the same thought in a different form. "I cannot step out of the ranks. I dare not leave. . . . *I must* have someone to give me orders. I must have another shoulder next to* mine." Doubtless it is the coarser motive which appeals to some: the fear of being removed from the Bolshevik patriciate to fall into the Soviet plebs.

Now, more than ever, all things are in flux, and he would be a bold man who would prophesy the direction in which the Party may develop. One thing seems certain: that the Russian people need, and will long need, a discipline which only its own best human material can supply, to replace (or must I say, supplement?) the harsher discipline which seems to be the alternative. In another chapter I shall discuss the reality, or the possibility, of actual democratic self-government: that third course which Americans and Britons, with their peculiarly fortunate experience of peaceful development and insulation, are prone to envisage as the political panacea for others as well as for themselves. In the meanwhile I suggest that the "Party" is most truly conceived as a Priesthood—a Priesthood of a Religion which is of this world, not of the next.

Chapter XVI

THE OPPOSITIONS WITHIN THE PARTY. THE DEATH OF LENIN. RIGHT AND LEFT OPPOSITION. THE THIRD INTERNATIONAL. TROTSKY'S ARGUMENTS

"No wonder my military work created so many enemies for me. I elbowed a way. I trod on their toes. . . ."

TROTSKY, *My Life.*

"With the exception of one intoxicated person, this meeting declares the medical officer of the Baths, Dr. Thomas Stockmann, to be an enemy of the people," All (yelling after the Doctor and his family as they go): "Enemy of the people! Enemy of the people!"

IBSEN, *An Enemy of the People.*

In his history of Literature in Revolution, Trotsky quotes with appreciation Boris Pilnyak's antithesis between the peasant and the spirit of the November Revolution.

"Peasant life is known—it is to eat in order to work, to work in order to eat, and, besides that, to be born, to bear and to die. Our Revolution is a rebellion in the name of the conscious, rational, purposeful and dynamic principle of life, against the elemental, senseless, biologic automatism of life: that is, against the peasant roots of our old Russian history, against its aimlessness, its non-teleological character, against the body and idiotic philosophy of Tolstoi's Karataev, in *War and Peace.* It will take decades to burn out Karataev's philosophy, but the process has begun."

Trotsky, who emphasised the necessity of a Plan for the economic life of Russia, was the champion of conscious design for life in general; and the simple, elemental, unconscious, unplanned existence of the peasants, living like a flock of sheep, following they know not what and know not whither, was an offence against the clarity, the lucidity, the consistency, which, for him, were the redeemers of human action. The peasant, and, along with the peasant, old Russia in general, obeyed the need of the moment, gave no thought to the morrow, trod the path in unconsciousness of any aim, followed its nose, we might say. Conscious purpose was something new, and, as Trotsky saw it, it came from the cities and the factories.

The place which was filled in the social system of the West by the middle class was filled, in Trotsky's view, by a petty *bourgeoisie*, the peasantry, which in its property-mentality resembled the middle-class, but lacked the political qualities of that class. The peasantry was capable of making a revolution, in order to satisfy its desire for the land, but capable of it only with the help and leadership of the proletariat of the towns, and, having made it, was incapable, owing to its attachment to its landed rights, of going on to the building of Socialism. The proletariat, the wage-earning workers of the town, would not only lead the Russian peasantry in the making of the revolution, but would find themselves in a dominant position in the new social and economic order, and would necessarily proceed to socialistic measures. But since the peasantry will be an uncertain and unwilling ally in the building of Socialism, the propertyless workers of the towns can only hope as it were to hold the fort, till the proletariats of the West join them in the completion of their task. The building of Socialism means a high degree of division of labour between the peoples of many countries: and the Permanent (or, as we should probably prefer to say, the Continuous) Revolution has for its postulate the achievement, at not too remote a date, of the World-Revolution, bringing all the proletariats into alliance and common action.

The November Revolution, as actually achieved, gave effect, up to a certain point, to Trotsky's theory. That is to say, it was carried out by the peasantry, who gave to the proletariat an opportunity to become installed in power. But the concessions made to the peasantry in the early land legislation, and afterwards in the New Economic Policy, show that this power was conditional only, and far from being absolute. So far, it was plain that the peasantry was not a reliable ally for the building of a Socialistic system. It was left for the future to disclose whether it could be converted into such an ally, or whether, for lack of such an ally, King Proletariat would have to await the establishment of a similar revolutionary régime in the countries of the West.

When, in 1927, Trotsky wrote *The True Position in Russia*, he logically conceded that the mechanisation of agriculture and the collectivisation of the peasantry would convert the latter into an instrument, by the aid of which the tasks of Socialist building could be performed. But he did not draw the conclusion, apparently implicit in this argument, that a World-Revolution was not essential to the establishment of Socialism in Russia. He did, in fact, retain the conviction that the attitude of the peasantry would not be such as to dispense with revolution elsewhere: and he continued to urge the necessity, as a *sine qua non*, of encouraging and supporting the World-Revolution. He retained this conviction because he believed that the Capitalist West was too strong for a Socialistic Russia, and would crush it by economic, if not by military, power.

The attitude to the peasantry was fundamental to the policies which Trotsky urged, in the long controversy which led to his disgrace and exile. For one who saw the peasantry as he saw it, the international alliance, the international division of labour, and the revolutions which alone could make them possible, were indispensable conditions of the achievement of Socialism.

Trotsky's opposition was very far from being the only one within the Party. Russia, where the gift of formulating general principle is a common one, exhibits when left to itself a particularly marked tendency to divisions of opinion. It was one of the things which Lenin fought when he established a Party on the basis of strict discipline. But the tree continued to put forth rebellious branches. On the eve of the November Revolution, and almost in the moment of battle, Zinoviev and Kamenev opposed the policy of insurrection, first won and then lost the majority vote, and, having lost, carried their protest into the non-Party newspapers. This was a divagation to the Right, again expressed, after November, by the opposition to the muzzling of the newspapers and the demand for a coalition of all Socialist parties. The discussion on the German Peace produced even more acute differences in the opposite direction, since the Left favoured a revolutionary war, in the confidence that military discipline and spirit could be restored and dissensions created in the ranks of the enemy by an appeal to proletarian enthusiasm. Bukharin, at that time a partisan of the ultra-leftist tendencies, joined with Radek, V. M. Smirnov and others, to set up an opposition journal, *The Communist*, which for months resisted the predominant influence of Lenin. Trotsky, who at first occupied an intermediate position, yielded to Lenin's arguments, and acquiesced in the temporarily disastrous peace—which to Lenin was no disaster, because he was still confident of the imminence of World-Revolution.

The New Economic Policy seemed a catastrophic surrender to the principles of Capitalism, and divided the Party fundamentally. Only the authority of Lenin prevented this division from finding expression in open and public opposition, and the Left's acceptance of the

N.E.P. compromise was always a grudging one, which sought every opportunity for struggling back in the direction of War Communism, and renewing the attack upon private trade and private profit. Whatever Lenin's view of the New Economic Policy may have been—and to me it seems clear that he regarded it as a temporary retreat, necessitated by the unexpected postponement of the World-Revolution—it was impossible that Trotsky should for long reconcile himself to such a compromise. It was a mixture of the individualistic with the socialistic economy, a combination of a free agriculture with an industry of which the citadels were held by the State. It was therefore incompatible with comprehensive planning, and Trotsky was from the outset an advocate of planning. He was not the originator of the idea, but it was his insistence that gave life to it. In 1923 he introduced a plan for the metallurgical industry, and in 1925 outlined a Five-Year-Plan upon a national scale, upon which an abortive draft for the period 1926-31 was actually prepared.

With Lenin the Revolution lost the dominating personality whom all tended instinctively to obey. When his influence was withdrawn the fissiparous tendency began to assert itself with more insistence. The New Economic Policy had involved a compromise in international politics as well as in internal affairs, and carried with it a species of truce between the rival worlds of Capitalism and the Revolution: a truce marked by the Soviet Government's participation in the Geneva Conference of 1922, and the agreement at Rapallo for co-operation with the Weimar Republic. The reduction of the Soviet Government's armed forces after the Civil War involved agreements with neighbouring States for mutual abstention from armed aggression. In the Europe of 1923, when the Curzon ultimatum threatened danger from the direction of Britain, there were reasons for desiring the firm establishment of that régime in Germany which had entered into friendly relations with the Soviet Government. The Germany of the Weimar Republic, humiliated by the Treaty of Versailles and by the policies which succeeded to it, seemed to the statesmen of the Soviet Union a fellow-sufferer in a world of menacing imperialism, and a natural friend, towards whom they were drawn by the necessities of their own position. These considerations clashed with others which sought the extension of the Revolution into a new sphere. When the French occupied the Ruhr in January, 1923, and the German mark fell to a figure which swept away all savings and disturbed all economic relations, Left Social Democrats and Communists formed a Cabinet in Saxony, and events appeared to point to an impending Communist revolution in Germany. There was much popular excitement in the U.S.S.R., and sympathy with the Communists in Germany ran high. It seemed as though a new Soviet Socialist Republic was about to be added to the Union. The ruling triumvirate—Stalin, Zinoviev and Kamenev—had to decide between Soviet support of the revolution and Soviet support of the existing Government. Karl Radek was sent to Germany, and he, or the Government which he represented, decided that the revolutionary movement in Germany must be discouraged: the German Communists received no countenance from the U.S.S.R.

This momentous decision was the ground of one of Trotsky's bitterest and most persistent attacks upon the policy of the Third International after the withdrawal of Lenin's influence. It was typical of the policies to which every normal Government is led by the actual pressure of international relations, and the criticism was typical of the uncompromising idealist. We do not find that Trotsky, in office, was in any way uncompromising. He told John Reed in 1920 that the Soviet Union could live in peace with *bourgeois* governments, and could even work with them, within broad limits. On September 30, 1923, he said that war would harm the German revolution, and that only that revolution which succeeds by its own strength is capable of life. Out of office, he became more and more convinced that the desertion of the German revolution in 1923 was a fatal error. But the dialectic of the situation, as a Marxian might have put it, had moved from the point at which it was a duty to seize every revolutionary opportunity, to another point at which it was desirable to support every political friend in a friendless world. Trotsky saw the situation as it had been: and perhaps Stalin saw the situation as it was. Lenin was too ill to have a voice in the decision.*

Ostracised by Europe—excepting Germany—and America, the Soviet Union naturally looked to Asia to redress the balance: to Asia, where she saw, in the dependent relations of the peoples to the Great

---

* The action, or inaction, in Germany, which is the subject of Trotsky's attacks, was technically that of the Third International rather than that of the Government of the U.S.S.R. In form, the Third International was the body to which the Communist Parties of all the world were affiliated, and from which the Communist Party of the U.S.S.R. took its instructions. In form, the Communist Party of the U.S.S.R. was only a guiding and inspiring element. In fact, the Party, or the heads of the Party hierarchy, were masters both of the Third International and of the Government of the U.S.S.R. When Trotsky attacked the Third International, he made no concealment that he was attacking the leadership of the Communist Party of the U.S.S.R. in international relations, and in particular that of its Secretary General, Stalin. The Third International was dissolved in 1943.

Powers, a reflection of her own recent relation to the class dispossessed by the Revolution. A Congress of Peoples of the East had been organised at Baku in September, 1920, for a holy war against British Imperialism. The Asiatic States were assured of the abandonment by Russia of all unequal privileges secured against them by the Government of the Tsars. Some of them seemed naturally linked to the Soviet Union by a common impulse of social revolution. She seemed to be at once a fellow-sufferer and a champion. This early feeling of sympathy gave place to disappointment, in proportion as the need of normal relations with the Great Powers ousted the revolutionary impulse to destroy their hold upon colonial and quasi-colonial territories. There was, in fact, a conflict between two tendencies in leading circles in the Soviet Union: the idealistic and the diplomatic. The second became increasingly dominant, until the first became little more than a concession to the sentiment of the extreme Left.

The failure of the Powers to return Shantung to China at the end of the war disillusioned the Chinese with Western political ethics, and made the way smooth for Soviet diplomatic successes. "Borodin's name is Lafayette," said Dr. Sun Yat-sen, describing the Soviet emissary to the Canton Government. The two were agreed on a policy of nationalism and anti-imperialism for China, which put revolution of the Russian type in the background as essentially premature.

In the winter of 1926-27, the Southern Chinese army, supplied with Russian officers and material, and obviously actuated by anti-foreign feeling, was advancing northwards to the Yangtsekiang, which was reached without serious opposition. The Western Powers had naturally taken alarm at the threat to the international settlement at Shanghai, and recognised the anti-imperalist character of the movement. General Chiang Kai-shek propitiated the Powers by wholesale executions of Communists and their sympathisers. It was plain now, if indeed it had ever been doubtful, that he was no friend to revolution, but a champion of Chinese nationalism. Stalin, who had desired a combination between workers and peasants and bourgeoisie to conduct a nationalist movement in China, found that the combination was shattered.

Borodin left China in July, 1927. The Communist remains of the Southern army were cut to pieces at Canton in December. The collapse of the policy of the Third International was followed by a marked anti-Russian reaction, in which the War-Lords at Peking and Shanghai vied in hostile demonstrations against the U.S.S.R. A new Chinese Government at Nankin severed diplomatic relations.

The reaction in China was encouraged by events in Great Britain. The first Labour Government in Britain recognised the Soviet Union in February, 1924, on condition of mutual abstention from interference in internal affairs. Negotiations for the settlement of debts followed, and it was agreed that the settlement should pave the way for a loan: an arrangement greatly disliked by the Conservative Opposition. The defeat of the Government, on the issue of the withdrawal of proceedings against a Communist charged with incitement to mutiny, was followed by a general election. During the campaign, the Press published a letter purporting to convey the instructions of the Third International, through its Chairman Zinoviev, to the Communist Party of Great Britain, regarding its tactics in the election. The document added that *work should be done in the British Army,* with a view to paralysing military preparations. There is internal evidence that this document was not an accurate copy of instructions given by the Third International, but it produced a great effect in Britain, where the Conservative Party was returned to power with a considerable majority. The policy of the new Government, culminating in the diplomatic rupture of May, 1927, was not friendly to the U.S.S.R.

In the meanwhile an understanding had been established between organised Labour in Soviet Russia and Great Britain. It had been found that the disunion between Communist and Social Democratic elements in the European Trade Unions made more difficult the maintenance of Trade Union standards in Great Britain, and it was decided to create a joint organisation. In April, 1925, the General Council of the British Trade Unions Congress ratified an agreement with the all-Russian Council of Trade Unions (not with the Communist International of Trade Unions, known as the Profintern) for the establishment of an Anglo-Russian Trade Unions Committee. The programme was for joint action against the encroachments of capital, against the outbreak of war, and for unification of the international labour movement: and there was a condition of mutual non-interference, which the Trade Unions Congress General Council afterwards held to have been violated by the Russians. British Trade Unions representatives in the Amsterdam International made a practice of espousing the Soviet cause. Soviet Labour showed sympathy with British Labour in its troubles, and offered pecuniary support in the General Strike of May, 1926, which the British Trades Unions' General Council declined to accept. But the miners, who continued their strike after the collapse of the General Strike, received the contribution of the all-Russian Central Council of Trade Unions to their strike fund. The British Government protested against the transmission of the money, but the Soviet Government declined to interfere. It has been suggested that the British protest would at that time have taken a more vigorous form but for the wish to exercise a restraining influence upon Soviet policy in China, where the revolutionary movement had not yet completely collapsed, and British interests continued to be threatened.

The Anglo-Russian Trade Unions Committee broke up because the Russians interfered in the strikes of 1926, abused the General Council for deserting the miners, and appealed to the British Trade Unions over its head. The British Government, having awaited the moment when the British position in China appeared no longer to be in peril, raided the Soviet Trade Delegation in London, and severed diplomatic, without severing commercial, relations with the U.S.S.R.

We know from a speech Stalin made in July, 1926, what he had expected from the understanding between the British and Russian Trade Unions. He wished for such an international organisation of the working class as would prevent, or embarrass, foreign intervention in the U.S.S.R. It is the same policy which, later on, took the form of the advocacy of the United Front between all sections of the Left, whether Communist or non-Communist. Both sides of the policy, the political and the industrial, broke down: and Russian aims received as serious a rebuff in Great Britain as in China. The Trotskyist opposition was not less critical of the alliance with the British Trade Unions than of that with Chiang Kai-shek and the Kuomintang.

These were not the only points at which Trotsky attacked the policy of the Third International. In May, 1926, Marshal Pilsudski, leader of the Polish armies and inspirer of Polish policies in 1920, who was, or perhaps I should rather say, had been, a Socialist, had become the virtual dictator of Poland. He drew his strength from elements of the population very different from those dominant in the U.S.S.R.: but the leader of the Communist Party in Poland declared him to be a champion of the town-workers and the peasantry, and called on the Communist Party to support him. This was done under the guidance of the Third International at Moscow, whose policy here furnished a close parallel to the case of the Kuomintang in China. The hollowness of the understanding between Soviet Russia and Pilsudskian Poland revealed itself in June, 1927, when the Soviet envoy to Warsaw was assassinated by a member of an anti-Bolshevik Society operating in Poland. The Soviet Government had already protested against the

toleration of anti-Soviet conspiracy. The Soviet Press now charged
the Polish Government with responsibility for the murder, and the
pending negotiations for a non-aggression pact between the two countries broke down.

This murder happened within a fortnight of the rupture with Great
Britain. It produced in the U.S.S.R. an impression of encirclement,
and intensified the fear of impending attack, for which the memories
of intervention between 1918 and 1920 gave a plausible basis. This
was the time when the proceedings of the Trotskyist opposition were
beginning to culminate in an open appeal to public feeling. The
danger of war was used, as it had been for some time past, to arouse
odium against supposed enemies of the Soviet Fatherland, and doubtless played a part in their expulsion from the Party, and commitment
into the hands of the Gay-Pay-oo.

I repeat that Trotsky had been substantially right in his forecast of
the course of the Revolution in Russia. It had gone straight to a dictatorship of the proletariat, supported by the peasants, but insecurely
supported by them. The remainder of his conception of the Permanent, or continuous, Revolution was yet to be fulfilled. He burned for
its fulfilment and chafed over every lost opportunity. It is this which
explains the bitterness of his criticism about Germany, about China,
about the British Trade Unions, and about Poland. The other threads
which ran through the web of his thought were: first, that the U.S.S.R.
must be industrialised, and industrialised with speed, in order to win
the support of the wavering peasantry with a supply of the goods
which were the price of its allegiance, and to strengthen the revolution
against attack, and secondly, that the economic activities of the revolutionary State must be co-ordinated by an authoritative Plan. There
was, I think, yet a third leading thought: that he, Trotsky, was the
hero of the masses, both party and non-party, and that to increase the
power of the masses was to secure to himself the means of carrying
the measures he saw to be necessary. I do not think that he was actuated by any Napoleonic ambitions, except in the sense that every
man who knows his own mind, and desires to have his own way, is so
actuated; but personal pride, leading to impatience of opposition, and
an unwillingness—in spite of all his brilliant pamphleteering—to explain himself in plain language to the plain man, were always among
the clues to his actions. Louis Fischer says that he "diagnosed, but
could not prescribe." In fertility of invention he was unsurpassed:
it is doubtful that his political judgment was of equal quality. He
was conscious of having no gift for political intrigue, or he despised

the arts which some employ for the attainment of their aims. Confident of great achievements and great powers, and of the popular appreciation of both, he stood haughtily upon his record. His rival pursued a different course, built up an organisation, used the mistakes of his adversary, and bided his time. He was helped by the spirit of caution, or timidity, or perhaps of weariness of adventure, characteristic of N.E.P., which made many unwilling to follow the brilliant, but possibly erratic, guidance of a genius too clever to be quite understood. I cannot, myself, after close study of Trotsky's recorded opinions, detect with certainty any ideological difference between the two men; but Stalin was an opportunist, where Trotsky was a theoretician, and Trotsky was earlier convinced of the paramount necessity of Planning and of rapid industrialisation, while Stalin stood—ultimately—for the conversion of the outside world to Socialism by the example of a successful Socialist State.

Along with the economic question, the issue of democracy within the Party, upon which many old Bolsheviks were in agreement with Trotsky, was also under debate. He addressed a complaint to the Central Committee of the Party (October 8, 1923), that party functionaries were being appointed from above—that a party bureaucracy was being created—instead of being elected from below, to an extent far greater than in the "fiercest moment" of War-Communism, when the dictatorship required special safeguards. He protested against the "18,000 revolutionary officials, in many of whom the habits of a superior caste are beginning to ossify." The controversy, deserting the ground of principles, at once reached personalities, and Trotsky was charged with personal ambition and pride. A compromise on a "new course" did not satisfy the Opposition: Trotsky appealed, or seemed to appeal, to youth against age for support to his contentions, and a conference of Party officials declared that the Opposition had given the word for the destruction of the Party staff. The question was never discussed on its merits, and the "Lenin push," which admitted to the Party nearly 200,000 workers, so altered the balance that the majority was no longer favourable to Trotsky.

A humorous, but characteristic, incident enlivened the debate when Trotsky, declaring his loyalty to discipline, said: "The Party is always right . . . one can only be right with the Party." The language awakened subconscious memories of the ingrained Orthodox conviction that truth is to be found in the congregation of the brethren where mutual love resides. For days, Communist circles in Moscow discussed, with an obstinately mystical and theological bent, whether *the Party is infallible:* till Stalin hinted that Trotsky had been making fun of them, and said that the Party often made mistakes.

This, I may take the opportunity of noting, has always been the line taken by Stalin, whatever lesser men may think and say. He makes mistakes, the Party makes mistakes, everyone makes mistakes. They must not cover up mistakes, but drag them to light, analyse them and provide against their recurrence. His advance is avowedly by trial and error.

In November, 1924, Trotsky republished some of his works, with an introduction entitled *Lessons of October.* This is a pamphlet of remarkable cogency and power, in form an analysis of Revolutionary history, in essence an attack upon the ruling triumvirate, with the lesson that success or failure depends upon the choice of the leader. The case of Germany in 1923 is shown to be parallel to that of Russia in the autumn of 1917. The leadership which the Third International should have given in the former case was lacking. The last words of the book summarise its intention:—

> "Bolshevism is not a theory (that is, not merely a theory): it is a revolutionary system for teaching revolution to the proletariat. And what does Bolshevising the Communist Parties mean? It means an education, *and a choice of leaders,* which will prevent them from missing the moment of their October."

A deadly insinuation, not to be forgiven by a triumvirate of leaders. The Government, which controlled the presses, kept back the book, and filled the newspapers with attacks upon Trotsky, on his theory of Permanent Revolution, on his under-estimation of the part to be played by the peasants, even on his work with the Red Army. (November, 1924.) A more effective blow was the reading of the letter which Trotsky had written in 1913 in criticism of Lenin. This letter had been seized by the Tsarist police, and Stalin, who had taken charge of the police archives when the Party came into power, had evidently noted its potential usefulness, and had it ready to hand. It was a broadside of poison gas against Trotsky's rapier: and the latter's reasoned demonstration to the Party that he had not ignored the peasants, nor despaired of Socialist construction, and not evaded Party discipline, was silenced by the general disapproval of his criticism of the newly lost leader. He was deprived of the post of People's Commissar of War, but an important economic office which included the chairmanship of the electro-technical board, was conferred upon him. (May, 1925.)

A factor of importance in the history of the Opposition was the illness of Trotsky and his prolonged absences from Moscow. He was ill and absent when Lenin died, did not attend Lenin's funeral, protested by letter, and not in person, against the building of his Mausoleum in the Red Square, and was still absent in the autumn of 1924 when the Press campaign was active against him. He again absented himself in the Caucasus in 1925, and visited Berlin for medical advice in 1926. Events move swiftly in the U.S.S.R., the very generations are shorter, the personnel of public life changes, memories are brief, or the persons who should remember give place to new. It is by reference to facts such as these that we must explain the evanescence of the popularity of a hero of the Revolution and Civil War, who had stood scarcely second to Lenin in the estimation of the people. It is not so much that the masses are fickle, as that everybody's business is nobody's business, and that organised publicity plays a necessary part in keeping popular memories alive.

The concentration of industry, the construction of State-credits, and the measures of rationalisation which had brought down industrial prices and ended the dream of creating resources out of the peasants' purchases from the town, had still left the question, which the exhaustion of reserves made urgent, of the means of finding capital for the revolutionary State. It inevitably raised the issue whether Socialism could be built in Russia alone, without the collaboration of the other peoples: and all questions thereafter, external as well as internal, tended to hinge upon the answer to this one. After a moment of hesitation, during which he expressed convictions which he was afterwards at pains to explain away, Stalin declared that Socialism could be built in a single country. He started with the assumption that the World-Revolution was postponed and Capitalism stabilised. He sought for protection against attack from a stabilized World-Capitalism in the support of the moderate groups abroad, of which the Kuomintang in China, the Trades Union Council in Britain, and, supposedly also, Marshal Pilsudski in Poland, were examples. He looked for resources within the U.S.S.R., and found them—very much as Peter Stolypin had found them two decades earlier—in the "strong and sober" among the peasantry, and he stood for an alliance with them. This was entirely in harmony with the spirit of N.E.P., which aimed at utilising the private desire for gain, as a means of restoration of the public economy. But reliance upon the prosperous peasants was combined with measures for controlling private enterprise in industry and trade. Observers in Russia in 1924 and 1925 were impressed with the vigour of the campaign against the *nepmen*, and with the deliberate stretching of the laws against them. Scheffer, a German journalist of distinction, went so far as to call 1924 the year of the second revolution. An immense number of small private enterprises were closed; such freedom as N.E.P. allowed was largely withdrawn; and these measures were accompanied by attacks upon surviving *bourgeois* culture, the closing of churches, the purging of libraries, and the exclusion of *bourgeois* children from the schools.

The policy of reliance upon the more prosperous peasantry was exemplified by the measures of 1925, which permitted the leasing of land and the hiring of agricultural labour. The workers of Leningrad took umbrage at the favours shown to the peasantry. Bukharin, in an article the outspokenness of which may have embarrassed the leader whose policy he intended to support, issued the blatant invitation to the peasantry to enrich themselves. The resultant controversy was hushed up by the Central Committee of the Party, but Zinoviev and Kamenev had taken alarm at Stalin's leadership in economic policy, and the Triumvirate (Stalin, Zinoviev and Kamenev) which had controlled the Soviet Union since the second illness of Lenin, was broken up.

Circumstances now brought Trotsky into alliance with Zinoviev and Kamenev. They feared the growth of power in the prosperous peasantry. He desired co-ordination, by plan, of all parts of the Soviet Economy, both industrial and agricultural, and actually sketched a Five-Year-Plan in 1925. At this time, planning was not in favour in official circles. Rykov made a speech about it at the end of 1923, in which he drew a picture of ringing up a "literary person and, literally in three hours, a plan was ready, with all its lines and circles and so forth. But this plan could in no way take into account the conditions of our market." The idea that something must take the place of *laisser faire, laisser aller,* in general economics, and that some authority must decide, if individuals were no longer to do so, had not yet won its way to general acceptance. The greatest contribution made by the Opposition, in this period of discussion and experiment, to the growth of a coherent system of Socialist economics, was the insistence upon the necessity of a fully comprehensive economic Plan. It won: but not before its most persistent advocate had trodden the path to exile.

In June, 1926, Trotsky, Zinoviev and Kamenev agreed upon a common platform. It is interesting, with reference to the Trotskyist trials of ten years later, to note that Karl Radek, Evdokimov, Rakovsky, Piatakov, Smilga and Smirnov were also among the leaders of this wing of the Opposition. It is hardly less interesting, with reference to

the same group of trials and the accompanying degradations and dismissals, to note the prominent position occupied, on the other side
of the controversy, by Bukharin and Rykov, at that time champions
of the Right wing.

The Opposition's policy in 1926 was a composite one, showing
plainly the need of concessions to unite different sections of thought.
In the province of foreign relations, it insisted upon energetic efforts
for World-Revolution, and it negatived the possibility of Socialism
in a single country. At the same time it advocated close links with
foreign capitalism, the use of foreign credits and of foreign technical
aid, the accumulation of a reserve of foreign raw materials, and the
stimulation of Russian industry by contact with the example of the
outside world. We can treat these aims as mutually compatible only
if we suppose the aim of World-Revolution to be postponed, at least
for a season. The strengthening of industry is demanded, but the
emphasis is on increased production, and on reduction of prices, by
the reduction of costs, and by the diminution of the spread between
wholesale and retail prices.

In this programme the peasantry, as an integral whole, is not looked
upon as a source of accumulation, a means of building up capital for
the Socialist State. A distinction is drawn between the prosperous
peasant, who is declared to be increasing in strength and to be using
his economic strength to oppress the poorer, and the rank and file
of the peasantry. All the means of the State are to be used to favour
the poorer peasant, who is to be relieved of taxation, while the kulak
is to be forced by higher taxation to surrender his accumulations of
grain. An interesting feature of the programme is that small-scale
peasant agriculture is to be ended as soon as the change is feasible,
and replaced by the organisation of collective farms. This is a reversion
to earlier projects dropped on the introduction of N.E.P. Until
collectivisation becomes feasible, the way for it is to be prepared by
increased co-operative production in agriculture and increased elec-
trification and mechanisation.

The programme makes much of the grievances of the urban workers.
The rationalisation associated with the policy of closing the "Scissors"
has unfairly reduced wages and increased unemployment. The hous-
ing-space for workers is inadequate. The workers are deprived of all
share and of all representation in the making of wage-bargains, and
the so-called collective agreements are not agreements at all, but unilateral instructions forced upon the Trade Unions. The differences
between wages are too great. Accidents in the factories are far too

common. Generally speaking, the programme of the Opposition turns its back upon N.E.P., with its reliance upon the acquisitive instincts ot individuals as a means of economic restoration, and faces once more the original revolutionary principle of a system based upon the worker and the poorer peasant, with active help for the realisation of the same principle in the world outside of Russia. Within the Party there is to be democracy; in the Soviets there is to be more rigorous control over elections, to exclude all *bourgeois* elements, including the prosperous peasants.

There is evidence that the programme had much support among the factory workers. The attack was a powerful one, launched along a wide front. But the Revolution had now created its own vested interests, and the fort was strongly held. The Opposition was accused of that worst of Bolshevik sins, of disbelief in the Revolution (as a Roman might have said, of despairing of the Republic), of lacking confidence that the Revolution could exist in isolation. Those in power declared that the Revolution was already victorious but not yet finally victorious, because of the possibilities of intervention from abroad: and they made vigorous use of the danger of war to create odium against their opponents. Many of the leaders of the Opposition (Trotsky himself, Zinoviev, Kamenev, Radek, Sokolnikov) were Jews. The Communist Party has always set its face against anti-Semitism. In April, 1928, the Central Committee issued instructions to the Party to proceed against anti-Semitic agitators, but discreetly, and in such a manner as not to give the impression that Communists are the particular champions of the Jews, or that the Government is a Government of Jews. This was an evident recognition of the survival of anti-Semitism among the people.

The Government took the sting out of some of the Opposition charges by measures of its own. A campaign of reform from within was launched in 1926 by Felix Dzherkhinsky, formerly head of the Cheka, who had succeeded to one of the vacant places in the supreme Triumvirate. In a series of speeches he condemned the consumption of reserves of capital, the famine of manufactured goods, and the lack of training for workers, and declared that the State was "smothered in bureaucracy." Rudzutak, the People's Commissar of Communications, attacked the administration of the Railways. "Papa" Kalinin declared that the rural Soviets were ossified, because so few took the trouble to vote, and that the Soviets both in town and country were increasingly dominated by persons of *bourgeois* sympathies. It was decided to cancel elections in cases of official interference, and where the proportion of voters fell below a certain minimum; and permission was given for the nomination of candidates outside the Party list. These measures are apparent concessions to the Opposition's demand for workers' democracy. It seems certain that attempts were made to effect conciliation, and that Stalin was prepared to go to considerable lengths to avoid a breach. There was a strong sentiment of *camaraderie* at this time, uniting all who had taken part in the early revolutionary movements, in spite of the bitterness of their disputes and the severity with which sentences of exile and transference to inferior offices were pronounced and executed. It was natural, *then*, to contrast the peaceable termination of apparently tragic quarrels with the murderous use of the guillotine against revolutionary rivals in the France of the eighteenth century. But the developments of a later epoch were such as to make any congratulation of the Russian revolutionaries upon this score obviously inappropriate.

In October, 1926, Trotsky, Zinoviev, Kamenev, Piatakov, Evdokimov and Sokolnikov put their hands to a document which looked like a treaty of peace; but it did not prevent them from continuing the struggle with Stalin, Bukharin and Rykov, now the ruling Triumvirate. It was not long before both Trotsky and Kamenev were expelled from the Politburo of the Party, and Zinoviev removed from the Chairmanship of the Third International. Karl Radek was dismissed from the headship of the Sun Yat-sen University at Moscow, because he shared Trotsky's views on revolution in China. There were fresh economic difficulties, with a widening of the "Scissors" in consequence of the scarcity of goods. The background of discontent revealed itself in the throwing of a bomb in Leningrad, and an attack on an officer of the Gay-Pay-oo at Minsk. The blows which the foreign policy of the U.S.S.R. received in 1927 in China, Great Britain and Poland, gave prestige to the Opposition by confirming its forecasts, and intensified the political strain. Zinoviev, who was not ordinarily remarkable for courage, addressed a non-party meeting at which he criticised the Central Party Committee, thus repeating his offence of October, 1917, when he carried Party affairs to the general public. Trotsky openly accused Stalin of betrayal of the cause of World-Revolution. A warning was given to Trotsky and Zinoviev by the Central Control Commission, and they ostensibly submitted to discipline. But when Smilga, a member of the Opposition, was transferred to a post in Siberia as a disciplinary measure, Trotsky saw him off from the railway station, and made a demonstrative speech.

Owing to the charges made against them of endangering the safety of the Socialist Fatherland when threatened by foreign attack, Trotsky and others signed, in August, 1927, a declaration that they would stand by the Government and the Party in the event of conflict, and would call upon the soldiers of the capitalist powers to desert and join the Red Army. Some of the Opposition leaders were occupying posts abroad (a favourite method of securing their isolation from the centre of opposition), and this declaration was signed by Rakovsky, Soviet ambassador at Paris, and by L. B. Kamenev, Soviet ambassador at Rome. In September, the Opposition sent to the Central Committee of the Party a statement of its case, to be published for the information of the members and discussed at special meetings in preparation for the Fifteenth Party Conference. The majority decided against its publication; whereupon it was mimeographed by I. P. Bakayev, G. E. Evdokimov, L. P. Serebriakov, and other members of the Opposition, who were brought to trial in 1936. The Gay-Pay-oo seized their press and arrested many persons. The substance of the document was elaborated into Trotsky's *Real Situation in Russia*, which purports to reproduce his speech on the motion to expel him from the Central Committee. This speech was not delivered, or was whistled and shouted down, but it stands as a record of the policy of the Opposition.

In the international and the internal economic spheres the policy of this abortive speech does not differ from that already described. World-Revolution is to be forwarded, there is to be an end of the policy of making allies in such quarters as the Chinese Kuomintang, the British Trade Unions Congress General Council and Pilsudskian Poland: but use is to be made of the capitalist governments to stimulate the growth of Russian industry. Internal policy is to be based upon the workers and the poorer peasants, not upon the *nepmen* and the *kulaks*.

The draft of the Five-Year-Plan for 1926-31 is criticised by Trotsky as inadequate, because it ignores all the potentialities presented by the position of the State as owner of nationalised land, banks, and industry, and does not deal drastically enough with the spread between wholesale and retail prices.

In Chapter V of *The Real Situation* the Soviet bureaucracy is attacked, not only for its size and cost, but for its tendency to develop social snobbery and to arrogate to itself the position of master of those whose servant it should be. In his later works, written in exile, Trotsky reverts again and again to the mischievous results of the growth of the great bureaucratic machine, with its conservative personal interests. He emphasises the subordination of the truly democratic organs, the Soviets, to this new official tyranny: and says that the objection to bureaucratic domination, the rule of the "apparatus," was the root of the opposition of 1924-27.

Next comes a chapter condemning the treatment of the minority nationalities, which are being deprived of the independent authority contemplated by the Federal Constitution. The evils of revived Capitalism and of bureaucratic domination, of which Trotsky has complained in Great Russia, tend to be at their worst (he says) in these outlying regions. The imported Communist and office-holder domineer and dictate over the native-born. The Council of Nationalities, intended to be a co-equal chamber in the Central Executive committee, is reduced to an inferior status.

One chapter is devoted to the Party, and one to the Communist League of Youth. The Party contains too few workers, too many officials, too many Social Revolutionaries and Mensheviks. Congresses and Conferences are summoned, without any preliminary free discussion, such as was always held under Lenin, of all questions by the whole Party. Old Party men are being replaced by Yes-men, who have not undergone the same hard experiences. One man at the top— the Secretary-General, for instance—counts for more than a hundred at the bottom. The subjection of the Politburo to the Secretariat, and of the Secretariat to the General Secretary, is an accomplished fact, and the dying out of democracy within the Party is accompanied by the dying out of democracy in general, in the Trade Unions, in the Soviets, and in all other non-party mass organisations. Lenin's precept that the General Staff must be supported by the honest and conscious will of the rank and file of the Army is forgotten. The controlling body must be reconstructed and organised, to make it a truly democratic force such as Lenin contemplated when he planned the Workers' and Peasants' Inspection.

The proportion of proletarians in the Communist League of Youth has fallen to just over a third of the whole, and there has been a recent lowering of the status of the young worker. The Opposition programme has evidently been devised to make an appeal to youth, and changes in these respects are demanded by Trotsky.

At this time scores of malcontents were visiting Trotsky in his office, where he still continued to be the head of the Economic Concessions Board, and a good deal of platonic sympathy was evidently felt in many quarters with his aims. He says that he had to pour cold water on the ardour of these emissaries, but he adds that the Opposition was preparing for the Party Congress by holding both secret and open meetings. One evening the Opposition seized the Technical College at Moscow (much as the Bolsheviks had seized the Kshesinskaya Palace at Petrograd in April, 1917) and held a mass meeting, which a crowd outside the building protected, while Trotsky and Kamenev spoke for two hours.

It is of some interest, with reference to the charges made at the Trotskyist trials of 1936-38, that the Opposition was charged with a royalist conspiracy at this time, as well as with assisting the military designs of foreign Powers. These charges played, or were intended to play, the same part in the strife of the parties as the incitement-to-murder accusations against Charles Stewart Parnell in the Irish Home Rule controversy, or the "German spy" stories against Lenin in July, 1917, or the burning of the Reichstag in the early stages of the Nazi campaign against the parties of the Left in Germany. The tendency to create odium against political opponents by exaggerating, if not actually fabricating, offences resembles the practice of propaganda against national enemies in time of war.

At the Anniversary demonstrations in Moscow on November 7, 1927, hundreds of the Opposition came out with banners and joined the procession in honour of the Revolution. Trotsky says these banners bore slogans, *not directed against the Party*, but worded as follows: "Let us turn our fire to the Right: against the *kulak*, the *nepman* and the bureaucrat." "Let us carry out Lenin's will." "Against opportunism, against a split, and for the unity of Lenin's Party." The Militia tore away the placards, Trotsky's car was fired upon by a policeman and similar action was taken at Leningrad, where Zinoviev had been busy.

It is not surprising that Trotsky and Zinoviev were at once expelled from the Party. They had broken every rule of party discipline in their open appeal to public support. On November 16th, Joffé, who was ill, and to whom sufficient means for undertaking a cure abroad had been refused by the Party, committed suicide, and his funeral was made the occasion of a further Opposition demonstration.

The Fifteenth Congress of the Party, in December, 1927, expelled Trotsky, Kamenev, Radek, Rakovsky, Piatakov, and many hundreds of lesser note. Of the 854,000 members of the Party 730,600 voted. Of these 724,000 supported Stalin and the Central Committee, 2,600 abstained from voting, and 4,000 voted for the Opposition. There is no reason to suspect these figures. Trotsky himself has stated in *The Revolution Betrayed* that the number of those who joined him was small. Zinoviev and Kamenev abased themselves, and along with thirty-six others, were readmitted to the Party in June, 1928. Trotsky himself was exiled to Central Asia in January, 1928, and excluded from the U.S.S.R. in January, 1929.

❊   ❊   ❊

It seems a far cry from Trotsky, who had urged the organisation of labour on military lines, to M. P. Tomsky, the president of the All-Union Central Council of Trade Unions, who had stoutly championed their claim to a freedom as complete as that of the Trade Unions in the United Kingdom. And yet there was a point of approach between the two. Trotsky made himself the advocate of democracy in the Party. Democracy in the Party involves very naturally the assertion of an important rôle for the Soviets and, equally easily, it passes on to a claim for independence in the Trade Unions. The programme of the Trotsky Opposition in 1926 included a protest against the so-called collective agreements, which are not agreements at all, but unilateral instructions forced upon the Trade Unions. In exile in 1931-32, we find Trotsky complaining (*The German Revolution and Stalin's Bureaucracy*) that the Trade Unions are deprived of all power to influence the relative proportion of consumption and saving: that is to say, to claim a larger part of the product for wages. He goes on to say that the participation of the workers in leadership will have a favourable influence upon production, and that Soviet Democracy is a living need. I do not stress unduly this ultimate similarity between the doctrines of a leader of the Left and a leader of the Right: but it obviously has some relevance to the events of 1936 and later, when Left and Right alike were swept into the net by the Department of Internal Affairs, which succeeded to the functions of the Gay-Pay-oo.

❊   ❊   ❊

I have found little space, so far, for any reference to the Opposition of the Right. It bulked less large in the period which we have been considering, because the leadership of the Party itself, at this time, stood so far on the right flank of politics. But there were already signs in the attitude of the Party in 1928 of a tack towards the Left. In proportion as this tendency developed, the Right Opposition became more restive. In June, 1929, Tomsky, who had demanded for the Trade Unions the right to defend the interests of their own members, was removed from the Presidency of the All-Union Central Council of Trade Unions. Bukharin had always held that it was possible to absorb, instead of destroying, the anti-Bolshevik forces in the villages, and the measures connected with the adoption of the first Five-Year Plan, the collectivisation of the farms, and the "liquidation" of the kulaks completed the breach between Stalin and his supporters on the Right. In 1930, Rykov, Bukharin and Tomsky addressed to the Politburo a memorandum showing that grain supplies would fail unless the policy was changed. The economist Kondratiev, who had collaborated with the three dissentients in the preparation of this document, disappeared into the hands of the Gay-Pay-oo. At the Sixteenth Conference of the Party, in 1930, Stalin attacked the Right deviators as representatives of the defeated classes. Bukharin, once a partner with Stalin in the Triumvirate and "the Party's supreme theoretician after Lenin," was dismissed from the Executive Committee of the Third International and from the editorship of Pravda. Tomsky was exiled from the capital. Syrtsov, who had organised a new opposition group, was charged with conspiracy and imprisoned. Rykov, "the old reliable Bolshevik," also a sharer at one time in the powers of the Triumvirate, was ousted from his post of Chairman of the Council of Commissars and replaced by Molotov. The Right Opposition then followed the Trotskyist Opposition underground.

Another form of Opposition within the Party came from Communists belonging to the non-Great Russian nationalities. Overtly, at least, their protests were made against over-centralisation and what has been termed Great Russian chauvinism, but I have more to say on this subject in the chapter dealing with the Nationalities of the U.S.S.R.

After his removal from the U.S.S.R. in 1929 Trotsky never bowed the knee, and did not respond to overtures, such as those which appear to have been made to him in July, 1936. His associates were more pliable, and most of them found their way back to the Party and to positions of trust, till the storm broke upon them again. Trotsky's later writings throw valuable light on his political aims. In The Soviet Union and the Fourth International he says that the last real Congress of the Bolshevik Party was the Twelfth, which took place at the beginning of 1923. All subsequent congresses were bureaucratic parades. No constitutional way remains for the removal of the ruling clique. Only by force can the bureaucracy be compelled to yield power into the hands of the proletarian vanguard. But the question of seizing power will arise for the new Party only when it shall have consolidated round itself the majority of the working class. A major historical test—which may be a war—will determine the relation of forces. The first Workers' State may fall. "But we wage our struggle from the standpoint of defending it. . . . The new International will offer the Stalinist bureaucracy a united front against the common foe."

In *The Revolution Betrayed* (1936) Trotsky's patriotic pride breaks through his partisan criticism, and he exultingly quotes the French technicians' report on the Red Air Fleet, which expressed "surprise and admiration." Envisaging the likelihood of war, he declares that, if the proletariat wins elsewhere, even the defeat of the U.S.S.R. will be only an episode. But no military victory will save the heritage of the Revolution if Imperialism keeps its place in the rest of the world. Nevertheless the Red Army is of extraordinary value, because it will give time for the development of the class-war in the imperialist countries. He condemns the recent policy of the Third International for its purely conservative policy of maintaining the world in status quo. The aim should be the creation of a United States of Europe: but not by adventurism nor by attempts to force the course of world events.

In a closing chapter he declares that a *new revolution is now ineluctable*. Delation and inquisition are devouring the society of the U.S.S.R. The workers detest the Bureaucracy. They abstain from action only because they fear to prepare the way for a capitalist restoration.

Trotsky then makes a reference to the assassination of Kirov in December, 1934, an outrage which had an important influence upon the course of events. He says that attacks on the representatives of power are important as symptoms, and that the assassination of Kirov was the most significant of these. He adds that individual terrorism is incapable of overthrowing the oligarchy. It is the aim of impatient or desperate men, generally belonging to the young generation of the bureaucracy. But, as under the autocracy, political crimes show that a crisis is at hand.

He continues that the task of the Fourth International—the new organisation created by Trotsky—is to prepare a new revolution and to place itself at the head of the masses, *in a favourable historic situation*.

It is an outspoken notification that Trotsky and the Fourth International will oust Stalin and make a new revolution, when the time is ripe for it. A war may provide the occasion. In such a war the Fourth International will defend the Soviet Union: but the intention of defending the Soviet Union is compatible with the making of a fresh revolution there.

Such a notification would set any ruler, any State, to work on measures of self-preservation. We cannot affect surprise that all who were within reach, and were supposed, by reason of their antecedents, to be sympathetic with Trotsky, were seized—after an attempt to arrive at an accommodation (by means of a meeting in Holland which was reported by the Dutch Press in July, 1936) had been made and failed. It is only a hypothesis, but I think it is a likely one, that the Government of the U.S.S.R. became aware that Trotsky was publishing, or about to publish, his *Revolution Betrayed*, with its ominous reference to the assassination of Kirov, and its threat of a new revolution; that it thereupon opened negotiations with Trotsky; and that when these failed it determined upon the general attack upon all surviving vestiges of Trotskyism within its reach. The attack included more than the old associates of Trotsky: for Tomsky committed suicide, and Bukharin and Rykov, both of the Right Opposition, were arrested. The prosecution, which continued from 1936 to 1938, alleged an alliance between Trotskyists, malcontents of the Right Opposition and the Red Army, and so-called *bourgeois* nationalists of the Ukraine, White Russia and Mahommedan Central Asia; treasonable negotiations with Germany and Japan; and conspiracy for murders, cession of territory to foreign powers, sabotage, and the restoration of capitalism.

When the oppositions went underground they became, by an internal logic of their own, more desperate and more dangerous. I disbelieve much of what was "confessed," or stated in evidence, in the trials of 1936-38: but close study makes evident an important nucleus of truth. Trotsky meant to make a new revolution when conditions should be ripe for it: and old revolutionaries who mean to make fresh revolutions do not sit with folded hands. They keep alive their old connections, are busy in making new ones, seek for agents and supporters, collect funds, exchange information, make alliances with others having similar objects, watch the course of international politics in order that the favourable moment may not be missed when it arrives.

Under the conditions of a constitutional country (not to be reproduced by the mere transportation of constitutional forms), the men of the Right might have become a constitutional conservative opposition, aiming at the absorption of *nepmen* and *kulaks* into a Socialist system, and at softening the transition for them. What actually happened to them is convincingly described in their own statements in March, 1938. Within the Party it was evident, in spite of their conviction that a wrong policy was being followed, that they could achieve nothing. The leaders were not to be disposed of by a vote. They must be ousted by more drastic means. First, it was to be done by insurrection, of the kind which the agrarian disturbances of 1929-31 seemed to make easily feasible. But the success achieved by collectivisation and by the operations of the first Five-Year Plan destroyed the hope of popular support for an insurrectionary movement. They turned therefore to the notion of a "palace coup," of the seizure of the Kremlin, to be carried out preferably in conjunction with foreign attack, and they began to pick up allies of every kind: the restless and ambitious soldier, the discontented nationalist, the Napoleonic police-officer with purely selfish aims and a head turned by arbitrary power. The logic of events carried them even into alliance with their opposites, who desired the same immediate end for altogether different reasons; and some of the new friends did things which others of them would, at the outset, have seriously disapproved. The dismemberment of the U.S.S.R. presented itself in the form of allowing particular constituent republics to secede by their own will from the Union; and the opening of the frontiers to the foreigner, in the form of allowing German or Polish troops to facilitate the secession.

Of the more serious offences charged and admitted, it is remarkable how much was merely contemplated, discussed and intended, and how little was actually done. There was much of "*imagining the death of His Majesty*," of designing treasonable intelligence and negotiation, and little specific evidence of performance or attempted performance. For the most part, we look in vain for dates and concrete instances. It is only when the terrible Yagoda, of whom something has already been said, comes upon the stage that murder passes from discussion into reality. Up to then, the conspirators seem to be wrestling with shadows. This is all the easier where action and thought are united so closely as they are in the Russian psychology. Close analysis of some of the statements, in particular of that of Bukharin, shows that an action, once shown to be a natural consequence of a particular thought, is conceived as already performed. The plotters readily admit responsibility for the action which should have followed upon the thought. It is part of the same mental habit which identifies planning with performance in the spheres of industry and agriculture. It is not that the union of action and thought causes the former invariably to follow the latter, but that there is an illusion of identity between them. The idea is familiar in the sphere of religion, where thought itself may be sin: but here we find it extended into jurisprudence, and a man pleads guilty to something of which the idea was present in his mind, though no overt act was committed.

Concerning Trotsky himself, there are some inferences to be drawn from the undiminished enthusiasm for the U.S.S.R. which his later speeches and writings make evident. It is very marked in a speech which he made at Copenhagen in November, 1932. He then declared that the results attained in industrial production were great, though there had been unfavorable developments in agriculture, and he extolled the rapid rise of merit to high places, and the careful preservation of everything which had been of value in old Russian civilisation. A couple of years later, in *The Soviet Union and the Fourth International*, he was declaring that even "the Stalinite apparatus" had its significance as the gate-keeper of the social achievements of the proletarian revolution: that there still existed the dictatorship of the proletariat, although a sick one. Even in *The Revolution Betrayed* (1936) he continued to say that Russia's industry had made enormous advances, while the capitalist States had advanced little or not at all. He fortified this statement with the particular observation that a comparison with Poland and the Baltic States, formerly the most advanced part of the Russian Empire, showed how great was the growth of the U.S.S.R.

So far as the internal situation goes, his most radical criticism is that, in spite of the advance made, productivity is still insufficient. From the insufficiency of productivity it follows that the U.S.S.R. has the form, not the substance, of Socialism. The evil lies in Trotsky's pet aversion, the bureaucracy, which paralyses the organisation. Because the product is too little, there is a scramble for that little, along with all the evils typical of a *bourgeois* State, and the bureaucracy appropriates power and comfort for itself. Thus, resources have not sufficed for the intended emancipation of woman, who had gone back, since rationing was abolished, to the wash-tub and the kitchen. Because production does not provide satisfactorily for all, the coercive State remains, to check the inevitable scramble, and liberty is subjected to regimentation.

As to the new Constitution of 1936, it involves (he says) the liquidation of the dictatorship of the proletariat, before the proletariat has merged into a socialistic society, for which the material basis of productivity has not yet been created.

In international affairs, his criticism is that the Third International now aims at neutralising the *bourgeoisie* by assuming the appearance of the guardian of order and, in taking that aspect, it becomes the thing itself. In one deadly sentence—the Soviets are becoming *bourgeois*.

The inferences to be drawn from all these considerations, some of them self-contradictory, must be read along with the events in Europe in 1936 and succeeding years. The Central European Dictators had ambitious plans which first revealed themselves in Spain. The widespread fear of Communism provided them with a system of concealed approaches to their objective, which ultimately proved to include an attack on the U.S.S.R. Trotsky had made no secret of his intention of bringing about a fresh revolution in that country. He, or his friends, were ready to hand as instruments of political intrigue. The Opposition of the Right, driven underground by the denial of freedom of expression, combined with the Opposition of the Left, by a manoeuvre which, however surprising, is not without parallel in history. However much falsity of detail there may be, the trials of the leading personages in 1936-38 were substantially justified by facts: and were probably the means of saving the U.S.S.R. from an attempted revolution which would have given to the Nazi Government an earlier opportunity.

Chapter XVII

STATE ECONOMIC PLANNING

> "The Russians have—at least since the beginning of the eighteenth century—been constantly mapping out . . . the country that lay before them, and advancing with gigantic strides according to the newest political theories."
>
> MACKENZIE WALLACE.

> "Nothing in Russia is ever done by cold design, unless it be by Jews and Germans. The whole of Russian history is a story of accidents."
>
> STEPHEN GRAHAM.

> "The slow and inconspicuous way in which great decisions in Russian history have often come of themselves."
>
> SIR BERNARD PARES.

State Planning, which is the subject of the present chapter, has naturally had to encounter the powerful criticism of orthodox economists, and has still to make good its claim, alongside of the financial budget that is now conventional in capitalist lands, to the respect and imitation of mankind as a device of better government. If it still appears a novelty, we may remind ourselves that the annual planning even of the revenue and expenditure of a State exercising very restricted functions is not of a hoary antiquity.

It is evident that the method by which we determine the choice between alternative uses of such labour, material and land as are available is vital to economic well-being. Man lives or dies, prospers or the reverse, by putting things into their right, or into their wrong, places. The controversy, or one of the controversies, between Individualism and Socialism centres upon the question: how is man to know which are the right places, and which are the wrong; how is he to distinguish the better from the worse use of his available resources? This question is abbreviated when we ask whether Plan or Price is to be the guide to economic action.

In the course of this controversy it is sometimes assumed that Plan is exclusively the method of Socialism, and Price exclusively the method of Individualism. The practical issue is less clear-cut. There is much planning in what we call the individualistic society, and much use of the mechanism of price in what we call the socialistic. But the planning in the individualistic society is not, except in a limited degree, done by a central authority, having the function of protecting the interests of the public in general: and the pricing in the socialistic society is not the outcome of the play of contending economic interests.

In the most individualistic societies which we know, the whole fields of public finance and taxation, of defence, of civil administration, of road- and bridge-making, of drainage, of primary and secondary education, except for Church Schools and for a limited number of well-to-do persons, of house-building for those who cannot pay competitive rents or cannot find accommodation with the help of private enterprise, are the subjects of planning by the State or by local authorities. The monetary system is planned by public or quasi-public bodies, which may nominally, but only nominally, be not responsible to the State. A part of the planning is done for annual periods, part of it extends over much longer periods. In war-time it is carried much further, and enters into most departments of life, controlling the means of production, distributing cargo-space by land and by water, raw materials and labour power, fixing prices, and making an equal division of food and other necessities in the public interest. This planning in the individualistic society is not limited to those departments in which there is difficulty in collecting remuneration for service rendered. The public planning extends to postal communications, sometimes to telegraphic and telephonic communications, to radio-telegraphy and broadcasting, and to public transport by railway, tram and bus.

Outside the province of peace-time planning in the individualistic society lie industry and trade in general. Here the State intervenes—by tariffs, subsidies, quotas and marketing boards, and by a monetary policy calculated, according to circumstances, to effect a general expansion or restriction of business—but, with rare exceptions, only to change the framework within which private interests operate. The planning of the actual operations is done by the private or quasi-private interests which produce or distribute the goods or supply the services.

If we examine another branch of economic activity—that of the hiring of labour—in an individualistic society, we find that planning plays a considerable part, but substantially less in the United States than in Britain. Employers' federations, on the one hand, and Trade

Unions and Trade Boards, on the other, exercise influence on the rates of wages, and limit the sphere of free, individual competition. A similar conclusion must be reached in respect to the rate of interest upon capital, where the planned monetary policy of the Central Bank is, within certain upward and downward limits, the effective factor. Land is locally often a monopoly, and in large towns, outside of special areas, rent is determined by the planned policy of the large estates, with the competition, all on one side, operating to increase the claims of the landowner.

If planning plays a large part in the individualistic society, prices play a large part in its socialistic counterpart. Since the second abolition of rationing in 1935 there has been a steady attempt in the U.S.S.R. at uniformity of retail prices in particular geographical zones, but with differences of prices between those zones. No wholesale market exists: but the prices at which materials and goods are exchanged between State organs and enterprises may reasonably be treated as wholesale prices. They are based upon the planned cost of production, with the addition of a commission or profit for every organisation through whose hands the goods pass, and of a turnover-tax which forms the largest portion of the State's revenue. Charges for rent are never included in cost of production, and charges for interest, in the strict sense, do not arise. But an allowance is made for the replacement of fixed assets, and the enterprises must surrender a share of their profits to the Bank from which they derive their investment capital.

In practice the wholesale price-fixing authority fixes only the price of certain standard qualities, and the prices of other qualities are negotiated between the enterprises concerned, on the basis of the standard thus set. In the case of agricultural produce, which is acquired by the Government (or by the Co-operative institutions) partly in the form of a tax-in-kind, partly in discharge of obligations contracted with the Machine Tractor Stations, and partly by voluntary sale in return for engagements to supply manufactured goods, the wholesale price—that is to say, the price at which the Government passes on the produce to the processing and exporting departments—appears to the present writer to be arbitrarily determined, subject to the ultimate necessity of adjusting retail prices to total incomes. At all events it has no discoverable relation to the retail prices obtained by the peasants in their private sales, or to the payments made by the Government to the peasants for their deliveries of produce.

Those wholesale prices determined, in the case of industrial goods, by costs of production, commissions or profits, and the turnover-tax, are planned on the basis of average costs in the whole of a given industry, not on the costs of the particular enterprise. It is thus quite possible for a particular enterprise not to recover its costs of production, and provision is made for the selling up of unsuccessful concerns at the instance of the Industrial Bank, whose business it is to finance them. This is not a meaningless provision, for standing orders require such virtual bankruptcies to be published, whether the sale of effects is, or is not, in practice enforced, and the student of the Soviet Press from time to time sees notices of them. The amount of the turnover-tax varies according as the Government desires to encourage or restrict a particular industry, and it forms a part of the wholesale price. Retail prices are zonally uniform: that is to say, zonally uniform in theory. But there are substantial fluctuations and local departures from the norm. Prices are sometimes put artificially low in order to encourage the use of particular products, or to get rid of goods for which there proves to be little demand. But the principle ordinarily observed in fixing them is that demand must be kept within the limits of supply. It may startle us to find ourselves back with the familiar language of the economic text-books. But there are only two ways of avoiding the necessity of adjusting the general level of prices according to the pressure of demand upon supply. One way is by rationing, which the U.S.S.R. abandoned in 1935. The other is by the principle of first come first served, which is a kind of rationing according to priority in the queue. While rationing existed, it was necessary to supplement it by putting high prices on the goods sold to the unrationed population, in order to equate the demand to the supply. In the alternative, the goods went cheap, and some of those who were prepared to pay the price went without, because the supply was exhausted before their turn came. But the aim is the provision of goods in order to satisfy needs, and the failure to provide them only showed that the Plan was inadequate, or not backed by sufficient industrial power. When rationing was abolished in 1935, and a simultaneous increase was made in the scale of wages, the Soviet Government showed that it believed the supply of goods to be enough to go round, at prices assumed to be reasonable with regard to the new level of income. When both supply (within the limits of industrial power) and income—which is potential demand—are controlled by the same monopolist authority, prices (though admittedly determined by the pressure of demand upon supply) become mere indices, and means of measurement. The Socialist State can change either or both the factors whose interaction determines price: and it is in this sense that Plan makes Price. On the other hand, Price makes Plan in an individualistic economy: in the sense that it is prospective price which leads the entrepreneur to his decisions.

The Socialist Government can control supply (to such extent as its industrial power extends) and can control the potential demand, which is represented by the general level of incomes. It cannot control the actual retail demand for any particular commodity, except by an artificial manipulation of price (like the draper selling off old stock at a sacrifice); and it is in respect to the retail demand for particular commodities that the consumer's choice is operative.

The greater part of the resources of the Government for the common purposes of the State is derived from the additions to the wholesale prices of which I have spoken above. If supply should ever catch up with demand, the natural law, which we have said is equally operative in a socialistic as in an individualistic society, that price is determined by the pressure of demand upon supply, would eliminate this source of income. The limit of demand for any particular commodity may, of course, easily be reached. But the notion that the limit of the demand for commodities in general can ever be reached seems to be due to a confusion between demand and effective demand. Man's appetite for the good things of life, including leisure, is reasonably assumed to be inexhaustible. It is only his poverty which causes him to go short. If it be true that a method of converting demand into effective demand has been found, there is no chance that supply will reach the limit of demand, or that the State will find itself deprived of its revenues from the turnover-tax, and from the difference between the price paid to the peasantry for food and the price charged to the processing and exporting departments.

Are we to suppose that the monopolist State will raise the price of necessities unduly against its people, or a section of them? The peasantry has on more than one occasion shown itself capable of very effective passive resistance, and the attempt to overcharge would be met by refusal to purchase, and by the withholding of food from the towns. The crisis which gave rise to Preobrazhensky's proposal to build up capital by this device was ended by measures of a character diametrically opposite to the raising of industrial prices. It is always true, in a sense, that a monopolist may use his power to raise his price excessively; but the Soviet Government would have changed its aims if it were guilty of this blunder, and would find itself back in the Food-War of earlier days.

In saying that it is the Plan which makes the Price in the U.S.S.R., I do not wish to convey that Price always conforms to Plan, but that it tends to do so, so far as control is complete. In one respect Plan governs Price in a manner quite unattainable in an individualistic society. Not only is the individualistic producer sometimes ignorant of what his competitors are doing; almost entirely unable to influence the incomes of his customers; and only able to direct their taste through advertisement and salesmanship; but he is bound to make his profit, if he makes it at all, in the one particular part of the field where his operations are located. The Socialist State not only controls incomes, through its control of wages, but it also deals with the whole, or virtually the whole, field of production. It can, if policy requires, lose in one part of the field, provided that incomings balance outgoings over the whole of it: and it actually follows this principle, not by allowing its individual departments to work ostensibly at a loss, but by subsidising their operations as policy requires. While the general level of prices must obey the general economic law, particular prices therefore become in great measure conventional prices, framed in the interests of general policy. Coal, for instance, is priced far below its cost of production, in the interests of industry as a whole; a policy which would only be possible to a private coalowner if largely subsidised on condition of fixing a low price for industrial purchasers.

It has been powerfully argued that, in an individualistic economy, Price is decisive, that is to say, that it determines both the amount and the direction of production and, in the form of interest, which is the Price of capital, it determines the volume of saving; that it is determined by competition, which cuts all costs to the bone; that it is, therefore, a perfect index to the choice between alternative uses of labour, land, and material; and that an economy which does not suffer its choice to be determined by Price must inevitably make the wrong choice, and pay the penalty in economic loss. There is no means of ascertaining the scale of this loss, but the implication is that it is fatal to the claim that a socialistic economy will excel an individualistic one in productivity—a claim upon which the success or failure of the former ultimately depends.

The case would be stronger if any completely competitive society were actually in existence, but the ideal competitive society does not exist. Von Hayek says that the world to-day is "just interventionist chaos." In the retail market competition is notoriously imperfect, owing to the ignorance and carelessness of many of the housewives with whom the business of retail purchases mostly rests. It follows that a portion of the loss which is anticipated in a socialistic system is already occurring in the individualistic one, and the difference between the two systems, as they actually exist, is, in respect to the economic advantages of free competition, rather one of degree than of kind. Indeed, we may with good reason suspect that the individualistic society has lost many of the merits of free competition, without acquiring those of collective planning.

Perhaps we may take the point of Professors von Hayek and Halm, to be this: that, in an economically satisfactory society, the decisions of separate individuals, each acting in his own field of vision, must carry more weight than decisions made by or for such individuals, combined in associations whether voluntary or compulsory. This process of decision by private individuals may legitimately be corrected or supplemented by decisions taken by certain types of combinations: the Federation of Employers, the Banking Corporations, the Joint Stock Companies and so on. But as soon as there is intervention by another group of combinations, in particular of the compulsory associations, the State and the Municipalities, mischief is done. It is the decisions of individuals and of voluntary associations of business men, taken in free competition with each other, which constitute consumer's choice, and ultimately determine relative economic values. The virtue lies in the conflict of individual wills, and, in proportion as deliberate organisation takes its place, the system falls short of economic effectiveness. It has the advantage of being self-regulating—an advantage which does not save it from miscarriages in the form of gluts and resultant slumps. The potentially effective demand and the potential supply go together into the calculating machine. A handle is turned, and out comes Price, the basis of a perfect compromise between rival desires—*so far as the desires have money behind them*. It is a beautiful device—or a beautiful accident— and we must sympathise with those who have learned to love it, and are asked to contemplate its abandonment. But a Socialist Government which determines all urban incomes, as well as prices, and comes near to controlling supply, at all events in respect to the upper limit, is not primarily concerned with the effectiveness of the demand— which it can itself, within limits, make effective—but rather with the maximum satisfaction of needs and desires, on the principles of payment for work done and of regard for the interests of the coming generation. It is precisely because the one system must wait upon the realised effectiveness of demand, while the other aims at making the demand effective, that the determination of values by a process dependent upon the existence of effective demand is irrelevant to the Socialist economy. The one registers facts, based upon the existing distribution of means. The facts are useful to the producer. He knows that his fur coat at a thousand guineas, and his lace nightgown at fifty, will find purchasers at those prices, and is encouraged to devote to similar confections more of "the scant means available for alternative purposes" of which the economists tell us. The other attempts to realise aims—that is to say, conscious and planned aims: and these will probably not include the disposal of the fur coat and of the lace nightgown.

One of the aims in the U.S.S.R. is to give freedom of choice to the consumer. The range can never be so wide as in a society where wide variations of wealth enable the rich customer to indulge an almost unlimited caprice. For the present, the industry of the U.S.S.R. is too busy in overtaking the demand of the State for the means of defence, and of the masses for primary necessities—plain food in abundance, substantial boots and clothing, and adequate housing—to give a great amount of attention to variations of individual taste. But the shops of the cities, which in 1937 exhibited a wide range of choice at a very varying scale of prices, demonstrate that the latter object is not ignored. The question which interests us in respect to consumer's choice is whether a planned system is necessarily incapable of respecting it. It has been powerfully argued that it is incapable: but the argument appears to start from the premise that plans cannot be, and are not, modified. In point of fact, they are very frequently modified. The asbestos engineer, Rukeyser, mentions five changes in the asbestos plan in the course of six months. Students of planning are aware that this was by no means an exceptional case. In both types of society the producer and the retailer make their guess, or their plan, of the consumer's desires and, if they err, have to sell their unpopular stock at a loss. Such sales are quite common in the U.S.S.R. In regard to that comparatively small number of commodities which are "made to order," it is possible, in the U.S.S.R. as in our individualistic society, to have recourse to the self-employers, whose economic function, as the Webbs have made clear to us, still survives. Generally speaking, it is no more difficult for a State or a municipal institution, than for an impersonal Joint Stock Company, or the management of chain stores, to meet the customer's wishes. Each must find, and train, the suitable personnel. Both may devise methods of remuneration which encourage skilful salesmanship.

It must be admitted that a special obstacle presents itself in the

U.S.S.R. in the form of a characteristic Russian contempt for retail trading, partly due to the essentially caste constitution of the old Kupyets or merchant class, and partly to the original revolutionary enthusiasm for manual productive work. It has also been made clear by recent investigation that the proportion of the population engaged on the work of retailing is far smaller in the U.S.S.R. than in Britain: from which we may infer a less degree of attention to the convenience of the retail customers. But the encouragement given to village Co-operative shops by Government and by the Central Union of Co-operatives, and the improved condition of the shops which has resulted, show that the importance of retail distribution is now better realised.

In so far as the system is successful in establishing freedom of choice for the consumer—and the practical difficulties will, of course, increase as the standard rises higher above the subsistence minimum—it will be possible to carry the process of economic valuation back from consumers' to producers' goods, and to obtain an economic criterion of the alternative uses of scant means at an earlier stage of the economic process.

Free choice of occupation is facilitated in the U.S.S.R. at present by the great unsatisfied demand for skilled labour and for technical qualifications, and encouraged by opportunities of training and of the chance of trial in a higher grade. There have been occasions when men of special qualifications or experience in one line, such for instance as railway work in 1931, have been required to return to it during a period of emergency. The introduction of the passport system for residents in the cities in 1932 has sometimes been represented as interference with the free choice of employment. Its aims appear to have been the prevention of overcrowding, with which the supply of new housing accommodation was unable to keep pace, and the relief of the pressure on the towns' supply of food. In April, 1933, owing to the heavy labour turnover in the mines of the Donets basin, arrangements were made which must have involved pressure to enter and remain in the mines. Demands for labour are often met by agreements between the administrations of Collective Farms and the managements of factories, and there is no reasonable doubt that the former exercise some pressure on their superfluous hands, if volunteers are not forthcoming.

In October, 1940, a system of industrial conscription was introduced under the pressure of political conditions, and, in order to diminish the attractiveness of literary education, fees were imposed for schools. Collective Farms and Town Soviets were instructed to select young men and women for the technical courses, and those upon whom the choice fell were required to take up the trade for which they were trained for a stated minimum period. These orders seem to show that the preference for industrial work, which was at one time marked, has given place to a liking for sedentary tasks.

At present, at all events, the U.S.S.R. is free from unemployment, and the choice of occupations is freer than in a country where young people must take the first job that offers, or risk finding none. I reserve for discussion elsewhere the question whether Planning or Price is the more favourable to human liberty. Here I will only pause to note that liberty is essentially a matter of balance. Each man, left to himself, takes so much of it, that he tends to impinge upon the liberty of others. The maintenance of the balance calls for organisation, and any tendencies towards anarchy, in the economic or any other sphere, inevitably upset this balance.

Whatever be our attitude to planning by public authorities, it becomes inevitable, in a greater or a less degree, in proportion as planning by private persons or by voluntary combinations ceases to give satisfactory results. Private armies, private navies, private road-making, private drains, private paving, private letter-carrying, in large measure also private schools and private hospitals, have ceased to be adequate. Private industry is debatable ground. In the pioneering period, when the object was to get increased production by any and every method, private industry was irreplaceable. But it has learned to live by providing employment for some and goods for some, without providing employment for all and goods for all. Many are cut off from the natural sources of subsistence, without obtaining access to the artificial sources. Many remain poor in the midst of plenty. It is too casual and fortuitous a method of meeting the needs of the enlarged community which it has helped to create.

❋   ❋   ❋

The need of planning was illustrated with particular force in Soviet Russia by the obvious mutuality of two economic functions. The supply of food inter-acts with the supply of industrial commodities. That alliance between peasant and town workers upon which Lenin insisted with so much emphasis is as inevitable in the economic as in the political sphere. Short food, short commodities: short commodities, short food. The peasant will not grow, or will not bring to market, a full supply, unless the handicraftsman has clothing and implements to give in return. The handicraftsman must go back to the land

and dig if the peasant does not give him grain. This is a platitude, no doubt, and yet a platitude upon the complete assimilation of which depends the understanding of Soviet Russia (and of much more beside). The two must work in mutual interchange, and maladjustment will bring about economic disease. Over-production on one side will set the world to burning or drowning its food, and so affect the remuneration of the food producer as to stop the sale of industrial commodities—since it is he who is the principal customer for them. Under-production on that same side, when it occurs, means famine in the towns, if not in the country also. The right adjustment means economic health: and the success or failure of economic policies is to be judged by the effectiveness of the adjustment. If we are to form an opinion of the deserts of the Soviet Government, which operates on a continent-wide scale upon the economic life of nearly 200 million human beings, it is essential to determine how it has set the balance between town and country.

And here we are confronted by diametrically opposite opinions, both purporting to establish their correctness by statistical demonstration. One, represented by the authoress of *Economics of Peasant Farming* (Oxford University Press, 1939), is that the State artificially widened the gap between the earnings of town workers and peasants in order to force the pace of investment in industry. The other, argued by E. Strauss in *Soviet Russia*, 1941, is that the peasant demand for modern means of production is almost completely satisfied, that supplies of manufactured consumption goods for the village were on the up-grade at least up to the end of the second Five-Year-Plan, and that "agriculture seems to be in a better position than industry, which has been fostered with so many exertions and which has now, to a certain extent, even become the basis of agriculture."

In Chapter XX and in one of my appendices I have tried to furnish material for a decision between these two opposite contentions. For the moment I only emphasise the importance, even the inevitability, of planning, if serious economic maladjustment is to be avoided.

❀ ❀ ❀

A definition of the national aim is an essential preliminary to planning. It may be planning for scarcity: as some capitalist planning must, inevitably, be—if it is to maintain the prospect of profit. There is the planning of Nazi Germany: planning for a maximum of armament and for the reduction of other peoples to a helot status. Russian planning, as its first prophets saw it, was to be planning to make an end of the backwardness of Russia. They had emerged from a war in

which the inability to create the apparatus of modern civilisation had
been emphasised by a virtual blockade, and had produced a humiliating military collapse. Whatever private industry might have done elsewhere (and in time of war it had been largely superseded), it had certainly not saved Russia. The Civil War had rammed home the lesson.
They were conscious of a weakness, not only military, but economic,
which the indefinite postponement of the hope of revolution abroad
made imminently dangerous. Internally they had an uncertain ally in
the peasantry, prepared to feed them *for a price*: and that price was
the supply of manufactured goods, for which native industry was still
inadequate. They realised that the final issue of the struggle between
Capitalism and Socialism depended on the capacity for victory in the
world's markets, and that the low productivity of Russian labour
threatened to be the fatal flaw in the armour of the Socialist Fatherland.

Trotsky, speaking in 1920 before the Third All-Russian Congress of
Trade Unions, in defence of his plan for the militarisation of labour,
said that it could succeed only on the basis of a single economic plan,
covering the whole country and all branches of economic activity.
The plan must be drawn up for a number of years, and must deal first
with transport and necessary supplies of food, raw material, and fuel;
secondly, with machine-building having the locomotive as its core;
thirdly, with machine-building in the interest of primary necessities;
and fourthly, with the production of articles of personal or secondary
significance. The living interest of all that is honest, class-conscious,
and inspired in the working-class must be excited in support of this
Plan. All energies must be concentrated upon it, there must be no
distraction of attention, no dissipation of forces, no waste of effort. This outline, made eight years in advance of the actual first Five-
Year Plan, is a very remarkable forecast.

The New Economic Policy—an interlude in which economic development, in agriculture almost entirely, and in industry to a very
large extent, was left to the individual appetite for gain—was the
antipodes of Planning: and the struggle of Trotsky and the Opposition
on behalf of planning was in essence an attempt for the premature
abrogation of N.E.P. The outline of a general economic plan, published in the summer of 1925, had a very modest scope. It aimed at
forecasting the development of private trade, particularly of agriculture, and at giving guidance to industrial enterprises in maintaining
the equilibrium which the "Scissors" crisis had shown to be precarious.
Annual control-figures continued to be published, and their binding

force upon State departments was increasingly emphasised. But this fell far short of the enforcement of a plan by the authority of a State having control of the processes of production and distribution.

The Plan, when it came, might have been, as the State Planning Department wished it to be, a mere forecast of probable attainments, based upon past experience and serving to co-ordinate the various branches of production and to prevent such disproportionate and one-sided growth as had been the cause of the "Scissors" crises. Actually it was more and yet less than this: it was of the nature of a production drive, a means of inspiring a whole people with the will to equip itself with all the instruments of civilisation. It aimed at rebuilding resources from the bottom upwards, the instruments of production, the agriculture that feeds the worker, the education that makes the most of the worker's brains and develops to the utmost his technical skill, the inspiration that gives the desire, as well as the power, to make the best of all opportunities in the pursuit of a great common aim. Man was to be remoulded for new tasks, stimulated to high hopes, encouraged to sacrifices.

The first outline of a Plan of this ambitious character was completed in March, 1927, but the examination of it lasted for more than two years. The Fifteenth Congress of the Communist Party adopted it in 1928, and the all-Union Congress of Soviets gave it formal approval in May, 1929. It was to run from October 1, 1928, at that time the beginning of the Soviet year, and the epoch of intensive production was thus inaugurated. It was adopted in its maximum variant, and it aimed at extending *the power to produce*, the means of production, not merely at increasing the supply of goods: with the object of bringing the Soviet Union nearer to the productive standards of capitalist enemies. That it co-ordinated the various branches of production, and prevented the disproportionate growth of some of them, is more difficult to establish.

Why was the leadership, which had resisted the pressure of the Opposition for the policies so clearly formulated in *The True Position in Russia* for the development of industry, the collectivisation of agriculture, and the co-ordination of the whole by Plan, now convinced that the moment had arrived for carrying these out? I think that the situation at home and abroad had become ripe for the change, which was, in effect, only a reversion, with increased energy and a new technique, to a suspended design. N.E.P. had replaced War-Communism, when the hope of alliance with the world-proletariat had been indefinitely postponed, and when the peasantry had plainly

shown its unwillingness to tide the Revolutionary Government over a
difficult interval. Up to a certain point, the position of 1927-28 was
parallel to that of 1921. The design of winning support for the
U.S.S.R. in a United Front of the proletariats, in China, in Britain,
in Poland, had broken down, and encirclement by hostile Capitalist
Powers seemed to be threatened. The peasantry was withholding its
grain, and it seemed as though its more prosperous elements might
soon be in a position to dictate their own terms. The difference between the two epochs lay in the increased strength and resources of
the Soviet Government at the later of the two dates. Both agriculture
and industry had recovered something like their pre-war standard.
The currency.had been stabilised, and a common denominator thus
provided for economic calculation. A serious rift had indeed developed
in the Party: but the leadership had shown itself powerful enough to
remove the dissentient element without the use of violence on either
side. It was no longer necessary to buy off opposition by vital concessions, as in 1921. It was possible so far to ignore the traditional individualism of the peasantry as to plan an agrarian revolution, far more
radical than anything contemplated in 1917-18. In other words, the
home front was secured: and cool heads and stout hearts could afford
to turn their attention to the grand aim of putting the material and
moral equipment of the Soviet Union on a par with that of its rivals
and potential enemies. These, as it seems to me, were the conditions
in which the first Five-Year Plan was set up as the goal of the ambitions of the people of the U.S.S.R. It was no desperate throw, made by
a gambler in a moment of difficulty and despair: but the seizing of a
favourable moment for the fulfilment of a cherished hope. For the
technique the leadership was indebted to the fertile inventiveness of
the Opposition, but it exercised its own political judgment in choosing the time for putting it into use. If Trotsky had gone bathing, and
Stalin had stolen his clothes, the clothes at least fitted their new
wearer.

＊　　＊　　＊

The aim was primarily one of defence, against capitalist boycott if
not against capitalist war, and against the pressure for the importation
of manufactured goods which must be the ultimate consequence of the
failure to produce them at home—with the resultant risks of debt and
enserfment. Since the power to produce must be extended to bring
the Union nearer to the standard of its capitalist rivals, heavy industry and the instruments of production were above all else to be developed. Light industry was not omitted from consideration, for it

was desired to raise the general standard of living by an increased supply of consumers' goods. But it was imperfectly realised that the demands of the urban worker are greater than those of the peasant, and the Plan did not give all that the prospective growth of the factory population required.

The actual working of the Plan was that of an enormous measure of compulsory saving, and of sacrifices far greater than had been contemplated, which substantially reduced the general standard of living for a time and, to hearts less stout and to wills less ruthless, might have seemed to presage ruin. For the capital required for the reconstruction of the U.S.S.R. was to be raised within the country, not borrowed from abroad. The penalty of foreign indebtedness would have been the sacrifice of that independence which it was the leading object of the Plan to achieve. With or without modern industrial equipment, the U.S.S.R. would have been enserfed to her creditors, if she had not paid her way by tightening the belts of her people.

Not in its first form, but in a later amendment, it incorporated the great and fruitful idea of new bases for the Coal and Metallurgical industries in Eastern Russia, and also the extension of the textile industry, hitherto limited to Great Russia, to Central Asia and Siberia, thus diminishing vulnerability to external attack, and giving to the non-Great-Russian nationalities a share in industrial development. How far-reaching were the consequences of this decision was shown indeed in the summer of 1942, when the old industrial areas were occupied by German armies.

❋ ❋ ❋

If we pick up, at random, any Russian newspaper of the period of the first Five-Year Plan when the strain was at its greatest, we receive an impression of ardent hopes, and of immense and general excitement, in which the sacrifices of individuals are forgotten by themselves as well as by others. The workers speak with their own voices and write with their own pens; on four pages of very poor paper, with very poor print, the vocal soldiers of industry shout themselves hoarse, with boasting, with exhortation, with criticism of failures, with challenges to Socialist competition, with offers of "tow-ropes" to less forward enterprises, with promises, with indignation. It happens to be an anniversary of the newspaper. Here is the Lenin factory of electrical apparatus, proclaiming itself the first-born of October, the giant of electro-technical industry, the strength of Bolshevik tempos, twice honoured with the order of Lenin, the active fighter for the Socialist reconstruction of rural economy, the sharpshooter of the undertakings

for Government grain-farms, the initiator of Lenin's great idea of mass
workers' control from below over Soviet bureaucracy. We seem to see
the giant slapping his bulging muscles, and challenging his rivals to
competition. He proclaims a two years' struggle for cleansing the personnel from bureaucrats, intriguers, rogues and opportunists and, in
honour of the journal's anniversary, promises to equip with electrical
transformers a workers' settlement and cultural buildings for the Capital: also to provide a magneto (evidently the magnetos had hitherto
been imported) for the Red Flag Tractor factory, "so that a Soviet
tractor may plough Soviet fields with a Soviet magneto." Then he
recites some of his triumphs: the initiation of the Third Soviet
loan, the equipment of the Moscow Airport, the equipment of the
Butter-centre with electric power; and calls upon the Editor to fight
implacably against divagations, whether to the Right or to the Left,
against recidivist counter-revolutionary Trotskyism and any compromise with it. The manifesto ends on this quasi-theological note.
The conciliar age of the Church is lined up with Messrs. Krupp and
Armstrong.

Next we come upon a grave article upon the problems of technical
construction in the Coal Industry, calling upon the whole mining
proletariat to devise machinery for those processes, such as freighting,
which are still conducted by primitive methods, and to bring Russian
coal-production to the second place in the world, alongside of England, and hope is held out of improvement of the material conditions of the miners, with socialistic settlements, schools, clubs, libraries, radio, baths, tramways, roads, telephones, so that they may be
placed on a level with the workers of the industrial centres.

More coal, more pig-iron, more steel, more machines, more oil, more
paper! Such are the headlines which take the place of the murders,
divorces, betting odds, and greyhound races, of our own newspapers.
The Boiler gang is short by fourteen boilers, and the quality of boilers
has deteriorated. There is plenty of seed but it hasn't yet reached the
farms, though the sowing season is upon us. The new beet-root
regions are very ill supplied with beet-seed. There are plenty of tractors, but no spare parts. The workers have proclaimed an all-union
muster roll of their own for the supply of spare parts. Cabbages and
potatoes for the factory! We have planted our own vegetable garden,
and challenge all others to Socialist competition to do the same. We,
the workers, guarantee Soviet fire-bricks for metallurgical work.

First raid of the Young Communist brigade. Post Office complaint
books examined. Officials show a stiff attitude to complainants. Com-

plaint book not given to complainants on demand. Five-day-period for anti-bureaucrats' light cavalry organised!

Milk, curds, and sour cream so adulterated as to lose both nutritive quality and natural flavour. Attention to sale of milk products on private market necessary. All inspectors will receive complaints of false weights and other breaches of orders regarding retail prices of necessities.

Short paragraphs announce, (1) a discovery of unpublished manuscripts of Goethe, (2) an advertisement for teachers of political economy, and a demand upon all undertakings and institutions to give up any of these whom they find in their employ, (3) the despatch of a medical mission to women and children in the Kirgiz country: *salaries by agreement*, (4) a Poster Exhibition in the Tretiakov gallery at Moscow, (5) a report of the current quotations of eight loans, State and Municipal, two of them lottery loans, (6) an advertisement of bile-powder—the only advertisement of any commodity which appears in the journal. This has the quality of *making the use of soap unnecessary* (soap is a deficit commodity at present), (7) a liquidators' announcement of the payment of claims against state concerns which have failed, (8) advertisements for two book-keepers; *salary by agreement*.

Then we are off again on self-criticism. Our correspondent complains of short production of coal in the Donets basin, there is absenteeism of labour on a large scale. Men are sometimes standing in queues for bread when they ought to be at work. For months the Co-operatives were feeding "dead souls" (non-existent customers), who swallowed thousands of tons of food. The portrait of a shock-worker in a coal-shaft is given, and details of the output at different shafts, some worse, some better than the plan, follow. Our correspondent at Cheliabinsk complains of too much dust in the coal produced there, and the consequent failure in the electric supply. The repair of locomotives on the Murmansk line is unsatisfactory, so the workers have instituted a system of marks for the work of different shops, and place them monthly in order of merit. A locomotive came back from the Vologda repair shop, after overhaul, with seventy defects.

And some more malpractices. A shaft in the North Caucasus coal administration attracted attention in two successive years by its exceptional output. It's a fake. Coal-dust was reckoned in, and old stocks were treated as new gettings. Sometimes the gettings were counted twice, once on coming from the mine and once after sorting. *The class origin of the conspiracy is clear.* The woman conspirator is the daughter of a man deprived of civil rights, and *her husband is a gentleman!* The Party and Trade Union leadership of the shaft slipped into the way of compromise with the class-enemy.

Follows a slashing attack upon the newspaper run by the Party Collective and Factory Committee of a flax and hemp mill. The editor of this minor organ does not know what was meant by Comrade Stalin's six points (see the chapter on "Old Stones in the New Building"), and his paper has no worker correspondents. (Worker correspondents are a very important part of the Soviet newspaper systems. Along with village correspondents, they keep the public in close touch with the newspapers, and the newspapers in touch with their public.) Why has no one yet thought of liquidating the fellow's illiteracy?

Next we have a page devoted to agriculture, with a great headline across it: "Quick collection of seed shows Bolshevik leadership": and a picture below showing the peasants of a collective farm examining and approving the seed for their spring-sowings. A priggish little townee describes his cross-examination of some up-country peasants, to discover how much they know of the organisation of their collective farm. "Don't know as how we can tell just how it is." "How many active workers are there?" Silence. "How many shock-workers?" Still complete silence. Our agricultural critic observes that this ignorance of farm problems is a serious sign—and we are left to imagine what the peasants said when they had got rid of him.

Someone has been in a hurry in Buriat-Mongolia, and has pushed a whole region into collectivisation. But the provincial Party Committee has censured the district Party Committee and put the matter right. Our Tashkent correspondent says a region of Uzbekistan is suffering from the absence on leave of certain Party leaders, so that the agricultural work does not begin till noon, and is pretty slack even then. There's too much talking in the Fergana valley: and in the region of Samarkand there is not a single collective in which the gangs of workers have been properly organised. Under the heading "The Red Tablet," certain collective farms on the lower Volga, in the North Caucasus, in the Tartar republic, in the Ukraine, and in the Chuvash region, are commended for having completed the collection of seed. Socialist competition is established between the different gangs of a collective farm near Simferopol. The cattle-breeding Trust is blamed for requiring a State cattle-farm to take more cattle than its completed preparations permitted: and is warned that the guilty must be held to their responsibility.

Stop speculation! Our Smolensk correspondent reports that our paper, price five kopeks, is being sold for fifteen, with a parcel of old useless magazines, and withheld from purchasers who will not take the lot. The railway station kiosks must be kept under proper control. Organisation of a department of the Academy of Sciences in the Far East! Delay in the repair of vessels on the Amur river! In the best-equipped basin at Blagoveschchensk there are twenty vessels less than the plan provides: but the less well-equipped Nikolaev has thirty vessels in excess of plan!

The administrator of a chemical depot at Nizhni-Novgorod, the full-powered attorney of the pedigree pig-breeding trust—there's a title for an ambitious man—and others, all members of the Communist Party, have been expelled from the Party for disposing of deficit articles in the private market, and for *relations with strange elements*. The Control Commission is passing the case on to the Public Prosecutor.

No attacks upon Government; no sex; no financial article, except the quotation of the loans and of rates of exchange; no reference to religion, churches, or clergy. Japan is very much in the news. Otherwise there is nothing "patriotic" or "Russian" or "national" in the paper; and no scandals, or crossword-puzzles. The sport is all in the Socialist competition for more output, and the heroes are all shock-workers. The beautiful ladies have shed their beautiful smiles, and are busy planting beet-root, or helping in the supply of deficit commodities.

Such was the pabulum of the newspaper reader in the final year of the first Five-Year-Plan: and so eagerly was it sought after that queues were formed at the newspaper kiosks. The Soviet Government carried the masses on a wave of enthusiasm, and made them forget that their belts sometimes needed tightening. But the strain had been enormous. When it was over, not much less than a third of the national income for four years had been put into compulsory savings —in other words, had been expended upon providing the instruments of future production, to the detriment of the present standard of living. Stalin made one of his rare but impressive speeches, declaring that the object of the Party had been to change the beggarly peasant-nag into a large-scale machine-industry, and that whereas there had been no ferrous metallurgy, no tractor or automobile industry, no construction of machine-tools, no serious up-to-date chemical industry, no production of agricultural machinery, and no aviation industry, all these things were now in existence, so that, from a weak country unprepared for defence, the U.S.S.R. had become a country prepared to defend itself against foreign attack. He declared that in the next five-year period there would no longer be any necessity of accelerating effort, and that they would be content with a yearly increase of 13-14% instead of demanding one of 22%. He claimed that unemployment had been eliminated, and the number of workers in large industry doubled, with increased money wages, and, not unnaturally, exulted in the contrast with the capitalist world, then in the trough of the worst depression that had ever affected it.

The Plan has well been described as a first assertion, in action, of the possibility of ending starvation and semi-starvation in the midst of potential plenty, of ending the coexistence of unemployed labour and unsatisfied consumers. But we must distinguish between the two aspects which are, in fact, confused together in the system of planning in operation in the U.S.S.R. Since it is to be Plan which determines Price, not, as in the theoretical conditions of a capitalist country, Price which determines Plan, the Russian Plan should discharge the function of determining the application of economic means to economic ends: in plainer language, should tell us how much capital, material and labour should be devoted to each branch of production, and should maintain the appropriate equilibrium between different objects. This is quite a different thing from a production drive, which seeks to get on with the job as quickly as possible in each of its sectors, without any particular concern with precise co-ordination, or even with exact calculation. It was natural to make the Plan a production drive as well as an estimate and a means of co-ordination, because demand, in the sense of need, is so greatly in excess of potential supply, in almost every line, that there seems no fear, for the present, of the actual over-production of anything. But this method of approach obscured the other object, of precise calculation and co-ordination. One of the results was the too rapid progress of the collectivisation of agriculture, before the supply of agricultural machinery, which was essential to the success of the collectivisation policy, was available. This involved discontent and resistance, which might have been averted, and important changes of plan, including the establishment of new centres for the manufacture of tractors.

In 1938 we find the Council of People's Commissars recognising the neglect of the aims of precise calculation and co-ordination, and insisting upon these aims as the most important problem of the State Planning Commission. But the nice adjustment of means to ends involved the existence of reliable statistics, and statistics, everywhere less reliable than could be desired, have always been a weak point in Russia.

In the critical days of the first Five-Year Plan and of agricultural collectivisation, there was an ominous restriction of the output of information on certain important points, and these restrictive tendencies grew more jealous as the threat of foreign attack grew more urgent.

However, though the U.S.S.R. keeps back some facts, of which it is aware, it is frank enough in admitting some very disconcerting information. There was no concealment, for instance, of the destruction of cattle, of the slowness of recovery in this respect, of the consequent diminution in meat products, of the continued low yield of the principal crops, for which we have to turn to India to find a parallel.

Statistics, where they exist, cannot afford a basis for a final judgment as to the quality of work. So far as quantities are concerned, a calculation by Maurice Dobb (*Soviet Economy and the War*, 1941) shows that the increase in production of certain important products between 1928 and 1937 (coal, oil, pig iron, steel, and cement) was 200-300%, while electrical power increased by 600%. These things have been achieved without foreign indebtedness, and along with a great reduction in the export of grain, formerly a prominent feature in Russian economy. The railway freight traffic in 1937 was five times heavier than it had been in 1913, and the number of passenger miles increased three and a half times. For the evidence of quality we can turn to the military records of the war, which must go far to convince the most sceptical.

That the three Five-Year Plans, the last of which was interrupted by the Nazi attack, were perfect, either in design or in execution, it is unlikely that anyone will contend. A different governmental machine might have done the job better. But the tremendous dynamic of that group of men which, having conceived and developed the idea, proceeded actually to put it on the map of realities, was unique. It will never again be possible, with an easy conscience, to relegate to cloud-cuckoo-land the notion that production and distribution for a great community may be based on something other than competitive price.

Chapter XVIII

THE OLD STONES IN THE NEW BUILDING

"We have to build with the bricks which Capitalism has left us. . . . The toilers have crushed Capitalism, but you cannot feed upon crushed Capitalism. You must take all the culture inherited from Capitalism and with it build Socialism: all the science, all the technique, all the knowledge, all the skill. And these things are in the hands and in the brains of the specialists."

LENIN, *Success and Difficulties of the Soviet Power.*

The Revolution was far less destructive of the material monuments of the past than has been commonly supposed. The survival of the statues of the Tsars—even that of Alexander III, to which a slighting inscription has been attached—and of historic buildings and collections, and the preservation of ancient icons (and, in many cases, their restoration to primitive beauty by the removal of barbarous additions) bear testimony to the truth of this statement. An instance of preservation, demanding considerable sacrifice in a period of acute fuel-famine, was that of the Imperial hot-houses at Leningrad, where many exotic plants still existed in 1935, and doubtless exist still. There has been, in fact, a tendency, and one which has grown rapidly stronger, to treat the achievements of bourgeois and earlier civilisations as a valued inheritance. Amid his bitter criticisms of the Stalinite period of the Revolution, Trotsky does not fail to award praise to the preservation, and wider dissemination, of the good things which the past has left behind. We are now to trace the workings of a like maxim in the spheres of industrial and financial administration.

Two-thirds of the way through the period of the first Plan, when some of the difficulties of that great reconstruction had become apparent, Stalin made one of his dramatic emergences from silence, and delivered to a conference of industrial managers and economic workers a sermon on the way to conduct their business. It was one of those frank enunciations of policy, delivered with complete disregard of all theory and all face-saving reticence, which give occasion to Western critics to acclaim the abandonment by the Revolutionary Government of its fundamental principles. He began by declaring that the Plan was developing in a lop-sided fashion, and that some branches of industry were forging ahead, while others were hanging behind. The backwardness was particularly marked in coal-mining and in metallurgy (as indeed it continues to be to-day). He called for a re-organisation of all ranks of the industrial army, and of commercial methods, in order to achieve that increased productivity which is a condition of the success of Socialism.

Low productivity—which is another way of expressing the backwardness of Russia—has been the root problem of the Revolution since the successful seizure of power. It is in the main an inheritance from the Tsarist period—it is rather Russian than revolutionary—but it was aggravated at the Revolution, partly by strained relations with the managing class, the technical intelligentsia, partly by the rebel mentality of manual labour, and the resultant necessity of creating a new labour discipline.

When Stalin made his "Six Points" speech on June 23, 1931, the increased demand for labour, caused by the first Five-Year-Plan, had put an end to unemployment and brought about a shortage of labour. The workers had taken advantage of the situation. "I have seen them laugh at a foreman who reprimanded them," writes Miss Ella Winter. Increased absenteeism and malingering, and even attacks upon the factory staffs, compelled the appointment in 1929 of a Commission to enquire into indiscipline. The Commission reported that it was due to the influx of fresh workers from the country, to the negligence and indifference of the technical and managing staffs, to the interference of representatives of the People's Commissariat of Labour, of Trade Unions, and of the Communist Party, in technical operations, and to the passive attitude of the Commissariats of Labour and of Justice to breaches of discipline. The powers of managers were thereupon strengthened, and steps taken to restore discipline. Tomsky, the steady advocate of Trade Union independence, was removed from the office of President of the All-Union Central Council of Trade Unions, and a purge took place of the Council's personnel (1929). The Sixteenth All-Union Congress of the Party (1930) made a final end of Tomsky's claim that each Trade Union was entitled to press for increased wages and improved conditions for its own membership, and declared that each must take part in increasing general productivity, as the one and only means of raising the standard for all.

Hostility and distrust towards managers and technical staff remained, though the workers had passed the humorous stage in which they expressed criticism by wheeling their administrators out in wheelbarrows to the rubbish-dump of the mill. One-man management was still not universally realised in fact. A controversy of long standing regarding the method and principles of determining wages was still not finally settled. The conditions of labour were not attractive, and there was perpetual "flitting" in the hope of finding better. There were grave complaints of irresponsibility in the treatment of machinery and tools. The costs of production remained unduly high, and the commercial management of economic enterprises was defective. Such were the conditions in which Stalin made his pronouncement.

THE BRAINS OF INDUSTRY

The old intelligentsia, the kin of Vissarion Belinsky and the "circles" of St. Petersburg and Moscow, was revolutionary in every fibre. It was academic, philosophical, literary, but it produced the fiery spirits of the seventies and eighties. The economic developments of Sergius Witte created, out of it or side by side with it, another, a new, intelligentsia, of managers, engineers and technicians. These were the men to whom the Revisionist Marxism of Eduard Bernstein, with its quietistic and anti-revolutionary philosophy, made its principal appeal. They had no sympathy with the Bolsheviks, dreaded the proletarian insurrection against authority, and withdrew from cooperation with the new power in the State. The lawyers refused to attend the new revolutionary Courts. It was almost impossible to fill with efficient holders the official posts outside the great cities. The flight of the telephone girls from the central office, on the day of its seizure, was typical of the general attitude of the white-collar worker. The *bourgeois* at the cross-roads, with his neck sunk in his collar, is the poet Blok's appropriate image. He was waiting for the upstart régime to come to an end. Madame Britnieva has put the same thing in other words:

"*Contrary to the first expectations of all reasonable people, these new-fangled persons who called themselves Bolsheviks had come to stay for some time, in spite of the complete chaos in every single branch of life which was the only visible consequence of their advent to power.*"

Lenin was conscious of the mischief, and pointed out that the proletariat had neither knowledge nor training for the building of industry and culture, and that the intelligentsia must be won to cooperation. The attempt, particularly effective in the case of the officering of the Red Army, was made to win them by offering openings to their ambitions, and by differential treatment. This aggravated the jealousy with which the proletarian regarded them. The masses, taught that physical labour was alone productive, and suspicious of the counter-revolutionary reputation of the managers and technicians, cherished their hatred, and welcomed every opportunity of revealing and punishing the offences of the suspected class. The dislike and the suspicion were mutual, as the diarists and novelists abundantly demonstrate. It is likely that some of the "intellectual" servants of Bolshevism neglected their work. Some may have done deliberate damage. Still more were suspected of doing it: and the failures, which must occur everywhere and in all enterprises, were represented to be deliberate. It is here that we must look for the explanation of that persecution of the white-collared which brought so much discredit upon the revolutionary régime. I shall here cite only two out of the numerous cases which occurred.

In December, 1930, Professor Ramzin, the leading expert in thermo-dynamics, and other Russians, were charged with economic sabotage, with the organisation of a secret political party, and conspiracy with a White émigré organisation in France to induce the French Government to invade Russia. This was the so-called Promparti (Industrial Party) trial, of which, and of its aims, the asbestos engineer, Rukeyser, has left us an account. He thinks the aims of the Government were to explain the breakdown of certain industries and the shortage of certain commodities, and to focus attention upon the foreign enemy, in order to divert it from mistakes at home. This explanation, by one who was in very close touch with industrial business, has a significant relevance to some later events. Professor Ramzin and others confessed to the charges. Six sentences of death were passed, but not carried out: and the sentences of imprisonment were reduced. In March, 1931, fourteen professors and State officials, including the well-known statistician Groman, who had pressed for lower estimates of production in the first Five-Year Plan, were brought to trial on a charge of conspiracy with Mensheviks, in the U.S.S.R. and abroad, for counter-revolutionary measures.

In his Six Points speech of June 23, 1931, Stalin referred to the Promparti trial, and said that wrecking had at that time been a sort of fashion. He recalled the panic in the right wing of the Communist Party in the early days of the first Five-Year Plan, when Rykov, Bukharin and Tomsky were shocked by the drastic action against the village capitalist; and explained that, at that time, determined suppression of all active wreckers was necessary. Now, however, the position had changed. The enemy was on the run, and a section of the intelligentsia, conscious of defeat, was ready to join the victor of the strug-

gle. He therefore called for greater consideration for the engineers and
technicians of the old school, and announced a truce with the intelligentsia, in order to win the co-operation of brains. At the same time
he insisted on the enormously increased demand for new brains to
direct the new centres of industry and railway construction which
the Five-Year Plan had called into being: and demanded an industrial and technical intelligentsia drawn from the working class.

For the first Five-Year Plan there was a shortage of 5,000 superior
engineers in industry and of 6,400 in transport; of 22,000 foremen and
overseers and of 12,000 subordinate railway technicians; of 13,000
agronomists, 200,000 tractor operators and 50,000 tractor mechanics.
No wonder that there has never been any unemployment of skilled
labour, or that there is a general pressure among workers to improve
their qualifications, since prizes such as these lie ahead of them.

The Desk and the Bench

Stalin called at the same time for the breaking up of unwieldy
amalgamations and for the decentralisation of management, while
retaining centralisation of control.

Boards of ten to fifteen persons (some of whom, said Stalin, might
be much better employed at work at the benches) were to be replaced
by one-man management. Chairmen and their deputies must get into
touch with their workers, and do more work in the field and less in
the boardroom. There is ample material to show how much this rebuke was needed.

Commercial Management

The existing sources, says Stalin, are no longer sufficient to provide the capital required by the developments of the Plan, which demand a new industry in the Urals, in Siberia, in Kazakstan, and a
new railway system uniting the West with the Far East. (This early
insistence upon the development of the East and the Far East shows
the prescience of the leader.) Heavy industry must become a new
source of accumulation of capital. At present it fails, for lack of good
commercial management. There is no check upon the cost of production, no check upon the credits granted by the Banks, no effective cost-
accounting to furnish a commercial basis of operations. In effect he
calls for the adoption of the devices of capitalist business, in the interests of an economy which has banished private profit.

But not quite all the devices, for there is one without which the
best cost-accounting is likely to be inefficacious: and this is a stable

currency, the true measure of expenditure and receipts. In June, 1930, there was no small change to be had in Moscow, silver and copper were being hoarded in spite of penalties, because of paper inflation. A rouble-note was being treated as equivalent to a ten-kopek piece. In 1931, on the black exchange at Berlin, twenty roubles were being offered for the dollar, and the rouble rate was to go considerably lower in succeeding years, though it never reverted to the astronomical figures of 1923, before the stabilisation. Without committing the reader to the opinion that the black exchange was the true mirror of the rouble's value, it is plain that its value was falling rapidly: and a changing medium is not an accurate measure for the purposes of cost-accounting.

Stalin was not among the theorists who said that money was tolerated only as a temporary concession in a transitional epoch. He laughed heartily at them in a speech which he made in January, 1934. It seems that there was, in the U.S.S.R., the same struggle between inflationists and deflationists as elsewhere, in spite of the absence of any large-scale private interest in the question, and Piatakov, the Chairman of the State Bank (later on, one of the sacrifices in the Trotskyist trials), was removed because he resisted the demand of the industrialists for the expansion of the currency. Under a régime of fixed official foreign exchange, and officially determined prices, such as that of the U.S.S.R., inflation does not take full effect except in the very limited open market, where its results, concentrated in a narrow channel, are correspondingly devastating: and it is easy to understand that Stalin was on the side of the industrialists, when he was preaching his sermon to the managers of industry. At a later date he told the world that the stability of the Soviet currency was secured primarily by the quantity of commodities which the Government puts into circulation at fixed prices: by which he meant that inflation is not inflation if it only supplies sufficient currency to deal with the actual volume of business.

He did not dwell upon bank credits, but he touched the subject, as was inevitable, for their influence upon commercial discipline, and on the reduction of the costs of production, is critical. All economic operations involve what we may call *hungry intervals*: the interval while the seed is in the ground, and before the crop is ready for eating or for marketing; the interval after the raw material has been supplied to the factory, and before it has been made into the finished goods; the interval after the goods have been sent to the trader, and before he has collected the price of them from the purchaser, and so on.

Short-term credit is that which fills these hungry intervals. In the type of society with which we are most familiar, the Bank accepts the custody of A's money, and lends it to B, to fill a hungry interval in B's operations. If B gets more than he needs to fill his hungry interval, or is allowed to keep it longer than his hungry interval ought to last, certain undesirable consequences ensue. Light come, light go, and B is careless about his costs; the pressure upon him for repayment being relaxed, he holds his goods for a higher price. The same operation being multiplied over a large number of Bs, there is too much short-term credit in operation, and the same thing happens which happens when there is too much currency—that is to say, there is inflation. The pressure of the Bank upon B is needed to maintain financial discipline. In the long run, if B is recalcitrant or unsuccessful, the Bank must be prepared to sell B up.

The Bolsheviks found that B, as a Trust or a Government enterprise, presented precisely the same problems as did B as a private *entrepreneur*. The hungry intervals were present and needed filling just the same: and Trust B, or Enterprise B, was just as prone to be careless about its costs, and to hold up its goods—more careless, in fact, because his own money was not directly at stake—as was Individual B, or Joint Stock Company B. We therefore see the Socialist State feeling its way towards a workable technique for short-term credit under State capitalism, and creating a system of control by the rouble.

In the United Kingdom there is a Credit Plan, operated by a Central Bank, which at some important crises dictates the financial policy of the State,* and on other occasions masks the responsibility of the rulers against attack. The Credit Plan is worked by raising or lowering the Bank rate on advances, and by purchase or sale of securities on the part of the Bank. It does not determine the share of individuals in the total amount of Credit, but it determines, within limits, what that total is to be. Individuals obtain, or fail to obtain, a share, according as they have, or have not, the required security to offer. The social value of the business for which the loan is granted is not a relevant question.

From January, 1930, the system of the U.S.S.R. has been to give a monopoly of short-term credit for industry to the State Bank and its forty-two regional head-offices. Commercial credit between different undertakings is forbidden. Bank credit is substituted for goods credit.

---

* This situation has, of course, been changed by the nationalisation of the Bank of England, and the extensive powers of government regulation of banking and credit operations.

At first the practice was to credit the seller of goods automatically, on proof that he had forwarded goods, and to debit the buyer with their value at the same time. This provided no check upon the costs of production, and no guarantee that the buyer was satisfied with the goods or their price. In 1931, before the date of Stalin's speech, the procedure was changed. On proof of an agreement between the parties, the Bank debits the buyer with the agreed value of the goods delivered to him. The adjustment between buyer and seller is made in the books of the bank, the seller having his outstanding loan reduced, while that of the buyer is increased, till the goods pass on to a third party. Industry is thus financed by advances limited to goods in process of production or distribution: advances which are treated as repaid as soon as a debit has been raised against the next stage in the series of exchanges. As soon as any doubt arises whether credit is being accompanied by production, the Bank is bound to make an investigation into the debtor's business. A law of March, 1931, gives the State Bank drastic authority for dealing with a defaulting State concern, which extends, in the final resort, to the sale of the effects of the defaulter.

There are complaints of a lack of elasticity in the system, and it is easy to imagine irritating delays. For instance—with an exception in favour of perishable goods—the railway authorities are forbidden to surrender goods till the State Bank has certified that the consignee has funds to pay for them. The Bank is expected to limit supplies of cash to wage-payments and to retail transactions. But there is a provision for an appeal against an order of the State Bank refusing credit to an organisation.

In practice some concerns do outrun the constable, but not, it would seem, by obtaining improper credits from the Bank. Complaints of arrears of wages, owing to the exhaustion of planned credits, from time to time make themselves heard.

Thus the hungry intervals of State enterprises in the U.S.S.R. are filled by planned overdrafts in the books of the State Bank, which acts as a universal clearing house: and the inflation of credits beyond the planned limit, except by a deliberate decision of the Government, is to all appearance impossible. Each buying enterprise has a motive for pressing for a reduction of the costs of each selling enterprise. Each producing enterprise has a similar motive—that of avoiding the discredit and possible loss of status and position, to which failure to keep within planned limits must lead. No long-term credits are given by the State Bank. There are four long-term banks which supply these—that is to say, which discharge the function of the money market in the United Kingdom. It is from this source that funds for investments are derived. Subject to the operation of the Plan, the long-term Bank doles out funds as the expenditures on construction, purchase of machinery and the like, occur and, on completion of the plant, credits the concern with the equivalent of the expenditure as assets. Technically speaking, the loan is unrepayable, and no interest is charged upon it. But the concern pays to the Bank a depreciation charge, which may be regarded as in essence the repayment of the loan: and it also contributes to the Bank 10% of the profits on its operations. These funds enable the long-term Bank to be a distributing agency for the financial requirements of industry.

There is an important difference between paying interest upon a loan, and paying a portion of the profits of the business created with its assistance. In the former case, the interest is a test of commercial success: if the concern's profits do not meet the interest, it must go under. In the latter case the concern is not automatically brought to reckoning by the inadequacy of its profit. In this respect also, therefore, the devices of the capitalist world are not fully applied to the cost-accounting of the U.S.S.R.

From a decree which issued a month after the date of Stalin's speech, it appears that the practice of applying short-term funds to capital investment, which led to the creation of frozen credits, still existed in the U.S.S.R. It was then prohibited. Whether the prohibition was effective is another matter.

The State bank not only keeps the banking account of each trust, but is the agency through which the Government inspects and supervises its operations. As soon as the flow of production ceases the defaulter must, if rules are observed, be brought up short by the collapse of his banking account. To this, I have only to add one qualification. The rigidity of rules in the U.S.S.R. is only equalled by the facility with which they are violated. The result is a somewhat capricious and uneven operation of the most important regulations, laxity alternating with meticulous insistence. Stalin himself has recently complained of the "soullessness" of the bureaucracy: but the bureaucracy has a way of suddenly and unexpectedly relenting. The "broad Slavonic nature," of which the poet Lermontov wrote, is still with us, and it still pardons evil where it sees its inevitability: but it grants, or withholds, pardon upon conditions which there is no foreseeing. I shall have occasion in the closing words of this book to point out that this instinctive elasticity has its good, as well as its bad, points. But in matters of finance there is something to be said for rigidity.

Directors can distinguish themselves and can earn honour and promotion by putting their enterprises upon a paying basis. By an order of April, 1936, each State enterprise receives 4% of the planned, and 50% of the unplanned, profit, for expenditure on the improvement of the social services for the workers engaged in that enterprise. It is true, no doubt, that the State, by manipulating price, can raise or lower profit on particular branches of industry. The fact remains that the incentive of profit exists in the Socialistic as in the Individualistic society, though the money which represents it does not pass into private pockets.

LABOUR

In the latter days of the Tsarist régime there were factory regulations without adequate staffs to enforce them; a law authorising the formation of Trade Unions, but an administration hostile to their formation; a government which, in the words of a former professor of the St. Petersburg University, had become the policeman of capitalism.

Urban labour was the mainstay of the Bolshevik Party. It was natural that it should expect to enjoy the Fortunatus' purse which it seemed to have won. The unwillingness of the technical intelligentsia to co-operate with the Revolution compelled the use of the operatives to keep watch upon the management. Workers' control of factories and the replacement of wages by subsistence allowances, calculated without regard to work done, were among the concessions made by the Revolutionary Government. But, at an early stage, the search for the elements of a new revolutionary labour-discipline began. Piecework was introduced into the metal industry, at the request of the Petrograd workers, in January, 1918, and soon extended to other workers in the capitals. Trotsky's proposals for a disciplined labour force went far in the direction of a militarised industrial system.

On the other hand, throughout the duration of the New Economic Policy the Trade Unions continued to struggle for the right to exercise functions similar to those of their Western prototypes, and in October, 1927, the Central Council of Trade Unions adopted a resolution declaring that the standard collective "agreement" issued by the Supreme Economic Council was an order addressed to State industrial undertakings, and not an agreement at all. The argument was that a sort of artificial wages-fund was fixed, over the heads of the Trade Unions, and that it left no room for bargaining. The demand for real consultation with the workers was again emphasised by the Central Council of Trade Unions in November, 1928.

A struggle was also in progress on the subject of piece-work. In 1928 the Eighth All-Union Congress of Trade Unions opposed a fresh extension of piece-work, and expressed a preference for collective bonuses. The managers thought there was danger of incorporating the extra pay in the standard rates, and of the consequent destruction of the incentive which the extra pay was intended to supply. Revision of the norms of output was ordered in 1929, but the difference between piece-rate pay and standard wage remained too high, because defects in technical standardisation made it too easy to exceed the norms.

The payment of Unemployment benefit was stopped from the last quarter of 1930, on the ground of the shortage of labour in State industry, and it was announced that the number of State workers and employees, which had been 14 millions in 1930, must be raised to 16 millions in 1931. Drastic steps were now being taken for the establishment of discipline. A crisis in railway transport in 1930 and 1931 was dealt with by compulsory recall to transport service of persons having technical experience, and by penal enforcement of railway discipline. In March, 1931, the principle of the adjustment of earnings to work was carried further by the abolition of limits upon additional earnings; in April, on the principle that he who works best shall be fed best, differential rations were prescribed for shock-workers—the udarniki who undertake more than the ordinary norms of work; in June it was ordered that all payments should be by results, with a progressive wage for those who exceeded a certain minimum of production, and that, in the case of work done by gangs, there should be differential payment within the gangs. The maintenance of conduct-sheets for workers, and the elimination from the working hours of the day of all occupations except work, had already been prescribed. In June, orders issued that a worker must go where he is sent; that he will be held responsible for his tools; and that wages are not to be paid in working hours. The operation of the seven-hour working day had been extended to all railway employees, and to the majority of the remainder: and the five-day continuous week, with every fifth day a holiday, was made widely applicable to most State undertakings. The prevailing signs, however, are those of a severe shortage of labour, and of measures for speeding up work. We are not surprised to learn that Government trusts were bidding against each other for labour, with offers of better wages and better living conditions, and that the "flitting" of labour from the less desirable forms of employment was a problem of grave urgency. There was precisely the same sort of competition for labour among Socialist managers that there had been in earlier centuries for peasants among the landed gentry.

Stalin declared in his "Six Points" speech that the old source of supply of labour, from the spontaneous overflow of the village, had been dried up by the improvement of rural conditions, and called upon economic organisations to re-establish the flow by entering into agreements with the managing bodies of the collective farms. The latter were to be induced to help by offers of assistance in various forms from the factories and mines. At the same time the need of additional hands was to be reduced by increased mechanisation. No direct call was made for what we have learned to describe as rationalisation, but it was a very obvious inference that rationalisation was desirable, and we shall see that the inference was actually drawn in practice. The evil of labour-flux was to be checked by the encouragement of the good workers, and in particular of the skilled workers, to stay where they were, instead of wandering in search of improved conditions elsewhere. There was no explicit reference to a severer discipline. The result was to be achieved partly by the improvement of supplies and of living conditions; and partly by an attack upon the principle of what Stalin called *equality-mongering*.

It is this denial of equality of remuneration which has occasioned and continues to occasion the greatest surprise among those who suppose that Socialism is necessarily egalitarian. Actually, there was nothing novel about the denial. In his *Critique of the Gotha Programme* Marx made it plain that equal distribution was not his primary demand. His aim was the establishment of a society which, by the very nature of its constitution, would do justice between all claims. The removal of the grosser inequalities, as of the exploitation of man by man, is implied in the aim of the classless society. But pending the attainments of complete Communism, when distribution is to be according to *needs*, because production will have reached a stage at which there is enough for all, the claim is for distribution according to *work*. There was a tendency, in the earlier period of the Revolution, to suppose that the final stage was already reached, or on the point of being reached, and to fix the remuneration of the workers accordingly. It was at the laxity of labour discipline, caused by this anticipation of a future achievement, that Stalin struck when he devised his condemnatory epithet, *equality-mongering*. Apt phrases stick, and this was one of them.

But the attempt to increase incentives by the adjustment of pay to the quantity and quality of work was largely frustrated by the system of rationing, and the accompanying variety of prices, which had been reintroduced in 1929. Rationing was a means of securing to the most important categories of the population—to factory-workers, school-teachers, office-workers and children—a minimum supply of necessities at a moderate price, at a time when supplies generally were short. It applied to bread, and (less regularly supplied) to meat, butter, groats, and finally to a number of other articles, including certain textiles, tobacco and cigarettes. Side by side with rationing, so-called Commercial shops of various types, some of them "closed," that is to say, limited to particular categories of customers, supplied similar articles at higher prices, but also in limited quantity. Shortly before the abolition of bread rationing in 1934, its ration-price was sixty kopeks per kilogram, while the commercial shops charged more than four times as much. Outside of the rationing and of the operations of the commercial shops was the open market, with unrestricted prices, which often ranged very high, and varied very greatly.

Under this system differences of money wages tended to lack practical significance. Income in excess of a certain amount could only be spent, if it could be spent at all, at such a sacrifice as deprived it of much of its value. It became a commonplace that privilege was worth more than wage, and since—for workers in the same ration-category—privilege was almost (but not absolutely) equal, the inequality aimed at by the differentiation of money-wage was all but non-existent. To achieve all that Stalin sought when he condemned equality-mongering, it was necessary to establish a rouble with equal purchasing power for all purposes, so that pecuniary incentives might have their full effect, and for that we are to wait till 1934-35, when rationing was abolished.

It was necessary also to arrive at a satisfactory solution of the problems of the wage-scale, which, for years past, had been exercising the best brains of the Soviet administration. Not all work is of a kind which can be remunerated by the piece, and time-work also requires encouragement. Wage categories, on a time basis, but varying according to skill, were devised, but they tended to become stereotyped, and therefore ceased to operate as incentives. The condemnation of equality-mongering is a sign that this controversy had taken a turn favourable to the claims of the piece-workers. The fact that a speech, dealing with so vital a question of industrial organisation as the principles of wage-payments, was addressed, not to Trade Unions, but to managers and economic workers, leaves us in little doubt as to the relative influence of the two in the decision of a question, which in effect was that of the distribution of an artificially fixed wages-fund between different categories of workers.

IRRESPONSIBILITY

Stalin passed from measures for ending the fluidity of labour to a criticism of irresponsibility. Here again he invented his own phrase, which it has become customary to translate by *depersonalisation*. No doubt he reckoned that it would stick better than a familiar word, and the event has shown that he was right. Depersonalisation means the negation of personal responsibility for work and the instruments of work. As the grand example, he pitched upon the five-day week, which had hitherto been regarded as the *ne plus ultra* of industrial organisation. With the five-day week the factories were permanently at work. The workers were on a rota, and got their holidays on different days. Each man worked four days, and had his holiday on the fifth. When his fourth day was over, he left his bench, his unfinished work, his tools for a successor. No one was continuously responsible either for work or for tools. Both were *depersonalised*. Stalin advocated a six-day week, with the sixth day a holiday for all, and a factory stoppage on that day. Workers, as well as managers, were to be made responsible each in his own sphere.

RESULTS OF STALIN'S SIX POINTS SPEECH

There were six principal heads with which Stalin wished to deal: the supply of labour; its fluidity; irresponsibility; creation of a working-class intelligentsia; attitude towards the old intelligentsia; management of industry on business principles. On these points he preached his sermon, and the obedient Press and wireless took it up, expounded and popularised it. The challenge from above was characteristic of Soviet methods. The oracle spoke, and every department set to work to give effect to its pronouncements. In lesser matters, the initiative may, and does, come from below. In greater, it comes from above.

We are now to see what the State machine made of the instructions. But first we must note that the Soviet Government was about to suffer a grave setback, which in great measure falsified the estimate of the success already attained. The bitterest part of the struggle over the collectivisation of agriculture, and the scarcity of 1932-33, was yet to come. The victories, which were believed to have rallied the intellectuals to the side of the Revolution, were not yet really won.

The speech was at once followed by a message signed by Stalin, Molotov, and Ordzhonikidze to all Party, Communist League of Youth, Economic and Trade Union organisations, regarding the position in the Donets coal-basin, which was the most important source of coal and iron, but also a classic example of ill-success in the organisation and productivity of labour. The output there was less than two-thirds of that planned, for the first half of 1931. The message required more mechanisation; the extension of geological research; better facilities for cleaning and sorting; personal responsibility of the manager for his pit, of the worker for his tools; more piece-work; better differentiation between skilled and unskilled work; attention to the quality of the work, both of individuals and gangs; more attractive conditions of labour in respect to food, housing, schools and workers' clubs; better training for technical jobs. Since the influx of labour from the villages had been checked by the improvement in rural conditions, the managing bodies of collective farms must be induced, by the offer of coal on favourable terms, to enter into agreements for its supply.

An All-Union Labour Conference which sat in November, 1931, began with complaints of the decline of the real wages of labour, and the suggestion of an all-round increase. This was not included in the Six Points, and was discouraged by the official representatives of the Commissariat of Labour. The Conference went on to the approval of piece-work and of the six-day week, instead of the unbroken five-day week condemned by Stalin, and agreed to measures of rationalisation —the reduction of hands and the exercise of a stricter discipline— apparently on the understanding that piece-work rates and harder work would increase the wages of those who remained in the factories, without involving any general increase. The impending rationalisation was evidently the keynote of the conference: and it was the assent to this that the authorities wished to obtain.

The persecution of the intelligentsia was not ended by Stalin's speech. The shooting of officers of the Agricultural Department in 1933, for supposed sabotage, took place immediately before the arrest of the engineers, British and other, in the Vickers-Maxim trial. There was a further trial, with eleven death sentences, of directors and officials of the horse-breeding trust, in 1934. But rival influences were at work after the speech. In August, 1931, engineers and specialists were placed on the same plane, in respect to living conditions, vacations, and the education of children, as the highest category of proletarian workers. In the spring of 1933 a Procurator, or Attorney

General, of the Union was invested with powers to supervise the legality of the proceedings of the Gay-Pay-oo, and released many prisoners. After the reorganisation of the Gay-Pay-oo in 1934, the Commissariat of Internal Affairs, which took its place, was deprived of the right to arrest engineers, and officers of the Red Army, without the Procurator's sanction. The new Constitution of November, 1936, makes the supervising authority of the Procurator a general one. *Pravda* of May 15, 1937, reports the revision of a sentence of five years' imprisonment passed upon an official of the Donets coal basin, who was found responsible for the output of inferior coal. The procurator demanded a thorough review of all cases of industrial crime in the past three years, and warned the Courts against the violation of revolutionary law. The year 1937 was one of alarms for managers and technical heads, as well as for Party men and administrators: but Professor Ramzin and other victims of the industrial party trial of 1930 received free pardons in 1938, and the importance of the intelligentsia in Soviet life was emphasised in the pronouncements on the equalisation of the franchise.

Lorwin and Abrahamson, two industrial experts who visited the Soviet Union in 1935, paid particular attention to the methods of technical training. They found a general urge for the improvement of qualifications, so that it seemed as though the whole country were at school. Sometimes the specialisation appeared to them excessive. In a speech of March, 1937, Stalin declares that his call "has given the Soviet Union tens and hundreds of thousands of splendid Bolshevik economic cadres." Littlepage, whose favourable opinion of the managers I have cited, says that the industrial worker has been constantly increasing his skill and his output since 1928: and this estimate is borne out by all the information received from the front in the war. The organisation of higher technical instruction was again overhauled in November, 1937, when instructors, hitherto employed and paid by the hour, were attached to particular institutions and provided with progressive monthly salaries, and the stipends of students were increased. It was now possible for a student to live on his stipend.

LABOUR AFTER JUNE, 1931

The number employed in large industry, building, and transport, when Stalin made his speech was just upon ten millions. In 1932 it was nearly twelve.

The general extension of mechanisation is notorious. We have precise figures of it for coal-getting in the years 1932-34 and for iron-smelting in 1933-35. In agriculture, particularly, the advance of mechanisation is very great indeed. A good deal of labour was set free for the increased Army, and for armament making, by these changes, as the census figures of rural and urban population clearly show (see Appendix).

There are many signs of rationalisation and of the tightening up of conditions of labour. At an earlier stage a general shortage had been combined with the employment of excessive numbers, and labour had also been undisciplined. The measures taken for restoring discipline were drastic. In November, 1932, it was decided that a man might be dismissed for a single day's absence without leave, and in December orders issued for the cancelment of the worker's ration-book on dismissal, and the co-operative shops in all the most important industries were transferred to the control of the managers of the works, with the evident intention of giving reality to the penalty. The passport system, familiar to Tsarist Russia, was reintroduced for Leningrad in 1931, and in the next year extended to other large cities, with the ostensible purpose of removing undesirable persons and those unconnected with industry or socially useful work (excepting invalids and pensioners). Substantial reductions of office staffs took place at the same time. It is evidently convenient to possess the means of limiting overcrowding and excessive calls upon the food supplies of the cities, and planning is facilitated by the authoritative determination of numbers. But the immediate aim of the passport system was to deal with the effects of rationalisation and the influx of unemployed persons from rural areas, at that time suffering from scarcity. We are not to understand that labour of good quality in the industrial centres was plentiful; but rather that rationalisation made it possible to pick and choose. A functionary called the *rationalisator* has made his appearance in the lists of Soviet employees. Though the passport system did not have all the effects expected, it appears that it checked the influx from outside. In April 1933 it was extended to other areas, including, evidently for political objects, a strip along the western frontier.

The six-day week gave place to a seven-day week, with a weekly holiday: the latter to a large extent suspended for the needs of defence.

An increasing use of piece-work, of premium systems, and of set norms of production, was noticed by Lorwin and Abrahamson in 1935. In large-scale industry, the proportion of work paid by the piece had been rather more than half in 1930: it was more than two-thirds in 1934. Generally speaking this method of payment was steadily extended, and the exceptional favour shown to shock-workers was carried further in the so-called Stakhanovite system. Here again the best information comes from Littlepage. Under the old shock-worker methods stress had been laid upon greater physical output by the individual worker. Stakhanov, a worker in the Donets Coal Basin, where low output had always been a subject of complaint, told the engineers and foremen in his mine that, if they would provide him with small tools and equipment and give him all the helpers he needed, he could get out many times more coal than he and the helpers could produce separately. Much time had hitherto been wasted by the disappearance of small tools and equipment, which—under the comprehensive description of "pipe-lighters"—had been very generally stolen. Part of the scheme was that engineers and foremen should be held responsible for keeping the gangs supplied with these articles. The rest was specialisation and organised co-operation of a brigade of workers combined with the piece-work wage.

The results of a severer discipline, or of more effective inducements to steadiness, show themselves, after 1932, in a remarkable drop in the figures of absence of workers for trivial causes, in some of the more important trades. But Labour flux—that curse of Soviet industry, for which the emblem of the grasshopper, and the opprobrious epithet of the "flitter," have been devised—continues extremely high. For years, including the year of Stalin's speech, it was, in a group of the principal trades, well over 100% of the total strength, and it was not till 1934 that it fell below that figure by a few points. In June, 1940, under the evident pressure of the needs of national defence, "flitting" was made punishable at the instance of the Central Council of Trade Unions. Both the decree itself, and the source of the proposal, are notable.

Of the general conditions and status of urban labour I have something to say in another chapter. One of Stalin's demands in his sermon to the managers was for an amelioration in the workers' conditions. Benefits, partly corporate, in particular for the Donets miners, who have received better housing and rest-homes, and partly individual, taking the shape of model dwellings for good workers, are from time to time announced. In the absence of statistical evidence of an increase in real wages, it seems that the material improvement has been rather for the capable and energetic minority of the workers, than for the rank and file. But all of them alike have benefited by increased security due to the ending of unemployment.

To sum up, the Soviet Government, on its industrial side, has learned to apply, in substance, most of the devices of its capitalist forerunners, but without allowing the accumulation of private fortunes.

Chapter XIX

THE END OF SMALL-SCALE AGRICULTURE.
COLLECTIVISATION

The idea that agricultural labour in the Russian village community should be collective can be traced to the Slavophils. Haxthausen, who first revealed to the Western world the existence of the Russian village community, hints at it. Leroy Beaulieu points out that, in a country of vast plains and in a machine age, the village community would adapt itself well to a system of large-scale cultivation by joint labour. Friedrich Engels, foreseeing the inability of peasant cultivation in France and Germany to compete with large-scale cultivation, formulates the task of the Communist as consisting in the transformation of individual production and individual ownership into co-operative production, and co-operative ownership, not forcibly, but by means of example.

The general Marxian outlook upon the peasantry was that capitalism, an inevitable stage of growth in the country as in the town, must live its life, and dig its own grave. The development of this stage was not to be hindered, but rather to be welcomed, as the necessary preliminary to the appearance of socialism. The first necessity was the destruction of the remains of feudalism, incarnate in the landowner. This would clear the way for the village capitalist, whose operations would create a rural proletariat, excite the class-war, and provide the weapon for slaying the slayer. No essential difference was conceived between the cases of town and country, so far as the conditions for the appearance of socialism were concerned. But Lenin had a double intellectual inheritance. On one side, and that perhaps the stronger, his brain descended from the Russian Populists. On that side, there survived in him memories of a Russian socialism, which gave the first place to the Peasant Commune and the Workers' Fellowship. With these memories went an impulse to active revolution and to militant measures, which the German Marxists and the Menshevik wing of the Russian Marxists missed. On the other side, he was a Marxist, with the Marxists conception that economic forces make for revolution, that the movement of their maturity cannot be forestalled, and that precocious attempts are to be condemned as mere adventurism. On the Populist side, he recognised the weight of the immense peasant mass.

On the Marxist side, he looked for leadership in revolution to the urban wage-earner, free from the bias which property gives. Out of this combination comes the conception of the alliance between peasantry and proletariat, the "dove-tailing" of the one with the other, which the Russian word for this alliance conveys. As Zinoviev put it in 1924: "The first new idea that Lenin introduced into Marxism was his outlook upon the peasantry . . . the union of a working-class revolution with a peasant-war."

I have already pointed out that Lenin had a double policy for the peasant: one which determined the ultimate aim, and another which fixed the tactics of the day. Even in 1901 we see that he aims at the replacement of small farming by large, and the full application of mechanised methods to agriculture. That was possible in two ways: either by the ousting of the small farmer and his reduction to the status of wage-earner, or by agricultural co-operation on a large scale. He was prepared for both or either, but the immediate task was something different. In deciding upon it, he followed the Marxist analysis. It is formulated in a very early number of *The Spark (Iskra)*, the first journal of the Russian Social Democrats. Social Democrats must use every opportunity of sending urban workers to country-markets and villages, to develop the antagonism, primarily, between landlord and peasant, and secondarily between rural employers and rural workers. Appeal must be made to the grievances of the peasant, and it must be brought home to him that a representative assembly is the remedy (for, at this time, the demand was merely for democratic institutions). There is no demand as yet for the nationalisation of land, for there is a possibility (a very near one at the crisis of the revolution of 1905) that the reactionaries will adopt this policy, in order to end peasant discontent at the cost of the landlords.

The peasant disturbances of 1905 showed the strength of the discontent in rural Russia, and Lenin changed his agrarian programme to one for the confiscation of all the land of the landlords. He recognised that the peasants might demand the distribution of the land among themselves, after the expropriation: thus defeating, or postponing, more far-reaching plans for the creation of large-scale cultivation. But, he wrote, "Every vegetable has its season": such a distribution may be temporarily inevitable, however little it may harmonise with a wise agrarian policy.

I need not follow him through each turn in his revolutionary tactics. I express the spirit of them compendiously by saying that he put the alliance of the peasants first among his aims: and was willing to wait upon their will in order to secure it. In 1917 he encouraged their seizure of the land, while urging that it should be an organised transfer, not a mere scramble by individuals. By this time the peasants themselves desired nationalisation, not as a means of forming large units of cultivation, but in order to end the exodus from the Mir which had taken place under the settlement of 1906-16: and Lenin, in consequence, abandoned his cautious attitude towards it. It was made plain by the Conference of Peasants Deputies in June, 1917, that the peasants wanted to use the new accessions of land as additions to their own holdings, and to redistribute the latter periodically in accordance with the ancient practice of the Mir.

After the November Revolution, the agrarian legislation of the new Government was a concession to this demand. The little group of Bolshevik and Left Social Revolutionary rulers "gave the peasant nag his head." It was a return to the dream which had danced in the village brain, at intervals, ever since the disappointment of the Emancipation decree. Live and dead stock was to be confiscated and distributed along with the land. Studs, cattle-breeding, and poultry farms were to become the property of the State. In this last sentence is the one vestige which the first decree contains of the policy of large-scale agriculture. After the dispersal of the Constituent Assembly a further decree was promulgated. It explicitly abolished private property in land, mineral wealth, water and forests. (February 19, 1918.) It left the local Soviets to make the redistribution, and defined the aims as including the "encouragement of collective-farming, as the more advantageous system in point of labour-saving and productivity, at the expense of individual farming, with a view to transition to Socialist agriculture." Beside these forecasts of future collectivisation, there is a cautious hint of future state-farms, contained in a provision that "Soviets may work lands by State-paid labour; though, generally and fundamentally, personal labour is the basis of the right to use land."

The speech with which Lenin accompanied this piece of legislation is significant. It was comparatively easy to overthrow the Tsardom and the power of the landowner. But now comes "the battle to secure the conquests of Socialist Russia and the communal tilling of the soil. Under no circumstances, of course, can such a change from small individual farming to common tillage be completed all at once. . . . But such a waste of human power and labour as is involved in small peasant economy cannot go on any longer. The productivity of labour and the economy of effort would be doubled and trebled in agriculture if, from the present disjointed individual system, we could pass to one of collective tillage." The speech is intimately relevant to the policy definitively adopted ten years later. "The struggle in the villages (says Lenin) was much more complex than in the towns. *We do not say of the kulak, as we do of the landlord or capitalist, that he must be deprived of all his property.* We say that we must break down his resistance to such necessary measures, as for instance the grain monopoly, which he refuses to observe, in order to enrich himself by the sale of surplus grain. In the case of the middling peasantry our policy has always been one of alliance."

Lenin goes on to say that a milliard roubles has been allotted for agricultural improvements, on condition that communal tillage be taken up, and that communal farms and state-farms are being created. But so long as Soviet industry continued to be unable to supply the village with manufactured goods, and above all with agricultural machinery, there was no means of establishing the material basis of the alliance of town and country, and no means of illustrating, in practice, the benefits of communal tillage. In 1921 there were 3,000 farms under communal tillage, as well as 10,000 cultivating fellowships on a smaller scale, but the New Economic Policy was a reversion to individualism: the General Land Code of October, 1922, specifically conceded the right to the alternatives of individual or collective cultivation, according to the decision in each case of the *Mir*; and such state-farms as existed were left without adequate financial support. On the other hand, agricultural co-operation—which differs from collectivisation in that co-operators receive only those associates whom they themselves approve—assisted the thriftier among the peasantry to increase production. This period was one in which the leasing of estates from poorer peasants and their cultivation by hired labour increased: and both these practices received official sanction in 1924, provided that the period of the lease should not exceed twelve years. In 1927 the whole of the so-called socialised sector of agriculture, including both state-farms and lands tilled communally, amounted to no more than 3% of the whole.

The question of obtaining assent to collectivisation was in reality the old one, constantly reappearing in revolutionary Russia, of the material basis of the economic link between town and country. When the "Scissors" was wide open, as it still was in 1926-27 and 1927-28, though not so wide open as in 1923-24, grain was withheld because there was no adequate reward for supplying it. Without a supply of commodities at reasonable prices, money was meaningless. Another phase of the same difficulty was the absence of machinery for economical large-scale cultivation.

On the part of the Government there was a consciousness of urgency. It was not only that the Powers of Western Europe constituted a military threat. There was also a profound realisation of an internal danger, so long as industry failed to furnish the countryside; a danger of irresistible pressure to abandon the monopoly of foreign trade, to admit the cheap goods of the West, and to accept the subordinate economic rôle of the inferior competitor: in the long run the victory of Communism or Capitalism depends upon the capacity for cheaper production. There could be no development of industry without an increased supply of food: and no increase in the supply of food without a development in industry. The circle was a vicious one, from which there was no escape without heroic measures. Stalin took those measures when he abandoned the New Economic Policy so far as to recommence the requisitioning of grain at fixed prices in 1927-28, launched the first Five-Year-Plan, and adopted as a part of it the active conversion of small-scale into large-scale agriculture. We have seen that this transformation of agriculture had been in the minds of the revolutionary leaders since the beginning of the century. The problem was to decide the moment for bringing it into effect. Lenin's statement, that this was a greater and more arduous achievement than the overthrow of the Tsar and the November insurrection, remained as true as when he made it.

❊   ❊   ❊

In one respect the difficulty was less than it had been. The process of differentiation in the villages had gone far enough to create an acute conflict of interest between the prosperous and poor. The poor peasant had to borrow animals and implements from the prosperous in order to cultivate his land and to pay unconscionable terms for the loan, either in labour or in a share of the crop. Non-economic holdings were numerous. The number of landless wage-earners in the village was as great as it had been before the Revolution. A government engaged in pooling land and resources might reasonably look for allies in those who benefited materially by the process. So, indeed, it proved; but less universally than might have been expected. The village is "dark": local influences are strong; people in these "bears' corners," away from the great concourse of life, are afraid of consequences; the man on the spot who has cattle and implements to lend, and money with which to pay wages, looms larger than the greater personage at a distance. The ordinary peasant admired, even if he hated, the successful neighbour and was inclined to follow his lead. There was some degree of solidarity in the village, and a power of common resistance to urban interference. The collective farm was a new thing, and humanity, most of all rural humanity, prefers the old until it becomes intolerable. "First we'll summer it, and then we'll winter it, and then we'll see," is the natural sentiment of the man who has followed the slow processes of nature, and witnessed her catastrophes.

But we shall fall into error if we suppose that the peasant, invited to pool holding and equipment, was a free yeoman accustomed to deal as he pleased with his own. Under the legislation of Peter Stolypin, one-tenth of the peasant allotments in European Russia had been consolidated into separate farms (1906 to 1916). The seizures of 1917 compelled many of the owners to return to the Mir which they had left. Between 1921 and 1926 there was a renewal of the movement towards separate consolidated holdings and the abolition of fragmentation into strips. But at the end of it, nine-tenths of European Russia preserved its separate strips, its open-field system, with the cattle of all driven over the stubbles of all, and, by consequence, its virtually compulsory three-field rotation. I cannot too strongly emphasize the facts that *old rural Russia survived till 1929*, and that it had a plan of cultivation, not a scientific plan, but a traditional one, which had played its part with the peasantry of Europe since the days of Charlemagne, and had become, as such things do, a fetter upon improvement. The holdings were too small and too ill-shaped to permit the use of machinery. The peasant depended on his own hands and the hands of his family, fortunate if he had a little nag to assist in the heaviest of the work. Co-operative production was indeed a palliative, but it needed a nucleus of means which the poorer lacked. It was this, and not the prosperous farm of a free yeoman, which the peasant was invited to pool. As ever, the young were quite ready for the adventure, though their elders might boggle over it. Among the material advantages offered by collectivisation were the remission of arrears, temporary exemption from levies, the supply of manufactured goods, and advances on a generous scale. Not every one, not even every peasant, is capable of being a good independent farmer, and collectivisation offered a differentiation of agricultural tasks, a measure of guidance, and a certain insurance against the accidents of illness and the incapacitation of the bread-winner; it saved the peasant from his normal obligation of attempting to be a business man as well as a tiller of the soil and—best of all—it held out a hope of ending the miserable plight of the cultivator without animals and implements of his own. On the other hand, it was not yet possible to offer the inducement of a liberal supply of machinery. In 1926-27, 10,000 tractors were imported; but the total number in all Russia cannot much have exceeded 20,000.

The Congress of the Communist Party which met in December, 1927, imposed restrictions upon the rights of hiring labour and leasing land, (and thereby struck a blow at the rural group which it had been Trotsky's aim to discourage). This was the same Congress that condemned him. It also advocated collectivisation "gradually but steadily, not by means of pressure, but by example and conviction." The adoption of this policy, along with the need of more vigorous measures for the collection of grain, soon brought the Government into collision with the more prosperous peasants—the class commonly described by the word *kulak*—and in January, 1928, a decree was passed to enforce the exclusion of *kulaks* from the village Soviet: a virtual revival of the Committees of the Poor which had governed the village in an epoch prior to the New Economic Policy. On the adoption of N.E.P., agricultural taxation had taken the form of cash imposts, presently amalgamated into the so-called single agricultural tax. The State depended for its supplies of foodstuffs and raw materials on a system of contracts with the peasantry, undertaking in return to provide with manufactured goods those who fulfilled their quota. In 1927-28 supplies were withheld by the peasants, either because the fixed price was too low, or because manufactured goods were not forthcoming. In March, 1928, a dictator of crops was appointed and compulsion was applied, with domiciliary searches, the closure of village markets and the erection of barriers to check the trade in grain. This was the abrogation of the right, conceded to peasants on the adoption of N.E.P., to dispose of their own produce. But the difficulty continued, and there was renewed friction between grain collectors and peasantry after the harvest of 1928. To meet the continued food crisis in 1929 energetic measures were taken, which included the recruiting of a volunteer corps of some 25,000 men, from the factories and the Red Army, to assist and accelerate the process of collectivisation. Anna Louise Strong has given us a lively description of the invasion by the zealots, accompanied by a miscellaneous crowd of helpers, of a village within convenient reach of the capital. Many, probably most, were entirely ignorant of the processes of agriculture: and we can imagine what the village thought of its visitors. The old people doubtless recalled stories of Antichrist and the Apocalypse.

It will not have escaped the reader's notice that the organization of the peasantry into collective units and the direct control of cultivation in state-farms were calculated greatly to facilitate the collection of the State's dues, whether in kind or in cash. These changes also made it far easier to apply mechanization, and the results of scientific research, to agriculture; and there was a natural expectation of increased production, as well as of improved collection, when the small unit had been eliminated. There was thus a direct connection between the introduction of large-scale cultivation and the removal of the difficulties of food supply for the towns; and the prosperous peasant, who objected to the pooling of his land and stock, and hoped to extract higher prices for his surplus products, was the principal obstacle to the attainment of both these aims. The atmosphere of the time is reproduced for us in Kirshon's play *Bread*, where we see the sanctimonious *kulak* making the peasants drunk, and persuading them to attack the party which has come to collect food. A fanatical nun is represented as inciting the attackers.

No doubt there were reasons of social policy for undertaking the great transformation, with all the risks and difficulties which were involved. The Party and the Soviet Government did not desire the survival of what was regarded as the *petit bourgeois* element of an individualistic peasantry. But far more convincing and urgent were the administrative and economic arguments. Above all, it was necessary to make provision for the renewal of the capital equipment of the Soviet State. Count Witte—if it had fallen to him to undertake such an operation—would have tided over the difficulty by means of a foreign loan; but the Soviet Government shunned commitments which were likely to compromise its independence, and preferred to pay for imported machinery by increasing agricultural exports. This involved arrangements for larger and more systematic deliveries from the peasantry. But, apart from any cornering of the produce to secure more favourable terms for its owners, it was calculated that the middling and smaller peasants were consuming half as much again of the grain as in 1913. This was in part a result of the breaking up of joint households and the increase in consuming units. In place of 16 million peasant households there were now 25. The increase was stimulated by fiscal arrangements which exempted the poorer households from taxation. The State generally lost something of its dues whenever a household was sub-divided, and the attempt to collect dues from many millions of separate units must, in any event, have been administratively difficult. This is what Stalin meant when he told the Party in April, 1928, that the number of farms must be reduced. The substitution of a limited number of collective farms for a much larger number of households was at once a convenient administrative device, and a means of taxing a large number of persons who were exempted under the poverty law.

There was prolonged hesitation before the final blow was struck. When it came, it was stunning in its impact. In January, 1930, the aims of complete collectivisation within three years, and of the "liquidation" of the kulaks, were announced. The latter meant that persons numbering, with their families, some five millions, were to be dispossessed of their properties, and in many cases driven from their homes. Apart from this tremendous decision, which can only be compared for ruthlessness with the wholesale removals of population by the ancient monarchies, or the expulsion of the Moors from Spain or of the Jews from Germany, it seems to have been intended that the process of collectivisation should be one of persuasion. But it was to be persuasion assisted by certain levers. The State had control of such tractors as were available, and the use of these was dependent upon the pooling of land and seed. The State had control of the supply of manufactured goods, and could use it to show favour or disfavour. The man who made himself prominent in resistance to the official policy ran the risk of finding himself classed as a kulak. This last was a consideration which weighed very heavily with the middling peasants, many of whom might easily be brought under the ban by jealous neighbours. The formal legislation followed, a month after the announcement, but the people had set to work in anticipation of the laws. The examples of 1905 and 1917, when the peasantry had sacked manor houses and seized property and (in the latter year) taken possession of the land, were followed in 1930. Hatred (perhaps jealousy, as much as hatred) of the prosperous kulaks created a zeal for collectivisation. Those who might have hesitated over so profound a change in the habits of a life-time were encouraged to the plunge by animosity against the success of unpopular fellow-villagers. Members of the Party, both local and urban, hung upon the flanks of the movement. But, for a time, it was entirely anarchical. Mrs. Strong says the great mass of the peasantry "moved like an avalanche into the collective farms."

What the order of liquidation meant, in the execution, may be gathered from Sholohov's novel Virgin Soil Upturned, where we see some of the villagers touched to the heart by the cries of the kulak's children, until they are reminded of the treatment which the kulaks have meted out to their debtors. Monkhouse saw some of the ousted

families. He heard tales of broken homes and vain search for employment. The older people were too terrified to talk. The children came
to him to beg.

It is a horrifying picture. The shock which the Western student of
the facts experiences is intensified by the suddenness of the blow.
Yesterday encouraged to increase and multiply the subsistence of the
family, to-day ousted from home and property, and exiled to a precarious livelihood. Similar, but less sudden, changes have resulted
from less violent agrarian revolutions elsewhere. The story of the
enclosures of common land in Great Britain, which substituted, over
a long period of years, large individual for common property, would
shock us too, if it had been concentrated into half a dozen seasons:
and the outlook upon the sanctity of landed property would be
different if we were more vividly conscious of its actual history.

When the formal law began to be enforced, the local authorities
appointed "testing commissions," whose duty it was to see that the
persons put forward as *kulaks* were really such, and that the demand
for their expulsion was a mass demand, and not dictated by personal
spite. But it was a wild winter, and it evidently shocked Mrs. Strong,
for all her strong sympathy with the Soviet Government. "There really
is too much anarchy," said the Communist with whom she discussed
the subject, and, characteristically, he laid the blame on the right wing
of the Party, which objected to drastic collectivisation. "*We expect
Government's decree soon. Then there will be more order.*" In the
meanwhile, he said, the Right had been delaying the precise formulation of the orders. Subordinates, full of zeal, or eager to distinguish
themselves, compelled unwilling acceptance of the complete pooling
of all property, including domestic fowls, threw the immemorial yards,
or gardens, of the peasants into the collectives, extended collectivisation to backward areas in the associated republics such as Buriat-
Mongolia, and removed church-bells and closed churches—these last
being apparently regarded as sanctuaries of the possessing class. It is
not surprising that there was retaliation in some places. Everywhere
a sinister consequence of collectivisation presented itself. *The people
killed their animals*; in particular, it seems, their young stock. This was
so general, and it so repeated itself in successive waves of destruction
as the process of collectivisation spread, that the simple explanation
of deliberate sabotage does not suffice. I see in it rather the naïve
assumption of each peasant, that animals for collective agriculture
would be supplied, and that he might as well make what he could out
of his own. Some killed animals because they feared that they would

be classified as *kulaks* if they had too many. Not only were milk and meat products reduced for years, but the manure supply, vital to the agriculture of the north central region, was dangerously diminished. Compulsory collectivisation was extended to the denomadisation of the wandering pastoral peoples in Kazakstan. Littelpage, as late as 1934, saw the smoke of the burning *auls* of the Kirgiz, and the empty pastures. Cattle and pigs had recovered their numbers by 1938, but sheep and goats still were short. The horse population, in part reinforced by mechanisation, was calculated in 1941 to have suffered a net loss of 8 million H.P. Another grave consequence was the removal from the soil of many of the most enterprising and industrious cultivators: for the so-called *kulaks* were by no means mere traders and money-lenders. The too rapid progress of collectivisation threw the Plan out of gear, compelled the curtailment of the importation of some things, and forced an increase in others and the opening of new sources of tractor supply.

The opposition of the Right had gone underground, and we learn from the revelations of the trial of March, 1938, that some of its members were talking of the "madness" of the Government, and building hopes of peasant revolt. But lest we should suppose that all rural Russia was in disorder, we have pictures, drawn in colours neither sombre nor garish, of some of the collective farms of this period, from the hands of Maurice Hindus and of Scheffer, a German journalist. Hindus describes the farm in his own village, which had evidently secured the best land in the redistribution between collectivists and individualists. The land included the finest pasture and the best water, and had been divided into eight fields for scientific rotations. Jealousy and carelessness were common in the management, and the best brains had gone to larger farms. But there was a real improvement in cultivation, and the Machine Tractor Station (M.T.S.) and the state-farm, both close at hand, helped with agricultural machinery. The collectivised peasants worked on the basis of wages, and were gradually introducing piece-work. Medical service was free, and there was maternity benefit for a month before and a month after birth. Here, as everywhere, there was a bitter cry for manufactured goods.

Scheffer, writing rather earlier, in September, 1929, describes a collective south of Saratov, on the Volga. It had a membership of over 1,000 souls, and an area of about 9,000 acres, of which half was under cultivation. It was hoped to deliver 1,600 tons of grain to the State. There was an elevator, which in the preceding year had handled about a tenth of the whole crop. Land and live and dead stock had been made common property, but the families lived and fed each in its own separate house. The surplus produce was divided according to the number of days of work done by each member of the collective, and approximate equality was attained by assigning the various tasks in turn to each. In anticipation of the annual accounting, cash-wages of 70 to 75 kopeks a day were paid in advance. A farming plan was laid out by an agronomist, who served more than one collective. The village was divided into brigades for the distribution of the work. The managing board contained, not only peasants, but also "rural intellectuals," for instance, teachers and factory workers, eager for distinction, who were sent to the farm by the Party in Moscow. Two former *kulaks* were members of the collective, having surrendered their possessions and paid entrance fees. Threshing was being done by Russian machines, with power furnished by the motors on American tractors. All this is a fairly close forecast of the forms which the collective farm took at a later date.

Littlepage, the mining engineer, who had his eyes open for the practical aims of industrialisation, saw that the expulsion of the well-to-do peasants would help to supply the labour market; and this, though only an incidental advantage, must have been one of the consequences which the authorities had in view. There was a reasonable expectation that the dispossessed would be absorbed by the development of industry under the first Five-Year Plan, and there has been in fact a net reduction of the agricultural population for which this absorption would account.

That serious excesses were committed in the first burst of collectivising zeal is made plain by Stalin's speech, known, like a Papal Bull, by its title: "Dizzy from success." (March 30, 1930.) It called a halt, and much of what had been done was now undone. Many full communes, which had pooled income and living as well as land and implements, took the opportunity of reverting to the intermediate status in which both living and income remain separate. Many peasants left the collectives in consequence of the liberty conceded to them. The speech was followed by the grant of half a milliard for credits to collectives, and by concessions to the propertied interest: in the division of the surplus product of the farms 5% was to be distributed to the members in proportion to the value of the property pooled by each. A definition was given of the status of *kulak*, to prevent wholesale extension of the application of the orders, and a limit of 3% was set to the proportion of the peasantry to be so described. The word was afterwards defined by a writer in the *Economic Review* as "a peasant who systematically employs hired labour, who possesses power-driven machinery such as a flour-mill or a wool-combing machine, who hires out such machinery or contracts to work on other farms, who rents out living quarters, who leases land for commercial purposes, or who receives unearned income of any kind." But it had been made clear that the canton Executive Committee was at liberty to change the interpretation according to conditions, and, in practice, we may take it that the description was made to cover all unpopular persons who had grown rich by village standards.

The sown area in 1930 increased by 7% over 1929, and the cereal harvest was 83 instead of 71 million tons: a remarkable result, considering the disorder of the spring. Michael Farbman travelled during the threshing season, and received the impression that the need for large cultivation and joint effort had taken root. He said that young people were attracted by the machines, and by the freedom from parental control which membership of the collective secured to them, and he noted that the Machine Tractor Station was a centre of activities for the young.

*　　*　　*

The Machine Tractor Station, always known by its initials M.T.S., was an adaptation to socialist ends of the practice, which had arisen among the middle and more prosperous peasants during the period of N.E.P., of lending animals and implements in return for the labour of the borrower or for a share in the crop raised by him. The Station provided machines, many of them horse-drawn at this stage, on condition of joint cultivation, and charged a share of the crop, or a money payment, for the loan. Agronomists and veterinary officers were attached to the Station, and courses of instruction, which the young people of the neighbourhood attended, were given there. In 1929 there was only one station. The gradual extension of these over increasingly wide areas, and their equipment with power-driven machinery of an increasingly effective type, have been the chief means of introducing the collective system to the people. By 1935 nearly half of the traction power required by agriculture was supplied by them, the tractors which were being newly put into use had been all, since 1932, of Russian make, and caterpillar traction was beginning to supplant wheeled traction on a large scale. The M.T.S., with its elevators and its stock of machines (by no means always protected by sheds or other coverings from the weather), and its skilled staff of experts, had become a centre of rural life and agricultural activity. Approximately there was one such to 60,000 acres of cultivation, and the total number was between 4,000 and 5,000, scattered over the length and breadth of the agricultural U.S.S.R..

Y. A. Yakovlev, the People's Commissar of Agriculture, of whose studies in rural economy I have already had a good deal to say, told the Sixteenth Congress of the Party (June-July, 1930) that peasants of the surplus-producing zone were already collectivised, to the extent of nearly half in the most important area, and to the extent of nearly a quarter in the rest of it. The size of the farms averaged over 3,000 acres in the former and under 1,000 acres in the latter. Two hundred M.T.S. were at that time established. The collectives owed two-fifths of their capital to the State, about a seventh of it was derived from the liquidated *kulaks,* and the rest had been the separate property of the members. He admitted the loss in the past year, owing to the slaughter of the animals, of a fifth of the beef-cattle, an eighth of the dairy cows, a third of the sheep, and two-fifths of the hogs, but did not dwell upon the consequences, or specify the loss of horses. He emphasised the remaining inequality in the collectives in consequence of the varying size of the yards, or garden holdings, known as *usàdba,* which are not pooled along with the peasant's allotments, but continue to be the separate possessions of particular families. On this last point, the Central Committee made the significant comment that the collectivised peasant should not be called upon to surrender all individualist habits and interests, or to give up his separate farming. The insistence on the pooling of the *usàdba* land was an error of over-zealous subordinates, never intended by the Government; and the determination of the Central Committee to retain a mixed system, partly individualistic, is an evidence of moderation. The private trade in food products, which was of the essence of N.E.P., was suppressed in 1929; but the markets were reopened in 1930 and have formed an important part of the Soviet system ever since.

There are interesting remarks upon the relations of the collectivised and the non-collectivised peasants. It seems that the latter had been penalised for holding out against collectivisation, and deprived of land which they had subjected to winter ploughing in anticipation of spring sowing, and that manufactured goods had been refused to them. The Central Committee condemns these proceedings, and says that all should be regarded as potential members of collectives, even though they have not yet joined. Those who deserted the collective, after the pronouncement of March 30th, ought to be readmitted, if they so desire, without penal measures.

Yakovlev's report says that the collective farms in surplus-producing regions should deliver to the Government, or to Co-operative organisations, from one-third to one-quarter of their grain in an average harvest, and more in a good harvest. This provision was embodied in contracts between the collectives and the District Union of Collective Farms, by which the latter bound itself to supply manufactured goods, to arrange credits, and to organise agronomic aid; engagements of which some were later assumed by the M.T.S. The theory at this time was that the collectives should yield up their surplus, after providing a necessary minimum contribution to common funds, assigning 5% to the remuneration of property contributed by the members, and setting aside enough for seed and the food of men and animals. The sale of produce to any except the Government and co-operative organisations was prohibited until 1932, when there was again a reversion, in part, to the fundamental principle of the New Economic Policy, allowing the peasantry to sell surplus direct to consumers. The labour of the members was remunerated by a dividend, according to the number of days' work done by each. It is added that there is no objection to the remuneration of members with large families according to the number of "mouths," if so desired. However, the provisions for what was virtually an interest on the value of property contributed, and for allowances for large families, afterwards disappeared from the system: and surplus was divided, after the share of the Government had been more precisely fixed in 1932, strictly according to the number of days' work, with some differentiation according to the social value of the work.

The wide prevalence of agricultural cooperation, in the strict sense of the words, had greatly facilitated the introduction of collectivisation. It had done its work, and its abolition is distinctly foreshadowed in Yakovlev's report cited above. The difference between the two is that co-operators choose their own associates, and presumably reject those whose qualities (or whose property contributions) they do not approve. But every local peasant man or woman has a legal right to join the collective, unless he belongs to one of the groups who were (prior to 1936) excluded from civil rights (*lishentsi*). The one provides for a select number: the other aims at providing for all, both good workers and bad, but with a difference of remuneration according to work.

The concession of the right to sell surplus, which was soon extended to vegetables, fruit, butter, milk, cheese and eggs, remained one of great importance, and it will be noticed that, in combination with the assertion of individual rights in the yards (*usàdba*), it converted the system of collectivisation into a mixed one, partly social-istic and partly individualistic, which it remains to this day. In order to give reality to the right of sale, markets were established in towns, at railway stations and at river ports, and the turnover at these was exempted from taxation.

The winter and spring of 1932-33, following the bad harvests of 1931 and 1932, was a time of food shortage and of struggle against opposition and discontent. In October Zinoviev and Kamenev, with eighteen others, were charged with organising a counter-revolutionary plot, and with using illicit presses to distribute their propaganda. Their actual offence appears to have been a demand for changes of policy, to overcome the difficulties of food-supply by obtaining assistance from abroad. They were expelled from the Party, this time finally. There was a general purge in 1933. The period has been described as one of severe famine, affecting a population of 50 millions, and causing 3 or 4 million deaths, and this description has passed into legend. As ex-plained previously, any suggestion of a calamity comparable with the famine of 1921-22 is, in the opinion of the present writer, who travelled through the Ukraine and North Caucasus in June and July, 1933, unfounded. The truth was probably stated by Kalinin when he said in June, 1933: "There are collective farms in the Ukraine and North Caucasus where the supply of bread does not suffice, or suffices with difficulty." Officials were placed on trial for the failure of the plans of grain collection, there were numerous conflicts between grain col-lectors and peasants, many stores of grain were destroyed by the latter, especially in the large area, having a population of 9 millions, known as the North Caucasus and later as Ordzhonikidze, in parts of the Volga basin, and in some districts of the Ukraine. Bands of vagrant peasants were plundering stores and trains. Resistance, generally pas-sive, was active in the North Caucasus, which had been a centre of mil-itary opposition during the Civil War. This territory was placed in January, 1933, under a special commission empowered to exact com-pulsory labour, and to evict, deport and punish, even with death, the resisters.

The removal of resisters, especially from the Kuban valley, a once prosperous tract largely inhabited by Cossacks recalcitrant to Soviet methods, included Communists and higher local officials and members of village Soviets who had made common cause with collectivist peasants. The mortality in particular villages subjected to these penal measures was very high, and is responsible for the high estimate which some have made of the general mortality over a larger area. Ukrainian villages which failed to deliver their quotas to the collectors were punished by the confiscation of all grains and the stoppage of relief supplies: a measure of ruthless reprisal which was doubtless the cause of some of the local mortality. Postyshev, an able Communist official, was sent to Ukraine to reorganise in that Republic the local Party, which was held to have failed in its tasks, and there was a virtual suspension of the Republic's authority. In July, 1933, the Ukrainian Bolshevik, Skrypnik, who had tendered great services to the Revolution, and was a member of the Central Committee of the Party and of the Politburo, committed suicide. The harsh lesson inflicted at this time—completely in harmony with Bolshevik methods, which are sharp, but mercifully short—seems to have put an end to all overt opposition both in the Ukraine and the North Caucasus.

All through this period the Soviet Government was wrestling mightily with every species of administrative difficulty. Trouble in the administration of the farms was caused by the short supply of qualified book-keepers, and consequent confusion over the distribution of the surplus. There were too few trained agronomists and technicians, and too few of the experimental stations whose function it was to provide the material for the scientific guidance of agriculture. In mere bulk—I say nothing of quality, which is always difficult to gauge—agricultural education of University standard had been multiplied twenty-five times since the Great War, and the number of experimental stations had been raised from 200 to nearly 1,600. Transport was presenting grave difficulties, and grain lay rotting at railway-stations and river-ports. "Policy sections" of selected Communists were appointed to deal with disorganisation on the railways in July, 1933.

Every period of stress in the U.S.S.R. claims its sacrifices or scapegoats. In March, 1933, thirty-five persons were executed for so-called sabotage in connection with the agrarian difficulties. All were officials of the Agricultural Commissariat and of the farms, and one of them, Konar, had recently been the Assistant Commissar for the U.S.S.R., but was now said to have been for thirteen years the secret agent of a foreign power. Zalogin, the Director of the Odessa Grain Trust, and five others, were tried for reserving too much grain for the use of the twelve state-farms under the Trust, and sentenced to ten years forced labour and five years deprivation of civil rights. I cannot pretend to be a judge of the facts of these painfully numerous cases. But I think that failure is often treated as a deliberate offence, and leading organisers sacrificed to general indignation—guided by that very dangerous thing, the revolutionary conscience.

By the beginning of 1933, 14½ million peasant-households had been included in collective farms, and the proportion collectivised ranged from 43% in White Russia to 80% on the Lower Volga and in the Crimea. Three-fourths of the 8 million horseless households which existed in 1928 had been absorbed. The extensive provision of machine-traction to peasants who formerly hired horses, or depended upon the muscle-power of themselves and their families, was a conspicuous gain of collectivisation: by this time, more than 80,000 tractors were available from nearly 2,500 M.T.S. Yakovlev's report to the Central Committee of the Party in 1933 steers clear of the painful subject of horses, but emphasises the value of the sub-farms in the collectives, which now had 5½ million large horned cattle and over 8 million pigs, sheep and goats. He severely criticises defective labour discipline, and blunders made in the work records upon which the remuneration of the members depends. He emphasises the leading function of the M.T.S., which must insist upon correct rotation and proper methods of cultivation in the farms of its charge. In a speech which Stalin made to a congress of collective farm workers two months later, stress was laid on the aim of making the peasantry well-to-do, without exploitation, and upon the opportunity given to the women to work on terms of equality with the men.

The harvest of 1933 yielded the best crop since the Revolution, and, in spite of difficulty in getting it in, it put an end to scarcity throughout the U.S.S.R. Favourable climatic conditions were the main cause, but the adoption of a fixed demand, in lieu of the vague stipulation for the surplus, contributed to the result, by encouraging sowings. Tension was relieved and, with more than two-thirds of the peasant households collectivised, collectivisation was virtually achieved. A less good crop in 1934 was more successfully carried home, thanks to mechanisation. This, and another good harvest in 1935, confirmed the victory. It was so complete that it became possible to amnesty a large number of the liquidated kulaks, who had done good work on the navigation canal between Leningrad and the White Sea.

By July 1, 1935, nearly 83% of the total number of peasant holders in the U.S.S.R. had joined the collectives, and, by the same date in 1936, just under 90%, and in the Ukraine the proportion was 91%.

The other section of the Socialist policy for agriculture, cultivation by paid labour on state-farms, can be dismissed with fewer words. The estates which were taken over for this purpose at the beginning of the revolutionary period were placed in 1922 under an Agricultural Trust, to the number of a thousand or so. They were not provided with adequate capital and equipment, and during the epoch of N.E.P. their reputation had sunk to a very low ebb. But some, especially in the Ukraine and the German Volga Republic, had done well. As part of the first Five-Year Plan it was decided to set up a Grain Trust to develop state-farms, and provision was made for 150 new ones, with some 12 million acres of land and a liberal financial grant, in Kazakstan, the middle and Lower Volga, Siberia, the Urals, the North Caucasus, the Ukraine and the Bashkir Republic. The aim of these measures was to raise an amount of grain equal to that provided by the prosperous peasants in 1927, which was a little over 1½ million tons. Some of the largest state-farms were set up in arid or semi-arid tracts, having a scanty population, and on lands which the agricultural officials of the pre-machine epoch thought incapable of profitable cultivation. The measure was virtually one of colonisation on lands hitherto left to pasture. In order to develop these new lands (from which often the horse or the sheep had been ousted) reliance was placed upon the speed with which the processes of agriculture could be conducted by means of machines, thus escaping the dry hot wind which is the bane of the cultivator in eastern and south-eastern Russia. Moisture was the desideratum, and the development of irrigation on a large scale would be slow and expensive, and perhaps not possible on the uneven lands of the steppe. It was hoped to secure the full benefit of the winter snow by winter plowing, after removal of the summer crop; and it was supposed that successive spring sowings of wheat, with no intervening fallows, except those of the winter months, would produce satisfactory returns. The areas of some of these farms were deliberately made enormous, so as to economise overhead charges. The *Gigant* (*Giant*) at one time contained 600,000 acres, and several of them varied from 80,000 to 160,000. The capital investment in buildings, machines, and road-making, was about 26 roubles per acre. At first the virgin soil produced returns substantially exceeding the average for the U.S.S.R. Nine and a half million acres, sown in 1929, yielded a net marketable surplus somewhat larger than the 1½ million tons which had been expected. To fill the gap in the ranks of trained agricultural workers, engineers and tractorists, training colleges and farming schools were built or extended on every farm.

The enterprise was carried far beyond the original intention. In the season of 1934, the state-farms were employing over 3 million persons, and were cultivating over 40 million acres, of which over three-quarters were under grain. They had nearly 1 million horses, 4½ million large horned cattle, 8½ million sheep and goats; their tractor park had a horse power of nearly 1¾ millions; and they supplied one-eighth of all the grain delivered to the State, and nearly an eighth of all the sugar-beet. But these figures convey only a part of the whole picture. There were about 10,000 farms, dealing with 228 million acres, of which the vast bulk was uncultivated land given over to ranching operations. They were administered by more than a dozen different departments of state, all but one of which (the Commissariat of State-farms) were mainly occupied with very different matters; and it was inevitable that they should be worked on very various principles and with very various degrees of success. The special Commissariat of State-farms dealt with 173 million acres, of which one-ninth part was cultivated, laid out in 2,179 farms, for grain, milk and meat, pigs and sheep.

The Commissariat of Agriculture for the U.S.S.R. had 531 farms extending over 17 million acres, nearly two-thirds of which was utilised for horse-breeding. There were also seed-farms, farms for cotton, flax, hemp, nitrogenous plants, rice, sub-tropical plants and silk, and farms for blood-stock (cattle, sheep and pigs). The blood-stock farms co-operated closely with the collective farms in the matter of animal-breeding, and the seed-farms supplied them with selected seed.

The Commissariats of Agriculture in the Constituent Republics had about 600 farms for vegetables, poultry, fruits, and vineyards. The Commissariat of Food industries had about as many farms for sugar-beet, vegetables, potatoes, tobacco, poultry, pigs, and essential oils, with a considerable area under glass. The attention paid to the essential oils, many of them employed in the manufacture of perfume, is an unexpected feature. In the middle of the scarcity of 1932-33 the city shops were well supplied with perfume, and it was stated to the present writer that perfumes were regarded as a necessity of hygiene. In 1934, 6,000 acres were devoted to the essential oils. It was a special con-cession to the female population.

The Commissariat of External Trade had twenty-eight farms, occu-pying 17 million acres, for silver foxes, Persian lambs, rabbits and other fur-yielding animals. That of Heavy Industry grew rubber substitutes over 130,000 acres. Thirteen million acres, under six different Com-missariats, were devoted to victualling various institutions, both co-operative and non-co-operative, including factory dining-rooms, and shops for the supply of particular departments. The farms in this category had hot-houses and land under glass; they grew more grain than anything else, but also vegetables, potatoes, roots and grasses, and they kept large horned cattle, pigs, sheep, poultry and rabbits.

They were by far the most numerous of all classes of state-farms, and their average area was small, not exceeding 2,000 acres. The unevenness of the arrangements for supply, favouring some and disfavouring others, must have been greatly accentuated by the existence of these auxiliary sources of food. A lucky factory or office would feed well, when others were going short.

Defects in organisation and management began to make themselves apparent as early as 1931. The harvest of 1931 on the grain-farms was a disappointment, and it was realised that the system of "monoculture," with strict specialisation on a single crop, must be modified by the adoption of regular rotations. The grain-farms were evidently too large for efficient management. They were divided up, and a decree of 1932 limited their size to a maximum of 108,000 acres, with subdivisions under assistant managers. Administrative opinion suggested 32,000 to 40,000 acres as the optimum size. The Six Points speech of Stalin, with its emphasis on cost-accounting (see Chapter XVIII) drew attention to the lack of arrangements for ascertaining how much of the resources of the State was absorbed in maintaining them, and what was the cost of their contribution to its grain and raw materials.

The excessive size of the great animal-breeding farms attracted animadversion in 1932. The herding together of large numbers of stock increased the danger of epidemics. "Cattle breeder" occupied over 63,000 square miles, and "Sheep breeder" over 46,000: more than the area of many a considerable province. These were broken up into more easily managed units. Among the blunders of the management, animals had been requisitioned before stockmen and stables were available. The names of delinquent officials were published, and thirty prosecuted.

"Policy sections," consisting largely of trained Party men from the Communist University at Moscow, were posted to the farms in 1933, and occasionally eclipsed the authority of local directors, or aroused the jealousy of local Communists. The directors were always Party men, relying upon their agronomists for expert knowledge, and transferred at short intervals from one post to another, sometimes in an office, sometimes in a factory, sometimes on a farm. All that they could contribute was general driving-power. For technical management, particularly for the larger farms, there was a dearth of trained personnel, and training had to be given rapidly.

It has been suggested that there is no reason why these farms should be expected to "pay," and that the habits, which still continue, of estimating results by current revenue and expenditure, with an allowance of 10% for depreciation of animals and machines and of 4% for buildings, with no addition on account of the value of the land acquired, is all that is necessary in a Socialist State, which meets all charges out of current income. I note in passing that 10% is an extremely low rate of depreciation to allow for animals, if not also for machines. On the general question, it is to be observed that a Socialist State, like every other, must know to what extent it is subsidising particular branches of its administration: and that no one more heartily endorses this principle than Stalin himself. In 1933 he declared that the state-farms—with the exception of a few dozens of them—did not "pay." He might have added that no one knows what their products cost the State. In 1929 the cost of their wheat per ton was calculated at 50 roubles, but no similar calculations seem to have been made after this date.

In 1934 the President of the State Planning Commission told the Seventeenth Party Congress that many state-farms, having better material and technical conditions than the collective farms, obtain considerably worse results than the latter: and he called for better organisation and management. This criticism set in motion a policy which has resulted in changes on a very large scale. At the end of 1935 the dissolution of a large number of the farms was announced. Those which remained were required to justify their operations on commercial principles, and were placed under the three Commissariats of State-Farms, of Food-Industry and of Agriculture. The land taken from them was transferred to collective farms. In June, 1937, the number of state-farms had been reduced to little more than 1,000, and 60 million acres had been taken from them out of the 228 millions of 1935.

In the absence of statistical details, which the Soviet Government has ceased to publish since 1935, I infer a very great reduction in the number and area of the grain-farms. It is probable that the animal-breeding farms remain substantially intact. Their value as a source of good stock was always very great, and their milking records were substantially better than those of the collective farms. Seed-farms and experimental farms doubtless continue as before. If these suppositions are correct, the changes indicate the partial abandonment of the design of large grain-factories, run by the State with paid labour, in favour of smaller units run by bodies of collectivised peasants, who divide the surplus produce among themselves. In other words, the new attitude to State-farms furnishes additional evidence of the triumph of collectivisation.

Chapter XX

THE COLLECTIVE FARM

"To do anything jointly, all in hugger-mugger, as they say, in such a way that you cannot bring the work done by each to a separate reckoning, is repulsive to the peasants. . . . They take very kindly to partnership work, when it is so divided that each receives the remuneration for his own share."

ENGLEHARDT, *From the Village*, 1872-87.

"To withdraw the use of steam-power suddenly will not have the effect of reducing us to the state in which we were before its introduction. There will be a general break-up and time of anarchy such as has never been known. It will be as though our population were suddenly doubled, with no additional means of feeding the increased number."

SAMUEL BUTLER, *Erehwon*.

Pavlovsky, the historian of Russian agriculture, said that peasant agriculture is not merely a means of livelihood: it is a way of life. For centuries it was both the means of livelihood and the way of life, for the overwhelming mass of mankind. Industrial life is a mere *parvenu* beside it, with many of the qualities, good and bad, of the *nouveau riche*. Until a comparatively recent date peasant agriculture made up nine-tenths of Russian life. Even in 1941, when industry had made great strides, over two-thirds of the population of the U.S.S.R. lived in villages, and a good deal more than half of the whole lived by tilling the soil. Since the beginning of the present century, the peasantry has more than once said No to the course of history. Its negative is greater than its positive strength. It might—tremendous thought— say No to Russian Socialism. Pavlovsky's sentence, which I have quoted above, adds that peasant agriculture does not lend itself to dramatic transformation.

Those who undertook to change the way of life of this half-awakened Titan were indeed armed in marble and triple bronze. He stirred, and muttered threateningly, in the crisis of the first Five-Year-Plan. The resistance with which he opposed the Germans gives cause for believing that the new institutions have won his support. But none of us can be certain even now that he may not strike out with those irresistible arms, and sweep them into a heap of fragments. Allowance being made for his lack of the qualities of leadership and organisation —for he is often the giant led by the dwarf—he is incomparably the greatest potential force on one-sixth of the world's land surface. I make no apology, therefore, for dealing at length with the things which concern him, and for making more of him and his way of life than of all the triumphs of industrialisation. The fate of Russia, and of all that part of the world which depends upon the fate of Russia, lies in the hollow of that callus-covered hand. If the rulers have discovered in collectivisation a way of life which can be made to harmonise with his instincts and to provide the satisfaction of his needs, their system will survive, and external enemies will fail to overthrow it, because of its internal strength. If he is submitting uneasily to a compulsion which irks him, the skipper must veer off upon another course, or Russia will again become the Land of Fragments depicted in Maya-kovsky's play. In this chapter, and the relevant appendices, I have set myself no less a task than to help my readers to a judgment on the chances of this supreme issue.

The observer of Russian historical life soon becomes conscious of a subtle distinction of values between townsman and countryman. The institution of serfdom will not account for the whole of this dis-tinction. There were household serfs quite familiar with the life of the towns: the earliest factories were worked by serfs. But the serf who paid his commutation fee and went off to work on his own account, generally in a town, reached an atmosphere of liberty unattainable to the man who stayed behind to work his master's land. The inferiority, or assumed inferiority, of the plough and sickle and flail and manure-cart seems to constitute the difference. The legal inferiority of the peasant, which survived into the twentieth century, leaves its traces even to-day, when the peasant has been placed by the Constitution of 1936 on a complete political equality with the townsman. The slogan of the dictatorship of the proletariat has not yet ceased to ring in our ears: and the status of the peasant as the ally, not the co-ruler, is not wholly forgotten. In the difference between the price paid to the peasant for his delivery of grain, and the price at which the Gov-ernment passes it on to the State departments, to be processed and exported, or consumed by towns and army, there is a large virtual land-revenue, or land-rent, through which the peasant pays at least one quarter—Hubbard says three-sevenths—of the whole State ex-penditure, in addition to his share of indirect taxation. In return he is secured in his collective rights in the land. Other boons he receives in less measure than the townsman—partly because nature and geography have scattered him over vast areas, whereas the townsman's life is by definition concentrated in a few accessible settlements. You will not find the peasant in the holiday homes and sanatoria with which the townsman is generously provided. His so-called cultural opportunities depend, even now, on what his local organisation, the collective farm, is able to do for him; and that varies immensely from one centre to another. The standard of maternity benefit for his wife is half-pay for a month before and a month after child-birth: the corresponding standard for the town-worker's wife is full pay for four weeks before and four after; in the case of the Red Army, the dependents' allowance in the village is half that in the town. These differences are typical of the surviving distinctions. Hitherto his work has been very different from that of the townsman: tremendous, back-breaking toil at certain seasons, when nature demands the completion of certain tasks at shattering speed, with long spells of demoralising idleness and sleep on the stove; as against hours, regular if long, under the watchful eye of manager or foreman. The machine has brought a relief from the excessive strain of ploughing and harvesting and carrying and threshing, but with it has come a new discipline, the need to spend the old leisure in agricultural or instructional processes unrecognised, or even unnecessary, before; the fixed hours; and the vigilance of the gang-master. He is a factory-hand working in the open air, and his work is piece-work, with payment varying according to output. But his furnace is the sun, his water comes from the clouds, nature is still his supreme arbiter, and the final payer of his wage.

The change to collectivisation has affected the social status of the peasant, and affected it in a direction different from that which we should have expected. In becoming, so to speak, a factory-hand, he might have lost some of the dignity of the permanent right-holder in his own allotment of land. But as earlier chapters in these studies have attempted to make plain, of dignity there was none. His work was "black" work, and, when he came to town, the factory-hand was his superior. Some of the memories of the time when he alone was subject to judicial and administrative flogging yet survived. The words for peasant, *muzhik*, and for peasant woman, *baba*, had nothing honourable about them. The new name for the collective farmer, *kolkhoznik*, barbarous though it may sound to the Russian scholar, has in fact more dignity. At the Peasant-house in Moscow they now serve the arrival from the country not with *peasant soup*, but with *kolkhoznik soup*. It is the same old soup, but the name gives it a social flavouring. In the collective farm, one peasant out of four holds an office or incumbency of some sort. He is a pig-breeding expert, or what not, and his wife is a dairy-woman, and in the women's group. That is very different from being a peasant, with the associations which attach to the old status and the old name. Collectivisation is a step up on the social ladder, and I err greatly if this has not been an element of importance in the acceptance of the change. It was otherwise, of course, with the prosperous peasant, who desired no such change; but the prosperous peasant, in his character of kulak, was condemned beyond reprieve.

But here I must interpolate an explanation. It is not prosperity that is condemned: one of the objects of the collective farms, as stated in their model statute, is to make the peasant well-to-do (zazhitochny). When Stalin addressed the Agricultural Combine Workers about their wages in December, 1935, he told them that the money was their own and they could spend it any way they liked. The prosperity which is derived from the exploitation of the labour of other persons, from usury, from buying cheap and selling dear, became a crime when the U.S.S.R. abandoned the principle of N.E.P. and entered upon the period of Planning. If we say that a man is at liberty to make all that he can by his own work, but nothing by the work of others, we lay ourselves open to the enquiry whether organisation, such as the captain of industry conducts in a capitalist society, is not itself work, and work of a very valuable order. The answer is that it is of high value but, in the socialist society, a man must not use his organising gift for his own personal profit, any more than he may use his exceptional nerve or muscle power to rob on the highway. If our supposed interlocutor objects that it was hard for the man who had been allowed, even encouraged, to use his organising gift for his own purposes one day, to be drastically punished the next day for doing the same thing, I shall have no reply to offer, except that revolutions are ruthless things, and that the effect on character of such sudden changes of fundamental principle is likely to be, for a generation or more, disintegrating. The organiser has to learn to use his organising power for the community, as the great military or naval commander does, and to be content with little more than the laurel wreath for his achievement.

The general conception of collectivisation is the conversion of peasant agriculture into a congeries of open-air factories of food and raw materials. But the new agricultural factory differs from the industrial factory, which was, in a certain sense, its model and prototype, because the workers in the former have permanent rights in some of the instruments of production, are entitled to a dividend instead of a wage, and use part of their labour in tiny sub-factories of their own, over the proceeds of which they have complete control. The system is, in fact, an ingenious combination of the individualistic with the socialistic farm, worked out by the favourite Bolshevik method of trial and error, which—we must remember—is still available to make alterations and corrections. How large and how far-reaching these alterations and corrections may be has been shown by the concession establishing fairs for the purchase and sale of cattle.

✳   ✳   ✳

The collectives are of three types. The simplest is a mere cultivating or herd-tending partnership, common among the nomads of Kazaks-tan, and found with some frequency in the North Caucasus, but otherwise occurring only on a small scale. At the other end of the scale is the full Commune, in which the members live together round a common dining-hall and kitchen, and have no separate belongings except trifling objects of personal use. Collectives of this type do not make more than 1% of the whole number. In the vast bulk of the collectives—those of which I write in this chapter—the work is com-mon, the rights in land and in live and dead stock are joint, the surplus product is divided among the members, the incomes are separate, and the members live, and, to a large extent feed, in their separate families and in their own houses. An important individualistic element in them is the small separate yard, or garden allotment, representing the old usàdba, ordinarily adjoining the living-house, and worked by the family. I shall use the expression collective farm for this common type of organisation only. It is the Russian Kolkhoz: a word which is be-gotten of the Western word collective, and the Russian word for a farm or economic establishment (khozyaistvo).

In the collective, thus defined, the land is the property of the State, but the members have rights of permanent enjoyment, subject to their legal obligation to admit other members who have the required qualifications. A cause of great satisfaction has been the distribution to the collectivised farms of certificates of permanent rights in the land accompanied by plans which show its area and boundaries. It is almost impossible to exaggerate the confidence which the receipt of these certificates has created. In the yard, or garden land—which for convenience I shall call simply the yard—attached to each household the right of permanent enjoyment is vested in the family. This yard was properly only from one acre to five, but larger yards are recognised in some areas, notably in the tracts where cattle-raising is the principal occupation. Abuses have been recently discovered which have led to a reduction of the area. It was found that some collective farmers (those of the Don valley were noted as particular offenders) were neglecting the collective work for the work of the yard, and the process of re-survey revealed the misappropriation from common land of no less than 100,000 acres. A minimum number of work-days on the collective lands has now been prescribed. A growing conviction that the collectivised peasants are giving too much time and industry to their yards and to cottage industry, and even to longer undertakings, including coal-mining, is noticeable.

The implements of cultivation belong generally to the State, so far as all power-driven and large-sized machinery is concerned, but the collective owns some large implements in areas to which the operations of the M.T.S. have not yet been extended, and all smaller and more primitive implements, and may be seen parading them at the rehearsal for the harvesting which takes place in June of each year. The horses belong to the collective. Of the other animals, some belong to the collectives, but most are kept in the sub-farms for animals, which form sections of the majority of collective farms—presumably to fix responsibility for the stock upon particular persons or groups. A very large proportion of the large horned cattle, and of smaller animals, are the property of individual collectivist peasants, who keep them in their yards and feed them on their own produce, and on the fodder which they receive as part of their dividends. It is a little-known fact, but one relevant to the prospects of cattle-rearing in the U.S.S.R., that 65% of the cows and calves and more than half of the pigs and sheep in the country are owned and tended by individuals. Of the remainder a large proportion are tended in the sub-farms by persons who are individually responsible for their charges, and remunerated in proportion to their success. The large element of individualism in the system, particularly in respect to cattle, has played a leading part in the reconciliation of the people to its collectivist features.

There are a quarter of a million of these collectives, occupying in 1935 94% of the whole cultivated area. The proportion which is collectivised is comparatively low in Georgia, Armenia, and in certain other areas. Elsewhere the percentage ran from 78 to 99 and, prior to the removal of the Germans to Asia, actually reached 100 in the German Volga Republic. In the surplus-food-producing centres, it was everywhere over 90: and in the Ukraine, as a whole, it reached 98.

The farm is not identical with the old village. It is often larger. Its average size varies widely in different regions. It is below 600 acres of cultivation in much of the Northern Agricultural belt, in White Russia, in the Trans-Caucasus, and in Mahommedan Central Asia. It runs up above 1,800 in the Ukraine, and twice or three times as high on the Middle and Lower Volga. For the whole country it averages 1,600 acres. The number of households in a farm averages ninety-five for the whole country: but here also the regional variation is great, from less than fifty in the Far East and the Northern Agricultural region, to 133 in the Ukraine, and 152 in the North Caucasus. The units of horse power (apart from the hiring of machines from the M.T.S.) available on the farm average fifty-two, but they go down in particular regions below half this figure. Nevertheless more than half the horse power used in agriculture was still provided by animals before the German attack. In 1935 less than three-quarters of all the cultivated area of the farms were served by the M.T.S. (Machine Tractor Station), with a substantially greater proportion in the more important agricultural areas, and a lower proportion in the north and centre. Nowhere is any but the heaviest of the agricultural work done by the M.T.S. There was everywhere a varying balance of heavy work which must be done by the people themselves, though they were for the most part relieved of the ploughing. The collectives had over 8½ million working horses, and an average of 29 acres of cultivation to every horse.

There are not less on an average than twelve working members of each collective to every 100 acres of cultivation. After making allowance, on the one hand, for the great amount of mechanisation which has been introduced into agriculture by the M.T.S., and, on the other, for the continuance of the elderly and invalid members and the employment of members on non-agricultural duties—we hear, for instance, of doctors, as well as veterinary surgeons and book-keepers, on the membership list, and a substantial amount of administrative work is also necessary on farms of this magnitude—the figures are indicative of rural under-employment. Three to five agricultural workers for every 100 arable acres, including permanent grass, are, I understand, found sufficient in Great Britain, except on glass and market gardens. The impression of under-employment is confirmed from other sources. There has been of late years a substantial reduction in the number of peasant households, and the existence of many abandoned houses has been noticed. The Census of 1939 showed a reduction of 5% in the rural population. Evidently a movement to the towns is in progress, in order to meet the demands of increasing industrialisation. Its extension will be economically advantageous at both ends. In the meanwhile it is clear that a remedy for rural over-population is being applied. Hubbard has criticised as uneconomical the widespread mechanisation which has been carried out: but one of its aims was to establish a pool from which labour for the towns could be drawn.

How much equality, and how much freedom, do the collectives give? What are their fiscal burdens? What has been their effect upon the livestock and upon the fertilisation of the soil with manure? What upon the land, and upon agricultural production? What upon the condition of the peasant both material and moral? How does the still surviving individualist farmer—now a rarity—carry on his economy? Has the new system come to stay or is it likely soon to be displaced by another? These are some of the questions upon which the reader will desire to have light.

Some degree of egalitarianism was forced upon the Bolsheviks by proletarian demands in the early period of the Revolution. But Marx was not egalitarian, and the Bolsheviks are not: and their non-egalitarianism is not something which has been unwillingly adopted by way of compromise, or surrender. True, it is contemplated that, on the attainment of the final stage of the classless society, when the growth of wealth, unhampered by the restrictions of a system based upon private profit, is expected to make feasible a virtually unlimited distribution of desirable things, the rule will be, from each according to his capacity, to each according to his needs. In the meanwhile, the rule is, to each according to his work, and he who does not work neither shall he eat: to which we must make the important addition that work is *provided*, and, under the new constitution, formally guaranteed.

As between the different farms, it cannot be said that the rule of equality according to work is actually operative. There are wide variations between the areas of cultivation per worker, and still wider variations in the advantages of climate, water, soil, and situation. This is only another way of stating the problem of the differential value of land and of the differential rent to which it theoretically gives rise. If we assume the existence of approximately equal industry and equal skill, and of approximately equal or insufficiently differentiated taxation, one corporation of collective farmers will grow rich, while another will remain poor. This is actually happening under our eyes. There are so-called "millionaire" collectives, whose income, translated into roubles, reaches hundreds of thousands, because they grow cotton or sugar-beet, or some other valuable crop, or because their cereal cultivation is exceptionally favoured by nature, or their vegetables and dairy produce are within easy reach of a great consuming centre. But an examination of average yields, as officially published prior to 1936, convinces us, without more ado, that the general lot is very different from this. Nothing less than a drastic differentiation of burdens would prevent the wide variation of prosperity from farm to farm. To what extent the Soviet Government has attempted to correct this anomaly we shall see when we come to the subject of taxation.

Within the farms, the principle of remuneration according to work is effectively observed. The collective farmers are divided into gangs or brigades, to each of which are allotted particular land, particular buildings, particular animals, particular implements; and further subdivision into links determines with precision the responsibilities of smaller groups. In some cases the land for which an individual worker is responsible may be seen marked out with wooden tablets. Within the group, the gang-leader appraises the work of links and of individuals, and there is a system of rewards and penalties according to results. The general scheme is one of payment by work-days, but the value of the work-day is determined by the social value of the type of work. A doctor, or veterinary surgeon, or book-keeper, who is a member of a collective, may be credited with two days or a day and a half for every day that he has worked. The valuation is determined by the general meeting of the collective. A standard work day is not very exacting, and a good worker may put in more than one between sunrise and sundown. A recent order of general application gives to the Chairman a lump allowance of 600 work-days, with an additional bonus of 250 roubles, if the requirements of the Plan are met in full. In the sub-farms which look after the animals there is a system of premiums, the milkmaid getting such and such a proportion of the milk, and so on.

The fund from which the payments are made might accurately be described as a dividend. It consists of the residual produce and cash which remain after the demands of the Government and of the M.T.S. have been met, and after setting aside certain funds such as the provision for next year's seeds, which forms a very large percentage of the total crop in Russia, owing to the extraordinary smallness of the yield. Subject to an exceptional provision for the rush of harvest work, there is, or there should be, no hired labour to be paid. A collective may employ an expert—for instance, a dairy expert—at an agreed salary, and it may employ paid builders. Otherwise the principle that no man must make a profit out of the labour of another is strictly enforced, or violated only at the peril of the transgressors. All the work must be done by the members and remunerated out of dividend.

The poet Nekrasov shows us seven peasants wandering far and wide, to discover Who can be happy and free in Russia. How much freedom is there now? The principal limitation is the Plan. I have already pointed out that there was a traditional plan—the three-field rotation —before the Bolsheviks invented Planning: and that it was virtually impossible for the individual to break away from it. The agricultural Plan of the present day, so far as the particular farm is concerned, amounts, in effect, to the device of a particular rotation, since the area of cultivation is limited by the land and resources available. The plan travels upward from the farm, and then back from the central planning authority to the farm again. The regional and local authorities, who deal with it on its way, have to translate it into terms of approved rotations, which, applied to the whole area with which they are severally concerned, will give the result demanded. If it is not agriculturally feasible, it will not be carried out and, despite a tendency to over-elaboration of detail, which has been recently diminished by dropping the attempt to prescribe the cultivation of particular cereals, pains are naturally taken to see that it shall be feasible, as well as to meet the requirements of the planning authority. On a big question, such as the rotation to be observed, the collective must, ultimately, submit to orders, after it has wrangled about its own share in the distribution of the areas to be devoted to particular crops. The frequent insistence by the higher authorities upon reasonable consideration for the opinions and requirements of the collective farmers suggests that they are often overridden by local agricultural authorities.

Normally, the plan is a reasonable thing, in which the cultivators have had their say. The worst which will happen to the collective farmers, if they fall short of requirements, is that they will go without some of the favours which the Government has to distribute; for instance, without a liberal share of advances, or the privilege of the cheap purchase of stock from the state-farm; and will have to pay their tax-in-kind on the total culturable area, though it be larger than the area sown and harvested.

On details of agricultural management, the General Meeting of the collective farmers has a large discretionary authority. This body has caught much of the primitive democratic spirit of the old Mir, while learning to submit to the rulings of a modern Communist chairman. In form, the latter is elected by the General Meeting; but the form is not a reality, and Chairmen are transferred from post to post at the discretion of the Government. I myself have met one who had been in charge of a glass factory before he joined the collective, and had just received orders transferring him to a brick factory. His successor, a woman, had been in charge of a Co-operative shop before she joined her new post as Chairman. Neither knew anything of agriculture. Their duty was to supply organising and driving capacity, and both appeared quite fitted to do so. The case may safely be taken to be typical of Bolshevik methods. There was no apprehension that the General Meeting of the collective might elect someone else to the chair.

The General Meeting elects out of its own members a managing committee for day-by-day business, and a revision or audit committee, which has the function of watching the accounts and scrutinising decisions. The records and accounts are kept by book-keepers, who are often very capable persons, men or women.

The collective must hire machinery from the M.T.S. of the region in which it is located, or deliver an increased amount of produce to the Government. It is conceivable that a collective might prefer to utilise surplus man-power for the heavy operations, if it were perfectly free to do so. We must recall, however, the extent to which animals and implements were hired from private persons before the establishment of the M.T.S., and the fact that the members of the collective, and not persons hired by them, would have to do the work, if the machines of the monopolist M.T.S. were not available. Mechanisation has very great advantages: among which the saving of agricultural time, in a country having a short open season, is the most important. It seems unlikely that the obligation to employ the M.T.S. is felt as a grievance, so long as the charges are substantially less than those formerly levied by the private lender, as I think they are. An effect of mechanisation, in the form which it has taken in the U.S.S.R., is to make the people closely dependent upon an official agency, as the inhabitants of an irrigated tract in Northern India are dependent upon the irrigation authorities, who decide "turns," and the dates of supply. Recent criticisms of Machine Tractor Stations by the People's Commissar of Agriculture are to the effect that they do not cover the outlay upon them, and that the machines are carelessly housed, or not housed at all.

For six or seven months of each year the collective farmers are prohibited from selling grain except to Government or to co-operative agencies. The object of this restriction is to prevent them from disposing of produce before the claims of the Government and the M.T.S. on the harvest have been met, and the necessary funds for seed and so on, set aside. Otherwise they have full liberty of sale. There exist no authorised wholesale dealers, and sales in large quantities, except to co-operatives or to government departments, would come under suspicion of illicit trading. Liberty of sale, in practice, means liberty of retail sale, and it may be exercised in collective markets or otherwise as each producer may find convenient.

❈   ❈   ❈

The member of the collective farm works under a discipline more closely resembling that of the factory than any to which the peasant, in his agricultural work, has hitherto had to submit. He must keep time, and satisfy the gang-leader, or he will lose his "work-day," if he incur no worse penalty. The People's Commissars' order of April, 1938, gives us a glimpse of the penalties which may be enforced. A man, or woman, who offends against internal order, may be punished by public admonition, by posting on the "black" board, by fine, by transfer to lower work, by being required to work for a period without remuneration. In the past, it appears that orders of expulsion have been passed by the Managing Committee, and even by the Chairman. Henceforth—if orders are observed—there is to be no expulsion from the collective except by the General Meeting, and by the vote of at least two-thirds of the members.

I turn to another form of restriction upon liberty: that of family life. Collectives receive women as full members on equal terms with men, and their statutes require them to give to women opportunities of advancement to work for which they are fitted, and to resist attempts to keep them in domestic subordination. The reality of such provisions depend upon economic conditions. The separate wage is of immense importance. I have been told, and I can readily believe, that the first actual reception of a solid dividend for the work done by the women, in solid rye and potatoes, was like the entry upon a new world, where each gazed on each with a wild surmise. A man said he had one complaint to make of the collective: *he no longer received his daughter's wages.* Female labour is very extensively employed on the farms, and the woman's dividend is one of the reasons why there has been acquiescence in collectivisation: *it has put the women on the side of the Soviets.*

Emancipation from household drudgery involves common catering, the crèche, the public laundry. The provision here is of course very uneven. Community kitchens and common catering are in operation for field-work at busy seasons. There are day-nurseries for the children, while the mothers are at work, and schools for the older ones. But these, like all other social arrangements in the village, are limited by the amount of the social insurance fund, and the extent of the building accommodation available in each case. In industry, Government is the employer, and sets aside as social insurance a stated percentage on the wages. In agriculture the collective farmers are self-employers. It is they who find the money out of the produce available after harvest, and there are wide variations in the prosperity, and therefore in the provision of social privileges and amenities, in different farms. On the other hand, we must not be misled by a crude comparison of percentages in the two cases. The percentage of 14% or more, in the case of industry, is a percentage on wages. The percentage of 2% or 3% in the farm is a percentage of the whole gross product of the concern. I feel no doubt, however, that the industrial worker does better out of his social insurance than the collective farmer does. Buildings in the collectives for schools, crèches and the like, vary very greatly. Sometimes they are very fine, the homes of former landlords and kulaks, sometimes very poor.

The woman has gained in liberty by her membership. The young people have gained also. It may be that the man, the head of the family, as we traditionally call him, has lost what they have gained. At all events he has less power over his family than he had. Custom and opinion still preserve to him a good deal of power, and the joint family-working of the "yard" gives him a sphere in which to exercise it. His position in society has gained in dignity for reasons already indicated.

※　※　※

We come next to the somewhat vexed question of the tax-burden, which is often stated by observers at a very low figure. The "single agricultural tax" in cash, which prevailed throughout the greater part of the period of N.E.P., was superseded in 1936 by an income-tax on collectives. But by far the most important part of the tax-burden is the "compulsory sale in the nature of a tax," which goes by the Russian name of Khlebopostavka. The contradictions which appear in the accounts given by different observers are due sometimes to the treatment of this compulsory sale as something other than a tax, sometimes to varying local experiences. Since a payment is made by the Government in respect to the compulsory deliveries it has been, not unnaturally, supposed that they constitute not a tax, but a sale. But the official description of them shows that they are in the nature of a tax.

There is a difference of opinion, among the investigators of Soviet conditions, between those who think that the régime has unduly favoured the peasant and those who think that it has disfavoured him. The present studies have been recorded in vain if they have failed to show that the general course of Russian history—with certain exceptions—has been to lay the greater burdens upon the peasant. It was he who was the predial serf, who did the "black" work, who, after emancipation, retained the inferior legal status, or had no legal status at all and submitted to beating by everyone dressed in a little brief authority. The "intelligents" who "went to the people" in the seventies of the last century were going against the stream. A quasi-religious sentiment took them to the peasant as to an oracle possessed of a mystical inspiration; but the peasant continued to be slighted and beaten and, for a long time, to be overtaxed and officially neglected. In 1902 and again in 1905 he awakened and gave signs of the same latent power which he had shown at rare intervals in earlier centuries, but with a new addition to it brought by strange allies. Henceforth he had leaders, who sought his alliance, and confirmed his strength with their own. But he was still not an equal, though he had come nearer to being one. Formal equality the Constitution of 1936 gave him. How near is the approach to real equality remains a question in dispute.

Light will be shed on this question if we can reach a secure conclusion regarding the distribution of the burden of taxation. This I have endeavoured to do in an appendix. For reasons there given, I think that the peasant pays between 15% and 18% of his gross produce in direct taxation in addition to the indirect taxation which falls upon him in proportion to his consumption. The direct tax is taken almost entirely in kind for a very good reason. You cannot tax a peasant in cash unless you provide him with a market: and the Russian *kolkhoznik* has a market only for a very small part of his produce. As to the direct impost of 15% to 18% of the gross produce, it shows the impossibility of escaping from certain economic laws. If land taxation is light, the person who enjoys the right of cultivation is placed at an enormous advantage over the rest of the community; and unless land taxation is differential, the man who is luckier in the soil, climate, and situation of his lot is better off than the man who is less lucky. In a state aiming at remuneration according to work, we naturally expect a system of land taxation which leaves as little as possible of the unearned income to any individual.

The impost is to be judged, as you would judge a rent-charge, by its amount, its distribution, and the elasticity of its assessment and collection. We are fortunate in having two standards by which to judge the severity of the 15-18% impost as a general average. The land revenue in British India, along with cesses for local purposes, comes, on an average, to something like the value of 12% of the product. But the Indian peasant, if a tenant, pays a rent which is probably double this percentage, and he is often deep in the books of the money-lender. We have another standard of comparison in a valuation of pre-war and post-revolution burdens on the Russian peasant made by Albert Vainstein and published at Moscow, under the auspices of the Council of Labour and Defence, in 1924. We there see the peasant of 1912 paying, in indirect as well as in direct taxation, 11.2% of all his income: a somewhat surprising figure, in view of the frequently repeated story of excessive taxation under the Tsarist régime. However, it must be remembered that, before 1912, not only the poll-tax, but also the redemption payments on account of emancipation from serfdom, had long been abolished, and that in this, as in some other respects, the Tsarist régime was not at its worst when the Revolution occurred.

According to Vainstein's calculations, the taxation of 1922-23 was about equal to that of 1912. We see, then, that the present rural taxation is more than the Tsarist taxation of 1912. But the peasant in 1912 was meeting charges on account of debt and of rent for additional land leased by him, which were out of all proportion to the loan-charges upon the collective farmer to-day.

Viewed as a tax or a rent charged for agricultural land by the proprietor State, 15-18% of the value of the gross produce is a moderate, but by no means a very low, charge. It does not justify the suggestion of E. Strauss in *Soviet Russia* that the peasant is favoured as against the urban worker. Criticism must be directed, not against the pitch of the charge, regarded as an average, but against its insufficient variation according to local conditions, for which I must again refer the reader to the appendix. The somewhat indulgent treatment given to the grower of the technical crops is justified, not only by the importance of industrial interests, but also by the desirability, from the agricultural point of view, of diminishing the still great preponderance of cereal crops, and of diversifying the range of cropping. The idea that the peasant receives exceptional favour is probably due to the comparatively high prices paid for the technical crops, the growing of which is not within the reach of the majority.

Taxation-in-kind, on a large scale, involves the existence of elevator or other storage accommodation, very widely distributed, and of arrangements, which only an organised Socialist Government can possess, for the preservation of perishables, and for putting them through the processes which fit them for the consumer. For instance, wherever there is a milk revenue, there must be creameries, or butter or cheese factories; where there is sugar-beet there must be sugar-boiling plant: and the kind-collecting Government must create all this machinery for processing or distribution, or organise its creation by Co-operative Societies. If we realise all the complexities of such a system, we shall not be surprised that collectivised agriculture, with taxation-in-kind, did not work smoothly from the outset. In a year of plentiful crops, such as 1937, complaints of inadequate storage, and of the resultant destruction of food by weather, are still insistent. But the People's Commissariat for Food Industry has done excellent work in creating the network of institutions and plants which was essential to the prevention of muddle and waste: and this organisation of supplies has contributed much to the improved food situation which has been so noticeable in the towns since 1933.

❄ ❄ ❄

The most important item in the needs of Russian agriculture is increased manuring, and this is closely bound up with an increase in live-stock. The Black-Earth zone lacks moisture more urgently than it lacks soil nutrients, but, in the long run, the elements taken from the soil by cropping require to be replaced. In the non-Black-Earth areas, where moisture is generally sufficient, manure has always been a prime necessity. Not only the reduction of stock, but also the disorganisation of the old methods of stock-keeping, caused by collectivisation, have affected the supply of farmyard manure of recent years; and have doubtless made important contributions to the general failure to increase the yields. The old methods of storage, collection, and carrying out of the manure, developed by long traditional practice, have had to be replaced by new ones which are not immediately effective. The potential supply is reckoned at 300 million tons, which, if it could be made actually available, would permit of the application of nearly a ton to every cultivated acre. Actually, 135 million tons of farmyard manure were applied in 1935. The British standard—applicable, of course, to a more intensive agriculture—is understood to be two tons of farmyard manure per acre, with artificials in addition, and with a leguminous crop ploughed in once in four years to restore vegetable humus. Very little use of cleaning crops is made in Russia. Without expecting conformity with the methods of an intensive cultivation such as the British, I think it clear that Russian agriculture has much leeway to make up: and that a very great increase in live-stock is essential to success.

A good deal of manure on the treeless steppe is burnt for fuel, and it is difficult to devise any means of checking this practice without extensive forestation. Factories have been set up for artificial fertilisers, and the supply is increasing fairly fast. There is an increasing production of phosphates, but the production of potash salts has only begun. Artificials are used almost exclusively for the industrial or technical crops, primarily for cotton and sugar-beet.

I have said enough to prepare the reader for the conclusion in the appendix, that agricultural yields in the U.S.S.R., always very low, do not show any unmistakable signs of rising higher. Doubtless, remarkable results are attained by Stakhanovite workers on particular farms, and there has been an increase in cultivated area resulting in an increase of gross produce. Otto Schiller, whose outlook upon collectivisation is not a favourable one, has recorded the opinion that in 1935, for the first time after a number of years, the bread supply was secured. There has also been a great extension of the area under the so-called technical crops, and the U.S.S.R. has become virtually self-sufficient in sugar, flax, and cotton, and to the extent of one-third, in tea. This, and the extension of fodder grasses, are great achievements. The harvest of 1937, after the serious disappointment of 1936, appears to have been a bumper, and that of 1940 was put by official speakers at a high figure. But the volume and quality of the crops depend almost entirely upon meteorological conditions, and the average yield per unit of area, as shown by the official figures published by the Soviet Government before 1936, continues generally stationary.* With a diminution of the manure supply, I do not see how anything better could have been expected.

❊   ❊   ❊

Collectivisation has contributed to the success of agricultural operations by the improvement, of which it has been the cause, in work-discipline. An equally important fact is that collectivisation enables the cultivator to concentrate on his job, instead of having to dissipate his attention over a number of different functions, including the financing of his farm and the buying and selling of implements and

---

* Sir John Russell in the *Journal of the Ministry of Agriculture*, February, 1938, cites evidence of a yield of sugar-beet per acre higher in 1937 than 1913.

produce. Collectivisation has also made possible the application to agriculture of the results of scientific research, to an extent hardly to be achieved in dealing with millions of separate holdings. Russian research work has won the admiration of scientists, and it is not being wasted by the pigeon-holing of its conclusions, as it often was in Great Britain. It has carried the wheat-belt further north, and defeated the shortness of the agricultural season by giving an earlier start to growth. Orders go through to the very bottom. When they are wrong orders, they cause extensive mischiefs, but the quality of the research work makes the prospect of judicious orders a promising one.

One of the most valuable influences upon agriculture has been the result, not of collectivisation, but of the increasing industrialisation of the country, which has created new, and enlarged old, centres of demand for dairy products, vegetables, and technical crops, and is slowly but surely diminishing the preponderance of cereals. Changes in this direction are particularly noticeable in the Leningrad, Moscow, Ivanovsk, and Gorky (old Nizhni-Novgorod) provinces. If the process of industrialisation continues, as appears likely, it is in this direction that we may look for the surest, if least spectacular, advances of Russian agriculture.

❋ ❋ ❋

If we now address ourselves to the question of the material prosperity of the peasant under collectivisation, we must begin by saying that it shows enormous variations, from what is wealth, by peasant standards, to what is poverty by any standard. Of the former type it is easy to find examples, because the rich collective is naturally the most willingly shown. Suffice it to say that the rich collective, with each member earning on the average 2,400 roubles a year, with half a ton of wheat, 600 lb. of vegetables, 300 lb. of potatoes, and 30 litres of wine, besides the earnings of his "yard," and taking in holiday lodgers into the bargain, actually does exist. That the average is something immensely less than this is an inevitable inference from known facts. Since cereal and other yields have not on the average increased, general material prosperity could be derived only from one or more of the following causes: a reduction of waste; an increase of cultivation in a ratio greater than the increase of population; a change of cultivation to more profitable crops; an increase of animal products; an improved market; non-agricultural earnings; a reduction in the prices of industrial goods, in terms of agricultural products; or a diminution of tax, rent and usury burdens. Under the head of reduction of waste, I have to note one wholly admirable result of mechanisation, in particular of the introduction of combine-harvesters. Hitherto there has always been a substantial loss of crop, caused by the breaking of the weather before it could be carried home. The combine-harvester has faults of its own, and will not wholly eliminate these losses. But, by the speed which it introduces into operations, it has reduced them. The complete elimination of this source of loss would raise the net supply by something like a fifth, and substantially enrich a large portion of the country.

The cultivated area within the present boundary of the U.S.S.R. increased by 25% between 1913 and 1935. The creation of the State-farms, on lands not previously under cultivation, accounts for nearly two-thirds of this. I do not know what proportion the 52 million acres recently taken from the State-farms was cultivated land, and how much of it was given to existing collectives, and how much to new ones created for the former employees of the State-Farms. I think it probable that the increase of the cultivated area of the peasants, partly by drainage of marsh, partly by the adoption of more scientific rotations, involving a smaller proportion of fallow than the old three-field rotation, and partly by surrender from the State-farms, has not been in a higher ratio than the growth of the rural population. No great projects of irrigation, on the scale familiar in Northern India, have been carried out, but some are in contemplation, and smaller projects are actually being carried out. In 1933, 1934, and 1935, 5 million acres in the non-Black-Earth zone were reclaimed from marsh, and probably the drainage of another 4 millions was completed in 1936.

As regards the cultivation of more profitable crops, the growers of cotton and sugar-beet have increased in prosperity. These crops occupy limited belts, well-defined by climate and physical conditions, and, in the case of cotton, very largely dependent on artificial irrigation. The extension of cotton-growing outside of irrigated areas has not so far given good results. Some increase of prosperity is probable in those northern and central regions where dairying, and the growth of vegetables, potatoes and technical crops, have recently developed. But three-fourths of the agriculture of the U.S.S.R. is still cereal. Gain has resulted from carrying the wheat-belt further north, into what has always been regarded as the deficit food-producing area: but otherwise conditions in the cereal areas are for the present stereotyped.

❋   ❋   ❋

It is plain that the average collective farmer, in order to make ends meet, must use to the utmost his yard and its produce: and we are not surprised to learn that, in the vicinity of towns, or where there are favourable market conditions, peasants have recently been taking great pains to develop their yards, which are the exclusive possession of the family. It is easy to see that an area of 1 to 5 acres (½ to 2 hectares) might in favouring circumstances become an important competitor with the claims of the collective; and Trotsky, who had his eyes wide open for all Soviet failures, said this was already happening. The taxation of collective farmers was revised in August, 1939, with the avowed object of discouraging it. But it can hardly be happening on a great scale, since the resources for glass, or other expensive methods of small-scale cultivation, do not exist except in the "millionaire" collectives. But, when we have emphasised the fact that prosperity is for a comparatively small number of collectives and that, for the vast majority, the *kolkhoznik* soup is still the same soup, both in quantity and quality, as the peasant soup was before, we have still to remind ourselves that—small though the increase in production continues to be—there have been important changes in distribution. What the *kulak* added to the common stock—it is hardly to be supposed that he added nothing—he has ceased to add. What he took from it, has gone back into it again. On an average, 15% of the property of the collectives is calculated to be derived from the *kulaks*. But this is not the whole of the redistribution which collectivisation has involved. The 8 million horseless households are now provided with horse-power, partly by the machines furnished by the M.T.S. and partly as co-sharers with their fellow collective farmers. The landless agricultural labourers, scarcely less numerous in 1928 than in 1916, are now partners on equal terms with the landed peasants, if their work is of equal value. These groups at least have made an important material gain.*

❊   ❊   ❊

That the village is "dark" and "deaf," and needs to be civilised by the influence of the town, is part of the Bolshevik thesis. The aim is "cultural"—which means urbanising in the etymological sense of the word—as well as economic. The model statute lays particular stress on raising the status of women, whose lot in rural Russia has always been a hard and degraded one. They are to be given every possible opportunity of advancement suited to their individual capacities. Attention is to be paid to hygiene. The statute requires the establish-

* See Appendix VI for a note on the present condition of villages investigated, by Dr. Shingarev, in 1902.

ment of barbers' shops, baths, plantations of fruit-trees, and other amenities. The system is criticised as loosening the family bond, by turning the wife into a "worker," and putting the cottage loom and spinning-wheel largely out of use; as making an end of national individuality along with peasant customs and costumes; as reducing the influence of the elders upon the children and, consequently, weakening the hold of religion. All three things are, in general, true, though the common interest in the yard, and the animals kept there, seems to me to counteract in part the tendency to the dissolution of the family bond. There is, in fact, a change from an old world to a new one, bringing its emancipations and its sophistications, destroying the picturesque uniqueness of village life, introducing a number of new occupations, teaching man to be machine-minded, opening up opportunities of promotion, and compelling an increase of literacy, because the business of administering a large farm cannot be carried on without it. The itinerant cinema and the autobus are active. The town is— whether for good or evil, or more probably for both—brought to the village. One of the consequences may be, perhaps already is, a diminution in the birth-rate of the villages.

❋   ❋   ❋

What, in the meanwhile, is the individualist peasant doing? He is not free to deal with his land as he pleases. Like the collectivised, he must abide by the Plan. But, as has always been the case in the food-importing section of agricultural Russia, agriculture is generally of subordinate importance to him. He is one of the "self-employers," doing only such farming as he must. As a farmer, his position is uncomfortable. The process of collectivisation has hitherto been a continuing one, involving changes as each additional batch of peasants decides to join. This means repeated redistribution, in which those who remain uncollectivised normally receive the worst and most distant land, allotted to them only for one agricultural year. The area and shape of their lots make it impossible for them to benefit by agricultural machinery, even if the M.T.S. were willing to supply it; their taxes and dues are, on paper, much higher than those of the collectivised, and they do not enjoy equal privileges in respect to loans from the State. Recent heavy taxation of their horses has evidently been aimed at the reduction of their openings in the carrying trade, which had been one of their remaining resources. It seems evident that the dissidents must soon be reduced to a still smaller residuum, or be driven into the towns. In fact, this process is already completing itself.

Must we conclude that collectivisation has come to stay? We have heard in recent years of the prosecution and imprisonment of Communists in the Yaroslav province—not an area in which collectivisation has been conspicuously successful—for conniving at reversion to individualist farming, on the ground that it was authorised by the Constitution of 1936. I do not think that the case is typical. Time is working for the new system: *vis inertiae* is beginning to be on its side. Otto Schiller, who closely watched Russian agriculture for many years, and profoundly dislikes collectivisation, said that the peasant does not object to the régime, as such, and blames the local official for his troubles. His feeling, he says, is one of resignation. This is not a feeling out of which combined resistance is likely to arise. A more dangerous threat to the system was that presented by the systematic evasion of which I have said something on an earlier page: 100,000 acres were misappropriated out of the common land to increase the area of the private yards in a single region, and many persons, including the local authorities, and the local Communists, must have connived with the law-breakers.

The support given to the Soviet régime in the war shows that it has the support of its people. As regards collectivisation, in particular, there has, of course, been grumbling, but apparently no specific grievance. There is no period of prosperity or freedom with which to contrast the present. The peasant has often been hungry, hungry for mere bread. Now he is, with some exceptions, poor, but not actually hungry for bread. The lack of manufactured goods is a recurrent irritation: but it has been like that, sometimes worse and sometimes better, for a generation, perhaps always, and it is probably less than in recent years. There is no landlord, and no *kulak*, upon whom to centre his jealousies and his hatred. Within his own collective, he sees all equal with himself, equal at least in that all get only what they earn. Outside the collective there may be groups of whom he is envious. He dislikes the official: but he has always disliked the official, a fussy person, making unintelligible demands, even if free from corruption. Taxation comes almost entirely out of a common stock. He is not conscious of paying it in person. There is no beating for him, as in the old days, if he fails. He still remembers, or is familiar by tradition with, the tremendous strain of harvest work, often without help from animal strength. Now that strain is taken off him by mechanisation.

The women have gained greatly in freedom and human dignity.

I do not think that a victorious Russia will abandon the system of collectivisation, which has given the advantages of *grande culture* without the incubus of landlordism, and has avoided the burden of peasant indebtedness, ordinarily so grave a feature of all peasant societies.

A good sign is that some of the Communists are beginning to study the details of agriculture, and learning to talk to farmers in farmers' language. Here is a scrap from a long speech by Khrushchev, Secretary of the Central Committee of the Party in the Ukraine, with the *voces populi* interjected: "You must have your coarse-wool sheep as well as your fine. A jacket from a coarse-wool Rumanian sheep is good for fifteen years' wear. (Applause.) I can't imagine what life in the village would be like without a sheep-skin jacket. (Laughter.) . . . You must do better with your buckwheat. Trophim Denisovich Lysenko (a famous populariser of new farming methods) says, grow millet instead. Millet? But what about your bowl of porridge? (Laughter.) And don't you want buckwheat for the sake of your bees? No honey this morning! What? (More laughter.)"

After this glimpse of a peasant crowd and its reception of a Communist's little jokes the official journal gives us a picture of the children of the *kolkhoz* practising their violins in a typical suburban drawing-room. Wonderful, past all whooping! This is the kind of collective farm which lets seaside lodgings to summer visitors. Need we tell the reader that there are not many such? Like the Press everywhere, the newspaper is irredeemably urban.

It remains for us to note the effect of the new system on the food supply of the towns and the provision of raw material for industry. Here we can register pure gain. The attempts to collect a land-tax from 25 million peasant households, many of them too poor to pay, or having incontrovertible claims to remission, and to obtain food and raw materials in return for manufactured goods of which the supply was always short and precarious, were evidently destined to failure. They have been replaced by collective claims upon the whole joint produce of a quarter of a million manageable units: claims of which the evasion is made all but impossible by the intimate participation of the Machine Tractor Stations in the harvesting of the crop. Regarded as a fiscal measure, collectivisation and its accompaniments have given a degree of efficiency undreamed of by the Tsarist, or the early Revolutionary Government. The towns are the direct beneficiaries, but the rural areas must ultimately benefit by the growth of industry to which these increased resources give the impulse. In the towns, the advance in material prosperity since 1933 leaps to the eye of the unprejudiced observer. The enriching fluids certainly pass from village to city. I look with some confidence for the return of the circulation from the heart to the members. I have already noted that that process has begun, in the increasing diversification of cropping in particular areas and the slow diminution of the predominance of cereals.

Chapter XXI

URBAN LABOUR

"There is violence in a system which compels a man to sell his work like merchandise, however capitalism may veil it: and in one which makes his material existence depend on people who demand particular convictions and beliefs from him. Real liberty demands an economic guarantee."

BERDYAEV, *Christianity and the Class War.*

"In Moscow, as a skilled factory worker, I should be a member of the ruling class, of the new aristocracy. . . . There's a very bright side, the facilities for rest and recreation . . . education, and the care they take of the children."

ARCHIBALD LYALL, *Russian Roundabout,* 1933.

Roughly speaking, and subject to important palliatives, in Great Britain, property is liberty: and the lack of it means dependence upon the will of those who have it, or of their paid assistants. This is mainly because property alone can give employment. Almost always there is a market for capital. Often there is no market for any but very special skill: and strength and skill perish while property survives.

Property alone can give employment, when the growth of population and the development of industrial civilisation have cut man off from access to the natural sources of subsistence. And property cannot always give it. It can give it, on a large scale, only if there is a market, at a satisfactory price, for the products of labour. Periodically this market fails, and the phenomena of large-scale unemployment appear.

It fails, in spite of powerful efforts, backed by diplomacy, and sometimes by war, to extend it abroad: and in spite of infinite ingenuity bestowed upon the arts of advertisement. Commercial rivalry, taking the form of cheap competition, accounts for something, but the principal cause is the deficiency of purchasing power. We are often reminded that a few more shillings in the hands of the Indian agriculturist or the Chinese coolie would rehabilitate Lancashire. That the same thing is true of the pockets of the British workman is less commonly mooted. The idea appears at intervals like an unquiet ghost, who finds no vacant chair, at the economic banquet, where business men are too busy with the *hors d'oeuvres* or the champagne to see it at all. The same man who would eagerly support a policy for the extension of foreign markets, and expend thousands on the advertisement of an alcohol, an amenity, or a convenience, takes a limited home-market for the great staples for granted. There is enough wealth in a limited circle to give profitable openings in a favourable season. The larger prospect of a nation-wide demand is overlooked: and a deliberate policy of increasing the incomes of all, if contemplated at all, seems like thimble-rigging. And yet it is plain enough that more work is capable of producing more commodities, and that more commodities are the essential pre-requisite of increased real incomes. Only the mechanism of market-exchange stands in the way.

In the meanwhile, it is necessary to restrict output, so that the smaller aggregate may find a market—it may be, and in the case of many luxuries and semi-luxuries it is, only among the wealthier section —at a price that pays the producer. Perishables—we would not exaggerate the extent to which this happens, it is sufficient that it does happen—are thrown away. Few plants, except for an emergency, work at full capacity.

The mentality of restriction spreads from the entrepreneur to the workman. The notion that there is a limited number of jobs, and that one must do nothing that might reduce the chances of one's fellows, takes root. Nevertheless we have been recently assured on good authority, in respect to the building industry, that the English worker produces about twice the volume that the Russian worker produces in the same time, and that the quality of the work of the Stakanovets builder would never be accepted in the United Kingdom. The Trade Unions fix the task, and fix it as low as their negotiating power will allow. Piece-work seems a trick to bring down time-rates. Interests seem—perhaps are—antagonistic, and profit-sharing a trick for the destruction of working-class solidarity in the struggle with the employer. All the essential conditions of a class-war come naturally into existence. To put the position at its best, the employer and the manager are the workman's opponents in the economic game. He and his fellows are on the defensive. He has no sense of "ownness" in the factory where he works. He knows how the boss lives, and he doubts the fairness of the sharing. When he himself has the advantage, he presses it ruthlessly. Why not? The boss will get rid of him whenever rationalisation makes it convenient to do so. In the meanwhile there is unemployment, a reservoir from which his place can be filled without difficulty unless he behaves himself: and unemployment, in the

anticipation as well as in the reality, is a hell for all who can think
and feel.

The millions of working-class homes are so many millions of separate
boxes, in which so many millions of women slave at millions of separate tasks, unaided by co-operation, and very little aided by mechanical device or electrical power; tugged at by children, and
burdened with children to come, till temper and nerves are frayed into
unnatural irritability: while the spectre of economic insecurity stands
always at the door.

I have done what I could not to exaggerate these characteristics of
British working life. They must be realised, if a just conception is
to be formed of the comparative advantages and disadvantages of the
life of the urban worker in the U.S.S.R. Let us begin by examining
the extent to which actual compulsion to labour—not merely compulsion by the prospect of starvation or semi-starvation as in Great
Britain—survives in the U.S.S.R. In doing this, I shall exclude from
my purview the subject of penal labour, which belongs rather to
prison management or criminal administration.

It is in respect to the timber camps of Karelia, and of northern
Russia generally, that allegations of compulsion have been most freely
made. A gifted journalist, who was excluded by the Gay-Pay-oo from
the timber camps, has told us that forced labour has been employed
in Karelia on a gigantic scale: but the enquiries of the Russian Timber
Committee of the British Timber Trade Federation, of the Central
Executive of the British Timber and Wood Workers' Union, and of
the Anti-slavery and Aborigines Protection Society (all in 1931),
rebut this statement. Albert Rhys Williams in *The Russian Land*
appears to be giving us a true picture, when he says that everyone
curses Northern Woods, the State exploiting department. "But, at
last, with many declarations of mutual esteem, the contracts are signed
and the season's work begins." The truth, as I gather it from the evidence, is that the exploitation of timber is not every man's job. It
requires some skill, and a good deal of strength; and a conscript force
would not be likely to deal with it in a satisfactory fashion. Commercial rivalry has exaggerated, if it has not invented, the charges against
the Timber administration of the U.S.S.R.

This is not to say that there is no compulsion of labour under the
Socialist Government. The practice descends from two, perhaps from
three, lines of ancestry. One is the immemorial usage of purely or
mainly agricultural countries, in which no general body of wage-labour

has yet come into existence, of calling upon the occupiers of land to deal with emergencies. For certain purposes, such as the seasonal repair of roads, there is actually no alternative, in primitive conditions, to the practice, and there is no more hesitation about turning out the countryside for such work than there is for a hue and cry after a thief. The *trinoda necessitas* of British history is a regularised and limited form of the usage. All that can fairly be asked is that such demands shall be limited to real emergencies, evenly distributed, and properly paid for.

Another line by which the compulsion of labour has established itself in the U.S.S.R. is the revolutionary principle: He who does not work, neither shall he eat.

Those who have experience of the employment of unwilling labour are aware that it seldom pays for its own food and lodging, and for the overhead charges of control and management. On a large scale it can only be used effectively for the simplest and most unskilled tasks, scavenging, earth-works, stone-breaking and the like. Though excellent carpets have been made in Indian jails, the business reduced the net expenditure on the convicts without completely defraying it. In this fact lies the true safeguard against the extensive employment of compulsory labour. It was made clearly manifest in the last days of serfdom. For any but the very simplest kind of unskilled task, it *does not pay*. But the Soviet Statute Book contains examples of the use of it. In the spring of 1930, there is to be "rigorous discipline in connection with timber-flotation, after the thaw," and labour is to be despatched from collective farms to "seasonal branches of the national economy—construction, floating, agriculture, loading and unloading." Demands for labour for loading and unloading of grain, and of export and import goods, are to have priority, and all unemployed persons (this refers to 1930) are to obey the call for work on these tasks, on pain of deprivation of unemployment benefit. Intellectual workers are included in this order. Labour organisations are to create voluntary brigades of shock-workers to work off accumulations of unloading and loading. As I have already noted elsewhere, the system of agreements with collective farms for the use of their surplus labour involves a measure of compulsion upon individuals.

There is yet a third form which compulsion takes, and that is the use of skilled workers as officials, liable to transfer from one place, and from one job, to another. A decree of October 20, 1930, empowered the authorities to send skilled workmen in unimportant branches of work to coal-mining, iron, steel, and construction enterprises. A little later, persons having technical experience of railway work were recalled to railway service, and in June, 1931, an order issued that a worker must go where he is sent. This would not strike a Western critic as a hardship in the case of a postal or a railway official, so long as the conditions of transfer were equitable and all its expenses paid. In proportion as the worker develops into a functionary, to be permanently provided for by the State which employs him, a further development on these lines seems to be perfectly logical. It is an abatement of liberty, paid for, as in the case of the official, by a guarantee of employment and pension. As a consequence, an apparently necessary consequence, of the relations between the Socialist State and the individual, it gives occasion for thought. But, if we desire that kind of liberty which consists in economic security, we must, it would seem, be prepared to sacrifice that kind of liberty which consists in doing what we please at the cost of economic security. Perhaps there is no such thing as doing what we please, except upon a basis of pecuniary independence. It is one of the middle-class illusions, which do not deceive the man who depends upon the wage of his daily labour.

There is, in fact, a radical contradiction between the British and the Russian type of liberty. A comparison of the status and functions of Trade Unions in the two cases will furnish further illustration. In spite of the attempt made in 1927 to limit its influence, the British Trade Union movement is truly representative of its members, and responsive to the sentiment of the majority of them. A majority of the workers are outside its ranks: but it is likely that its existence confers advantages on more than its members. It is, so far, as free from official and social influence as the British affection for rank and distinction will allow any British movement to be. It honestly aims at the good of its members: that is to say, it seeks the improvement of conditions, the increase of pay, and the lightening of toil. It does not aim at the increase of output and, indeed, appears to be indifferent to this consideration. This is because the increase of output is conceived as advantageous to the employer, and as not advantageous, possibly disadvantageous, to the worker, as involving a reduction in the number of available jobs. The advantage to the community as a whole, including the worker, of increased output, is obscured by the system of distribution.

After a long struggle, beginning with the attempt in the early days of the Revolution to achieve the Syndicalist ideal of industrial and social control by the Trade Unions—an ideal very close to that of the Anarchists—the Trade Unions have settled down in the U.S.S.R. as organs of the State. Membership has long ceased to be compulsory, but the subscription (1% of pay) is so small, and the advantages of membership so obvious, that the movement covers 80-90% of the whole body of urban workers in all categories.

It has been notorious that elections to Trade Union offices in the U.S.S.R. were influenced, if not actually dictated, by authority, but, since the introduction of the new Constitution of 1936, Stalin has insisted upon secret voting, and it is probable that these orders have been generally carried out, with such reservations as are implied in the dominant position of the Communist Party. But it is in the functions, rather than in the organisation, that the difference between the British and the Russian Trade Union reveals itself.

The All-Union Joint Trade Union Congress, and its elected Central Committee, have inherited the functions of the former Commissariats of Labour in the Union and the Constituent Republics, and a portion of those of the Workers' and Peasants' Inspection. If we assume them to be actually democratic in constitution, not only all working-class institutions, including all branches of social insurance, but all factory inspections, and all labour recruiting, are controlled by representatives of the workers themselves. We have the authority of the Webbs for saying that the collective bargaining with the agencies of production, which is carried out by the All-Union Congress of the individual trades, in consultation with the Central Trade Union Committee, is a reality and no mere form. That it was not always so, we learn from S. Zagorsky's work on Wages, published by the International Labour Organisation in 1930. What we there see is an allotment of available funds by agreement between central authorities, followed by a distribution of them over particular industries and undertakings, in consultation with the Trade Unions. In September, 1929, there is a definite ruling that no one can demand an increase in funds determined by the central authority for providing increments in wages. It does not appear that there has been any essential change of procedure since. The officials of the Central Trade Union Committee sit down with the officials representing the various Commissariats, and the State Planning Committee. The clerks bring up the figures, showing how much is available for wages. When the accuracy of the calculation is verified, that amount becomes a sort of artificial wages-fund, out of which claims are to be met. The rest is merely a question of distribution.

This is all most reasonable: but it is not bargaining, in the ordinary sense of the word, which implies the possibility, on each side, of withholding something from the other. The assumption in the U.S.S.R. is that a Trade Union is to protect, not wage-rates in its particular industry, but the earnings and conditions of all the wage-earners: and this is to be achieved by a general increase of productivity which gives a larger surplus for distribution. Therefore, as it appears to me, there is no bargaining. Beside the width of its functions as the manager of working-class institutions, and of social insurance, and the controller of factory inspection, the Russian differs from the corresponding British movement in two important particulars: it is not a potential organiser of strikes, and it seeks to stimulate productivity and to raise technical proficiency—that is to say, it has, as one of its aims, co-operation with the Employer State in the increase of output.

There is no law which prohibits strikes. There were seven as recently as 1929-30. It is argued that they are unnecessary because, with the end of the exploiting class, there is no enemy party. The workers are one with the Workers' State, and can have no interest that conflicts with it. The enquiry which precedes the formulation of the collective "bargain" is an ascertainment of facts, not an examination of claims. The amount available for the wages of the worker is the whole balance of the State's receipts after the needs of public expenditures have been met. Simple arithmetic admits of no dispute. That the State may be making demands for military defence, for the adornment of the capital, or for other purposes which to some may seem excessive; that there may be differences between different groups of workers regarding the division of the product, after all exploitation has come to an end; that there may be tyranny of the whole as against the part, of the majority as against the minority, of a favoured minority as against the majority: these contingencies do not enter into consideration.

Can we feel satisfied that the interests of the worker are safeguarded, when the organisation which should protect him is, by a fundamental assumption of the system, precluded from protecting him by strike— in other words, from enforcing its power of bargain by withholding the labour which is the subject-matter of the bargain? The Russian answer is: Yes. Liberty is secured to the class when its fundamental interests are secured. And the fundamental interests are something corporate, of course. In his early days of power Trotsky himself put the case thus, as between the Party and the general body of workers. "In the substitution of the power of the Party for the power of the working class, there is in reality no substitution at all. The Communists express the fundamental interests of the working class." And of course, there was no minority, no fraction, no individual, to be taken into account. The true liberty of the individual would be realised in a complete economic security, setting him free for the development of his personality in the classless society.

S. Zagorsky made plain to us the actual course which the Trade Unions were taking, when he wrote in 1930, to support the claim of their members. They played their part, of course, along with the manager of the factory and the local representative of the Party, as the *Troika* for the decision of industrial disputes. But, since there was no possibility in the final resort of withholding labour, they did not play it as responsible negotiators. They satisfied the men by asking for too much, and referred the unsettled differences to the Court of Arbitration: passed the baby, if we may be pardoned for using the language of the market-place. In this shifting of the responsibility of decision, we note a characteristic Russian weakness—which drastic punishments only aggravate.

The notion of the Trade Union movement as a co-operator with the State in the stimulation of productivity is shocking to the fundamental sentiment of the British Trade Unionist, who conceives his duty to be in the direction of protecting the worker against the normal tendency of the employer to exact a larger task. The Russian conception is framed in the interest of the community as a whole, which certainly stands to gain by increased output, and cannot be enriched without it: while the British is framed in the interest of the worker, whom the employer must not be permitted to exploit. The encouragement of the pace-maker in Russian industry is carried very far indeed. The shock-worker, who increased his output by sheer power of muscle, and enjoyed the best conditions as the reward of his achievement, has been succeeded by the *Stakhanovets*, of whose function something has already been said elsewhere in these studies. The peculiar danger of piece-work is that this method of remuneration will be used to bring down wage-rates by alteration of the norms. This is actually occurring, and we are not surprised at hearing of discontent among those who cannot stand the pace, and even of murderous attacks upon Stakhanovites. The British worker, from his own peculiar point of view, as one who seeks to checkmate efforts to hasten the pace, would probably call them blacklegs.

The city shops are filled with articles of luxury and semi-luxury for which the average wage is certainly unable to pay. One of Mrs. Seema Allan's correspondents at Moscow wrote in 1937 with enthusiasm about the varieties of bread, jams, jellies, canned fruit and vegetables at attainable prices. She added that dress material of every kind, from calico to velvet, was available, but at very high prices; and that stockings could be had at prices ranging from 70 kopeks to 20 roubles a pair (from two pence to four shillings!), "not as good as foreign, but can be worn." It is an inevitable inference that the new super-piece-workers are buying many of these things, and that society is being transformed by the growth of a new kind of sectional prosperity, having, indeed, a better claim than the old, because it is graduated according to work, but creative of new jealousies. There seems to be nothing to protect the worker against the temptation to exhaust prematurely his reserves of strength. At the same time we must recognise that the norms of production in Russia are extremely low: and that the only way of raising them to something approaching the Western standard is to begin by utilising the willingness of the few to do more work, or to organise their work better.

It is low productivity which, next to the dread of foreign attack, continues to be the fundamental anxiety of the U.S.S.R. There is a call in official quarters for a collective Stakhanovism, and the inefficacy of the individual record-breaker, as a means of increasing general productivity, has recently been emphasised. Stalin himself insisted on it in his speech of March 5, 1937, to the Central Committee of the Communist Party. Among other "rotten" mistakes which he there enumerated was a boastful confidence in the achievements of the Stakhanovite workers. In April, 1937, the journal of the all-Union Communist Party wrote of the continuing backwardness of the country both in the quantity and in the quality of the product.

Something is needed which will effect an escape from the contrary faults of the British and the Russian Trade Union systems, which will amend the former by taking account of the community's need of increased production, and the latter by protecting the worker against overstrain. In the meanwhile we can only register the fact that the Trade Union movement in the U.S.S.R. does not defend the individual against overwork. In too many cases he protects himself by an invincible slackness, confident of the difficulty of replacing him in a society which needs all hands.

But we shall leave a wrong impression if we stop at this point. There are plenty of Russian workers who care nothing for their work: the proportion of labour turnover and the large number of "flitters" prove this. But a very general characteristic is a pride, of *ownness* if not of ownership, in the factory and the job. Frau Koerber, who enrolled herself as a worker in the Putilov factory at Leningrad in July, 1931, "continually had the impression of being on a visit to the women workers, because they seem so like hostesses anxious to show their guest all the new household arrangements." Mrs. Margaret Cole made a similar reflection. "The factory is my father," sang the Communist poet. The aim of making the factory a social centre, as well as a place of work, has been deliberate. The best of the modern factories are surrounded by workers' settlements having a complete equipment for all needs: schools, hospitals, clubs, theatres, baths. They remind me of British Public Schools in their *esprit de corps*. The sense of *ownness* goes deep. "You would think they owned the country," wrote Knickerbocker: "maybe they do, and maybe they don't: but they think so, and I have never seen the slave who thought he was the boss." To help the completion of the Moscow Subway, workers gave up their holidays, and embarrassed the organisers with their volunteer assistance. It is the team-spirit, raised to a higher power, and operating in a wider field.

It is likely that Russians have a special aptitude for a communal feeling of this kind. It is very noticeable in the theatre, where the perfection of acting is sometimes achieved by perfect drilling and combined effort, without the prominence of particular stars. It is not new, for Turgeniev in his *Sketches of a Sportsman* has given us an example of it in the old world of serfdom. Extended to a larger sphere, it becomes devotion to the State.

A fourth form of compulsion was established in October, 1940 in the restriction of the choice of employment by a proportion of the young people. Some of them are selected by the Committees of collective farms for industrial training, and required to remain for a period in the trade to which they are allotted. Virtually this is industrial conscription, and the compulsion is fortified by the charging of fees in secondary schools where a more general education is given. This step was taken as a part of the measures for national defence, and may or may not represent a permanent policy.

Alongside of the possibilities of compulsion to be exercised by the Employer State, that State has formulated a fundamental principle for the defence of the status and dignity of the worker. There was a moment when the well-to-do peasant was permitted to hire labour as well as lease land. This was before Stalin and the Communist Party decided on that dramatic turn to the Left, which is associated with the first Five-Year-Plan and collectivisation. It is still permissible to pay a "hired girl" for domestic tasks. We must take note, however,

that the employer of a "hired girl" for domestic work does not make
a profit out of her labour: and it is the making of a profit out of the
labour of others which is the head and front of the offense of exploitation. Collective farms may pay experts to help them with their agriculture, masons to do their building work, and extra labour in the
emergencies of the harvest season. With these rare exceptions, the
employment of one person by another is against the law. The State
and the public agencies subordinate to the State have a monopoly of
employment: and "exploitation," which means the enjoyment of the
profit of one man's labour by another, is forbidden.

Is the worker better off when his only exploiter is the Employer
State or the Employer City or some such public body? It depends in
part upon the sense of *ownness* of which I have spoken above. Materially he is no better off. He may even find it harder to resist pressure,
when the opposite party has all the weight of public authority. But
if he feels himself one with his public employer, his position gains
immensely in moral dignity. And let no one suppose that a gain in
moral dignity and self-respect is not desired by the working man. Even
where the sense of *ownness* is less strong than it is in the U.S.S.R.,
the position of the public employee has its attractions. There is a
justifiable assumption that caprice will be less arbitrary, and public
opinion more powerful. Whatever be the sentiments, good, bad, or
indifferent, which prompt the preference, I believe it to be general.

The dictatorship of the Proletariat—that is, of the wage-earner un-
corrupted by the mentality of property—though so obviously not to be
literally realised in the sphere of high politics, has been no meaningless phrase in the U.S.S.R. "They are a cocky lot," wrote Knickerbocker. They have had reason to be cocky, elevated as they were to
the position of the dominant class, from which the Revolution had
ousted the remnants of feudalism and the nascent *bourgeoisie*. "She's
no worker," protested a disputant, justifying his rudeness to a
woman in the tram. To be of worker stock was an asset in the struggle
for favour and promotion. "You were born with a silver spoon in your
mouth because you happen to be a proletarian," says the disappointed
son of a senator in the play to the woman student who has been
elected to an Assistant Professorship on the strength of her qualification in the Workers' Faculty. The whole of the ration system, twice
established, had for its object the securing of the town worker's food
and clothing when food and clothing were short. There are signs that
this unquestioned dominance of a class is coming to an end. On the
one hand, it is being divided by the special pay and privileges of the

champion worker. On the other hand, the new Constitution threatens a new equality in politics of the worker and the peasant. But an honourable status, satisfactory to the sense of human dignity, has been secured by the Revolution to the Russian worker in virtue of his work.

※ ※ ※

The Trade Union, along with the Factory Committee, which is a section of the Trade Union in a particular undertaking, is no longer a potential fighting machine, but an instrument for the improvement of output. The aspect of the Trade Union as an agent in the enforcement of labour discipline was emphasized in the closing days of 1938, by legislation which halved the insurance benefits of workers who were not members. But the Trade Union is a forum for the complaints of the worker, and a channel through which the Government addresses him on questions of social policy. It can generally secure the dismissal of an unpopular manager, it can prevent the unjust dismissal of a worker. It assists in the decision of disputes, without having more than a moral force behind its contentions. It administers the Factory-inspection laws. It administers social insurance, some milliards of roubles annually, a sum enormously in excess of the contributions to Trade Union funds derived from members. The worker does not contribute to the fund for social insurance and social services. Since the sum for expenditure is taken out of the total set aside for the payment of wages, by agreement between the Central Council of Trade Unions and the Commissariats concerned, it has been argued that he pays indirectly the whole of it. I will not attempt to follow this argument into all the vistas which it opens. At all events the worker is not aware that he contributes, any more than he is aware that he pays the tariff charges which form part of the British fiscal system.

Social Insurance, in general, does not cover the self-employers, and therefore excludes the peasantry, both individualist farmers and members of collective farms. These last have their own arrangements, in the form of a percentage of net produce put aside by each farm for social objects. Since there is wide variation in the productivity of the farms, there is also wide variation in the provision made for these objects. For urban employees there are sickness and medical benefits and old-age benefit at sixty years: and mothers receive full pay for two months before, and twenty-eight days after, confinement. With a view to the improvement of labour discipline and the discouragement of labour-flux, the statutory annual holiday with pay may be taken only after eleven months of continuous service in one and the same enterprise, and incapacitation pensions vary according to the number of years last worked continuously in the same enterprise. Measures were taken at the same time, 1938, to enforce the full statutory working day, and to compel the vacation of workers' dwellings in the event of resignation or dismissal. These pills were sweetened by a provision that the economies resulting from the changes should be expended in workers' dwellings and other amenities, and new honorific distinctions carrying pecuniary benefits were instituted.

There are admirable rest-homes at the seaside and in the mountains, but they do not suffice for more than a small portion of the working population. Children enjoy a large share in these good things, and the children's holiday camp, or a party of children marching off to train or boat for a summer outing, is generally a model of kindly and effective organisation. There are still beggars upon the Russian streets and at places where travellers resort, so the wage and the social insurance do not cover all cases. Prostitution has been very greatly diminished, by the extensive employment for women and equal pay for equal work, but luxury prostitution has made its appearance, along with expensive shops and wide inequality of piece-work wages in the cities. It seems that the existence of luxuries unattainable to the ordinary wage inevitably breeds this phenomenon, which is less simple than that of the hungry woman offering herself for the means of livelihood.

The absence since 1930 of a cost-of-living index, and of family budgets, and of every statistical provision for calculation of the value of real wages, stands in the way of effective generalisation on the general standard of living, even in the towns. I am aware of no possibility of improving, in principle, upon the method adopted by Colin Clark in his *Critique of Russian Statistics*, 1939.

A consideration not to be ignored is that there is a subjective, as well as an objective, element in poverty. What the Russian was able to buy with his wage in 1934 was purchasable in England for a wage below the poverty line in that country. It does not follow that he felt the pinch of poverty in anything like the degree represented by the difference in the figures. His living and eating habits are, traditionally and to-day, far less expensive than those of his opposite number in London. He gets as many calories, and possibly as good a supply of vitamins, out of a much cheaper type of food, and he pays, for accommodation which does not shock his sense of decency or even of comfort, an immensely lower rent. Sir John Russell has calculated that the Plan for 1937, assuming its fulfilment in respect to food (and the harvest of that year was exceptionally bountiful, quite unparalleled in the agricultural history of revolutionary Russia), would have given to each inhabitant of the U.S.S.R. quantities of meat, eggs, milk and milk products, margarine and fish, somewhat less than half of those consumed per head in Great Britain; about one-third of the amount of sugar; twice the amount of flour; and 160% of the weight of potatoes. These figures illustrate the radical difference in the standards of diet in the two countries—standards the relative cost of which is only partially relevant to the respective degrees of well-being.

Life generally is simpler and nearer to nature. The differences in diet make a smaller wage go further. But it is in the item of rent that the advantage of the Russian over the British worker is most marked. The housing of workers, by comparison with that of Britain, is on the average bad. In Moscow there is, on the average, only 45 square feet of space (not including kitchen, passage, lavatory, bath and staircase) for each individual. But it is important to get the right perspective. It is with countries like India, and with Tsarist Russia, that the comparison should be made.

In seeking our perspective we have to recall that excellent communal arrangements, in the form of catering establishments, day crèches, workers' clubs, parks for rest and amusement, cheap entertainments, have been provided on a handsome scale in the cities. The money value of the benefits from all social services has been calculated at 34.5% of the individual wage, whereas it is probably about 16% of it in England. The bad home, which for the majority of Russian city workmen takes the place of a good one, is at least inexpensive, and the rent does not swallow a sixth of the whole family income, according to the British example, but rather the thirtieth part.

To return to the respective real values of the Russian and the British urban wage: the comparative inefficiency of retail distribution in the U.S.S.R. has become, since the abolition of rationing, more than ever relevant to the question. I feel no doubt that inconvenient access to retail supplies lowers the real value of the cash-wage.

In 1928 the International Labour Office concluded that the real value of the Moscow wage was then exactly 50% of the English. There is no evidence that it represented any greater proportion of the latter in 1934, after which date the data for the comparison come to an end. (After 1935 the Russian annual compilation known as *Socialist Construction* ceased to be published, probably from the fear of giving economic secrets away to Germany.) Colin Clark has cited figures (he is careful to call them provisional) which show a rise up to 1937 both in agricultural and industrial output, and an increase between 1934 and 1937 by as much as 42% in the average income of the working population taken as a whole. I have attempted, in Appendix IV to this study, to show what the Russian urban wage was capable of purchasing in 1937-38.

Outside of wage and price statistics, and of those propagandist statements which naturally awaken the suspicion of the enquirer, there are some indications of an increased divisible product in the U.S.S.R., and of an increasingly efficient method of securing the share of the cities in that product. The export of food has substantially diminished, and the waste of food has been greatly reduced by the operations of the Commissariat of Food, and the processing and storage of meat, fish, milk, grain, vegetables and fruits which have been consequences of the collection of revenue-in-kind. The growth of industry cannot be estimated in figures, because of the uncertainty and variation of the value of the rouble: but it is quantitatively very great. There is rather more food, and a good deal more of the product of industry, per head of the population. So far as the urban population goes, the arrangements for supply have, in gross, and with some reservations due to bad retailing, been immensely improved by the efficiency of the collection of the revenue-in-kind. There are net gains, and the gains have gone partly to the growers of industrial crops, but mainly to the cities: partly in the form of public amenities, partly in that of an improved standard of living.

The Russian worker, like the British, has his share in the machinery of the workers' State brought periodically home to him by the exercise of his vote, both for the Soviets and for the Trade Union organisation. The practices of issuing instructions to representatives, of receiving reports from them, and of recalling them if their conduct of public business is not satisfactory, are calculated to give to representative institutions a reality which is lacking to them for the working-man in Great Britain, unless he is a particularly active politician. In both cases they contribute something to the worker's self-respect. Whether the contribution is greater in the one case than in the other, I am doubtful. In both there are considerable potentialities for the exceptional man, not much for the rank and file.

There was a statutory seven-hour day, which was later suspended to meet the needs of defence. It must be understood, in respect to this and to everything else in the U.S.S.R., that the laws show what the law-makers would desire, rather than what they are actually able to enforce. That the ordinary time-worker in the factory

—that is to say, the mass of the urban workers—got the benefit of the seven-hour restriction, there is no reason to doubt. But in April, 1933, the newspaper *Labour* was complaining of the disregard of the time rule in the Donets mines. The working day underground was officially six hours: but some miners were working between twelve and eighteen a day without extra pay, in consequence of the disorder in the wage system. I take leave to doubt whether anything less than a workers' organisation independent of, or at least secure against interference by, the Employer State will put an end to abuses of this sort.

Unemployment

Under-employment in the rural areas is, in a certain sense, inevitable so long as the agriculture continues to be predominantly of the type which requires very great reinforcement of labour in certain seasons, and fails to give employment to it during the remainder of the year. Cereal cultivation, still three-quarters of the whole, is of that type. The situation was relieved at one time by rural industries. Some of these were inevitably killed by the competition of the factory. Others survived it, but the Bolsheviks underrated their importance, and tended for a time to tax them out of existence. The mistake was discovered by 1932, when Molotov declared that handicraft industry can and should provide a share of additional products for the local markets, and also supply industry with subsidiary articles and with building materials. The self-employers, largely outside the towns, are now a recognised subsidiary source of supply, and local industries, under the control of local Soviets, also contribute.

In Britain there are approximately three to five agricultural workers to every 100 acres of arable, if land permanently under grass be included. In the U.S.S.R. there are approximately twelve able-bodied rural workers to every 100 arable acres. The two sets of figures are obviously not comparable: for from the second are to be deducted the handicraftsmen, and a number of persons who are doing, in the collective farms and elsewhere, work of an administrative or clerical character, who would not be reckoned as agricultural workers in Britain. On the other hand, agriculture is now mechanised in the U.S.S.R. to a great, and increasing, extent. We cannot but conclude that, judged by the British standard, there is very great under-employment in the rural areas of the U.S.S.R., all the greater, because there is so much less of the glass and truck-farming which occupies a large proportion of the labour in Britain.

It is not only inevitable, for the present, that there should be under-employment in rural Russia: it is also actually desirable, while the country is in the process of rapid industrialisation. The rural underemployment is the reservoir from which the growing needs of the towns are to be met. We should therefore welcome the indication of rural depopulation, the diminution in the number of peasant households, and the large number of deserted buildings, to which some have pointed as indications of rural decay. A process, economically advantageous, is transferring population to the towns. It is far from being completed.

Skilled labour has never suffered from unemployment in the U.S.S.R. But before, and during the first two years of, the First Plan, there was much unskilled unemployment in the cities, probably attributable to the influx of peasants.

In 1932 there was a reappearance of the symptoms of unemployment: to be explained by the combined effects of rationalisation in industry and of scarcity in certain rural areas. Actually the facts point, simultaneously, to shortage of labour, and the excessive employment of superfluous hands—in other words, to bad organisation of labour.

The secret of preventing mass unemployment lies in the power to make demand effective: in other words, to confer purchasing power as well as to put commodities on the market, and to make the one process a necessary correlative of the other. Those who talk of producers improving their markets by increasing the wages of their workers are feeling after the truth. If all producers did it, and did it simultaneously, they would actually improve their markets. But in proportion as they attained to identity and simultaneity of action, they would be simulating the action of the Socialist State, which is able to regulate income as well as supply.

Does this mean that every need will be met? No. The art of production is not yet sufficiently advanced. Does it mean that every variety of taste will be catered for as in the luxury shops of London, Paris and New York? No. A great deal of mere caprice, always the privilege of the few, will necessarily be eliminated from the range of choice. Does it mean that there will be no failures and blunders, no forced sales of unwanted commodities, no miscalculations, no woodenness of application, and no resultant losses and suffering? There will be all these things.

The claim is that the true technique has been discovered, not that it will always be unerringly applied, and that it leads to the ending of mass unemployment. In this, a by-product of the Socialist experiment, lies what is perhaps the greatest claim of the U.S.S.R. to the gratitude

of mankind. The chief misery of working-class life is economic insecurity. With adequate social insurance, and a technique which promises the end of industrial unemployment, that misery is at an end:
until war destroys the foundations of society.

To sum up a comparison of the pre-war conditions of Labour in
London and in Moscow: the Russian worker produces much less; has
a much smaller real wage, and more uniformly poor accommodation;
he pays one-fifth of the London rent; he gets holidays with pay (which
the British worker is only now beginning to get); he makes no direct
contribution to social insurance; and he enjoys important communal
amenities without payment. His wage and his conditions of work are
protected, less by Trade Unions than by the absence of unemployment, which makes him a valuable asset. There are no Trade Boards,
and the minimum wage is almost a dead letter. Trade Union protection in London is far from general, but it is supplemented in certain
trades (those most liable to exploitation) by Trade Boards, which enforce a minimum wage.

For the children of the London worker, the chance of being below
the poverty line (that is, of having less than the indispensable necessities) is one in eight. In old age, the chance of being below the poverty
line is one in six; the chance of having bad house accommodation is
one in three. The Russian worker enjoys greater security in respect
to his children, whose health, schooling, and holidays are extremely
well looked after. There is no material for a comparison of the conditions in old age.

❋   ❋   ❋

Widespread fear, which has no parallel in Britain, has existed, perhaps still exists, in Russia in the class which is called upon to make
decisions. This fear and these anxieties do not extend to the workers
in the U.S.S.R. The Russian worker is freer than the British from
anxiety, because of the absence of unemployment. He stands higher
in the comparative scale of human values, and has no example of disproportionate luxury before him (except in so far as the Stakhanovets
or the Soviet bureaucrat begins to set it) to give him a sense of inferiority. He has no cause (other than personal indolence) for restricting
output, and has a feeling (which the British worker lacks) that he is
working for himself. His wife works hard, but is economically freer,
and is largely emancipated from household drudgery. He lives in an
obviously advancing and improving world, which breeds hope.

Who shall say how the balance dips? I believe that, given the material minimum required for subsistence, the moral and mental considerations are the more important. In spite of Unemployment Benefit and Unemployment Assistance, security is one desideratum in Great Britain: and status is another—for status, for the undistinguished mass, too obviously depends upon property. Here is the missing half of liberty for the British worker.

Chapter XXII

RELIGION IN THE REVOLUTION

"Russians are always apocalyptic or nihilist. . . . The spirit
of the people could very easily pass from one integrated faith
to another integrated faith, from one orthodoxy to another
orthodoxy, which embraced the whole of life. . . . And there
always remains, as the chief thing, the profession of some
orthodox faith: this is always the criterion by which membership of the Russian people is judged."

BERDYAEV, *Origins of Russian Communism.*

The early Orthodox Church, making no distinction of spiritual and
temporal authority, identified itself with a Messianic mission of the
Russian people, in which Holy Russia was the God-bearer. The
Church played a heroic part in the national history.

The Schism (Raskol) of the seventeenth century marked a turning
point. It was the beginning of a breach in the tradition of unity. The
quarrel revealed itself as a movement of rudimentary nationalism, and
threw the official Church into a new subjection to the State. The
process of change was thereafter rapid. Peter the Great hastened it by
putting the Patriarchate into commission under a lay Procurator.
Catherine the Great confiscated the land of the monasteries, and the
completeness of the fall was made manifest when Gregory Rasputin—
neither priest nor monk, but a mere Imperial favourite with the affec-
tation of a Divine Mission and the reality of a debauched life—made
high ecclesiastical functionaries, and canonised saints by his influence
upon the heads of the State.

Against this degradation of the official Church there was a volume
of protest from its lay defenders. But, in the words of Merezhkovsky,
" the holy words of the Scriptures, in which we (the laymen) heard
the voice of the Seven Thunders, sounded to them (the ecclesiastics)
like catechism texts learned by heart." The Church had become a
department of the State, and participated in its incompetence and corruption. The extension of Orthodoxy was a branch of the policy of
Russification, and was thrust upon unwilling dissentients. The Church
was an oppressor as well as a worldling. Only individuals stood out
from the mass as true pastors and true saints.

Karl Marx regarded the organised Churches as enemies to social revolution. In Imperial Russia the state of the Orthodox Church confirmed, for the revolutionary parties, the inferences which Marx had drawn. Not only this or that Church, but religion in general, assumed the aspect of a defender of oppression: and philosophical theories which might appear to justify the intellectual demand for a transcendental cause became outworks of the hostile citadel, to be conquered and demolished. That is why, when the Social Democratic Party at the Communist school at Capri was toying with Mach and Avenarius, and the "god-building" which seemed to be the inevitable accompaniment of their philosophy, Lenin intervened with his insistence upon materialism.

His book on Empirio-criticism was no mere essay in philosophy. It was a battering-ram to level fortifications behind which he saw the oppressor sheltering; and it is as an instrument for the destruction of ideas hostile to the Revolution that anti-religious propaganda and anti-idealist philosophical teaching have been employed by the Communist Party.

Dialectical materialism, which repudiates idealism but retains the dynamic principle, must displace religion. Without the materialism on the one hand, and the dialectic on the other, we fall, according to the Communist outlook, into fatal error.

The teaching of the Godless is no mere negative. There is an actual substitute for religion, though it does not receive the name of religion and, if religion is necessarily the recognition of the transcendent, is not religion at all. One integral faith can only be driven out by another. Mere scepticism, mere negatives, cannot serve as battering-rams. In the heresies to be avoided, on either side of the truth, we are conscious of an atmosphere like that of the early Councils of the Church whose decisions took shape in the Creeds. Idealism means reaction: mechanism, without the dialectic, means fatalism and inertia.

The representatives of the Orthodox renaissance, among whom Nicolas Berdyaev and Sergius Bulgakov are the most remarkable, are well aware of the causes of Communist hostility to religion, and conscious of the lines along which a concordat might be won. Bulgakov accepts the division between Church and State, assures us that Orthodoxy is not the guardian of capitalism, and protests only against the Russian Communism of to-day, as denying the freedom of personality. In a very different sphere of life and thought from that occupied by the labours of Berdyaev and Bulgakov, there are some priests who are cultivating Communist favour by colouring church doors and crosses red, and by emphasising the proletarian origin of Jesus the carpenter, of Paul the tent-maker and of Simon Peter the fisherman.

When Nazi Germany made the attack in June, 1941, the acting Patriarch of the Orthodox Church blessed the Russian cause, and it is probable that Orthodox priests and Orthodox believers are as patriotic as the rest of the population.

National Churches in the non-Great-Russian nationalities were encouraged by the Soviet Government. In the Ukraine there arose a Pan-Ukrainian Orthodoxy which gave an outlet to nationalist as well as religious aspirations, and is described as being directed at first as much against Moscow as against Roman Catholic Poland. The new Church here was declared to rest upon the principles of congregationalism (sobornost) and of the will of the Ukrainian people, and a lively description is given by N. Brianchaninov, a historian of the Orthodox Church, of the consecration of a Metropolitan of Kiev and his bishops by the laity, no bishop being available for the purpose. All the people present in the Cathedral of St. Sophia "laid their hands upon one another's shoulders: those who were in the front row laid their hands upon the shoulders of the priests"; and the priests laid their hands upon the Metropolitan. A further process of consecration was carried out by the elective Rada (the Ukrainian equivalent of Soviet). Thus the ancient principle of congregationalism (which remembered that the Holy Ghost at Pentecost descended upon all the people and not merely on the Apostles) was here carried to the point of conveying the Apostolical Succession to the Episcopate by the hands of the laity.

The Russian Dissenters (Raskolnik) had enjoyed the reputation of the most sober, honest, and steady element in the Great Russian people. Their ideal was an autonomous Church managed by the faithful, and the election of the clergy. The Union of the Godless has no information regarding them: but we catch glimpses of them among the prisoners whom the Yugoslav Socialist, Ciliga, met in his wanderings from jail to jail. One of them was a member of one of the Biblical Sects, or possibly an Old Believer, who described to Ciliga a mutual aid association which his people had set up to cover the urban population outside of the factories and the trade unions. Ciliga says that these communities live a sort of innocent underground existence and, when possible, elect as their heads persons who stand high in the Soviet administration. This sidelight is valuable because it shows that religion has gone under the surface. M. Ciliga—I give his statement for what it may be worth—says that the Church has succeeded in modernising itself, and is one of the most powerful and secret forces in

Russia. This is almost certainly an exaggeration, except as regards the dissenting sects: which are, I suspect, still an underground influence of importance.

*   *   *

Islam, like Eastern Orthodox Christianity, is a social or collectivist religion, in which truth is conceived as residing in the congregation; and 'ijma'a, the consensus of the faithful, takes a place similar to that of sobornost in Orthodoxy. The concordant decisions of the general assemblies are regarded, at least by the Sunnis, that is to say, by the bulk of the Mahommedans outside of Persia, as equal in authority with the Koran: though interpretation has in practice become ossified. There are some 18 million Mahommedans in the U.S.S.R., in very different stages of development, religious, social, and economic. Except among the Kirgiz, whose Mahommedanism is superficial, religion is intimately intertwined with social custom and the way of living, and it would be difficult to separate religious from social and customary life. Arabic, as the language of the Koran, occupies a position similar to that of Latin in the Roman Catholic Church, and Hebrew among the Jews. There is a chief ecclesiastical directorate of the Muslim Faith in the U.S.S.R. having its headquarters at Ufa, whose pronouncements are in some degree recognised as binding upon the faithful.

The Tsars maintained the local theocratic rulers in Central Asia, and the Mahommedan Courts, civil laws and customs, but refused recognition to local languages. The principles of the Soviet Government are to encourage the local languages, in which Arabic is, of course, not included; to instal native administration when the personnel becomes available; to exercise control through the Communist Party; and to attack native customs inimical to the approved social policy, which includes the emancipation of women. This attack upon native custom, together with the nationalisation of land, affecting the livelihood of the ministers of religion and the religious law, brings the Soviet Government into collision with Mahommedan sentiment. Armed risings in Central Asia have been frequent, and the so-called brigandage of the Basmachi, who are Mahommedan irreconcilables, has been an almost chronic phenomenon. The murder of women who have made themselves prominent in the movement of emancipation is not infrequent.

The Mahommedan social and economic system in Central Asia was more firmly rooted than the corresponding system in Christian Russia. The landlords were smaller men, who lived on the land and maintained a closer touch with their tenants and farm-hands. The tenants, with their share in the crop, and the farm-hands, paid in kind, were interested in the system. There was a free-masonry between all these and the representatives of Koranic learning, and religion was inseparably a part of social life. On rumour of active nationalisation, all combined to drive flocks and herds to safety, and the nomad part of the population was virtually secure against effective interference. Only on the irrigated lands, where cotton and rice grew, was the rural population intimately accessible to the demands of alien authority. In the towns the Bolsheviks seem to have recognised the limits set by popular feeling to communist principle: for the bazaars are active, with little or no pretence of the public control of trade, and Asiatic merchants freely infringe the State's monopoly of import and export.

However, the jurisdiction of the Cadi in the towns has been ousted by salaried judges sitting alongside non-professional assessors. The veil and the bride-price are discouraged, but exist. It is likely that the mullahs continue to some extent to enjoy the proceeds of endowment lands, after the latter have been nominally merged in collective farms or in the more individualistic partnerships which are common in Kazakstan. Only a very active and ubiquitous administration could change these things or prevent the teaching of the Koran in the yard outside the mosque. It is reported that in Adjaristan, the portion of Georgia which adjoins the Black Sea at Batum, the mullahs deliberately fixed the hours of their Koran schools so as to clash with those of the Government schools: and made it necessary to instal religious sections in the curriculum of the latter, in which the mullahs were invited to give religious instruction. The Bolsheviks have retained some of the native Russian faculty for concession when resistance becomes unwise.

On the Volga, in Azarbaijan, and in the Crimea, Mahommedan custom had struck less tenacious roots or had already lost strength. In the Crimea the veil has disappeared, and the girls are attending the secular schools and joining the Communist League of Youth. At Bakshi Serai, formerly regarded as a hotbed of reaction, only three mosques remain, out of a former total of thirty-three. Azarbaijan was the first Mahommedan State to replace the Arabic alphabet with the Latin, and to adopt legislation for the emancipation of women. Owing to the oil industry, it is permeated by cosmopolitan influences. In the Tartar Republic on the Volga, now prosperous and setting an example in agriculture, little resistance to anti-religious propaganda is encountered. But, generally speaking, there is a kind of strength in mere backwardness, which has made Islam a more thorny plant to handle than Christianity has thus far shown itself to be. To a large extent the old social and religious leaders continue in control, under new titles, and occasionally we catch glimpses of them behaving very much in the old way.

In 1926 the Soviet Government so far recognised the religious authority of the Mahommedan ecclesiastical centre at Ufa as to allow it to send a delegation to Mecca, for the general Islamic Conference convened by Ibn Sa'ud to make proposals for the future administration of the Holy Places and for the conduct of the annual Pilgrimage, a matter of extraordinary interest to the whole Mahommedan world. Its attitude at the time contributed to the reinforcement of the position of the Sa'ud. It was the first Government to recognise the title of King of the Hejaz assumed by him, and the first to raise its Consular representative to the rank of Minister.

✳　　✳　　✳

There is no objection of principle to the election of a head to an autonomous Church. In 1933, with the acquiescence of the Soviet Government, a body of some eighty ecclesiastics and laymen, some of whom had returned from abroad for the purpose, elected a new Katholikos and a Holy Synod for the Gregorian Church of Armenia, at the ancient ecclesiastical centre of that country.

It is to be noted that the laws regarding religion are not federal laws, but republican laws. In the R.S.F.S.R.—that is to say, in by far the greater part of the Union, including some Mahommedan areas, such as Bashkiria, Crimea and the Tartar republic—the legal status of religion is laid down in the Law of 1929, and is now as follows. Registered congregations of adult citizens may use the churches and the articles required at their religious services—which include stores of candles, wine, oil, coal and money necessary for the religious ceremonies—and may make collections and receive voluntary donations, but only from registered members, and only for purposes connected with the maintenance of their Church, property and service. They must accept liability for maintenance and insurance and for the payment of local taxes. Local taxes are leviable on the Churches, but not federal or republic taxes. They cannot make compulsory levies, establish central funds, or own property. All central funds and property that existed before have been confiscated. In the second place, they must not propagate religious doctrine outside the limits of the registered congregation, and their priests must limit their activity to the area of their own congregations. We shall see that this prohibition is not always observed. In the third place, the law prohibits religious instruction in any State, public or private educational institution: it provides that such instruction may only be communicated to adult citizens, and only at special courses of religious instruction given by Soviet citizens, and only by special permission obtained in each case from the authorities. This means that there can be nothing corresponding to Sunday Schools. Only in the family can the young receive religious instruction. Another provision directed against the organisation of the Churches is that communities and groups must obtain permission before holding general meetings—that is to say, presumably, of members of more than one registered congregation: and district and national conferences, if formed, are not juridical persons, and cannot own property or enter into legal agreements. The Churches are also debarred from welfare work for their congregations.

Summarised in a sentence, the position now is: freedom of conscience for the adult individual, together with the right to impart religion personally to his own offspring, but, otherwise, no pecuniary or other means of making an appeal to the public or of influencing the younger generation, and no ecclesiastical organisations, beyond the individual congregation, except for purely consultative purposes and by the sanction of the temporal authority. The organisations of the Churches have, however, not been broken up, and there have been numerous instances since the attack by Germany of the continuing activity of these organisations. The Government is unfriendly, but, if persecution means the punishment of persons on charges of believing, or of holding or attending religious services, there has been no persecution.

I have myself observed a tendency to convert the Anti-God Museum in the Cathedral of St. Isaac at Leningrad into an *anticlerical* Museum, and the Commissariat of Education has closed the anti-religious faculties at the Universities. Trotsky, writing in 1936, described the present attitude of the Soviet Government to religion as one of "ironical neutrality": and he suspected that this was a preliminary step towards making use of the Churches as a support for the existing régime.

A picture of the position of religion in Soviet Russia was given in April, 1937, by Yaroslavsky, President of the Union of the Godless. He estimated that a third of the adult population in the towns and two-thirds in the villages were still believers. It was untrue that there were no believers except among the old. Among believers there were many persons loyal to the Soviet Government. But many decline to work on Sundays and on Holy Days, and many workers and collective farmers served as members of the Church Soviets. In 1897 there were 295,000 persons employed in the offices of religion, of whom 7,638 were priests. In 1936 only 79,000 were employed in the offices of religion, of whom only 948 were priests. According to the latest figures there were 30,000 registered religious congregations, with 8,338 churches, synagogues and mosques. The buildings were said to have considerable incomes and good choirs, and to be not badly decorated. But the newly created industrial towns, such as Magnitogorsk, Karaganda, and Stalinsk, had no places of worship. There were thirty-seven surviving monasteries.

The teaching of atheism in the schools remains universal: and believers continue to be debarred from membership of the Party. But the dismissal of school teachers and of other functionaries for the exercise of religion is prohibited by law, and the constitution of 1936 has abolished the disfranchisement of the priest and of other office-holders of religion. Church Soviets, for the management of Church affairs, are general in rural areas.

I have myself attended religious services including a baptism by immersion. It is untrue that they are restricted in any way.

There is a word to be added here regarding the Jews. Freed by the revolution from all their civil disabilities, they have fallen into a new religious disability, along with the followers of the other cults. Hebrew, which is to them what Arabic is to the Mahommedans, because it is the language of the Bible and the Talmud, but not the vernacular in use in their homes, was discouraged as being a vehicle for the teaching of religion. But the appearance of a secular literature in Hebrew has destroyed the basis of this unfavourable discrimination, and the works of Mayakovsky and of Pushkin have been translated into it. Zionism is frowned upon for political reasons. There is a particularly prosperous Synagogue at Moscow, with paid seats and an income of eight hundred thousand roubles. There is no anti-Semitism in the Soviet Government, but it occasionally shows itself in the people.

Regarding Buddhism, or that mixture of Buddhism and Shamanism and Animism which is to be found among Mongolian citizens of the U.S.S.R., the policy is the same, but enforcement presents difficulties even greater than in the case of Islam. We see the Kem or Medicine-man, of the Oirat country, in trouble with the Soviet authorities, partly because he is a Kem and partly because he is a kulak: and we see vigorous and effective efforts being made, through the Institute of the Northern Peoples at Leningrad, to equip the most promising members of the nomad tribes with the literacy, the Communism, and the irreligion, which are the Bolshevik equivalents of missionary training. A strong resemblance between the officer corps of the Salvation Army and the instructors at institutions of this type is the most vivid impression left upon my mind; so that I ask myself, when departing from them, what is the effective difference between atheism and theism; and do the gods of one revelation become the devils of the next, as they seem to have done in the passage of the Aryan invaders out of Persia into India; or is the essential feature of all Religion this, that it turns the eyes of man to something greater than his individual self?

I approach with diffidence the question—which naturally presents itself in different aspects to those who do and those who do not believe—whether a revival of religion in the U.S.S.R. is to be anticipated. Actual persecution would revive it, but persecution is not the Bolshevik method. The movement represented by Berdyaev and Bulgakov is a powerful bid for such recovery. But the possibilities are wider than this. What do we mean by religion? It has taken a thousand forms. The essential feature seems to be an ideal, expressed in myth or ritual or prayer or mystical communion or ascetic exercise, of an entity or an aim *above and beyond visible humanity, but accessible to it.*

Every religion leaves the ground of ascertained knowledge to imagine this ideal. The Communist holds that there is no knowledge except that which is verifiable by experiment or by experience: but he, too, leaves the ground of ascertained knowledge, when he makes his flight to the hypotheses of the classless society and the redeeming mission of the socialist fatherland. "The Thing came first, and the Thought came after," and yet there was an ideal burning in the hearts of those first revolutionaries, and, paradoxically, the Thought did come first, however passionately they might repudiate the sequence. The early Christians, observes Julius Hecker—but we are not sure that he himself satisfies the canons of the stricter dialectical materialism—were driven by an inner urge which they called God within us, or the witness of the Holy Spirit: and something of the same order is to be observed in the Bolsheviks. He might have added that Orthodoxy, perhaps in consequence of the influence of the Platonic Idea upon the Eastern Fathers, sees in the visible world a reflection or a symbol of a spiritual entity elsewhere, a spiritual entity which it is the task of the Church to reflect with an ever closer approach to perfection: and that the search for a meaning in history, a straining for a vision of the picture to be realised, which is a noticeable characteristic of Russian thought, has its origin here. The pre-existent idea, to which the reality must be brought to conform, is present to the Bolsheviks in their conception of a classless society, and of the oecumenical mission of Russia.

Berdyaev, in *The Russian Revolution*, analyses the psychological tendencies in Russian Communism, and traces some of them to Christian Orthodoxy. He does more than this, as everyone must do who would draw the picture faithfully. He goes back to the origins: to the conception of a Messianic mission for Orthodox Russia, growing up perhaps in the struggle of Christian against Mongol, and taking shape in the fifteenth-century notion of Moscow as the Third Rome, destined to give to the world what the first and second Rome and Byzantium had failed to give. The Schism, the *Raskol*, of the seventeenth century was the protest against a betrayal of this Messianic idea, when the Church surrendered to the Greeks over the question of ritual; to the Greeks who were envisaged as having themselves betrayed the Church, when they yielded to Western error to buy succour for Byzantium against the Turk. There was a second betrayal when the Orthodox State, along with the Church which had become its servant, failed either to advance alongside of the West or to fulfil the Slavophil ideal. Then came the *second Raskol*, the nineteenth-century Schism of the intellectuals who found themselves as much divorced from contemporary life, as conscious of a gulf between themselves and both rulers and people, as had been the dissenters of the seventeenth century. The intelligentsia, whether Westernisers or Slavophils, whether revolutionaries or no, were exiles in their own land, looking either to an ideal past or to an ideal future. The influences of both met and intertwined in the development of the Populist revolutionaries: and the sons of priestly families, with vivid memories of early religious training, played a large part in it. Berdyaev finds in them the sense of sin, the tender conscience, the profound compassion for human suffering, the passion for social justice, the capacity for self-sacrifice, the ascetic contempt of worldly goods, the religious questioning of the value and justification of culture in a world of sin and suffering, the maximalism demanding from man effort and sacrifice without compromise, and the expectation of an apocalyptic ending in revolution or a Last Judgment—which the early days spent in intimate familiarity with the teaching of Orthodox Christianity might be expected to inspire. In their irreligion—for the revolutionary intelligentsia of the nineteenth century were irreligious, though the Slavophils were champions of the Faith—he sees a mere inversion of religious motives and of religious psychology into a non-religious or anti-religious conviction: so that the spiritual energy of Religion flows into social channels. In the anarchist Michael Bakunin he sees the belief in a Russian and Slavonic mission for bringing about a cataclysm of destruction, in which the old sinful world shall perish and a new one—a kingdom of God upon earth—arise upon its ashes.

Marxism introduced certain other elements into Russian Socialism: the idea of class war and the psychology of a conquering class which had been oppressed and felt the resentment of oppression, but also the conception that man is capable of leaping out of the realm of necessity into the realm of freedom, and in this last Berdyaev finds an echo of the idea of spiritual liberty which he regards as specifically Christian. For him the anti-religious psychology of Communism is a religious psychology *turned inside out*.

The echoes of religious thought in the brain of the anti-religious Communist ring yet further, if more faintly, in that strange passion for confession and self-humiliation which the trials of the Communists fallen into disfavour have revealed to a puzzled world. At the very root of the Russian conception of religion lies the idea of a brotherhood of the faithful, in whose mutual love resides the revelation. For the Roman Catholic, nurtured in an ecclesiastical system which has borrowed the autocracy of the Roman Empire, the Holy Father is the ultimate authority, and under him the priesthood is the interpreter. For the Russian Orthodox, notwithstanding the solitary supremacy of the Emperor both in Church and State, truth was republican, and was to be sought in the communion of the Orthodox brethren—laity as well as clergy: for it was not only upon the Apostles, but upon the disciples too that the Holy Ghost descended at Pentecost. It is the doctrine of *sobornost*, congregationalism, as I venture to translate it. What excommunication is to the pious Catholic, that, to the Orthodox, is separation from the congregation of the brethren, in which truth and love alike reside. He must seek restoration by the abjuration of all errors and the confession of all sins. *Outside of the congregation he cannot be right.*

The religious conception of the presence of truth in the congregation passed to the Communists.

The revolutionaries of the nineteenth century proclaimed their deeds with pride and defiance. They were conscious that the congregation of the faithful was with them. But the majority now is on the side of the Government: and the offender, alone in an agony of isolation from the brethren, confesses all, and more than all, in the humiliation of his soul.

There are others, of course, who obstinately refuse to confess: and these are not brought to public trial, because their appearance will not make for edification. It is not every man in whose brain the old tune rings so compellingly.

※　　※　　※

If Communist psychology has in it much that is Christian and Orthodox in its origin, Orthodox Christianity, on its part, prepared the way for some of the conceptions of Communism: and nowhere more clearly than in its vision of a Kingdom of God upon earth, of a transfigured universe made perfect for the Second Coming. The period of wars and revolution which precedes it is the period of apocalyptic preparation.

The survival of religious habits in thoughts and action does not mean that the Bolsheviks are likely to become Christian: but merely shows what persistent "residues" these habits are. On the other hand, the notion that there is a pattern somewhere stored up, to which it is desirable to make the life of man conform (such, for instance as the pattern of the classless society), carries with it a conception of teleology which is, in essence, religious: and is hardly reconcilable with the materialistic doctrine that the deed comes first and the thought comes after. That the Bolsheviks have an ideal is not to be denied, and latterly they have used language which at least admits the word to their vocabulary.

Communism has been the inheritor of much. It has also added much of its own. Orthodoxy trained the heart, but not the will. The sense which Communism has brought to its adepts, that man has the power to make his own history, has steeled the will. The philosophers are able to demonstrate to us that materialism is incompatible with the free will. On this basis, the Communists should be lacking in willpower: but I cannot discover any such deficiency. On the contrary, an immensely optimistic energy is characteristic of them. They themselves would probably tell us that it is the dialectical element in their materialism which makes the difference, and that the philosophers are thinking of a mechanistic materialism.

It is vain to discuss whether Communism is itself a religion. What is more important is to notice that Communism possesses certain of the qualities which have caused religions to spread. Chief among these is an aim (which in the case of Communism is the service of Man) inspiring devotion and creating unity, and linking together the generations in a communion—we must not say of Saints.

Finally, to descend to a different plane of thought, there are the possibilities of ecclesiastical politics, from which the solid benefits of toleration may be extracted. The concession to the Polish Army in the U.S.S.R., of its own Roman Catholic chaplains, and the placing of the French Catholic Church at Moscow at the disposal of the Roman Catholic community there, are happy omens. The clergy ceased, under the Constitution of 1936, to be disfranchised. Victory over Germany, achieved by the help of the Western Powers, will give to the U.S.S.R. a new sense of security, which will make precautions against internal opposition less urgent, and diminish anti-clerical feeling. In the meanwhile, it appears that new sects of an evangelical type have emerged during the last decade in Central Russia. Religion—the passionate yearning of Man for something greater than his present solitary self—will yet find many and various expressions; not all of them other-worldly.

Chapter XXIII

THE BACKGROUND OF THE NATIONALITIES:
UNITY AND DISUNITY

It may be that the Russian peasants could have built a State, as the Old Believers built an organised though necessarily limited community. But in fact, as history presents itself to us, they stopped in the initial stages of organisation, and the upper storeys of the social edifice were added not by their hands but by others, out of materials strange to them: and the two parts of the work never formed a united whole. Different peoples have actually exhibited widely different aptitudes for the development of social and political institutions. Some stop for tens of centuries at the family, and some pass on to the clan or the caste, and find their limit for long periods at that stage, though military empires may bring them artificially together in much larger groups. Some have built the city-state, and some only the village community. We are familiar to-day with a number which have, ostensibly at all events, grown into nation-states. But this stage of growth is sometimes apparent only, and the organic unity which the nation-state should have attained is, in varying degrees, incomplete.

The Great-Russian people found no difficulty in the formation of certain primitive aggregations: the patriarchal family, and communes of villages and even of larger units. Beyond these there was never an organic unity. In spite of a unity of language which varies very little over hundreds of leagues, it remained in essence a confederation of village communities governed by a common head, by means of an administrative system imposed from above. There are, in fact, two conflicting streams of tendency active at different levels. One, which may be loosely described as associational, brings the Russian people together to work out a common economic and social life, in the family, the Mir and the partnership of cultivators or artisans. The other— it might reasonably be called anarchical, in so far as it is inimical to the consolidation of the State—forces the primary units away from further organic union. It is no accident that the most widely famous of Russian writers repudiates the State. He is giving literary expression to the subconscious conviction of the mass of his fellow countrymen.

Perhaps all humanity is, socially speaking, both centripetal and centrifugal. It needs its loves, and it needs its hates, or at all events cherishes both, and each seems necessary to the other. The difference, at different epochs, and among peoples with different histories, lies in the point at which attraction is replaced by repulsion: the limit of social aggregation at which it ceases to seem virtuous to give mutual aid and begins to seem virtuous to make mutual war. The British people—subject to certain incipient achievements of a higher order, such as the tenuous bond which unites the Empire, the attraction of the French Canadians and the Dutch Boers, and the inchoate, much more doubtful, attachment of the Indian peoples—reaches its associational limit at the nation-state. But we do not forget the past existence of a narrower bond of attraction in the Heptarchy of Anglo-Saxon England and in the separate kingdoms of England and Scotland; and we still see international anarchy, only slightly modified by a precarious agreement of peace and co-operation between nations. The Russian people ceased to be associational, and began to be anarchical, before it had completely reached the stage of the nation-state. Whether a difficulty in becoming a nation may make it easier to take the further step of forming an association which crosses national lines, we can only speculate. But the claim has been made, and before the Revolutionaries of November set for themselves the definite ideal of a World-State.

The two agents which supplemented, or replaced, the organic growth of the Russian people towards nationhood were the Orthodox Church, in first place, and the Autocracy as its defender and guardian. When the Church was divided by the Schism in the seventeenth century, unifying influences were gravely weakened. The Tsar was the Orthodox Tsar, the people were, par excellence, Orthodox, and the fact that their religion seemed to consist only in the due performance of prescribed rites did not impair its character as the bond of nationhood. The identity of the religious with the national bond explains the efforts made to bring all within the religious fold. Dissenters were regarded as Orthodox who declined to perform their religious duties, and subjected to compulsion as such. Jews became Russians, immune from all disabilities, as soon as they became Orthodox. Uniats, who accepted Papal Supremacy while observing the Orthodox rite, were, from the State's point of view, as serious a stone of offence as the Roman Catholics, until they became Orthodox. Roman Catholics were the worst treated of all the unorthodox confessions, because they owned the supremacy of a foreign spiritual head, and therefore lacked the essential bond of Russian nationhood. All along the doubtful and shifting frontier between the Russian and Polish races, it was Orthodoxy or Roman Catholicism which in practice determined the question of race.

One of the consequences of the position, as I have described it, is that the Revolution, which made an end of the State Church as well as of the Tsar, left the new rulers with the task of creating a new bond of association. They found it first in class, and hoped to have made it international. The frustration of this expectation has now taken them back to the task of building a new nation. I shall here sketch very briefly the background of the chief nationalities other than the Great-Russian. The Great-Russian kernel of the State constituted less than half of the population under the Tsar. The non-Great-Russian peoples were numerically the more important, and they supplied forty-five per cent of the armies which fought for Russia during the First World War. They differed widely in history and conditions both from Great-Russia, and one from another: and a picture which excluded them from view would give the impression of a closer approach to unity and less marked class divisions than actually existed in the Russian Empire.

To some extent, and generally in the west, the non-Great-Russian peoples were the inheritors of cultures superior to that of the Great-Russians, and were materially richer. This was very marked with the Finns, Germans, Poles, Armenians, and Georgians. The Ukrainian method of living was better than that of the Great-Russians, and the long association with Polish influences had introduced touches of western civilisation. The Mahommedan Khanates of Central Asia had an older culture, and a more advanced agriculture, with an immemorial system of irrigation. Except for the Caucasian mountaineers, the Mongolians, and the nomad tribes of the north, the Great-Russians were not governing their admitted inferiors: and there was little about Great-Russian culture of that attractiveness which sometimes explains an unexpected tolerance of unfamiliar influences.

The policy of the nineteenth century Tsars towards the nationalities had certain general characteristics. It disfavoured the non-orthodox confessions, particularly Roman Catholicism. It discouraged the use of the local languages for official business, the press, and education. It tended to exclude the non-Great-Russian areas from the operation of certain beneficial legislation: for instance, of that which established Rural Councils. But the policy of Russification, which meant, in general, Russia for the Great-Russians and for those willing to be assimilated to them by the adoption of the Orthodox Confession, began with Alexander III. Up to that time the policy of the Tsars is not to be regarded as always and everywhere unfavourable to the nationalities. On the contrary, the position of Poland under Alexander I, with her constitution and national army, was a reasonable ground of jealousy to Russia herself. Finland retained her "Constitutions," her Diet, language, and army, till the reign of Nicolas II.

In the Baltic provinces there were internal contradictions, which put part of the population on the side of the Tsar, and the Russian Government had improved, or attempted to improve, by its policy the advantage which these contradictions gave. Broadly speaking the western appendages of Imperial Russia contained both a dominant and a plebeian nationality, and the Imperial policy was to support the plebeian against the dominant. The upper class was German or Polish: the lower, Esthonian, Lettish, White-Russian, Ukrainian; the upper, Lutheran or Catholic: the lower, Uniat (that is to say worshipping according to the Orthodox rite but accepting the supremacy of the Pope) or Orthodox. In Esthonia, Livonia and Latvia the German descendants of the Knights of the Sword had been installed since the thirteenth century as conquerors and landlords among a subject population. The German barons were faithful supporters of the Tsarist administration, and their estates were like agricultural factories. Alexander I emancipated the serfs without giving them land, and the villages, like the towns, were largely populated by wage-earning labourers; were in fact, in the language of the Marxists, already proletarian. The clergy, first Catholic, then Lutheran, afterwards in part Orthodox, were on the side of the masters.

The part played in Tsarist Russia by the Germans, and in particular by the Balts of the maritime provinces, is a historical factor of immense importance. Though little more than one per cent of the total population, they occupied, towards the close of the nineteenth century, a very high proportion of the places in the upper ranks of the civil and military administration. Figures cited by Hans von Eckardt show that they held a third or more than a third of the administrative offices in the Imperial Council, the Senate, the Ministry of Foreign Affairs, the Ministries of Domains, Communications, Marine and War, and in the Posts and Telegraphs. Germans were also very prominent in business and in estate management. The spirit of the Russian bureaucracy was more German than Russian, in a meticulous insistence upon detail, and in an inelastic conscientiousness, both of which appear foreign to the Russian nature. Some of the differences between St. Petersburg and Moscow, which attract frequent notice, are attributable to the large German element in the former.

The dynasty itself was German, and the Empresses and Grand Duchesses traced their origin in many cases to the petty courts of Germany. German policy thwarted Slavophil hopes at the Berlin Congress of 1878, after the Russian armies had arrived almost within sight of Constantinople. The history of Wilhelm II's relations with Nicolas II contains more than one example of the former's exploitation of the latter, including the extortionate commercial treaty of 1904. By 1914 the stage was evidently set for an outburst of anger against Germans within and without the Russian Empire.

❋   ❋   ❋

Russia has no physical boundaries in the west unless the Pripet marshes can be so regarded, and no clearly ascertainable racial limits in that direction. Between the Vistula and the Dnieper, and even further east than the Dnieper, the ebb and flow of Polish-Lithuanian and Roman Catholic influences have confused history and complicated political and social conditions. In the Ukraine the nobility and upper clergy became Roman Catholic, while the population was Orthodox. In White-Russia the upper stratum was Polonised, and the Russian serf stratum either became Roman Catholic, or accepted spiritual subordination to the Papacy while retaining the orthodox rite, that is to say, became Uniat. When the kingdom of Poland was disrupted, the Poles retained a historical claim to provinces in which the facts of race, religion and language pointed, doubtfully but predominantly, to a Russian affiliation. During Poland's struggle for the restoration of national existence, this doubtful claim has been the determining factor. Great-Russian sentiment was outraged by what seemed an unjustified attempt to dominate Russian lands, and gave vigorous support to the Tsarist policy of Russifying Poland herself.

In the meanwhile, industrialisation in Russian Poland proceeded far more rapidly than in Russia. Wealth increased and factory labour became organised. A new middle-class party combined anti-socialism and anti-semitism with Polish nationalism. At the beginning of the twentieth century Russian Poland was far richer and further advanced than the dominant neighbour, with a much larger proportion of urban centres and of railway communications, and a more menacing clash between capital and labour. Resistance in Poland to mobilisation for the Japanese war was the beginning of the revolutionary movement in Russia. The Polish workers struck unanimously when the news arrived of Bloody Sunday in St. Petersburg: and martial law in Warsaw called forth the second general strike in Russia in November 1905. In terroristic outrage on the one hand, and in the activity of police repression on the other, Poland surpassed Russia. In the counter-revolution Poland was almost continually under martial law. But by far the most powerful element of discontent was nationalist, not socialist.

In the second Imperial Duma the nationalist middle-class party of Poland supplied a particularly able group of members, headed by Roman Dmowski. Its nationalism did not extend to a demand for separation: and the later history suggests that the Tsarist Government would have been well advised if it had made this party one of its points of support. But nationalism, in any form, neutralised, from the point of view of that Government, the merits of a conservative attachment to property: and Stolypin's revised electoral law cut down the number of Polish representatives in the Third Duma by more than half.

Whatever causes of complaint the Poles might have against Tsarist Russia, they were, as nationalists, far more afraid of German efficiency than of Russian unwillingness to make concessions. When, at the beginning of the First World War an undefined self-government was promised to Poland by the Grand Duke Nicolas, the Poles of Russian Poland ranked themselves definitely on the Russian side of the quarrel.

White-Russia, with a population of some seven million White-Russians, Great-Russians, Poles, Jews and Lithuanians, is a land of much bog and swamp, with a generally poor soil. It has a language of its own, resembling Ukrainian, but affected by Polish contacts. The separation between the three Russian nations, Great-Russian, White-Russian, and Ukrainian, appears to date from the time when Kiev lost the control of the Dnieper to advancing barbarians, and the Great-Russians retired into the forests to mingle with the indigenous Finns. The marshes of the Pripet, as effective a separator of peoples as seas or high mountains, divide the White-Russians from the Ukrainians to the south of them.

White-Russia has been unfortunate in her history as well as in her soil. The brutalities of serfdom were aggravated by the alien faith and spirit of proprietors who were either Poles or Polonised Russians and Lithuanians; and all non-agricultural pursuits were monopolised by Poles and Jews. Under Tsarist rule, poverty and ignorance prevailed. Outside of the capital, Minsk, there was not a single hospital. The people were so crushed that they never expressed national aspirations and when, at the Revolution, federal autonomy came, with the right of using the national language, it came almost as an unasked gift.

If Poland lost something of its unity of sentiment by the partitions of the eighteenth century, the Ukraine, "the frontier," has never been suffered to form a political unit. It has not even any linguistic or racial name of its own, but its language is sufficiently separate to be mostly unintelligible to the mere student of Russian. If the linguistic test be applied, it stretches from the neighbourhood of Lvov, in present-day Poland, to Krasnodar, in the North Caucasus province of the U.S.S.R., and includes the present Carpatho-Ukraine and a former portion of the Roumanian kingdom, as well as the Polish and Russian Ukraine. There is a recognisable common culture, much subdued and impoverished in Carpatho-Ukraine (formerly known as Ruthenia). Both in Poland and Russia the villages of the Ukraine have a similar appearance, a brighter, more cheerful look, with white-washed adobe huts, trees and gardens, than those of the Great-Russians. The people seem happier. The women exchange chaff with the passing traveller. There is more of song and play and dance. Trifles, such as the existence of finger-posts on the roads, point to a greater interest in life, and more time and means to attend to it. On the other hand, the country slides easily into brigandage and anarchy. The raids of the Krim Tartars, and the life of the island stronghold of the Zaporozhian Cossacks, a centre of savage and war-like freedom which held its own for generations against Pole and Turk, have left their mark. For centuries the "frontier" was the theatre of raid and counter-raid, and the alternate prey of different neighbours.

A counter-reformation at the end of the sixteenth century made the nobility and upper clergy Catholic, while the people remained Ortho-dox. A treaty of 1667 gave Kiev and all of Ukraine east of the Dnieper to Russia, while the rest, with all of White-Russia, went to Poland. Before that date, Poland held the territory on both sides of the Dnieper, and her influence, and that of the Roman Catholic religion which she professed, have brought a western infiltration. The Ukrain-ian outlook is to Galicia and the west. It was a Ukrainian Bishop who assisted Peter the Great with his reforms, when his own ecclesiastics looked glumly upon them. The Ukrainian National Church was more popular and less authoritative than the Orthodox Church of Russia. There was more individualism than in Great-Russia, and the village Communes at an early date lost the right to redistribute the land, which thus became heritable household property. But the Ukrainians are a rural people, and the towns are almost monopolised by non-Ukrainians: Great-Russians, Jews and Poles.

The Tsar made war upon the language and treated Ukrainian pub-lications with great severity. As a result the Ukrainian movement took extreme revolutionary forms. The first Congress of the Social Democratic party of Russia took place at the instance of the Kiev Fighting-Union for the Liberation of the Working Class. The first serious disturbance among the peasants took place in the area of small holdings and congestion in the north-eastern Ukraine. The first general strike, that of 1903, was in Southern Russia, including the Ukraine. In short, the Ukraine was prominent in revolutionary enterprise, very largely because nationalist-Ukraine feeling was outraged by Tsarist policy. The Russifiers could not leave their passion for religious unification behind them, and when the Russian armies—coming as deliverers—occupied Galicia in 1915, the Grand Duke Nicolas, who was commander-in-chief, was disgusted by the arrival of a trainload of Orthodox clergy to convert the Uniats, when he had hoped for munitions. But it does not appear that, except in very limited circles, there was any desire in Russian Ukraine for political separation, or any demand that local autonomy and freedom of language would not have satisfied.

The line of demarcation between Great-Russia and Ukraine is difficult to draw. The Donets basin is filled with workers from outside, many of them Asiatic in origin; Kharkov is alien in spirit to the Ukraine, and it has been estimated that not more than half of those shown in the statistics to be Ukrainians have any stable or convinced sense of nationality. Of the surplus-producing agricultural regions of Russia, the Ukraine makes up a third, and the anthracite, iron, and manganese of the Donets basin constitute a large fraction of the mineral supply of Russia. When the irritation of interference is not a grievance, Russian literature and the civilisation of the cities exercises an attraction. It was a Ukrainian, Gogol, who penned the famous patriotic description of Russia as a swift troika rushing ever onward. The Germans were so sure of Ukrainian separatist sentiment that they tried to organise Ukrainian legions; but they were disappointed in the results.

❀ ❀ ❀

The Jews of Russia are mainly residents of the south-west and west, for a historical reason. The Kings of Poland and the Dukes of Lithuania, who between them commanded, at one time and another, all of White-Russia and most of Ukraine, made it their policy to encourage the Jews. At the partition of Poland, these invaluable builders of commerce and the arts were allowed to remain in their old homes and in the Black Sea provinces conquered by Catherine the Great, but not to settle in the rest of Russian territory. This is the origin of the Jewish Pale. Their treatment by the Tsars varied, but it must be understood that it was the religion, and not the race, which was placed under dis-

ability, and that the Jew who became Orthodox was at once assimilated to the orthodox population. When the disabilities were in force,
the pressure to accept conversion was strong. We hear of all Jews in
receipt of Government bursaries being registered as Orthodox, and
of converts obtaining free divorce from their Jewish wives. Alexander
II gave them access to schools and professions and allowed them to
settle outside the Pale, but they remained ineligible for public service.
Alexander III, in accordance with his general policy of Russification,
limited them to towns within the Pale, excluded them from the Bar
and from technical schools, and restricted them to a maximum percentage in the Universities and Secondary Schools. They were not
allowed to own land. The residential restriction did not apply to Jews
with University degrees, to merchants paying a certain minimum tax,
nor to craftsmen inscribed in a workers' fellowship. Readers of Trotsky's autobiography will recall that rich Jews like his father—a prosperous wheat rancher—did well enough. Those who administered the
law made exceptions for those who could pay, and the severities re-
coiled upon the Government by making its officials corrupt, as well
as by driving the Jews wholesale into the ranks of the revolutionaries.
They were the first to form a Social Democratic organisation of their
own, and they provided many leaders to the Bolsheviks: though the
notion that the Bolsheviks are Jews is a myth.

There is a special irony in the persistence of anti-semitism in Russia,
because of the enormous influence which Judaism has had upon
popular habits of thought. Possibly in consequence of the presence of
the civilised tribe of the Khazars, who were Jewish converts, in southern Russia, Judaism greatly affected the Russian masses in the eleventh
and twelfth centuries, and the Church was obliged to combat it, as it
combated Catholicism in the thirteenth century. In later times we
find the doctrines of Count Leo Tolstoi far closer to Judaism than to
Christianity: and Rozanov was powerfully influenced by the Old Testament outlook upon life.

※   ※   ※

The Cossacks were men of many races, having an origin, as communities, similar to the legendary origin of Rome. They were runaway
slaves, runaway serfs, broken men and outlaws of every sort, who gathered together in asylums of which the Zaporozhian fastness on the
Dnieper was the most famous. For long they were embodiments of
anarchy, for ever seeking the weakest and least troublesome masters, if
it was necessary to have a master at all. The modern groups are those

of the Don, the Ural, the Kuban and the Terek. Time and the policy
of the Tsars have reversed their old function. From being frequent
rebels they became the instruments of the autocracy. They were organised in military colonies, holding their lands by a military tenure,
and paying no taxes. As a whole their lands were much in excess of
those of the peasants. They were privileged persons and looked with
contempt upon the peasants, workers, and students, to whom they
were called upon from time to time to apply their whips.

✵   ✵   ✵

The Caucasus, and the country south of it, was and is a macédoine,
out-balkanising the Balkans by its variety of faiths, languages, and
races. In the post-revolutionary distribution of territories, which aimed
at the encouragement of local language and racial sentiment, the country north of the great range of mountains contained one autonomous
republic, Daghestan, six autonomous regions, and one autonomous
district (Circassian). In the mountains, and to the south of them,
are three main republics, which, by the constitution of 1936, were elevated to the constituent status. These are Christian Georgia, Christian
Armenia, and Mahommedan Azarbaijan. But, in Christian Georgia,
Adzharians, who speak the Georgian language, have the Turkish culture and follow the Islamic confession. Adzhar and Abkhazia are
autonomous Soviet Socialist republics included within the Georgian
constituent republic. The Nakhichevan autonomous Soviet Socialist
republic is included in the Azarbaijan constituent republic, and so is
the Nagorno-Karabakh autonomous province. Under the administration of the Tsars there was no recognition of these distinctions.

The trans-Caucasus territory is, for its size, immensely the most
valuable part of Russian territory. The principal wealth is the oil of
Baku, but other minerals, including manganese, are produced in
Georgia, and the semi-tropical productiveness of the country gives to
Russia grapes, lemons, tea, and the growths of more southern climates.
The tract is also the seat of an old civilisation and an old intellectual
life: and it contains in the great city of Baku a kaleidoscope of races
and an Americanised centre of business and proletarian life hardly
inferior to Moscow and Leningrad themselves.

Georgians have a proud and ancient history, and their nationalism
is one which merely federal liberties do not satisfy. But their country,
of very great value in itself, is also necessary to Russia as the highway
to the Baku oil, and Georgia was forced to accept Russian protection
by the menace of the Ottoman Empire.

There were two proletariats in Georgia. One of these was Oriental,

living by the carrying trade and by odd jobs: what we might call a
coolie element. The other, largely Great-Russian, the wage-earners in
industry and the railway workers, formed a sort of élite of labour, and
naturally became a stronghold of democratic sentiment. Numerous
Trade Unions were formed during the Revolution of 1905: but were
mercilessly repressed during the reaction which followed. There was
a part brigand, part Georgian-patriot, part Social-Democrat, movement, inspired by the name of Shamil, the Caucasian patriot who, in
the fifties of the nineteenth century, held the Russians at bay for
years. At the head of this was Joseph Dzhugashvili, famous by the
name of Stalin, "the man of steel." His father was a Georgian of the
trading class, his mother belonged to a small Ossetian mountain
tribe. Trained in the theological seminary of Tiflis, and expelled from
it for his interest in Marxian studies, his revolutionary activities in the
late nineties were already enterprising, and he organised the first
Caucasian workers' strike on the Tiflis tram-ways. His experience of
the Caucasian macédoine, its mountain fastnesses, its city streets, and
not least its jails, marked him out as the revolutionary expert on the
question of nationalities. He made his first Marxian study of its in-
tricacies as early as 1913, and then laid down the principles which have
survived into the present-day practice of the Soviet Government.

Before the Revolution, Tiflis was the political capital of all the
trans-Caucasus country. It was also an intellectual centre which produced many political thinkers, mostly of the Menshevik complexion.
Trotsky called Georgia "the heart of the Menshevik Gironde." The
Social-Democratic fraction of the Fourth Imperial Duma, which was
sitting at the outbreak of the Great War, chose a Georgian Menshevik,
Tchkeidze, as its leader. It voted against War Credits, and Tchkeidze
read the Zimmerwald manifesto for peace in the Duma. There was an
elevation about these Georgian Socialists which gives a favourable impression of the national character: brave to a fault, large-hearted, song-
ful, jovial; a little given to the drinking of wine.

Not only in the trans-Caucasus, but throughout the territories of the
non-Russian nationalities, the proletarian élite in the towns and on
the railways were not natives of the land. They were mainly Great-
Russians, partly Germans, Poles and Jews, forming a sort of natural
garrison for cities and communications, to which social forces gave an
anti-national and pro-Russian unity and a spirit of Great-Russian
chauvinism. In newly acquired Central Asia, the indigenous peoples
continued to live in their own cities, and the "European" element
occupied separate settlements alongside of these, as in the Canton-

ments and Civil Stations of British India: but the "European" element included more than officials, soldiers and well-to-do merchants. It is in the exportation of their wage-earning workers to dependencies and conquered territories that the Russians have followed a method different from that of Great Britain. In Siberia the townspeople and the civilised elements generally have been Great-Russian: often political exiles respected for their high-culture, and rarely having the desire for separation from Russia.

Towns exercise an immense influence upon the client countryside, and the presence of these quasi-garrisons, in key positions among the non-Great-Russian nationalities, tended to prevent the growth of effective separatist movements. A movement which is purely rural may be embarrassing, but it is not likely to be permanently disruptive while the towns hold. This factor would have exercised an even greater influence, if Great-Russian industrial jealousy, before the Revolution, had not stood in the way of the wider distribution of industries in the territories of the nationalities.

In Mahommedan Central Asia the Tsarist Government maintained the native Khans in their rule in Khiva and Bukhara, but "sat upon the head waters" of the rivers which supplied the means of agriculture and of life. As in the Caucasus and on the Volga, Russian and Mahommedan towns were and are separate. In the areas of direct Russian rule, the Cadi and the Mufti continued to dispense Koranic law. The veil and the bride-price, and Islamic custom generally, were sacred. The official staffs and the official language were Russian, and even the names of the streets were written in Russian. But, if rules were strict, practice was judiciously neglectful. Schools were supposed to be Russified, but the pupils of the Koranic school continued to drone out the sacred texts to the supervising Mullah. The official missionary of Orthodoxy made his rounds, in all the dignity of pectoral cross and vestment: but the local administrator knew the danger of him, and kept him harmless.

In 1905 an Association of all-Russian Mahommedans was joined by Crimean Tartars and by Kirgiz and Turks of Turkestan. The Young Turk revolution in the Ottoman Empire encouraged the spirit of Mahommedan nationalism, always strong in Central Asia: and it seems likely that the desire for autonomy here comes nearer to a demand for separation than in any of the other non-Russian nationalities. There is a strong cultural movement among Mahommedans generally, and the Tartars on the Volga show a cultural superiority, particularly marked in their agriculture, to their Russian neighbours.

What is it that any of us actually love when we feel the sentiment which we call patriotism? What is it with us Britons, for whom there is an ancient and very concrete unity to attach our affections? Very few of us know, still less love, classes other than our own: we are jarred and offended by trifling differences of speech and manner; often our overseas brethren are a trial to us. When we experience the feeling of love of country, do we call up before us its historic Head, the land and the features which it owes to nature and art, the white cliffs, the green meadows, the woods and the streams, the noble monuments and buildings lovely or familiar to our affections, the far-scattered sister-lands of the commonwealth: or a complex including all this and more, the history and the institutions and the glorious potentialities of betterment which they hold for the men and women who share their inheritance with us? A few, a very few of us, may have this wide vision, and these only in moments of exaltation. We must have the small change of the grand emotions, symbols to which we may attach our affection: the Union Jack, the map painted red, perhaps a calf-love for the figure of Britannia on a penny, surely loveliest of women, if anyone had time to look at her. And perhaps we must have something to hate, before we can love with single heart.

What, for the Russian, were the symbols of the grand emotion, for these are what make it possible for men in the mass to feel? The Church was difficult to visualise behind the somewhat gross figure of the parish priest: but some no doubt retained in memory the blue and gilded and star-spangled domes of some shrine, or the magic vision of Kiev seen from the eastern bank of the Dnieper. The Orthodox Tsar was the great emblem of unity, but the trust and love had somehow gone out of the picture which he presented to his people. The land meant much to poet and seer: for the mass, if she had a personality at all, it was that of a hard step-mother and task-mistress, under the long sameness of her robe of white, or the monotony of brown and grey; though veined with perennial rivers, decking herself like a bride at the sudden inspiration of spring, and wearing such glorious jewels as the city of Moscow seen from the Sparrow Hills. The rivers indeed awakened affection and had a personality of their own, Volga for all Great-Russians, Dnieper for the Ukraine, Don for the Cossacks: and Moscow was a true centre and symbol.

But patriotism, if in the making, was still incompletely made: a weaker thing than the solidarity of class which the common life of the factory had developed in the city workers. There at least was a tangible and material unity. Elsewhere, if I read the signs aright, there was hardly even a common hate.

Chapter XXIV

THE SOVIET TREATMENT OF THE NATIONALI-
TIES: UNITY AND DIVERSITY

"The hunger for knowledge displayed by the most primitive
peoples in the Union."

KURT LONDON, *The Seven Soviet Arts.*

Stalin in one of his early pamphlets on Nationality detects the essential likeness between Nationality and Religion, and asserts the natural
right of man to both. However much the idea of tolerance may have
been violated in the pressure of the daily struggle, it represents at bottom the Bolshevik attitude to both religion and nationality. Both are
substitutes for something which is regarded as better and greater. For
Religion there is to be no encouragement, but a cold toleration. For
Nationality there is to be something warmer than toleration, and, as
I shall endeavour to show, a Soviet patriotism has been brought into
vogue by the dangers of external attack, while the corporate sentiment
of the minor nationalities is nursed by appeals to sectional pride.

Religion and national sentiment sometimes meet inseparably in
the way of life of a people. In the mass of the Jews the two appear to
be identified. The case of Islam is similar, though more obviously
modified by the existence of underlying national distinctions anterior
to conversion. In Eastern Europe the identity extends beyond these
two examples. On the doubtful racial borderland between Poland and
Russia, a Pole is a Pole because he is Catholic, a Russian is Russian
because he is Orthodox. Among the Balkan peoples it was the national
Church that kept the nationality alive. The spirit of nationality is in
essence the love of a greater self. But there are other and rival devo-
tions, and other and rival greater selves, contending with the national
devotion and the national self. Setting on one side for the moment the
religious devotion and the religious self, we find, in a very cursory examination of recent European and American history, that Socialism
has created a loyalty which crosses the boundaries between nations,
and sometimes comes into conflict with the spirit of nationality. I
need not dwell upon this new rivalry. It is embodied in the successive
Internationals, illustrated in the fraternal relations between Interna-

tional Labour, and recorded in much revolutionary history. I lay stress upon it here because the conflict between the devotion to class and the devotion to nationality explains much that is otherwise unintelligible in the course of Russian events. It takes two forms, and appears equally under the aspects of opposition between the national and the international, and of opposition between the minor nationality or minority and the federal state.

The general Marxian view which passed on to Russian Socialists was the internationalist standpoint, which regards national self-determination with suspicion. The reason why we hear so much in Russian controversies of "*bourgeois* nationalism," as a mark of the counter-revolutionary, is that there is a conviction that not the workers, but the middle class, aspire to national self-determination, in the sense of political separation. Cultural autonomy, on the other hand, which means the use of one's own language in schools and courts and public affairs, along with the encouragement of national literature, drama and art, is the legitimate ambition, and harmonises completely with the international ideal.

The Russian Empire grew outward from a Great-Russian nucleus till more than half its subjects and nearly half its armies were non-Great-Russian. After the loss of Russian Poland, Finland, the Baltic Provinces and Bessarabia, the U.S.S.R. contained, in 1926, 182 ethnic groups speaking 149 languages. If we ignore the smallest groups, there were thirty principal nationalities. Half of the causes of the revolution had been found in the policy of the Tsars towards their non-Great-Russian subjects. That policy was not a mere caprice of the Autocracy. It had the warm support of the most influential groups, military, official, social and industrial, and of the Great Russian quasi-garrisons of officials and skilled workers cantoned in the cities of the subject peoples. It was a policy of Russification, religious, cultural and linguistic, and, in great measure, of Russia for the Great-Russians. "The name Russian means Oppressor, to the Bashkir," said Lenin, when addressing the Communist Party in March, 1919.

The sentiment of Great-Russian national chauvinism, which had ranged itself behind the Emperors Alexander III and Nicolas II in support of the policy of Russification, survived the Revolution. The Revolutionary leaders found the human material, which was to serve the purposes of socialist uplift in the minor nationalities, infected with an overbearing nationalism of its own, and likely therefore to provoke a responsive growth of local separatism in them. The unevenness of material and cultural development which the Imperial régime had left behind it made the search for civilising agencies in local sources difficult and slow. The leaders themselves, in the days before they came to power, had been concerned, not with the urgent day-by-day realities of administering a hungry and anarchical people, but with higher and remoter problems, such as that of replacing national-ism by internationalism, and with securing allies for the revolutionary task by the promise of freedom extending as far as the right of seces-sion. These things played an important part in the early period, when cessions of territory and authority had less significance than the preser-vation of existence and the winning of friends by the reversal of un-popular policies. But a scheme of permanent relations between ma-jority and minorities, in a State made strong for defence against ex-ternal enemies, was yet to seek: and it was mainly from a man who had personal experience of a *macédoine* of religions and nationalities that the elements of such a scheme were derived.

The man was Stalin, the son of a Georgian father by an Ossetian mother, who had spent his boyhood in the streets of Tiflis, had been educated in its theological seminary, done his early revolutionary work there and in Batum and Baku, and won intimate knowledge of the prison in the last-named place, where he once underwent the punishment of running the gauntlet among the prisoners. The *macédoine* was the Caucasus, out-balkaning the Balkans by its variety of faiths and races. In the post-revolutionary distribution of territories, for which Stalin himself was mainly responsible, account had to be taken (it is perhaps too early to say that it no longer has to be taken) of deadly quarrels between Georgians and Armenians, between Ossetians, Adzharis and Abkazians against Armenians, between Tar-tars on the one hand and Russians and Armenians on the other: not to mention some scores of different languages, and the jarring remnants left by the successive dominations of Persian, Turk and Russian. It is not surprising that Stalin viewed without illusion the prospect of national cultural autonomy for Chechens and Ingushes and other similar Caucasian tribes, or that he had a realistic outlook upon the problem of autonomy for Georgia. He was a member of a minority within a minority, and he knew what those who claim liberty for themselves may do to others who make a similar claim.

In 1913, as mentioned in the preceding chapter, he made a Marxian study of the question of nationalities. In this he traces the idea of nationality to a *bourgeois* source, but claims that it must be respected as long as it lasts. He rejects the plan of registering nominal lists of all who claim to be members of a particular nationality wherever resi-

dent, and of assigning to each of the bodies, thus voluntarily constituted, a protective institution which will look after their religious,
cultural and educational needs. The Jews, the one nationality which
lacked altogether at that time a territorial basis, he expects to become
assimilated to the local populations. The general question is to be
dealt with by complete equality of personal rights for all, including
freedom of conscience, and freedom of movement (which the later
Romanov Emperors denied to the Jews): along with cultural autonomy for definite territorial units. He strongly opposes the national
organisation either of the Party or of the Trade Unions, which must
continue on an international basis, on pain of dissolution into separate
units. In general, he insists upon the adjustment of a nationalities
policy to the changing needs of the times: upon an opportunist rather
than a dogmatic solution of particular problems.

Stalin, as I read his brochure of 1913, is for tolerance, but not for
the perpetuation of backward cultures. He classes the idea of nationality along with religion, as something to which all peoples have a right.
But—and this is a reservation of great significance, in view of the later
development of the nationalities policy—the Social Democracy, as it
was termed at that time—in other words, the Party—must agitate
against bad institutions, and resist whatever is contrary to the interests
of the proletariat. As to the right of secession, that must depend upon
the needs of the time. There is no express reference to federation,
but the idea of federation was implicit in the contention that the Party
and the Trade Unions must remain on an international basis instead
of being split up among the nationalities.

The actual policy of the Soviet State to-day, as carried out in practice, whatever the difference of form, corresponds very closely with
the outline sketched by Stalin in 1913: it has been filled in by the provision of opportunities for the realisation of the promised equality.

When the Revolution of November came, Stalin was the natural
choice for the tasks of the Commissariat of Nationalities. The declaration of November 15, 1917, announced the equality and sovereignty of
the peoples of Russia, and their right to self-determination, extending
to secession and the formation of independent States; the abolition of
all national and religious restrictions; and the free development of
national minorities and ethnographical groups inhabiting the territory
of Russia. But the revolutions had given to the victorious party, in-
stantly expectant of the accession of new peoples to the revolutionary
cause, a new outlook upon the question of nationalities. It was necessary to provide a form of union for the expected allies of the Soviets

from outside Russia. Equality and sovereignty, which means no more than confederation, even if they mean so much, must be replaced by a more definite bond. In January, 1918, it was announced that the Soviet Russian Republic was constituted on the basis of a free union of free nations, as a federation of Soviet National Republics: and Stalin wrote a new essay, justifying the conception of Federation by the international character of the Revolution. The argument is that the nationalities question has now ceased to be one of particular struggle against national oppression, and has become a general one of the liberation of nations, colonies, and semi-colonies (including such countries as China) from the greed of imperialism: and that the November Revolution has opened the way to that liberation.

The bitter struggle which preceded, and followed, the signature of the ruinous treaty of Brest-Litovsk with Germany revealed the depths of the national Russian sentiment that survived in Marxian minds: and the losses of territory, permanent and temporary, which took place between 1918 and 1920, by depriving Great-Russia of most of her food and fuel, read a new lesson to the revolutionary leaders. It was demonstrated that the Ukraine and the territories north and south of the Caucasus, if not others of the border countries, were indispensable to the very existence of the Russian State. It was easy to argue further that Great-Russia was equally necessary to these countries, in order to protect them against exploitation by the imperialism which had shown itself greedy for their resources. Stalin wrote a third essay, in 1920, in which he plainly said that so-called independence for the smaller nationalities of old Russia was an illusion. The course marked out for the nationalities is provincial autonomy, but a provincial autonomy allowing wide variations of form and scope. Even mere treaty relations, he says, such as those existing at that time with (Soviet) Azarbaijan, the principal source of oil, were admissible. A point upon which he insists is that respect must be shown for religion as well as for national feeling, and he vigorously condemns what he calls the shock-tactics of the Great-Russian Chauvinists in endeavouring to force conformity upon the outlying peoples. Mutual confidence must be created by destroying the remains of feudalism and privilege; by conferring those economic benefits which the policy of the Tsarist Government had limited to Great-Russia; by employing local men for local duties; and by giving scope for national education and for the national theatre. Autonomy, he said, is not a mere temporary evil to be eliminated as soon as possible. On the other hand, the whole tenor of his article is to show, what the actions of the Soviet Government have always made clear, that the interests of the revolution and of Socialism, assumed to be identical with those of the masses, come first, and that no breakaway will be tolerated.

At the end of 1922 the Russian Soviet Federative Socialist Republic agreed, together with the Ukraine, White Russia, and the Trans-Caucasus Federation, to a federal union. The result was the formation of the Union of Soviet Socialist Republics in January, 1924. At the end of that year the Soviet Socialist Republics of Uzbekistan and Turkmenistan, created by an ethnical rearrangement of the Mahommedan States of Khiva and Bokhara, together with the imperial Russian conquests in Central Asia, entered the Union, and in 1929 the separate Soviet Socialist Republic of Tajikistan was formed for the Shia Mahommedans of Uzbekistan. Under the constitution of 1936 the Trans-Caucasus Federation was broken up, and, in place of it, its three Soviet Socialist Republics, Azarbaijan, Georgia and Armenia, joined the U.S.S.R. as constituent Republics. Two new Soviet Socialist Republics, Kazakh and Kirgiz, also became at that time constituent Republics of the Union. The acquisitions of territory made in 1939-40 raised the number of full constituent republics to sixteen. But this fact is very far from presenting a full picture of the framework of the Union. There are numerous autonomous Soviet socialist republics (A.S.S.R. is the common abbreviation) and autonomous provinces and national regions, exercising functions which, in the cultural and educational field, are of importance, and help to satisfy the instinct of nationality for small territorial units.

While the Union was still in process of formation in 1923, the Party adopted a Resolution which recited the difficulties and explained the ultimate aim.

One embarrassing survival which is specified in the resolution is the conviction existing among many Soviet officials that the Union is not a federation of equal states, but a transitory stage towards unification: and the consequent attempts of the Commissariats of the predominant partner, the R.S.F.S.R., to dominate the autonomous Commissariats. So far from justifying such encroachments (of which it is not difficult to find examples to-day), the Resolution declares that the Union of the constituent republics is the first step towards the creation of the future World Soviet Socialist Republic of Labour. Here we see the Party, in a mood of World-Revolution, envisaging the addition to the U.S.S.R. of a German Soviet Socialist Republic and—who knows how many more—to complete that assemblage of the continents of which the five-pointed star is the symbol. The attitude is relevant to the question here under consideration, for the prospect of such poten-tial additions inevitably influenced the outlook upon the minor nation-alities.

The Constitution of 1924 reaffirmed the right of secession: and declared that the sovereignty of each constituent republic should be restricted only to the extent specified—in other words, that all residu-ary authority belonged to the constituent unit (as in the United States of America), and not to the federal Union. To both of these assur-ances, then and always, there was an implied limitation—the all-union unity of the Communist Party, and of the Trade Union organisations.

The Party is very strongly centralised in Moscow, and it is from this centre that the driving force takes its direction. It is certain that the right of secession is one which could not be enforced.

The Sixth Congress of the Third International, meeting in Septem-ber, 1928, reaffirmed the right of secession, the complete equality of all nationalities, and the duty of combating all remains of chauvinism, national hatred and race prejudice: and broadened the nationalities policy by the express addition of provisions for the creation of *oppor-tunity*.

Since equality is not equality when the potential competitors start differently equipped, and since some of the minor nationalities are in fact backward in varying degrees, the resolution pronounces for assistance to those which lag behind. Another clause is an unmistak-able echo of Stalin's strictures of 1913 on the folly of encouraging the survival of unworthy cultures. The guarantee given to the national cultures is to be accompanied by a proletarian policy of developing the content of such cultures. By this time we have reached the com-plete theory of *constructive levelling* which is characteristic of Soviet policy towards the nationalities.

But Great-Russian chauvinism remained, as it remains to-day, and in July, 1930, Stalin attacked it once more. He defined its errors as the disregard of differences of language, culture and manner of living; the adoption of the objective of unification; the destruction of na-tional equality of rights; and encroachment upon the national admin-istration and the national press and schools. On the other hand, he stigmatised the contrary deviation of local nationalism, as an attempt to "shut oneself up in one's own national mussel-shell . . . not to see what brings the working masses of the Soviet Union closer together and unites them, and only to see what can keep them apart." He de-clared for a culture national in form and Socialist in content, ulti-mately merging in one, Socialist both in form and content, with a common language, when the complete ultimate triumph of world-wide Socialism is achieved.

A particularly interesting question is whether the U.S.S.R. has discovered, and put successfully into practice, a method of dealing with less advanced nations which enlists their co-operation by allaying their jealousies, and differs fundamentally from the imperialism of European colonising powers. There is a further question applicable particularly to nationalities, such as those of the Ukraine and Georgia, which claim a civilisation equal or superior to that of the predominant partner. How far is their sense of equality satisfied, and their national pride reconciled to their constitutional and actual status? Upon the answers to these questions must depend a large part of our estimate of the value of the federal organisation and of the reputation of Stalin as a statesman of the first rank. We shall see that no absolute answers can yet be given. We must look to tendencies rather than to conclusions.

The claims of nationality are sometimes of a character to be satisfied by the equalisation of the rights of individuals. It seemed at one time that the Jews of Russia would be content with the removal of their disabilities, and the right to live where they pleased: but their ambitions, perhaps under the stimulus of the Zionist movement, have now extended further. Generally speaking, however, the nationalities of Russia have a territorial basis, greater or smaller, and make corporate claims, ranging from national autonomy in some form, to the right to a separate cultural existence in respect to language, literature, art and education, the right to a proportionate local provision for education and economic advancement (in particular in respect to railways and industries), and the right to the local employment, not only of local residents, but of natives. Sections of them have had organisations abroad, for the most part in Paris, claiming independence, and there have been, particularly in Asiatic Russia, vigorous separatist movements, of which that under Enver Pasha, in 1922, for the unification of all Turkestan, was perhaps the most determined. Occasional incidents, such as the murder of Abid Saidov at Bokhara in 1930 for giving evidence on behalf of the Soviet Government, reveal the underground workings of "bourgeois nationalism" and a whole section of the prosecution's case against the "Rights and Trotskyist bloc" in 1938 was devoted to plots in the Ukraine, White Russia, Kirgizia and Uzbekistan, for separation from the Union. But the signs of popular support for such movements are scanty. The expression "bourgeois nationalism" is applied to everything which over-emphasises the fact of the separate corporate existence of any nationality, and the assumption is made that claims such as these proceed from the remains of the "liquidated" classes, and not from workers and peasants. It is probable that this assumption is on the whole true.

To summarise the aims which the Communist Party has set before itself: The first is to convert all the peoples, not into Russians, which was what the later Tsars desired to make them, but into builders of Socialism, and ultimately into willing members of a Communist society. In every society an attempt, more or less conscious, more or less organised, more or less efficient, is made to fashion man according to a particular pattern. This, indeed, is the aim of all education and of all forms of moral discipline. A great part of what we mean by liberty is the right of individuals and associations, parents, school teachers, Churches, newspaper proprietors, to mould humanity according to their own plan. In a society such as that of the United States of America or the United Kingdom, the State, as such, takes a very small share in the process, but in the U.S.S.R., the whole of the work of "making Man" falls upon the State and its agents, including the Communist Party. This is not the whole of the difference between the position of the State as an educator in the two sections of the modern world. In the United States of America and the United Kingdom the aim is to adjust the character and habits of men to the conditions of an existent society based upon property. In the U.S.S.R. it is sought to change man and his habits, and to create, by doing so, a new type of society. The task is thus immeasurably greater, and it falls upon a single totalitarian agency, which has repudiated the traditional co-operation of the Churches, and itself controls, directly or indirectly, the whole of the Press.

Granted the premise, which is that one bent is evil and another one is good, it is impossible to surrender the function of guidance to persons who have a different conception of what the bent should be. The magnitude and difficulty of the operation, and the extent to which it is conducted in the minor nationalities by nationals of the major one, account for some of the friction which is produced by the process. Owing to the close relation, at some points, between religion and nationality, on the one hand, and between communism and religion, on the other hand, the task presents some of the difficulties of a religious mass-conversion. This is particularly evident in the case of the Islamic peoples, and no doubt a portion of the conversion will, in fact, be superficial. Education, in the widest sense, starting from the young Octobrist in the lowest class in the seven-year school, travelling upward to the Pioneer and the higher school, still further to the Communist League of Youth, the technicum and the university, and continued in the propaganda of radio, theatre and press which accompanies Soviet man and Soviet woman through life, is national in form and socialist in content and, alongside of the activities of the Communist Party, one and indivisible in discipline and inspiration, is the means by which Great-Russian and Georgian, Ukrainian and Tartar, Armenian, Uzbek and Yakut, are to be moulded to the standards of the new society.

Economic considerations have to some extent run athwart of the aim of placating national sentiment. The U.S.S.R. has been divided into economic regions, in order to give local unity to economic policy, and these economic regions are not conterminous with national boundaries. In Central Asia, for instance, there is a single economic region, having its headquarters at Tashkent, which is not the capital of any of the constituent republics, but is admirably situated as a centre for the organisation of the production of cotton and for the textile industry. The Economic Council of this area deals with irrigation, river transport, cotton, silk, local coal and grain, and Asiatic health resorts: in other words, with all the most vital economic problems and with the recreation of the workers. The Ukraine, on the other hand, is divided into two regions, one agricultural and one industrial. We owe to Batsell (in *Soviet Rule in Russia*) the knowledge that a struggle was in progress for three years between the Tartar and the Chuvash autonomous republics, on the one hand, and the economic region having its headquarters at Samara on the middle Volga, on the other: and that it was necessary to effect a compromise by special administrative arrangements. Another dispute arose from making White Russia (a separate Constituent Republic, with all the susceptibilities appropriate to the status) a part of an economic region having its headquarters at Smolensk in the R.S.F.S.R. That the principle of economic regionalisation should have been extended, in this way, to the constituent and autonomous republics shows that their authority in economic matters was not regarded seriously, and confirms the conclusion at which I arrive in a later paragraph, that real autonomy, except in linguistic and cultural matters, does not extend very deep or very far. Nevertheless there is a genuine aim, which I put in the second place after the primary aim of making a Socialist, and ultimately a Communist, commonwealth: to get rid of all causes of friction between the nationalities.

One of the methods of achieving this elimination of friction in

Central Asia has been the revision of boundaries on lines corresponding with ethnical and economic conditions. The purely political demarcation of Khiva, Bokhara and Korezem has been replaced by a delimitation which separates mountaineers from plainsmen, nomads from settled agriculturists, Shia from Sunni Mahommedans. But the principal expedient has been that of social and economic levelling, levelling up, as well as levelling down, levelling both for the individual and for the corporate body of each of the nationalities. The only historical parallel, and that an incomplete one, with which I am acquainted, is that of primitive Islam, which admitted all races and all colours to the full privileges of Islamic brotherhood and intermarriage, retaining the unconverted in a status similar to that of the disfranchised under the pre-1936 constitution of the U.S.S.R.

When the old régime did not actively disfavour non-Russians (as by depriving them of their lands for the establishment of Russian settlers), it, at all events, took no pains to secure for them equality of opportunity. There was no deliberate provision of economic opportunity to the outlying sections, and this is what the revolutionary government has supplied: partly in the interests of general economic development, partly in pursuance of the policy of equalising the nationalities. The establishment, over the whole Union, of Machine Tractor Stations, which have mechanised uniformly a large part of all the operations of agriculture, is an instance of the combination of both of these aims. But the most striking example of the new policy is the creation of cotton-spinning and cotton-weaving in the Central Asian Republics, which were formerly purveyors of raw material to the centre. The vested interests of the imperial régime would hardly have allowed this assertion of equality.

It is in the overriding of the vested interests, whether of workers or of entrepreneurs, that the merits of a levelling authority, no respector of classes or persons, reveal themselves. The later Tsars were autocrats in name; but they were chary of offending their capitalists. The British Government, under a system of unevenly distributed democracy, in an Empire partly parliamentary, partly bureaucratic, must inevitably do more for that section of its people which commands the vote than it does for the voteless section. When Lancashire is at odds with a non-self-governing colony, the odds are that Lancashire wins, and that Imperial Preference makes the market safe for the British producer. This may be politically convenient, but it does not strengthen the bonds of affection in the Empire. The Communist rulers are subject to no such weakness, and they do in fact aim at even-handed justice and equality in the economic sphere for all peoples alike. Industries are very generally making their appearance in areas formerly devoid of them, and there is no preference for the interests of one nationality over those of another, wherever the natural facilities for economic development exist or can be stimulated.

Generally speaking, the official attitude towards the older national cultures is a very appreciative one. The work of the thirteenth-century Georgian poet, Rustaveli, was the subject of general interest and ovation at his seven hundredth and fiftieth anniversary, and it has been translated into many of the local languages, with the evident aim of giving to all the nationalities a sense of a common inheritance in the monuments of each. As much was made of Rustaveli, and his "Knight in the Tiger Skin," as had been made of Pushkin some months before. As pointed out in a later chapter, the aim in recent years has been to create a Soviet patriotism equally distinct from a purely national one and from internationalism: and the events of the war seem to show that the effort has met with success.

※   ※   ※

The theatre and the film are regarded as powerful means of popular education: and the national theatre and the national film receive generous encouragement. The U.S.S.R. is divided into film areas on the basis of nationality, in order that the cinema may be adjusted to local needs. We hear, for instance, of a film exhibiting at Tashkent the evils of polygamous marriage. The smallest national section now has its theatre. A play in the Karelian (closely similar to Finnish) language was first presented in December, 1937. Non-periodic literature is published in seventy-three languages. Dictionaries of a scholarly quality (sometimes the occasion of a good deal of pedantic squabbling) begin to fill the shelves.

The extension of linguistic, cultural and other autonomy into very small territorial aggregations is well illustrated by the treatment of the Jews. Biro-Bidzhan, a region in Siberia somewhat larger than Palestine, and believed to be capable of supporting 50,000 families, 40,000 of them in agriculture, has become an autonomous province, with its own mainly Jewish provincial executive committee, under the Constitution of November, 1936. Since there is a non-Jewish population, the economic and educational administrative units are not exclusively Jewish. But the Jews have thus ceased to be a non-territorial minority, like the gipsies, and have a small territorial home of their own. On an even smaller scale they have a quasi-territorial status in European Russia also: in the Crimea, White Russia and the

Ukraine, there are numerous Jewish Soviets, conducting all their transactions in Yiddish, which is the vernacular of the Russian Jew. Jewish Soviets exist wherever there is a considerable Jewish group. In the Ukraine a minimum population of 1,000 Ukrainians or 500 non-Ukrainians is entitled to form a Soviet: and a minimum of 25,000 Ukrainians or of 10,000 non-Ukrainians a regional Soviet. A conception of the nature of this regional autonomy can be formed from the fact that the Jewish regional Soviet in the Kherson district had a Jewish Police Commissioner, with a small Jewish jail. There is a considerable number of lower judicial courts in the Ukraine and White Russia where the business is conducted entirely in Yiddish; there are Jewish police at Kiev and Odessa, and a Jewish registration office for marriage and divorce at the latter place. The wide concession of territorial autonomy to small national groups in the Ukraine has been made the basis of a charge by Ukrainian nationalists of deliberate weakening of Ukrainian nationalism by the Soviet Government. This is the familiar difficulty of the minority within the minority.

The Soviet Government encourages Yiddish, as the actual vernacular of Russian Jews, and the Jewish theatre in the U.S.S.R. makes use of this language. The large number of Jews employed in the public offices—it is particularly marked in White Russia and the Ukraine—and in such institutions as those of socialist retail trade, is responsible for some growth of anti-Semitism in the U.S.S.R., and also perhaps for the fancy that the Soviet Government is predominantly one of Jews. The Soviet Government has set its face firmly against anti-Semitism, and punishes anti-Jewish outrages with severity. It is itself charged with anti-Semitism, because of its repression of the Zionist movement: but is, in fact, neither pro- nor anti-Jew, but gives to the Jewish the same encouragement which it gives to other nationalities, while discouraging the separation which appears to be involved in Zionism.

✳   ✳   ✳

The Soviet of Nationalities, which is one of the two co-equal chambers of the Supreme Soviet of the U.S.S.R. under the constitution of 1936, is a device, similar in principle to the Senate of the U.S.A., for securing the equal representation of Constituent Republics as such, and of smaller autonomous units. Each Constituent Republic (with twenty-five deputies), each autonomous republic (with five deputies), and each national region (with one deputy) is represented in this chamber. Smaller numbers were proposed in the first draft, but were deliberately increased by an amendment aiming at making the numbers of the two chambers approximately equal: so as to give to each of them equal weight when joint sessions are held. Another amendment of importance was made at the same time. The first draft provided for indirect election of the members of the Soviet of Nationalities through the Supreme Soviet. It was amended by the substitution, for indirect election, of direct election by the citizens of each unit. Another amendment improved the standing of the Constituent Republics in the Presidium of the Supreme Soviet of the U.S.S.R. The Presidium had eleven (now sixteen) Vice-Chairmen, each of whom, by a convention, is the Chairman, either of the Presidium of the Supreme Soviet of a constituent republic, or of the Council of People's Commissars of the same. The original draft, which had provided for a smaller number of Vice-Chairmen, was amended to provide one for each constituent republic, and so affirm the equality of all the Vice-Chairmen in the Presidium. The care taken to ensure the equality of the smaller national units between themselves is evidence of Stalin's personal vigilances. If the actual opportunity and power which are given by the membership of the Supreme Soviet and the vice-chairmanship of its Presidium are small, the dignity is considerable, and is at all events equal for all: and the smallest constituent republic is coequal with the largest in at least one of the two chambers. The increase made in the proportion of the number of deputies to the population in the Supreme Soviets of the smaller constituent republics is another evidence of this case. For instance, whereas the R.S.F.S.R. has a Supreme Soviet consisting of one deputy to every 150,000, Ukraine has one to every 100,000, Georgia has one to every 15,000, Kirgizia has one to every 5,000 and so on. There is no doubt that Stalin's heart is in the success of his nationalities policy; and equality, both corporate and individual, by removing jealousy eliminates friction.

✿   ✿   ✿

Friction there has often been, particularly in the Ukraine. A vigorous effort at conciliation of that Republic was made between 1922 and 1929, when the Soviet Government aimed specifically at "Ukrainisation" of the official language and the administration, against the contrary inclination of Great-Russian zealots. Ukrainian separatists abroad allege that this effort was neutralised by the wide establishment of regional autonomies for non-Ukrainian minorities, and by wholesale Jewish colonisation in the Crimea and the south. The Ukrainian-speaking population is one of peasants, and measures which caused discontent among peasants in general were particularly resented by national sentiment in the Ukraine. In 1930 a member of the Ukrainian Academy of Sciences was imprisoned for forming a society of liberation, and the Academy was closed. The allegations against the Soviet Government include neglect of industrial interests, export of necessary food in periods of scarcity, and depletion of Ukrainian finance in the interests of the Union. One of them—that the Donets mineral area has been separated from the Ukraine—is evidently based on the fact, already mentioned, that the Ukraine has been divided into two economic regions, one agricultural and one industrial: but it is misleadingly stated. The friction took a very serious form at the time of the struggle over collectivisation. In July, 1933, N. A. Skrypnik, an old collaborator of Lenin, Commissar of Education in the Ukraine, and a member of the Central Executive Committee of the U.S.S.R., whose sixtieth birthday had been celebrated as a State ceremony, protested against the agrarian policy, was called upon to recant, and committed suicide. There were many lesser sufferers on the same account. The purge of 1933 disclosed the presence, as chairmen of the collective farms, of a number of the old officers of the nationalist chief Petliura: and the Commission, returning a month later, after the expulsion of these undesirables, found them again at their posts. About a quarter of the Ukrainian Communists were expelled at this purge, the average for the whole Union being a fifth. In 1935 there were disturbances, with numerous attacks on tax-collectors, Communist agitators, newspaper reporters, chairmen of collective farms, factory foremen and shock workers, and one district chief of political police. This outbreak may have been purely economic, but the line is difficult to draw. In 1937, Lyubchenko, chairman of the Council of People's Commissars in the Ukraine, committed suicide to avoid arrest as an enemy of the U.S.S.R. and a betrayer of Ukrainian interests; Postyshev, who had been a sort of hero of Bolshevisation in the Ukraine since the difficulties over collectivisation, was disgraced; and a general clearance made in the upper ranks of the Ukrainian Communist Party.

In White Russia *Pravda* gave a picture of the purge of 1933, particularly in the region of Vitebsk, where were found many adherents of the Zionist and Jewish Bund parties, along with Social Revolutionaries and National Democrats.

In the Mahommedan areas nationalist movements, such as *Milli Istiklal* (National Independence), in Uzbekistan, have often been active, and have invaded the local sections of the Party. In 1934 Nusratulla, the Chairman of the Central Executive Committee in Tajikistan, was removed on charges of having pursued an unduly nationalistic policy in that republic: and replaced by Rahimbayev. Other Tajiks were also degraded. In 1937 Rahimbayev was in turn disgraced on a charge of supporting the Mahommedan mullahs and of diverting public funds to the mosques. I will not weary the reader with a full list of similar incidents in the constituent and autonomous republics in 1937; but the cases of Lokola, a former chairman of the Executive Committee in Abkhazia, and of nine high officials in Soviet Azarbaijan, convicted of a plot to murder Stalin, and executed, deserve notice. The Terror was at least as active in the constituent Republics generally as in the R.S.F.S.R., and separatist movements played a great part in the trial of March, 1938. But Hitler's attempt in 1941 to rouse the Russian Mahommedans to a Holy War on the German side were met by an appeal from the Mufti Abdurrahman Rasulev to Muslims throughout the world to give aid to the U.S.S.R. The events of 1941 showed that the separatist movements, in spite of jealousies and sore places, were neither strong nor widespread.

Anna Louise Strong, a good observer, writing in 1930, found no traces of race prejudice in Central Asia, where she saw Russians and Uzbeks sitting down together in the co-operative dining-room: but the same was true of the pre-Revolutionary period. Littlepage tells a startling, but convincing, story of the Kirgiz outside a hospital during a typhus epidemic flipping lice at the nervous Russian out-patients, and describes a sort of inverted national snobbery which favours the Asiatic against the European, and puts the former into places for which they are not really fit. As regards the peoples of the macédoine of the Caucasus, John Lehmann, after a stay of some months in 1937, sums up his opinion by saying that "there seems little reason to question the claim of the local authorities that, in the face of the advance in education and material welfare, old tribal jealousies are rapidly dying out." He adds that the vendetta was hard to eradicate, and that in upper Svanetia there were 600 deaths from this cause between 1917 and 1921, but between 1930 and 1932 two only. My own experience in another part of Asia leads me to regard this achievement as unusually rapid. Lehmann also thinks that the quarrel between Tartars, Armenians and Georgians has been ended by the socialisation of the three constituent republics. It may be so: but I prefer to await further evidence.

I arrive at these paradoxical conclusions: that the constitution gives little or nothing in the way of actual power to the constituent bodies which are parties to the federation; that the political system is one of intense centralisation, particularly in the vital sphere of finance; that the concessions to local language and culture give a very large part of what national feeling most desires; and that there is such an absence of favour to particular nationalities, and such a constructive effort to make their equality real, that national jealousy and friction are diminished, though not yet eliminated. It is not, except in the sphere of language, liberty: but national *amour propre* is placated; and levelling *up* is in active operation. The Soviet Government has, in fact, reverted to a system more familiar in Asia and in the Balkan Peninsula than in western Europe, which gives cultural, without political, autonomy; but the Soviet Government has added an element of active encouragement which is all its own. To those nationalities which are only emerging from primitive nomadism and were, under the Tsarist régime, threatened with extinction, the policy brings pure gain. To those such as the Central Asians, who occupy an intermediate place in the order of civilisation, it offers a compromise which is likely to keep discontent within manageable limits. For Ukrainians, Georgians, Germans, there is a measure of relaxation in the strait waistcoat of the centralised state, and an end of certain much-felt grievances. Experience of the consequences of national self-determination in practice makes it reasonable to doubt whether anything better was possible.

Like many other things in the U.S.S.R., the policy for the nationalities is not that miracle of completed performance which the propagandist would have us believe, but it is an immense improvement upon the Tsarist policy, and a genuine achievement on the part of its creator, Stalin. I think that other Governments have something to learn from it, particularly in respect to the device of cultural autonomy for peoples not sufficiently advanced to exercise political autonomy, and in respect to the active *levelling up* of the economically backward.

Chapter XXV

THE NEW RESPECTABILITY

"All things are in flux."
HERACLITUS OF EPHESUS (sixth to fifth century B. C.).

"Russia is full of respectable married people, just as anxious
to do well in their jobs and help their children to get a good
start in life as their counterparts in the U.S.A. A new kind
of respectability is emerging, which sometimes seems almost as
extreme in one direction as the previous ideas in the other."
LITTLEPAGE AND BESS, In Search of Soviet Gold.

The task of the November Revolution, as seen by the men who took
part in it, was the seizure of power by a hitherto oppressed class which
would use it to create a classless society, in which each would work
according to his capacity and receive according to his needs. Those
who did not fancy that industry was a Fortunatus' purse, into which
all could dip without exhausting it, perceived clearly that the central
problem was that of production, and, less clearly perhaps, that a long
period of time must elapse before the necessary stage of productivity
could be reached. An indispensable condition of the attainment of
that stage, in the eyes of all, was the world-wide division of labour
which would result from the anticipated world-wide revolution. For
the rest, the discoveries of physical science were to achieve the conquest of matter, and machines, owned and operated by a public authority in the interests of all, were to take the place of the slaves and
serfs and wage-earning proletariats upon which earlier civilisation had
depended. The workers were to become the lords of the machines.
There was cold, there was hunger, there was danger from within and
from without: but there was a happy certainty of victory, made possible by the close approach of the moment when the barriers would go
down, and the rush of brethren from abroad would relieve the proletarian citadel.

In this imagined world, the Third International represented the
aspirations of the proletariats to emancipation from the chains of
capital, and of the colonial peoples to freedom from imperialist oppression, and it met each year at Moscow, the centre of a new world of
hope, to determine the policies for effecting these deliverances. De-

feats, political and other, were no worse than the return of workmen after an unsuccessful strike, submission to the inevitable by men confident of an early resurrection. There were no alliances except of proletariat with proletariat. In such a world nationalism was merely a weakness to be tolerated, a stumbling-block of superstition. The coercive state was necessary so long as cupidity demanded an unfair share of the world's wealth for a class or for an individual: but that would come to an end with the removal of the fetters upon production; the problem of distribution, which had so greatly exercised earlier Socialist thinkers, would solve itself; and men—their reasonable requirements freely met—would cease to snatch advantage and to need restraint. The coercive state would wither away. In the meantime, the armed workers, when each day's work was done, would, like the Twelve in Blok's poem, patrol streets and factories, watch over public security, and enforce the proper discharge of public business: or stand forth to protect the achievements of the revolution against attack from within or without. Great establishments of civil functionaries, like regular armies, seemed part of the paraphernalia of a bad old world, vanished for ever into the limbo of nightmares. . . .

At the twenty-first anniversary of the November Revolution, the Union of Soviet Socialist Republics was an organised state, immensely more efficient and more powerful than the one which it overthrew; exercising all and more than all of the coercive functions of its predecessor, with a military machine as regular, as elaborately equipped, and more numerous than that of any power on earth; paying no more than lip-service to the idea of world-revolution; in close association with capitalist powers, a member of the *bourgeois* League of Nations, seeking in its relations with the outside world the advantages of peace and profitable trade. In building up gigantic projects of State-controlled industry and agriculture, this State had created a host of functionaries, 70,000 of them employed in the one task of tabulating its statistics.

The "Party," once a handful of men and women, steeled to endurance in the school of hardship and exile, had grown to two millions, who occupied all the best and many of the second and third best places in the state: an influential inner ring having a vested interest in things as they are, and enjoying more privilege and more comfort (though not more wealth) than the rank and file of the population. The vision of the armed workers, taking care to see that officials are servants and not masters, had faded away through the ivory gate of dreams. The Soviets themselves, though they had bequeathed their name to the new state, had ceased to be the constituents of the supreme legislature, now remodelled on the lines of a *bourgeois* parliament. The Third International had held only one full meeting since 1928, and was represented by a permanent Executive Committee issuing its instructions to rigidly disciplined national Parties, and following a policy of defence of the Socialist Fatherland. In the discharge of this function, it must help to defend the capitalist states which are the allies of the Socialist Fatherland, and to maintain order among their African and Asiatic subjects. It had gone through a phase in which it ordered the affiliated parties to support the moderate non-Communist Left of the *bourgeois* countries, once condemned as Social Fascists. Lip-service continued to be paid to the idea of world-revolution, but the former engine of change and overthrow was harnessed to the Foreign Office of a world-power, in competition with other world-powers like itself.

It had taken two decades to bring these developments thus far: and they had worked themselves out, not by any new turn, but rather by the prolongation of a curve which began to diverge from the straight line of theoretical principle from the first moment of the seizure of power. The curve was inevitable as soon as the Soviet Government came into contact with the obstinate realities of existence in a *bourgeois* world. The divergence had taken place, not with a mathematical precision, but with a wavering oscillation, as rival forces pulled this way and that: but the dominant influence acted always in the direction which, at the end of the period, we see to have been taken. The result is hateful to the surviving idealists of an earlier period, who tell us that the Soviets have become *bourgeois*: and the intransigence of Trotsky and the bitter struggle associated with his name were the historical issue of the contradiction. But there could have been no reconstruction of industry and agriculture by the State without an army of civil functionaries: and there could have been no safety in a predatory world without a military machine of quantity and quality similar to that of dangerous neighbours, and without alliances and contacts incompatible with a policy of the encouragement of revolutionary movements. I think that Trotsky, if it had been he and not Stalin who had triumphed in the struggle of 1924-27, would have done very much what Stalin has done, and that his earlier actions and writings, when he was himself in power, afford ample proof of this. The task of Socialism is a task of organisation and construction: and there can be no organisation and no construction without the employment of the available human material. Armed workers, giving their spare time to the job of building and defending a new world, cannot take the place of military experts, equipment, and training, of administrators, statisticians and clerks. That the servants should tend to become masters, should develop bureaucratic tendencies as the phrase goes, is the critical difficulty of all social organisation. The simple course is the quasi-anarchical one of *laisser faire, laisser aller*, which permits the individual to use his organising gifts for his own purposes, that is to say, to dominate his fellows who lack those gifts. When we have decided that this is neither justice nor wisdom, we must take our risk of being dominated by those who should be servants of society, and use our brains to find a solution of the peril. The existing régime in the U.S.S.R. is not without expedients for keeping the Party man and the official in their places, as the periodical purge, and the trials and the expulsions of 1936-38, sufficiently demonstrate.

In external affairs the first great compromise was the Peace of Brest-Litovsk, signed against the will of a majority of the Central Executive Committee, who desired the continuance of war with Germany in the belief that it would spread the revolution. In the bitterness of the struggle over it, the Left, then including Bukharin, plotted to kidnap Lenin. The strategic retreat of the New Economic Policy—accompanied by an analogous change in international relations—was made possible by Lenin's overwhelming authority: but the suicides of ardent spirits marked the disappointment with which it was received. When, in 1924, Stalin formulated his theory of Socialism in one country, the death of the aspiration to world-revolution—except as something to be reached by a slow process of universal conviction—and the development of nationalism in the international revolutionary state, were already within sight.

The struggle between the original internationalism and the nationalism which has taken its place has been a long one, and has been fought with varying fortunes. The history of the Third International is a compendium of this struggle. Brought into existence because the Second International had betrayed the International cause by its support of national war in 1914, it began its career as the avowed champion of World-Revolution: and it was the enthusiasm of one of its meetings which sent the Red Armies to defeat outside Warsaw. It made a concession to compromise when it damped down the revolutionary spirit in Germany in 1923, and further concessions when it endorsed the policy of friendly alliance with moderate parties abroad, with the Kuomintang in China, the Trade Union Congress in Great Britain, Pilsudski in Poland: still more when it adopted the policy of the United Front in 1935. But its schools for Asiatic and colonial propaganda were directed against the Powers with which the Soviet Government desired friendly relations, and its extraordinary plan made in 1928 for a Negro Republic in the United States of America was a direct challenge. The long delays between its plenary meetings (after the one held in 1924 there was an interval of four years, and after the one held in 1928 there was an interval of seven) seemed to proclaim lukewarmness or neutrality. The signature of the non-aggression pacts, including a clause against intervention in foreign countries on account of their internal condition; the entry into the comity of nations signalised by the endorsement of the Kellogg Pact (1928); the acceptance of membership of the League of Nations, appeared to repudiate subversive designs. But, even in 1934, the permanent organisation of the Third International was engaged on plans for the encouragement of revolution in three European countries, one of them on terms of intimate political association with the U.S.S.R.

The accession of Italy in November, 1937, to the anti-Comintern pact, already signed by Germany and Japan, called forth a pronouncement, addressed to the peoples of the world, in which World Revolution takes a place entirely subordinate to the defense of the U.S.S.R., as the Fatherland of Socialism, and of Republican Spain and Nationalist China, against Fascist attack. This was followed by a declaration by the Chairman of the International that the workers of capitalistic countries should judge each State by its relations with the Soviet Union, not by its relations with Socialism in general. In effect, this declaration waved the aim of proletarian revolution for those countries which stood with the U.S.S.R. against the dictatorships of Central Europe and the Japanese Empire. Molotov, delivering his report at the ceremonial session of Party and non-Party organs in the Great Theatre of Moscow on November 6, 1937, formulated the now ruling theory regarding World-Revolution. He said that it had already begun with the revolution of November, 1917: not by the sudden fall of the whole chain, but by the successive fall of individual links. Since November, 1917, the proletarian revolution had become the support of all really progressive movements of the popular masses, *even though not purely communistic*. "Now," he said, "it is the support also of the struggle of the toilers *for their democratic rights against the fascists,* and of the weak countries for their national independence against imperialistic aggression."

In spite of the puzzle which was set the rest of the world by the Russo-German Pact of August, 1939, the policy of the Third International from 1935 was to bring about a United Front throughout the world of all the left and leftward forces and to use them for the protection of the U.S.S.R., the Fatherland of Socialism, against the apprehended attack of those Powers, in particular Italy, Germany and Japan, which were either, by definition, hostile to the tenets of Communism, or prepared to use Communism as a pretext for aggression. Thus the Communists of Great Britain received instructions from Party headquarters, before the General Election of 1935, to support the Labour Party, and sought, without success, to establish intimate relations with that organisation. The Popular Fronts in Spain and France were among the consequences of this policy. Nothing more is heard of the agitation, once so active, in the Asiatic colonies of Great Britain and France for the emancipation of their peoples from the Imperialist yoke; and pains are taken to reassure the representatives of actually or potentially allied states against the apprehension of Communist interference.

And yet the toasts of the Central Committee of the All Union Communist Party for the twentieth anniversary of the Revolution, as given to us in the Party newspaper on October 30, 1937, included minute libations to the old gods: "Proletarians of all lands! Oppressed peoples of the colonies! Up with the flag of Lenin–Stalin, the flag of the victorious Socialist Revolution! Long live the proletarian revolution in the whole world! Long live the Communist International: the leader and organiser of the struggle against war, fascism and capitalism! Long live World Communism."

Every Government of the Left has a further Left, which it cannot ignore; a section which is shocked by compromise, suspicious of concession, impatient of backsliding. A portion of it may be frankly hostile, and may necessitate measures of the kind applied to the followers of Trotsky. But thought is subtle, and its influence penetrates beyond the avowed opposition. It is necessary to placate and neutralise this leftward thought. That is why the Soviet Government was careful to continue to uphold the Third International, as well as to use it as the instrument of its own Foreign Office, while it supported the existing régimes of the Powers from which it hoped for support. It hopes that the world will become Communist, as the Pope trusts that it will become Catholic: but the result is now to be attained by conversion, not by subversion, and, in accordance with Molotov's metaphor, by the gradual slipping of the links off the chain. Communism is to conquer by its superior productivity: a contingency which the capitalist, presumably, does not contemplate.

But before I consider further the relations between the Soviets and the so-called capitalist States, I have something to add as to the replacement of the internationalist ideal by an entirely new Soviet Patriotism. Precisely how wide and how deep was the sentiment of Great-Russian patriotism in the pre-revolution state, it is not easy to say. Patriotism of the *State* was perhaps neither wide nor deep. Patriotism of a mystical entity, of Mother Russia, may have been both. What seems certain is that the minor nationalities of the Empire did not share it.

In the preceding chapter I have shown that these lesser peoples, their cultures and their economic interests, have been matters of special concern to the revolutionary régime.

A step of profound significance—for the Cossacks were instruments of the Tsarist administration, a large part of the strength of the White armies in the civil war, and the most obstinate opponents of the collectivisation of agriculture—was the re-establishment of Cossack regiments in the Red Army. And a patriotic Cossack song from the opera in Sholohov's *Virgin Soil Upturned* figured prominently in the Soviet Press in the Anniversary week. Along with the Law of 1935 which abrogated the exclusion of the children of the disfranchised from the higher educational institutions, and with the provisions of the constitution of 1936, the inclusion of the Cossacks in the Red Army was an invitation to all classes to co-operate in the service of the Soviet Fatherland. The moral and political unity of the peoples of the U.S.S.R. was strongly emphasised in the speeches of the twentieth anniversary of the Revolution. Soviet patriotism is inculcated by a new turn in the teaching of history, for which Stalin himself gave the cue by a brochure addressed to the writers of text-books. Patriotism both of the whole and of the parts, of the constituent Republics as well as of the Union, is included. Mingled with announcements of record output of potatoes and pig-iron, of roads in the sub-arctic regions, of new water supplies and public baths for cities, of chess champions and polar fliers, with enormities of Trotskyist and Bukharinist enemies and Fascist machinations, we find the poems and portraits of Georgian and Armenian and Tartar minstrels and poets, and notices of a new archæological magazine which throws light upon the pre-history of the peoples of the U.S.S.R., and an account of the recovery from the bottom of the river Bug of a cargo-boat which must have carried Ukrainian corn to Greece 3,000 years ago, when Jason was setting forth to Kolchis to find the Golden Fleece. From February, 1938, the form of oath for the Red Army has been changed, and the soldiers now pledge their faith as citizens of the Soviet Union, in lieu of the older international pledge.

In 1933 a schoolmaster was dismissed from his post for making too much of Kutusov and Bagration, the heroes of the Napoleonic war. It was counter-revolutionary to cherish the portraits of Tsarist Generals. In June, 1938, the Press was insisting on his restoration to his school. He had become the remembrance of a Russian triumph.

Patriotism has its obverse in xenophobia, and foreign consulates in Russia are cut down, and foreign associations, even those for purely beneficent purposes, are excluded from Russian soil. Statistics are suppressed; suspicion becomes more painfully obtrusive on all hands; official reticence is carried to a point which seemed morbid, until we learned in June, 1941, that foreign attack was not mere fancy.

How real were the grounds of apprehension and how effectively had the patriotism of the Soviet peoples been aroused to meet the danger, we learned in the next months.

The aim of the Soviet Government in its relations with foreign Powers was dictated by its experience of the intervention of 1918 and 1919, by the announced intentions of the man who controlled the vast might of the German Reich, by the ambitions of Japan, and by the willingness of a third Power to share in the spoils. These things caused the Soviet Government to look for helpers where they were to be found. It needed time for development, and needed peace. It was eager to combat depression and restore economic order in capitalist countries, because the world is its customer and supplier. It courted foreign opinion, and sought to disarm foreign suspicion and prejudice. One of the aims of the new Constitution was to give evidence of liberal and democratic sympathies.

✻ ✻ ✻

Stalin desired peace: but he firmly expected war. Having regard to Hitler's own announcement of his intentions in the Ukraine, and to the actual course of the world's history since Japan attacked Manchuria in 1931, he had the best of reasons for expecting it.

Why then did he miss the opportunity of confronting Hitler with the prospect of war both on the east and on the west, by accepting the overtures of the British Empire and the French Republic for joint defence of Poland against attack?

As I see the political position, Stalin made one great miscalculation; and another minor one. His policy was entirely realistic and self-regarding; and he did not believe—having regard to the history of appeasement in Europe—that Great Britain and France could be trusted to stand against aggression. In the light of events we may reasonably agree that he had good reasons for these doubts in the case of France. He was wrong about Britain. But Britain was far away and not a land Power. He therefore thought it best, in the interests of the U.S.S.R., to gain time to strengthen his military position. And, as a part of his measures for this, and knowing something of the pounce of a mechanised German Army, he sought to put as great a distance as possible between his advanced posts and the potential enemy, that more time might be given for the assemblage of the Russian reserves. Time was of the essence of his defence plan, and it was apparent that, while the Germans were ready, Russian mobilisation would be a comparatively prolonged process. The facts entirely justified this forecast. The minor miscalculations were as to the willingness and power of the Finns to defend themselves, and perhaps also as to the rancour with which they would resume the fight as soon as opportunity should present itself. But in the facts of the war we have the justification of the policies Stalin followed.

❆   ❆   ❆

The new consciousness of the need of consolidating strength at home changed the outlook upon the family, the basic institution of the new as of the old State. Neither Lenin nor the Communist Party in general desired that anarchy in sexual morals with which the revolutionary epoch began. Both Lenin and his wife, Mme. Krupskaya, spoke and wrote against it. It was part of the general collapse of the framework of society and the State which characterised the great overturn; and I repeat that the business of the Communist Party, far from being the business of destruction, was that of reconstruction upon the ruins, social, economic and political, of old Russia. The Marxian outlook upon Woman was upon a being whose personality had been sacrificed to the tasks of reproduction, child-rearing, and household drudgery: who must be rehabilitated by an economic emancipation. She must cease to be a mere instrument for the creation of a future generation, and become the equal companion of Man, as well as the mother of his children.

It is a delicate adjustment which determines the true balance between woman as a personality and woman as a mother. A little too much this way, and she is Aspasia, free to love and to leave. A little too much the other way, and she is the drudge.

There were always many millions of the second type, of whom social history is silent. But the early period of the Revolution rather favoured the first, with effects which were not inconsiderable in the towns.

There was absolute freedom of divorce at the will of either party, and the right to abortion, so long as it was performed under authorised conditions. These things, combined with the widespread employment of women as wage-earners and social and political workers, and the encouragement of communal life in the forms of public catering and arrangements for the public care of children, were not favourable to the family. Plans even went so far as to envisage the establishment of children's towns, in which—as in the so-called "public schools" of England—the parents would have minimum concern with their off-spring: but at this point nature rebelled.

The danger of attack from Germany and Japan brought home the necessity of a nation made strong by its teeming millions, while some reduction in the speed of the annual increase, caused by the spread of urban notions to the rural areas, suggested the possibility of a future falling off. It is an interesting fact—the more curious be-cause of the high place taken by the Θεογοκος, the Mother of God, in Orthodox Religion—that Woman has in Soviet Russia no consort status. She is dependent for her place in society on her own achieve-ments. The wives and families of the leaders are rarely mentioned. But the Party and official Press made much of a visit paid by Stalin to his mother in Ossetia. It was an announcement that the family was an object of Bolshevik respect. The lesson of the debt of politeness due from young to old began to be inculcated by the Press and educational authorities. It was not unneeded; for youth was, and continues to be, not too respectful to its elders. The League of Youth received a brusque intimation that it was their juniors, and not their seniors, whom they were to instruct. In 1935 the Party and the Government initiated a campaign against the practice of abortion, and ultimately enacted legislation which made operations unlawful except in cases of danger to life or health. Other clauses placed obstacles in the way of divorce; increased the amount of alimony payable for a child; and offered substantial premia for large families.

While the new law was under discussion, there was a remarkable outburst of criticism, largely from women, against the limitation of abortion. This was grounded upon the low standard of family incomes, the lack of housing accommodation in the cities, and the inadequate supply of nursery requirements, from perambulators to baby's bottles. It came from women of all groups, teachers, students, factory workers, office employees and collectivised peasants. Nothing could have been less like the platitudes of laudation—along with judicious criticism of selected details—with which the columns of the Press are normally occupied. For once, the female population of the U.S.S.R. was fully vocal, and there could be no doubt at all what it wanted.

The Soviet Government has its ear very close to the ground, and may have been aware that the men did not fully sympathise with their women on this issue. Hindus suggests something of the kind when he tells us that Russians do not want their birthrate interfered with, because they expect war. Men are also less acutely sensible of the inconvenience of large families than are women: for reasons which I need not emphasise. The bill went through, and the *head of the Planning Commission*—this is a characteristic touch—announced that the U.S.S.R. would have a population of 300 millions by 1975.

In so far as woman continues in the prison of domestic duty, her economic equality is incomplete, and it is economic equality upon which emancipation ultimately depends. She has gained, and continues to gain, by the right to divorce, which has made an end of the legal right of property in her as a chattel; by the large openings for industrial employment; and by the system which makes her a co-sharer and a dividend-drawer in the farm; by the enforcement of the law of alimony for children; and by the communal provision for family-catering, for mechanised washhouses, and for the care of the young, so far as these last in practice extend. The housewife, and the woman who is a mother, now figure along with the worker and the woman worker, the collective farmer and the woman collective farmer, the Red Army man, the man of the Red Fleet, the Government employee, the member of the working intelligentsia, and the old-age pensioner, and separate from all of these, as two of the groups of which the citizens of the Soviet Union are made up. The two aims, of a largely increased population, and of the emancipation of woman, will continue to be mutually contradictory, until a further development of economic strength makes possible a vast extension of accommodation in maternity homes and in institutions for the reception and charge of young children, and of the supply of mechanised laundries and of the requirements of the civilised nursery. In the meanwhile, as a part of its policy for the strengthening of the family, the Soviet Government strikes at the sexual perversions, formerly treated with legal tolerance; and we hear of persons excluded from the Communist Party on the ground of successive divorces.

※   ※   ※

The children have always been regarded as the treasures of the Socialist State, and, in periods of want, they and their education have been the first charge upon scanty resources. It is a part of the new developments that all the children, whatever their social origin, should be equally treated. Stalin himself gave the key note when he declared that sons were not responsible for the offences of their fathers. In the Budget for 1937 education was the next largest item, after Defence, and a very close second to it. After an interval of experiment, the Bolsheviks have learned not to put too great a strain upon the children, and to abandon educational eccentricities which had attracted them in the early stages. Discipline, uniforms, examinations, certificates, a place for classical studies, learned titles, have all come back into the schools. A touch of priggishness betrays itself now and again: *Pioneer Truth* had made light of the children's habit of jumping up behind motor cars and so getting free rides; adult *Truth* rebukes it for this levity, and particularly for some verses in which fun is made of the children who climbed on to a car in the hope of a ride, and found the chauffeur was asleep inside. Are the examinations not at hand, and are there not more serious subjects to occupy the pages of the juvenile journal? Mr. Gradgrind is not solely of British nationality. But his appearance in Russian dress may be no more than a reaction against the spirit which encouraged the child to write to the public press when his mother whipped him.

*　　*　　*

I have suggested that latter-day Communism—the Communism which reconciles itself with the stage of socialism in one country— hopes to establish its œcumenical claim by its superior productivity. To what extent does it rely, as N.E.P. relied, upon the incentive of personal gain? There are those to whom it seems that the system of piece-work wages, carried to the pitch it reached in the case of the Stakhanovite super-piece-workers and the other champion producers, represented a new stage of retreat from principles. It is a part of the model statute for collective farms that its members are expected to become well-to-do. The definition of the legal rights of collective farmers in their own yards and the product of their yards and in their dividends, after the dues of Government and of Machine Tractor Stations have been met, tends in the same direction. There are inequalities from farm to farm, and a number of farms have actually reached the so-called "millionaire" status. One of the earliest advertisements (as distinct from political propaganda) which appeared in Moscow was that of the Savings Banks. The newspapers publish with pride the rising amounts there deposited: and every *plage* and holiday resort has its branches for the convenience of depositors. The law allows of the inheritance of wealth, subject to a very drastic scale of death duties; government loans offer an opportunity of investment free from inheritance tax; and there are even a few individuals who live upon the interest of them. The successful artist or novelist may almost be called rich on the proceeds of his royalties. Town households which keep maids, and have country cottages for summer *villegiatura*, are pretty numerous. There was a pleasant suggestion of leisure in the great prominence given in the news—before the Nazi invasion—to sports: skating, tennis, ski-ing, hiking, hockey, parachute jumping, and *phut-bol*. The shops were fairly full of semi-luxury goods at substantial prices. Model department stores in the cities would pack your purchases in paper and deliver goods to your address. Advertisements of sports goods, musical instruments, photographic apparatus, paints and perfumes, superior soap, preserved foods, sweet biscuits, and articles the appearance of which suggests wedding presents, occupy space in the newspapers and public vehicles. One advertisement showing an extremely respectable family in a well-furnished room, with book-case, sofa, sofa-cushions, dining-table, chairs, and electric light shade, and urging householders to insure their furniture, clothing, and musical instruments, *auto-transport*, etc., irresistibly suggested to me Maxim Gorky's story of the man with the smug ideals, who realised his ambition of the *red armchair*, in which he might sit and read the newspaper to his wife and children.

The differences in the emoluments of the better-paid workers and technicians have combined with the position of the *sovburi*, as the people call them—the huge administrative and clerical staffs—to create the semblance, which bids fair to develop into the reality, of a middle class. In the upper ranks of the Red Army, and in official circles, there is a return to Tsarist manners, and you may see the gentleman, *en grande tenue*, bowing over the lady's hand, or kissing it at the end of a dance. The excursion steamers on the new Moscow Volga Canal advertised three classes of fares.

Lest I should convey a false impression, I hasten to emphasise that the new economic inequality is not the inequality of the West, for the gambling of the Stock Exchange, and of financial manipulation, is unknown, and one man cannot make money for himself by organising the labour of others, or establish a factory or a commercial business involving the employment of paid labour, or the buying and selling of commodities. Make all that you can by your own labour, but nothing by the labour of others, and nothing by trade, is, in brief, the law of the land since the end of N.E.P. Nothing approaching the waste and ostentation of the fashionable quarters of London, Paris and New York exists in the U.S.S.R. If there is any "law of conspicuous waste" in operation in the U.S.S.R., it is not for the individual, but for the city and for public institutions.

* * *

Side by side with the growth of inequality between the rank-and-file workman on the one hand and the official and the better-paid technician on the other, there has been a closer approach to equality between the larger categories of the population. The abolition of rationing and the establishment of zonally uniform prices (1934-35) deprived the urban workers of a privilege which they had enjoyed since the early days of the planning period and, in spite of the additions made to cash wages, did actually reduce the real wages of that group as a whole. I shall deal in the next chapter with the constitution of November, 1936: but I must note here that it too was, in theory at least, a political leveller, destroying the class-basis of indirect election by class-organs, and substituting a supreme legislature of the parliamentary type, equalising the franchise for town and country, and putting an end to the disfranchisement of particular classes. All this was, in effect, an invasion of the "dictatorship of the proletariat" by a principle of an entirely different kind. The Society of Old Bolsheviks, which was founded in 1922, with a membership qualified by at least eighteen years' service in the Party, and playing the part of a sort of Elder Statesmen, consulted on large issues, felt very strongly on the subject of this essay in equalisation. It was dissolved in May, 1935, while the draft of the constitution was still in embryo. It is likely also that the abolition of the Communist Academy (founded in 1918) and its absorption, in February, 1936, in the all-Union Academy of Sciences, founded by Peter the Great, aimed at forestalling opposition to the principles of the new constitution.

There are some other indications that the drafters of the new constitution sought to introduce something more closely resembling what the Western democrat regards as a normal democratic constitution. One of these is the importance attached to the non-party element in the list of candidates for election to the Supreme and the local Soviets.

As pointed out in the succeeding chapter, the 1936 Constitution, which goes into so many and such meticulous details regarding the system of Government, says practically nothing about the "Party" which guides and controls the working of the whole. Until after the Nazi onslaught, it was true to say that Stalin himself had no place in the Constitution. He was merely the General Secretary of the Communist Party; and not a part of the Government recognised as such by the document which purports to define its character. But while he was still outside of it, he was, as he remains, the unquestioned head of the State, and these were some of the things which the Press and people were saying about him: He is the leader, the teacher, the friend, the father, the saviour. The others are merely his counsellors and pupils. It was the Stalinite Five-Year-Plan, Stalin's constitution, Stalin's block of party and non-party citizens, and it was a Stalinite exploit which the heroes of the drifting floe in the Arctic Ocean accomplished. He is always at his post, always on the captain's bridge, always handling the true compass: he is the giant, the genius of political reason and unbendable will, his name is the symbol of our victories, and the war-flag of our people. To all he is precious, to all he is familiar, to each one he is the close friend, for all he is hope and strength and guidance on the dangerous and difficult path from oppression to freedom and happiness. He is fearless in fight and merciless to the people's enemies, like Lenin: free from every kind of panic, like Lenin; wise and unhurrying in the decision of complex problems, like Lenin. He *loves his people* (sic) as Lenin loved it.

His name passes into legend, and I append to this chapter a translation of a poem, which tells a sort of good St. Wenceslas story about him. It makes a bizarre foreground to the Moscow trials of 1936-38: but this seemingly impossible combination of the people's father and friend, with the executioner of political opponents, is what actually reveals itself. The warm broad smile, which films and photographs show to us, is a reality, confirmed by recent close observation. He loves a homely proverb or a quotation from Gogol, the Russian Dickens. He has no command of literary Russian, and talks in short sentences, shifting from one leg to another, or walking up and down, while the people roar with delight at every sentence. It is not fear that makes this enthusiasm. It is the men in responsible places who have cause for fear. The rank and file are happy with their hero, and confident that he is their friend.

In March, 1937, he made a characteristic onslaught upon the bureaucracy, and described it as *soulless*. *Krokodil*, the Party's comic paper, plays a part similar to the famous "Labby" of England's Victorian days, in lashing official abuses and ridiculing indolence and inefficiency. The editors would not do this if they did not know that Stalin chuckled over their criticisms. Both the Bureaucracy and the Communist Party—now not easily to be distinguished from it—suffered severely in the storms of 1936-38. The Sovburi, as the people call them, the Soviet bureaucrats, now constitute a vested interest, making for conservatism, as all vested interests do, and Stalin doubtless feels the necessity of keeping both the "Party" and the official staffs in a proper subjection to control.

The great Russian rulers—Ivan the Terrible, Peter the Great, Catherine the Great—have not been fortunate in their successors. The burden of autocracy can hardly be lifted on lesser shoulders. If I may be pardoned for attempting to raise a corner of the veil which covers Stalin's inner thoughts, I suggest that his Constitution of 1936, with the accompanying hints of a desire to construct a true democracy, show that he has no successor in whom he is able to repose full confidence, and that he seeks to protect his people against the consequences of a less able rule than his own. It may be that S. M. Kirov, murdered in 1934, was his provisional choice, and that the extraordinary consequences which followed upon Kirov's death are explained by the blow then given to Stalin's plans.

* * *

The theatre is to the Bolsheviks what the Church was to the Orthodox. The liturgy of the Church re-enacted the holy mysteries, and its decorations represented them for the better understanding of the congregation. In doing this it *caused the great events to happen anew*: did not merely give a theatrical representation of them. The Church could not have tolerated irrelevant or distracting matter in its services or its paintings and did in fact observe a very rigid convention in respect to both. Similarly the Bolsheviks required their dramatists and producers to show to the people the great events and the characteristic life and aims of the Revolution. This is the key to certain demands which, without it, seem to show an unreasonable rigidity of outlook. But the audiences wanted relaxation and amusement. They did not want, if I may so put it, to be always in Church. Man can endure the heights for a time, but he cannot live on them. I think that the changing history of the Russian theatre is to be explained by these two things: the insistence on a revolutionary liturgy, and the self-protective reaction of the philistine public, who prefer to see *Charlie's Aunt*,

A change in popular taste accounted for the temporary eclipse of the promising young composer Shostakovich. His music for the opera of *Lady Macbeth of Mtsensk* was admirably expressive of the action of the drama. But there were no *tunes* in it, and people much prefer something which they can pick up and hum over. A review, in the Communist daily, of a ten days' musical festival held to commemorate the twentieth anniversary emphasises the need of a Soviet

symphonic classic, of something national, bright, gay and melo-
dious. It contrasts C. Prokofiev's complete failure in his "formalistic"
fourth symphony, with the success of later compositions in which he
had corrected his former style. Now, it seems, he has attained to a profound simplicity and truth, and shown us what a *Soviet composer*, a
serious musician and a great master, can achieve—when guided by
instruction.

We should go wrong if we were to suppose that the guidance which
brings about these changes is merely official. The public make their
own demands upon the artists, and press their own tastes. Readers and
playgoers write to playwrights and authors and urge their own requirements with no uncertain voice.

It was not for nothing that the Tretiakov Gallery in Moscow selected for its special 1937 Exhibition the works of the painter Surikov,
a well-known nineteenth-century realist. It is simple, crude, broad-
canvassed, historical stuff, with a tang of sensation in it, something
which everybody can understand. Many visitors to Moscow have
probably carried away a recollection of *The Morning of the Execution
of the Streltsi*, and the picture of *Ivan the Terrible's Murder of his
Son*, by another artist of the same school: and perhaps are Philistine
enough to sympathise with the popular taste which likes such graphic
representations.

A change, essentially similar, has made its appearance in architecture. The straight up-and-down buildings of glass, concrete and steel,
which have been irreverently described as band-boxes, have given place
to a showy, luxurious, pseudo-classical style, which I may, I hope without offence, describe as nineteenth-century *bourgeois*. The new
Worker's Sanatorium at the sea-side resort of Sochi, opened at the
twentieth anniversary of the Revolution, is a fine example of this re-
lapse. It is Hans Andersen's Goblin, weary of adventure and hungry
for comfort, settling down to "take porridge with the huskster." But
architects continue to be enthusiastic over the large opportunities and
generous expenditure of Russian planning. In looking at the new Moscow with its glorious spaces, one is reminded of the Athens of Pericles.

Let us not forget that the terrible Gay-Pay-oo started dance clubs
for the young people—to keep them out of mischief—and sanctioned
jazz. Man cannot remain for ever on the stretch; any more than Apollo
can always bend the bow: and one of the things which has happened:
to the Russian people is that they—of course before the German
attack in June, 1941—felt the need of relaxation after effort.

The Soviet novel has been returning, since its revival in 1924, to that close concern with the individual human being and the springs of his action which characterised Leo Tolstoi and the great masters. There was an interruption of this current in the period of the first Five-Year Plan, with its summons for the enlistment of literature under the banner of economic progress. But, after Maxim Gorky returned to the Soviet Union in 1932, the demand was for Socialist Realism. That is very far from signifying mere photographic realism. There must be in it a buoyancy, an optimism, a mood of prophecy; it must imagine and forecast the future triumphs of Socialism: must be, in short, not Realism at all, but, rather, a romantic conviction in the light of which the present is to be transformed. For this new Art, misgivings and doubts are treason to the truth. The artist must be whole-hearted in an assured faith. He is no longer asked to comply with a social command, to depict the victories of cement-making or wheat-growing. But he must be inspired with a general vision of the success of the tasks upon which the Soviet Union has entered. It is an echo of the conviction that man can make his own history.

Fortunately for the artist, there is here no minute prescription with which he must comply under threat of ostracism. But he is not free to mope, to doubt, to plunge into introspection. As Mr. Hannibal Chollop informed Mark Tapley, "We must be cracked up, sir. We are a model to the airth, and must be jist cracked up, I tell you." He continues by saying: "Our backs is easy ris. We must be cracked up, or they rises, and we snarls." But there is a vagueness in the requirement, which leaves a wide range of choice. Sholohov has satisfied it with his *Virgin Soil Upturned*, although he was not insensible to the tragedy of the *kulak's* dispossession and deportation. Stalin himself has sometimes proved more reasonable than the lesser members of his constellation. It was at his instance that *The days of the Turbins* was restored to the stage, although the singing of the old Russian national anthem, *God Save the Tsar*, was part of the performance, and the sympathies of the audience were enlisted for White officers.

In the drama and the film, as in the novel, the individual human being has come into his own, and the interest is in his character and its expression in action: no longer in that mystical entity, the mass, as it was when such productions as *October*, and *Turk-Sib*, were the approved form of Cinema art. *Chapayev* (issued in November, 1934), the simple story of a hot-headed, stout-hearted partisan leader, and of the political Commissar who guides him to wisdom, is a film with a hero. *Circus*, the story of a white woman who defies American convention against miscegenation, and wins the sympathy of the many races of the U.S.S.R., despite the machinations of a villainous German, combines the representation of the heroic individual with the theme of the fascist enemy. It had a success only second to *Chapayev*. *The Last Night*, a picture of Moscow on the eve of revolution in November, 1917, might have lent itself to the mass treatment of an earlier epoch of film-production, but is actually full of individual characters distinctly developed. The same thing shows itself in the theatre, where Okhlopkov, a young producer, made a great success of *Aristocrats*, a play with the theme of the building of the Baltic-White Sea Canal by criminals of all types. Pride in the work, and in his own contribution to it, works a change in each individual, differing according to each character. It is no mass conversion.

The emphasis on the personality of individuals, characteristic of latter-day Soviet literature and art, found its analogue in the character-pictures of the candidates selected for the election to the Supreme Soviet which figured in the Press. Tractorists, collective farmers, smelters, miners, men and women, not necessarily Stakhanovites and by no means all Communists, were depicted, along with their large-scale portraits, to each being allotted over a third of a newspaper page. There was an insistent suggestion that similar honour was attainable by each and all who learn to do a job well: but the individual did emerge in distinction from the mass, and was made interesting for his own sake. Orders and decorations for good service are bestowed as lavishly as under the Tsarist régime. Stalin and his inner circle of councillors appear on banners and posters with wearisome repetition. If one of them ceases to figure before the eyes of the public, it is an ominous sign, and a warning that his favour is diminished. *The anonymity is gone out of Soviet life*, and the heroes and martyrs are buried, if not in the wall of the Kremlin, at least in that of the Novodevichi monastery, with tablets commemorating their names and achievements.

Annexure to Chapter XXV

THE BOY IN OUR VILLAGE

The little boy is ill.
  Death sits on his pillow.
His mother's heart will break.
  The earth sleeps under the rain.
The autumn leaves fall:
  There is no sap in them,
It is evening, and the village
  Lies far away in a sleepy hole.
The son is dying, the boy,
  The hope, the joy, the delight.
The father grieves sorely,
  There is lead on his heart.
He looks at the child
  And sees the greyness,
The greyness that is darkening
  The bright face.
It seems, it is already going out,
  The young flame of the eyes,
They are already growing cold,
  The little fingers.
A doctor! But a wise one!
  He wrings his hands.
Help, help, is needed,
  Such as is not in the village.
A rare, a cruel, chance,
  And no doctor to help.
The father goes out in the street,
  He goes with weary feet.
The sleepy telegraph man
  Opens his hatch.
The father writes, in agitation:
  "Moscow,
    Kremlin,
      To Stalin."

493

And forth flashes a telegram
   Across the fierce whistle of the wind:
It flies over the hills
   A short and plain one:
It lights up the trees in the woods,
   With its voice like a spark.
The telegram knocks at Kremlin Gate,
   Stalin receives it,
And sorrow, the sorrow of a father,
   Gives a squeeze to his heart.

But Death sits beside the boy.
   Measure her strength!
It is she who triumphs. All is over.
   Give up, be silent, yield.
She knows not that Stalin
   Means a struggle with Death.
She knows not that Stalin
   Means Life for us.
Not a moment is lost:
   Stalin gives the order.
Hurry, scurry, the telegraph men
   Send off the telegram, and lo!
The mechanics wake up the pilot:
   And, while it is night at Kazan,
The doctor enters the cabin.
   The aeroplane flies into the sky.
The aeroplane rushes over the clouds,
   The messenger of the Great Friend.
Louder, nearer, the engine,
   Speaks its message of gladness.
The mother flies to meet it.
   Death cowers in the corner.
The doctor enters the room:
   He rolls up his sleeves.
He says gently to Sister:
   "See that all is in order!"
He says to the parents:
   "Father and mother, not another tear!"
The old man, fearless and wrathful,
   Begins to wrestle with Death.

And the boy falls into sleep:
   And Death sneaks away.
There it is, Stalin's heart,
   His life, and his work.
He leads to great happiness
   The peoples of my land.
Foresees the storms and the wars,
Gives their marching orders to the pilots,
Saves the life of the child,
   The boy in our village.

Chapter XXVI

THE CONSTITUTION OF 1936

"But it is an easy thing for men to be deceived by the specious name of Libertie: and, for want of Judgment to distinguish, mistake for their Private Inheritance, and Birthright, which is the right of the Publique only. . . ."

Hobbes, *Leviathan.*

"Communism has no idea of freedom as the possibility of choice, but only as the possibility of giving full play to one's energy when one has chosen which way to turn."

Berdyaev, *The Russian Revolution.*

"In the Soviet factory where I worked, every single change in production or administration was the subject of the widest and most heated discussion among the workers. . . . From the floor came not only criticism, but constructive proposals. The rank and file contributed enormously to the reorganisation of the factory. If this isn't democracy, I don't know what the word means."

Clarence Hathaway, quoted by Joseph Freeman
in *An American Testament.*

Certain fundamental assumptions underlie the Constitution of 1936. It is assumed that a basis, economic, social and political, has been created, a solid foothold upon which the advancing commonwealth can establish itself, till a further step forward can be taken in the passage through the slough of difficulties. We should be wrong if we were to assume the attainment of a permanent goal. There is, for instance, no pretence that the Communist ideal: *from each according to his ability, to each according to his needs,* is yet within grasp. That is attainable only when production has so increased as to make possible the satisfaction of all reasonable needs. So long as there is less than enough, whether of objects of enjoyment or of leisure, to go round, there remains the possibility of differences over the distribution, and the need of the coercive State to prevent the scramble and the furtive misappropriation which characterise Capitalistic conditions. The State still exists. As Article I makes plain to us—if we needed the assurance —it has not withered away. It is a Socialist State: not yet a Communist Society knit by purely economic and social bonds.

And yet, it appears certain things have become possible which were not possible hitherto, because the material basis for them has now come into existence. The danger from the dispossessed classes has so diminished that it is safe to admit them to a franchise, universal, equal, direct and secret, for all the elective organs of the State. The peasant, always a potential danger to the socialistic ideal, and from time to time able to dictate departures from it, is so far reconciled to the process of collectivisation and its results that it has ceased to be necessary to withhold from him the right to equal suffrage alongside the urban worker. Certain rights, very far from realisation in the capitalistic societies, notably the right to work and the right to leisure, can now be proclaimed: because confidence is felt in the existence of a material basis for their realisation.

※　　※　　※

Any forecast of the value in practice of this new Constitution, with its significant fundamental assumptions, must begin with an estimate of the reality of those assumptions. It is obvious, for instance, that the Government of the Soviet Union bound, as every Government must be, to self-preservation as its first duty, will not tolerate subversion by the newly enfranchised of the fundamental principles upon which its existence is based. It is even more obvious that the declaration of the right to work will become meaningless if economic conditions do not permit of its fulfilment. We must look therefore, in the first place, not to the intentions of those in power, but to the correctness of their estimate of the stage at which the U.S.S.R. has arrived: and that is to be judged by a review of all the conditions. That is why I have left the constitution nearly to the end of my study.

※　　※　　※

The events which followed upon the promulgation of the Constitution did not justify an optimistic forecast either of the abatement of internal political difficulties or of the attainment of economic security. Still less did they appear to promise the permanence of that international peace upon which depends the direction of resources to useful ends, and even the stability of the régime itself.

The Soviet Government declared itself beset by internal enemies, hampered by intentional as well as by merely negligent injury to production, and threatened by the treachery of highly placed military commanders. The Party itself was said to be full of spies, and ceaseless internal vigilance was a condition of survival. The excellence of the intentions with which the new Constitution had been formulated would not save it, in circumstances such as these, from becoming a dead letter. The Communist Party receives a passing reference in the Constitution of November, 1936, in a clause providing for liberty of association. The clause affirms the right of combining in public organisations, and, among others, "for the most active and conscientious citizens from the ranks of the working class and other strata of the toilers of uniting in the Communist Party of the U.S.S.R., which is the vanguard of the toilers in their struggle for strengthening and developing the socialist system, and which represents the leading nucleus of all organisations of the toilers both public and state." It is again mentioned in the chapter on the Electoral System, where Communist Party organisations are specified among those having the right to nominate candidates for election. Otherwise the Communist Party is outside of the Constitution of November, 1936, as it was outside the previous Constitutions. In fact, it has a separate Constitution. And yet the Communist Party is by far the most important element in the government of the U.S.S.R.—so important, that it comes near to being an *Axiocracy*, a government of the most worthy citizens. The fact that these vast functions are outside the document compels us to regard the new constitution with a qualified conviction.

At the outset, therefore, of our examination of the constitution we find, first, that its reality is dependent upon favouring circumstances, and secondly, that power actually resides elsewhere than in the authorities for whose establishment it makes formal provision. Such contradictions are not unique. Both in the United States of America and in the United Kingdom, the uneven distribution of wealth, and the resultant social influence, contradict in practice the theory of democracy: and the ruling class or group is, in fact, something other than the elected representatives of the people, although it ordinarily makes a scrupulous use of constitutional forms. It is not therefore in a written constitution, or even in an unwritten constitution as expounded by constitutional students, but in the political practice of the adepts, that we must look for the realities of the distribution of power. This is not less, but possibly somewhat more, true of the U.S.S.R. than of the Western democracies. At the basis of the institutions of every state there lies a fundamental principle. In the West it is private property, in the U.S.S.R. it is socialised property: and in neither will democracy be permitted to violate the fundamental principle. In the one case the Communist Party is the guardian and guide, in the other the same functions are exercised by a more fluid, less tangible entity, of which wealth is the most easily recognisable characteristic, but having behind it the forces of tradition and inertia. The one desires change, the other desires continuity. Both may be said to drive,. the one on a new road, the other on an old one: and both unmistakably occupy the driver's seat and hold the whip.

What emerges is that, in attempting to interpret any particular clause of the constitution, there is a reservation to be made. Chapter I affirms the structure of society, which no one will be permitted to change or to attempt to change. All the rest of the document must be understood as subject to this fixed fundamental determinisation, which transcends all rights. The preambles to Articles 125 and 126 are equally significant. Freedom of speech, Press, and demonstration, are guaranteed "in accordance with the interests of the working people, and *in order to strengthen the socialist system.*" And the right of association is affirmed "in accordance with the interests of the working people, and for the purpose of developing the *organised* self-expression and political activity of the masses of the people." The rights do not exist independently of these considerations, and are nullified where they run counter to them.

※   ※   ※

There was a constitution for the revolutionary State in 1918, followed by a federal constitution in 1924 for the four republics which formed a union then. It was during the discussions of this federal constitution that the name of the Union of Soviet Socialist Republics originated, the order of the words indicating the type of the new State. It is Soviet Socialist, not Socialist Soviet, as sometimes erroneously written, and each of its constituent members is Soviet Socialist too. The Soviet is—perhaps we should now write, was—an essential institution of the system. In its origin it was a class institution representing the soldiers or sailors of a particular unit, the workers of a factory or mine or unit of transport, the peasants of a village. For the lowest tier of the Soviets, election was direct. In and above the lowest tier, it was indirect, each successive tier making the choice for the one next higher. The principal virtue of the Soviet was its spontaneous growth from the indigenous practice, by which the workers who had left the village for the factory chose their mouthpieces and headmen. The voting was naturally open, by show of hands. The propertied classes, who had no place in the workers' gatherings, were naturally disfranchised in the constitution built upon these gatherings. It was as natural for the peasants' Soviet to be based upon a territorial unit, the village, as for the workers' Soviet to be based upon a production unit, the factory: and when, in 1918, the Congress of Peasants' Soviets was combined with the Congress of Workers and

Soldiers' deputies to form a united Congress, each retained its then existing number, so that an inequality of representation came into existence for historical reasons. There was no division of powers in the primitive Soviets, and no division of them in the Constitutions which were based upon these.

Two features which bear the imprint of the primitive institution: the instructions which the electors gave to the man or woman of their choice, and the power of recall which they exercised when dissatisfied with the delegate—both eminently favourable to the reality of democracy—have been preserved in the constitution of November, 1936. It is the practice to make a documentary record of the instructions, and of the extent to which they have been fulfilled. Recall became common after a campaign in 1929 for popular vigilance, and, in his one and only election speech in 1937, Stalin emphasised the right, and bade the voters watch their delegates closely, and keep them to their duties.

The other characteristic features of the Soviet system—the class composition, the indirect election by open voting, the disfranchisement of class groups, the constituency based upon a production unit, the inequality between peasants and urban workers, the combination of legislative and executive powers—have been abandoned in the new instrument, whose makers set before themselves a parliamentary model, with territorial constituencies, universal, equal, direct, and secret suffrage, and the division of powers into legislative, executive, and judicial. We have no difficulty in seeing at a glance why some of these practices have been given up. Open voting was originally a form of protection against secret influence by class enemies. Later it became a means of exercising pressure upon voters for the defence of vested interests. The inequality between peasants and urban voters became an anomaly, in proportion as the town was carried to the country, and the farm became an open-air factory. The actual disappearance of an employing class eliminated the reason for class-disfranchisement.

❊   ❊   ❊

It was the Seventh All-Union Congress of Soviets in February, 1935, which formally took up the question of a new constitution. That it was only the seventh, after more than eighteen years of revolutionary government, is a point to be noticed at the outset. In the numerous and long intervals between sessions, the work of legislation and of passing budgets had fallen upon the Central Executive Committee, in so far as it had not been appropriated by other authorities.

The Seventh All-Union Congress of Soviets appointed a Drafting Commission, and Stalin himself became its Chairman. The draft was published in all the languages of the Union, in numbers sufficient for each adult to have easy access to it: and subjected to a drastic popular examination. The amendments proposed ran into many thousands, but they were almost entirely amendments of detail. The draft was then introduced in November, 1935, by a report from Stalin himself to the Eighth Special Congress of Soviets, which consisted, to the extent of more than a quarter of its membership of non-Party persons, and, to the extent of a fifth, of women. He said that the victory of Socialism—not of Communism—was now a fact, and that the frontiers between the different categories of the population were disappearing: that the working class was no longer a proletariat, because it now owned the instruments of production: that the peasantry, now collectivised, was a new peasantry: that the intelligentsia, springing now for the most part from workers and peasants, was a new intelligentsia: and that the multi-national state, consisting of equal nations, was now successfully established. He dealt with the amendments by excluding all recitals of historical facts and declarations of intention, as out of place, and by postponing matters of current legislation for consideration by the new organs when brought into existence. There remained a couple of score of relevant amendments, which he proceeded to discuss. Of the great majority he recommended the rejection, for reasons which he gave. He pointed out, for instance, that the Chairman of the Presidium of the Supreme Soviet ought to be elected by the Supreme Soviet, because, if he were elected by the whole population, as the amendment suggested, he would enjoy excessive power. It was plainly not intended that a sort of President of the United States should be brought into existence. He also gave reasons for refusing to forbid all religious rites, which a zealous anti-religious critic had proposed, and said that the clergy and members of the formerly hostile classes ought not to be disfranchised, because some of them were no longer enemies, and because the admission of inability to protect the State against such groups would argue weakness. Only in four instances did he advise acceptance of amendments. Three of these concerned the interests of the constituent republics. The fourth was a proposal for the creation of a new Peoples Commissariat for Defence.

No one questioned any of these recommendations, there was no discussion, and the whole project, with the approved amendments, was passed with enthusiastic acclamation, after a number of speeches of a laudatory kind had been delivered by members of all types, ranging from highly placed functionaries to famous milkmaids—famous, of course, for milking records—and factory workers who had won renown by excellence in productive work. All of them spoke on a single theme, the theme of Socialist achievement carried out under the unequalled leadership of Stalin. Cossacks said they had been called Free Folk, but only now did their really free life begin. A middle-aged woman said she had received the Order of Lenin for the 672 calves she had raised: and now she was going to raise 800. All of them, in terms of factory, farm, or federal republic, said "The country has changed so that we cannot even compare it with the past. You can't see anything that resembles the old life any more."

All, of course, were delegates and said what their constituents wanted them to say. The unanimity, the enthusiasm, the hyperbolical exaggeration of achievement, were eloquent of the power of mass-suggestion. The truth is wonderful, but not so wonderful as this. But the assembly gave a demonstration of that passion of fusion in one pæan of praise and thanksgiving which is characteristically Russian, and closely connected with the traditions of Orthodox Christianity. "Behold how good and pleasant it is for brethren to dwell together in unity!" sings the Psalmist. It was a congregation of praise and thanksgiving.

❋　　❋　　❋

There is every sign that earnest thought has been given to the provisions of the new constitution, and that it has by no means been treated as a piece of "spectacle-wiping": which is the Russian expression for what we call eye-wash. The short interval between the confirmation of the draft by the Congress of Soviets and the election of the new Supreme Soviet, with its two chambers, was filled with organising and propagandist work of a quality which entirely belies the Russian reputation for easy-going slackness. With one exception—the substitution of thirty-seven new names for candidates who had fallen out of favour in dominant circles, thirty-seven, that is to say, out of a total well over 1,100—the Government kept strictly within the limits of its own law. Forms have been carefully observed, and the observance of forms is important. One other criticism—that the Russian speeches delivered in the constituencies were not translated into the local vernaculars—has some significance, but it is the only one that I find occasion to make.

Of course, there were mistakes, as indeed there are in the conduct of British elections, in spite of a long experience. *Pravda* was righteously indignant at a mistranslation of the name of the Constitution into the Georgian language—an error very likely to catch the eye of Stalin. It also did not like the use in Tajikistan of a primitive method of calculating ages. So-and-so was described as 4 Dog: which meant that he was fifty-one. The figure 4 meant that he had gone through four complete twelve-year-cycles, and reached the third year of the fifth, which was named after the Dog. A decade or so more and he would have been a monkey or a hedgehog. The supply of paper and envelopes —at one time a subject of some anxiety—was vigilantly watched by peripatetic correspondents. Careless and backward committees were exposed and pilloried daily. Explanations of the way to claim the vote and how to exercise it were published and republished. The arrangements in the voting cabins, and the right of illiterates to take a friend in with them, were fully described.

The great day of the election was a holiday for the whole of the U.S.S.R. Not only is the U.S.S.R., by reason of the rapid growth of its population, a younger country than any in the West: but the minimum age for the vote, both for men and women, is eighteen; and the atmosphere of enthusiasm which had been brought into existence gave a particular stimulus to the young. Tarantass, ox-cart, camel, aeroplane, reindeer, dog-teams, skis, horseback, brought the millions to the booths. One story of a pair of brothers, who came in by night to vote at 6 a.m. and get back to take their turns at the well, carried one into the arid places of Asia. In Buriat Mongolia the old swore they would be in before the young, and achieved their promise. Lighthouse men came in to Kronstadt by icebreaker. Man-of-war's men got into a dinghy, moored to the ship, and did their secret voting thus. Polling was arranged in long-distance trains, in passenger ships, in hospitals, sanatoria and maternity homes. Outside voters were met by welcoming parties at the railway stations and cast their votes in the waiting-rooms, converted into booths for the occasion. There were "Welcome" notices outside the polling-booths in the cities, and the officials turned out to meet the early arrivals, who had gathered in long queues. It was a January day, and there were snow-showers, followed by bright sun, in Moscow: a raging blizzard in Franz Joseph Land: semi-tropical sunlight at Baku: and a torchlight procession through the Arctic night somewhere in the north. Concerts and dances followed the recording of the votes. Everywhere, it seems, the festival spirit prevailed, and the people kept order for themselves. We hear nothing of any drinking. Enthusiastic country people in Moscow burst into lyrical hyperbole: Moscow, capital of the world! Moscow

with the ruby stars on her Kremlin! Stakhanovite workers announced
new records.

It was another of those demonstrations of unity, of fusion of the
brethren and the sisterhood into a congregation of love, which Russians express by the word *sleetnost*. The sentiment of fusion into a
greater unity has a real significance in the Bolshevik code. In Afinogeniev's play *Fear*, Elena, the champion of innovation in the physiological laboratory, declares that "our politics is to transform people.
Feelings that were considered innate are now dying out. Envy, jealousy, anger, fear are disappearing. *Collectivity, enthusiasm, the joy of
life, are growing. And we will help these new stimuli to grow.*"

When the votes were counted and the results announced, it appeared that of 93,639,458 Soviet citizens entitled to vote, 90,319,346
actually voted: a percentage of 96. Of the 1,143 deputies elected, 855
were Communists, 288 non-party. One hundred and eighty-four were
women.

Five hundred and sixty-nine seats were filled on the Council of
the Union, 574 on the Council of Nationalities. Something like 354
workers and peasants were returned, 120 Red Army and Navy men
and aviators, seventy-eight who might be classified as intelligentsia—
that is to say, white-collared men who are not officials. And fifty-one
members of the Commissariat of Internal affairs, the present title of
the political police.

※   ※   ※

Two features in this election will present puzzles to students of
affairs in the United States and in the United Kingdom. In the first
place, there was only one "Party." In the second place—a still more
startling fact—with insignificantly few exceptions, there was only one
candidate for each vacancy. Why, then, all the expensive and troublesome machinery of an election, over a country of enormous spaces and
indifferent communications: and why the chorus of happy jubilation
over the successful, almost unanimous, return of the unopposed?

I have written the preceding chapters in vain if I have failed to convey to the reader the radical difference between the Communist
"Party" and any political party known to Britain or America. The word
Party, applied to the former, is indeed a complete misnomer. The
Communist Party is an Order of men and women vowed to the realisation and defence of the fundamentals of the Soviet State. It comes
near to being a priesthood of a religion of this world. Since there is
no intention of tolerating any challenge to the fundamentals, there

is also no intention of allowing any alternative order to champion alternative principles. To find a parallel, we must imagine a State, having, not merely a national Church, but an exclusive National Church, with a monopoly of spiritual influence and authority, to which no rival is tolerated by the national law. The Communist Party in the U.S.S.R. has very few resemblances to a political party as we understand it, but it has many resemblances to a Church claiming universal dominion, and realising that dominion within national limits. In the political sense, the U.S.S.R. tolerates no parties at all.

Stalin, contrasting the party system of the West with his own, told us that the question which he expected the electors to put to the candidates in the U.S.S.R., were such as these. "Have you or have you not built a good school? Have you improved living conditions? Are you a bureaucrat? Have you helped to make our labour more effective, our life more cultured?" In other words, the party label is unnecessary, because the fundamental requirement of the acceptance of the Socialist system is taken for granted, and the candidate will be accepted or rejected on his personal record and qualifications. The part played by the party system in the United Kingdom, in consolidating the strength of the executive, is unnecessary in the U.S.S.R., because the real strength of the executive in the latter is independent of the elected bodies.

We come to the second and startling difference between the election in the U.S.S.R. in December, 1937, and what appears to the Western mind a normal election. In an insignificantly small number of constituencies more than one candidate stood for election. Generally there was only one candidate in each. What might seem to be the real work had been done when the nominations were completed.

The election turned entirely upon the right of nomination. In the United Kingdom any ten electors can nominate a candidate: but there is a pecuniary check upon nomination in the requirement for a deposit of £150, which the candidate will forfeit if he does not secure a stated proportion of the votes polled. The constitution of the U.S.S.R. demands, of course, no pecuniary guarantee, which would be contrary to the spirit of its institutions: but Article 141 restricts the right of nomination to public organisations and societies of working people; Communist Party organisations; trade unions; co-operatives; organisations of youth; and cultural societies. Individuals, and groups not organised in any of these forms, have no right of nomination. Paramount influence is thus secured to those controlling the approved organisations and societies, in particular the Communist Party. The

Communist Party did not use this advantage to prevent the nomination of non-party men and women. On the contrary, a particular emphasis was laid upon the alliance of party and non-party citizens and, as already noticed, a considerable minority of the latter obtained nomination and election. But the Communist Party had its instructions to be watchful of the antecedents of those proposed for nomination. It was at this point that the directional power exercised by the actual government of the country came into effective operation.

What the rulers wanted was to convey the impression, both abroad and at home, of a united people: in order to discourage aggressors, by diminishing their hopes of division and discontent, and to inspire confidence among native supporters. The way to achieve this result was to call forth an outburst of popular enthusiasm, and to give an example of successful organisation. It could not have been done by compulsion. If there was compulsion, it was a compulsion exercised by the people themselves, drawing the minority into the vortex of their own excitement. The remarkably good harvest of 1937 helped greatly. Full stomachs and full bins created the conditions of general jubilation, and displayed the Government in a halo of the rosiest light. Many of the leading candidates told the electors plainly that the merits of this or that candidate were irrelevant. What was wanted was the universal acclamation of the victory of Socialism and its achievements; a union-wide recognition of the first occasion in the world's history on which workers and peasants have been masters of their own country; a general rejoicing in the completeness of the defence against foreign aggression, in the escape from the snares of "Trotskyist-Bukharinist-Rykovist wreckers," in the superiority of the Stalinite constitution over the sham democracies of the west, in the attainment of the equal status of workers and peasants, men and women (whether the latter be workers or housewives), and working intelligentsia, in the escape of the lesser peoples from the "prison-house of nationalities," in the elevation of work to a glory and heroism. This people has a genius for a cosmic emotion, which makes of them a mystical unity; and they responded to the call with a self-abandonment in which there was something dionysiac.

To have felt and realised, though for a moment, this generous excitement, and to have given expression to it in the quasi-sacrament of the nearly unanimous vote, was a contribution to political education which is likely to have some practical value. One of the results of the campaign, it was noticed, was the sudden emergence of unsuspected talents and energy. Unknown persons found themselves, not necessarily as candidates but as political workers, capable of influencing and organising their fellows.

The Supreme Soviet, which has exclusive power of legislation for the U.S.S.R., is elected for a term of four years and is to hold an ordinary session twice a year. Its members enjoy a conditional immunity from prosecution and arrest. It elects its own Presidium and sets up the Council of People's Commissars, which between them constitute the official Executive. It has no executive powers of its own; and its Presidium has no legislative powers, but issues what are known as decrees: for instance, confers distinctions and honours, and declares general or partial mobilisation. There is thus formal separation of the legislative and executive authority. At the first session in January, 1938, each member of the Supreme Soviet elected permanent commissions for legislation, budget, and foreign affairs. The two Chambers sitting jointly elected a Presidium, with Kalinin as its President, and eleven vice-chairmen, one from each constituent republic. Molotov, chairman of the old Council of Commissars, was then asked to form a new Council, and his selections were confirmed by the Supreme Soviet. The Supreme Soviet then adopted certain changes in the constitution. The territories included in the different constituent republics were more fully specified; three new People's Commissariats were created, one of them being a separate ministry for the Fleet. Of another amendment of greater constitutional importance I shall have something to say below. Three members rose in succession to criticise particular branches of the administration. Zhdanov, while acknowledging the services of Litvinov, then Commissar for Foreign Affairs, complained of the Foreign Office for the weakness of its policy in Japan and in France. The latter country, he said, was tolerant of anti-Soviet activities incompatible with the position of a loyal ally. He also objected to the foreign consulates in the U.S.S.R., as being more numerous than the consulates maintained by the U.S.S.R. in foreign countries: and made severe comments on the administration of both Water-transport and Art. Another critic attacked the Commissariat of Justice, and in particular the People's Commissar of Justice, Krylenko, for spending his time in mountain-climbing and chess-playing, instead of attending to his duties. A third blamed the committee which dealt with the collections-in-kind of agricultural products for inadequate storage arrangements which, in a year of plentiful harvest, left large quantities of grain exposed to the weather. All these criticisms might have been spontaneous, but I think that soundings had been taken before they were publicly made. The extent to which the Supreme Soviet will become a forum for the ventilation of popular grievances still remains to be seen.

The status and functions of the Presidium of the Supreme Soviet have some peculiar features. Its members are elected by the Supreme Soviet, to which it is accountable in all its activities. But there is no express provision for the removal of any of its members by the Supreme Soviet: and it actually survives (Article 55) the Supreme Soviet to which it owes its existence, and is authorised to dissolve the Supreme Soviet (Article 47) in the event of an irreconcilable difference between the two chambers of the latter. It is apparently to be permanently in session: it convenes sessions of the Supreme Soviet, dissolves it at the end of its four-year-term in ordinary course, and fixes new elections. *Even when the Supreme Soviet is sitting,* it interprets laws made by that body, and may rescind orders and decisions of the Council of People's Commissars of the U.S.S.R. and the Councils of People's Commissars of the constituent republics in case they do not conform to the law. By an important amendment to the Constitution to which I have already referred, it is also empowered to declare martial law. These powers approach so closely to legislative authority, that the difficulty of summoning the Supreme Soviet at short notice in an emergency will supply a plausible reason for extending them to actual legislation.

※　※　※

Experience of democratic politics makes it natural to ask where the power of the purse resides in the new constitution. The annual budget is a "law," and it may be that every project of taxation is a "law," requiring to be passed by a majority in both chambers. It may be—but there is no express constitutional provision to this effect—that appropriations of funds for specific purposes will have to be made by the Supreme Soviet. But in 1937 direct taxation constituted only 3.7% of the total revenues of the U.S.S.R. Indirect taxation, taking effect by additions to prices, was over 86% of it. This distribution of taxation is no casual accident, but an inevitable condition of a State in which there is no private wealth to tax. One of the political consequences is that the so-called power of the purse rests almost inevitably with the Government. Robson has noticed that out of 100,000 instructions given by the electors in Moscow to their representatives in 1934, not one complained of extravagance or demanded a reduction of taxation. I think they were not fully alive to the fact that the money came out of their own pockets, because only a small fraction of the taxation was either direct, or collected in the form of a local *octroi.*

The Supreme Soviet discusses the budget, and both Chambers have appointed Budget Commissions, but it seems unlikely that we are to look to the power of the purse for a guarantee of its independence and of the reality of its supremacy.

❀ ❀ ❀

In the final resort, the defence of private rights rests everywhere upon the Courts of Justice and, as the Courts depend in large measure upon the proper presentation of cases, upon the legal profession which practises in them. It has been said that a poor man in the Western democracies can only be sure of his rights if he can find a lawyer who will take up his case without fee. In the U.S.S.R., charges of political conspiracy or outrage are tried under a special law of 1934, passed immediately after the murder of Kirov, which assigns the cases to a so-called military tribunal and denies the right of appeal. It is usual for the accused in such cases to be bitterly attacked by the Press and by public associations and virtually condemned before trial. The Presidium of the Supreme Soviet now has legal authority to declare martial law (which has sometimes been defined as the will of the military commanding officer). Chapter IX of the Constitution must be read subject to these reservations.

In cases which do not threaten the fundamental assumptions of the Constitution, People's Associate Judges, a kind of non-professional assessors, participate in the trial. All professional judges are appointed by elected bodies, except those of the People's Courts, who are elected by the citizens of the district by universal, direct, equal and secret vote. The accused is guaranteed the right to defence. Article 112 provides that the judges are independent, and are subordinate only to the law. Subject to the reservations to be made as regards political offences, I believe this constitutional promise is likely to be observed. The treatment of ordinary crime in the U.S.S.R. is as considerate as that of political crime is ruthless.

In adding to the declaration of the rights of citizens (Chapter X) a statement of the guarantees for their exercise, the Constitution has shown conspicuous originality. Earlier declarations of rights—the rights to life, liberty, and the pursuit of happiness, or whatever the formula may have been—have left the means of exercise to the arbitrament of economic and other conditions. Here we find, for the first time, the explicit recognition that the value of rights depends upon the means of exercising them: which should make it difficult for the drafters of future constitutions to stop short at an abstract recital, which keeps the word of promise to the ear and breaks it to the heart.

If the guarantee in the U.S.S.R. is, in the nature of things, incomplete, the economic organisation of society none the less gives a measure of reality to it which is lacking elsewhere.

The statement of rights includes the right to work, and the right to rest and to security in old age and invalidity. The equality of women with men—a difficult achievement, because both nature and traditional habit assign particular tasks to the female sex—has been brought nearer to realisation by the ending of unemployment, and by a measure of provision for the special needs of the housewife and the child. The equal rights of all citizens, irrespective of nationality or race, are proclaimed: and for these, as elsewhere pointed out, provision has been and is being secured by the extension of economic opportunity, as well as by cultural independence.

We come next to certain rights, the exercise of which is more obviously limited by the fundamental determination of the State to establish a socialist system. Freedom of speech, of the press, of assembly and meetings, of street processions and demonstrations are stated to be "ensured by placing at the disposal of the working people and their organisations printing shops, supplies of paper, public buildings, the streets, means of communication, and other materials requisite for the exercise of those rights" (Article 125). These are not rights of individuals, but rights of "the workers and their organisations," and the exercise of them depends upon those who control the organisations in the interests of the class. Next follows the article regarding the right to unite in public organisations, which is limited in such a manner as to exclude the formation of political parties other than the Communist Party. Inviolability of the person, of homes, and of the secrecy of correspondence, is guaranteed: but is to be understood always as subject to the same overriding political considerations which govern the safeguards upon judicial proceedings.

It was constantly repeated by press and platform during the election period and after it that the constitution was the most democratic in the world. Kalinin made a speech on this point which throws much light on Russian ideas. It is vain to discuss the question without a preliminary agreement on the meaning to be assigned to the word democratic. It is probably the most equal constitution in the world, because it, or the conditions in which it is promulgated, eliminate the inequalities caused by varying economic conditions. That it enables a majority of the Russian peoples to change its rulers without the use of force, or the violation of the law, is plainly untrue: and this provision of a constitutional channel for the changing of rulers is what democracy generally means to the Western mind. It is unlikely, however, that the vast mass of the Russian peoples ever dreamed of such a channel. What they earnestly desire is economic security and an economic and social levelling, and these, it seems, in large measure they have.

Differences of means remain because of the considerable variations in the remuneration of work: but these are trifling in comparison with the enormous inequalities produced in the United States and the United Kingdom by the private ownership of land and of the instruments of production, which enable the individual to levy tribute on his fellows. The social constitution in these countries enables the man who has the organising gift to use it entirely for his own benefit. The claim for the Soviet system is that it makes the organising gift the servant of the community. This is what Stalin meant when he said: "We did not build this society in order to restrict personal liberty, but in order that the human individual may feel really free. . . . Real liberty can only exist where exploitation has been abolished, where there is no oppression of some others, where there is no unemployment, and no poverty. Only in such a society is real, and not paper, personal and every other liberty possible." It will be said—and with perfect fairness—that, in so far as these conditions have actually been achieved, and even Stalin does not claim their complete achievement, they are antecedent to the paper constitution, which has only created a machine and put good intentions into solemnly attested language.

I shall not quarrel with this statement of the case. Perhaps all rights, everywhere, are independent of the paper on which they are recorded: and, if they were not independent of it, would not actually exist. In the Soviet Union there is, in fact, a kind of democracy which is altogether sui generis: so that the man is master where in Britain he is the dependent, though his mouth is closed on some things where in Britain he can speak his mind. One of the most wholesome features of the Soviet system—having its origin perhaps in the immemorial discussions of the Mir—is that, on what we may call the lower planes of public affairs, a vigorous democratic system is actually in existence, and has been encouraged by the revolutionary government. It is the actual truth that the factory, the farm, the steamer, the office, the shop and the mine, are run under the perpetual criticism of the workers, who freely express their opinions and suggestions through the medium of the wall-newspaper and the factory committee. The dwellings of the workers are managed by committees chosen by the workers and responsible to them, with no interference from distant estate-agents or investment-holders. At a conference of the High Schools, attended by representatives of the pupils as well as by teachers and persons engaged in educational administration, a girl student's complaint of the attitude of teachers towards questioners received sympathetic attention, and was taken up warmly by the Press. Members of the outside public are associated with local bodies for many purposes, for instance for the details of town-planning. The function of patronage (*sheftsvo*) exercised by factory in respect of village, and by associations in respect of certain public departments, carries interest and influence into wider spheres. I am not certain that the procedure of the Party Purge is intended to survive. Hitherto it has given to everybody the opportunity of publicly ventilating grievances against all but the most highly placed. So many officials are Communists, that a purge of the Party came near to being a purge of the bureaucracy. However cavalierly constitutional forms may on some occasions have been treated, important measures have sometimes been submitted to free public discussion for long periods before adoption by the legislature. This is true not only of the two measures of 1927 and 1936 affecting marriage and the family, but also of the momentous decision of 1929 regarding the collectivisation of agriculture. I do not say that public opinion had its way on all these occasions, but it certainly had a good hearing: and a good hearing is something which is highly appreciated.

What I have called democracy on the lower planes of public affairs may, or may not, be a preparation for democracy on the higher planes. Among the pre-requisites of successful democracy, and perhaps most important of them, is knowledge. When Abraham Lincoln said that you could not fool all the people all the time, he had in view an order of society in which knowledge was generally accessible to the seeker for it. This implies not only a literate people (which is virtually achieved in the U.S.S.R.), but also a maximum of freedom of expression and ventilation of opinion. The latter is not only not existent in the U.S.S.R., but is impossible to be conceded, so long as the aim of the Government continues to be the remaking of the habits of man in a new image. It is easy to concede it in the United Kingdom or in the United States, where the aim is, not radically to change man, but to perpetuate his adjustment to a long-established order of society. Natural inertia may be trusted to neutralise the preaching of innovators, when innovation is the thing that is dreaded: and the thinkers may without danger be left to publish their thoughts. But an accompaniment of the attempt to educate man into a new attitude towards life must be the direction of all overt utterances towards that aim, and the stifling of all that runs counter to it. The socialistic habit of mind is not yet sufficiently established to resist the impact of contrary teachings and, because the U.S.S.R. does not dare expose its citizens to the possible infection of reaction, it puts a check upon that freedom of thought, without which the knowledge necessary to the exercise of democracy upon the higher planes of public affairs is not to be had.

Each Constituent Republic has its own constitution, modelled upon that of the Union, with the differences made necessary by the federal character of the latter: and the elections were held everywhere in June, in an atmosphere resembling that of an English Bank Holiday, amid music, dancing and rejoicing—with results which reproduced the unanimity of the elections for the Union.

❊   ❊   ❊

I have been drastic in my examination of the Stalin constitution: and I do not, in fact, find any reason for expecting it to establish anything like what the West means by democratic institutions. Freedom—or so it seems at present—is to be divided between East and West in mutually exclusive fractions: the one getting such freedom as depends upon economic equality, and the other such freedom as legal and political equality may be capable of creating. I do not infer that the new constitution in the U.S.S.R. is of no importance. Forms, if they are not too flagrantly violated, have a way of adding unto themselves some measure of reality. The constitution has already done something to inspire the sense of unity in sundered millions, to stimulate the political education and ambition of youth, to create self-respect where there was none before, to open up reservoirs of unsuspected ability: and it may yet prove to have established a forum for the effective ventilation of grievances. The provisions of this constitution that every deputy is bound to report to the electors on his work, and on the work of the Soviet of which he is a member, and may at any time be recalled by decision of a majority of the electors, are devised for the purpose of maintaining the living link between electors and representatives. In the meanwhile we have glimpses of the local deputy raising questions of the timing of trains, the shortage of housing accommodation, and the unjust dismissal of workmen, on behalf of local complainants. We also see him going on tour in a mountain constituency and criticising the absence of provision against erosion by mountain torrents, the slowness of local mails, and the inadequacy of the supply of articles of prime necessity, and enunciating the important principle that officials should travel about the area of their charges, in order to acquaint themselves with actual conditions. Here he puts his finger on one of the expedients for holding bureaucracy in check.

The new constitution, it must be repeated, will not enable the Russian peoples to change their rulers without the use of force or the violation of law. In this power, existing in differing degrees and in differing forms in the U.S.A., the United Kingdom, much of northern and western Europe, in the British Dominions, and in germ also in British India, consists the essence of Democracy. It is not complete, even in the so-called democratic States, because of the weighting of the scales in favour of wealth. In such degree as it exists, it contains the secret of peaceful political growth. It makes possible the distinction between opposition to the Government and enmity to the State: for lack of which, independent thinkers grow into traitors, and differences of opinion become potential revolutions.

The constitution of the U.S.S.R. is not democratic, in spite of the document. Nor indeed do the conditions make democracy possible. What is aimed at is, a discipline which shall remake man in a new image, and the co-operation of the patient in the process of remaking. The Russian people is at school.

But democracy itself is in flux: and is to be respected rather for its potentialities than for its achievements. The missing half of it—the economic half—is still to be supplied in the West. The long isolation of Russia from the West, and of the West from Russia, has kept the two halves of Democracy apart from one another. Are we to witness the coming together of the two in a complete whole? Only wishful thinking can answer, with conviction, Yes.

Chapter XXVII

PERSONALITY OUT OF COLLECTIVISM

"Russia has from time immemorial been the country of the impersonal collective idea. The realisation of this idea was the aspiration of the Church, as well as of all the sects opposed to the Church, and of all the intellectual, cultural, and social currents."

RÉNÉ FULOP-MILLER, *The Mind and Face of Bolshevism.*

"In all matters in which state interests are supposed to be involved, the rights of individuals are ruthlessly sacrificed."

MACKENZIE WALLACE.

"Bolshevism is but the extension of the individualist doctrine of the rights of man from the political sphere to the economic. Far from being the opposite of Individualism, it is its consistent fulfilment."

OTHMAR SPANN, *Der Wahre Staat*, 1931: as quoted by Karl Polanyi in *Christianity and the Social Revolution.*

"The principle of personality can in no way stand and develop on the soil of materialism."

BERDYAEV, *Origins of Russian Communism.*

"Once he has done with the anarchic forces of his own society, Man will set to work on himself in the mortar and crucible of the chemist. For the first time mankind will regard itself as raw material, or, at best, as a physical and psychic half-finished product."

TROTSKY, speech at Copenhagen, November, 1932.

"What a double-armed power this Russian revolution is: how on the one hand it stifles, and on the other hand it redeems, personality! Whether it does the one or the other, depends upon whether one is an enemy and non-conformist, or a ward and supporter, of the new dispensation."

MAURICE HINDUS, *Red Bread.*

No one has ever questioned the lack, in old Russia, of the sense of human personality. Russia—old Russia, at all events—fused her people into a congregation, which jointly received the gift of an undivided and indivisible spirit, radically different from the spirit of individuality.

There has been no similar unity of opinion regarding the influence of the doctrines of Communism on the growth of human personality. Some, like Berdyaev, in the quotation at the head of the chapter, hold that Communism is incompatible with appreciation of the value of the individual. Others—dating back to the framers of the Communist Manifesto of 1849—defend the opposite contention, and declare that it favours personality, by eliminating anxiety for daily bread, and setting man free for other concerns. The question at issue is a vital one. Perhaps it is the question of questions, for any and every society.

Let us begin by making up our minds what we mean when we talk of personality. It is easy to see what we mean by the absence of it. Gleb Uspensky, the story-teller of humble Russian life, wrote a tale in which he described the peasant as living under "the power of the land," and responding to the external stimulus of the daily needs of agricultural life, a life which is still dominated by the caprices of nature; foreseeing, indeed, the goal of the harvest, and the outcome of the primitive plan of the three-field rotation, and to this extent in advance of the amœba which obeys the calls of hunger, reproduction, and fear as from moment to moment they present themselves: but unable to transcend the routine and look *from outside* upon himself and his destiny, still less able to use himself for the fulfilment of conscious purposes of his own. In untranslatable language, he describes this mass of beings living *splosh* (the Russian word), in huggermugger, as Shakespeare might have said; in indistinguishable and promiscuous confusion: and has a vision of them as fish running together into a net, by an unconsidered impulse of common instinct. If this was true of the common man, much more was it true of woman, doubly imprisoned between stove and threshold, cradle and cooking-pot.

Let us now attempt to define the quality or faculty which was missing or latent in Gleb Uspensky's peasants, who lived *splosh*: but present in a greater or less degree in some of their contemporaries. For it is the spread of this quality or faculty to wider circles—or its restriction to narrower ones—under the impact of the new attitude to life that we are attempting to investigate.

Plainly it is something which is related to social life: and it must have an element of balance in it, discouraging A from the aggressive attempt to development at the expense of B, and encouraging co-operative effort. But since society is not always and everywhere the same, and ought to be susceptible of variation and evolution, the desiderated faculty or quality must also have an element of elasticity, to fit itself for change. At its best, it should include that capacity for man to "set to work upon himself" to change himself, which Trotsky postulates in the quotation from the Copenhagen speech set at the head of this chapter. A balance between freedom and discipline is evidently involved: and a hereditary caste system is unfavourable to that which we are seeking. But if one can imagine a distribution of functions in which there was no arbitrariness or fixity, but each fell into his appropriate place by a conscious appreciation of rightness, it would seem that the development of personality had gone far and wide in such a state.

Perhaps personality means the faculty of finding and recognising your own place and work in society, and of pitching your choice as high as your powers permit. This involves a corresponding function on the part of society—of facilitating and not obstructing the recognition and the choice.

This definition brings us very close to T. H. Green's,* of "the quality in a person of being consciously an object to itself," and it will give us a working basis for the investigation of this final chapter, which I have called Personality out of Collectivism. What is there in Soviet Communism which favours, and what is there in it which retards, the conscious search of each for his and her true place?

Whether it be the call of a divine being, or man's own reading of his powers, which is to enable him to find and realise his personality seems to make little difference in practice, since it is he who, whether as an individual, or the obedient son of a church, or the disciple of an institution which keeps his conscience for him—the Communist Party, for instance—must interpret the call, or divine the summons. In the case of the U.S.S.R., which is here under investigation, there exists an analogue of a priesthood, which undertakes a task similar to the keeping of consciences by certain of the churches, and helps the individual to find his duty. In this respect the position of the Soviet citizen is less like that of a Protestant Christian, who reads his own conscience for himself, than that of a Roman Catholic, who submits himself to ecclesiastical guidance. This makes easier the adjustment of self to society: but an adjustment which is rather the acceptance of a discipline, than that conscious self-harmonisation with one's fellows and their needs which is what I understand by the development of personality.

❋   ❋   ❋

* *Prolegomena to Ethics.*

Socialism is still in the making, and still on the defensive. It is inevitable that Russia should be in a sense *at school*. The more complex the society, the newer the type of behaviour which it demands, the more extended and elaborate the functions of the Government: the more difficult is the adjustment of the individual, and the harder the task of finding his place; and the more probable it becomes that conformity will be the result more of an external discipline than of an inner harmonisation. When to these things is added a rapidly changing law, or a law which changes on principles not readily intelligible to the masses of men, the difficulty of self-harmonisation is increased, and the chances of the disintegration of personality multiplied.

Anything like caprice in the dominant régime is unfavourable to personality: and autocracy, even in the strongest and ablest, has a tendency to caprice.

If we desire to see how Communist rule has affected and how it is likely to affect the development of human personality, we must look, in the first place, at the conditions which were superseded by the Revolution, and not at the conditions existing in western Europe or in the United States. As I see the Revolution, it was as though a people, hitherto submissive to the demands of a Solomon and a Rehoboam, had cried: To your tents, O Israel; and had decided, as Tolstoi wished them to decide, that they had no more need of the State. It was the collapse of a social order, leaving ruin, upon which one group alone possessed the faith, the courage and the discipline for the task of rebuilding. The Communists did not overthrow the Tsars. The structure gave way, from inherent defects, when shaken by military defeat. The anarchy which followed was in essence the same which has followed the break up of other empires. But it was made shorter, and predatory forces were to some extent kept off the carcase, by the emergence of an organised force which took up the task of reconstruction.

❋   ❋   ❋

We must not build theories upon the supposed tendencies of a materialistic philosophy or upon deductions from the teaching of Karl Marx. A philosophy, like a religion, has profound effects upon the thoughts and actions of a people. But it is the actual philosophy, or the actual religion, which exercises influence: and the actual philosophy of the modern U.S.S.R. is something to which Karl Marx and dialectical materialism have made a contribution, but which is made up of other elements, including those of Orthodox Christianity and traditional Russian sentiment. We can only discover what Communist rule has done, and is likely to do, by an examination of facts, some of which are directly attributable to the new régime, while others are only indirectly a product of it.

Assuming a normal proportion between the sexes, the most radical fact in any group of human beings is its average age. Nearly half of the present population of the U.S.S.R. is under twenty-one years of age, and nearly two-thirds of it is under twenty-nine. Only a third of it has anything but a very young child's recollection of what went before the Revolution, and only a third of it has passed the first flush of youth. At the census of 1931, half the population of Great Britain had reached or passed the age of twenty-nine. If hope and energy and susceptibility to fresh impressions are pre-eminently characteristic of youth, we must be prepared to find more of these qualities in the U.S.S.R.: and more sobriety in Great Britain. The former is the younger country, in the most literal sense of the expression.

I shall not beg the question of the permanent end of unemployment, and will merely note here that the U.S.S.R. continued to show every sign of industrial boom at a time when the condition of the United Kingdom, and still more that of the United States, threatened recession. The combination of youthfulness with equality of opportunity and a wide variety of openings gives reality to the optimism on which Soviet ethics insist.

The conditions of the U.S.S.R. at the present day have points of resemblance to those of middle America, at the time of Horace Greeley's "Go west, young man, go west!" A vast estate, long neglected, is being opened to enterprise: and methods of exploitation, which are not new to the capitalist countries, but come with all the freshness of gigantic toys to the naïveté of young Russia, are put at its disposal. This old world of Scythians and Mongols and immemorial nomadism is transformed: and deserts and moss-covered sub-Arctic wastes are yielding their secrets, as the Oceans yielded theirs when Vasco da Gama and Columbus dared to leave the shore. What the age of discovery did for Western Europe—leaving the East untouched—the twentieth century, with its motor transport, planes and wireless, is doing for Asia, and for Russia which is its vestibule. Visitors to an earlier Russia carried away with them an ineffaceable impression of the boredom which was for ever on the lips and in the yawns of the young people of those days. There was a sort of self-contempt, bred from a sense of lack of direction. The examples and the leading were bad, and energy was frustrated. But that is changed, because youth is able to do what its self-respect approves as good, has found the service which is freedom—and because particular pains are taken to bring to the front the right men and women, a point in which the old régime failed notoriously.

The first question for every Government which would have peace and happiness at home is: what can you offer to youth? And to this question the Soviet Government has the best of answers. Life itself is become an adventure, and a hopeful one. The size and variety of the U.S.S.R., with its many peoples and languages and cultures, all frontierless and open as the United States of America for unbroken thousands of miles, provide a sensation of limitless space which neutralises the effect of the virtual prohibition of foreign travel.

The pioneering is pioneering with a difference, of course. A powerful Government travels with the emigrant and, by the might of organisation, makes possible triumphs that were beyond the reach of the unaided individual. For most of the peoples, the world has grown smaller: even in America the sense of unlimited space for development has been disappointed: only in the U.S.S.R., during the last two decades, has the world grown larger and more satisfying.

The gain is as great, by comparison with the past it is greater, for women than for men. The enormous demand for labour of every kind, but more particularly for skilled labour, for school teachers, doctors, dentists, engineers, farm managers, sea and river navigators, to which the forward policies of the Revolutionary Government have given occasion, has raised women to a new status. In 1936 over 8 million women were occupied in different branches of State, economic and cultural life. There were 184 of them in the Supreme Soviet elected in 1937.

This has been found compatible with the encouragement of motherhood—a marked contrast with the British system, in which marriage is, for the woman, a cause of exclusion from certain important occupations, particularly educational. Not only generous social services and the absence of the complex due to property, but also the social attitude towards motherhood, as a function valuable to the State, are favourable to the mother: and the house-mistress, *domokhozaika*, takes place, along with the female worker and collective farmer and employee, among honoured citizens. We are here in a region in which statistical demonstration is impossible: but I suspect that the facility for marriage and the absence of discouragements to child-bearing constitute points of real superiority in the Soviet social system over the British. Taboos of more kinds than one obstruct the frank and unbiased consideration of this subject, in which religious teachers ought to be prepared to co-operate with sociologists and doctors, statisticians and psychologists, but most of us are conscious of the presence in our midst of a phenomenon as morbid as that of the child-widow in India, and more widely spread.

Self-fulfilment in respect to all the functions of humanity is necessary to health: and love, and the child, are even more radically important than the job and the gratification of ambition. We Westerners still wear our ill-fitting fig-leaves of the law, of family and succession to property, of puritanism and romanticism, and force upon youth an external conformity from which it tends more and more to break away. In the result, because sexual ethics are not adjusted to human needs, sexual practice tends towards anarchy. That Bolshevik Russia has arrived at a perfect marriage law is very improbable. It has, in fact, made important changes in it during the last few years. But in repudiating the notion of a divine origin for rules which demonstrably lack all sanction except that of expedients for local and transient phases of society, it has cleared the ground which the West has left cluttered, and made a contribution to the wholesomeness of life.

The morals of Bolshevism are hostile both to asceticism and to dissipation. The latter is a waste, a diversion of human powers which society needs for a better purpose: and the ideal—we must use the word—is an active one, an ideal of cheerful work and cheerful play, such as Maxim Gorky envisaged when he drew his picture of Nil in *The Townsmen:* with no introspection, and no aloofness; no seeking for solitude: a life lived in public, where every man feels another shoulder next to his, and loves to feel it so. The State is a jealous State, which makes a totalitarian demand upon every faculty and every act of man, and claims to know his thoughts. There must be no escape from life, whether it takes the form of suicide, or of flight from the U.S.S.R., or of recourse to those forms of art which serve as opiates. The artists must, as Stalin once put it, be engineers of human souls. If a man seeks to walk alone, his path is an uneasy one.

❋ ❋ ❋

For those who find the adjustment to social life hard to compass, I suspect that family life, at its best, furnishes a valuable help to the growth of personality, by providing as it were a recognized escape into a more sympathetic *milieu.* It seems to be the normal field for the operation of that principle of *withdrawal and return,* to which Toynbee has pointed as a beneficent influence in life. The rehabilitation of the family, to be completed later on by the improvement of housing accommodation—still notably deficient—is a favourable influence, therefore, on the conditions of Soviet Russia.

✳   ✳   ✳

It was part of the Bolshevik code never to conceal, or slur over, a defeat or a mistake: but to drag all facts to light and analyse them, so as to win the full value of the lesson. There have been some remarkable confessions of error, of which Stalin's "Dizzy from Success" speech was perhaps the most striking. Kalinin has a particular gift for disarming opposition by these acknowledgments of mistake. "Of course we make many mistakes," said he in October, 1919, when White armies were threatening the capitals: "because we did not learn to rule before. But we cannot place at our head a wise man of another class, because he will betray us." Another confession was made by him when the policy of agricultural requisitions was changed in 1921. The people of Russia understand a confession: and it is a way of establishing brotherly relations with them which has contributed to the successes of the Soviet Government. The criticisms of Public Departments which are an almost daily feature of the Soviet Press represent the small change of the habit of confession by Government. But alongside of this frankness there are some suppressions of fact, when fact might be discouraging to national optimism, and some making of scapegoats. The full figures of the harvest of 1936, which was a partial failure, have never been published, though from our Western standpoint the failure was nature's work, not the Government's. Condemnations of the Railways, of Retail Trade, and of other departments of the administration, are generally accompanied by the statement that Trotskyist–Bukharinist–Rykovist saboteurs have had too free a hand and must be checked. The constant instilment of suspicion against enemies, unknown and only vaguely imagined, must have a deleterious effect upon national character. It is the present-day Russian equivalent for that diversion of popular anger upon the Jews which was the corresponding device in Nazi Germany. It has the excuse of civil war mentality, but it is none the less mischievous for that.

How much of individual freedom is there in the U.S.S.R.? If freedom means a share in choosing his own masters, the ordinary citizen lacks it, in spite of the Constitution of 1936. If it means security against the application of extraordinary laws and extraordinary procedure when he is charged with a political offence, he has none of it. Democracy, as I have tried to make plain elsewhere, exists only on the lower planes. A man, or a woman, may criticise the factory management or any of the party rank and file, but must keep his mouth shut about

the higher policy and the higher politicians, unless very careful soundings have been taken in advance. In the United Kingdom and the
United States it is the other way round: caution about the boss, complete freedom to say the worst of the President or the Prime Minister.

In so far as freedom means a facility for self-fulfilment, a power, as
well as a right, to pursue the ends which have his wholehearted approval, the citizen of the U.S.S.R. stands better. That there is more
planning by the State, and less planning by the individual, may cramp
the personality of the born captain of industry, who cannot reconcile
himself to placing his powers at the disposal of the community, as a
statesman or a military commander does. The man of the rank and
file has no opportunity anywhere of planning anything more than the
disposal of his own income, and not much of that. In the U.S.S.R. his
real wage is small, but he has a very high degree of economic security.
So far as we are able to judge at present, he runs no risk of mass unemployment, and the social services guarantee his subsistence in sickness
and old age. He has no need to go cap in hand to his brother-man for
work, and his factory committee (or the absence of unemployment)
protects him from wrongful dismissal. There are others with higher
wages than his, perhaps even eight or ten times as great (unless he is
one of the super-piece-workers), but there is no obtrusion of unbridled
luxury to remind him of an inferior status, and none of that swollen
wealth which represents in reality both economic and political power
over fellow-beings. He has as much (or as little) property as his Western analogue, and an equal facility for savings, and greater communal
amenities. He has opportunities for self-improvement, and may fit
himself for more important work if he has the capacity for it. He lives
in a society which honours labour, and does not honour money-
getting. The dignity of toil has a meaning here, outside of the books
of the Sunday-school moralists, and his toil is what he has to contribute
to the common pool. Sometimes, unless he is one of the "flitters," he
has a sense of ownness in his factory and his job. If he is a collective
farmer, he probably has some special task on the farm which gives him
a sense of improved status. There is a genuine significance in that
verse of the Internationale which declares that he who was naught
to-day is all. It is a life which admits of a solid self-respect, and the
power to retain self-respect is a large part of liberty.

❊   ❊   ❊

Let us consider for a moment, from the point of view of the development of personality, the change which has been made by the collectivisation of the farms in the position of the peasant. He was a man-of-

all-work, not only a cultivator and a manager of beasts, but a buyer and a seller, a man of business on a small scale. But both nature and tradition compelled him to a narrow routine. The "power of the land" was upon him, and punished every weakness with hunger. Not only must he obey the course of the seasons and adapt his minute economy to their caprices; but the ancient procedure of his fellow-toilers, partly helping, partly thwarting, but wholly restrictive, prescribed and enforced each detail of his practice.

As a member of a collective farm, he is less of an all-round manager of a tiny agricultural business and more of a specialised functionary, with no individual responsibility for the success of the concern on its business side, and no anxiety regarding debt. As before, the general lines of work are laid down. The main difference is in a certain variety in the choices of occupation which lie before him. He is no longer called upon to do a little of everything and, almost inevitably, to do some of it ill, for he is one partner in a joint task, and there is a reasonable likelihood that different parts of it will be allotted according to capacity and liking.

There is room for difference of opinion as to the way in which this change may be expected to work. Expressed in one sentence, it is a change to specialisation of function: accompanied by a sharing of the burden of financial responsibility. Leisure, or at all events a measure of freedom from responsibility, seems more likely now than before. The fact that there is more scope for choice seems to me to favour the development of personality.

❊　　❊　　❊

And now as to the place of the citizen in the world of politics. He must keep his mouth shut about the higher policy; and the desire to open it on this subject is likely to be speedily suppressed, when it takes a more determined form than ordinary grumbling. One of the consequences of the ubiquity of the Party is that discontent is discovered and nipped in the bud. There is grumbling, of course, when things for one cause or another go amiss, and sometimes there is discontent of a more serious kind. What happens to the man or woman who dares to become a mouthpiece on such occasions? The answer is to be sought in the history of the series of judicial trials and administrative expulsions and dismissals which continued between 1936 and 1938. The protest may have so much popular support behind it, or may so commend itself to superior authority by its evident reasonableness, that the particular wrong will be amended. We see this happening in the occasional unexpected interventions of Stalin himself, to support a person aggrieved by the conduct of an intermediate authority: and in the occasional dramatic reversals of a course of action which has created a general sense of injustice. There is an element of luck, almost an element of caprice, in these instances of successful resistance: the same kind of luck, the same kind of caprice, which we naturally associate with every despotic system, with Haroun-al-Rashid making his midnight visitations in Bagdad, with the disguised Kalinin making purchases of bad soap in a careless store. Otherwise, the man who has the courage to take a stand apart from or ahead of his group, and to assert his own canon of right and wrong, or is suspected of having it, is likely to be victimised.

He is victimised in other countries beside the U.S.S.R., but the terrible charges of counter-revolutionary activity, or of association with Trotskyist-Bukharinist-Rykovist spies and traitors, which serve as heavy artillery against the rebel mentality in the U.S.S.R., and involve a virtual excommunication, are not available to crush resistance, and sympathy with resistance, in the United Kingdom or in the United States.

The worst of these thunders are certainly reserved for persons who occupy responsible positions, and for the managing group. If the rank and file of the workers were generally endangered by the Terror, the régime would be in peril. It is because they are confident that the scourge is directed against offending Communists, or against the technical intelligentsia, that they remain indifferent to it, and even manifest sympathy with the executioners.

The modern intelligentsia is no longer the sedentary, literary, philosophising discussion circle of a Russian Bloomsbury. In the early twentieth century that type was already being supplemented or replaced by a technical intelligentsia, brought into existence by the needs of incipient industrialisation. At the present day it is largely of proletariat or peasant origin, trained in the schools and technicums of the Revolutionary period: and it ranges from the doctor, the agronomist, the schoolmaster, the engineer and the manager, to the white-collared (or black-coated) workers, who keep the books and do the clerical work. But despite the quick passage, both upward and downward, which characterises Soviet life, and the general spread of education—levelling distinctions—the difference between the brain-worker and the manual worker continues to assert itself, and continues to be something tangible and recognisable. Fraulein Koerber gives us a glimpse of it in her account of the investigation into factory conditions by what was then the Workers' and Peasants' Inspectorate.

"Workmen don't mind this inquisition. They just confess to mistakes. But an intellectual thinks it is terrible to be spied upon and questioned and called to account." And a doctor comments upon this: "*No citizens of the Soviet Union have private lives.*" The sensitiveness of the old intelligentsia has been inherited by the new: and it is the symbol of a separation from the rank and file. This explains why the Terror was not a Terror for the latter. As regards the principal delinquents, the leaders of the "Trotskyist–Bukharinist–Rykovist–*bourgeois*–nationalist—counter-revolutionary" conspiracies, the people accepted with a religious faith what the newspapers told them, and clamoured— long before the trials were completed and the accused found guilty— for the blood of the traitors. There were signs, at one moment, of a reawakening of the old Russian pitifulness, which could not bear the execution of criminals by formal sentence of Court: but these were rapidly organised out of existence by a nation-wide demonstration of gratitude to the political police. As to the minor offenders in industry and agriculture, there was no sense of unity between them and the rank and file. I have dwelt upon this subject here in order to explain my own conclusion that fear has not affected the psychology of the masses. But the impression is given that when anything goes wrong, no matter what the cause, scapegoats will be found and sacrificed without mercy, and that any general movement of sympathy for the victim will be diverted by a barrage of organised propaganda: vilification of the accused, or glorification of the instruments of his punishment, or both; and that not one man, just and tenacious of purpose, will dare to stand firm against the people taught to clamour for the predetermined sentence.

The terrifying efficiency of organised propaganda, eliminating truth by calculated suppression and misrepresentation, and dinning the prescribed formulas into the ears of millions prepared for their reception by universal education, is ominous of a more complete regimentation than any merely negative censorship. The Tsars only played with the control of thought: their worthy and somewhat somnolent (not to say thick-headed) censors passed the most transparently subversive suggestions. The greatest innovation of the Bolsheviks in the "bears' corners" of old Russia is an efficient administration. Their orders go right through to the bottom. They have harnessed the writers and artists themselves to their censorship: they have secured an effective monopoly of truth, and filled the market with their own brand of the article, and the smuggler of the precious commodity has little chance of competition with merchants in whom all powers are concentrated.

I must not leave this subject of propaganda without a *caveat* against the assumption that it has no analogue in the West. There are some uncomfortable things to be said about the domination of private interests there also. Outside of the newspapers (as well as in them) Western propaganda takes the form of commercial advertisement. It stares from every hoarding, loads every postman, and, in the United States, even occupies a portion of the ether. Taking this Western propaganda in the mass, it immensely exceeds that of the U.S.S.R., and its aims are more blatantly sectional or selfish. However, propaganda in the U.S.S.R. has the uniform aim of confirming the foundations of a Socialist state: and it lacks the saving virtue of self-contradiction.

It is plain that man is *at school* with the Communist Party in the U.S.S.R., and is being taught, supposedly for his own good, a particular set of lessons: and that the process involves the employment of nearly the whole machinery of art and literature, press, radio and platform. Other systems of government, and other social or religious systems, have attempted a similar control. What differentiates the Communist system is the greater thoroughness with which it postpones liberty of thought to a scheme of human happiness—or perhaps I should say, of human justice. It would seem that the deliberate intention to remake man upon a new pattern inevitably postulates, in a greater or less degree, such a restriction of liberty, and that the restriction can only be brought to an end when the remaking is complete.

To what extent are breaches in this monopoly of access to the mind of man suffered to exist? The Churches are discouraged, and have no right to spread their teaching. The national cultures and languages, on the other hand, are encouraged, and might make some breach in the panoply of Communistic teaching: but it is insisted that culture shall be socialist in content, even though it be national in form. The film is almost purely propagandist. The visiting of foreign countries, once the source of a large part of the education of a whole class, is rarely permitted. The presence in the U.S.S.R., for extended periods, of foreign subjects is almost entirely prohibited, and there is increasing strictness in respect to visas even for temporary visitors. But the schools teach at least one foreign language, and the classics of all tongues are published in hundreds of thousands, with no apparent restriction upon content. With certain exceptions—for instance, those of Count Tolstoi's writings which directly preach anarchy—there is no ban upon the classics of Russian and other Soviet national literature: and of these, too, hundreds of thousands of copies are published. Regarding the Soviet national literature of to-day, there was a considerable degree of freedom in the period preceding the epoch of the Plans. Between 1928 and 1932—that is to say, before the return of Maxim Gorky to the U.S.S.R. —the Association of Proletarian writers ruled with a rod of iron, and insisted upon the appropriate literature of the Plan: so that a knowledge of cement-mixing and paper-making and of the principles of retail supply became for the Soviet writer an important accomplishment. The milder yoke of Socialist Realism, which means little more than a roseate outlook upon the achievement and the promise of the U.S.S.R., succeeded to these four years of rigorous social demand. But in 1937 artist after artist fell victim to new criteria of idea and performance. What I have said of literature is equally true of the drama and of dramatic production, in which some old favourites fell into disrepute for reasons at which I have sometimes been unable to guess. In all this an element of caprice and unforeseeability makes itself apparent.

I think it probable that the artist has never been wholly free. He has always stood in need of a patron. Whether his patron was a Greek City State, or a Renaissance Pope, or a British merchant desiring to perpetuate his virtues in a flamboyant dedication, or his bodily properties in a picture or a statue, or a first-night public in quest of a mild pornography to soothe brains wearied by office and counter, he had to accept orders. But sometimes a Benvenuto Cellini played the part of a spoiled child of genius, and insisted upon his own way even against a king; or a Thucydides wrote history to be a possession of all men for ever; a John Bunyan wrote his *Pilgrim's Progress* in Bedford jail out of pure zeal; a Fra Angelico painted, on his knees, the saints as the spirit showed them to him. How much of work such as this would find its way into existence against an inquisition so all-pervading as that of the U.S.S.R.—for an inquisition it is—I cannot pretend to guess. There would certainly be less of it, and some of it would be diverted into less spontaneous channels. The world would be the poorer for the loss of it. The artist and the thinker help man to know himself. If personality grows partly by man's knowledge of himself and of his surroundings, every diminution of the freedom of artist and thinker must tend to retard its growth.

Here we arrive at the most serious criticism which I have to make of the Soviet Government. A few, a very few, persons in every age and every country, possess the gift of adding to man's knowledge of himself and of the world in which he lives, of scattering the living seed of thought and understanding. To take away the wings of the artist and the thinker is to incur the danger of an arrested civilisation. This is not, of course, the Bolshevik view. Thought is conceived as conditioned by social and economic relations, and the individual expresses only what these relations have put into his mind. The deed comes first, and the thought comes after. There will be change in the thought when existing contradictions have resulted in a new synthesis of the relations.

And yet—man is capable of making his own history. This, if not pure Marxism, is at least pure Marxism as understood in Russia: and the idea has been as the blast of a trumpet, summoning sluggard men to battle. How to harmonise it with the rival conception that the deed came first and the thought came after, let philosophers dispute. Somehow the lion has contrived to lie down with the lamb, and Hercules of the Seven Labours has been able to identify himself with the fatalist. I can only, in all diffidence, suggest that it is the dialectical element in materialism which has made the miracle possible: while continuing to cherish a private conviction of my own that the Russian is not a philosopher at all, but rather one who uses all the philosophies to justify a moral passion for the regeneration of mankind, and the fulfilment of the Messianic mission of Moscow. This is why there is no real danger of this people becoming obsessed by dogma, despite the rigidity of their quasi-philosophers. When they find that a rule does not fit life, they give the preference to life: in other words, fall back upon more primitive and enduring convictions. Their gift for breaking rules will save them from being pedantic. For the same reason Planning will not hurt them: for they will change the Plan whenever it has gone amiss. This is what has been called "the broad Slavonic nature." But it is not race that has made it. The illimitable spaces of Europasia —there is no line of distinction between the two continents or between Mongol and Slav, they mingle naturally and imperceptibly—have created the tolerance and the all-humanitarianism in a melting-pot of peoples. There was room for all.

On this note I close. It is not the satisfying note of prophecy; but rather one of confidence in the character which these conditions must create, when they enter into alliance with the new conviction that man is able to make his own history. Fate gave to this people a great inheritance; and they have learned to believe that they can dominate it.

APPENDICES

I. Census of 1939

No detailed Census report has been published. But it is known that the figure of total population is 170 millions, and that subsequent additions of territory raised it to about 190 millions before the outbreak of war in June, 1941. The particulars given below are of the 170 millions shown by the Census.

The town population was 17.9% of the whole in 1926, and 32.8% of the whole in 1939. The rural population showed an absolute decrease of 6 millions. These facts reflect the progress of industrialisation.

Of the 170 millions, sixty-one are children under fifteen, and seventy-one are men and women between fifteen and thirty-nine. Youthfulness is thus a characteristic of the population. Over 45% of the population are under twenty years of age.

88.2% of the males, and 66.6% of the females, are literate.

49.73% of the population are workers by hand and brain in urban and rural areas. 46.9% are collective farmers and co-operative handworkers, 2.6% are individual farmers and hand-workers. The proportion not occupied in any gainful employment is 0.04%.

The northern nomads known as Nentsi (formerly called Samoyeds) co-operated well in the Census and travelled down to meet the enumerators. This evidence of co-operation with the régime is of interest.

II. Budget of 1937

(All figures in millions of roubles.)

REVENUE

1. Turn-over tax				76,795
Including: Heavy Industry			8,860	
Light "			11,382	
Food "			20,387	
Spirits "			6,190	
Committee for collection of agricultural products			24,106	
State Trade			2,605	
2. Deductions from profits				6,304
Including: Heavy Industry			1,331	
Light "			829	
Timber "			37	
Food "			1,800	
Local "			542	
Undertakings of Agricultural Department			40	

II. Budget of 1937—Continued

Ditto of State Farms Department	30
Rail Transport	687
Undertakings of department of Internal trade ..	175
Committee for collection of agricultural products	58
Undertakings of department of external trade ..	37
State credit institutions	245
Organs of State Insurance	319
Other disbursements	170

3. Income tax and other taxes on undertakings and organisations:

(a) Tax on non-trading operations	390	
(b) Income tax on collective farms	530	
(c) Tax on State farms	46	
(d) Others	6	
Total		972

4. Receipts from State Insurance		3,700
5. State loans:		
(a) By subscription	4,375	
(b) Savings banks	1,200	
(c) From State Insurance	400	
Total		5,975
6. Direct taxes:		
(a) Agricultural tax from collective farmers and individual peasants	650	
(b) Town tax for cultural needs	1,465	
(c) Village tax for ditto	530	
Total		2,645
7. Other revenue:		
(a) Import duties	860	
(b) Revenue from coinage	15	
(c) " " timber	180	
(d) Miscellaneous	622	
Total		1,677
Grand total of Revenue		98,069

EXPENDITURE

A. State Economy:		
Industry		12,397
Including: Heavy Industry	5,217	
Defence "	2,328	
Light "	1,603	
Timber "	1,274	
Food "	1,042	
Local "	375	
Cinema "	163	
Agriculture		9,059
Under Commissariat of State Farms	2,064	

II. Budget of 1937—*Continued*

Under Commissariat of Agriculture	6,790	
Grant for mineral fertilisers	205	
Transport and communications		8,533
Including: Commissariat of Communications	4,698	
Ditto of Water Transport	1,133	
Northern Sea Route	580	
Roads (Commissariat of Internal Affairs)	831	
Civil Air Fleet	301	
State trade, supply and collecting organisations		3,035
Commissariat of external trade		19
Committee of Reserves		1,697
Moscow Metro		458
Hydro-meteorological service		128
Miscellaneous		3,875
Total of State Economy		39,585
B. Social and Cultural Measures		26,604
(a) On State budget direct	10,870	
(b) Through local budgets	15,734	
Including:		
(1) Education	18,270	
(a) On State budget direct 7,842		
(b) Through local budgets 10,428		
(2) Health	7,528	
(a) On State budget direct 2,472		
(b) Through local budgets 5,055		
(3) Physical culture	97	
(a) On State budget direct 44		
(b) Through local budgets 53		
(4) Protection of labour	710	
(a) On State budget direct 511		
(b) Through local budgets 199		
C. Commissariat of Defence		20,102
D. " " Internal Affairs		2,699
E. " " Justice and Procuration		149
F. Administration		1,618
G. State Loans		2,579
H. Banks of long-term investment		1,382
J. Reserve funds of Union and constituent Republics		1,855
K. Miscellaneous		544
Grand total of expenditure		97,119
Excess of revenue over expenditure		950
Total		98,069

I have not full details of the budgets of the years following 1937.
The following abstracts show, in milliards of roubles, rapidly rising
proportions and totals of expenditure on defence.

The abstract for 1938 provided for a total expenditure of 121, of which 23 was for defence (19%).

The abstract for 1939 provided for a total expenditure of 154, of which 40 was for defence (26%).

The abstract for 1940 provided for a revenue of 184, and an expenditure of 180, of which defence accounted for 57, nearly one-third, and culture and health for 43.

The abstract for 1941 was:—

Revenue 216, including:		Expenditure 215, including:	
Turnover-taxes	124	Industry	39
Assessment of profits	31	Agriculture	13
State Insurance	10	Transport and communica-	
M.T.S. income	2.6	tions	6.5
State loans	13	Education	26.6
Taxes and duties levied on		Health	11
population	12	Social maintenance	3.4
		Defence and Navy	71

The expenditure on defence and Navy exceeds that of 1940 by 26.3%. It is nearly one-third of the whole: though the whole includes expenditure on industry and agriculture.

III. What the Industrial Wage in the U.S.S.R. could Purchase in 1937-38

Stalin told the 18th Party Congress that the annual average wage of the industrial worker amounted to 66 roubles per week in 1938. An addition, certainly a larger proportion than in pre-war London, is to be made to this sum to arrive at the family earnings, because of the extensive employment of women. Colin Clark's calculation of 23 dependents to 19 workers gives approximately $1\frac{1}{5}$ dependent to each worker. I take a statistically average family as consisting of two workers and $2\frac{2}{5}$ dependents, total $4\frac{2}{5}$. The wage will be 112 roubles per week, if 70% of the principal wage be allowed as the wage of the second worker.

They will pay

R. 0.75 in income tax.

R. 2.25 in State loan (virtually compulsory).

R. 2.65 in house rent (4% of the wage of the principal earner).

The two wage-earners must be assumed to take twelve mid-day meals in the factory canteen, since factory feeding has in recent years been made compulsory. The cheapest meal consists of a bowl of soup, of the solid Russian type, made from cabbage and potatoes, with bread. The newspaper *Industriya* gives 0.78 rouble as the price. I deduct from the income R. 9.36 on this score, and also R. 1.20 for tram fares, assuming 5 kopeks per journey for twenty-four journeys. This leaves R. 96 out of the wage of the two workers.

The following food prices are quoted from newspaper statements at various dates in 1937 and 1938, and at various places on the main railway lines in European Russia:—

Black bread. R. 0.83-0.85 per kilo. A kilogram is a little over 2.2 lb.

Rye and wheat flour (evidently of superior quality). R. 1.30-4.40 per kilo at Kharkov.

Wheat flour. R. 1-1.50 per kilo at Armavir.

Potatoes (perhaps a wholesale price). R. 0.40-0.65 per kilo at Armavir.

Lard. R. 13-14 per kilo at Moscow.

Butter. R. 15-17 per kilo at Moscow. R. 15-24 per kilo at Armavir.

Milk. Prices varying from R. 1.20 to R. 1.75 per litre, at Leningrad, Moscow and Armavir. A litre is a small fraction over a quart.

Eggs. Prices varying from R. 0.30 to R. 0.45 each at Kalinin (the old Tver) and Armavir.

Sugar. Prices varying from R. 3.50 to R. 4.50 per kilo.

Cabbage. R. 1 per kilo at Moscow.

Other food prices of 1937 and 1938 for which I have no record of the documentary authority are:—

Pork. R. 10-11.50 per kilo.

Salt Herrings. R. 8-9 per kilo.

Cucumbers. R. 0.40 per kilo.

Margarine. R. 12-14 per kilo.

Tea. R. 60 per kilo.

Beef. Second quality, R. 8-10 per kilo.

It will be seen at a glance that tea and meat are beyond the reach of the average wage-earner as a part of the normal diet. It is evident that he does not use lard, or butter, or margarine. I have little doubt that the fat he does use is sunflower and hemp oil, both comparatively cheap. These, together with black bread, potatoes, cucumbers, cabbage, milk and eggs, and perhaps salt herring, are the articles of food ordinarily within his reach.

A warning must be given against the practice of certain writers (e.g., of Paul Haensel in "The Public Finance of the U.S.S.R.," published in *Tax Magazine*, 1938) of translating rouble prices into their American or English equivalent, on the basis of the officially fixed rate of exchange. The rouble is enormously over-valued, and the prices arrived at by this method are very misleading. Jacob Miller, who lived for a year in Moscow in 1937, calculated it to be worth 2d.* for the purchase of clothing, 3d.-4d. for food bought in shops, 4d.-5d. for canteen meals. In 1935 and 1937 the traveller found it pretty safe to assume that his rouble had a purchasing power of 2d. or 2½d., though he had acquired it at a cost five times as great.

A kilogram of bread per diem is not more than a sufficient ration for a working adult. But since the adults get bread with the factory meal, and the children probably get it with their school meal, I shall allow half a kilo for each of the individuals, adult and non-adult, making:—

15½ kilos for the week: cost at R. 0.85 per kilo	R. 13.20
Half of that quantity of potatoes at R. 0.65 per kilo	R. 5.0
Food other than bread, on the basis of Colin Clark's estimate......	R. 24.0
Fuel on the same basis	R. 4.0
Light	R. 4.0
Total	R. 50.20

Jacob Miller, to whose personal experiences in Moscow throughout a year of employment in the office of the Planning Commission much weight must be attached, calculates that in 1937-38 a Moscow worker's family would consist of two earners and three dependents, total five persons: and that its expenditure at London prices would amount to about 42 shillings per week. That is a trifle above the *London Life and Labour* poverty line of 38s.-41s. His calculation of "income" allows, over and above wage, for "other income," which means un-avowed payments by factory management in order to secure labour which is in scant supply. He puts the family income at 120 roubles a week, including this "other income," and not including social benefit, classified under the head of social wage.

IV. Taxation of the Peasant in Kind and in Cash

The principal authorities consulted by me on this subject (all in Russian) are:—

Financial and Economic Manual of Information of the Collective Farm: compiled by E. M. Gailis, S. S. Maslov, and N. P.

* The English penny—1d.—worth 2 U.S. cents at pre-war par of exchange, probably had a purchasing power, as regards manual workers' expenditure, equivalent to something over 3 cents in the United States. *Ed.*

Sidelkin. State Publishing House of Collective and State-farm literature. Moscow, 1936.

Agriculture of the U.S.S.R. Annual. Volume 1935. Edited by A. I. Muralov and others. Published by the same State Publishing House. Moscow, 1936.

Money Impost on the Income of Collective Farms. By Liubarsky and Khmelev. State Finance Publishing Department. Moscow, 1937.

Socialist Construction. Annual volumes published in 1935 and 1936. (No later publication to date.)

By far the greater proportion of the taxation of the peasant of to-day is in kind, and takes the form of compulsory deliveries paid for at a very low conventional price. This is officially described as a "compulsory sale in the nature of a tax." The relation of the conventional price to the actual value cannot be determined by ordinary methods, because there is no wholesale trade in the produce other than that conducted by the Government itself, and it would be obviously inappropriate (even if it were in practice feasible) to make use of the retail prices at which the peasants dispose of their small available balances in the collective markets and elsewhere. I have therefore taken the prices at which the Government passes the produce on to its own departments (such as the Commissariats of Food and Export Trade) as representing the wholesale prices which the peasants might hope to obtain in a non-socialist economy. On this basis they obtain, for their compulsory deliveries of cereals, about one-eighth of the wholesale price.

When the system of agricultural taxation in cash which prevailed during the period of the New Economic Policy was brought to an end by the closure of the free market in grain, and by changes in the value of money which destroyed the fiscal significance of the "single agricultural tax," the Soviet Government reverted to what was virtually a system of requisition under the name of "contracting." In January, 1933, this system was replaced by the levy in kind on the more important agricultural products, which continues to-day: and the markets were opened for the free sale of the balance by the peasants. The demand is not for a fractional share of the product, but for a stated quantity per unit; the quantity varying, in the case of cereals, in different parts of the country within limits represented by the figures 1 to 5: with provision for reduction, and even for remission, in the case of serious failure, but otherwise rigidly fixed. The unit on which the levy is calculated was not, in 1934-35, the unit actually cultivated, but the unit planned for cultivation. Thus, an acre of planned cultivation with grain in the Crimea was assessed to a compulsory delivery four or five times as great as an acre planned for grain in the North of Russia or in the Trans-Caucasus territory: with a score of intermediate charges in other areas. In all cases the tax-payer received, in 1936, 120-130 roubles per metric ton for wheat, and 60-100 for rye and the cheaper cereals—which is about one-eighth of the wholesale price as defined above. If we call the compulsory delivery of cereals x, the tax upon the peasant under this head was ⅞ x.

Since cereal cultivation still accounts for three-quarters of the whole of Russian agriculture, we shall reach an estimate of the burden of taxation in kind upon the peasant, if we are able to ascertain what ⅞ x was in 1934 and 1935.

A similar system was applied also to potatoes, sunflower and fodder grasses. The price paid for potatoes in 1935 was 40 roubles per metric ton, and that for sunflower seed 80-150 roubles. The individualist peasants, who have not accepted collectivisation, were penalised by a higher levy. There was also a higher levy in Central Asia for irrigated land, which is naturally expected to produce a higher yield.

The demand applies equally to the crops grown by collective farmers on their own yards or garden plots and, in the case of potatoes, was levied on them at a higher rate than on the collectivised lands, though not at so high a rate as on the individualist peasants.

Other taxes in kind were levied upon meat, milk and wool, but not on skins: and collective farms, collective farmers (in respect to the animals kept in their own yards) and individualist peasants, were all liable for these imposts. Deliveries of meat might be made, alternatively, in live animals: namely, in large horned cattle, sheep, pigs, rabbits, hens, geese, ducks and guinea fowls. Within the collective farms there are sub-farms for the charge of animals, in order to fix the responsibility for them: and each such sub-farm must deliver a prescribed weight in respect to each brood animal; and each collective farm household must also deliver a stated weight. For the sub-farms, the rates were: 30 kilo. for each cow, 120 for every brood sow, and 8 for every ewe of one year and more; reduced by one-third in Central Asia, the Trans-Caucasus, the Far East and Kazakstan. The rate of payment by Government was 1½ roubles per kilogram. The obligation to deliver milk was scaled at the highest figure for the dairying villages in the provinces of Leningrad and Moscow, where individualist peasants were required to deliver as much as 250 litres (that is to say 255 quarts) annually for each cow, with lower rates for collective farmers. The conventional price was approximately 8-12 kopeks per quart. The rate of delivery for wool ran up as high as 3½ kilos for collective farms and collective farmers, and to 4 kilos for individualist peasants, for each merino sheep of the best breed. I have no information of the conventional prices paid for wool by the Government: but all these items of animal produce are on a similar footing, as parts of a tax-in-kind on which there was no pretence of paying more than a fraction of the full value.

There remain the "technical" crops—cotton, flax, sugar-beet, hemp, tobacco, coarse tobacco (*makhorka*)—which continue to be dealt with by a system of so-called "contracting." The purchaser being the monopolist state, but a monopolist state which has, for the present at all events, an unlimited need of these products, prices are determined by the consideration that a motive is to be given to the peasant for adequate attention to them. Cultivation is encouraged by premium prices for deliveries in excess of contract: and by particularly high prices in areas where the crop is a novelty. Thus, sugar-beet was priced at 60 roubles per metric ton in the Far East, in Georgia and Armenia, and 50 roubles in the Kirgiz and Kazak constituent republics: but at half or less than half these prices where the crop was well established. The prices paid for cleaned cotton ranged, according to quality, from 805 to 1,758 roubles per ton for American, and from 1,560, to 3,960 for Egyptian. Flax ranged from 2,000 to 4,000 roubles per ton.

I lack all data for comparing these conventional Government prices for technical crops with the prices at which the Government passes on the produce to its industrial departments. On April 20, 1938, cotton was selling at 9.05 cents per pound at New Orleans, or roughly 200 dollars per metric ton. If the rouble is worth 6 cents, 200 dollars represents a price of 3,333 roubles, nearly double the conventional price paid by the Government of the U.S.S.R. for cleaned cotton of the American type. Thus the price for cotton was far more favourable to the peasant than was the price for cereals: and I suspect that the case would be found to be similar with the technical crops. There was, and is, a definite policy of high payment for crops of this category.

I turn back to the calculation of the burden on cereals and to the ascertainment of the value of ⅞x in 1934 and 1935.

Official figures enable me to state with *almost* arithmetical correctness the proportion of the cereal crop of the collective farms which was delivered to Government in discharge of the obligation of "sale in the nature of tax."

1930.	1931.	1932.	1933.	1934.	1935.
27.5%	36.8%	27.5%	21.6%	19.5%	19.4% (approx.)

As the new system of taxation was introduced from 1933, I take the average of the three latest years, which is just over 20%.

I wish that I could claim that 20% $= x$. Unfortunately the official figures combine repayment of seed loans with compulsory deliveries, and I have no means of dividing the two. I can only say that it is improbable that in any particular year the repayment of seed loans exceeded 5% of the total: and then fix x tentatively at 19%. Thus I make ⅞ x $= 16.6\%$, and suggest that this percentage of the gross cereal crop goes in taxation in kind.

There still remains a source of error. For, the demand being not a particular fraction of the whole, but a fixed amount per unit, the larger the harvest the smaller the proportion. If the harvest of 1937 was anything like as good as is reported, the tax burden on cereals in that year was proportionately less than 16.6%, and may even have been down to 12% or 13%. This would bring it very near to the average of land revenue and cesses in British India. As to the non-cereal products, in the absence of data for precise calculations I can only say that I feel sure that the burden of them was lighter than on cereals, because the conventional price paid to the peasants was higher, as indicated by the figures for cotton.

There remain the cash taxes, which are specified in the Budget (Appendix II); the income tax on collective farms, introduced on July 30, 1926, and replacing the former cash tax calculated on the planned savings of the current year, which fell with undue severity on cereals; the agricultural tax on collective farmers in respect to their yards or garden plots, and on individualist peasants; and the village tax for local purposes: which, taken together, figure in the budget for 1937 at 1,710 million roubles. This is rather more than 7% of the amount derived from the Committee for the collection of agricultural products (see Appendix II), which represents the difference between Government's payments to peasants, and the credits taken against the processing and trading departments. It will suffice to raise our figure of 16.6 to 17.9% in order to arrive at the approximate direct burdens upon the peasant in a year not differing greatly from the triennium 1933, 1934, 1935.

A change in the method of rural taxation was made in 1939-40. In

lieu of an assessment varying according to the area of planned cultivation, the Soviet Government adopted the system of varying the
assessment according to the potential culturable area of each farm.
I can make this statement clearer by saying that the collective farm
was to pay in accordance with what it was capable of doing, rather
than what it actually proposed to do. But in distributing the assessment over the farms, the Government aimed only at getting the same
aggregate of products as before, though by a changed method. It
seems unlikely, therefore, that my calculation of the proportions taken
by the Government is disturbed by the change.

Baykov is quoted by Dobb as arriving at the figure of 15% for a
typical collective farm in 1938. I have pointed out already that the
figure for the earlier years was liable to variation according to the
volume of the crop. If the reader concludes that the compulsory
delivery of crop is something like 15-18% of the gross yield (not including, of course, the extra deliveries on account of the service done
by the M.T.S.), but that the collective farm which has a considerable
area of technical crop, beet, flax, or cotton, bears a lighter burden than
this, he will probably get as near to the truth as Soviet statistics will
permit.

General taxation is almost entirely indirect, and, in so far as the
peasant is a purchaser of commodities, he pays this general indirect
taxation in addition to 15-18% of direct. Must we infer that he is
unfairly carrying a double burden? If we regard him as the proprietor
of the land, entitled to the use of it without paying any equivalent
of rent, the answer to this question is, Yes. But this conclusion would
lead very far. Since the value of the land differs enormously, according
to climate, soil, and access to markets, the right to the use of it without payment would involve inequalities of fortune, unearned by personal effort, incompatible with a Socialist society.

What is wrong with the fiscal system of the U.S.S.R., in respect to
land, is not that the average impost is excessive or that the peasant
pays a double share of taxation, but that the range of differentiation
(from one to five) is inadequate for a country so vast as the U.S.S.R.,
and that the provision for failures and partial failures is insufficiently
elastic. The Government has been very generous with its advances for
agricultural purposes: arrears of repayment are a constant subject of
complaint: and arrears have twice recently been remitted by general
orders, which apparently ignored local conditions.

Theoretically the individualist peasant pays considerably more than
the quantities levied upon the collective farm. The excess is far greater

than the 10% which is usually cited by Soviet officials, as may be seen by reference to any of the notifications reproduced in the *Financial and Economic Manual*. But I think it doubtful whether the whole of the excess is actually collected. It is far less easy to discover the cultivation of an individualist, who does not, ex *hypothesi*, employ the Machine Tractor Station. At least a part of the excess is an insurance against concealment. On April 19, 1938, the Council of People's Commissars animadverted on these irregularities. They said that the individualist peasants use their horses for the private carrying trade and must henceforth pay a horse tax: that they do not deliver meat to the State, and their obligations are often transferred to the collective farms, which are more amenable: and they are often engaged to labour on collective lands at rates of pay higher than those of the "work days" received by collective farmers.

V. Other Obligations of the Peasant

Apart from taxation, the Collectives sell, at a price fixed substantially above that for compulsory deliveries, part of their produce to co-operative organisations, in consideration of the supply of manufactured commodities on favourable terms. This was a very small item in 1932 and 1933. In each of the years 1934 and 1935 it amounted to 3½ million tons—less than a quarter of the amount of the compulsory deliveries. From the year 1938 the price paid by the Co-operatives for this grain varies very widely, according to the amounts delivered: a higher price per unit being paid for a larger quantity. The price, at its highest, is much below what I have assumed to be equivalent to a wholesale price in a free market: but, so far as wholesale purchases are concerned, Government and the Co-operatives are monopolists: and it is probable that the collectives could not find retail purchases for the whole of their surplus. If we could be sure that the alternative of sale in the open market actually existed—which is unlikely in areas distant from consuming centres—it would be possible to infer from these sales, at a low price, to Co-operative institutions in return for the supply of commodities, that the "scissors" was very wide open against the growers of food and raw materials, and that they were therefore glad of every opportunity of obtaining manufactured goods on reasonable terms.

A milling charge of 10-12%, which was levied on all grain brought to the State mills, has been recently abolished.

The report of the People's Commissar of Agriculture in January, 1938, showed that the bulk of the ploughing in 1937 was done for the collective farms by the Machine Tractor Stations. The proportions were nearly two-thirds of the ploughing for spring crops, including both the preliminary winter ploughing and the ploughing before the sowing: and more than three-quarters of the ploughing for winter crops. In 1935 the M.T.S. did a sixth of the spring sowing, a fifth of the winter sowing, nearly a quarter of the harvesting of grain, nearly half of the harvesting of sugar-beet, and more than half of the threshing of cereals. They did no cotton-picking and practically none of the harvesting of flax. Except in ploughing and threshing, the greater part of the operations of agriculture is still not mechanised, and half of the traction power is still animal.

The services of the M.T.S. have been paid in kind since 1933, and in varying fractions of the total crop. On cereals and sunflower, the fraction is a smaller one in the case of a smaller crop, a larger one in the case of a larger crop.

Some figures given by Otto Schiller and reproduced by Miss Warriner in *Economics of Peasant Farming*, Chapter IX, convey the erroneous impression of excessive taxation of the peasant, because they combine payments to the M.T.S. (which are payments for services rendered) with tax payments, and also because the percentages have been wrongly calculated or wrongly copied. I reproduce the table below, with the percentages correctly calculated. The figures are in millions of hundred-weights.

	1932.	1933.	1934.	1935.
1. Harvest in the ear	1,334	1,714	1,706	1,756
2. Grain losses in harvesting	341	492	408	324
3. Harvest in granary	993	1,222	1,298	1,432
4. Sales and deliveries by collective farms, including payments to M.T.S. as well as tax payments to the State	376	481	538	601
5. Percentage of (4) on (1)	28	28	32	34
6. Percentage of (4) on (3)	38	40	41	42

Schiller thinks that, in a plentiful year, the charge made by the M.T.S. amounted to more than 20%. But in the aggregate the deliveries to the M.T.S. for work done make a much smaller proportion than this. There are now nearly 6,000 M.T.S., but there are still many farms not served by them, or only partially served. In 1935 a shortage of gasoline interfered with the completion of winter ploughing. If the charge upon the harvest on account of work done by the M.T.S. should ever reach the general level of 20%, it will still be much lower than the proportion charged in the period of N.E.P. by the private persons who then made a practice of hiring out their animals and implements to the poorer peasants.

Another charge upon the peasant, which cannot be classified with taxation, is the compulsory insurance of his house. A peasant's house upon which the insurance charges remain unpaid for three years is forfeited to the Government. This is a measure designed to provide against the ruinous consequences of fires among mainly wooden buildings.

VI. An Account of Rural Conditions near Voronezh at the Beginning of the Twentieth Century

The Soviet Government has republished a volume which forms an impressive record of rural conditions in the Black-Earth zone in the neighbourhood of Voronezh at the beginning of this century.

A certain Dr. Shingarev, employed by the Voronezh Provincial Council, supervised a local investigation, and published a report of it in a brochure to which he gave the name of *The Dying Village*. His description of two villages on the river-bank is of great value to the economic historian, though he deliberately omits from it all information about the local gentry and what he calls the "large-scale economy" of their business affairs, which, it is obvious, played a considerable part in the lives of the peasantry of the neighbourhood.

There was a school building capable of holding a hundred pupils and even a few boarders, but it was poorly attended, and, whoever it was who presented the building, he did not complete his gift by providing any books or educational apparatus, nor did the *Zemstvo* itself, it seems, think of making such arrangements.

Reading between the lines, I guess that the employee of a local body, who found occasion to criticise the impoverished circumstances of the people and the inadequacy of their holdings, was judiciously taciturn about the rich proprietor who enjoyed the rents and proceeds of the "large-scale economy."

The family had held the property since A.D. 1619, and it was one of their earliest acquisitions on the River Don. They were probably nonresident. All particulars about ecclesiastics, church servants, and the few town craftsmen who lived in the villages, are also excluded from the report.

The description is very minute, but I have summarised its main features in the paragraphs which follow, because of the light which it throws on the life of the peasant of the Black-Earth zone in the beginning of the twentieth century. Two adjoining villages are concerned, one of which was economically somewhat better off than the other; but, for the sake of brevity, I have made no distinction between the two.

They lie on the left bank of the Don, 16 miles from the town of Voronezh, where the nearest railway station is, and they are close to a main road. For this and other reasons (particularly the amount of outside employment which the people obtained) they were not typical rural villages. At the Census of 1897, there were 161 households with 1063 persons. They were Orthodox Great Russians, but they were collected together by a proclamation of the proprietors inviting tenants to present themselves, and they were of various origin. This proclamation probably dated from the early eighteenth century. At the Emancipation of the Serfs they accepted "pauper holdings" of one quarter of the norm, and therefore never paid any redemption dues and never lived entirely by agriculture; at all events, never by cultivating their own land. The total "pauper" allotment for the two villages amounted to 864 acres, for 395 census "souls": perhaps 800 persons. Though the area is in the Black-Earth zone, the soil is river-sand over clay and limestone. Between the date of the Emancipation (1861) and 1884 the people did not plough their own land at all. They used it for rough pasture, for hay and wood-cutting. They rented their arable from the local landowner at less than a rouble an acre; say, 1s.8d.* In 1884 rents rose suddenly by 150 per cent in consequence of the general development of the Black-Earth zone, which was now filling up with colonists. The margin of cultivation went down, and the people of these two river-side villages began to plough up their waste and to reduce their hayfield and their wood (and, with these their cattle also).

An unusual feature which made its appearance in 1894 was that, in one of the two villages, the communally owned arable land was entirely merged in the individually owned yards and gardens, which Russians call usàdba. The lands of this class have recently played an important part in agrarian history because they threatened to monopolise the labour which Communist policy desired to direct to the collectivised farms.

* Forty cents, United States, at pre-war par of exchange.

The rough pasture, the hayfield, and the wood (that is to say, the peasants' wood) continued, when Dr. Shingarev wrote, to be enjoyed by the two villages jointly; but they did not make much out of these sources of subsistence. According to the Report, each "soul" obtained, every second or third year, half a load of small brushwood, five to ten thin stakes of wood, 3 to 6 cwt. of hay. The last was of poor quality, because the cattle were admitted, by the decision of the *Mir*, to the common hayfield till May 9th, and it was only after this date that the grass was allowed to grow.

The rye grown on the arable came to 1½ to 4½ cwt., the millet to 1 to 3 cwt. for three or four "souls." A small area of the better land, which had been mortgaged, grew melons.

A working man's daily ration being at least 2 to 2½ lb. of rye, it will be seen how small a contribution to the needs of these villages was made by their allotment of land. But Dr. Shingarev, who wishes to prove that increased allotments will cure the troubles of the Russian cultivator, demonstrates by statistics the superior economic position of the family which has the larger area of allotment land, as opposed to rented land.

The direct taxation due from each "soul" to the State and the *Zemstvo* was less than a rouble (say 2s.) annually. But State Insurance charges were heavy, and amounted in 1901 to more than the whole of the other direct charges. At that date there were heavy arrears on the taxes due to the *Mir*. These arrears were mostly a legacy from the past, when the *Mir's* rate, formerly one rouble per revision soul, had been reduced to one-eighth of that amount, but without the remission of arrears. They amounted to over 2,400 roubles for the *Mir's* rate and over 900 for insurance payments. Fire insurance has always been important in Russia, owing to the prevalence of wooden buildings and the frequency of conflagrations, and it had recently been made compulsory.

Except for rent of land, there was very little indebtedness to private persons. Presumably there was very little credit to be had. At this period there were no co-operative societies or co-operative banks. There were two small retail shops, having a trifling turnover, and an annual fair.

Increasing impoverishment since 1884 was indicated by the figures for horses and cows. In the former year 133 owners had 222 horses and 182 cows; in the latter year 158 owners had 209 horses and 129 cows. The only kind of animals which increased in this interval was sheep.

The obvious deficit in grain was made up partly by renting land.

The standard rent was rather less than 2 roubles an acre (say 4s.), or a slightly smaller amount in cash, plus about 7½ loads of manure delivered on the landlord's land. These payments in manure had considerable importance in an area in which animals were few, and sufficient moisture was present in the river valley to make manure valuable, if not essential. Manure was so scarce that none of it was used for fuel, though this use of it is normal in a great part of Russia, where wood is as deficient as it is in the Don valley.

The deficit in straw—a very important commodity where it is the main source of fuel, bedding for humans and animals, and roofing—was partly made up by buying the stubble from the landlord's estate, at the rate of about 20 kopeks an acre. Wood is necessary to the baking of bread, and the people had not enough wood for this daily need. But there was a large "Economic Forest" belonging to the landlord; and the villagers, heckled by the investigator on this subject, could only tell him with sheepish grins: "The baking must be done: so we go to the *Bàrin* (gentleman) in the forest; he has got wood rotting." In other words, they stole wood.

There were seventeen households only, out of 159, whose grain lasted from the end of one harvest to the time for sowing the next. All the rest had to buy grain, and thirty-nine households did not cultivate their allotments at all.

It is hardly necessary to explain that much of the livelihood was derived from wage-earning occupations. Nearly a third of the men were so occupied in the neighborhood, and about one-sixth of them outside it. A much smaller number of women were thus employed: but in both sexes the numbers tended to rise. The large-scale agriculture of the landlord gave occupation both to men and women, but stone-quarrying, a dangerous and unhealthy occupation, with no sort of provision for occupational disease or accident, was the main local industry apart from agriculture. Grain- and wood-carrying was common, and some had recently taken to dealing in these commodities on their own account in a small way.

An agricultural labourer by the year received 60 roubles (say £6) for a male, 36 roubles (say £3 12s.) for a female, plus food. Day labourers who found their own food got from 20 to 40 kopeks (say from 5d. to 10d.) for males, from 15 to 30 kopeks for females, according to the season: the summer day, at harvest time, being eighteen hours, with three hours off for food. The figures sound unbelievable, but they are correctly reproduced from the report, and I do not doubt them. The stone-quarries worked by the piece, and part of the pay was given in kind. This makes it difficult to say what the earnings were.

A peculiar feature of the village life was the practice of taking foster-children to nurse, either at breast or bottle, from the Zemstvo's Orphan Asylum at Voronezh. Our medical investigator traces an increased mortality among the children of the foster-parents to this practice. Syphilis plays a considerable part in his report. High mortality among the foster-children seems to be due rather to ignorance than to criminal neglect. Up to 1897 the Zemstvo had no inspectors to ascertain how its nurselings were doing. Adult food was always given at six months of age—presumably to all the children, and, our doctor says, no wonder that many died. Some were adopted by the foster-parents, and a few were accepted as full members by the Mir, "for a drink of vodka"—an incidental observation which illuminates the practical working of the village community, and the small value attached to the share of a "soul" in the economic advantages of its land.

A detailed investigation of the dietary in comparison with the theoretical norm (itself by no means a high one) worked out for the Voronezh Province as a whole showed a great deficiency of fats. The doctor considered that one of the two villages was suffering from fat-hunger. He was surprised to find that many households had to go entirely without cabbage, cucumbers, and milk. The lack of meat did not surprise him: but these three items did, and considering the large part played by cabbage and cucumber in the Russian village, there was ground for surprise. The consumption of sugar per person per annum was 2½ oz.; that of tea less than ½ oz. There was no drink-shop in either of the villages, and the consumption of vodka per person per annum was two-fifths of a gallon. Evidently these things were luxuries for an occasional holiday.

The history of the villages was marked by occasional famine (e.g., 1891), conflagration, and epidemics among human beings or animals. Diphtheria and abdominal typhus were the principal forms of infectious disease. On the opposite side of the Don, and 3 miles away, was the hospital for in- and out-patients, at which our friend the investigating doctor was stationed. Even in the flood season boats plied across the river. But the hospital had no accommodation for syphilitic patients, who had to go to another place 8 miles away, and often could find no free beds there. A crèche was established at the insistance of the Russian Society for the Protection of the People's Health, and in 1900 a special branch was added by the Society for Resistance to Contagious Disease for syphilitic children. The distribution of milk to children under 3 years of age was also begun under the auspices of the first-named society. The people were suspicious of the crèche, and the charitable societies apparently wearied of well-doing. It is noticeable again that the Zemstvo did not take up the work.

Malaria was common in both villages. Along with this fact we read that each village has a pond formed by damming a small stream on its way down to the Don. It is in these ponds that the cattle drink. The dam is formed of dung (sic), which all the householders bring each spring when the floods have gone down. Dead horses and cows are skinned, and sometimes carried out and left to the dogs, but sometimes buried in the house-yard. A horseless house-owner lost seven cows in succession—from an unspecified disease—and on each occasion buried the carcase in his yard.

In one of the two villages there were no privies: in the other there were eight. Excrements were left in the outer passages of the house (izba, generally of wood), and eaten by swine, dogs and fowl.

General features of the living-houses were that they were closely packed together, small in air-space, smoky and yet not sufficiently warm, poorly lighted, entirely without ventilation, and in many cases old. There were only two beds (both wooden) in the whole of one village; one belonging to a carpenter and one to a stone-mason. The stove, benches, shelves, and the floor were the sleeping places. In the vast majority of the izbas the cattle wintered inside.

Our doctor has the true scientific passion for statistics. The ordinary red and the Eastern black cockroach were observed in 90% of the dwellings, but bugs only in 15.5%. This fact gives occasion for an interesting observation. *The bug is a natural aristocrat.* He does not like the miserable bedding of the poor man. The black beetle is most democratic. But there is a point at which he too draws the line because there is too little food to be got. The peasants have a saying about the most extreme poverty: "There are no black beetles there."

Of the male population rather less than one-third in one village and less than one-sixth in the other could read and write. The proportion of literate women was far smaller, and in one village there was not even one. But, it must be added, these figures are a good deal higher than they would be in a similar Indian village. As in India, the people did not believe in the value of instruction for women. Those who are familiar with the Indian village will recognize many other resemblances.

The doctor says that these are typical villages of the Black-Earth zone at the beginning of the twentieth century. This is true, I think, with one reservation. The people made a bad choice when they accepted the "pauper" allotment of one quarter. They took it for granted that the low standard of rent would remain unaltered, and that there would be a chance for renting more land for new mouths. But their population increased, from the time of the Tenth Census in 1858 to the investigation made in 1891, from 828 to 1,151, and their expectation of cheap land was disappointed. In other respects these villages, being near to sources of non-agricultural employment, were rather favourably situated, and there are signs of an urban, or rather a suburban, habit.

A casual observation informs us of the existence of a higher standard of comfort in the "manufacturing" villages; by which the doctor means those in which cottage industries were practised. He says that the rural villages investigated by him lack "the window curtains, photographs, and flowers in vases" which are seen in the industrial villages. The absence of all decoration (except the Icons in the corner above the table) is a feature which strikes him.

In a note written in 1907, Dr. Shingarev quotes from the report of a Committee which dealt with the overcropping of the lands of the Black-Earth zone. "Since the Emancipation, the woods have been cut down (owing to the extension of cultivation), the streams have become shallow or have disappeared, drifting sands have invaded the fields, the hayfields have been ploughed up, the fields have broken away into ravines, and, instead of once fertile lands, gullies, watercourses, landslips and even precipices, have made their appearance: the land has lost fertility, its productiveness has fallen, the natural wealth is exhausted, and the people are impoverished." The contrast, he said, was marked between the brilliant financial condition of the Empire, and the progressive ruin of the peasant masses. A writer in the magazine *Russian Wealth* said that many of the peasants who lacked land or had non-economic holdings were in similar condition: "which represents a whole section of the lower strata of our economy."

The historian, Pavlovsky, of *Agricultural Russia on the Eve of Revolution*, taking a more general and wider view than the doctor, has analysed for us the economic troubles of the peasant at this time. Perhaps they could be attributed compendiously to the lack of a more intensive agriculture, having more scientific rotations, and that in turn to the as yet inchoate industrialisation, insufficient to provide the demand for a greater variety of crop. Where dairying or flax-growing had established itself, there was a comparative local prosperity. Pavlovsky says that a great rise in population was accompanied by an increase, but not a proportionate increase, in the productivity of peasant agriculture. To these facts let me add, quoting the words from the report of an Official Commission of 1897, that "nowhere are the relations between employer and employed so strained as in agriculture."

The rise of agricultural prices which began in 1896 should have been beneficial to those who produced in excess of their requirements: but most peasant cultivators, particularly in the area of deficit cereal production, are outside that category, and suffer, in a greater or less degree, from high prices. Every peasant tends to sell after harvest, when prices are low, and to buy at sowing time, when they are higher. Only a high development of co-operation, which was still lacking, can save him from the consequences of the attempt to combine marketing with agriculture, which is the normal lot of every farmer who has left subsistence agriculture behind. The cash nexus is inevitably cruel to those to whom arithmetic is still a mystery.

The peasants themselves, and many of their champions like Dr. Shingarev, believed that they were robbed of their land, and that more land was the remedy for their troubles. Their purchases of land, with and without the help of the Peasants Bank, were enormous, as the figures of ownership of different categories in 1877-78 and in 1905 show:

The totals, in millions of acres, are:—

	1877-78	1905
Acres held as peasants' allotments (Nadyel)	314	347
Area held by gentry	194	125
Area held by peasants (other than allotments dating from the time of emancipation)	12½	78

After 1905, when there was a panic among the gentry and a great increase in sales of land, this passage of land to the peasant class became even more rapid, and it was accompanied by very extensive emigration to Siberia, assisted by the State.

But the figures will convey a misleading impression unless it is understood that the category of "peasant" represented a legal, not an economic status. Many of the purchasers who figure as peasants in the statistics were well-to-do land holders who were peasants only in name: as was Hor in Turgeniev's story.

The troubles of the peasant in the period preceding the revolution of 1905 were not only economic. A good deal of the "black" status of a social inferior had survived the Emancipation. A memorandum recorded in 1898 by Count Witte for the information of Nicolas II gave a list of his grievances. They included arbitrary punishment (generally corporal), arbitrary restrictions on leaving the home-village, the lack of legal definition of rights and duties, and even of laws of peasant inheritance, and oppression by the Land Captains and other officials, who treated him literally as they pleased. He was not precisely a member of a depressed class like the lower castes of India, for there was no religious distinction, and no barrier to intermarriage even while serfdom still existed: but in some respects his case was worse than theirs, and urgently demanded a radical amendment.

※　　　※　　　※

The Soviet Government has published an account of the present condition of these two villages. They are changed beyond recognition: but close study of the volume reveals that the land at the disposal of the two villages is now six times what it was. The changes are therefore due to the transfer of land from the landlord to the peasants, rather than to the transformation of the system of farming. Additions to the land on this scale were exceptional, for the average gain to the peasants did not exceed 20%.

INDEX

For main location of principal topics, see Table of Contents.
Last names only are given, as Lenin, Stalin, unless there is need for particularisation.
Book titles are italicised.

Abkhasia, see Caucasus
Abortion, 483-4
Abrahamson, 363-4
Abundance, economics of, 249
Ackermann, Madame, 92, 107
Adzhar, see Caucasus
Afinogeniev, *Fear*, 281, 504
Agriculture, see Collective farm, Collectivisation, Kulak, Mir, Peasant, State farm, App. II, IV-VI
Agriculture of the U.S.S.R., App. IV
Aksakov, Konstantin, 58, 61, 64
Aladin, Labour group in 1st Duma, 131
Alexander I, 9, 168, Ch. XXIII
Alexander II, 90, 144, 155, Ch. XXIII
Alexander III, 56, 142-3, 154, Ch. XXIII
Alexéev, General, 172, 210-11
Alexis, Tsar, Greek tradition in liturgy, 58
Allan, Mrs. Seema Rynan, 295, 419
Amsterdam International, 307
Anarchism, 68, 75-6, 102-4, 124, 136, 204, 227, 297, 417
Anglo-Russian Agreement, 251
Anglo-Russian Trade Union Committee, 307
Animism, 438-9
Anti-Comintern pact, 478 *et seq.*
Anti-Semitism, see Jews, Pogroms, Ch. XXIII
Aquinas, St. Thomas, 106
Arakchéev, 9
Archangel govt., 215
Aristotle, 106
Armenia, 143, Chs. XXIII-IV, 480, App. IV
Artel, 28
Arts and Architecture, 489 *et seq.*
Artsybashev, *Sanin*, 166
Asch, Sholem, *Three Cities*, 289
Asia, Central; Central Asian Republics, Chs. XXIII-VII, App. IV
Austria, Chernyshevsky and, 71
Avenarius, 135, 137, 432
Azarbaijan, see Caucasus
Azev, 145

Bakayev, 317
Baku, general strike, 1903, 142
Bakunin, 64, 74, 75-9, 103, 116, 118, 128, 133, 441
Balkans, 457, 459
Baltic Provinces and States, 143, 148-9, 161, 222, 325, Chs. XXIII-IV
Banking, bank credits [see also State Bank], Ch. XVIII
Baring, Maurice, 133, 140, 150, 152, 155, 279, 283
Batsell, *Soviet Rule in Russia*, 466
Baykov, 541
Beaulieu, Leroy, 366
Belinsky, Vissarion, 64-9, 71-2, 81, 350
Bell, The, 70, 76, 118
Bely, Andrei, 166
Benedictines, 55
Bentham, Jeremy, 5
Berdyaev, 1, 25, 53, 63, 100, 106, 109, 127, 136, 412, 431-2, 439-41, 496, 515-16
Bernstein, Eduard, 126, 350
Bessarabia, 458
Biro-Bidzhan, 468
Bismarck, xii
Black Earth zone, 22, 28, 30, 35-6, 147, 162, 215, 238, 240, 248, App. VI
Black Hundreds, 150, 152-3, 156, 160, 166, 174
Black Partition, 89, 90
Blok, Alexander, *The Twelve*, 108, 210, 350, 475
Blockade, allied, see France, Great Britain, Japan, United States
Bogdanov, P. A., 135, 137
Bolshevik, see Communism, Marxism, Menshevik, Social Democrats, Revolutionary Government, November Revolution, Lenin, Stalin, Trotsky
Bolshevik Central Committee, 1917, 191
Borisov, 178
Borodin, 306
Breshkovskaya, Co-op. Bank and School, 79
Brest-Litovsk, 203, 211-12, 477

Brianchaninov, *The Russian Church*, 60, 433
Britnieva, Madame, 215, 350
Bubnov, 193
Buchanan, Sir George, 167, 175, 177, 190, 194
Buddhism, 438-9
Bukharin, xiv, 202, 256, 275, 288, 291, 299, 303, 313-14, 316, 321, 323-4, 351, 477, 506
Bulgakov, 50, 136-7, 432, 439
Bulygin Constitution, 147-8
Bunge, Nicolas, 142
Bureaucracy, see Lenin, Stalin, Trotsky, Eckhardt
Buxton, Roden, 231, 234
Byron, Lord, 5
Byzantium [Constantinople], 1-4, 13, 52-3, 58, 61-2

Canteens, factory, App. III
Capital, capitalism, 220, 223-5, 233, 253-4, 274-6, Chs. XVII-IX, 432, 448, 496-9
Capital levy, 1919, 227
Capital Punishment, 189, 283-5
Capitalism, State, 220, 253
Capri communist school, 137
Carpatho-Ukraine, 450
Carr, E. H., 110
Catherine, Empress, 4, 8-9, 18, 161, 168, Ch. XXIII
Caucasus, Chs. XXIII-IV, App. IV
Censorship, 56, 87, 155, 176, 257, 526
Census, 17, App. I
Chaadev, 65, 98, 136
Chamberlain, 184, 189
Chechens, 459
Cheka, see Police, political
Chekhov, 90, 125-6
Chernov, Victor, *Constructive Socialism*, 90-1; 135, 184, 187-9, 209, 236, 297
Chernyshevsky, *What Is to Be Done*, 64, 70-73, 95, 136, 294
Chiang Kai-shek, 306, 308
Chicherin, 202
China, 306-9, 312, 316, 340, 461, 477
Chkeidze, 138
Christianity, Eastern, see Church, Orthodox
Chrysostom, Saint, 59
Chuprov, M., 163

Church, Anglican, and Orthodoxy, 55
Church, Gregorian, 436
Church, Orthodox, 2, 4, 6, 7, 13, 35-6, 52, 59-60, 97, 99, 143, 149, 206-7, 289, 299 Chs. XXII-IV, XXVII
Church, Protestant, 59-61, 97, Chs. XXIII-IV, 517
Church, Roman Catholic [see also Rome], 3, 4, 54, 58-61, 68, 97-9, 143, 145, 156, Chs. XXII-V, 517
Church Soviets, 438
Chuvash republic, 466
Ciliga, 433-4
Circassia, see Caucasus
Civil War, see Czechs, Denikin, Intervention, allied, Koltchak, Makhno, Petliura, Skoropadsky, Samara govt.
Clark, Colin, *Critique of Russian Statistics*, 424, 425-6, App. III
Class-struggle [see also Marxism, Communism], 116-17, 120, 138
Classless society, see Belinsky, Marx, Marxism, Soloviev, Stalin
Coalition Govt., 189
Cole, Margaret, 421
Collective Farm, 221, 233, 236-7, 262-3, 270, 275, 314, 335-6, 344, 359, 362, Chs. XIX-XX, XXVI-VII, 523-4, App. II, IV, V
Collectivisation [see also Collective Farm, State Farm], 17, 198, 233, 238, 262-3, 267, 270, 275, 285, 314, 344, 346-7, 359, 362, Chs. XIX-XX, XXVI-VII, App. IV-V
Colonial peoples, see Great Britain, Nationalism, Stalin, Third International
Colonisation, internal, 36, 154, 165, 384
Commune, Paris, 79, 133, 205-6
Communes, independent [peasant], 58, 366
Communism, communist party, communist govt. [see also Marxism, Messianism, Socialism, November Revolution, Revolutionary govt., Soviets, Third International; Marx, Engels, Plekhanov, Lenin, Stalin, Trotsky, Bukharin, Kirov, Rykov, Zinoviev, Berdyaev], 128-9, 192-3, 202-3, 207-9, 212, 219, 228-30, 235, 239-41, 244, 251-8, 265, 274-7, 279-80, 285-300, Chs. XVI-XXVII
Communist International, see Third International

Communist Manifesto of 1849, 118, 516

Consensus of the congregation, see Sobornost

Constituent Assembly, 146-7, 149, 183, 185, 188, 193, 196, 203, 205, 207-10, 215, 297, 368

Constitution of 1936, 116, 214, 325, 363, 389, 417, 423, 438, Chs. XXIV-VI

"Constructive levelling," 463, 511

Consumer, consumer's choice, Ch. XVII

Contemporary Magazine, 65

Co-operative Bank, 270

Co-operatives, 28, 36, 67, 144, 154-5, 180-1, 221, 233, 236-7, 241, 259-62, 268-71, 297, 314, 329, 335, 343, 364, 366-7, 398-9, 403, 505, App. V

Cossacks [see also Zaporozhian], 6, 58, 175-6, 177-90, 196, 210, 211, 227, 381, Chs. XXIII-V, 502

Cost of living, see Standard of living

Cost-accounting, 225, Ch. XVIII

Cottage industries, 33

Council of People's Commissars, Nov. 8, 1917, 196

Creameries, Siberian, 271

Credit control, Ch. XVIII

Credit Societies, see Co-operatives

Crimean War, 69

Crops, industrial and technical, Ch. XX, App. IV

Currency management, Ch. XVIII

Curzon, Lord, 304

Czecho-Slovaks, 212-13, 227-8, 244

Daghestan, see Caucasus

Dairying, see Mir, Peasant, Collective Farm, Collectivisation, App. IV

Dan, 195

Das Kapital, 118, 124

De Toqueville, 12

Debts, Foreign, 206

Defeatism, in 1st World War, 138-9

Defensism, liquidationism, Our Dawn, 138

Deficit-Russia, Ch. II; 222

Democracy [see also Lenin, Stalin], economic versus political, 14; local, 20-1, 1936 Constitution, 510-11

Denikin, 210, 217, 227-8, 242-4, 272

Dialectical Materialism, 112-116, 138, 432, 518

Diderot, and Catherine the Great, 18

Diet, 30-2, 424-5, App. III, VI

Dillon, Dr., 146

Dissenters, religious, Chs. XXII-III

Distribution, less important than production, 123

Divine Wisdom, The, in Russia and the Universal Church, 99-100

Dmitry, Grand Duke, 172

Dmitry of the Don, 53

Dmowski, Roman, 449

Dobb, Soviet Economy and the War, 347, 541

Dobroliubov, 70

Dolgorukov, Prince, 282

Don Cossacks, see Cossacks

Donets basin, see Ukraine

Dostoievsky, 51, 62, 64, 65-66, 70, 74, 77, 83, 88, 92-7, 100, 103-8, 135-6, 166, 170, 284

Drought, see Famine

Dualism, philosophical, 138

Duma, 131, 134, 137-9, 147-9, 152-3, 159-60, 164-7, 170-1, 174, 176-7, 181, 190, 210, 279, 449, 454

Duranty, 198

Dzherkhinsky, 193, 202, 204, 315

Ecclesiastical courts, 56

Eckhardt, Hans von, 447

Economic Council, Supreme, 225, 246

Economic Councils, local, 225

Economic regions, 466

"Economics of Peasant Farming," 337

Education, expenditure, App. II

Effective demand, 331-4, Ch. XVII

Elizabeth, Empress, 4, 283

Emancipation of serfs, 10, 24-30, 141, 149, 161, 168, 183, App. VI

Empirio-criticism, 135, 432

Employment, unemployment, see Trade Unions, Labour, Ch. XXI

Employment, choice of, 335-6

Empress, see Tsaritsa

Empress Dowager, 167

Engels, 110-15, 118-19; Germany in 1848, 134; Peasant Problems in France and Germany, 233; 293; 366

Engelhardt, women and flax cultivation, 34; village priests, 35

Enver Pasha, 464

Equality, see Mir, Peasant, Ch. II, Marx, Marxism

Esthonia, Chs. XXIII-IV
Evdokimov, 313, 316

Factory, Marx on, 140
Factory Committees, 228
Family, the, 483 et seq.
Famine, 29, 30, 238, Ch. XIII
Farbman, Michael, 378
Farms, see Collective Farms, State
   Farms, collectivisation
Fascism, see Germany, Italy, Japan,
   Spain, Molotov, Stalin, Trotsky
Fathers and Sons, Turgeniev's, 70
Fedin, Konstantin, Cities and Years,
   216
Fellow Travellers, Trotsky on, 257
Figner, Vera, city and agrarian terrorists,
   89
Finland and Finns, 149, 156, 160, 190,
   222, Ch. XXIII, 482
Fischer, Louis, 289, 309
Five-Year Plans, Chs. XVII-XX
Food [see also Diet, Famine] deficit
   and surplus zones, Ch. II; 214-15,
   222, 238-40; 261; App. III-VI
Fourier, 72-3, 92, 95
Fourth International, 321-2, 325
France, 4, 16, 218, 227-8, 244-5, 304,
   351, 479, 481-2, 507
Freedom, divided between Western
   democracies and U.S.S.R., 14; lower
   plane, 20; Marxist doctrine, 122-3;
   liberty of the subject, outlook on law,
   155; and labour, 414-17; 1936 Con-
   stitution, 499 et seq.; Ch. XXVII
Freeman, Joseph, 496
Fulop-Miller, Mind and Face of Bolshevism, 515
Fyodorov, N., Philosophy of Common
   Work, 105; 135

Gailis, E. M., Financial and Economic
   Manual of the Collective Farm, App.
   IV
Galicia, 450-451
Gandhi, 103, 297
Gapon, Father, 97, 145
General Strike, 1903, 142, 144; 1905,
   146-8, 156
Geneva Conference, 1922, 304
Georgia [see also Stalin, Chkeidze, Na-
   tionalities], 146; Chs. XXIII-IV; 480;
   App. IV
German Social Democrats, 125

Germans, Germany, 4-5, 8, 13, 16, 19,
   59, 123, 126, 149, 173, 176, 190-2,
   201-3, 211-12, 227-33, 251, 285,
   288-9, 304-5, 309, 324, 326, 337,
   366, Chs. XXIII-V
Gladkov, Cement, 217, 246
Goethe, 138
Gogol, 13, 69, 257, 451, 489
Gorky, The Townsmen, 124-5; 137,
   147, Down and Out, 168; 216, 486,
   491, 521, 528
Graham, Stephen, 154, 327
Great Britain, 4-5, 215, 227-8, 242-5,
   251, 282, 304, 306-9, 312, 316, 340,
   354, 362, 375, 403-5, 412-14, 416,
   424-30, 455, 465, 467, 479, 481-2,
   498, 504-5, 511-14, 519-21, 523, 525,
   App. III
Great-Russians, Chs. XXIII-IV
Greek influence [see also Church, Or-
   thodox], 3
Greeley, Horace, 519
Green, T. H., Prolegomena to Ethics,
   517
Green International, 91
Grigorov, Leonid, the "Popular Judge,"
   273
Grimm, and Catherine the Great, 18
Groman, W. C., 186, 351
Guchkov, Alexander, 153, 167, 171

Haensel, Paul, App. III
Hague Court, 168
Halm, Prof., 333
Handicrafts, Ch. XXI
Hathaway, Clarence, 496
Haxthausen, Baron, 23, 32-3
Hayek, Von, 332-3
Health, App. II
Hebrew Prophets, 110
Hecker, Julius, 439
Hegel, 65-6, 68, 74-5, 111-2, 135-6
Heraclitus, 113, 474
Hereford, Prof., 110
Herzen, 9, 64, 67-70, 72, 75-6, 118
Hildebrand, Pope, 294
Hindus, Maurice, Red Bread, etc., 268,
   376, 484, 515
Hippius, Zinaida, 106
History of Revolutionary Ideas, Her-
   zen's, 68
History of Social Thought, see Razum-
   nik, Ivan
Hitler, Adolf, 481

Hobbes, Thomas, *Leviathan*, 84, 496
Holland, admired in Peter the Great's time, 4
Holy Alliance, 9
Holy Name, see Imasliye
Holy Synod, see Synod, Holy
Hubbard, 389, 395

Ibsen, 15, 107, 301
Imaslaviye movement, 106
Immanentists, 135
Income-tax, see Taxation
India, comparisons with U.S.S.R., 247, 290, 297, 347, 398, 402, 406, 415, 425, 439, 455, App. IV, VI
Individualism, Ch. XVII, 492-3, Ch. XXVII
Individualist peasants, see *Mir*, Peasants, App. IV
Industrial and Technical crops, Ch. XX; App. IV, VI
Industrial Bank, 330
Industrialisation [see also Five-Year Plans], 157-9, Ch. XVII, App. II-III
Ingushes, 459
Insurance, town workers', 224; peasants, 236; social, 400, 417, Ch. XXI, 423; state, App. II, VI
Insurrectionism, see Bakunin, Lenin, Zinoviev, Kamenev
Intelligentsia, Chs. V, VII, XVIII, XXII, 525 *et seq.*
International Labour Office, 425
"International Social Democratic Alliance," 77
International, Third, see Third International
Internationalism, see Marxism, Communism, Socialism, Messianism, Nationalism, Third International
Intervention, Allied, see France, Great Britain, Japan, United States
Iron and steel, 1887-98, 141
Iskra, 129, 367
Islam [see also Mahommedans], 245, 434-6, Ch. XXIV
Italy, 3, 16, 19, 288-9, 478
Ivan the Great, 2
Ivan the Terrible, 3, 5, 6, 18, 53, 151
Ivan III, 52
Ivanov, Vyacheslav, 136, 166

Japan, 128, 140, 143-5, 147, 227-8, 285, 323, 345, 448, 479, 507

Jesuits, 55, 128, 168
Jews [see also Jewish Social Democrats, Pogroms], 150, 155, 159, 315, 438, Chs. XXIII-IV
Joffé, 319
Justice, revolutionary, 1918, 207

Kadet party, 131, 134, 152, 188, 190, 208, 282
Kaledin, 196
Kalinin, 197, 202, 244, 262-3, 381, 507, 510, 522, 525
Kamenev, 191-3, 196, 201-2, 207, 287-8, 303, 305, 313-17, 319-20, 381
Kant, 127, 135-6
Kartashev, Society of Religious Philosophy, 105
Katkov, 88
Kazakh S.S.R., Ch. XXIV, App. IV
Kellogg Pact, 478
Kerensky, 126, 166, 170, 186-90, 193-6, 204, 209-10, 215, 222, 280, 284
Khalturin, Stepan, Northern Union, 1878-9, 80; 129
Kharkov, 1902 peasants' revolt, 28
Khomiakov, Aleksei, 56, 59-61, 64, 93, 95, 100
Khrushchev, 410
Kiev, early, 1; Slavophils and parliament of, 58
Kirgiz S.S.R., Chs. XXIII-IV, App. IV
Kirov, 19, 285-8, 296, 322, 489, 509
Kirshon, *Bread*, 278, 299, 373
Kishinev pogrom, 145
Knickerbocker, 421-2
Knox, Major-Genl., 172, 230
Koerber, 525-6
Köfod, M., and Stolypin's agrarian reform, 162
Kolkhoz, Kolkhoznik [see also Collective Farm Peasant], 390-2, 401-10
Kollontai, Madame, 202
Koltchak, 217, 228, 242-4, 297
Koltsov, 82-3
Konar, 382
Kondratiev, 321
Korea, 143-4
Kornilov, 188, 196, 210
Krasnov, Genl., 227
Krassin, 202, 245
Kremlin, Fight for, in November, 1917, 196
Krestinsky, 290
Krim Tartars, 2, 450

Krokodil, 488
Kropotkin, Prince, 204
Krupskaya, 203, 482
Krylenko, 507
Kulak, 17, 19, 28, 180, Ch. XIV, 317, 319, 323, 369, Chs. XVIII-XX, 439
Kuomintang, see China

Labour [see also Marx, Marxism, Communism, Trade Unions, Proletariat], Chs. XVII-XXI, XXIII-IV, App. II-III
Labour opposition, 1920, 229
Labour Party [see also Trade Unions, British], 306-7
Land Decree of, Nov. 8, 1917, 222
Land distribution, 1927, 264
Land Settlement, Stolypin's, 164, 235
Land-Committees, in 1917, 183, 185, 189, 265, 272
Landmarks, 136
Latvia, 161; Chs. XXIII-IV
Lavrov, Peter, *Historical Letters*, 78; *Forward, People's Will*, 79, 118
League of Nations, Ch. XXV
Left Social Revolutionaries, 195, 208-9, 280, 368
"Legal Marxism," 118, 126, 128
Lehmann, John, 472
Lena gold-fields, 1912, 166
Lenin, 1, 13, 88, 115, 124, 128-9, 130-4, *Materialism and Empirio-criticism*, 137-8; 142, 147, 186, 188-9, 191-4, 196, 199-203, 206-8, 212, 215, 219, 223, 228-9, 232-3, 235, 240, 244, 251-8, 263, 273, 279, 293-4, 297, Ch. XVI, 341, 348, 350, 366-70, 432, 458, 477, 479, 482, 488, 502
Leo XIII, 125
Leontiev, Konstantin, *World Socialist Revolution under Orthodox Autocrat*, 97
Le Play, 258
Lermontov, 69, 356
Letts, 149, Chs. XXIII-IV
Leveller [see also "Constructive Levelling"], Autocrat as, 169, 291
Liberalism, 153
Liberalism, English, 10
Liberals [see also Kadets], 12, 130, 134-5, 153
Liquidationism, 138
Lithuanians, 3, Chs. XXIII-IV

Littlepage and Bess, *In Search of Soviet Gold*, 278, 290, 363, 365, 376-7, 472, 474
Litvinov, 203, 245, 507
Liubarsky and Khmelev, *Money Impost on Collective Farms*, App. IV
Livonia, Chs. XXIII-IV
Lokola, 472
London, Kurt, *Seven Soviet Arts*, 457
London Life and Labour, App. III
Lorwin, 363-4
Ludendorff, and Ukraine, 214
Lunacharsky, 135, 137, 196, 257
Lutherans, see Baltic Provinces; Church, Protestant
Lvov, Prince, 181, 187
Lyall, Archibald, 412
Lyeskov, satire on missionizing, 57
Lysenko, 410
Lyubchenko, 471

Mach, Machians, 135-7, 432
Machine Tractor Stations [M.T.S.], 267, 329; Chs. XVIII-XX; 467; App. II, IV
Makhno, 204, 227, 298
Manchuria, Southern, 144
March Revolution, 181-2, 297
Marx, Karl, 14-15, 71, 77-8, Ch. VII; *Critique of Gotha Program*, 136; 140, 142, 199, 218, 252, 273, 297, 359, 395, 431-2, 518
Marxism, Marxists [see also Communism, Socialism, Bukharin, Lenin, Plekhanov, Stalin, Trotsky], 83-7, 233, 237, 257, 263, 275, 305, 366-7, 441, 447, 458, 482, 518, 529
Maslov, S. S., App. IV
Materialism, Dialectical, 112-6, 138, 432, 518
Maximalists, see Socialism
Mayakovsky, *Mystery Bouffe*, 16; *Land of Fragments*, 389, 438
Mensheviks, 123, 128-9, 130-4, 139, 146, 149, 186, 208, 210, 212, 219, 244, 318, 351, 366, Ch. XXIII
Merezhkovsky, D. S., 50, 105-6, 109, 136, 431
Messianism [see also Third Rome, Slavophils, Marxism, Berayaev, Bulgakov, Dostoievsky, Khomiakov, Nietzsche, Scyths, Soloviev], 218-19, Ch. XXII, 529
Meyendorff, Baron, 209

Meyerhold, 257
Mikhailovsky, 74; *Notes of the Fatherland*, 81; *What Is Progress*, 84, 85-9, 93, 126-7
Miliukov, Paul, 153, 176
Miller, Jacob, App. III
"Milli Istiklal," 471
Minin and Pojarsky, 5, 6
Mir, 11, Ch. II, 61, 67-9, 71, 82, 84, 121, 131, 135, 163-4, 181-5, 189, 233, 235, 237, 263-4, 273, 275-6, 368-9, 371, 397, 511, App. VI
Mirsky, Svyatopolk, 145
Mohammedans, Mohammedanism, 15, 205-6, 245, 323, 434-6, Chs. XXIII-IV
Molotov, Vyacheslav, 203, 321, 362, 427, 478, 480, 507
Monasticism, Orthodox, 55
Money Impost on Collective Farms, App. IV
Mongols, 2, 3; Chs. XXIII-IV
Monkhouse, 33, 185, 204, 374-5
Moscow, 2, 8, 9, 63-5, 133, 146-52, 196, 211, 490
Moscow Art Theatre, 126
Muralov, A. I., *Agriculture of the U.S.-S.R.*, App. IV
Muralov, N. I., 290
Muslims, see Mohammedans

Nagorno-Karabakh, see Caucasus
Nakhichevan, see Caucasus
Nansen, Fridjof, 249
Narkomvnudel, see Police, political
National Democrats, 471
National Socialism, 150
Nationalisation [see also Collectivisation, Marxism, Communism, Socialism, Lenin, Stalin, Trotsky, Social Democrats, Social Revolutionaries], 222-5, 235, 367-9
Nationalism, nationalities, Chs. XXIII-IV
Nazis, Nazi govt., see Germany
Nechayev, 76-7, 128
Nekrasov, N. A., 1, 81-2, 397
Nemirovich-Danchenko, 126
Nepmen, see N.E.P.
New Economic Policy [N.E.P.], 17, Ch. XII, 239-42, 262-3, 265, 270-1, 281, 302-4, 310-14, 317, 319, 323, 338-9, 357, 369-70, 372, 378-80, 384, 391, 400, 477, App. IV-V

Nicolas I, 5, 9, 55, 67-76, 204, 279, 283
Nicolas II, 36, 142-144, 149-151, 161, 170-4, 182, 203, 213, 448
Nicolas, Grand Duke, 149, 172, 449
Nietzshe, 106-8, 120, 137
Nihilism, 63, 67, 70, 73, 74, 88
Nikon, Patriarch, 57-8
Northern Peoples, institute, 439
Northern Union, 80
Nosar, Khrustalev, 132
Notes of the Fatherland, 80-1
November Government, see Revolutionary Government
November Revolution, 191-5, 198, 204, 206, 211, 261, 273, 280, 301-3, 368, 460-1, 474-5, 518
Novgorod the Great, 1, 2, 58, 258-9
Novoe Vremya, 142, 147
Nusratulla, 471

O.G.P.U., see Police, political
Obschina, see *Mir*
October Manifesto, 147-9, 151, 156
Octobrists, 165, 167, 171
Oecumenical Council, 57
Okhrana, see Police, political
Old Bolsheviks, 487
Oppositions, the [see also Bukharin, Kamenev, Lenin, Rykov, Stalin, Trotsky, Zinoviev, etc.], Chs. XV-XVI
Ordzhonikidze, 286, 362
Oriental Churches, 3
Orthodox Autocrat, see Church, Orthodox, and under names of Tsars
Orthodox Church, Orthodoxy, see Church, Orthodox
Orthodox revival [see Church, Orthodox, Bulgakov, Berdyaev, Khomiakov, Soloviev], Ch. XXII
Ossetians, see Stalin; Chs. XXIII-IV
Ottoman empire, Ch. XXIII
Otzovists, see Ultimatists
Owen, Lancelot, 181

Pale, Jewish, 451
Paléologue, Maurice, 50, 130, 157, 172, 174
Palmer, Rev. Wm., 55-6, 59
Pares, Sir Bernard, 156, 327
Paris communist school, 137
Party, The, similarities to lay Church, 20; and democracy, 21

Patriarchate, see Church Orthodox, "Union of the Russian People"

Pavlovsky, *Agricultural Russia on the Eve of Revolution*, 179-80, 388, 550

Peasant [see also Collective Farm, Collectivisation, Mir, Serfdom], 12-13, 17, 24, 148, 151-2, 162-5, Ch. X, 213-15, 218, Chs. XIX, XX, App. IV-VI

Peasant Bank, 36, 142, 149, 154, 162, App. VI

Peasant Deputies, All-Russian Congress, 184, 186

Peasant Union, in Moscow, 1905, 147

People's Army, of the Volga, 209; of the Don, 210

People's Commissars, Council of, Nov. 8, 1917, 196

People's Will, 89-90, 120, 122

Peoples of the East, Congress, 306

Permanent Revolution, see Trotsky, Lenin, World-Revolution

Peter the Great, 4, 6, 7, 8, 18, 54, 57-8, 65, 96, 150, 211, 283, 291, Ch. XXIII

Petersburg Fighting Union, 1895, 124

Petliura, 218, 227-8, 243, 471

Petrograd [see also Saint Petersburg], 175-7, 181-2, 186, 193-4, 214, 216

Philosophical Academy, 257

Piatakov, 290, 313, 316, 319, 353

Pilnyak, 104, 301

Pilsudski [see also Poland], 308, 312, 477

Pisarev, 73

Pius IX, Encyclical to Eastern Churches, Eastern Patriarchs reply, 59

Planning [see also Five-Year Plans, Lenin, Rykov, Stalin, Trotsky], 19-20, Chs. XVII-XX, 529

Planning Commission, Chs. XVII, XIX, XXI, XXV

Plato, Platonism, 106, 278, 439-40

Plehve, von, 144-5, 151

Plekhanov, George, *Black Partition*, 89; *Socialism and the Political Struggle*, 120; *Our Disagreements*, 121-4; 129, 137-8, 141

Plotinus, 110

Pobiedonostsev, 56, 96, 143, 149, 169

Pogroms, 56, 144-5, 150, 160, 283-4

Pokrovsky, 179

Poland and Poles, 3, 54, 71, 76, 88, 143, 145-6, 156, 171, 174, 217, 222, 228, 243, 245, 308-9, 325, 340, 433, Chs. XXIII-V, 477

Polanyi, *Christianity and the Social Revolution*, 515

Police, political, 204-5, Chs. XV-VI, 362-3, 504, 526

"Police Socialism," 97, 128, 144-5

Politburo, 286, Ch. XV

Poll tax, 1882, 36

Poltava, peasants' revolt, 1902, 28

Poor, Committees of, 213

Popular Fronts, 479 et seq.

Population, App. I

Populists, 26, 33, 68, 70-2, 74, 80-88, 90, 121, 124, 126-8, 141, 145, 297, 366, Ch. XXII

Port Arthur, 144, 146

Portsmouth, Peace of, 144, 159

Positivism, 136

Postyshev, 382, 471

Potemkin, battleship, 133, 146

Pravda, 129, 139, 155, 203, 208, 240, 277, 321, 363, 471

Preobrazhensky, 331

Press, restriction, 1917, 207

Price system, see capitalism, N.E.P., Socialism, Ch. XVII, App. III-IV

Priests, Parish, 55-6, et seq.

Procopovich, 246

Production, more important than distribution, 123

Productivity [see also Five-Year Plans], Chs. XVI-VIII

Profintern, see Trade Unions

Prokofiev, 490

Proletariat [see also Communism, Lenin, Marx, Marxism, Plekhanov, Stalin, Tomsky, Trotsky, Trade Unions, etc.], 116-17, 119, 235, 298, Chs. XXI, XXV

Promparti, 351

Propaganda, 526-7

Protestantism, see Church, Protestant

Protopopov, 174, 176-7

Proudhon, 75

Provisional Gov't, 1917, 182-4, 186-90, 194-5, 208-9, 221-2, 235, 247, 272, 284

Pugachev, 6, 8, 38

Purges, 1936-8, 232, et seq.

Purishkevitch, 172

Pushkin, 96, 438, 468

Rachmanova, Madame, 217, 243
Radek, 200, 290, 303, 305, 313-16, 319
Rahimbayev, 472
Rakovsky, 290, 313, 317, 319
Ramzin, Prof., 351, 363
Rapallo, 202, 251, 304
Raskol, Raskolnik, 2nd Raskol, Chs. XXII-III
Rasputin, 153, 170-4, 176-7
Rasulev, Mufti Abdurrahman, 472
Rationalisation, Chs. XVIII, XXI
Rationing, Ch. XVII, 360, 487, App. III
Razin, Stenka, 6, 38
Razumnik, Ivanov, History of Social Thought, 15, 86, 90, 107-8, 124
Red Army [see also Lenin, Stalin, Trotsky, Voroshilov], 200, 229-32, 350, 363, 481, 486
Red Guard, 188
Redemption dues, remitted, 1905, 38
Reed, John, 305
Religion, see Church, Protestant, Roman Catholic, Orthodox
Religious Philosophical Society, 105-6
Rent, App. III, VI
Republic, proclamation, Council of, 190; 209, 213
Revelations, Book of [see also Messianism], Rozanov, 97
Revenue, App. II
Revolution of 1905, 133, 136, 141, 146, 153-4, Ch. XXIII
Revolutionary Government, 196, 199, 204, 207-11, 214-15, 217-18, 220, 222-5, 227-9, 233, 235, 237-9, 242-6, 248, 261-2, 265, 268, 276, 283, 286, 293, 340, 348, 410, 460-1, 520
Robson, J. J., 508
Roman Catholic, see Church, Roman Catholic
Romanov, Tsar Michael, 5, 54
Romanov, Metropolitan Philaret, 5, 54
Romanovs [see also Alexander, Alexis, Ivan, Peter, Nicolas], end of, 212-13
Rome [see also Church, Roman Catholic, Third Rome], 3, 4, 54, 58, 97
Romania, 450
Rozanov, V., 97, 105, 136, 452
Rudnev, V. A., 185
Ruduzutak, 315
Rukeyser, 334, 351
Rural Councils, 37, 88, 145, 175, 182

Russell, Sir John, 404, 424-5
Russia, Holy, see Messianism; Ch. XXII
Russian Church, The, Nicolas Brianchaninov, 60
Russification, Chs. XXIII-IV
Russo-German pact, 478 et seq.
Rustaveli, Knight in the Tiger Skin, 468
Ruthenia, 450
Rykov, A. I., 192, 196, 203, 207, 275, 291, 313-14, 316, 321, 323, 351, 506

Sadoviev, 220
St. Petersburg [see also Petrograd; St. Petersburg Soviet], 131-3, 141-2, 145-9, 152, 211, 447
St. Petersburg Soviet, 1905, 131-3, 147-51, 156
Sakhalin, 144
Saltkov-Schedrin, The Solovlev Family, 81
Salvation Army, 439
Samara, S.R. govt., 214, 216, 246
Sa'ud, Ibn, 436
Saving, compulsory, Ch. XVII
Savings Banks, 485
Sazonov, 172
Scheffer, 313, 376-7
Schiller, Otto, 404, 409, 543
Schism, see Raskol
"Scissors, The," 179, Ch. XIV, 338-9, 369, App. V
Scyths, 15, 107-8
Self-employers, Ch. XXI
Semyonov, Sergei, 217
Serebriakov, 290, 317
Serfdom, see Foreword, Author's Introduction, and 6-11, 13, 18-19, 23, 24-6, 141
Sergei, The Holy, 53
Sergius, Grand Duke, 146
Shamanism, 438-9
Shamil, 454
Shestov, 15, 105, 107
Shingarev, Dr., 183-4, 208, App. VI
Shlyapnikov, 228-9
Sholohov, Virgin Soil Upturned, 374, 480, 491
Shostakovitch, 489
Siberian Co-operatives, 155
Sidelkin, N. P., App. IV
Sketches of the Fatherland magazine, 65

Skoporadsky, Hetman, 214, 227

Skrypnik, 382, 471

Slavonic, 4

Slavophils, 8, 23, 26, Ch. IV, 64, 66-9, 71, 74, 76, 95-6, 109, 136, 150, 211, Ch. XXII, 448

Smilga, 313, 316

Smirnov, V. M., 303, 313

Smith, Adam, 5

Sobornost, 50, 52, 58-9, 99, 105, 135-6, Ch. XXII

Social Democrats, 18, 124, 128-9, 131, 133-4, 138-9, 208, 212, 233, 367, 432, 450-1

Social-Fascists, Ch. XXV

Social insurance, 400, 417, Ch. XXI, 423

Social Revolutionaries [see also Social Revolutionaries of the Left], 90, Constructive Socialism, 91; 126, 130-1, 135, 145-6, 184-6, 196, 208-15, 219, 222, 236, 244-6, 297, 318

Social Revolutionaries of the Left, 195, 208-10, 280, 471

Socialism, Socialist State [see also Marx, Populists, Social Democrats, Social Revolutionaries, Stalin], 5, 66-8, 71-3, 80, 86, 90, 95, 111, 119, 124, 126, 131, 134, 144-5, 163, 165-6, 184, 187-8, 190, 195, 197-8, 206, 213, 217, 219, 221, 223-5, 235-6, 239, 251-3, 256-7, 261, Chs. XVI-XIX, XXII-VII, App. II-V

Socialist Construction, App. IV

Socialist Fatherland, 476 et seq.

Sokolnikov, 290, 315-16

Solòmin, Turgeniev's, 80

Soloviev, Russia and the Universal Church, 98-101; 105, 108-9, 126, 135-6, 166, 284

Southern Union of Workers, 80

Soviet Communism: A New Civilisation, see Webb

Soviet Constitution, 1918, 213; 1936, 116, 214, 325, 363, 389, 417, 423, 438, Chs. XXIV-VI

Soviet of Nationalities, 469-70

Soviet of Workers' Delegates, St. Petersburg, 1905, 147-9

Soviet Patriotism, Chs. XXIV-XXV

Soviets, Congress of, 1917, 192-3, 195-6; 1918, 218

Soviets, and Soviet Gov't, 131-3, 141, 147, 151, 181, 183, 188-92, 196, 209, 212-13, 245, 304

Soviets, village, canton, district, 272-3

Sowing Committees, 265-6

Spann, Der Wahre Staat, 515

Spencer, Herbert, 85

Spiridonova, Madame, 209

Stakhanovism, 365, 404, Ch. XXI, 485

Stalin, 17-19, 35, 134, 139, 193, 196, 200-3, 230, 256, 285-8, 291-2, 296-9, Ch. XVI, 340, 344-6, 348-56, 359-63, 365, 370, 373, 377, 383, 386-7, 391, 417, 420-1, 454, 457, 459 et seq., Ch. XXV, 487-9, 491-5, 500-2, 505, 511, 513, 521-2, 524-5, App. III

Standard of living, 30, 424-30

Stanislavsky, 126

State Bank, 254, 270, 354-6

State Farms, 233, 235-7, 259, 262-3, 275, 342, 344, Ch. XIX

State-control of industry, 1917-18, 223

Statistics, 276, 424-6, 475, App. I-IV

Stepnyak, 89

Stolypin, 19, 29, 149, 154, 160-7, 172, 178, 180, 235-6, 243, 262-3, 274, 279, 371, 449

Strauss, E., Soviet Russia, 1941, 271, 337, 402

Strikes [see also General Strike, Lenin, Police Socialism], 144, 146, 166-7, 176

Strong, Anna Louise, 255, 372, 374-5, 472

Struve, Peter, 106, 126; Critical Observations, 127; Landmarks, 136; 245

Sturmer, 172, 176-7

Sukhomlinov, 170

Sun Yat-sen, 306

Sun Yat-sen University, 316

Supreme Council, Allied, 245

Supreme Economic Council, 225, 246, 357

Surplus Value, 116-17

Surplus-producing region, see Agriculture, Collectivisation, Mir, Peasant, Collective Farm, State Farm

Sverdlov, 193, 201-3, 206, 208

Syndicalism, 229, 416-17

Synod, Holy, 54, 57, 145, 171, 173

Syrtsov, 321

Tajikstan, Ch. XXIV

Tapley, Mark, 491